METTERNICH'S GERMAN POLICY

VOLUME II:

THE CONGRESS OF VIENNA, 1814–1815

METTERNICH

An engraving of 1830 from a drawing
done by Friedrich Johann Lieder, probably during
the Congress of Vienna

METTERNICH'S GERMAN POLICY

VOLUME II: THE CONGRESS OF

VIENNA, 1814–1815

BY ENNO E. KRAEHE

PRINCETON, NEW JERSEY

PRINCETON UNIVERSITY PRESS

1983

Copyright © 1983 by Princeton University Press
Published by Princeton University Press,
41 William Street, Princeton, New Jersey 08540
In the United Kingdom: Princeton University Press,
Guildford, Surrey

Library of Congress Cataloging in Publication Data will be
found on the last printed page of this book

This book has been composed in Linotron Baskerville

ISBN cloth 0-691-05186-0
ISBN paper 0-691-10133-7

Clothbound editions of Princeton University Press books are
printed on acid-free paper, and binding materials
are chosen for strength and durability.
Paperbacks, although satisfactory for personal collections,
are not usually suitable for library rebinding.

Printed in the United States of America by
Princeton University Press, Princeton, New Jersey

To Laurence and Claudia

PREFACE

IN THE preface to Volume I of this study I explained that it began
as an introductory chapter to a work on the German Confederation
but then went astray, extending only to the defeat of Napoleon in 1814
and making Metternich's German policy the central subject. Despite
this chastening experience, I miscalculated again. Intending a second
volume carrying the story to 1820, I assumed that the existing literature
would sustain a chapter or two on the Congress of Vienna and open
the way for surveying the less well mapped terrain ahead. Instead, I
found that despite its fame, the great congress had not been as well
served by historiography as I had supposed, suffering on the one hand
from mere anecdotal accounts and on the other from works which,
though serious and often indispensable, have been dominated by contemporary preoccupations of various kinds.

Among the comprehensive works on the congress the most obvious
example of the latter type is Charles K. Webster's *The Congress of Vienna
1814–1815* (London, 1919), admirable in many ways but hastily written
to provide guidance for the British delegation to the Paris peace conference in 1919. Harold Nicolson's *The Congress of Vienna: A Study in
Allied Unity, 1815–1822* (New York, 1946) was not written for official
purposes but still addressed itself, as the title indicates, to a major
concern prevalent after the Second World War. Similarly Henry A.
Kissinger's *A World Restored: Metternich, Castlereagh, and the Problems of
Peace 1812–1822* (London, 1957), though more profound, viewed the
congress mainly as a laboratory for testing certain political theories
relevant to his generation. The best book on the subject remains Karl
Griewank's *Der Wiener Kongress und die Neuordnung Europas 1814–1815*
(Leipzig, 1942), a work of sound original scholarship, but even it is
marred by anti-Semitism and affected by its times at least with respect
to its title, which suggests that the author hoped for his study a use
comparable to that of Webster's 1919 work: as a guide for German
officials in organizing Hitler's "New Order." Significantly, when Griewank published a revised edition in East Germany in the 1950s he
changed the title to *Der Wiener Kongress und die europäische Restauration*
(Leipzig, 1954) bringing this much at least into line with Marxist historiography, which still views the congress mainly as a ruling-class
conspiracy against popular aspirations—paradoxically continuing the
national and liberal biases of the nineteenth century.[1]

[1] E.g., Karl Obermann, "Der Wiener Kongress 1814/1815," *Zeitschrift für Geschichtswissenschaft*, XIII (1965), 474–492; L. A. Zak, "Die Grossmächte und die deutschen
Staaten am Ende der napoleonischen Kriege," *Zeitschrift für Geschichtswissenschaft*,

Special aspects of the congress have fared better, as witness Webster's *The Foreign Policy of Castlereagh 1812–1815* (London, 1931) and Charles Dupuis's *Le ministère de Talleyrand en 1814*, 2 vols. (Paris, 1919–1920) to take two of the best examples, and, for our present purposes, Heinrich Ritter von Srbik's *Metternich der Staatsmann und der Mensch*, I (Munich, 1925), which for a general biography is surprisingly thorough on the congress. On Germany the most direct ancestors of my work are W. A. Schmidt, *Geschichte der deutschen Verfassungsfrage während der Befreiungskriege und des Wiener Kongresses* (Stuttgart, 1890), and Hans-Joachim Hartmann, *Das Schicksal der preussischen-österreichischen Verfassungsvorschläge . . . auf dem Wiener Kongress* (Göttingen, 1964), the former the pioneering work published posthumously by Alfred Stern, the latter a recent dissertation in the field of jurisprudence but more concrete than works of that type usually are. Without them and dozens of other monographs, especially recent studies in social and constitutional history, a work of synthesis like this one would not have been possible.

And yet, in confronting the literature from the points of view developed in my first volume, I was so struck by the incongruities that I decided to plunge back into the archives not only to seek new material but also to reexamine relatively familiar documents, little realizing that I would end by breaking the congress down into its constituent events and reassembling it in a more chronological form than is usual with a topic of such complexity, where many different series of events occur simultaneously, now intersecting, now diverging. Unfortunately the historian's medium does not allow him to say a dozen things at once, the way the composer of music can, but only by striving toward this ideal can he approximate the rich texture and vibrance of events as experienced by human beings. This is not to deny the value of seeking deeper meanings if our imperious time-bound intellects so insist, but the first priority is to set the record straight, to concentrate on what happened, not what should have happened.

In the years since the appearance of Volume I, I have become more than ever an advocate of what I would call "microhistory," which is really no more than a self-conscious empiricism that seeks to relate the events of a period, physical and mental, to each other rather than to norms imported from afar. There is always, of course, a subjective element supplied by the historian, but there is no reason why, with long immersion in the sources, his mind-set cannot be shaped as much

---

XIX (1971), 1536–1547; L. A. Zak, "Iz istorii diplomaticheskoi bor'bi na Venskom Kongresse," *Voprosy istorii*, III (1966), 70–82. See also Andreas Dorpalen, "The German Struggle against Napoleon: The East German View," *Journal of Modern History*, XLI (1969), 485–516.

by the assumptions of the past as by his own times. The practical difficulties are greater, but in theory there is, I am convinced, no epistemological problem attending the understanding of the past that is not equally obtrusive in trying to explain how we know the present. Strangely, the development of photocopying has rendered important service in this regard. We are no longer permanently bound by the first impressions that govern note-taking on a single swoop through the archives but can return again and again to the more important documents, reinterpreting them in the light of new insights gleaned from the period itself—taking time to read the fine print, as it were.

This confession of faith may betray an uneasy feeling that, for all my obsession with detail, this study contains a goodly number of conjectures, hypotheses, and leaps of imagination. The truth is that the surviving documentation relating to the Congress of Vienna is disappointing, especially in the case of Austria. In daily contact with the emperor, Metternich wrote relatively few reports and thereby almost by default permitted Talleyrand and Castlereagh (whose own reports home are far from exhaustive) to dominate the interpretation of the congress for posterity. Another problem is Metternich's *modus operandi*, which found him usually reacting to the initiatives of others, whose policies often require more analysis than his own. At times it even seemed to me that a study centered on him was not the best vehicle for expressing what needed to be said about Germany and the Congress of Vienna. It was characteristic of the man, however, that despite the difficulty of keeping him in focus, he emerged as the central figure after all. But as Metternich well knew, there is danger in explaining oneself too much. The principal claim made for narrative history, after all, is that it is understandable without the mediation of a high priest. Let us proceed to more important things.

I have never traveled with a retinue like that attending Metternich, but along the way I have received comparable assistance, all of it cheerfully given and gratefully received. A stipend from the Duke-North Carolina Cooperative Program in the Humanities in the summer of 1965 enabled me to begin research in Vienna; grants from the American Council of Learned Societies in 1969 and 1973 and from the National Endowment for the Humanities in 1973 and 1980 enabled me to complete it. Generous leaves from the University of Virginia were likewise essential, and my thanks go out to all concerned, including Charles L. Flanders, whose counsel and technical assistance cleared the way through many a bureaucratic jungle.

Next we come to the custodians of the past, the archivists and librarians, who make a study such as this possible. Given the subject of this work, the repository most used was the Österreichisches Staatsarchiv, whose general director at the time of my investigations was Professor Dr. Hanns Leo Mikoletzky, while the director of the Haus- Hof- und Staatsarchiv branch was Dr. Richard Blass. The successor of the latter, Dr. Anna Hedwig Benna, Dr. Anna Coreth, and Dr. Leopold Auer were also graciously helpful, as was Archivrat Anton Nemeth, who on numerous occasions over the years has dropped his own work to rush to my assistance. At the Státní Ústřední Archiv in Prague, where the Metternich family papers are deposited, I benefited not only from the hospitality and expertise of the director, Dr. Josef Görner, and Section-Chief Dr. Jaroslav Honc, but also from a splendid index to the Metternich papers just then completed by Dr. Antonin Haas. Nor can I leave Prague without a word of thanks to Dr. Maria Ullrichová, who introduced me both to the Metternich collection and to the many charms of the beautiful city on the Vltava.

Elsewhere I was given similar warm receptions, for which I wish to thank Dr. Carl Haase, director, and Dr. Gieschen of the Niedersächsisches Hauptstaatsarchiv in Hanover; Dr. Gönner, director, and his staff at the Hauptstaatsarchiv in Stuttgart; Dr. Heinrich Waldmann, director of the Zentrales Staatsarchiv in Merseburg; Dr. Professor Paul Zinsmaier, director, and his staff at the Generallandesarchiv in Karlsruhe (in particular the photography department, which rendered legible documents written in invisible ink); the staff of the Bayerisches Hauptstaatsarchiv in Munich for microfilming; Professor Dr. W. Kohl, director of the Staatsarchiv in Münster; and Mr. Kenneth Timmings, at the time Director of the Search Rooms of that treasure trove, the Public Record Office in Chancery Lane. In some cases the material I examined originated after 1815 and was not used in this volume, but thanks are due now regardless of the fate of the next volume.

I salute as well the front-line troops that have sustained me not on a single mission but steadily on a daily basis over the years: the staffs of the Alderman Library of the University of Virginia and the Louis Round Wilson Library of the University of North Carolina, as well as my research assistants over the years, Keith Mostofi, George L. Vogt, Timothy R. Walton, and most recently Lawrence Sondhaus, who supplied more than his share of time and ingenuity to the preparation of the final manuscript. Alderman Library was not content with providing reference and lending services but purchased aggressively in the antiquarian markets to supply countless volumes that have now been on my own shelves so long that I sometimes forget that they do not belong to me. For typing assistance I am indebted to the Center for Advanced Study at the University of Virginia and the Department of History, which allowed me at times to monopolize its secretarial skills, especially those of Mrs. Ella Wood. Iris Hunter typed the appendices from exceedingly rough originals, and Cristina W. Sharretts generously contributed her time and artistic gifts to producing the map.

Fondly I look back on a morning of discussion with Professor Heinz Gollwitzer of the University of Münster; a luncheon in Vienna with Professor Karl Otmar Freiherr von Aretin of the Technische Hochschule in Darmstadt; a day in Bielefeld as the guest of Professor Wolfgang Mager; a pleasant drive to Freiburg with Dr. Philip Mattson, director of the Wilhelm von Humboldt Brief-Archiv in Heidelberg; some five years of stimulating correspondence with Paul R. Sweet, professor emeritus at Michigan State University; and years of consultation with my friend, Guillaume de Bertier de Sauvigny, of the Institut Catholique in Paris. The last two, as well as Professor Paul W. Schroeder of the University of Illinois, have read all or part of my manuscript with critical acumen and unsurpassed knowledge of the period but of course no responsibility for my shortcomings. Sadly, Professor Robert A. Kann, a reader of the manuscript for Volume I, died before I could request his assistance again, but his friendship has influenced the final product all the same. Professor Sweet's second volume on Humboldt, *Wilhelm von Humboldt, A Biography* (Columbus, Ohio, 1980), though it appeared after much of my manuscript was written, has influenced my thinking in many ways that cannot be precisely documented. The same is true of other masters such as Srbik, Webster, Gerhard Ritter, and Heinrich von Treitschke. With a few exceptions I have resisted the temptation to burden the notes with a running commentary on their classic works.

Finally, if there is anyone more relieved than I am that the work is done at last, it is my wife and children, who teased but never criticized and cheerfully bore privations along the way. Thank you all.

Charlottesville
August, 1982

CONTENTS

ABBREVIATIONS USED IN FOOTNOTES

I HAVE endeavored to make most abbreviations intelligible on their face, but the following, which consist only of initials, perhaps require the reminders provided here.

BD   Charles K. Webster, ed. *British Diplomacy 1813–1815. Select Documents Dealing with the Reconstruction of Europe*. London, 1921.

GSA   Geheimes Staatsarchiv, Munich.

HHSA   Haus- Hof- und Staatsarchiv, Vienna.
  StK.   Staatskanzlei section of above.

HSA   Hauptstaatsarchiv, Stuttgart.

NP   *Aus Metternich's nachgelassenen Papieren*. Edited by Prince Richard Metternich. 8 vols. Vienna, 1880–1884.

NSHSA   Niedersächsisches Hauptstaatsarchiv, Hanover.
  Cal. Br.   Calenberger Briefschaftsarchiv section of above.
  Dep.   Deposita section of above.

PRO   Public Record Office, London.
  F.O.   Foreign Office section of above.

SUA   Státní Úsdřený Archiv, Prague.

VPR   U.S.S.R., Ministry of Foreign Affairs. *Vneshniaia politika Rossii XIX i nachala XX veka*, 1st ser. 8 vols. Moscow, 1960–1972.

ZSTA   Zentrales Staatsarchiv, Merseburg.

METTERNICH'S GERMAN POLICY

VOLUME II:

THE CONGRESS OF VIENNA, 1814–1815

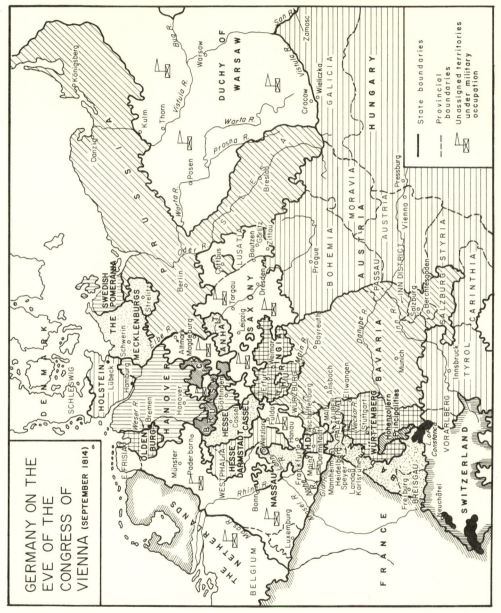

GERMANY ON THE
EVE OF THE
CONGRESS OF
VIENNA (SEPTEMBER 1814)

State boundaries

Provincial
boundaries

Unassigned territories
under military
occupation

Map drawn by Cristina Sharretts

CHAPTER I

PARIS IN THE SPRING

A CONVENIENT way of analyzing Austria's basic security interests is to imagine concentric circles with Vienna as their center marking out zones of varying importance to the survival of the monarchy. So long as Bohemia, Hungary, and the Austrian crown lands were intact, the monarchy could be said at least to exist and by the standards of the early nineteenth century to exist as a great power, though not on a par with France or Russia. In this sense the Peace of Schönbrunn in 1809 had brought the monarchy to a bare subsistence level. Beyond this minimum lay territories perhaps not necessary to the simple existence of the monarchy but of such transcendent strategic or economic importance that they had to be acquired if possible, regardless of the internal complications they might cause. Although the relative priorities might be debated, these territories were the Tyrol, which covered the Brenner Pass; the Salzburg-Inn District-Passau complex, which covered the Danube; Galicia with Cracow, which commanded the Carpathians and the Moravian Gateway; and the Illyrian provinces, which gave access to the sea and included the Croatian military frontier. Each of these areas had thresholds, so to speak, constituting a zone where it was imperative that Austrian influence preponderate, whether by annexation, dynastic union, or alliance. Lombardy-Venetia was in this zone as were Bavaria, West Galicia, and possibly Saxony. Still further out from Vienna was a zone where indirect Austrian hegemony was desirable, yet dispensable provided that no other great power established itself there. In this category were Germany, Italy, Poland, and the Ottoman Empire.

It should be emphasized that this model judges Austrian interests strictly from the vantage point of the state—its power, its security, its independence. It does not consider dynastic ties, sentimental yearnings, ethnic diversity, social values, or even the practical problems of internal administration. It is unconcerned with desires to repossess Emperor Francis's boyhood home in Tuscany; to preserve the social order; to restore the papacy to its former glory; to perpetuate the tradition of Kaunitz, say, or of Joseph II; or to keep the faith with former subjects, loyal still, in Belgium, the Breisgau, and the mediatized estates in Germany. These concerns might or might not be compatible with sheer interests of state rationally considered, and they most certainly related to reasons why many cared whether the monarchy existed or not. Nevertheless, they were luxury considerations, always

3

to be evaluated in terms of the means available once the elementary conditions of security and independence had been established. The model, moreover, incorporates possible contradictions and invidious choices. Could one take the Tyrol, Salzburg, the Inn District, and Passau from Bavaria and still keep her as an ally? Could one rely on Piedmont to check France while wrangling with her over Lombardy? Was the integrity of Saxony compatible with the good relations with Prussia that were essential to stability in Germany? No policy could succeed perfectly on all fronts; still, Metternich saw it as his task to realize as many of these objects as possible and to integrate Austrian interests with a European order that would reinforce and preserve them.

The European order—here was the overriding concern, the outer framework that was the great legislator of limits and opportunity, the concern that set the former Rhinelander apart from (one could fairly say above) most other Austrians of his generation. One might conceivably achieve every goal dictated by the model, but how long would the system hold in a Europe where France and Russia were allies or Prussia was a Russian puppet? Metternich's celebrated European outlook acquired much embellishment along the way, some of it genuine, much of it rhetorical, but the foundation of it all was neither more nor less than an appreciation of the remote interests of the monarchy upon which those closer to Vienna depended. It was a vision possible perhaps only for a man of his unique experience. He knew what independence was, from the full enjoyment of it, which he had witnessed as an ambassador in Napoleon's Paris, to the complete absence of it when he took over as foreign minister in Vienna, his options confined to "tacking, evading, and flattering." The contrast remained forever imbedded in his soul.

Tacking, evading, and flattering were habits he never outgrew. The less necessary they became, however, the less dignified they seemed to be, and that is why Metternich's critics were forever scandalized by his seeming neglect of affairs, his love of fêtes and frivolous conversation, the time he idled away planning trysts and penning amorous letters. Yet that was his peculiar way of relaxing and surely no less proper than, for example, the high-minded Wilhelm von Humboldt's notorious lust for lower-class girls, a passion freely, indeed exultantly, indulged in along the allies' line of march.[1] There is a difference between acting at random and constantly making adjustments in means for the sake of ends not readily apparent to the casual onlooker, the impatient

[1] On this surprising side of Humboldt see S. A. Kaehler, *Wilhelm von Humboldt und der Staat*, 2nd ed. (Göttingen, 1963), 59–64.

colleague, or the disappointed petitioner. The one overriding objective, the ultimate determinant of all his regional policies, including his German policy and even Austria's own territorial claims, was the establishment of an independent European center as the bulwark against the hegemony of France or Russia or, worse, the joint imperium of both. Such equilibrium was the elementary condition of Austrian independence, and from this goal his gaze never wandered, not during the grand mediation of 1813, not during the War of Liberation or the peace negotiation with France, not during the Congress of Vienna or anything that followed.

Increasingly he referred to Russia and France as "the perturbatory powers," not, it should be emphasized, because of their social and political systems, but because of their long records of seeking expansion at the expense of the weak and disorganized center. For years Austria had defended that center almost single-handedly, and in so doing had brought about her physical and financial exhaustion. Unable to bear the burden alone, she now needed the help of "the conservative powers," that is to say, those states which, like Austria herself, were presumed to have a primary interest in a stable, balanced international order regardless of what their domestic institutions were or what political ideologies they professed. The most important of these was England, and Metternich lost no time, once Castlereagh had arrived on the continent, in instructing his ambassador in London, Count Maximilian von Merveldt, on how to explain the plan there.

This principle of the conversation of order [he wrote], which should be the true maxim of state for the two monarchies, is for Austria the natural consequence of her geographical situation, for England the condition of her freedom of commerce and easy access to all the countries that form the basis of her national prosperity. . . . Placed between the great monarchies of the east and west of Europe, they are called to hold the balance between these masses, which are drawn constantly toward the center, to contain them within proper limits [*justes proportions*], and to prevent a rapprochement between them such as has once already threatened Europe with complete ruin by crushing the intermediate states.[2]

To this combination, Metternich went on, should be added Spain and Portugal, as counterweights to France, and Holland, Prussia, the German states, and even the Ottoman Empire to complete the grand alliance of the center.

[2] Mett. to Merveldt, 21 Jan. 1814, extr. in Charles Dupuis, *Le ministère de Talleyrand en 1814*, 2 vols. (Paris, 1919–1920), II, 295. (Throughout, familiar and frequently cited names will be abbreviated where no confusion results.)

Metternich left room in his system for Napoleon, provided he would accept the limits of France's monarchical frontiers. Indeed, as argued in the previous volume of this study, he hoped to the very end to save Napoleon, partly for Habsburg dynastic reasons but even more because, given Alexander's intent to overthrow him, Napoleon was now the best guarantee that France would be both strong and anti-Russian. True, Metternich intended that his intermediate system would be strong enough to discourage or even to withstand a union of the flanking powers, but until the system was actually built, it was imperative to keep the two apart. The fall of Napoleon, who believed to the end that Austria could not abandon him, thus created a situation of danger and uncertainty. Which was worse: a France in anarchy and dissolution, suddenly removed as a counterweight, or a France intact and seeking salvation by throwing herself on the generosity of the tsar? As with the European center, so with the installation of the Bourbons, a long transition was in store, and the ugly prospect was that the coalition partners would now rush in, each endeavoring to place his own imprimatur on the character and policies of the successor regime. The control of France was the key to all else. The contest with Alexander was in the open at last.

It would seem that Metternich's most consistent course, the one offering a natural opening for asserting Austrian influence in Paris, would have been the establishment of a regency under Marie Louise. This was the favorite plan of loyal Bonapartists, including most of the army and indeed almost anybody else who had reason to fear the return of the Bourbons. Napoleon himself opted for this solution, if only at the last minute. An immediate upsurge of Austrian influence and the long-term possibility that the emperor Francis's grandson would ascend the throne of France—should this prospect not have dazzled the man who in 1810 had himself conducted the Habsburg princess to Paris? In one of the most profound decisions of his career he gave a negative answer. Part of the trouble was in the timing. By the time solid offers in this direction came from Napoleon, Metternich was already drinking to the Bourbons. What credit would Austria have if she changed course daily, like the wildly fluctuating bourse in Vienna? There were more enduring considerations as well. Metternich did not confuse external symbols with reality. The mystique of Napoleon was not transferable; it was his alone, and even as he himself maintained, it required the stimulus of continual victory to be sustained. At bottom, however, considerations of diplomatic alignment were most important. A solution of this kind would be considered a concession to Austria's own particular interests, something to be subtracted from her other claims. It would also be an exceedingly poor precedent to set before Alex-

ander, whose aspiration to form a dynastic union with a restored Poland was commonly taken for granted.[3] Finally there was England. A
Bourbon France, which had been Castlereagh's hope from the beginning, would, if warmly embraced by Austria, strengthen the bond
between London and Vienna; and a bond with the impervious rock
across the channel now seemed more reliable and more predictable
than any French connection could be. For these reasons Metternich
not only did not encourage the regency movement; he took every
opportunity to dissociate the Habsburgs from the Bonaparte cause,
even, alas, at the cost of family anguish comparable only to the original
sacrifice of 1810.[4]

Thus, although expecting a struggle for influence in France, Metternich did not mean to start it himself. While fearing Franco-Russian
entente, he intended no exclusive ties of his own with France. He would
be satisfied if the new regime was reasonably stable, reasonably independent, and relatively inactive in its external relations. If France stood
still, so to speak, he could pursue his goal, described to his subordinates
at home as "the establishment of a solid system combining Austria,
England, Spain, and Prussia, to which system I undertake to gain the
complete adherence of Bavaria as a bulwark against France."[5]

By an accident of war Metternich, along with Castlereagh, Hardenberg, and the emperor Francis, was stranded in Dijon while the tsar
and the king of Prussia found themselves with Marshal Schwarzenberg
at the headquarters of the main allied army which took Paris. Given
the meek devotion of Frederick William and the subordinate position
of the allied commander, it was Alexander who shone in solitary splen-
dor at the grand military review on the Champs Elysées and received
the full force of acclaim and adulation from the war-weary populace.
He alone could speak for the allies in dealing with both Napoleon's
emissaries and Talleyrand's senatorial provisional government. Where
solemn interallied understandings existed, he could interpret them;

[3] Cf. *ibid.*, I, 243. I think Dupuis exaggerates the specifically anti-Russian impulse
in Metternich's reasoning on this particular issue, but the point is valid nonetheless.
[4] Guillaume de Bertier de Sauvigny, *The Bourbon Restoration*, trans. Lynn M. Case
(Philadelphia, 1966), 31; Alfred von Arneth, *Johann Freiherr von Wessenberg*, 2 vols.
(Vienna and Leipzig, 1898), I, 188–196; Charles K. Webster, *The Foreign Policy of
Castlereagh*, I (London, 1931), 243; Clemens Lothar Wenzel von Metternich-Winneburg, "Autobiographische Denkschrift," *Aus Metternich's nachgelassenen Papieren*, ed.
Prince Richard Metternich, 8 vols. (Vienna, 1880–1884), I, 198 (hereafter cited as
Metternich, *NP*); Wilhelm Oncken, *Das Zeitalter der Revolution, des Kaiserreichs, und
der Befreiungskriege*, 2 vols. (Berlin, 1886), II, 788–817; and Dupuis, *Talleyrand*, I,
190–192 and 243–245.
[5] Mett. to Josef von Hudelist, 24 May 1814, Vienna, Haus- Hof- und Staatsarchiv,
Staatskanzlei, Interiora, Fasc. 78, pp. 239f. (Hereafter the Haus- Hof- und Staatsarchiv in Vienna will be indicated by HHSA and the Staatskanzlei section by StK.)

where there were none, he could improvise his own. He was the man of the hour, the liberator of Europe, the benefactor of mankind.[6]

At first the group in Dijon was content to leave matters this way. Castlereagh, the author of the Bourbon restoration, doubted its popularity and preferred to have the tsar appear to bear the onus of it. Metternich was not so sanguine, but Austria faced a situation of unique delicacy. In a capital that was idolizing the hero of Moscow the sight of Emperor Francis, the man who had bartered his daughter away in 1810 and was now turning on her family, was likely to arouse disgust or perhaps refurbish the hopes of those who still favored a regency under Marie Louise. For this reason and for the sake of his own dignity Francis believed that when he entered Paris, it must be as the sponsor of the Bourbons, with the count of Artois, surrogate for Louis XVIII, at his side. When Francis's offer to this effect was refused—did the Bourbons need anyone to vouch for them?—his next plan was to have Metternich induce the king's brother to invite him to Paris as a gesture of gratitude. Such maneuvering took time, and in the absence of news there seemed no need to rush. Metternich was able to write his adored friend, Wilhelmina von Sagan, duchess of Courland, about his love of repose and his "envy of people who are always in motion and never feel." Even the hardworking Humboldt kept one of the town strumpets in his room while applying his pen to the working draft of a German constitution. Dijon, he confided to Metternich, was the best of places "because of the complaisance of the women."[7]

Then the news began to trickle in from Paris, first of the capitulation of the city on 30 March and then of the manifold activities of the tsar. Everything indicated that although he did not flatly violate interallied understandings, he far exceeded his mandate. It was quite in order, for example, to issue a manifesto declaring that the French themselves should determine their form of government. Nothing, however, required him to grant in advance an allied guarantee of whatever constitution they might adopt, let alone to encourage the Senate "to give France strong liberal institutions in line with current ideas," or to permit his own general, Count Carlo Andrea Pozzo di Borgo, and his own foreign secretary, Count Karl Nesselrode, to sit on the committee of

---

[6] Typical descriptions are those of Talleyrand and Baron vom Stein. See Charles M. de Talleyrand-Perigord, *Memoirs of the Prince de Talleyrand*, trans. Raphaël Ledos de Beaufort, 5 vols. (New York and London, 1891–1892), II, 121–123; and Stein to his wife, 10 April 1814, in Heinrich Friedrich Karl Freiherr vom Stein, *Briefe und amtliche Schriften*, ed. Erich Bozenhart/Walther Hubatsch, 10 vols. (Stuttgart, 1957–1974), IV, 692–694. (Hereafter cited as Stein, *Briefe*.)

[7] Webster, *Castlereagh*, I, 246. Dupuis, *Talleyrand*, I, 259; and Mett. to Sagan, 7 Apr. 1814, in Maria Ullrichová, ed., *Clemens Metternich—Wilhelmine von Sagan: Ein Briefwechsel 1813–1815* (Graz and Cologne, 1966), 241f.

twenty that was drafting a new constitution. Similarly, whereas the allies were agreed on the boundary of 1792, Alexander could not resist adding that they would do still more since "the welfare of Europe" required France "to be great and strong," a declaration that led many Frenchmen to expect the Rhine frontier. Toward Napoleon, long the archenemy, the tsar was equally generous, offering him the island of Elba in full sovereignty, an annual allowance of 2 million francs, and the retention of his imperial title. Metternich, who had contemplated an island in America, was aghast at the thought of having the restless genius just off the shores of France and Italy, a rallying point for subversive movements of all kinds and in easy invasion distance of the mainland. It was time to get to Paris and to try to repair the damage.[8]

Metternich, Castlereagh, and Hardenberg left Dijon on 7 April and arrived in the capital in the evening of the 10th, an Easter Sunday. Though Metternich's entries into the City of Light were never political triumphs, Paris in the spring still had its charms. The boulevards, he observed, were full of carriages and well-dressed people mingling cordially; everywhere there were hussars and cossacks, ladies wearing masks, friends greeting one another, and Napoleonic marshals suddenly sporting the white cockade of the Bourbons. Rushing immediately to the tsar's quarters, which were in Talleyrand's private residence, he found a host of familiar faces—Talleyrand, representing the provisional government; Armand Caulaincourt, Marshal Michel Ney and Marshal Alexandre MacDonald, all speaking for Napoleon; and the tsar himself with Nesselrode at his side. They had already agreed on the terms of a treaty and needed only the signatures of the ministers just arrived. Scanning the draft handed him by the Nesselrode, Metternich found the reports about Napoleon's fate confirmed and equally generous terms for his family included. Marie Louise was to receive the duchies of Parma, Piacenza, and Guastalla for herself and son. Most of the others were to receive annual allowances, and even Napoleon's stepson, Eugene Beauharnais, viceroy of Italy, was promised "a suitable establishment outside of France." The Polish legion, still at Fontainebleau with Napoleon, was to be free to return home in honor with all standards and decorations—this at Napoleon's insistence, to be sure, but who could doubt that the legion would thereby pass into the service of Russia? "Do you know whom your fine emperor likes best in the world at the present time?" Metternich asked Sagan: "The Bonapartes. He would give them the impossible if he could."[9]

[8] Dupuis, *Talleyrand*, I, 190–192, 247–259; and Bertier, *Bourbon Restoration*, 40. Text of the tsar's manifesto, which was drafted by Talleyrand, in Albert Pfister, *Aus dem Lager der Verbündeten 1814 und 1815* (Stuttgart, 1897), 230.

[9] Metternich's "Autobiographische Denkschrift," in Metternich, *NP*, I, 199–201; and Mett. to Sagan, 13 and 21 Apr. 1814 in Ullrichová, ed., *Briefwechsel*, 243 and

Metternich welcomed the arrangement for Marie Louise, and Austria had no exclusive interest in most of the other provisions, though the tsar's patronage of Prince Eugene was to generate future difficulties in Germany. Even the clause about the Polish legion was more an omen than an immediate threat. On the issue of Elba, however, he and Castlereagh pressed the argument far into the night, but to no avail. In the end both ministers concluded that a rupture of negotiations or a unilateral démarche by the tsar were greater dangers still. "The marshals must deliver the act to Napoleon this very night," said Alexander in a tone that suggested ultimatum. Shortly after midnight the treaty was signed and sent to Fontainebleau, where Napoleon affixed his signature the following day.[10] "If I had been here three days sooner, it wouldn't have happened," Metternich wrote again to Sagan of the decision on Elba. "I tell you your fine emperor has made a lot of boners and behaved like a schoolboy who has escaped from his teacher. Now that the teacher has returned, things will go better."[11] The prediction was accurate enough: things did go better though not necessarily because of the teacher's return.

To counteract both the persistent regency movement and "the isolated course that Alexander has adopted," Metternich obtained the invitation that Francis had requested and implored him to come to Paris at once. There was no chance of duplicating the tsar's triumphal entry, but the resourceful foreign minister, lover of pageantry that he was, did his best. Disregarding his master's desire for privacy as he faced reunion with his daughter, Metternich arranged what he called "a spectacle," making sure that the entry would be "solemn and not incognito." Accordingly, when Francis arrived on 15 April, he was met by the count of Artois at the head of the mounted national guard; with him were the tsar and the king of Prussia. A grand military review featuring several smart Austrian units was held in the Place de la Révolution, after which came a reception at the Senate. There Francis listened to a speech of welcome written by Napoleon's former minister, Joseph Fouché, and made a response composed by Metternich, a hom-

---

249. On the Polish legion, cf. Friedrich von Gentz's memorial on Poland in Alfons Klinkowström, ed., *Oesterreichs Theilnahme in den Befreiungskriegen* (Vienna, 1887), 391f.

[10] Metternich's "Autobiographische Denkschrift," in Metternich, *NP*, I, 199–201; Mett. to Emperor Francis, 11 Apr. 1814, in *ibid.*, II, 469f.; Castle. to Lord Liverpool, 13 Apr. 1814 in Charles K. Webster, ed., *British Diplomacy 1813–1815* (London, 1921), 175–177 (hereafter cited as *BD*). Text of treaty of Fontainebleau in Leopold Neumann, ed., *Recueil des traités et conventions conclus par l'Autriche avec les puissances étrangères, depuis 1763 jusqu'à nos jours*, 32 vols. (Leipzig and Vienna, 1855–1912), II, 450–456.

[11] Mett. to Sagan, 13 Apr. 1814, in Ullrichová, ed., *Briefwechsel*, 244.

ily that emphasized his twenty-year struggle against the principles that had desolated the world.[12]

Observers at the time considered the performance a failure, tasteless in its lack of concern for Marie Louise and an insult to the senators, most of whom had espoused revolutionary principles at one time or another and were now so incensed that they refused to record the speech in their minutes.[13] Such criticism missed the point. The spectacle was intended to dramatize the break between the Habsburgs and the Bonapartes and align them in the public mind with the returning Bourbons, for which reason Metternich in the next few days ignored Marie Louise's pathetic avowals of love for her husband and advised the emperor to send her back to Vienna, the sooner the better.[14] Nor is it easy to believe that Metternich was so inept a speechwriter. Here was rather a deliberate reminder that the Senate was not the sole authority in France and that the constitution drafted under the auspices of the tsar still needed to satisfy the principles of the returning dynasty. If feelings were hurt, so much the better. Let Alexander flatter the Bonapartists and court the French nation; Austria would sponsor the Bourbons, and one would see who won out in the end.

Indeed, there was no way to outshine the tsar. Even in affecting to yield first place to the Austrian emperor he called attention to himself and to the difference between his own charm and elegance and the dour personality of Francis, who preferred all the while to be with his daughter. Superficially this ascendancy of Alexander continued. Everywhere he spread good will and flattery, praising Gallic civilization, paying tribute to French military glory, and reminding Frenchmen that Russia alone of the conquering powers had no territorial or financial claims, not even stolen artworks to be recovered. What he did have in abundance, however, were sisters (four to be exact), one of whom, Grand Duchess Anne, he assiduously offered as a bride to the duke of Berry, heir to the French throne. Moreover, what Alexander did not say others could say for him. There was his old tutor, Frédéric La Harpe, to vouch for the tsar's devotion to the Enlightenment and liberal principles. There was, again, Pozzo di Borgo: who could better dramatize the tsar's message of brotherhood and reconciliation than this old Corsican foe of the Bonapartes now serving in both the Russian

---

[12] Mett. to Francis, 13 Apr. 1814, extr. in Dupuis, *Talleyrand*, I, 260; *ibid.*, 260–262; and Humboldt to his wife, Caroline, 15 Apr. 1814, in *Wilhelm und Caroline von Humboldt in ihren Briefen*, ed. Anna von Sydow, 7 vols. (1907–1918, reprinted. Osnabrück, 1968), IV, 311f. (hereafter cited as Humboldt, *Briefe*).

[13] Dupuis, *Talleyrand*, I, 262; and Albert Sorel, *L'Europe et la révolution française*, 8 vols. (Paris, 1885–1904), VIII, 334f.

[14] Egon Cäsar Conte Corti, *Metternich und die Frauen*, 2 vols. (Zürich and Vienna, 1948–1949), I, 439–442.

army and the Senate's constitution committee and preaching the doctrine of Franco-Russian entente? There was as well the Polish patriot, Prince Adam Czartoryski, chief architect of Alexander's Polish plans, who provided a Russophile leadership for the still numerous Poles, many of whom did not go immediately home but stayed on in Paris to lobby for a restoration of their kingdom. Only one of the tsar's old confidants of the war years was a liability in Paris: Baron Heinrich Karl vom Stein, the German patriot, who looked on with disgust as "this corrupt, shameless, and dissolute French race already abuses the emperor Alexander's generosity and goodness."[15] Stein's loss, however, was Talleyrand's gain.

It is not necessary to impute malevolence or calculation to all that the tsar did, to deny the spirit of magnanimity in his moves, or to question his humanitarian interests. On the contrary, the more benevolent he was the more overwhelming his ascendancy might be; Napoleon too had had grand visions, and these had helped him to conquer the continent. The pursuit of high ideals is no more exempt from the play of interests than is the pursuit of power. The difference is that the idealist is usually more indifferent to the interests of others. The others in turn take the opposite view, for the best way to combat virtue is to represent it as deception and hypocrisy. And so it was that in a contest for influence in France, Russia, with fewer claims than the rest and physical remoteness, was in a position, like Woodrow Wilson a century later, to set the standard of generosity high and at every turn to expose the pettiness and rapacity of the others. "This consideration was the deciding factor," said Friedrich von Gentz afterwards in explaining the moderation of the final peace terms.[16]

Although Alexander's generosity was directed at France as a whole, the particular beneficiary was the provisional government, which Talleyrand and the tsar alike expected to continue in power, transformed somewhat under the constitution that the Senate committee had drafted even before Napoleon's abdication. This draft evolved into the famous Constitutional Charter, but its contents bear repeating here if only because many of the Rheinbund sovereigns quickly came to appreciate it as a model for their own efforts to fend off counterrevolution in Germany. The Imperial Senate and Legislative Body were to be perpetuated and expanded, the one by the admission of additional peers from the traditional nobility, the other by a complicated system of election based on a narrow franchise of wealth. The existing judicial and administrative systems were to be left intact and officials kept in

[15] Stein to his wife, 10 Apr. 1814, in Stein, *Briefe*, IV, 694.
[16] Gentz to Karadja, 13 June 1814, in Klinkowström, *Oesterreichs Theilnahme*, 368.

their posts. The civil rights of Frenchmen were defined and safeguards inserted to prevent reprisals against supporters of previous regimes. Significantly, Metternich, who was apprised of this document almost on his arrival to Paris, was on the whole satisfied. Even under the duress of the preceding month he had himself acquiesced in the Bourbon restoration only when assured that there would be no counter-revolution, which he feared would begin the revolution all over again. His first impression was that the constitution was much like the English, "very constitutional and monarchical."[17]

The choice of words was prophetic, for as time went on it became clear that where he stressed the monarchical, Talleyrand and the tsar emphasized the constitutional, regarding the document as the expression of a national will that was to dominate the crown. Until the arrival of Louis XVIII himself on 3 May it was their interpretation that prevailed, sobering testimony to the supremacy of Bonapartism over true royalism. Our concern with these familiar facts of French domestic history is their effect on diplomatic alignments. No one could be certain, but in the simplified projections of the day a strong monarch was equated with an anti-Russian, a strong senate with a pro-Russian orientation. Count Ernst Münster of Hanover considered the trend to senatorial supremacy "more dangerous than the French boundary question,"[18] and Gentz, hearing of these developments from a distance, was as usual more pessimistic than his chief. "I would rather have kept Napoleon himself with the frontier of the Rhine and the Alps," he complained from Vienna, "than experience the complete triumph of all false and pernicious principles under the guise of restoring the Bourbons."[19] Metternich, meanwhile, was not the active participant in French politics that Alexander was, but his stake in the Bourbons grew apace, becoming increasingly intrinsic rather than merely a matter of building bridges to England. The primacy of the diplomatic motive, however, remained. Almost by accident he who had been the leading champion of Napoleon was now in the camp of traditional monarchy, while Alexander, once the implacable foe of Napoleon, was aligned with his late followers.

Regardless of the outcome of the internal jousting, which for the remainder of April ran in favor of national, as opposed to monarchical sovereignty, the position of France as a power continued to improve. All the allies were worried that unrest in the country might upset everybody's calculations; all were witness to skirmishes between the

---

[17] Mett. to Francis, 11 Apr. 1814, Metternich, *NP*, II, 472.
[18] Münster to Prince Regent, 20 Apr. 1814, in George Herbert Count Münster, *Political Sketches of the State of Europe from 1814–1867* (Edinburgh, 1868), 152.
[19] Gentz to Mett., 24 Apr. 1814, in Klinkowström, *Oesterreichs Theilnahme*, 325f.

populace and the occupation authorities; all wanted normal relations as soon as possible; and all were concerned about the sizable garrisons of Napoleonic veterans still holding outposts beyond the frontier of 1792, some as far off as the Elbe and the Oder. They included some of the most fanatical, and it was hard to tell whether they would be more dangerous in Germany and Italy or back home in France as disaffected losers. Talleyrand was the ingenious author of the notion that both the peaceful capitulation of these troops and their subsequent reconciliation to the Bourbon monarchy could be facilitated by allowing them to march home in honor in exchange for the evacuation of sacred French soil. On 23 April an armistice was signed on this basis, the French boundary being provisionally defined as that of 1 January 1792. A similar arrangement for the transfer of a French fleet then in British hands at Antwerp was generally agreed to, even by Castlereagh, but vetoed by Lord Liverpool in London.[20]

Although the exchange of troops went on over a period of weeks, the armistice marked a new stage in great-power relations. Among the allies the evacuation of France removed one of the last elements of military necessity holding them together. There remained, to be sure, a formidable ring of armies on the French frontier, but their effectiveness would henceforth depend on the voluntary collaboration of conventional diplomacy, specifically a willingness to observe interallied obligations under the Treaty of Chaumont. For France itself the armistice marked the attainment of parity as a negotiating power, a status implicitly acknowledged in the concomitant decision to make the peace with France in some sense preliminary[21] and to follow it up with a general congress, to which, according to Castlereagh, "we propose to admit the French ambassador."[22]

[20] Dupuis, *Talleyrand*, I, 265–267; Castle. to Liverpool, 19 April 1814, in Robert Stewart, Charles William Vane, 2nd marquess of Londonderry, *Memoirs and correspondence of Viscount Castlereagh*, ed. Charles Vane, 3rd marquess of Londonderry, 12 vols. (London, 1848–1853), IX, 473 (hereafter cited as *Castle. Corr.*). Text of the convention in Neumann, *Traités par l'Autriche*, II, 457–461.

[21] The matter is best put this way because the sources do not make clear whether there was to be a *preliminary* treaty followed by a *definitive* treaty with France and then a general congress for the European settlement or whether the definitive treaty with France was to form part of the congress business. This ambiguity pervades both the "Protocole d'une conference du 13 avril 1814" in U.S.S.R., Ministry of Foreign Affairs, *Vneshniaia politika Rossii XIX i nachala XX veka*, 1st ser., 8 vols. (Moscow, 1960–1972), VII, 647f. (hererafter cited as *VPR*), and Castlereagh's report to Liverpool on the conference, 13 Apr. 1814, *Castle. Corr.*, IX, 459–461. Subsequent events and the tradition shaped by them are the main basis of the first assumption; the language, however, seems to favor the second interpretation, which would mean that what became known as the Treaty of Paris of 30 May 1814 was originally intended to be preliminary and that the congress was to be in close association with it. As it happened, of course, the Hundred Days made the treaty "preliminary" in a sense that no one had foreseen.

[22] Castle. to Liverpool, 19 Apr. 1814, in *Castle. Corr.*, IX, 472f.

Although subject to various interpretations, this last proviso is perhaps the best key of all to the shifting diplomatic alignments. Only a few weeks before, Alexander had agreed to a program of moderate war aims designed to keep France strong only on condition that she be excluded from a voice in the peace settlement beyond her frontiers; if France must be left intact, he had insisted, she must be a diplomatic cipher.[23] Castlereagh at the time considered this a harsh demand to make of a great power, and later, at the Congress of Châtillon, Caulaincourt had tried to circumvent the disability by proposing a two-stage operation: first a peace for France and then a general settlement "in order that we not be excluded and at the same time that the conclusion of peace not be delayed."[24] Now, only about five weeks later, this is precisely what the allies were offering, and no one with more enthusiasm than the tsar. In view of the fact that he continued at Paris the same silence he had kept before—at Reichenbach, at Teplitz, at Frankfurt, at Troyes, and at Châtillon—about his specific demands in Poland, the reasonable assumption was that he now expected a grateful France under Talleyrand's direction to support him when all the powers were assembled and no distinctions drawn between victor and vanquished.

Metternich, conversely, who had once visualized himself presiding over a congress as the grand mediator between east and west, now began to discount the future congress as a mere formality, a ceremony "less for negotiation than for signing."[25] France must be committed to a congenial European settlement before the congress took place, or, to use the phraseology of the draft treaty that he put forward for discussion on 9 May, the purpose of the congress would be to regulate "the state of future possessions of each [power] and their relations among themselves in conformance with the treaties and engagements that they have mutually contracted."[26] But how to induce the French government voluntarily to surrender the voice in a European settlement that it had so long and so sedulously pursued? The leverage Metternich found was not specifically Austrian but lay rather in the hands of his allies. England still held numerous colonies scheduled for return to France, and these could be withheld as bargaining material, a tactic that Metternich implored Castlereagh to adopt. The other advantage Metternich had was that Prussia's need for a settlement was even greater than Austria's. Britain, in possession of colonies, Austria

---

[23] Cf. Vol. I of this study, 289–317 (hereafter cited as Kraehe, I).
[24] Caulaincourt to Napoleon, 15 Mar. 1814, as quoted in Karl Griewank, *Der Wiener Kongress und die Neuordnung Europas 1814–1815* (Leipzig, 1942), 60.
[25] Mett. to Hudelist, 24 May 1814, HHSA, StK., Interiora, Fasc. 78.
[26] Text in Dupuis, *Talleyrand*, I, 343.

with a large army in northern Italy, and Russia, her military buildup going forward in Poland, already occupied the bulk of the territories they claimed. Not so Prussia, which held a part of the Rhineland but not Saxony or any of Poland. Despite the close bond between Frederick William and Alexander, moreover, the Russian alliance had a peculiar flaw in that the major Prussian advocates of the alliance—patriots and army officers for the most part, the very men who had inspired the headlong drive to Paris and who were now the toast of Europe—were also the main advocates of a harsh peace. The latter in fact were outraged at the boundary of 1792 and recalled that Alexander had once mentioned the cession of Alsace, whereas he was now pledged to leave France with even more than the boundary of 1792.

These considerations, together with Hardenberg's own uneasiness about the Russian advance into Central Europe, created the conditions for close collaboration at a time when a Franco-Russian entente seemed imminent. Castlereagh, who would have preferred to leave everything but the peace with France to the general congress, complained of the lack of progress, which he attributed both to bickering about the boundary question and to "the strong desire felt by Austria and Prussia to bring both Russia and France to some understanding upon the main principles of the continental arrangements, in a secret article or otherwise, previous to our stipulating away our conquests. . . ."[27] Here we have another reversal. At the Congress of Châtillon the outline of a general settlement had been shown to France as a courtesy, a preview of what she could expect if she made peace but without obligation on her part. Now "the main principles of the continental arrangements," when and if agreement was reached among the allies, were to be demands that she must meet in order to have peace, binding obligations that she must help enforce. The one constant, however, was that now as then the signature of Russia was as important as that of France.

As explained earlier,[28] the allies were already pledged among themselves to certain rudiments of the general peace settlement. As listed in the secret articles of the Treaty of Chaumont and other instruments, these included a Spain restored to the Bourbons, an independent Holland, enlarged by the annexation of Belgium, an Italy of independent states, a Swiss federation under great-power guarantee, and a "Germany composed of sovereign princes united by a federal bond that shall assure and guarantee the independence of Germany." The one glaring omission was a precise statement on the future of Poland, but even the other terms required elaboration and refinement, notably in

[27] Castle. to Liverpool, 5 May 1814 in *BD*, 180. Cf. Griewank, *Wiener Kongress*, 61.

[28] Kraehe, I, chap. x.

regard to drawing geographical boundaries and, in the case of Germany, an explication of the term "federal bond" as well. The colonial settlement, also unspecified, was another omission, and Metternich hoped to use this to enforce on France a commitment to support his interpretation of the other points—this, as noted, in contrast to the negotiations at Châtillon, where she was merely shown the articles as a courtesy, not asked to join in imposing them. In this way, France would continue on the sidelines until the allies settled these questions among themselves. The Congress of Vienna must not extend the dismal legacies of Teschen, Regensburg, and Tilsit.

CHAPTER II

PEACEMAKING AND THE FUTURE
OF GERMANY

A S Metternich turned his attention from the prospects on the Seine
to the vast space between the Vistula and the Rhine, the outlook
for a strong and independent center seemed more remote than ever.
A voiceless France was better than a vote for Russia but no substitute
for the counterforce that Napoleon had once provided. That force
must now be supplied by Britain and Prussia, but the former conferred
her favors on both central powers alike, and the latter aimed at a
European center built more around her than Austria. With France
removed from the equation Hardenberg in truth now occupied the
pivotal position of mediator between Austria and Russia. This shift in
alignment, moreover, was accompanied by growing unrest in that kal-
eidoscopic world of the third Germany where, as in France itself, the
forces of restoration engaged in continual skirmishing with the established governments of the Napoleonic period and where millions of
"souls" waited uneasily from one day to the next wondering where
new boundaries would be drawn and who their new sovereigns would
be.

Metternich had all along based his German policy on the existing
governments, seeing in them the foundations of order and political
calculability, the only alternatives to anarchy and unrestrained contention among the powers. Now those governments were under heavy
attack: by the mediatized houses,[1] which drew renewed hope from the
fall of Napoleon; by Baron Stein, who used all the resources of his
Central Administrative Council to harass "the petty despots," as he
called the ruling princes; by Hardenberg, who believed that their weakness augmented Prussia's strength; and by countless sentimentalists
and former officials of the Reich, who dreamed of returning to the
good old days before Bonaparte. Morally the Rheinbund regimes bore
the stigma of long collaboration with the tyrant, and Metternich's wartime arguments that their military resources were essential to the allied
cause no longer applied. Each day that passed without a settlement in

---

[1] I.e., those imperial princes, counts, and knights who had once held their estates
directly from the emperor but under the Rheinbund had been subordinated to the
sovereignty of another prince formerly no more than their equal. Imperial princes
and counts, as members of the peerage, were called *Standesherren*, a term for which
there is no exact translation and that will hereafter be used without italics. See
Kraehe, I, 315–318.

Germany increased anxiety, undermined stability, and increasingly embarrassed Metternich's defense of these regimes.

Paradoxically, one of the results of the intensified struggle was a reversal of attitudes toward the Rheinbund Act of 1806. To the mediatized nobility this document had always loomed as the instrument of their suffering and degradation though in fact it contained important safeguards of their rights: notably local administration of justice, control of manorial facilities, tax exemption on a par with members of the ruling houses, and criminal trial only by one's peers. In the heyday of the Rheinbund these provisions had been violated often enough, as in the egregious case of Count Johann Philipp Stadion, whose income was impounded by the king of Württemberg, but cases of compliance had been common too, notably in Baden and here and there in North Germany wherever traditional patterns of life remained relatively undisturbed. Now that the Rheinbund was gone, however, these safeguards were sorely missed, for the ruling houses, once the principal beneficiaries of the Rheinbund Act, suddenly found themselves free from even its mild restraints and acted accordingly. Anticipating the vengeful restorative trend that was in fact taking place as Napoleon staggered to his fall, they rushed to complete the administrative centralization of their states before new controls could be imposed by the allies and inconvenient territorial exchanges enforced.

In Württemberg King Frederick continued his notorious ways, prolonging his harassment of Stadion and driving his own brother to beg Stein's help in redressing his grievances. In self-imposed exile in St. Petersburg, Duke Alexander of Württemberg brooded over an appanage the king had cancelled and demanded compensation—even a mediatized property, he told Stein, so long as it was not under the sovereignty of his brother. "Let one ask his brothers, the house of Hohenlohe, Count Stadion, or Prince Metternich," the duke added, "and so many others who have the misfortune to live under the *Landeshoheit* of Württemberg, if my worries are unfounded or not."[2] More significant were the complaints raised against Grand Duke Charles of Baden, for they signaled a change of policy by a house that had heretofore enjoyed good relations with its mediatized subjects. With territorial disfigurement imminent and future federal regulation uncertain, Charles belatedly set about integrating his lands and consolidating his controls. Thus, illustrious princely families like the Loewensteins and the Leiningens lost their patrimonial powers, and found their officials ousted and their bailiwicks reorganized under state direction.

[2] Alexander of Württemberg to Stein, 4 May 1814, in Stein, *Briefe*, IV, 759f. The term *Landeshoheit*, though often equated with sovereignty, actually implied in usage derived from the Holy Roman Empire a limited fealty to the emperor and certain restraints in the treatment of subjects.

Wertheim, the seat of the Loewensteins, was occupied by the grand duke's troops, and a councilor of the prince was arrested for publishing a pamphlet critical of the Rheinbund regime. As a result of the experience, the privy councilor, Baron Franz von Gärtner, who brought the news to Metternich and the others at Dijon, became a believer in freedom of the press. Stein, who did not respond to every petty complaint, in this case implored Hardenberg to intercede directly with the grand duke.[3]

The situation in the South was exacerbated by the ferocious determination of Stein and his recruitment chief, Otto Rühle von Lilienstern, to organize a Germany-wide popular militia or *Landsturm*, based on the demanding Prussian model. The *Landsturm* incorporated elective local defense committees, and was divided into districts with the martial name of *Bannerschaften*, which often cut across state boundaries and challenged the existing state authorities, even to impeding their regular military operations. In Münster's disapproving words, the program violated the accession treaties and treated the princes as nothing better than "amnestied enemies." There was a strong impulse of revenge in these arrangements, for the command of such districts fell with conspicuous frequency on mediatized noblemen. In Nassau, for example, where the reigning duke, Frederick William, managed to keep things in his own hands by declaring his son the *Bannerherr*, Rühle did everything in his power to have him removed in favor of the prince of Wied-Neuwied, one of the duke's most truculent mediatized subjects. Grand Duke Louis of Hesse-Darmstadt took a similar precaution, but Rühle ignored him and appointed the count of Erbach, who thereupon tried to rally support by telling the people of Erbach that they were no longer bound by the grand duke's tax and conscription laws. Louis won out in the end because the allied powers backed the sovereign princes, but not before it came to open violence in Erbach and covert resistance in the other mediatized lands of the state. All in all, it was a portentous sight: a mediatized count standing at the head of his subjects as their military leader, their *Bannerherr*.[4]

In North Germany conditions, though less turbulent, were more unsettled still. There whole governments had disappeared—Westphalia, Berg, the grand duchy of Frankfurt, and the French regime in the northwest—without successor states yet filling the void. The fate of large areas such as Saxony, Posen, and the whole left bank of the

---

[3] Gärtner to Stein, 29 Mar. 1814, and Stein to Hard., 14 May 1814, in Stein, *Briefe*, IV, 674 and 790 respectively.

[4] Kraehe, I, 247–249; Münster to Stein, 13 Mar. 1814, Stein, *Briefe*, IV, 634–635; Baron Marschall von Bieberstein to Stein, 11 Mar., and Baron Johann von Türckheim to Stein, 9 Mar. 1814, in *ibid.*, IV, 626–628 and 611–612; and Julius Reinhart Dietrich, "Hessen-Darmstadt auf dem Wiener Kongress und die Erwerbung Rheinhessens," *Quellen und Forschungen zur hessischen Geschichte*, IV (1917), 220.

Rhine, was still undetermined. As a result most of North Germany was subject to martial law and the controls of Stein's administrative department. Even for Germany as a whole it is no exaggeration to say that more people than not were unsure of who their future rulers would be or what kind of government they would have. The lands of the mediatized nobility alone accounted for a population of 1,202,662, approximately equal to that of Württemberg.[5] The surviving Rheinbund states in the north, most of them small, felt particularly menaced by this situation and feared that in the coming reorganization they were almost certain to be mediatized. To forestall this fate Princess Caroline of Schwarzburg-Rudolstadt and Crown Prince George of Mecklenburg-Strelitz turned to Humboldt for support, the man known for his pride in the diversity of German culture and his interest in preserving the fragments of history. Their best protection, he replied, was to avoid arbitrary acts and accept some limits on their authority under a German constitution—which was not quite what they wanted to hear.[6]

Both these sovereigns had the good fortune to live outside Stein's jurisdiction. Prince George Henry of Waldeck and the duke of Anhalt-Bernburg, by contrast, had to deal with agents of the administrative department and engaged in constant bickering with them over the rights of the *Ritterschaft* and other subjects. The prince of Waldeck in fact, though he had no mediatized nobility to contend with, seized what he considered to be his last chance to emulate his South German colleagues in replacing an old-style constitution based on the estates with a more centralized regime. In an edict of 28 January 1814, he abolished all tax exemptions and bypassed the estates in setting up what was called the French system of taxation, which emphasized the personal income tax rather than the property tax. The estates complained, and Stein threatened the prince with intervention by "higher authorities" if he did not mend his ways. Waldeck, with a population of 50,000, was not important in itself, but episodes of this kind strengthened the hand of those who advocated allied action to halt "arbitrary" deeds and to reassure subjects that their rights would be protected and their wrongs righted regardless of who their future sovereigns might be.[7]

Under such pressure Metternich had long since retreated from his original position that a future German league should be little more

[5] Statistics and commentary in a memorial of Count Solms-Laubach, 5 May 1814, HHSA, StK., Kongressakten, Cart. 6, p. 201. Curiously enough, Solms himself understated his case, using Hesse-Darmstadt (pop. 541,000) rather than Württemberg.

[6] Humb. to Princess Caroline, 9 Dec. 1813, 25 May and 2 Aug. 1814; to Staatsminister Oertzen, 8 May 1814; and to Prince George, 27 Aug. 1814, all in Wilhelm von Humboldt, *Wilhelm von Humboldts gesammelte Schriften*, ed. Albert Leitzmann and others (1903–1936; reprint ed. Berlin, 1967–1968) XVII, 36–39 and 64–72.

[7] Dalwig to Stein, 3 and 11 May 1814; and Stein to the prince of Waldeck, 24 May 1814, in Stein, *Briefe*, IV, 752f., 790f., and 818f. respectively.

than an extended system of alliances among equals with no powers over the internal affairs of its members.[8] He was now committed to the principle that certain supervisory powers, still to be defined, should be concentrated in a directory composed of the larger states, usually taken to be Austria, Prussia, Bavaria, Hanover, and Württemberg, the last-named at the insistence of the tsar. Metternich was also on record as endorsing a resolution adopted by the allied ministers on 23 March that condemned arbitrary measures against the mediatized houses, and he himself proposed that Count Friedrich Christian Solms-Laubach, head of the Association of Mediatized Houses, draw up a list of the rights that should be guaranteed to his constituents. The other allied ministers agreed, insisting as well that a public declaration of allied endorsement should follow.[9] Metternich's initiative is surprising, especially as he really hoped to limit action to confidential warnings to the sovereign princes, but he evidently felt sure that he could prevent a public manifesto if it ever came to that. Besides, in times of raging emotions and righteous indignation bills of particulars take time and tend to bring people down to earth.[10]

In the two weeks in Dijon following the adoption of the resolution, the principal ministers, immersed in the war and the negotiations with France, left the German question to lower-level discussions, mainly between Münster and Humboldt. Count Stadion probably participated for Austria, but there is no record of his contribution or even whether he was authorized to speak officially, for when it came to the German constitution Metternich preferred to let others make proposals.[11] Stein was apparently too busy with the affairs of the Central Administrative Council to play an active role, but a constitutional draft he had written in Chaumont in early March served as a starting point. Its main features were a four-power directory with Württemberg excluded, a federal

[8] Münster to Castle., 8 Feb. 1814: "Prince Metternich, who formerly considered interference in these matters to be inadvisable, is at present convinced of the necessity of securing [the rights of the estates] by the Laws of the league," enforcement to be by the courts of each of the directing powers. This report in Niedersächsisches Hauptstaatsarchiv, Hanover, Dep. 110 A, III, No. 2. (Hereafter this repository will be abbreviated NSHSA. The designation Hanover, Dep. 110 A refers to the private papers of Count Ernst Herbert von Münster-Derneburg.)

[9] Kraehe, I, 317.

[10] Solms-Laubach to Münster, 31 [Dec. probably] 1814, in NSHSA, Hanover, Des. 91, No. 20. This is a letter of transmittal for his memorandum, "which I wrote in May of this year at the instance of Prince Metternich." On private warnings see Nesselrode to Mett., 23 Mar. 1814 in Prague, Státní Ústřední Archiv, Rodinný archiv Metternišsky, Acta Clementina, Correspondance politique Autriche, Cart. 3, folder 59–A, p. 3. These are the Metternich family papers in the state archives of Czechoslovakia, which will hereafter be cited as SUA, Prague. Correspondance politique will hereafter be rendered as Corr. pol.

[11] Cf. Hellmuth Rössler, *Österreichs Kampf um Deutschlands Befreiung*, 2 vols. (Hamburg, 1940), II, 201f.

legislature composed both of governmental envoys and of deputies from the estates, and a detailed bill of aristocratic rights. More spitefully he proposed that ruling princes live solely on their private revenue without a civil list.[12] Münster, who visualized Hanover, when restored, as an old-fashioned hierarchy of traditional orders (*Ständestaat*), sympathized with the rights of noblemen, but as the minister of a crowned head himself, he refused to give up civil lists or to grant the representatives of subjects seats side by side with the envoys of their sovereigns.

His main concern, however, was to counteract the influence of his powerful Prussian neighbor by adding Württemberg, Holland, and Switzerland to the directory. Württemberg's place was in any case assured "because the tsar desired it" and morally justified by the military exploits of Crown Prince William, while the inclusion of Holland and Switzerland as members of the confederation was recommended in many quarters to protect the German flanks. Regarding the rights of subjects Münster's ideas did not differ much from Stein's except possibly for a greater interest in freedom of the press (which, however, despite his Anglo-Saxon associations, he apparently considered compatible with the continuation of preventive censorship). Rather than listing those rights, however, he enunciated a principle, one that was to be much cited in the days ahead. In point of law, he argued, the abolition of the supreme imperial constitution did not free monarchs to rule as they pleased because the constitutions within their lands remained intact, retaining their old validity and providing the most sensible basis for discussions. Sovereignty, the seeming gift of the Rheinbund Act and the accession treaties, was being eroded by tricks of definition.[13]

Humboldt, meanwhile, looking beyond the contents of a German constitution to the leverage for securing its adoption, was anxious to link the project to the intended declaration of rights, hoping thereby to bind the allies to a comprehensive program all at once. Without a brief description of the future constitution, he argued, a declaration might arouse exaggerated hopes in the populace at large and needless anxieties among the sovereign houses. Accordingly, he proposed that as a minimum mention be made of a directory, a military organization,

[12] Text in Stein, *Briefe*, IV, 612f. Cf. Kraehe, I, 316f.

[13] Münster's memorandum of 31 Mar. 1814, Dijon, in Zentrales Staatsarchiv, Historische Abteilung II, Merseburg, 2, 4.1. I, No. 1454. (This archive, which houses the old Prussian State Archives, will hereafter be cited as ZSTA, Merseburg, as officially requested.) The memorandum is summarized in W. A. Schmidt, *Geschichte der deutschen Verfassungsfrage während der Befreiungskriege und des Wiener Kongresses*, ed. Alfred Stern (Stuttgart, 1890), 131–141; and Karl Friedrich Brandes, *Graf Münster und die Wiedererstehung Hannovers 1809–1815* (Urach, Württemberg, 1938).

a federal court, a guarantee of provincial estates, freedom of the press, religious equality, and special consideration for the mediatized houses. Russia and England, he added, should be designated guarantors of the confederation even as France and Russia had been in the later years of the Reich. In a ten-point bill of rights he included *habeus corpus*, an independent judiciary, the rights of emigration, of university attendance and state employment anywhere in Germany, and again freedom of the press, the last within the limits set "by a just and reasonable censorship" to assure uniform standards in Germany. The remaining four points pertained to the traditional rights of the mediatized houses only. All in all, the public was to be told "that the allied courts are working continuously to let Germany have a constitution as much like the former one as possible," different only so far as existing practical realities required.[14]

As previously explained,[15] however, Humboldt was more than a sentimental restorationist; he was a Prussian statesman. In a project drafted for confidential use by the cabinets only[16] he rejected Münster's plan for the directory, ignoring the tsar's interest in Württemberg and making Holland and Switzerland allies of the confederation rather than full-fledged members. Next, by assigning Austria and Prussia two votes each while Bavaria and Hanover were to alternate in possessing one or two, he in effect salvaged the principle of an Austro-Prussian condominium which had been the essence of his December plan. This concept was then to be reinforced by dividing Germany into four districts called *Kreise*, each administered in executive and military affairs and to some extent in judicial matters[17] by one of the directors, the Kreise of Bavaria and Hanover, however, being limited essentially to their own territory. All states were to be represented in a federal diet (in which the directorial states among them would have a majority) and all enjoined "to institute or reestablish provincial estates," with power over taxation, government borrowing, an annual accounting, and the right of remonstrance against administrative abuses, the aim being to approximate the rights once enjoyed by the estates under the Reich. For the mediatized houses Humboldt favored special privileges

[14] "Mémoire préparatoire pour les conférences des cabinets alliés sur les affaires de l'Allemagne," Apr. 1814; and "Exposé des droits de tout sujet Allemand en général et des Princes et Comtes médiatisés en particulier," in Humboldt, *Gesammelte Schriften*, XI, ed. Bruno Gebhardt (Berlin, 1967–1968), 204–211 and 217–219. Last quotation from p. 208.

[15] Kraehe, I, 272–275.

[16] Text in Humboldt, *Gesammelte Schriften*, XI, 211–217.

[17] All states with a population of less than 100,000 would have to allow their subjects access to the supreme court of the *Kreis* director. Because the term *Kreis* in this connection has a special meaning fundamental to this study, I shall henceforth import it into English.

under federal guarantee but only within existing states, not in the form of restoring their previous autonomy.

Humboldt's ideas may be justly admired as constituting an ingenious effort to reconcile traditional imperial institutions with Prussia's drive for equality to Austria, and indeed many of them eventually found their way into the Federal Act of 1815. How liberal or how national they were is another matter, best left for the time being for others to dispute.[18] In the immediate situation, however, progress was slow, especially after discussions were removed to Paris, where other problems competed for attention. By the end of April Münster could report "the willingness to admit Württemberg to the directory," but he and Humboldt continued to disagree about the preponderance of Austria and Prussia on it, Münster favoring absolute equality of all members together with a rotating chairmanship, which Hardenberg himself had once promised him.[19] On the related issue of Switzerland's connection with the Bund the two were closer together, but they encountered the opposition of those who favored simple neutrality for the Alpine cantons. The argument was made, probably by the Russians, that Germany could not hire enough Swiss mercenaries to justify Switzerland's renouncing the right to export troops to any country that wanted to pay for them. "The plan of the German constitution," Münster had to report, "remains nearly the same as that proposed at Langres"—that is to say, agreement only that Germany would be a confederation.[20]

Neither was the promised declaration of rights forthcoming. On 5 May Count Solms completed his statement on the matter, but it was not really a bill of rights. It was rather a long constitutional treatise and legal brief tracing the history of the iniquities visited upon the mediatized houses and explaining why it was "not possible that Europe be returned to the footing of 1789 and Germany alone remain at the status quo of 1813." The very nomenclature was nostalgic. Germany formed "a sovereign Reich," headed preferably by an "hereditary Kaiser," and only as a last resort by a directory. The diet was a *Reichsrat*, the sovereign princes *Regenten*, and states again *Länder*, in which the mediatized houses formed "a special class." The problem was how to reconcile princely sovereignty with limits on its exercise, and Solms

---

[18] E.g., Marianne Goerdeler, *Die Reichsidee in den Bundesplänen und ihr geistiger Hintergrund* (Weida in Thüringen, 1943); Friedrich Meinecke, *Weltbürgertum und Nationalstaat*, 5th ed. (Munich and Berlin, 1919), 192–205; Bruno Gebhardt, *Wilhelm von Humboldt als Staatsman*, 2 vols. (1896; reprint ed. Aalen, 1965), II, 24; Kaehler, *Humboldt und der Staat*, 250–279.

[19] Münster to Castle., 8 Feb. 1814, NSHSA, Hanover, Dep. 110 A III, No. 2.

[20] Münster to Prince Regent, 27 Apr. 1814, in Münster, *Political Sketches*, 160; Same to same, 17 Sept. 1814, extr. in Dupuis, *Talleyrand*, II, 325; and Humboldt's memorial, "Über den Anschluss der Schweiz an Deutschland," 2 Aug. 1814 in Humboldt, *Gesammelte Schriften*, XI, 136–139.

was zealous in his search for precedents, finding them in everything from a letter patent of Louis XIV to the count of Hanau in Alsace in 1701 to the Rheinbund Act of 1806. Solms was probably the first systematically to articulate the possibility of turning the hated Rheinbund Act to advantage, holding that it transferred to the sovereign princes certain powers previously exercised by the sovereign Reich but did not essentially infringe the traditional powers of the mediatized houses within their own domains. The pillars of the Rheinbund, he held, did not consider themselves any the less sovereign for accepting these limits and recognizing Napoleon's right as protector to enforce them from above. Why should the allies voluntarily grant them more? In fact, Solms concluded, the Act would have served tolerably well if Napoleon, in return for troops, had not encouraged the new sovereigns to ignore it. It should be emphasized that Solms was not so much judging the validity of the Rheinbund Act as seeking in it a restrictive definition of sovereignty that could then be applied to the accession treaties. The argument resembled Münster's thesis about the continuity of the territorial constitutions dating back to imperial times; it was more realistic, however, because it assumed the validity of the accession treaties, of which the principal author was Metternich.[21]

More clearly focused on the specific rights of the mediatized houses was a memorial by Gärtner, likewise drafted by request "of the higher-ups," though we do not know whom. Personal rights on his list (which future developments compel us to give here in some detail) included free choice of residence and state service anywhere in Europe, the inviolability of family compacts and inheritance laws, the title of "ruling lord," the abrogation of all fealty to a sovereign prince, complete exemption from personal and household taxes, and privileged treatment in courts of law, with the right of appeal to "a supreme German tribunal." Public rights amounted to the exercise of virtually all local government, including regulation of schools, churches, foundations, mines, and forests; control of records and domain and chamber accounts, and courts of both first and second instance. In regard to the all-important financial settlement, the Standesherren were to recover all rents, dues, regalian fees, and other income enjoyed before 1806, except for the so-called *Kontribution*, the special tax that in the Reich had been levied for Kreis and imperial defense and always kept in a separate account. The list was comprehensive, aiming at the restoration of the old privileges as well as the abolition of such irritating Rheinbund legislation as requiring a certain period of residence each year in the sovereign's capital. The premise was that if these rights could be guar-

---

[21] "Idee des Grafen Solms-Laubach über Deutschlands künftige Gestaltung," Frankfurt, 5 May 1814, in HHSA, StK. Kongressakten, Cart. 6, pp. 189–222.

anteed, it would not matter so much what participation the mediatized were granted in the day-to-day operation of the future Bund. Though not officially submitted at the time, the memorial defined the official position of the Association of Mediatized Houses.[22]

Solm's treatise was completed 5 May, Gärtner's by 16 May. If Metternich had merely been waiting for some way to reconcile the rights of the mediatized with the terms of his treaties, he, or more likely Gentz, could easily have pieced together enough material from these works to sustain an allied declaration. Despite his initiative in the charge to Solms, however, he had of course never favored a formal allied declaration, partly because of the substantive issue but even more because he preferred to keep all matters pertaining to a German constitution in the hands of the German powers themselves. We shall not claim for him a full appreciation as yet of the dangers lurking in the doctrine, later derived by the tsar from the Holy Alliance, that all the great powers had a universal right of intervention in other states, but clearly the seed was there. Even Hardenberg soon lost interest in an allied guarantee, choosing instead to build up Prussia's following among the Standesherren through private assurances "that no class of German estates or subjects will be injured in their rights."[23]

From the beginning Metternich had been less interested in the contents of a German constitution than in its acceptability to all concerned. Obviously he was not by nature hostile to the mediatized houses, for which his father was a leading lobbyist, but, as will become clearer as we go along, he thought that there was a better way to approach the problem. The mediatized houses, he believed, should avoid purely symbolic challenges to the sovereignty of their rulers, should yield patrimonial rights in reasonable measure to the claims of modern centralized administration, and instead concentrate on their true interests, which were mainly the right, realistically modified if need be, to the traditional revenue from their estates and above all the recognition of their *Ebenbürtigkeit* or equality of birth, the key to advantageous marriages with any of the sovereign houses. The Rheinbund sovereigns, in their turn, would be well advised to make concessions precisely in order to forestall external coercion, whether from the allies or from the future German league. In the meantime there was more important business.

The state most capable of resisting a program of restoration was Bavaria. In their campaign to fend off federal controls her rulers were

[22] Johann Friedrich Hoff, *Die Mediatisiertenfrage in den Jahren 1813–1815* (Berlin and Leipzig, 1913), 18–27.
[23] Quoted by Wolfgang Mager, "Das Problem der landständischen Verfassungen auf dem Wiener Kongress 1814/15" *Historische Zeitschrift*, CCXVII (1973), 319, n. 56.

fond of comparing her to Sardinia-Piedmont, which faced no such prospect. The states were about the same size and were both considered powers of the second rank. Both had common frontiers with Austria and were so situated as to function as buffers against France. Both held or coveted territory claimed by Austria, and both aspired to roles as independent European powers finding their safety solely "under the protection of the grand European equilibrium," to use the words of the Bavarian king, Maximilian I Joseph.[24] The main difference was psychological. Bavaria was an established state with a long record of Bonapartist loyalty, including Princess Augusta's marriage to Eugene Beauharnais; Piedmont was just being restored to the king of Sardinia. The fact that the latter went on to the greatness of national leadership whereas Bavaria was overshadowed by Prussia should not cause one to make light of Wittelsbach ambitions or to ridicule in Munich the *Realpolitik* that one admires or finds natural in Berlin. In the spring of 1814 Bavaria, with a population of 3,800,000 and an army of 70,000, stretched from Bolzano in Italy to the Saale River north of the Main in Germany. She controlled the Brenner Pass and a stretch of the Danube running from Passau on the Austrian border not far from Linz to the outskirts of Ulm, widely considered in military circles to be the best point at which to make a stand against armies debouching from the defiles of the Black Forest, Although the Austrian army had transit rights through the Tyrol, Bavarian authorities ruled the entire land.

From the beginning of the war Bavaria, even more than Prussia, had been the key to Metternich's German policy. Prussia after all held no territory claimed by Austria, and given the current uncertainty about the Polish and Saxon questions, she could not supply a fixed reference point for further calculations. One had to start somewhere to bring order out of the chaos, and Metternich was convinced that whatever else happened in Germany, it was imperative to remove Bavaria from the Austrian lands and compensate her generously in the region of the Rhine-Main confluence, making her both a bulwark against France and a counterweight to Prussia. If an alliance was possible, so much the better, but a friendly, satisfied neighbor was an elementary necessity, even, as we shall see, at the price of sacrificing local Austrian claims.

Accordingly, one of the first interviews that Metternich saw fit to grant after signing the Treaty of Fontainebleau was with Field Marshal Prince Karl Wrede, commander of the Bavarian corps under Schwarzenberg and now the official envoy in the Austrian negotiations.

[24] King Max to Wrede, 4 May 1814, extr. in Dupuis, *Talleyrand*, II, 322.

Wrede's dispatch case contained a text of the Treaty of Ried of the preceding year, which specified that in exchange for the cessions necessary "to assure the two states a suitable military line," Bavaria would receive *complete* compensation in *contiguous* areas at her convenience.[25] The king and his first minister, Count Maximilian Joseph Montgelas, would have preferred to keep exactly what Bavaria then held, but as preliminary sparring both in Munich and allied headquarters early in 1814 had indicated that at least the Tyrol must be retroceded, they were prepared with alternatives.[26] Wrede's instructions contemplated five contingencies based on possible Austrian demands. The details are not important here, but one common feature is of interest: namely, an extreme aversion to coming into contact with France. If Salzburg could be kept, Bavaria would refuse territory on the left bank of the Rhine entirely; if Salzburg must be ceded, the first choice of compensations would be the right-bank Palatinate, the second Mainz and Speyer, providing a bare foothold on the left bank and leaving room for another state to be interposed between Bavarian lands and France. Only if these could not be had and, additionally, if Alsace remained with France and was thus not available for partitioning between Baden and Württemberg, could she consider taking the left-bank Palatinate on the French border. This was the fifth and least desirable of her options. Bavaria no more than the great powers desired the role of buffer against French revanchism. Montgelas nominated Baden for this part, in one of his plans proposing to transfer the grand duke bodily to entirely new lands in the Rhineland.[27]

Metternich's conduct of the interview was characteristic, containing the customary rhetorical promise of good faith, a warning against dealing with others, encouragement to hope for much, and a certain vagueness about Austria's own demands. Bavaria, he said, should receive the grand duchies of Würzburg and Frankfurt, and even Mainz, a point mentioned in only one of Montgelas's five contingencies. Würzburg was available because of the impending transfer of Grand Duke Ferdinand of Habsburg back to his homeland in Tuscany, and Frankfurt had been vacant since the abdication of Karl Theodor von Dalberg, Prince Primate of the Rheinbund. It encompassed not only the city proper but also the former bishoprics of Aschaffenburg, Fulda, and Hanau, and the town of Wetzlar. Handsome acquisitions in their own

[25] Kraehe, I, 211.
[26] Count Karl von Hruby to Mett., 23 and 29 Jan. and 22 Mar. 1814; and Montgelas to Mett., 3 Feb. 1814, in Anton Chroust, ed., *Gesandtschaftsberichte aus München 1814–1848. Abteilung II: Die Berichte der österreichischen Gesandten*, 4 vols. (Munich, 1939–1943), I, 18–22.
[27] Wrede's instructions of 24 Feb. 1814 in Adam Sahrmann, *Pfalz oder Salzburg?* (Munich and Berlin, 1921), 29–32.

right, the two duchies would give Bavaria a frontier as far north as the Lahn River, put her in complete command of the Rhine-Main confluence, and provide her a substantial hinterland from which to provision the great fortress at Mainz with its immense garrison of 50,000 men.[28]

Mainz, indeed, was the heart of the plan. Countless memoranda of the day called the fortress "the key to Germany," and this was true vis-à-vis France as well as between North and South Germany. In Prussia it was the standard view that with Mainz in her hands South Germany "would be compelled to join the Prussian system."[29] In Austria the same assumption prevailed, especially in the army. "Mainz in Prussian hands is dangerous for us to a much greater degree than it is useful for Prussia," wrote Schwarzenberg some time later, and General Peter Baron von Duka, a confidant of the emperor, agreed, adding that the danger was not direct but consisted of the irresistible pressure that could be exerted on the South German states. For such reasons Metternich had first cleared the plan with Castlereagh before broaching it to Wrede. Thus the inclusion of Mainz in his offers was gratuitous, less a matter of finding indemnities for Bavaria than of building her up to forestall Prussian domination of this strategically vital area, and, what is equally significant in the light of future developments, to do so without using Austrian troops.[30]

As for Austria's demands on Bavaria, Metternich informed Wrede simply that the emperor would claim the status quo of 1805. This was a perfectly legitimate reference to the formula adopted among the allies in the Teplitz treaties of the preceding year; the formula itself, however, was ambiguous. Strictly speaking, it meant, as far as Bavaria was concerned, the retrocession of Vorarlberg, the Tyrol, and Passau, all ceded by Austria in the treaty of Pressburg of 26 December 1805. But what about Salzburg and Berchtesgaden, which Austria had *acquired* by the same treaty and kept until 1809? In that first interview Metternich deliberately left Wrede with some optimism in this particular regard, though in general the Bavarian soldier was loath to part

[28] Wrede to King Max, 12 Apr. 1814, extr. in Dupuis, *Talleyrand*, II, 89; Sahrmann, *Pfalz oder Salzburg?*, 26.

[29] Protocol of a Prussian conference of 29 May 1814. Text in G. H. Pertz and H. Delbrück, *Das Leben des Feldmarschalls Grafen Neithardt von Gneisenau*, 5 vols. (Berlin, 1864–1880), IV, 694–697. Cf. Stein memorial of 12 May 1814, Stein, *Briefe*, IV, 682; and Hard. to Castle., 27 Aug. 1814 in Karl Griewank, "Preussen und die Neuordnung Deutschlands," *Forschungen zur brandenburgischen und preussischen Geschichte*, LII (1940), 276–279.

[30] Memorials of 16 Jan. and 5 Feb. 1815, in HHSA, StK., Kongressakten, Cart 8, pp. 54–69; and Münster's report of 13 Feb. 1814 as cited in Kurt Krausnick, *Ernst Graf von Münster in der europäischen Politik 1806–1815* (Bielefeld, 1936), 43 and n. 476.

with Passau and even clung tenaciously to parts of the Tyrol. In subsequent conversations, however, Metternich was more precise, explaining that the status quo of 1805 was only a norm for population and area, that Salzburg was on the list but that Passau might be sacrificed in favor of the Inn and Hausrück districts, which Austria demanded in any case. Indeed, such were the Austrian demands that, had they been candidly presented at Ried, Bavaria might never have joined the coalition at all or done so under Russian protection. There was some risk of the latter even now, but Metternich was under pressure both from the army, which consistently put strong frontiers ahead of political alignments, and from the Reich restorers, who would have cut Bavaria back to her boundaries of 1802 if they could. Besides, he was still confident that he could find enough objects of compensation to the northwest of Bavaria to satisfy his would-be friends in Munich. Wrede, for one, was captivated by Metternich's charms and really thought he would make good.[31]

The Austrian claim to Salzburg, in combination with the armistice of 23 April with France, which implied that France would keep Alsace, reduced the Bavarian options to case five. While new instructions were being drafted on this basis, however, Metternich injected a new complication. In those somewhat indeterminate days before Napoleon's abdication he had evidently encouraged King Max to believe that his son-in-law, Prince Eugene, would be established in Italy, probably in Parma. By the time the prince abdicated, however, in Milan on 16 April, most Italian territory, Parma in particular, had already been awarded, and Eugene himself apparently had had enough of Italy. Metternich, in order to ease his problems there, suggested both to Wrede and the regular Bavarian envoy, Baron Johann Baptist von Verger, on about 20 April that Eugene be established in a German territory and placed under Bavarian sovereignty. Wrede was outraged. Such an establishment, he feared, would be counted against Bavaria's compensations whereas a true sovereignty in Italy would not only be a net gain but would also preserve a European standing of sorts for the house of Wittelsbach. His orders were "to refresh Prince Metternich's memory on this" and now that Parma was lost, to seek Genoa instead. Going over Metternich's head, he protested to the tsar, to Castlereagh, and even to Emperor Francis. All were sympathetic, for Eugene was much respected, but it was clear that a final determination must await the general settlement in Italy and Germany.[32]

[31] Wrede to King Max, 12 Apr. 1814, cited in n. 22 above; and Alexander Winter, *Karl Philipp Fürst von Wrede als Berater des Königs Max Joseph und des Kronprinzen Ludwig von Bayern (1813–1825)* (Munich, 1968), 133–136.

[32] Sahrmann, *Pfalz oder Salzburg?*, 33; King Max to Wrede, 13, 20, and 25 Apr.

One measure of the importance Metternich attached to the Bavarian negotiation was that he kept it tightly in his own hands. In the parallel negotiations with Prussia, on the other hand, he assigned an important role to Count Stadion, his predecessor as foreign minister and now his immediate subordinate as well as frequent critic. This procedure is the more remarkable as it was the territorial reconstruction of Germany that divided the two most. Stadion was incorrigibly suspicious of the Francophile government in Munich and believed that coercion alone would bring it and other courts to accept subordination to a strong central authority. His solution was to outflank them by concentrating the compensations of the two powers in the west, Prussia taking most of what later became the Rhineland, Austria taking the Breisgau from Baden and a broad connecting corridor from the lands of Bavaria and Württemberg. In this way, he believed, Germany could maintain a vigilant watch on the Rhine, the middle states would be hemmed in, Austria would recover her old status as a German power, and Prussia would be amply indemnified without taking Saxony.[33] Metternich, on the other hand, was flexible in regard to Saxony, preferred appeasement to coercion in dealing with the lesser states, and, like the Prussians themselves, disliked a common frontier with France.

Even so, his position is hard to pin down. If he thought that in the end Austria must acquiesce in regard to Saxony, all the more reason to sell dearly by taking a strong stand now. For that Stadion was the man. Metternich's attitude toward the Breisgau is less clear. The only explicit disclaimer he made at the time was an assurance to Baron Eugène François de Vitrolles, a representative of the Bourbons, that Austria had no desire for direct contact with France.[34] On the other hand, Hardenberg, as we shall see, continued into the Congress of Vienna to think that Austria would take the province, and Metternich himself in the next few years hung on to an Austrian right of reversion by inheritance. A corridor at the expense of Württemberg and Bavaria he did eventually reject, but the Breisgau itself he did not. He no doubt considered it expendable but only in relation to the larger settlement. Thus, the differences between the foreign minister and his agent were more contingent than rigidly set. Hardenberg may have received conflicting testimony from the Austrian camp, but there was no harm in this. On the contrary, Metternich's supreme concern was the Polish question, and until he knew the Prussian stand on it, he could not make final decisions about either his goals or his strategy in Germany.

1814, extr. in Dupuis, *Talleyrand*, II, 83–85; and Gentz to Karadja, 26 Apr. 1814, in Klinkowström, *Oesterreichs Theilnahme*, 329f.

[33] Kraehe, I, 270ff.

[34] Oncken, *Zeitalter der Revolution*, II, 780.

What does seem certain in any case is that when Hardenberg unveiled his famous "Plan for the Future Settlement of Europe" on 29 April, it was not sprung on the Austrians as a surprise but rather incorporated as many of Metternich's wishes as he could accommodate.[35]

This plan, the first comprehensive proposal presented by any of the powers, was a bold attempt to break the log jam in Paris and achieve a European settlement before France should regain a voice in it.[36] Understandably Hardenberg's first concern was the reconstruction of Prussia, but he did his best to accommodate the formal demands, the interests, and even the whims of the other powers, counting and distributing people with prodigious feats of arithmetic and double-entry bookkeeping that precisely balanced debits and credits down to the last soul. France, he postulated, the generosity of the tsar notwithstanding, must be bound strictly to the boundary of 1792, but the other powers should receive not merely what existing treaties promised but either what their sacrifices in the long struggle against tyranny entitled them to (England and Russia) or what was necessary "to maintain the equilibrium and their own independence" (Austria, Prussia, Holland, and Sardinia). Thus Austria was to emerge with 1,644,000 more souls, Prussia with 602,827, more than each had had in 1805, not including a number of mediatized lands, which the chancellor always counted separately because their souls were seen as laboring more for the privileged Standesherren than for the more distant sovereign, who received only residual revenue from such properties. These territories, as we shall see, he intended to absorb by other means.

In Poland Hardenberg proposed a boundary running from the headwaters of the Soldau River straight across to the great bend in the Warta and thence along the Warta to the environs of Cracow. The line thus encompassed much more than the mere strip connecting East Prussia and Silesia stipulated in the Treaty of Kalisch; the stout fortress of Thorn was included, and the Warta line was well to the east of the Prosna River, the line that Prussia ultimately received. In Saxony Prussia was to receive all but a small portion set aside at the tsar's behest for his brother-in-law, Duke Charles Augustus of Saxe-Weimar, the kingdom retaining its identity and Frederick William taking the title, King of Prussia and Saxony. Elsewhere Prussia was to receive Altmark, most of Magdeburg, and adjacent pieces on the left bank of the Elbe; a large mass in the west that included Nassau, Berg, Cleves, and Mark

[35] Cf. Münster to Prince Regent, 27 Apr. 1814, in Münster, *Political Sketches*, 159f. wherein he reports that Hardenberg's conferences with Stadion enabled him "to complete this morning the plan he will propose for adoption."

[36] Text in Karl Griewank, "Preussische Neuordnungspläne für Mitteleuropa aus dem Jahre 1814," *Deutsches Archiv für Landes- und Volksforschung*, VI (1942), 342–360.

on the right of the Rhine; and a strip thirty miles wide on the left bank from Wesel near the Dutch border down to and including Mainz. The fortress at Erfurt and Swedish Pomerania were other projected acquisitions, the latter by purchase from Denmark if necessary.

Taking into account Prussia's losses in Poland, her claims may not have been scandalous in a mathematical sense, but they in fact necessitated the reconstruction of all North Germany. The king of Saxony was assigned a synthetic territory called Münster-Paderborn, ranked as a duchy though the king was to retain his royal title. Hanover was to be reborn, with the Prussian midwife supplying 300,000 souls to add to the remnants of the stem lands. The territory in the triangle formed by the French, the Dutch, and the Prussian frontiers was to be divided among Baden, Hesse-Darmstadt, and the house of Nassau-Weilburg and Usingen, the rationale being that the duke of Nassau would really prefer to give up his traditional seat on the Rhine in order to be next door to his kin in Holland. The wrench for Baden would be almost as great, leaving of her existing territory scarcely more than the original margraviate and extending her frontier with France from Strasbourg to Luxemburg. The blow was justified, Hardenberg argued, by Baden's obligation under her treaty of accesion to make sacrifices "for preserving the independence of Germany."[37] Actually, he contended, the grand duke would come out ahead, not only because he would gain 20,250 in population but also because in the new lands he would possess "both sovereignty and proprietorship," whereas most of the lands to be ceded were the proprietary domains of mediatized houses, a distinction clearly echoing the philosophy of Solms and Münster. These arrangements for the left bank of the Rhine together with the extension of the Netherlands to the barrier fortresses and a part of Luxemburg, including the fortress, would give Prussia an imposing buffer backed by her own strong positions at Mainz and Wesel and her control of the Rhine.

Hardenberg was equally generous to Austria, recognizing all her claims and more, depending on whether Stadion or Metternich was making them. In Poland these included the districts of Zamość and Tarnopol, lost in 1809, and Cracow with its environs, a region essential for covering the Moravian Gateway, the direct invasion route to Vienna. This was short of the simple return to the full partition of 1795, which was Metternich's ideal, but it met Austria's minimum requirements and together with the Prussian claims would have produced an adequate frontier for the whole of Central Europe. In Germany Hardenberg offered all the provinces already mentioned in the Bavarian

37 Kraehe, I, 238.

negotiations (Tyrol, Vorarlberg, Salzburg and Berchtesgaden, Passau, and the Inn and Haustrück districts) as well as the corridor to the Rhine coveted by Stadion. Indeed, he offered more, on his charts extending Austria's frontage on the Rhine as far north as Strasbourg and enlarging the connecting corridor by mediatizing the Hohenzollern principalities of Sigmaringen and Hechingen with their 53,000 inhabitants. Was there calculated mischief here, giving Austria a common frontier with France while sheltering Prussia behind a wall of middle states? Probably not. There is no evidence that Hardenberg was ever insistent on this point; it is more likely that, influenced by Stadion, he thought of himself as acceding to Austrian wishes in a spirit of amity. The sacrifice of the Hohenzollern principalities was no doubt intended as an especially generous gesture—even if also an ominous token of the concept that Metternich had always resisted: Hardenberg's longstanding predilection for a north-south partition of Germany.

Nowhere, however, was Austrian influence on the Prussian plan more conspicuous than in the treatment proposed for Bavaria, for critical though the chancellor was of Metternich's appeasement policy toward the South German courts, he nevertheless made every concession that he deemed consistent with Prussia's own interests. His plans met every requirement of the Treaty of Ried, providing for a net population gain of 25,000 and keeping all compensations in contiguous areas, the latter to be accomplished by awarding her parts of Hesse-Darmstadt and the northern part of Baden (the region known as the Main-Tauber district) to connect with the left-bank Palatinate across the Rhine. Other concessions included Würzburg and Aschaffenburg as well as the renunciation at long last of Prussian claims to Ansbach and Bayreuth "however much the king regrets having to refuse the wishes of the inhabitants of these old Brandenburg provinces." Even the left-bank Palatinate was delimited in such a way that Bavaria would acquire the fortress of Landau and yet avoid direct contact with France. These were generous terms, but they fell short in two ways, one probably negotiable, the other not. The negotiable point, negotiable at least between Hardenberg and Metternich though perhaps not for Wrede, concerned the grand duchy of Frankfurt, only one part of which, Aschaffenburg, did the chancellor assign to Bavaria, whereas Metternich wanted her to have the whole state. The crucial, unnegotiable defect in the plan was the omission of Mainz and any territory necessary for access to it. The Bavarians had no great desire to assume the expenses of maintaining Germany's mightiest fortress, but they did desperately want to keep the Prussians out and control the mouth of the Main. Otherwise, as Wrede was soon to complain to his king, "all the possessions that your majesty can acquire in Franconia would be commercially without value."[38] This was an exaggeration perhaps but still valid testimony to the storms brewing in this critical sector.

The unresolved question of the German constitution Hardenberg reserved mainly for a later state paper, but what he did say on the subject was clear enough. The confederation, he wrote, should above all have "a military system strong enough to maintain the independence of the *corps germanique*," but beyond that it should conduct foreign affairs, administer justice, regulate commerce, and govern the relations between sovereigns and their subjects. The last was especially emphasized in the plan inasmuch as Hardenberg intended that many of the lesser sovereigns of the late Rheinbund would be "assimilated to the mediatized"; therefore, he said, it was only right to improve the status of the princely houses in this category. This was a none-too-subtle concession to the conscience of Europe at a time when he was announcing that Prussia herself intended to take over some twenty previously mediatized properties as well as the hitherto sovereign states of Waldeck, Lippe-Detmold, Reuss, and Schwarzburg.[39] These lands, which would indirectly add another 611,800 to her population gains, were "to be tied to Prussia according to principles still to be determined for the small princes and estates that belonged to the Confederation of the Rhine."[40] Apart from Hanover and Prussia herself, the only sovereign states assured of survival in North Germany were Oldenburg, the Mecklenburg duchies, Saxe-Weimar, and Saxe-Coburg, all with close dynastic ties to the tsar. It is easy to understand the panic that overcame the rulers who were either earmarked for mediatization or not mentioned at all.

The Hardenberg plan overall was neither accepted nor rejected; it was simply another, if unusually comprehensive, step in an ongoing negotiation. The British objected to the frontier of the Mass for Holland, but otherwise Castlereagh clung to the role of mediator between Austria and Prussia, the better to encourage them to stand up to the tsar. Münster postponed a trip to London in order to join Hardenberg, Humboldt, and Stadion in a further attempt to fill in the missing parts regarding a German constitution; it was soon agreed, however, that

[38] Wrede to King Max, 12 May 1814, extr. in Dupuis, *Talleyrand*, II, 76.

[39] These four states were singled out because they represented "new" houses dating their *Landeshoheit* only to the seventeenth century. We shall hear more of this new device for reducing the ranks of the sovereigns. Hardenberg's aides provided him with lists that carefully distinguished old from new lines. See ZSTA, Merseburg, 2.4.1.I, No. 1454.

[40] This cryptic language was no doubt taken by readers of the time to be a euphemism for simple mediatization. As we shall see later, however, it was more likely an allusion to a different scheme, under which these lands, sovereign and mediatized alike, would technically belong not to the Prussian state but to a Prussia-directed Kreis, with a status inferior to that of the larger members of the Kreis.

this task must be deferred till the meetings in London or even till the Congress of Vienna itself. Hence the official statement that was later incorporated into the treaty with France bound her to no more than what had been provided in the Troyes formula about a German league. Rumors about a tight German confederation, however, continued to cause unrest among the middle states.[41]

The tsar, to whom the plan was presented about 5 May, flatly rejected the arrangements for Poland and with each passing day seemed to increase his demands, this despite the entreaties of Baron Stein that he join Hardenberg in forcing the plan on Austria as the basis for negotiations. While refusing still to present a plan of his own, he yet denied all of Austria's claims and most of Prussia's, so that Thorn, Cracow, Zamość, and much of Posen would fall under his scepter should he eventually be crowned king. From the Tarnopol district he vowed he would cede Austria not one village. Count Münster, one of the few sources for these developments, was alarmed enough to warn the Prince Regent about the possibility of a new war and to await demobilization of the armies before pressing negotiations too far.[42]

Metternich's response to the Prussian plan is as obscure as his influence upon it. It was the general impression in Paris that the Austrians opposed the destruction of Saxony but that if it came to this, they must take a portion too: namely a strip that included Dresden. This belief is in line with Stadion's well-known stand as well as the emperor's later avowals that he would do everything for Saxony except go to war.[43] The fact that Metternich had once before offered Saxony, albeit in different circumstances, suggests a more flexible attitude, especially as Hardenberg's solution of the Polish question now at last contained the quid pro quo that he had always insisted upon: a strong frontier for both the central powers. Yet there was one more piece that had to fall into place before Saxony could be conceded, and that was Mainz. On this issue Metternich was adamant, once again offering the fortress town to Bavaria and secretly proposing that Bavarian troops take possession of it when the French moved out.[44] Despite this, the Austrian

---

[41] Münster to Prince Regent, 5 May 1814, Münster, *Political Sketches*, 165f.; Humb. to Oertzen, 8 May 1814, Humboldt, *Gesammelte Schriften*, XVII, 64; Humb. to Caroline, 13 May 1814, Humboldt, *Briefe*, IV, 330; Webster, *Castlereagh*, I, 282ff.; Rössler, *Österreichs Kampf*, II, 202; and Pfister, *Lager der Verbündeten*, 259.

[42] Castle. to Liverp., 5 May 1814, in Webster, *BD*, 180; Zak, "Grossmächte und die deutschen Staaten," 1543; Stein's memorial of 12 May 1814, Stein, *Briefe*, IV, 782–784; and Münster to Prince Regent, 5 May 1814, Münster, *Political Sketches*, 163.

[43] E.g., Wrede to King Max, 28 Apr. 1814, and Just to King of Saxony, 6 June 1814, in Dupuis, *Talleyrand*, II, 72 and 80. Cf. Johann Heilmann, *Feldmarschall Fürst Wrede* (Leipzig, 1881), 412.

[44] Münster to Prince Regent, 15 May 1814, in Münster, *Political Sketches*, 70;

minister saw fit to tell his deputy in Vienna, Baron Josef von Hudelist, that a close accord existed with Prussia, suggesting perhaps that he expected ultimately to end all difficulties by trading Dresden for Mainz and thereby complete his front against Russia. Hardenberg too seems to have been optimistic. "Russia alone is to blame," he later insisted, "that we did not reach agreement in Paris and London."[45]

The issue of Mainz aside, Hardenberg's liberal proposals for Bavaria opened new opportunities for dealing with her. On 6 May Wrede submitted to Metternich his new instructions, which, disregarding some assorted bailiwicks and border adjustments with Württemberg, differed from the Hardenberg plan mainly in demanding Mainz and the entire grand duchy of Frankfurt, of which Hardenberg had offered only Aschaffenburg. Frankfurt was no small matter, to be sure, but, as suggested earlier, there was margin for compromise. On 11 May Metternich handed Wrede a counterproject, the notable feature of which was acceptance of Hardenberg's limits on Frankfurt but the inclusion of a few more left-bank parcels to facilitate contact with Mainz. His own contribution was Austria's renunciation of Vorarlberg with all that that entailed for Stadion's dream of a corridor to the Rhine. Followed literally, it would have removed Austria from the river even above Lake Constance. Otherwise his demands remained the same: Tyrol, Salzburg, and the Inn and Hausrück districts. Wrede conceded these last pending final settlement of the French boundary, which rumor had it, would leave Landau with France. He demanded other parcels as well, all except the principality of Isenburg too small to enumerate.[46]

Then Metternich himself increased the stakes, bringing Prince Eugene into the equation again. The prince, as it happened, had arrived in Paris two days before and reiterated his preference for an establishment in Germany.[47] Bavaria's new provinces could provide it, Metternich told Wrede. Those on the Austrian list would yield twice the revenue of the old, he argued, and from these the king could easily provide the 600,000 francs of annual revenue to which the prince was entitled. Wrede protested, complaining of the expenses of maintaining the fortresses at Mainz and Hanau and the loss of salt mines if Berchtesgaden should be ceded. Perhaps if Zweibrücken and Saarbrücken

---

Winter, *Wrede als Berater*, 138; and Gentz to Karadja, 21 and 24 June 1814, in Klinkowström, *Oesterreichs Theilnahme*, 430.

[45] Gentz to Mett., 12 May 1814, in Klinkowström, *Oesterreichs Theilnahme*, 341; and quotation by Oncken, *Zeitalter der Revolution*, II, 834, n. 1.

[46] Sahrmann, *Pfalz oder Salzburg?* 33f.; and King Max to Wrede, 29 Apr. 1814, extr. in Dupuis, *Talleyrand*, II, 90.

[47] Carola Oman, *Napoleon's Viceroy Eugène de Beauharnais* (New York, 1966), 390–392.

were added. . . .[48] And so it went, to no conclusion; for as long as Mainz could be offered only as a good Austrian intention and not as a guarantee, what more could be done? In the negotiation with Bavaria nothing, but toward Prussia Metternich reverted to a harder line: the whole grand duchy of Frankfurt for Bavaria, Vorarlberg remaining with Austria.[49]

Throughout the talks with Wrede Metternich, imparting another dimension to the territorial issue, urged the Bavarians to help their cause by ameliorating the lot of the Standesherren. The existing system in Bavaria, based on a special edict of 1807 and the constitution of 1808, was moderate in comparison with the harsh practices of Baden and Württemberg; with a few improvements, Metternich pleaded, it could become a model for the rest of Germany, thereby obviating pretexts for outside intervention and giving Bavaria a moral and psychological edge in the fierce struggle over territory. The less revenue, for example, that the court in Munich extracted from each mediatized property, the more of them she could reasonably claim when calculating the compensation due her. In some border areas, moreover, the preferences of the resident Standesherren themselves might make the difference.[50]

Wrede was so impressed that he drafted a program on his own that would have restored certain patrimonial rights and ended such discriminatory practices as excluding Standesherren from the estates assembly and from holding certain public offices. Montgelas and King Max, however, saw such concessions as opening wedges to the gradual dismemberment of the state and refused even into the Congress of Vienna to depart from the standards of 1807–1808. Indeed, they bolted in the opposite direction, accelerating work on a new constitution designed to outflank the local elites by still more centralized administration and, though creating an assembly of estates, making it a mere ornament on the tree of bureaucratic absolutism. What matters here, however, is the clear demonstration of Metternich's preference for diplomatic pressure rather than federal coercion in treating the problem and his concern that this most important state enhance its prestige in the eyes of German restorationists.[51]

---

[48] Wrede to King Max, 12 May 1814, extr. in Dupuis, *Talleyrand*, II, 91f.

[49] Münster to Prince Regent, 30 May 1814, Münster, *Political Sketches*, 183. Münster, a close but second-hand source, would not be enough to prove the harder stand toward Prussia. My conclusion is based additionally on the reappearance of Vorarlberg in Austria's share and the essentials of Frankfurt for Bavaria in the subsequent treaty (see below, p. 50f).

[50] Winter, *Wrede als Berater*, 182–185.

[51] *Ibid.*, 185; Ernst Rudolf Huber, *Deutsche Verfassungsgeschichte seit 1789*, 5 vols. (Stuttgart, Berlin, Cologne, and Mainz, 1957–1978), I, 321f.

Since so much depended on Bavaria, it is small wonder that the Austrian minister had little to say to the other South German envoys. Baden was represented in Paris by Baron Karl von Hacke, an unabashed Francophile, whose main concerns were to hang on to the Breisgau, to dull Bavaria's appetite for Baden soil, and to avoid compensations on the left bank of the Rhine.[52] If Metternich had really reached a final decision to renounce the Breisgau, here was his chance to make a friend. Yet there is no record of talk to this effect either from him or from his chargé d'affaires in Karlsruhe, Ritter Hermann von Greiffenegg. On the contrary, Greiffenegg not only shared Stadion's strategic views about Swabia and the Breisgau but passionately believed that the men of this region excelled all others in mettle and should once again have a chance to serve in the Kaiser's armies.[53] In the absence of instructions from Metternich, he was hardly the one to set the grand duke's mind at rest. In fact, Charles in the coming weeks remained in a state of shock, one minute crying in despair that he would sell the whole state to Bavaria for a million and a half guilders a year and the next vowing that he would not surrender the Breisgau even if Francis gave him Bohemia for it. That his internal policies meanwhile were under attack by Stein only increased his misery; territorial estates, he insisted, would take all the fun out of being a sovereign.[54]

Württemberg's envoy in Paris was Count Heinrich Karl Friedrich Levin von Winzingerode, who had entered the city in the retinue of the tsar. He too saw little of Metternich, probably because he faithfully reflected his king's penchant for fanatical loyalty to an ally of the moment, in this case Alexander, who had replaced Napoleon in his affections. King Frederick was one of those who assumed that Austria would back the regency movement in France and immediately rushed into the opposite corner. "All events show," he wrote to Winzingerode in mid-April, "what a stench Austria makes as she tries to salvage the inheritance of the grandson. I entrust myself rather to the steadfastness of Tsar Alexander and the revulsion of the nation toward this offspring of dubious ancestry"—a remark itself of dubious ancestry, coming as it did from the father-in-law of Jerome Bonaparte.[55]

[52] Marie Glaser, "Die badische Politik und die deutsche Frage zur Zeit der Befreiungskriege und des Wiener Kongresses," *Zeitschrift für die Geschichte des Oberrheins*, n.s. XLI (1928), 269–275.

[53] See his memorial "Ueber die Vorteile welche der Besitz Oesterreichischen Länder in Schwaben dem Kaiserstaat gewähren könnten und müssten," Karlsruhe, 15 May 1814, HHSA, StK., Diplomatische Korrespondenz, Baden, Fasc. 10.

[54] Greiffenegg to Mett., 28 June, 17 and 28 July, 6 and 12 Sept. 1814, HHSA, StK., Diplomatische Korrespondenz, Baden, Fasc. 10.

[55] King Frederick to Winzingerode, 14 Apr. 1814, extr. in Pfister, *Lager der Verbündeten*, 235.

Encouraged by Alexander's previous support for a seat on the directory of the projected German league, Frederick hoped that the tsar, his nephew, would assume the leadership of the league and choose Württemberg as the "frontier bulwark against France" and a counterweight to the Austro-Bavarian bloc. Such a role, he held, would justify an increment of population of 75 percent or about 1,000,000 subjects, a goal to be reached by regaining the exclave of Montbeliard and annexing much of Alsace. These reveries were soon shattered, but the king's appetite, ever on a par with his corpulent physique, turned to Germany for satisfaction, especially to morsels not yet mediatized. It was no pleasant assignment, but Winzingerode did his best. In time he found access to Nesselrode only to be told that the tsar would do what he could "but to raise you to the same level as Bavaria will be difficult." At length too Winzingerode on 16 May finally talked with Metternich, who was still less encouraging, insisting that Württemberg could be compensated for losses but not enlarged.[56]

As the days passed without decision the middle-state envoys, excluded from the councils of the powers, grew increasingly exasperated at the preoccupations of their respective patrons. "I tried three times," Winzingerode reported, "to call on Messrs. Nesselrode, Wolkonsky, and Anstett, but to no avail. The first is always with Monsieur Talleyrand, the second always in church with the tsar, offering up prayers of thanks, and the third spends all his time at the tavern."[57] In like vein, the blunt and guileless Marshal Wrede, who seemed to believe that Munich was the capital of Germany, could not comprehend Metternich's dalliance and increasing vagueness. "One drinks, one eats, one dances, one watches theater and fireworks, but the discussions do not move forward at the desired pace," he observed with perhaps less wit and elegance, than, later, the prince de Ligne expressed it.[58] But how could they move forward as long as Alexander, as hardboiled in private as he was magnanimous in public, refused on the one hand to state his program for Poland and on the other inspired the Poles in Paris to believe in miracles? For Metternich evasion, vagueness, and keeping all options open seemed the only way to proceed.[59]

Then a ray of light appeared from a barely foreseeable source. On 3 May Louis XVIII arrived in Paris to assume his throne and face at last the man who had expelled him from his Russian sanctuary in 1801 when appeasing Bonaparte was the order of the day. Despite his obesity

[56] Pfister, *Lager der Verbündeten*, 236–258, quoting the persons referred to.
[57] Quoted in *ibid.*, 236. Baron Johann von Anstett was a Russian diplomat in Germany, Count Peter Wolkonsky a Russian general.
[58] Quoted by Sahrmann, *Pfalz oder Salzburg?* 34. Slightly different version in Webster, *Castlereagh*, I, 283.
[59] Cf. Dupuis, *Talleyrand*, II, 43–45.

and an attack of gout which had delayed his trip, he managed to keep a regal bearing that somehow overshadowed the circumstances of his recall. He sat while Talleyrand stood. He made light of a Romanov-Bourbon marriage. He preceded the tsar through doors and at dinner assigned him to an inferior chair. He accepted the homage of the army chiefs and the Legislative Body but treated the Senate with contempt. The senators had thought to withhold recognition until he had accepted their constitution; now they accepted his assumption of sovereignty and with it the necessity of negotiating the constitution.[60] The rebuff was a stunning setback to the tsar, for he had personally undertaken to argue the Senate's case to Louis. Alexander in fact never recovered the lost ground. His French policy was going the way of his German policy the year before, when he had first aligned himself with the national resistance movement only in the end to have to deal with the ruling princes.

As the review of the constitution proceeded in the course of the month, his influence on it waned, and though the new government gladly accepted Russian aid in the peace negotiations, it was not with the gratitude that everybody had expected but rather with hauteur and the assumption that France deserved as much. Metternich, who spent several hours with Louis shortly after his arrival, himself was surprised at such presumption and admitted that the king had "decided views" that differed from his own. In the long run, however, who could rejoice more than he if France pursued an independent course? The maintenance of a low profile, the inconspicuous but steady support of the one Bourbon cause where Alexander had tried to support all causes, seemed at last to be paying dividends.[61]

The new turn in French politics came just when the debate on a European settlement was reaching the impasse into which the Hardenberg plan had thrown it. The result was a slight shift in the balance of risks. With less to fear from a Franco-Russian entente and more to fear from another ugly exposure of interallied differences, Metternich and Hardenberg now conceded that the negotiations with France must proceed, regardless of what stipulations could or could not be included in the treaty. Accordingly they abandoned their strategy of holding the colonies for ransom and allowed England to resume the colonial negotiation while the four powers together engaged France in trying to resolve the other issues.[62]

[60] J.P.T. Bury, "The End of the Napoleonic Senate," *Cambridge Historical Journal*, IX, no. 2, 1948, 165–189.
[61] Bertier, *Restoration*, 52–65; Metternich, "Autobiographische Denkschrift," *NP*, I, 202.
[62] Dupuis, *Talleyrand*, I, 340.

Even now, however, Metternich did what he could to bind France in advance to at least such elements of a European settlement as could then be advanced. When the first formal conference between Talleyrand and a full complement of allied ministers took place on 9 May—so long had peace negotiations lagged behind—it adopted as the basis of discussion an Austrian draft in twelve articles.[63] The fifth of these contained a revised version of the program first adumbrated at Langres and Troyes, later placed in the Treaty of Chaumont, and submitted to the French at Châtillon merely for their information. How little progress had been made since! Germany was still to be "composed of independent states united by a federal bond," Italy "divided into independent states," Spain restored under Ferdinand VII, Switzerland given independence under guarantee of all the powers; and Holland, under the house of Orange, was to receive unspecified aggrandizement with the proviso that there must never be a personal union between the Dutch and a foreign crown. This last stipulation, a demand of Talleyrand but generally favored by the allies as well, was the only substantive addition since Châtillon. Also new was a preamble stating explicitly that the king of France *fully adhered* to the views and intentions of His Imperial and Royal Majesty and of his allies."[64] If only a clause on Poland could have been included.

In other articles the Austrian draft proposed a complete amnesty for partisans of previous regimes and made provision for the Congress of Vienna, as previously noted, so as to emphasize its ratifying rather than its negotiating function. Article III listed the territorial increments beyond the frontier of 1792 as promised by the tsar. These would have added 500,000 to France in population and were made possible by straightening the frontier here and there and awarding her such former enclaves as Avignon, Montbeliard, Saarlouis, and Salm, the last three of which had German claimants. Landau, a French enclave before 1792, was also included. Finally, there was an article that in effect modified the common principle of international custom that debts hypothecated on the assets of a province should go with the province when it changed hands; in Metternich's version this was still true of debts incurred for local purposes but not of those contracted for national spending and inscribed in the great ledger of the French public debt. For further consideration of these proposals two commissions were established at that same meeting of 9 May, one for the boundary question, the other for financial affairs.

On 12 May Talleyrand sent his official reply. It was on the whole conciliatory, as he maintained in a personal note to Metternich, but it

[63] Text extracted in Dupuis, *Talleyrand*, I, 341–343.
[64] Article V. Italics mine.

took advantage of every opening. To the statement on Germany it added a stipulation that the confederation of states "cannot have at its head the sovereign of any of the great states of Europe." Metternich personally struck this passage from the document,[65] not because he necessarily intended to make Francis emperor of a restored Reich but because Talleyrand was here straying into the area reserved to the allies. Still, although the French minister did not contest the matter, he had perceived that anything he was asked to adhere to was necessarily negotiable. In another maneuver affecting Germany the French note proposed that the numerous endowments that Napoleon had established for his followers in the ceded territories be among the financial burdens to be transferred with the land. The major beneficiary would have been Dalberg, who had an establishment at Regensburg that he hoped to retain under the king of Bavaria. Similar cases, however, abounded in North Germany, especially in the provinces once part of the kingdom of Westphalia, where the old electoral domains of Hanover had been divided among French generals.[66]

In the ensuing discussions Metternich found himself for once the mediator between unusual combinations. On one side were the advocates of firmness, Castlereagh and Hardenberg, both with a vital interest in maintaining the integrity of the Belgian and German frontiers and each with a special problem as well. In Castlereagh's case this was the abolition of the slave trade so clamorously demanded at home. For Hardenberg there was the peculiar urgency of having France repay the debts incurred by Napoleon for services rendered in past campaigns. On the other side were the French themselves—the dexterous Talleyrand, the loftily presumptuous king, the restless, bellicose marshals—abetted in most matters by the tsar. With varying mixtures of genuine concern, conscious deception, and veiled threat, they spoke gloomily of the revolution that was bound to come if France yielded a single fort, made good on a single contract, or released a single painting from the Louvre. The French public, they maintained, had been promised an increment not of 500,000 people but 1,000,000. To meet this figure they demanded a new line against Belgium, all of Luxemburg, and even Kaiserslautern. The proposition caused consternation on the boundary commission. After days of inconclusive wrangling the commissioners sent the issue back to the ministers, requesting that Metternich and Talleyrand settle it privately between themselves. Metternich, with his keen appreciation of the specious, insisted that population totals were incidental to a sound frontier but that if France was concerned about public opinion, the allies would

[65] Griewank, *Wiener Kongress*, 61, n. 91.
[66] Dupuis, *Talleyrand*, I, 344f. and 372.

allow her to announce any figures she pleased "without anyone ever attempting to verify them."[67] In the final compromise France received, instead of territory in Belgium and Luxemburg, a connecting link with Landau, a part of Savoy, and the strategically important village of Gex in Switzerland.

On the financial issues Talleyrand was especially tenacious. Since his own income from Benevento, an enclave in the kingdom of Naples, was at the mercy of Joachim Murat, he could well imagine that the army would be further alienated from the regime if the marshals were deprived of their Westphalian benefices; at best France herself might have to make good their losses. Still, the sums involved were small in comparison to what the allies demanded in settlement of the war debts owed by the Napoleonic regime to former allies: 130 million francs to Prussia alone. In rebuttal the French commissioners pleaded that the Bourbons, as the main victims of Napoleon, were assuredly not responsible for his debts, a remarkable contention, observed Count Münster, for a regime that insisted it had valid title to the artworks acquired by the late emperor. The Prussians were insistent, however, as they had the most to lose—in contrast to the Russians, who having only negligible claims, supported France in the matter, on at least one occasion through the personal intercession of the tsar. Metternich and his representative on the commission, Baron Johann Philipp Wessenberg, tended to remain neutral, not wishing to antagonize Hardenberg, yet being unwilling to leave the French field to Alexander. It was Castlereagh who broke the deadlock, proposing that France pay reparations for private damages but no governmental claims. Metternich then completed the compromise by inducing the French at last to renounce claim to the foreign endowments. For the sake of public opinion, however, this stipulation, like several others that Talleyrand alleged to be inflammatory and dangerous to the regime, was relegated to the secret articles of the treaty. Talleyrand's further demand, however, that the treaty carry a preamble praising the French army was rejected.[68]

Throughout the negotiations the tsar usually sided with the French, and Metternich once again laid the trouble to his affinity with the old Bonapartists, still dominant in the government. These, he maintained, harbored "pretensions that Napoleon himself, at the height of his success, would not have pressed so far" and set the tone even for the king. "The complaisance that Russia exhibits," he advised Merveldt in Lon-

[67] French commissioner Osmond to Talleyrand, 24 May 1814, in Dupuis, *Talleyrand*, I, 355.

[68] Münster to Prince Regent, 23 May 1814, Münster, *Political Sketches*, 177f.; and Dupuis, *Talleyrand*, I, 359–374.

don, on 18 May,"—far less toward the newly restored sovereign than to the government officials with whom she has mainly dealt—amplifies this tone, which we and Lord Castlereagh alone manage to keep within reasonable limits." All the more reason then, he went on, to stand fast by the established policy of building up the European center: "Everything in these first moments of calm and discussion of mutual interests confirms us in the conviction . . . that our close union with England, Holland, Prussia, and the states of Germany will succeed in preventing too intimate a rapprochement between Russia and France, toward which, as we foresaw, these two governments will trend from now on."[69]

Under these circumstances the pursuit of a European settlement to be incorporated in the peace treaty seemed no longer merely futile but dangerous. "The present terrain is in no way suited to this negotiation," wrote Metternich in a progress report to Hudelist, "because it is too much under the influence of all these wretched Polish Frenchmen and French Poles."[70] Castlereagh, who had never been sanguine about success in Paris, had in fact some time before devised an eminently simple means of excluding France: by transferring the general negotiation to London, where he could be the mediator. Originally he had invited the tsar to a largely nonpolitical victory celebration, but distressed at the latter's soaring popularity, he had then decided "to dilute the libation to Russia" by including Francis and Frederick William.[71] Although Metternich and Stadion both implored the emperor to accept, Francis decided to send Metternich in his place. "I have very much encouraged this plan," Castlereagh reported home on 15 May, "as his presence in London would enable us (Hardenberg and Nesselrode being also there) to decide finally on several important points previous to the Congress of Vienna."[72] Metternich himself was pleased with the prospect. "We are completely at one with England," he continued to Hudelist; "the Russian travesty has reached new depths. . . . In this way for the first time will my fondest idea be realized of establishing a system based on the central powers and having the sea powers quite naturally aligned with it. As far as possible I will extend the system to the Porte. . . ."

Thus freed from the burden of a dozen competing negotiations, those with France went forward to a conclusion. The final draft of the

[69] Mett. to Merveldt, 18 May 1814, extr. in Dupuis, *Talleyrand*, I, 353f. and II, 297.

[70] Mett. to Hudelist, 24 May 1814, HHSA, StK., Interiora, Fasc. 78.

[71] Castle. to Liverp., 20 Apr. 1814 in Webster, *BD*, 178f.

[72] Castle. to Liverp., 15 May 1814, in Arthur Wellesley, First Duke of Wellington, *Supplementary Despatches and Memoranda of Field Marshal Arthur, Duke of Wellington K.G.*, 15 vols. (London, 1858–1872), IX, 72.

treaty[73] contained the agreements already described though with slightly different wording in many cases. In Article VI France recognized the interallied agreements relating to Holland, Germany, Italy, and Switzerland much as the original Austrian draft had defined them. In the case of Germany the actual phrasing was: "the states of Germany will be independent and united by a federal bond." Italy by contrast, was to be "composed of sovereign states." In the secret articles France further recognized the Dutch annexation of Belgium at least as far as the Maas, the division of the left bank of the Rhine among Holland, Prussia, "and other German states," the right of the allies to determine the future status of Switzerland, and several other decisions deemed too deleterious to French morale for publication. The Franco-Austrian version of the treaty additionally made secret provision for returning documents relative to Belgium and the Holy Roman Empire that Napoleon had carted away from the archives in Vienna.

Regarding the all-important question of a French voice in the general affairs of Europe, the treaty was somewhat ambiguous. On the one hand, Article XXXII, which provided for the Congress of Vienna, made no distinction among the participants, stating merely that "all the Powers that have been engaged on one side or the other in the present war" should send plenipotentiaries. On the other hand, the first secret article, a preamble to the others, specified that the disposition of the territories renounced by France "and the relations from which there is to arise in Europe a true and lasting system of equilibrium shall be regulated at the Congress on bases concluded by the allied Powers *among themselves* and according to the general provisions contained in the following articles." The main question here is whether the exclusion of France was limited to the topics explicitly treated in the secret articles (which amounted to the border territory renounced by France) or whether the exclusion was meant to apply literally to any question affecting the European equilibrium: e.g., Poland. If the latter, French participation would be almost meaningless unless it was further argued that while the allies might lay down general principles, they could not impose any precise final terms. Both interpretations have been advanced in the literature but the matter remains speculative.[74]

[73] Text of Franco-Austrian treaty in Neumann, *Traités par l'Autriche*, II, 462–476. Slightly different text of Franco-Russian treaty in Fedor Fedorovitch Martens, *Recueil des traités et conventions conclus par la Russie avec les puissances étrangères*, 15 vols. (St. Petersburg, 1874–1909), XIV, 238–260.

[74] Oncken, *Zeitalter der Revolution*, II, 838f. argues the latter; Jacques-Henri Pirenne, *La Sainte-Alliance: Organisation européenne de la paix mondiale*, 2 vols. (Neuchâtel, 1946–1949), I, 56–59, the former. Pirenne even makes the far-fetched contention that France implicitly recognized the Russian claim to Poland—in flagrant contradiction to Talleyrand's position later. The dispute is sterile, but for what it is worth, I believe Oncken has the better of it.

At the time Talleyrand considered the secret articles a humiliation, but that would have been his attitude in either case. If anybody wanted a broader role for France, it would have been Alexander, but even he could not be certain that an independent France would support him on Poland. Metternich's opinion, however, can hardly be in doubt. Summarizing the understandings shortly before the treaty was signed, he emphasized that France had recognized everything stipulated in interallied treaties regarding Italy and Germany and "French renunciation of every direct influence outside of her new and old boundaries."[75] Although the latter leaves "direct influence" undefined, it sounds on the face of it broadly exclusionary and consistent with Metternich's hope that he and Castlereagh would solve the main problems in London and that the Congress of Vienna would be "less for negotiation than for signing." It is still another irony in this period that Metternich and Castlereagh were eventually to be the ones to avail themselves of the loopholes in the treaty, not Alexander.

The knowledge that France would not be a factor in the forthcoming talks in London was indeed an advantage, but how much better would the situation not be if Austria and Prussia could appear there united, their major problems solved? With this thought in mind Metternich, Hardenberg, and Castlereagh in the last days of May made one last effort to break the deadlock on Saxony and Mainz. The British proposed that Mainz belong to neither Prussia nor Bavaria but become "a fortress belonging to the German line [sic] in general," maintained and garrisoned by the German states collectively.[76] The idea was not new, but as an unwelcome compromise and a complicating factor for the German constitution it had never gained serious consideration. Metternich himself did not favor it and continued his campaign to obtain the fortress for Bavaria. On the other hand, he openly retreated on the Saxon question, assuring Humboldt that it was "natural" for Prussia to seek a large part of that state and even, as Humboldt reported it, did "not feel as much repugnance as previously to the idea that we should have the whole of Saxony."[77] Metternich also agreed with Hardenberg on the need to stop unrest in Germany and promised that the agenda of the Congress of Vienna would include the regulation of relations between rulers and subjects and a few other "social questions running across all Europe."[78] The king of Bavaria too eased

[75] Mett. to Hudelist, 24 May 1814, HHSA, StK., Interiora, Fasc. 78, p. 40.

[76] Münster to Prince Regent, 15 May 1814, Münster, *Political Sketches*, 171. In all probability an error in copying in this version changed "ligue" to "ligne."

[77] Quoted in Gebhardt, *Humboldt als Staatsmann*, II, 55. Cf. Griewank, "Neuordnung Deutschlands," 251, n. 1.

[78] Mett. to Hudelist, 24 May 1814, HHSA, StK., Interiora, Fasc. 78; Münster to Prince Regent, 30 May 1814, Münster, *Political Sketches*, 183.

matters slightly by agreeing at last to have Prince Eugene established on Bavarian soil—to be sure, with the proviso that others pay the 600,000 francs that had been promised as a pension.[79]

Metternich, who had earlier, in ballroom and antechamber, in conference and in soirée, put off Marshal Wrede with pleasant assurances, now gave him grim promises of action. Individual opinions among the Austrian leaders cannot be documented, but the consensus is fairly well established: the awards of Warsaw to Russia and of Saxony to Prussia they would vigorously protest, but for Mainz they would threaten war.[80] On 29 May the emperor gave orders to settle the issue in twenty-four hours, and Metternich scheduled a meeting of allied ministers for 6 p.m. of that day.[81] Thus alerted, the Prussians hastened to fix their own position. At a conference that same day attended by Hardenberg, Humboldt, and the generals Neithardt von Gneisenau, Hermann von Boyen, and Karl Friedrich von dem Knesebeck, it was decided to yield somewhat for the sake of larger goals. Mainz *and* Saxony, they agreed, could be had only at the cost of incurring eternal Austrian hatred and intolerable dependence on Russia. On the other hand, they were sanguine that if they did not insist on Mainz, Austria would acquiesce in most of their other plans for Germany. Interestingly enough, they did not insist that Hardenberg crudely try to trade Mainz for Saxony but rather gave him various options, including the federal fortress solution for Mainz with a joint Austro-Prussian garrison, and cutbacks in Bavarian gains along the Main. They also attached great importance to acquiring Fulda, the better to facilitate exchanges with Hesse-Cassel and thus to create an uninterrupted corridor to the west. The possibility of obtaining Saxony by transferring the king to a territory in Italy was listed almost as an afterthought, as a maximum quid pro quo unlikely to be granted—unlikely because the one thing the conference dismissed out of hand was awarding Mainz to Bavaria.[82]

Whether the four-power meeting took place as scheduled on the 29th or later hardly matters. The fact is that, plagued by the details involved in the signing of the peace treaty with France, the ministers could not produce the European settlement, or even the German settlement, for which they had yearned. The best they could devise was a provisional plan that established zones of occupation pending final settlement in London or Vienna. Nevertheless, Metternich did not come away empty-handed, for as Nesselrode reported later, it was expressly understood "that so far as possible, the provisional govern-

---

[79] King Max to Wrede, 29 May 1814, extr. in Dupuis, *Talleyrand*, II, 88.
[80] Just to Einsiedel, 6 June 1814, extr. in *ibid.*, II, 80.
[81] Wrede to King Max. 29 May 1814, extr. in *ibid.*, II, 78.
[82] Protocol of conference of 29 May 1814. See n. 29 above.

ment of each province ceded by France would be placed in the hands of the power to whose permanent possession it would in all probability fall."[83] On this reassuring basis Bavaria became the only German middle state to share in the occupation duties, being assigned to police Würzburg and Aschaffenburg on her own and to divide with Austria the occupation of the area south of the Mosel on the left bank of the Rhine. The territory north of the Mosel between The Rhine and the Maas went to Prussia, that west of the Maas to the British and Dutch. Presumably Bavaria would now release Tyrol and Vorarlberg, but even more important to Metternich was the recognition of the Mosel as the dividing line between North and South Germany, this being a modification in Austria's favor of Hardenberg's plan of April. Austria and Bavaria now had the right of way to dispose of their left-bank zone at their mutual convenience. Less gratifying was the disposition of Mainz. In accordance with one of Hardenberg's options, the fifth German army corps at Mainz under Duke Ernest of Saxe-Coburg was to turn the fortress over to a temporary garrison made up equally of Prussians and Austrians, a delicate arrangement that was to last longer than anyone then imagined. This device put Mainz in the same kind of no man's land as the nearby grand duchy of Frankfurt (now minus Aschaffenburg) which all along had been under the jurisdiction of Stein's administrative department but with an Austrian field marshal as governor. Thus did disagreement narrow but harden as Austria and Prussia confronted each other at the confluence of the Rhine and the Main.[84]

Despite the provisional character of the above, Metternich now felt sure enough of his ground to make formal commitments to Bavaria. Under the pressure of his imminent departure from Paris he was able in one final round of talks to bring Wrede to terms—to be sure, by glossing over in silence a few disputed points such as Berchtesgaden and Füssen. By a convention which they signed on 3 June,[85] Austria was to receive the Tyrol, Vorarlberg, Salzburg, and the Inn and Haus-

[83] Nesselrode to Alexander, 24 June 1814, in *VPR*, VIII, 27.

[84] "Protocole de la conférence des quatres puissances alliées," 31 May 1814, in Martens, *Traités par la Russie*, III, 168. Also Austro-Prussian agreement of 13 June 1814 in Neumann, *Traités par l'Autriche*, II, 477f.; and "Composition des corps d'armée" of Nov. 1813, in Georges Frédéric de Martens, *Nouveau recueil de traités . . .*, 16 vols. (Göttingen, 1817–1842) I, 631. Cf. Mett. to Francis, 23 June 1814, in August Fournier, "Londoner Präludien zum Wiener Kongress," *Deutsche Revue*, XLIII (1918), no. 1, 214.

[85] Texts in Neumann, *Traités par l'Autriche*, II, 480–484, and Comte d'Angeberg, *Le congrés de Vienne et les traités de 1815*, 4 vols.. (Paris, 1864), I, 179-183, are serviceable but incomplete, omitting the crucial third point entirely. See Sahrmann, *Pfalz oder Salzburg?* 35f., who found the original in the Munich archives, which corroborates the text in Wellington, *Supplementary Despatches*, IX, 355–357.

rück districts, the first two immediately in conjunction with the Bavarian occupation of Würzburg and Aschaffenburg, the others only when a definitive settlement was reached. In return Austria promised to obtain equivalents "and even more insofar as she has the means and circumstances permit." Specifically Austria undertook "to use her best offices" to obtain 1) the city and fortress of Mainz with as much left-bank territory as possible, 2) the old Rhenish Palatinate on both sides of the Rhine, and 3) Wetzlar, the town and fortress of Frankfurt, and the county Hanau, all these being, like Aschaffenburg, parts of the former grand duchy of Frankfurt. The absence from this list of Fulda and several other fragments of the duchy no doubt means that in his talks with Hardenberg Metternich had conceded them to Prussia and hoped still to reach an accommodation on that basis. In another provision, less significant for its subsequent application than for the light it shed on Metternich's thinking at the time, any small principalities that might interrupt the contiguity of Bavaria's holdings were to be mediatized.

On the surface the convention seemed to be a typical piece of Metternichian sleight of hand, making concrete awards to Austria while holding out to Bavaria nothing but promises. Even Würzburg and Aschaffenburg were not explicitly awarded her in permanence. Montgelas in Munich was outraged when he saw the text and ever after maintained that Wrede's military bluntness on the one hand offended his adversaries and on the other allowed him to be taken in by the deceitfulness of the diplomats. The truth is different. Until Metternich had settled with the other powers, he could make no promises of other people's territory. Nor can one question his good faith; every territory proferred was scrupulously considered in the light of Austrian interest and the state of the negotiations with Prussia. Metternich may have been overly optimistic, but he had good reason to believe that he could make good. If Wrede had to be content with Austria's good offices, he also protected himself by insisting that Bavaria release lands to Austria only when her own equivalents were in hand. Emperor Francis was also displeased, especially at the exclusion of Berchtesgaden with its valuable salt mines. "The treaty with Bavaria is bad," he said simply,[86] and Metternich had to justify himself. Not a word in it, he explained, was more definite than those in the Treaty of Ried. In the dangerous transitional period it was imperative to have something fixed. "We have a single firm basing point in our relations with Germany," he said. "This point is Bavaria." Without the agreement, he maintained, she "would have been thrown into a sort of wavering which Russia and

[86] Mett. to Francis, 3 June 1814, with Francis's marginal note in HHSA, StK., Vorträge, Cart. 195, April-June, pp. 171–172.

51

Prussia quite naturally would have used to strengthen themselves in all respects that would have detracted from ours."[87] It was a familiar argument, the routine rejoinder to the critics of his appeasement policy: if we do not, our rivals will. And that is why Wrede, among the first with whom Metternich spoke in Paris, was also the last. Around midnight of the day the convention was signed, Metternich set out for London, pressing upon the emperor before he left "the necessity of maintaining a military posture that will command respect."[88]

[87] Mett. to Francis, 25 June 1814, in Fournier, "Londoner Präludien," no. 2, 26f. See also Robert Landauer, "Die Einverleibung Salzburgs durch Österreich 1816," *Mitteilungen der Gesellschaft für Salzburger Landeskunde*, LXXIII (1933), 3.
[88] Mett. to Francis, 3 June 1814, HHSA, StK., Vorträge, Cart. 195, pp. 173–174.

CHAPTER III

STALEMATE IN LONDON

"I AM still destined for adventures that are too great to allow me to expect a moment of repose," Metternich wrote to Wilhelmina von Sagan several days before departure. "London will be torture for me, and this torture will be followed by a new series of tortures."[1] If the allusion was to physical exhaustion, to the din and dash of the past months, to the all too familiar jolts of the highway, we can well believe him. A midnight departure from Paris by coach, a meal the next day in Amiens with Hardenberg and Humboldt, who chanced to be there at the same time, pulling into Boulogne at 5:30 in the morning, a five-hour crossing to Dover, an overnight ride to London, and an early morning arrival there on the 6th—this was hardly the repose one might expect in the soft glow of victory and peace. It was a faster pace than that kept by Hardenberg, who arrived with his king and the tsar several days later, by which time the Austrian minister, a reputed procrastinator, had already presented the prince regent with the Order of the Golden Fleece and the uniform of an Austrian regiment bearing his name and had dined with him at a soirée that lasted till three o'clock in the morning.[2]

Life continued at that tempo: mornings filled with official ceremony, invitations to countless luncheons, supper between eight and nine, and balls only just beginning at eleven at night.[3] On June 14 there was a trip to Oxford to receive an honorary doctorate, with dinner at Christ Church and quadrilles at the town hall afterwards. Three days later there followed a dinner at the Guild Hall in London, the most sumptuous repast in English history to that time and remembered in the country much as the Viennese remembered their congress. Participants in both celebrations agreed that if the one in London was not so protracted, it was more intense and exhausting. Fatigued Metternich no doubt was, but who could believe that this way of life was really torture? Ironically the one painful development in his personal life was the arrival of Sagan herself, bringing with her as she did a spirit of defiance that he was scarcely accustomed to in such circumstances. Searingly jealous of a younger and dashing rival, Prince Alfred von Windisch-grätz, he demanded that she forsake all others while he continue in

[1] Mett. to "A Russian Lady," 1 June 1814, extr. in Dupuis, *Talleyrand*, I, 402.
[2] Mett. to Sagan, 8 June 1814, in Ullrichová, ed., *Briefwechsel*, 257; and Mett. to Francis, 12 June 1814, in Fournier, "Londoner Präludien," 1, 205.
[3] Humboldt to Caroline, 14 June 1814, in *Briefe*, IV, 349.

the comforts and benefits of his marriage to Eleonore. It was a one-sided offer of a sort that he would never have made as a diplomat, at least not to an equal. The duchess was more than an equal, and she refused. The torture was genuine, for Metternich was in raptures over the woman and admired her intelligence, though not enough evidently to give up family and career for her. She in turn, a favorite of Alexander as well, was adept at arousing fits of jealousy and despair that dogged the minister far into the Congress of Vienna, to the disgust of his associates, who blushed to see their leader mooning away like a young Werther.[4]

This distraction aside, Metternich, who shortly before had boasted of all that he had achieved for his age, pursued his social and professional duties with finesse, taking it for granted that they were one and the same. In London he followed the same pattern as in France, lavishing attention upon the crown, standing foursquare with the government, and shunning contact with the political opposition. Especially did he stay out of the marital strife between the prince regent and the princess Caroline, a scandal that was rocking the country. Indeed, at a time when much of England considered him a loathsome beast, the prince regent was genuinely touched by Metternich's attentions. Who else in those days was calling him the arbiter of Europe?[5] Now the biting critic of the Jacobins, now the charming flatterer, the Austrian minister cut a brilliant swath that the emperor Francis could not have matched and did much to restore the prestige he had once helped Austria to lose by the sacrifice of Marie Louise.

Gentz no doubt exaggerated when he called Metternich's performance "un chef-d'oeuvre de perfection," but he was right in adding that it was enhanced by "the coolness that from the first days set in between the emperor Alexander and the prince regent."[6] The tsar in truth, like Metternich himself, brought his Parisian practices across the channel with him. There was the same play to the galleries, the same affinity with the political opposition, the same attempt to capitalize on the hero-worship to which the English were unusually susceptible at the time. There was a difference, however, for whereas in Paris the calculated slights had originated with Louis, in London Alexander himself was the author of gratuitous insults. To begin with, he brought with him as his personal guest Henry Brougham's friend, Prince Czartoryski,

---

[4] Corti, *Frauen*, I, 450–453, who believes Sagan flatly demanded marriage; and Dorothy Gies McGuigan, *Metternich and the Duchess* (New York, 1975), 300–304, who is more circumspect.

[5] Webster, *Castlereagh*, I, 292.

[6] Gentz to Karadja, 9 July 1814, in Friedrich von Gentz, *Dépêches inédites du chevalier de Gentz aux Hospodars de Valachie*, ed. Graf Anton Prokesch von Osten, 3 vols. (Paris, 1876–1877), I, 90.

whom Castlereagh had once requested to leave allied headquarters.[7] Then he refused the quarters reserved for him at St. James in order to be near his sister, the recently widowed Grand Duchess Catherine, in the Pulteney Hotel. There, in the center of London, he sought the plaudits of the same crowd that spat at the mention of the prince regent. Catherine, meanwhile, was even more disagreeable, rejecting with little grace the marriage proposals made to her by the duke of Sussex and the duke of Clarence, joining with Czartoryski in promoting the Polish cause with leaders of the Whig opposition, and stridently declaring her dislike of the musical performances that were the staple of royal entertainment. At the Guild Hall banquet she stopped the operatic music entirely and only sullenly agreed to have "God Save the King" go on.[8]

It is hard to comprehend such behavior, for the tsar and the duchess were not boors, certainly not "the barbarians of the North," that the prince regent was beginning to call them in emulation of the Central European practice.[9] And even if they had been, they might still have made a hit; crusty old Marshal Blücher did so for all his barracks humor, and the cossack general, Matvei Platov, a virtual wild man from the steppes, was likewise lionized. Perhaps the tsar's experience with continental monarchies induced him to believe all monarchs unpopular (as George was), all opposition disloyal (as the Whigs were not), and both ever grasping for leverage wherever it could be found, in this case in the blessing of the savior of Europe. Or perhaps it was an uneasy sense of challenge, an upswelling of the same acute sensitivity that had caused the Tilsit accords to be signed in the middle of the river Niemen. Here he was, in the capital of the country that had fought for two decades only to emerge physically unharmed, financially sound, and dominant on the sea, a counterpoise to landlocked Russia from India to the Dardanelles, from Malta to the Gulf of Finland. Britain was not, like France, a pawn in the game; she was the "other side." Once before, in the War of the Second Coalition, victory over France had been impeded and then reversed in part by a common Anglo-Austrian dread of the Russian advance, whether in Germany or the Mediterranean. Did Alexander feel such a rivalry now under a sunless English sky that belied the month of June?

However that may be, it is a fact that the plummeting star of the Russian visitors hit bottom on an issue that combined international

---

[7] Kraehe, I, 301; and Marian Kukiel, *Czartoryski and European Unity 1770–1861* (Princeton, N.J., 1955), 116.

[8] Harold Nicolson, *The Congress of Vienna: A Study in Allied Unity 1815–1822* (New York, 1946), 116.

[9] Mett. to Francis, 25 June 1814, in Fournier, "Londoner Präludien," 2, 24f.

politics with internal meddling. This was the projected marriage of the English Princess Charlotte to the Hereditary Prince William of Orange. The enterprise was an integral part of Castlereagh's concept of a secure continental beachhead, and he had sedulously nursed it along for many months despite displays of fickleness on Charlotte's part and obstruction by the Whigs, who saw in the affair a means to support Charlotte's mother against the prince regent. At one time the tsar had thought of Catherine herself as a suitable bride for William, but with the announcement of Charlotte's betrothal in February, 1814, Catherine lost interest and in that same month broached the possibility of a match with Archduke Charles of Habsburg, the hero of Aspern, whose merits had come to her attention in Prague the preceding summer.[10] Nevertheless, the rebuff was keenly felt, and the prospect of the marriage of two great fleets was a setback for the tsar's policy of supporting the smaller seapowers against Britain. There is little doubt that Catherine, in collusion with her brother, came to London with the express purpose of sabotaging Charlotte's marriage and substituting the grand duchess Anne, the sister previously turned down by the duke of Berry. As many other factors also combined to break the royal engagement, it is difficult to measure the extent of Catherine's influence, but her antics in this regard, especially her intimate chats with the wavering Charlotte, which carried the contest into the very citadel of her hosts, offended the British sense of fair play and forced Castlereagh to admit to an angry parliament that his work lay in ruins. To make matters worse, it was well known by now that the tsar's first stop after leaving England was to be The Hague, where the Orange family took for granted that the hand of Catherine or Anne would be offered. Metternich for his part could well rejoice that Austrian prestige was rising "in measure as illusions disappear," but he so far shared Castlereagh's fear of Russo-Dutch union that he broached the possibility of an Austrian bride for the prince of Orange.[11]

But Catherine's matrimonial schemes did not stop there. Out of consideration for her father-in-law, Peter (later the duke) of Oldenburg, she was in no hurry to marry, but this sense of decorum did not impede a warm correspondence with Archduke Charles, who increasingly returned her compliments.[12] The exchanges were not passionate

---

[10] Catherine to Alexander, 26 Feb. 1814, in *Correspondance de l'empereur Alexandre Ier avec sa soeur la Grande-Duchesse Catherine, Princesse d'Oldenbourg, puis Reine de Wurtemberg 1805–1818*, intro. Grand Duke Nicolas Mikhailovitch (St. Petersburg, 1910), 169–171; Johann von Bourgoing, *Vom Wiener Kongress* (Brunn, Munich, Vienna, 1943), 239; Kraehe, I, 304.

[11] Mett. to Francis, 12 June 1814, in Fournier, "Londoner Präludien," I, 205; and Webster, *Castlereagh*, I, 299–303.

[12] Münster to Prince Regent, 9 May 1814, in Münster, *Political Sketches*, 169.

by Metternich's standards, but when his police agents in London intercepted a letter of hers, he sensed an opportunity. Any of the tsar's other sisters he might have considered hardly worth the effort, but Catherine's influence on her brother, there for all to see, was worth having on Austria's side. Then the tsar himself sent for him in order to speak of his sister's feelings and to inform him that a courier was already en route to obtain the permission of the empress mother. Metternich doubted that the tsar had reached a decision, but convinced that "the grand princess is henceforth very definite about the whole matter," he urged Francis to act without delay. "I consider it desirable in the present situation," he concluded in an urgent dispatch of 12 June. The emperor, however, though willing to take Catherine into the family, preferred that the bridegroom be the Archduke Palatine Joseph, whose wife, also a Russian princess, had died. Because of this difference he agreed to await Metternich's return to Vienna before proceeding. There the matter rested except for one thing: in Portsmouth Catherine met the dashing young general, Crown Prince William of Württemberg.[13]

Experienced marriage broker that he was, Metternich knew as well as anybody that a great power seeks dynastic unions more to reinforce friendly relations than to redress bad ones. No marriage of itself was going to solve the Polish problem, which was the main purpose of the London conference, if conference it was. In this regard London quickly became a disappointment, worse terrain in some ways than Paris had been. For the first time Metternich realized the full extent of Frederick William's "unprecedented bent for giving in" to all the tsar's ideas. "The most important question of the moment," he reported to the emperor, would probably be settled in short order if "there were some way of counting on the personality of the king." Hardenberg himself shared Metternich's views but other "Prussian heads begin to heat up" in their impatience to do what was necessary to lay hold of Saxony.[14] Meanwhile, the Polish cause gained new adherents in Parliament—not, certainly, through the grating campaign of the tsar but through the quiet efforts of Czartoryski. His cause at any rate was his own; he could merely shrug his shoulders and smile when asked why Poland should not be restored as an *independent* state, a solution with which he was already identified through an article published earlier in the year by his friend Brougham. Officially Czartoryski favored combining the duchy of Warsaw with Russia's Polish provinces under the Russian

[13] Mett. to Francis, 12 June 1814, in Fournier, "Londoner Präludien," 1, 208; Bourgoing, *Wiener Kongress*, 241f.; and Corti, *Frauen*, 1, 455–459.
[14] Mett. to Francis, 12 June 1814, in Fournier, "Londoner Präludien," 1, 205–210.

crown, but neither he nor any other Poles in London left much doubt that they hoped someday to sever the Russian connection. This indeed was the only way to appeal to British liberals, and it was on this basis that Sir James Mackintosh and George Ponsonby raised the question in the House of Commons, arguing that all the ills of Europe, including the French revolution, could be traced to the first partition of Poland.[15]

Metternich had often said as much, but under existing circumstances the flare-up of a true restoration movement in Parliament only added to the prevailing uncertainties. For this reason, he told the emperor, it was best not to bring the issue into the open. For a change, it is Metternich's reports that are almost our only source, and these speak of three-power ministerial conferences held to decide how best to face the Russian challenge: whether to allow Britain as the power least involved to speak for the group or let each power take its own part.[16] Reading between the lines, it is not difficult to see Metternich pleading for British initiative in a joint démarche, Hardenberg begging off because the king ties his hands, and Castlereagh, for fear of breaking up the alliance, refusing to go beyond the role of honest broker, especially as he privately shared his countrymen's sympathies for a Polish restoration.

His advice was to try to outbid Alexander by calling for a completely independent Poland, which he was certain the tsar would have to reject. Metternich was not prepared for such a drastic cure, for even if the tsar did back down, there was no predicting the effect of such an offer on the Poles themselves. It was a risk that looked safer from afar than on the scene, a gamble better held in reserve until all hope for Prussian cooperation was gone. Nevertheless, since this worst case was ever a possibility, the Austrian minister welcomed a means of coping with it and later tried to interest the French government in the idea.[17]

Alexander in the meantime had his own problems and did not press for a decision. Although he adhered to his original demand for the whole of the duchy of Warsaw, minus a small strip for Prussia, he had not yet decided whether to call it Poland, what kind of constitution to give it, or whether and to what extent to add to it the Polish provinces of Russia. He had led the Poles to believe that he wanted to accomplish all these goals, but his Russian advisers, headed by Nesselrode, almost unanimously implored him to desist. Soundings at home took time, and meanwhile the Russian army in Poland continued to grow. He

[15] Dupuis, *Talleyrand*, II, 144–152; Kukiel, *Czartoryski*, 116f.; Kraehe, I, 300; and T. C. Hansard, ed., *The Parliamentary Debates*, XXVIII (London, 1814), 453 and 849 (sessions of 29 June and 27 July 1814).

[16] Mett. to Francis, 12 June 1814 in Fournier, "Londoner Präludien," 1, 205–207.

[17] Webster, *Castlereagh*, I, 318–320; and Mett. to Merveldt, 6 July 1814, extr. in Dupuis, *Talleyrand*, II, 174f., n. 3.

could wait, and so too, for lack of agreement among themselves, must his allies. Metternich thereupon abandoned his plan of concluding a settlement in London and spent his remaining time there trying to strengthen his ties to England and Prussia. In the meantime, he advised the emperor, Austria's best hope was to keep the army strong. "If we command some respect," he said, "we shall prevail in the matter; otherwise the Russian emperor will go his own way without giving us a thought or honoring us with a glance."[18]

In accepting the delay, Metternich believed that the Congress of Vienna would nonetheless begin soon, and this remained his assumption even after Castlereagh had to ask for extra time to explain the break between Charlotte and William to Parliament. By a new schedule adopted on 16 June the four ministers agreed that they would meet in Vienna in early August to prepare decisions for the consideration of the powers signatory to the Treaty of Paris; these in turn would present their program to a plenary meeting of the congress on 15 August.[19] Then the tsar surprised everyone, including Nesselrode evidently, by suddenly announcing that he could not wait so long, that he must return home at once, and could only arrive in Vienna in late September. Castlereagh, who had created the situation, could hardly object. Metternich, however, fearing that the tsar would use the time "to take a definitive stand in Polish affairs," made angry protests.[20] On 20 June he met privately with Hardenberg and Castlereagh and won their support for a joint remonstrance: if the congress had to be postponed, the tsar must at least promise that in the interval "the existing provisional state of things not undergo any change," and that nothing be done to prejudice the decisions of the congress. There was really no way to refuse a demand of this kind, and so Alexander, in departing London on 22 June, left orders for Nesselrode to give the required assurances and vouch for his appearance in Vienna by 27 September.[21]

In drafting a declaration to this effect,[22] Nesselrode insisted that the record show Castlereagh rather than the tsar responsible for the delay, but who could complain about that? Metternich had brought about a freeze of the status quo, and if he was still concerned lest the postponement cause more unrest in the occupied areas, the new situation had its advantages. Exposure to anti-Polish sentiment at home, as Nesselrode pointed out, would be good for the tsar and removal from the

---

[18] Mett. to Francis, 12 June and 23 June 1814, in Fournier, "Londoner Präludien," 1, 210f.

[19] Dupuis, *Talleyrand*, II, 117–120.

[20] Mett. to Francis, 23 June 1814, in Fournier, "Londoner Präludien," 1, 212.

[21] Nessel. to Alex., 24 June 1814 in *VPR*, VIII, 27f. Texts of protocols of the conferences of 16 and 23 June 1814 in Dupuis, *Talleyrand*, II, 117–120.

[22] Text with date of 22 June 1814 in *VPR*, VIII, 25.

tsar's influence good for Frederick William. Moreover, the preliminary conference of the four ministers, which was rescheduled for 10 September with Nesselrode's consent, would now be held not only beyond the reach of Talleyrand but outside the immediate influence of Alexander as well. It would be a great advantage, Metternich advised his own emperor, to be "the only monarch in the vicinity of the negotiation" in the interval. "Metternich's disposition seems to have improved since the declaration," reported the Bavarian observer, Baron Hubert von Pfeffel.[23]

The postponement of the congress had one important side effect, of concern to all but especially to the Austrians. This was the threat to the existing balance of military forces posed by the imminent expiration of the Treaty of Chaumont, at least of those clauses which related to the late campaign against France; the twenty-year mutual assistance pact against future French aggression of course remained in force. The obligation of each power to maintain a force of 150,000 men had ceased with the signing of the peace treaty.[24] Thereafter troop levels were determined mainly by the convenience of each power and the continuation at wartime levels of the British subsidies, which, however, were to expire: on 31 July for Austria and Prussia, on 30 September for Russia, these intervals having been projected to cover the costs of returning the armies home. If a Polish settlement had been reached in London, the dates would have sufficed, but now Metternich faced two months of extreme danger with no assurance that the emperor and his hard-pressed financial officials in Vienna would be willing or able to fulfill Austria's occupation duties and still maintain the flow of troops into Galicia and Bohemia that his reports urgently advised. To make matters worse, Britain, still engaged in transporting troops to the battlefields of North America, was as anxious as the Austrians were to dismantle a war machine on the continent. Russia and Prussia, on the other hand, their territorial claims still unrealized, could be counted on to maintain their forces at full strength—approximately 200,000 each according to Metternich's calculations. How galling, moreover, to think that in the same two-month interval the Russians would continue to receive "return money," as it was called, which could be applied to their military buildup in Poland. Clearly fair play and common prudence dictated a renewal in some form of the Chaumont arrangements.[25]

[23] Mett. to Francis, 25 June 1814 in Fournier, "Londoner Präludien," 1, 215f.; and Pfeffel to Montgelas, 26/27 June 1814, in Dupuis, *Talleyrand*, II, 138–141.

[24] Kraehe, I, 303f. Text of treaty of Chaumont in full in Martens, *Traités par la Russie*, III, 155–165.

[25] Mett. to Francis, 28 June 1814, in Fournier, "Londoner Präludien," 2, 28; and John M. Sherwig, *Guineas and Gunpowder* (Cambridge, Mass., 1969), 323–327.

Since it was Castlereagh's aim to reduce commitments as much as possible, a simple extension of the Chaumont treaty was out of the question. What emerged instead was a military convention that omitted outright subsidies altogether but cut the military obligation of each power by a proportionate amount: namely, to 75,000 men, just half the Chaumont level and in effect eliminating the troops heretofore supported by the subsidies. Since England retained her previous option of substituting cash for her contingent or portions thereof, there was available an extra amount to support the other contingents at levels above 75,000, the annual rate being twenty pounds sterling for each infantryman and thirty for each cavalryman and his equipment.[26] Ostensibly these forces were deemed necessary to preserve order in the occupied zones until the final settlement, but the omission of any reference to France and the inclusion of a pledge "to employ these armies only in common accord" betrayed clearly enough that the powers involved distrusted each other most of all. If Castlereagh viewed the pact as a pledge from the tsar "that he would not attempt to settle his difficulties by the sword,"[27] it was no less true that Alexander gained some protection against a hostile combination that included France. At Portsmouth at the time, he quickly approved Nesselrode's conduct and allowed the document to be signed on 29 June.[28]

Metternich's satisfaction was more mundane. He had promised the emperor that he would never sign a military convention without his authorization; he did so now, he explained, in order to avoid exclusion from the optional subsidies expected from Britain, for apart from a force of about 22,000 in Belgium the British intended to discharge their obligation with cash. Austria's share, he estimated, would be about £30,000 per month, enough to support about 15,000 men. Uninformed at the time about the exact deployment of the armies, he calculated that Austria must keep at least 40,000 in Italy, 30,000 in Galicia and Moravia, and 10,000 on the Rhine—a total of 80,000, enough to meet her obligation and still receive a subsidy to cover the excess. All in all, the figure of 75,000 suited Austria's situation better than that of any other power. Still, Metternich held an Austrian force of 80,000 or so to be the absolute minimum, acceptable, if at all, only because of Bavarian assistance in the occupation and because "dem-

---

[26] Text of convention of 29 June 1814 in Neumann, *Traités par l'Autriche*, II, 188–190. Although Castlereagh at Chaumont had reckoned the subsidy the equivalent of 50,000 troops for each ally, the formula in fact yielded 75,000, the difference probably being due to the lower cost of continental troops. See Castle. to Hamilton, 10 Mar. 1814 in *Castle, Corr.*, IX, 335f.; and Treaty of Chaumont, Art. IX.

[27] As Webster, *Castlereagh*, I, 296, maintains.

[28] Pirenne, *Sainte-Alliance*, I, 79, imputes deliberate calculation to the tsar in this regard, overlooking that he had no part in initiating or negotiating the convention.

onstrations" did not need so much stuff behind them as real military campaigns. "I cannot recommend enough to your majesty," he reported, "to persevere in the most formidable military posture till the conclusion of the congress. Only in this way can the latter have a salutary outcome—but also with these measures I can vouch for such an outcome."[29]

Meanwhile, though definitive settlements in London were now out of reach, the quest for private understandings and strategic advantage went on. Once the Polish problem had been shelved, the question that next sprang to the fore was the future of the Netherlands. Anxious to counteract the tsar's expected blandishments in the Hague and to prove to the house of Orange that the flightiness of a young lady should make no difference in the relations between mature powers, Castlereagh went out of his way to shower honors on the hereditary prince and was determined to deliver Belgium to Orange rule as swiftly and completely as possible.[30] To turn the Anglo-Dutch troops in Belgium over to Dutch command was no problem under the terms of the occupation agreement, but formally to invest Prince William with the direction of the provisional government, to do so in a way that explicitly made the move preparatory to permanent union, and to spell out the terms of its realization required the further cooperation of the powers.

Of these the first in line was Prussia, because of her direct territorial and strategic interests. As noted earlier, Hardenberg's plan of 29 April had provided for a Dutch-German boundary along the Maas, Dutch possession of the dangerously exposed fortress Luxemburg, and a perpetual alliance between the Netherlands and the future German league. None of these did Castlereagh relish, but around the middle of June he and the Prussian minister reached an understanding. Without specifying what territory was meant, Hardenberg apparently agreed to the immediate transfer of the Belgian provisional government to the prince of Orange under terms previously negotiated by the British envoy in The Hague, Lord Richard Trench Clancarty.[31] Castlereagh

[29] Mett. to Francis, 6 July 1814 in Fournier, "Londoner Präludien," 1, 31. Metternich's estimates were conservative; in reality the Austrian troop levels were far higher during this period.

[30] Webster, *Castlereagh*, I, 302f.

[31] This matter must be stated with circumspection because the authorities disagree about the dates of the protocol concerned. D'Angeberg, *Congrès*, I, 182, gives 14 June. Neumann, *Traités par l'Autriche*, II, 484f. and Georges Frédéric de Martens, *Nouveau supplément au recueil de traités . . .* , 3 vols. (Göttingen, 1839–1842), I, 330f. date the conference 14 June but the signing of the protocol 21 June—in Paris, which is certainly wrong. Nesselrode in his report of 24 June (in *VPR*, VIII, 22f.) says the protocol was of that date, as does Fournier, "Londoner Präludien," 1, 133, n. 1. A conference on 14 June seems unlikely because the principal ministers were taken up with festivities in Oxford that day, but otherwise all the dates may have

in turn consented to the incorporation of the Orange share of Luxemburg in the German league, the fortress itself to become a federal
fortress maintained by the league as a whole. A similar status was
indicated as a *possible* solution to the problem of Mainz, the tentative
language reflecting Hardenberg's conviction that this solution was still
only a last resort.[32] Thus the Netherlands were to be closely linked to
the defense system of Germany while remaining for the bulk of their
territories entirely free of military commitments to Germany. Münster,
who signed the protocol on 15 June in behalf of Castlereagh, had his
own reason to be pleased since any association of the Netherlands with
the confederation aided Hanover in counterbalancing Prussia.[33]

Metternich's interests in these developments were less direct but
serious all the same. Castlereagh's plan for Mainz was a disappointment
but nothing new and certainly not yet binding on either Austria or
Bavaria—or Prussia either for that matter. In regard to Belgium Austria's only problem was how to withdraw as gracefully as possible.
There, as in Germany, she was faced with a restorative movement based
on the traditional estates. In the spring the latter had bombarded allied
headquarters with petitions pleading for a return to Austrian rule; for
despite bad memories of Joseph II, their fear of the Dutch, of Protestants, and of business competitors was greater still. Since Metternich
had already signed Belgium away at Troyes in February, he could no
more heed their wishes than he could those of the mediatized houses
in Germany. To allay anxiety as much as possible, however, he also
induced his allies to issue a guarantee of the Catholic religion and
other Belgian interests and to place an Austrian general, Baron Karl
von Vincent, in charge of the occupation.[34]

Vincent's position was awkward in the extreme, being reminiscent
of old Franz Georg Metternich's mission twenty years before.[35] In
political matters subject to the immediate authority of Stein's administrative department and in military affairs having to depend on Dutch,
English, and Prussian troops, he yet had daily to deal with a populace

---

some validity, reflecting different phases of the discussion. In any case the texts are
the same and the issues not in doubt.

[32] Karl Griewank, *Der Wiener Kongress und die Neuordnung Europas 1814–1815*
(Leipzig, 1942), 120, n. 67.

[33] Text in full in Dupuis, *Talleyrand*, II, 123f. Cf. Webster, *Castlereagh*, I, 293, who
exaggerates the definitiveness of the agreement.

[34] Mett. to Vincent, 29 March 1814, with protocol of conference of 13 Mar. and
Austrian declaration of 14 Mar. in Herman Theodor Colenbrander, ed., *Gedenk-
stukken der algemeene Geschiedenis van Nederland van 1795 tot 1840*, 22 vols. (The
Hague, 1905–1922), VII, 329–331; "Note verbale adressée aux députés belges," 14
Mar. 1814, in *ibid.*, 92. Also G. J. Renier, *Great Britain and the Establishment of the
Kingdom of the Netherlands* (London, 1930), 240–285; and Herman Theodor Col-
enbrander, *Vestiging van het Koninkrijk 1813–1814* (Amsterdam, 1927), pp. 149–193.

[35] Kraehe, I, 13f.

that still expected the Habsburgs to evince an interest in its fate—where in fact their only interest was to curry favor with Castlereagh and to see to it that in letting go of the provinces they also wrote off the debts still chargeable to Austria from that quarter. A further difficulty for Vincent came from the Prussians, who were slow to remove their troops back across the Maas and made unusually severe requisitions in the area.[36]

Throughout, Metternich consistently backed the British, advising Vincent to resist Prussian interference and support Clancarty's terms of union, which provided strong safeguards for the equality of the two countries but, at Dutch insistence, made no concession to federalism or provincial privileges as the Belgians desired; the articles rather maintained the same rigid centralism that Metternich condoned in the Rheinbund states. The internal structure of the new state was not of course his main concern, but it underscored once again the dissociation of his policy from the old Reich and its privileged estates. So complete was the break that in the final agreement, which the allied ministers signed on 21 June, they expressly handed the provisional government to the prince of Orange "by virtue of their right of conquest" with no mention of Austria's previous possession. In this way the former debts were buried forever and the Belgians denied a voice in their destiny.[37] With Vincent's departure from Brussels an old liability was at an end, but himself of Lorraine origin, the general could not forgo the comment that "the mass of the people and the great majority of the Belgians are painfully affected by seeing themselves separated from Austria and not being able to relax in the thought of returning to the mild rule of the august house."[38] Metternich was used to talk like this from the Breisgau, but coming from the rich provinces that had rebelled against Habsburg rule in 1789 and made a fool of his father in 1794, such professions of devotion would hardly have moved him even if his hands had not been tied.

Metternich's renunciation of Belgium was more than a means of courting Britain; it was in itself an Austrian interest, for which, moreover, Castlereagh had long before delivered a quid pro quo: the preservation of France as a great power. Saxony was altogether different. Here the particular Austrian interest was its preservation as a buffer, which most Austrians were unwilling to sacrifice even in the interests of the general European equilibrium. Metternich stood almost alone

---

[36] Renier, *Britain and the Netherlands*, 251 and 267–271.

[37] Mett. to Vincent, 1 May 1814, in Colenbrander, *Gedenkstukken*, VII, 333f.; and Renier, *Britain and the Netherlands*, 255–257. Text of the eight conditions in Colenbrander, *Vestiging van het Koninkrijk*, 181f. See also n. 33 above.

[38] Vincent to Mett., 3 Aug. 1814, in Colenbrander, *Gedenkstukken*, VII, 339.

in his belief that the sacrifice should be made if necessary, but only if first assured of Prussian collaboration in Poland and her compliance with respect to Mainz. Since neither condition could be met in London, he could not give in on Saxony. Although the question was never officially on the agenda, it would appear that informally he urged Hardenberg and the Saxon king himself to be satisfied with part of the kingdom. The context of such remarks, however, is very nebulous. When General Karl Friedrich Ludwig von Watzdorf, the Saxon envoy in London, raised the issue of 19 June, Metternich advised against either a protest or a demand for the termination of Prince Repnin's provisional government. On the other hand, unlike Hardenberg and Alexander, who avoided Watzdorf entirely, and Castlereagh, who was cool, the Austrian minister treated him with respect as the represent-ative of a legitimate sovereign whose fate was still undecided. Austria, he said, was outraged at the king's unprecedented detention as a pris-oner of war and would back his personal situation by all means short of war. This sounded like strong support; in reality the statement merely reiterated what the emperor had often said and amounted to a warning that Austria would not single-handedly fight for Saxony. In several interviews between 19 and 26 June Metternich advised the general to appear in Vienna with plenary powers and request admit-tance to the congress.[39]

This advice has sometimes been adduced as evidence of duplicity and even proof that Metternich's offers to Hardenberg were never sincere. The truth, however, is that his handling of Watzdorf was perfectly correct: uninspired and conventional, perhaps, but friendly, solicitous, and candidly noncommittal, as the situation required. The Prussians meanwhile were more distrustful of the tsar, who persistently rejected their pleas to transfer the administration of Saxony to them. If the occupation assignments were meant to presage ultimate posses-sion, why should Saxony be different from Belgium, Alexander's so-licitude different from Castlereagh's, the right of conquest applied in one place and not another? Stein raised these questions, and so did Humboldt. "I may be wrong and judge too harshly," said the latter of the tsar a few weeks later, "but I always ask: why not leave the admin-istration of the land to us? . . . It can only be to keep in his hands what basically belongs to us already and thereby make us dependent on him." Whether Humboldt was genuinely surprised at the tsar's stand

[39] Dupuis, *Talleyrand*, II, 124–138 with copious extracts from Watzdorf's reports; Walter Kohlschmidt, *Die sächsische Frage auf dem Wiener Kongress und die sächsische Diplomatie dieser Zeit* (Dresden, 1930), 60f.; and Hard. to Mett., 7 July 1814, in HHSA, StK., Kongressakten, Cart. 7. Cf. Gentz to Karadja, 21 June 1814, in *Dépêches inedites*, I, 78–84.

or merely trying to arouse Hardenberg's suspicions, the fact remains that the tsar had no more reason to deliver Saxony on credit than did Metternich. Besides, he wanted to reserve substantial parts of the kingdom for his in-laws, the duke of Weimar and the duke of Coburg. The result in any case was to link the Saxon and Polish questions more closely than ever and to defer both till the Congress of Vienna.[40]

With the adjournment of the stalemated territorial disputes, it was possible to deal with the German constitutional question in a deliberate way and at the highest level. Metternich had "regular conferences" with Hardenberg in hopes of "adjusting our views on the subject in advance of further deliberations." Progress evidently was considerable; he promised the emperor he would be able to submit the main outlines on his return and called the plan they were working on "the only one really feasible." He also referred to "temporary measures" that were under consideration for "ameliorating the lot of the subjects in the smaller despotisms of central Germany." Unfortunately the circumspect foreign minister added no substance to these tantalizing lines and thus left us to deduce what we can from a ten-point outline that Hardenberg showed him during their conversations in London.[41]

Building on Humboldt's earlier suggestions, the chancellor began with the familiar idea of a directory consisting of Austria, Prussia, Bavaria, Hanover, and Württemberg, but whereas Humboldt had thought to assure the preponderance of Austria and Prussia by arbitrarily assigning them more votes and immensely larger Kreise to head, Hardenberg simply divided Germany into seven Kreise with Austria and Prussia in charge of two each and casting votes accordingly. He also proposed a rotating chairmanship, a major concession to Münster though watered down by a seven-step cycle, which meant that the two powers between them would preside four out of seven years. The directory or council of Kreis chiefs, as it was called, was to exercise the executive powers of the confederation, make war and peace, and have a right of consultation in the internal affairs of the states within certain limits to be determined. In the Kreise themselves each chief was to

[40] Hard. and Stein to Alex., both 21 June 1814, in Stein, *Briefe*, v, 26ff.; Humb. to Hard., 23 July 1814, in *Gesammelte Schriften*, XVII, 65f.; and Martens, *Traités par la russie*, VII, 156, referring to the tsar's instructions for his plenipotentiaries at the Congress of Vienna.
[41] Mett. to Francis, 25 June 1814, in Fournier, "Londoner Präludien," 2, 24. The ten-point outline, undated, is in ZSTA, Merseburg, 2.4.1.I, No. 1559, pp. 77–79 (original in Hardenberg's hand) and pp. 80f. (copy), and is the source of the following. The presence of another copy, in NSHSA, Hanover, Des. 91, No. 23, pp. 21–24, indicates that Münster was also privy to the negotiation. The summary in Gebhardt, *Humboldt als Staatsmann*, II, 121f., is incomplete and misses the crucial significance of the document. For full text see Appendix A.

supervise the military and police, "administer public security," enforce federal and Kreis law, provide a supreme court for the whole Kreis, and preside over the Kreis assembly.

For the lesser states Hardenberg proposed a council of princes and estates, those with a population above 100,000 casting whole (*viril*) votes, the rest being grouped into curiae in which several of them would share a vote. Together the two councils were to constitute a federal diet, but they were to meet and vote separately, their differences being composed by a conference committee drawn from both. Each Kreis would likewise have an assembly, presided over by the Kreis chief and consisting of all secular princes who had formerly sat in the old Reichstag. Only those with populations above 100,000 were to keep their own armies, tax their subjects, administer higher justice, and otherwise govern within the limits allowed by federal law. All the rest, some twenty-one in number, were to have no armies, only residual taxing powers (that is, a claim to what remained after the Kreis chief had skimmed off his share), and a police and judicial function confined to the local level and exercised under the supervision of the Kreis. They would retain, however, such ancient sources of revenue as the regalia. Technically, this arrangement would not have constituted mediatization but only because the victims were to be subordinated through the machinery of the Kreis and not by the imposition of the Kreis chief's sovereignty.

At the same time Hardenberg meant to elevate the already mediatized houses to this same status, and to do so he had to strain the accession treaties to the breaking point. The passage in question, soon to be referred to as the "onerous" clause, permitted limits to be placed on the sovereignty, independence, and territorial integrity of the acceding states if "necessary in peacetime for preserving the independence of Germany."[42] Heretofore this clause had been construed mainly as a reference to the projected federal institutions and certain territorial exchanges necessary to the military security of the Bund. Even Hardenberg, in his master plan of April, had painstakingly calculated the deserts of each state on the basis of existing population. What he now proposed amounted to a unilateral revision of the treaties: not existing population but the scale of 1803 must be the norm, whether or not the "independence of Germany" was involved.

Since Hardenberg never wholly abandoned this position and returned to it at the Congress of Vienna, it is essential now to see in his own words how he put it to Metternich in London.

---

[42] See Kraehe, I, 238.

Justice speaks loudly for the mediatized [he said]. Regarding the possessions of the *Länder* the standard that should be adopted is the state of possession fixed by the Imperial Recess of 1803 after the peace of Lunéville, exceptions to be made only where the general good so requires or at least is not harmed by them. Baden, Darmstadt, Nassau, Sigmaringen cannot complain if the mediatized bestowed on them through Napoleon's dispositions are taken from them. . . . Let us assign the mediatized to the Kreise and thereby join them to the states of the Kreis chiefs as the present situation demands. *In this way they become* eo ipso *equal to the small states that belonged to the Rheinbund, and that is fair and right.*[43]

From these avenging pronouncements Bavaria and Württemberg were to be exempt, partly because of their more favorable treaties and their status as Kreis chiefs, but also because Hardenberg never intended their Kreise to extend beyond their own territory. They would keep their existing mediatized lands but would be required to grant their proprietors the same rights that the other mediatized houses received through the Kreise. For them the system would be an instrument not for making indirect annexations but for sabotaging control over portions of territory they already possessed. Even the former imperial knights, though Hardenberg pointedly refused to restore them, were to be privileged members of federally guaranteed diets, or Landtage as these bodies were traditionally called.

Apart from the startling assertion of the territorial scale of 1803, the most striking feature of the chancellor's thinking at this time is the strong emphasis on the Kreise at the expense of unity at the top. A supreme executive organ consisting of five members alternating in the chairmanship was inherently cumbersome, and its collective powers, aside from that over war and peace, were meager in comparison to those each Kreis chief would exercise individually, another issue that was to come up again at the Congress of Vienna. Ordinary justice, for example, was to reach its apex not in a federal supreme court (which the Prussians later proposed mainly for the protection of the estates and mediatized houses) but in the five separate high courts of the Kreis chiefs. In similar fashion the clauses about the lower house related mainly to its composition, its powers being vaguely limited to a share in promoting the general interest, a much more modest role than Humboldt had visualized for it. Indeed, there is discernible in these provisions an undercurrent of disagreement in the Prussian camp. In his plan of December, 1813, which proposed a four-power directory but no Kreise, Humboldt had explicitly warned that any attempt to

[43] The ten-point outline, as in n. 41 above. Emphasis mine.

ameliorate the lot of the Standesherren by mediatizing the smaller sovereigns would inevitably lead to the creation of four or five large states which could not maintain German unity for long. "Guarantees of internal rights and a common court would be unimaginable," he had written, "and all the mediatized princes would very soon lose their rights to the encroachments of the larger governments."[44] Humboldt at the time probably had absorption into actual states in mind, but the chancellor's Kreise pointed in that direction too.

Once again it is clear that Hardenberg was less interested in an attenuated influence over all Germany than in an iron control over the North, for apart from Hanover's modest Kreis, all the rest of North Germany would have been caught in the nets of Prussia's military command, her supreme court, her executive and police agencies, and her Kreis assemblies—all this without counting the mediatized and associated lands in her population totals. Prussia no doubt had the capability to impose her control; at issue was the permission of Europe to do so. No wonder the chancellor felt constrained to add (whether sheepishly or defiantly, we do not know) that "nothing in this is contrary to the treaties concluded in Frankfurt."[45]

Was this the plan that Metternich described as the only one really feasible? It seems unlikely. Both its informal style (Hardenberg occasionally used the first person) and its extreme substance indicate rather that the outline was a position paper standing near the beginning of their dialogue, though not perhaps without some roots in previous exchanges of views. On this assumption let us examine a quite different draft that Hardenberg completed over the next three weeks, two of them spent almost constantly in the company of Metternich. In this more polished project of forty-one articles[46] the directory was expanded to include the grand duke of Baden and the elector of Hesse as codirectors of Kreise, and the sovereign prince of the Netherlands for his German territory, the chairmanship being rotated through a twelve-step cycle. Although Austria and Prussia retained their supremacy with extra votes if they stood together, the larger directory in fact expanded Vienna's opportunities to put together anti-Prussian combinations. Moreover, as now projected, the directory would have no legislative function, and though its members were to join the lower assembly with extra votes, they could prevail only in the unlikely case that they were united among themselves.

At the same time a much sharper distinction was drawn between the

---

[44] Humboldt, *Gesammelte Schriften*, XI, 109.

[45] Ten-point outline as in n. 41 above.

[46] Text in Stein, *Briefe*, v, 841–852. First brought to light and published by Griewank, "Preussen und die Neuordnung," 269–276.

small states and the mediatized houses. Gone was the arbitrary distinction between states above and below 100,000 in population; even the houses of Reuss, Waldeck, Lippe, and Schwarzburg, previously consigned to Prussian sovereignty, were now, in Hardenberg's terminology, to be "conserved as immediate members of the federation."[47] Only one still surviving state, Liechtenstein, was singled out for mediatization, and a listing of Standesherren privileges was reserved for separate negotiation later, except to say that these families should constitute the first estate in each state under an estates-type constitution (*landständische Verfassung*); in short, they would not be autonomous Kreis estates (*Kreisstände*) or in any other way "*eo ipso* equal to the small states that belonged to the Rheinbund." Regarding the internal organization of the Kreise, only military affairs and the procedure for appealing judicial decisions were discussed; of Kreis executive powers, Kreis diets, and seats for all the former Reichstag members there was now no mention; in fact, the powers of the individual Kreis chiefs, previously spelled out in detail, were no longer enumerated at all. Clearly all these changes were in the direction of less status for the Standesherren at one level and for the Kreis chiefs at another—in short, greater equality among sovereigns, exactly the principles Metternich would be expected to defend.

This is not to say that all these changes can be traced to Metternich alone or that Hardenberg's retreat accommodated the Austrian position completely, only that it gives some idea of the probable course of debate. Metternich had long since accepted a directory in principle and some distinction between large and small states, including further mediatizing if necessary. The difference between a severe centralism exercised by the two great powers and a loose federalism was mainly a quantitative matter: how large a directory, how many Kreise, and with what powers? The deletion of a bill of rights for the Standesherren is especially significant, for Metternich's report to the emperor, cited above, actually indicates a certain concern about small-state despotism but mainly as an interim problem quite separate from the making of a permanent constitution.[48] The least Metternichian article was the provision for *landständische Verfassungen*, always synonymous with infringed sovereignty; but viewed as substitutes for the Kreis estates of the previous plan, such arrangements seem by comparison a step backward toward the status quo, especially as allowance was to be made for variations in local conditions. In arguing along these lines, the Austrian minister, if true to form, no doubt assured Hardenberg that their aims

[47] Hardenberg's "Mémoire supplementaire," of the same date, relating to the territorial settlement. See n. 55 below.
[48] See above, n. 41.

were alike but that it was better to take one step at a time, relying on the force of circumstances to bring the other states into line rather than provoke panic and resistance by explicit announcements. Given his self-assurance and unfounded optimism regarding other matters at this time, he could easily have construed their efforts as focused on "the only plan really feasible."

That Metternich and Hardenberg considered themselves divided mostly by details about proportion is further indicated by another witness: Humboldt. Though not always present at the ministerial conversations, he knew in general that there would be no final decision in London. Anxious that a draft constitution nevertheless be prepared in advance of the congress, he urged Hardenberg to try to arrange for a meeting of the five largest German states—never, be it noted, including Saxony—in Vienna by 1 August at the latest. These states would constitute a "preparatory committee for the German constitution" and would deliberate on the basis of guidelines laid down by the four allied powers. The choice of these particular states, he emphasized, was merely an expedient and was not to prejudice the ultimate composition of the directory. Given his preference for an even smaller directory, this is additional evidence that the issue was much disputed in London.[49]

At the same time he proposed that the powers prepare for the committee a list of the guidelines "which could still be taken into consideration before our departure from London." This too was full of generalities.[50] There would be a permanent league of princes, membership

[49] Humb. to Hard., 26 June 1814, in *Gesammelte Schriften*, XI, 219f.

[50] "Bases pour servir de norme au travail du comité préparatoire," text in Schmidt, *Verfassungsfrage*, 157f. Schmidt, thinking only in terms of the development of Humboldt's ideas, places this undated memorandum *before* the "Mémoire préparatoire" of April, the main reason being its brevity and lack of detail. The possibility that it followed the more elaborate paper and was reduced to generalities for purposes of negotiation did not occur to him. My main reason, however, for linking it to the letter to Hardenberg of 26 June is the expression "comité préparatoire," which was so new that Humboldt called attention to it in the letter itself: he would admit to this "Comité préparatoire de la constitution Allemande (car c'est ainsi que je le nommerais)" only the ministers of . . . etc. In the April memorandum, by contrast, the committee was called "Comité qui sera chargé de la rédaction de la Constitution Germanique." It is also worth noting that between December, 1813, and April, 1814, he knew exactly whom he wanted on the directory (Austria, Prussia, Bavaria, and Hanover) and would not at that time have left the issue open as if he had not decided. Griewank, "Preussen und die Neuordnung," 246, n. 1, is even more confused. He makes no reference to the memorandum, but realizing that something is needed, he places the "Mémoire préparatoire" in this slot, saying flatly that Schmidt had misdated it. Schmidt's argument for April, however, is irrefutable though Dijon, not Paris, was the place of origin. The original documents are filed in an order corresponding to Schmidt's and Griewank's errors (ZSTA, Merseburg, 2.4.1.I, Nos. 1454 and 1559) but whether this order fooled the authors or the authors misled the archivists is difficult to say.

in which would be determined by the size and antiquity of holdings and other reasonable considerations. "A small number of these princes" would form a directory, with certain powers to be determined, but among them would be that over war and peace, with all the wholly German states barred from waging their own wars. There would be a diet in which all members could vote. The Kreis principle was affirmed but no number of Kreise given; only states of a certain size might exercise military and judicial powers, but where to draw the line was still to be negotiated. Humboldt included a federal court but avoided a key controversy by denying it authority in disputes between princes and subjects; the rights of the latter were to be decided later. It must have pained this scholarly man to reduce his ideas to such generalities, but this was no time to philosophize about the nature of government. Now he was mapping out a plan of action, seeking to place the authority of the great powers behind at least the foundations of a German constitution. His primary concern had to be the existing consensus as far as he could perceive it, and that is what makes his diluted guidelines a credible key to the state of the debate as the sojourn in London drew to a close.

As a plan of procedure, however, Humboldt's advice was disregarded. Although both Metternich and Hardenberg favored a great-power guarantee of a German league once it came into being, as per the Treaty of Paris, they had no intention of allowing other powers a hand in determining its particular structure. Humboldt's course was all too reminiscent of the Imperial Recess and Tilsit. Instead of endorsing his guidelines, Hardenberg preferred to deal directly with Metternich, promising that he would draw up a definitive plan and send it to Vienna for review. By the middle of August, Metternich estimated, they would "together have the plan of the German constitution cleared up" and be in a position to draw the three middle states into the proceedings, probably by inviting them to send plenipotentiaries to Vienna. Then, on 10 September Hardenberg would appear, along with Castlereagh and Nesselrode, to settle territorial questions. About 1 October the monarchs would arrive to put the finishing touches on their work.[51] This was more than a schedule; it was a grand strategy, a strategy that left Metternich as the mediator between Prussia and the middle states. Just as the tsar would not be present when the ministers discussed Poland, so would the chancellor be absent from the discussions on Germany. Humboldt, to be sure was scheduled to arrive in Vienna on 1 August to resume his duties as the Prussian ambassador, but neither his rank nor his role in the previous bilateral

[51] Mett. to Francis, 28 June 1814, in Fournier, "Londoner Präludien," 2, 28.

negotiation would enable him to stand up effectively to the middle states if Metternich did not.[52] It was the strategy of grand mediation again, this time in miniature.

Metternich left London on 30 June in good spirits over the results of his sojourn, especially his role in undermining the prestige of the tsar. "We still have a storm to ride out but I'm not afraid of it," he wrote the emperor. "Here again we stand at the head of the good cause; the principles we proceed from are unassailable and will surely withstand the battle against the mad ideas of the Russian emperor." For this battle the journey itself offered many opportunities. He traveled in the company of Hardenberg and Humboldt, spending some seventeen hours becalmed on the English Channel and learning to sleep in a hammock; whether the German constitution was discussed we do not know. Coaches were waiting at Boulogne to take the group to Paris, where they arrived on 2 July. Humboldt went on to join Frederick William in Neuchâtel, Switzerland, while Metternich had another five days with Hardenberg in the French capital.[53]

This time too was well spent. News had just arrived of an ill-considered trip that Marie Louise had made to the waters of Aix-les-Bains in Savoy, and good royalists were quick to see in it the beginning of a Bonapartist plot. Metternich believed the episode "would come to nothing, like a shot in the air," but he chided the emperor for allowing it to happen and begged him to keep his daughter home till after the congress. Nervous about the loyalty of the army and suspicious of Austrian policy in Italy, the French king needed all Metternich's reassurances that the Habsburgs had abandoned the Bonapartes forever, and who could do this better than the author of the original dynastic bond? Metternich in his turn was sensitive to any sign of Franco-Russian entente, and on this score he was completely satisfied. He was astonished at what he found of the tsar's trafficking with the Jacobins in France, which seemed deliberately aimed at the undermining of Louis' throne. A two-hour conversation with the king on 6 July convinced him that "between this and the Russian court there exists far more tension than rapprochement and that in the future negotiations we shall witness the singular phenomenon of all parties without exception standing up against the Russian system." This much he jubilantly wrote the emperor, but he was as well anxious to get the news back to England that the king endorsed the strategy to be used. He

[52] Humb. to Caroline, 30 June 1814, in *Briefe*, IV, 363. Throughout the congress, Humboldt, though a plenipotentiary to it, remained vis-à-vis Austria merely the Prussian ambassador and keenly resented his inferiority to Metternich, the foreign minister. Humb. to Caroline, 9 April 1815, *ibid.*, IV, 523f.

[53] Mett. to Francis, 5 July 1814, in Fournier, "Londoner Präludien," 2, 29f.; and Humb. to Caroline, 2 July 1814, in *Briefe*, IV, 365.

agrees, Metternich told Merveldt, that if the tsar insists on proclaiming "a Russian Poland, we shall have recourse to all means, even if necessary, that of declaring an independent Poland in order to prevent it."

Since France of all powers actually preferred a Polish restoration, which for Austria could only be an act of desperation, Metternich probably broached the notion more as bait to keep France neutral than as an invitation to join a bloc. To remove all doubt on this point, he cautioned General Vincent, who arrived in Paris a few weeks later as the new chargé, to refrain from any negotiation. "We hope," he explained, "that all these reasons together will prevent France for the present moment from playing an active role in Europe." A central bloc against France *and* Russia, not a triple alliance with Britain and France, remained his goal.[54]

For this reason he continued his close relations with Hardenberg, trying to narrow the gap between them. By now he had at last convinced the chancellor that Austria would refuse a corridor to the Breisgau at the expense of the South German states, whereupon Hardenberg reduced the compensations he had earlier visualized for these states on the left bank of the Rhine. He also withdrew the proposal for mediatizing the Hohenzollern principalities, assigning them instead to a Kreis to be led by Württemberg. According to his figures the refusal of the corridor meant an outright sacrifice for Austria of 440,000 souls, but it did not include abandonment of the Breisgau itself. "From what Prince Metternich tells us," Hardenberg reported in his revised plan, "Austria will be satisfied with a part of the Breisgau," the sacrifice of a connecting link being made "to facilitate the settlement in Germany."[55] Six weeks later Humboldt similarly advised that the dispute between Metternich and Stadion was not over the Breisgau itself but over the value of a corridor to it, which was not worth antagonizing the South German courts.[56] An unsupported foothold on the Rhine

[54] Mett. to Francis, 5 and 7 July 1814, "London Präludien," 2, 29–32; Mett. to Merveldt, 6 July 1814, extr. in Dupuis, *Talleyrand*, II, 174, n. 3; Mett. to Vincent, 8 Aug. 1814, extr. in *ibid.*, 304. Cf. Griewank, *Wiener Kongress*, 68.

[55] Hardenberg's "Mémoire supplementaire" of mid-July in ZSTA, Merseburg, 2.4.1.I, no. 1570, pp. 44–45. I am indebted to Griewank, *Wiener Kongress*, 119 and n. 65, for supplying a title and an approximate date for this memorial from a note of Humboldt's. I accept this even though Griewank's reading of the document missed the clear reference to Austria's retention of the Breisgau. The terms "Breisgau" and "a part of the Breisgau" were used interchangeably in this period to denote a territory of between 140,000 and 150,000 in population.

[56] Humb. to Fred. Wm., 20 Aug. 1814, in *Gesammelte Schriften*, XI, 151. Cf. Heinrich von Srbik, *Metternich, der Staatsmann und der Mensch*, 3 vols. (Munich, 1925–1954), I, 204, who believes Metternich wanted the Breisgau all along; Rössler, *Österreichs Kampf*, II, 186, who doubts it; and Karl Otmar Freiherr von Aretin, *Bayerns Weg*

presented problems to be sure, but within the framework of a joint Austro-Baden Kreis, which was then in the planning, the arrangement would have seemed more tenable than if the province had remained nothing more than an isolated outpost. One thing is now certain in any case: whether for his own reasons or by orders of the emperor, Metternich wanted the Breisgau. As we shall see in the course of the next year, however, his position on this or almost any other particular province depended on the shape of larger combinations. Strong and friendly neighbors and their relationship to the overall German order came ahead of purely local advantages in his priorities. He did not intend to repeat Cobenzl's unseemly jousting with Munich and Stuttgart over the remnants of Swabia.

In regard to Saxony Metternich reiterated his pleas that Prussia be satisfied with part of the kingdom, but in vain. "I see no possibility of arranging Prussia without the possession of Saxony in its entirety, and my duty imposes the law on me in this regard," the chancellor replied, adding that any compensation offered the king must now be in Italy, specifically in the three legations of Ravenna, Bologna, and Ferrara, which the pope had once voluntarily ceded to France, making them conquered territory to be disposed of as the allies wished.[57] It was no better with Mainz. Hardenberg argued his case with a long memorandum drafted by Knesebeck and reiterating that the base was too important to the defense of North Germany and the Netherlands to be entrusted to a state of Bavaria's modest military resources. In fact, he went on, "no power in the world is capable of maintaining it at full strength from its standing army alone."[58] Hence a rational system of reinforcements would require her to bring Nassau, Berg, and the two Hesses into her Kreis system, and that, he warned, would be fatal to any Austro-Prussian cooperation. It was, in short, a thinly disguised restatement of Prussia's constant preference for a partition of Germany along the Main—however much Hardenberg referred to "our system" and insisted that the two powers were so closely bound that Austria could only benefit from her partner's strength. There is no reason to doubt the chancellor's sincerity; Metternich talked in this vein too. Two hours before leaving Paris he left a bon voyage note, reminding Hardenberg to send "the outline for Germany" as soon as possible and promising a counterproject in return. "We will certainly come to terms amicably," he said.[59]

---

zum souveränen Staat (Munich, 1976), 158, who believes Metternich flatly renounced the province at this time.

[57] Hard. to Mett., 7 July 1814, HHSA, StK., Kongressakten, Cart. 7, p. 556. Cf. Mett. to Hudelist, 13 June 1814 in Fournier, "Londoner Präludien," 2, 33.

[58] Text in HHSA, StK., Kongressakten, Cart. 7.

[59] Mett. to Hard., 7 July 1814, in Griewank, "Preussen und die Neurdnung," 268f.

It speaks well for the staff work of the mobile section of the State Chancellery, headed by Baron Franz von Binder,[60] that the foreign minister was able to keep so tight a schedule on the road home. Leaving Paris probably in early morning of 8 July, he passed through Strasbourg on the 11th and reached Bruchsal near Karlsruhe on the 12th.[61] Here, in a palace taken over from the prince bishops of Speyer, the tsar was at last spending a week with the empress Elizabeth, who had come from St. Petersburg to meet him and visit her brother, Grand Duke Charles. The tender sentiments of a family reunion, however, did not greatly reduce the coming and going of couriers, emissaries, and petitioners wherever the tsar happened to be. La Harpe was among them and Baron Stein, who had come from nearby Frankfurt to rail once more against the petty despots "who spare only those who flatter their prejudices—in Darmstadt the comedians and musicians perhaps, in Stuttgart the court favorites and the wild boars." Russia, he pleaded, must use her influence to impose constitutions on them.[62]

Though Metternich was thus only one among many vying for the tsar's time, he received his share, which he chose to devote to Poland rather than Germany. According to the accounts he gave later to the Prussians, he found Alexander, who was surrounded at last by dyed-in-the-wool Russians, strangely undecided about his course, even desirous of reaching an accord with Austria then and there. The comforting statements of Castlereagh, Hardenberg, and Louis XVIII still loud in his ears, however, Metternich was wary of any maneuver that might isolate him from his friends. He therefore took his stand on the London pledges that nothing was to be done to prejudice the issue before the congress and contented himself with detailing to Alexander the unrest, the suspicion, and eventually the war that were sure to come from rekindling a hotbed of unrest in their midst. Resorting to flattery, he asked the tsar if this was really the monument he wanted to his glorious role as the peacemaker of Europe. Bruchsal was not the Palace Marcolini in Dresden, but the effort to inculcate a sense of limits in an ambitious man was reminiscent of the meeting with Napoleon only a year before; for Alexander deeply believed that a grateful Europe should present him with Poland in recognition of his contribution to her liberation. In the end this obsession was to count more with the tsar than his fear of the united front that Metternich was preparing against him. For the moment, however, Metternich, who

---

[60] Josef K. Mayr, *Geschichte der österreichischen Staatskanzlei* (Vienna, 1935), 12.

[61] In the interests of accuracy even on small points, these dates reflect adjustments necessary to eliminate inconsistencies and physical impossibilities in the records— the result no doubt of fatigue, haste, and the failure to note date changes at midnight. All-night travel was much commoner than one would suppose.

[62] K. Waliszewski, *La Russie il y a cent ans. Le régne d'Alexandre Ier*, 3 vols. (Paris, 1924), II, 266; and Stein to Alex., Bruchsal, 9 July 1814, Stein, *Breife*, v, 58–60.

had an equal faith in the efficacy of superior combinations, concluded at Bruschal that "this sovereign has backed away from his idea up to a certain point" and proceeded on his way with renewed hope.[63]

Late the following day he stopped in Ludwigsburg for a meeting with King Frederick of Württemberg, who as it happened had just rushed back from an audience with the tsar at Heilbronn. Neither conference made a discernible imprint on the written record,[64] but the spectacle of the king of Württemberg shuttling between the tsar and the chief of the Ballhausplatz had a symbolic significance that should be noted here. The king's primary concerns were territorial aggrandizement and the political independence of his state, which he considered threatened by the Austro-Bavarian alignment and even more by the future German Confederation, rumors about which Winzingerode duly reported from Paris and London. In London Metternich had spoken encouragingly of expansion in the direction of Baden "if Russia did not object,"[65] and he probably continued in this vein in Ludwigsburg. Regarding the Confederation he was now in a position to say that Württemberg would be consulted and would share in the directory. If he in fact did so is conjectural, but it hardly matters. Nothing he said could have drawn Frederick back from the project that was ever closer to his heart: a league of German states under the protection of Russia.

Even before the Heilbronn meeting had been arranged, King Frederick and his minister-president, Count Ulrich Lebrecht von Mandelsloh, were busy setting the stage. Traveling in the tsar's entourage, Winzingerode spoke coyly to Nesselrode about the importance of finding "a third power" to protect the German states against Austria and Prussia. Nesselrode was unreceptive, acknowledging that the two German powers were indeed threats to stability but professing to have no idea what third power might be available as an alternative protector of a German confederation. Mandelsloh regretted his envoy's guarded language and begged the king all the more to use his "radiant eloquence" on the tsar.[66] Meanwhile, right at home a less obtuse pupil had been found: Count Yuri Alexandrovitch Golovkin, the Russian

[63] Mett. to Zichy, 1 Aug. 1814, HHSA, Gesandtschaftsarchiv, Berlin, Fasc. 60, folder 1 (printed in August Fournier, "Zur Vorgeschichte der Wiener Kongresses," in *Historische Studien und Skizzen* [Vienna and Leipzig, 1908], 314–318). Also Humb. to Fred. Wm., 20 Aug. 1814, *Gesammelte Schriften*, XI, 146–148. I have found no more immediate reports of the interview.

[64] I.e., beyond preparations for them and reports that they took place. See *Le Moniteur universel*, 24 and 25 July 1814, pp. 823 and 827. Metternich erred slightly in telling Francis that he met the king in Stuttgart.

[65] Winzingerode to King Frederick, 21 June 1814, extr. in Pfister, *Lager der Verbündeten*, 265.

[66] Mandelsloh to Fred., 11 and 12 July 1814, in Hauptstaatsarchiv, Stuttgart, E 70, Fasc. 20, No. 1. (Hereafter this archive will be cited as HSA, Stuttgart.)

envoy in Stuttgart, who saw the plan as a golden opportunity for his country. An astounding memorandum bearing his signature and the date of 3 July stated the case.[67] With the recovery of France, so his argument ran, the German states would once again be caught between her and Austria, but with the latter now oriented more toward Italy, France in the long run would dominate the area, Prussia being preoccupied with North Germany and too weak to compete. True, the Treaty of Paris called for the independence of these states in a confederation, but divided as they were, they would never become united, viable, and independent without outside support. From their point of view Russia, being distant and impartial, could best perform this role. She, in turn, now more a part of Europe than ever before, could hardly wish to see either France or Austria in control. It was "in the interest of Russia that a barrier, military and political, be placed between Austria and France and that she be in direct contact with the states destined to form that barrier." At the start, Golovkin continued, the league should be composed of Bavaria, Württemberg, Baden, Hesse-Darmstadt, Frankfurt, and Nassau, but others, including Switzerland, perhaps, would join later. Mutual guarantees of cooperation and protection were the essence of the plan; there was no talk at all about directing powers, Kreise, the rights of subjects, federal courts, and the like, not even a federal diet. For King Frederick it offered the best of all worlds. Except for the emphasis on Austro-French rivalry rather than Austro-Prussian collaboration, which was his chief worry at the time, he could not have prepared a better scheme himself. Indeed, no more than a week after the Heilbronn meeting the much-traveled Winzingerode was on his way to St. Petersburg with official instructions that took this same line, directing him to pursue a "Union Russo-Germanique."[68]

If there was actual collusion between Golovkin and the king, however, it did not cover everything, for the Russian envoy, much like Metternich himself, tended to separate the problem of a German confederation from that of immediate relief for the mediatized houses. In another memorandum of the same date, in fact, he spoke up for "the justice and necessity of reestablishing constitutions in the several German states," a task he would assign to the four allied powers.[69] Since such a step would have been anathema to Frederick, no matter what agency was employed, it is difficult to visualize the relations between the two men. Perhaps Golovkin did not understand the contradiction the king would see in the two positions. Perhaps he considered

[67] "Des rapports politiques de l'empire de Russie avec le Midi de l'Allemagne," text in *VPR*, VIII, 35–41.

[68] Erwin Hölzle, *Württemberg im Zeitalter Napoleons und der deutschen Erhebung* (Stuttgart and Berlin, 1937), 163f.

[69] Text in *VPR*, VIII, 45–50.

himself a mere conveyor of local views, in the first case those of the king, in the latter those of the numerous Standesherren in Württemberg. Or it may only have been that Golovkin, whose intellect Metternich later loved to ridicule, was momentarily under the spell of Stein, with whom he was in correspondence.[70] Be that as it may, the king himself meanwhile pressed other approaches to the tsar, urging Crown Prince William to divorce his wife so that he might marry Catherine, and begging his daughter, also named Catherine, to divorce Jerome Bonaparte, once a highly prized son-in-law but now an intolerable embarrassment.[71]

From Ludwigsburg Metternich went on to Munich for a similar meeting with King Max Joseph on 15 July, but again there is no record of what was said. He left the following day, and this time it was to head directly home—home to Baden-bei-Wien, where the family was spending the summer, and then to Vienna itself and the State Chancellery building, which he had not seen for over a year. Here, in the evening of the 20th he was given a tumultuous reception, one that strained the musical resources of even that extraordinary city; the combined forces of the Hoftheater and the Theater an der Wien sounded forth the Prometheus overture of Beethoven and a specially written cantata by Josef Kinsky and Johann Vieth, whose mighty choruses filled the night air high above the Ballhausplatz:

> Welcome thou, who on thy tongue
> The golden words of concord bore
> And saw that discord all dividing
> Did not on wings of mock'ry soar.
>
> Welcome thou, who aided sword
> To consummate the greatest deed.
> With joyous cries of thanks the world
> Applauds thy wise and steadfast lead.
>
> May legend show thee to the future
> As a model for the great,
> And midst the heaps of broken statues
> May yours rise up intact and straight.[72]

The Prussians had their Blücher, the Austrians their Metternich.

[70] Stein to Golovkin, June 1814, in Stein, *Briefe*, v, 47f.
[71] This Catherine, however, stood by her husband; the pair only asked to be let alone with an establishment similar to that promised Prince Eugene. See Pfister, *Lager der Verbündeten*, 244f.
[72] Metternich, *NP*, 1, 262–264. Selection and translation of the stanzas mine.

CHAPTER IV

DRESS REHEARSAL IN BADEN

S EVENTEEN miles south of Vienna, about two hours away by
carriage in Metternich's time, lies the charming town of Baden,
entrance to the network of footpaths that follow the Helenental, a
favorite haunt of Beethoven and Schubert and countless romantic poets.
Famous for its baths since Roman times, the town was a popular summer resort, not so international in character as Carlsbad, say, which
was more centrally located in Europe, but frequented by the Austrian
court and aristocracy and especially convenient for officials who might
commute to the city to keep a hand on affairs. The emperor himself
was frequently in residence, though he spread his time over other
retreats as well. The summer of 1814 was unusually festive there, the
ranks of the regular visitors being swollen with guests from abroad
and from the more distant provinces of the monarchy, all with interests
of various kinds in the forthcoming congress.

Metternich thus found in Baden an ideal place to set up headquarters
for the next two months. He could get to the State Chancellery as need
arose, yet was shielded from importunate visitors who hesitated to
disturb the prince's well-deserved vacation. At the same time Baden
offered the social diversion that seemed a growing necessity for the
deceptively insouciant Rhinelander who seemed always to put pleasure
before business. Back with the princess Eleonore and the children, yet
scarcely tied down by them, he was free to visit whom he wished and
to choose his own callers on his terms. Country houses, walking trails
and bridle paths, roulette wheels and decks of cards, the wines of
nearby Gumpoldskirchen and Vöslau—these too were diplomacy's tools,
and with them the foreign minister was able at Baden to stage a dress
rehearsal for the Congress of Vienna.

Not surprisingly, one of the first to pay his respects in Baden was
the Saxon envoy, Count Friedrich Albrecht von der Schulenburg.[1] To
him Metternich essentially repeated the message he had earlier given
Watzdorf in London: Austrian interests certainly favored the preservation of Saxony, but Prussia could muster equally good reasons for
her side. The one objective consideration was the illegitimacy of the
seizure, and Austria would continue to brand this "a political crime,"
hoping that if Britain and France did likewise, moral pressure would
cause Prussia to desist. Austria, however, could not "wage war on all

---

[1] Kohlschmidt, *Sächsische Frage*, 61.

Europe." It was "a matter of knowing if Prussia and Russia were willing to go to war on this issue and what assistance the former would receive."[2] The great French authority on these events, Charles Dupuis, has called the sincerity of these words genuine but a "sincerity completely Platonic" inasmuch as Metternich had already decided on the cession of Saxony not only to avoid war but simply for the sake of an Austro-Prussian accord.[3] The judgment is more clever than accurate. Even if Metternich in his own mind had come to this conclusion—an assumption that rests mainly, as we shall see, on the misreading of a crucial document—the foreign minister could not act independently of the emperor, and Francis at the time still insisted that his maximum concession would be a partition of Saxony between the two powers, and even that only as an alternative to war. By Metternich's own calculations, moreover, based as they were on the indeterminacy of Prussian policy, a flat rebuff to Schulenburg would have been premature. Again Metternich's words were within the bounds of a prudent but honest reserve probably not beyond the talents of the average diplomat. Schulenburg at any rate was under no illusions; he knew that there was no rescue by Austrian efforts alone.[4]

Metternich's main occupation meanwhile was to sort out the impressions of the days since London, fill in missing information, and clear his strategy with the emperor.[5] Although Alexander's utterances about Poland had been ambiguous, one had to assume that he would demand the whole duchy of Warsaw minus a strip for Prussia, which could be as much as Posen in its entirety or only a small part of it. There was also the strong probability that the tsar intended to resurrect the name of Poland with the title of king for himself and a national constitution administered by Grand Duke Constantine. Despite Alexander's own statements to the Poles that at least some of Russia's Polish provinces would be transferred to the new kingdom, there is no evidence that

[2] Schulenburg quoting Metternich in a private letter to his brother-in-law, Count Detlev von Einsiedel, the king's chief minister, 2 Aug. 1814, extr. in Dupuis, *Talleyrand*, II, 308f.

[3] *Ibid.*, II, 307. Emil Lauber, *Metternichs Kampf um die europäische Mitte* (Vienna and Leipzig, 1939), 150f.

[4] Dupuis, *Talleyrand*, II, 309f.; and Kohlschmidt, *Sächsische Frage*, 61f.

[5] For lack of any record of Metternich's oral reports to the emperor on returning home, we must rely primarily on a long analysis that he sent to his ambassador in Berlin, Count Stephan Zichy, on 1 Aug. 1814, a memorandum on the Polish question attached to this, and a memorial of 18 Aug. 1814 on Poland by Gentz. Metternich's marginalia on this last indicate his general endorsement, but differences, too, can be detected by comparing all three documents. The first two are published in August Fournier, "Zur Vorgeschichte," 314–319; the originals are in HHSA, Gesandtschaftsarchiv, Berlin, Fasc. 50. (Hereafter Gesandtschaftsarchiv will be cited as Ges. Arch.) The Gentz memorial is in Klinkowström, *Oesterreichs Theilnahme*, 384–399. In subsequent citations only the document and page nos. will be given.

Metternich considered this possibility at the time. Rather he thought it proof of the tsar's folly that in restoring a national Poland he would create a monster which, far from radiating gratitude, would not rest until it had reconquered all the Polish lands still in Russian hands.[6] There was, of course, no comfort in this prospect, for an assault on Austria and Prussia, probably with Russian encouragement, would no doubt come first, resulting for Austria not merely in "the certain loss of one of her most valuable provinces" but in the probable subversion of Hungary as well.[7] Prussia meanwhile would lose territory and find East Prussia isolated and at the mercy of Russia.

As Metternich pondered the situation, as he related it to the reports of Russian agitation in Italy and the Balkans and to the tsar's courting of the anti-government forces in France and Great Britain, he was more than ever convinced that Alexander fancied himself another Napoleon, "seduced by the new style of glory which he hopes to win by conferring his protection on so-called liberal and philanthropic ideas."[8] As a result, the prevention of a constitutional Polish kingdom, the torch that could set all Eastern Europe ablaze, moved steadily upward on Metternich's scale of priorities. If Alexander would be content with the title Grand Duchy of Warsaw, Austria and Prussia, he advised Hardenberg, could afford to acquiesce in Russian aggrandizement "on the most liberal scale."[9] If this expansion could be confined to the right bank of the Vistula, with Warsaw on the left bank thrown in for good measure and Austria regaining Zamość, that would be fair enough; if not, then at least Thorn and Danzig for Prussia and Cracow for Austria must be held at all costs. But if Alexander insisted on baptizing his new lands the Kingdom of Poland, the only alternatives would be war or recourse to declaring an independent Poland under the sponsorship of the great powers. In the extreme case, even the boundaries of 1772 might be tendered, but Metternich's first hope was that the Poles would be satisfied with the territorial scope of the Duchy of Warsaw and focus their revisionist ambitions on Russia.[10]

Still, all these grim contingencies were to be avoided if Alexander could be persuaded to listen to reason. Perhaps it was not too late. Starting with the Poles themselves all reports indicated bitterness at the rigors of the Russian occupation, which imposed ever greater requisitions to supply the expanding Russian army. The native Polish army under Jan Dombrowski meanwhile languished; some recruits deserted

[6] Mett. memorandum on Poland, 319.
[7] Mett. to Zichy, 316. Cf. Gentz memorial, 396.
[8] Mett. to Zichy, 316.
[9] Mett. memorandum on Poland, 318.
[10] Gentz memorial, 398; Mett. to Zichy, 316.

to the Austrians, and Dombrowski himself was soon to resign.[11] Severe food shortages necessitated a ban on exports, and although this caused hardship in Galicia, Metternich was delighted that in the process the Russians inadvertently delineated the frontier in Austria's favor.[12] As to the powers, Metternich knew that he had the backing of England, at least on the boundary question, although according to Merveldt's reports, Castlereagh did not share his anxiety about reviving the name of Poland if the tsar wished it.[13] Bourbon France seemed safely immune to the tsar's blandishments, for which reason Vincent's orders were to attempt no more than to preserve her neutrality lest a more active policy arouse the latent Russophile sentiment still rife in government and army.[14]

The key to the situation was Prussia, and though Metternich could offer nothing new, he did his best to represent previous concessions as verging on reckless abandon, impatiently begging Hardenberg for his detailed plan for Germany and reiterating assurances that there were no fundamental differences between them. Regarding Mainz this was probably true. Explaining the situation to his ambassador in Berlin, Count Stephan Zichy, he alluded to "a middle way," no doubt the federal-fortress solution, which the Prussians grudgingly accepted as their last choice, though he probably still had a Bavarian rather than a mixed garrison in mind. In regard to Saxony Metternich's appeal was positively eloquent. "Whatever considerations which in other circumstances would cause us to fear the extension of the Prussian monarchy on our northern frontier," he continued to Zichy, "whatever our regrets at the destruction of an ancient monarchy, so often serving our interests and the balance of power in Germany, *the acquisitions of Prussia in Saxony will encounter no obstacle from our side.*"[15] This is the passage that Dupuis construed as an outright offer of the whole Saxon state.[16] It was not. In the context of the dialogue running through that summer the words "acquisitions in Saxony" could only have meant the partitioning of the state discussed in Paris on the return from London. Hardenberg, as we shall see, was unimpressed and saw nothing new in Metternich's overtures.[17] Nor did Metternich even intend a dé-

---

[11] Humb. to Fred. Wm., 20 Aug. 1814, in *Gesammelte Schriften*, XI, 146. Cf. Theodor Schiemann, *Geschichte Russlands unter Kaiser Nikolaus I* (Berlin, 1904), I, 112f.

[12] Mett. to Francis, 7 Aug. 1814, HHSA, StK., Vorträge, Cart. 195, pp. 85f.

[13] Merveldt to Mett., 15 Aug. 1814, extr. in Dupuis, *Talleyrand*, II, 282.

[14] Mett. to Vincent, 8 August 1814, extr. in *ibid.*, II, 301–309.

[15] Mett. to Zichy, 1 Aug. 1814, pp. 315f. Italics mine.

[16] Likewise Fournier, "Zur Vorgeschichte," 304f., and Lauber, *Metternichs Kampf*, 150.

[17] Zichy to Mett., 12 Aug. 1814, in Fournier, "Zur Vorgeschichte," 320. For explicit confirmation see Hard. to Reinhold Otto von Schoeler (the Prussian envoy in St. Petersburg) 26 Aug. 1814 (ZSTA, Merseburg, 2.4.1.I, No. 992, pp. 1–4), wherein

marche at this point. Although Zichy was to emphasize at every opportunity that alliance with Prussia was "the basis of our policy," he was scrupulously to refrain from any negotiation lest it appear that Austria had no faith in existing understandings. In this way the long directive to Zichy, dispatched on 1 August, clarified the state of the argument and left Metternich to hope that, back home in Berlin, Hardenberg might round up support and even counteract "the personal ascendancy that the Emperor Alexander exercises on the mind of the king."[18]

There remained one more avenue, and that was to Russia herself. What had Alexander's homecoming done for him? Reports coming into Baden and Vienna invariably called the restoration of a Polish kingdom "anything but popular,"[19] but how was the tsar reacting? Were Metternich's impressions of the Bruchsal audience correct? Was Alexander indeed drawing back? Would he resort to military force? Did he have any secret understandings with other powers? Did he encourage the agitators from Italy or the agents of the German middle states who were flocking to St. Petersburg to solicit protection? The Ballhausplatz needed answers. Austrian spies, meanwhile, had intercepted letters between Grand Duchess Catherine and Prince William of Württemberg, with all that they portended for Metternich's hopes of a match with Archduke Charles. Her attitude, too, needed to be investigated, and it was mainly for this reason that the man chosen for a special mission to the Russian court was the sophisticated and charming Field Marshal Baron Franz von Koller, who had won Catherine's trust and affection while officially attending her in Prague the summer before, again in London, and lately in Franzensbrunn, the Bohemian spa where she was still vacationing.[20]

Ostensibly the purpose of Koller's roundabout journey to Franzensbrunn and Petersburg was to invite Catherine to the congress and to assist the tsar in his travel preparations. Both objects required personal approval as well as autograph letters from Francis, who was then on an inspection tour of the Austrian crown lands. As a result, although

---

the chancellor describes the Austrian demands as consisting of a slice of the Erzgebirge and possibly Dresden.

[18] Mett. to Zichy, 1 Aug. 1814, 314.

[19] This and following from "Instruktion für den ... Freiherrn von Koller," 16 Aug. 1814, HHSA, StK., Russland III, Cart. 41, pp. 1–6 and 14.

[20] Bourgoing, *Vom Wiener Kongress*, 238–242; Corti, *Frauen*, I, 458f; and Fournier, "Zur Vorgeschichte," 309. See also Countess Nesselrode to her husband, Franzensbrunn, 19 Aug. 1814, in Charles Robert Comte de Nesselrode, *Lettres et papiers du chancelier comte de Nesselrode 1769–1850*, 11 vols. (Paris, 1904–1912), V, 196–198; and Count Hardenberg to Münster, 3 Aug. 1814, in August Fournier, *Die Geheimpolizei auf dem Wiener Kongress* (Vienna and Leipzig, 1913), 108.

Metternich decided on the mission about 1 August,[21] he could not complete Koller's instructions until he had met with the emperor a full two weeks later in the imperial castle at Persenbeug on the Danube. The agenda at Persenbeug, to be sure, included more than the Koller mission, but given the urgency of the events scheduled for September, the delay is difficult to explain. Whatever the reason, the field marshal set out on 18 August, in such haste that he neglected to take the usual travel documents and gather receipts, so that later Metternich had to petition the emperor personally for his reimbursement.[22] Such was the opulence of Francis's court in the midst of the Congress of Vienna.

Once the new appeal to Hardenberg had been dispatched and the Koller mission decided upon, waiting replaced action on those fronts, and Metternich turned his attention to other things. Sagan was ever on his mind, and as if obedient to an inner law, within hours of signing the directive to Zichy on 1 August he found himself roaming the streets with Gentz, expatiating on her insistent demands until three in the morning.[23] Occasionally business in Vienna called, and he used these opportunities to watch over the remodeling of his house in the Rennweg, where he was already planning to hold a spectacular fête on the first anniversary of Leipzig.[24] No detail about the congress was beneath him. What other minister would have thought to establish a government warehouse for the storage of foreign wines so that all guests might have duty-free the kind to which they were accustomed?[25]

Family affairs also required attention. The principality of Oschsenhausen in Württemberg, the house of Metternich's compensation for the loss of Winneburg-Beilstein, was not only burdened with debt but was deteriorating under the harassment of the king of Württemberg's disruptive officials. To complicate matters, Metternich's sister, Pauline, was in love with the king's brother, Duke Ferdinand, who requited her affection but could not gain King Frederick's consent to an inferior union, especially as she had no property of her own. Some months before, Metternich had pledged his personal credit to a Viennese bank to save Ochsenhausen, but his long-term solution was to sell the property outright. Hoping in this way both to sever all ties with Württemberg and to improve Pauline's prospects with an appropriate dowry, Clemens's sister and mother agreed with him, only to find that old Franz Georg, the father, dreaming still of lavish indemnities for the

[21] Count Hardenberg to Münster, 3 Aug. 1814, as in n. 20.
[22] Mett. to Francis, 4 Dec. 1814, HHSA, StK., Vorträge, Cart. 196.
[23] Friedrich von Gentz, *Tagebücher von Friedrich von Gentz*, 4 vols. (Leipzig, 1873), I, 287f.
[24] Cf. McGuigen, *Metternich and the Duchess*, 308.
[25] Mett. to Francis, 9 Aug. 1814, HHSA, StK., Vorträge, Cart. 196, VIII, pp. 98–100.

Standesherren, insisted on returning home, home to the fief that had once raised him from count to prince in the imperial hierarchy. Eventually Pauline married Ferdinand and Ochsenhausen was sold, but not until Franz Georg's death in 1818, by which time it was clear that there, in Baden, Clemens had correctly assessed the postwar prospects of the mediatized houses. Metternich took his share of gifts and loans along the way, but his refusal to cultivate this private interest, which he could honorably have done, was a mark of realism, loyalty, and integrity for which he was more often criticized than admired.[26]

Italian affairs occupied him much in Baden, his principal success being the appointment of his trusted aide, Baron Johann von Wessenberg, as vice-president of the Central-Organisierungs-Hofcommission, the special board then being set up to govern all newly acquired provinces. Partly Metternich was venting his anger at having been ignored in the establishment of the commission.[27] Mainly, however, he hoped through Wessenberg to restrain Josephinist bureaucrats from heedlessly imposing Habsburg institutions on the new peoples; his German policy did not include Germanization. Instead he favored a looser administration, one catering to local conditions, utilizing existing organs, and assuaging popular sensibilities. He did not intend to appear at the peace congress with provinces in revolt before they had been officially awarded. Wessenberg agreed, and it was probably owing to his brilliant reports of early August on his mission to Italy that Metternich assigned him to German affairs as well and made him his deputy at the Congress of Vienna.[28]

Meanwhile, the most urgent need was to put the chancellery itself in order. The minister had lived out of trunks for over a year, and the main business of his department had been handled by a hastily organized mobile section (*Reiseabteilung*) that followed the chief in an assortment of coaches and wagons strung out in a column and carrying paper, seals, portable desks, cipher books, and other equipment, even a portable field press, used to print bulletins and copy for the *Oesterreichischer Beobachter*, the newspaper maintained by the chancellery.[29] Back home at last, the mobile section had to be reintegrated into the whole operation and new assignments made. A considerable expansion of staff was also needed. With the breakup of Napoleon's empire dozens of independent states had reappeared with which diplomatic relations must be restored; former missions had to be reopened and new

[26] Corti, *Frauen*, I, 418–422; Srbik, *Metternich*, I, 455.
[27] Mett. to Francis, 30 July 1814, HHSA, StK., Vorträge, Cart. 195.
[28] Humb. to Hard., [13] Aug. 1814, in *Gesammelte Schriften*, XVII, 68; and Arthur G. Haas, *Metternich, Reorganization and Nationality, 1813–1818* (Wiesbaden, 1963), 42–51.
[29] Mayr, *Staatskanzlei*, 11f.

ones created. Austria's own territorial expansion, moreover, would bring with it a proliferation of internal agencies—the Central- Organisierungs- Hofcommission was only a beginning—with which the chancellery must coordinate its efforts.[30]

Not only new personnel but the best was Metternich's goal, and he spoke for diplomats everywhere when he told the emperor:

> There is no well ordered state where the department entrusted with the conduct of external negotiations would not at all times enjoy preferred treatment. The reason for this is partly in the importance and intricacy of these transactions, where a mistake can often cause incalculable and irremediable consequences for the state, and partly in the resulting necessity of employing only men of oustanding talent, proven experience with affairs, and reliability. Such men must assume great responsibilities, take pleasure in the strains and difficulties of official duty, and forgo almost all the pleasures and recreations that other state officials enjoy, especially in social matters— and for all that, without having the same prospects for advancement as the latter.[31]

There is a note of cynicism here, the implication that promotion comes mainly through intrigue practiced at home, but the dominant chord is pride in the diplomatic corps, the elite service in the state.

Metternich also deemed the time propitious for a reorganization of his ministry. During his five years in office he had gradually changed from a system of dividing the work by country and region to one based more on function, recapitulating in this respect the normal evolution of all administration in the period. By 1814 the chancellery was divided into three sections, the first dealing with major political-diplomatic affairs, the second with routine matters such as accrediting envoys, ratifying treaties, preparing state documents, processing financial and legal claims, and issuing passports. The third section was primarily in charge of internal affairs, maintaining liaison with other government agencies at both the imperial and provincial levels. Still, the lines of demarcation were blurred, sometimes in ways that only the Austrians could have devised. The third section, for example, was in charge of ceremonies, etiquette, and the affairs of the imperial household, all of which had ramifications abroad, while the Academy of Fine Arts and the Oriental Institute were responsibilities of the second and first sections respectively, reminders that historically the State Chancellery was considerably more than a foreign office.[32]

[30] Mett. to Francis, 12 Aug. 1814, HHSA, StK., Vorträge, Cart. 195, p. 117.
[31] *Ibid.*, 118.
[32] Mayr, *Staatskanzlei*, 13–14 and 27f.

87

What Metternich now proposed was a simple division into two co-ordinate sections, one dealing exclusively with external correspondence at all levels, the other with internal liaison, each section to be headed by a *Staatsrat* (councilor of state), the highest ranking title in the Austrian system short of minister or other department head. Each section would have as well its own director, a kind of executive secretary, its own dispatch office and record office, and a hierarchy of court councilors, councilors, secretaries, and *Konzipisten*, the last being officers, usually experts in their fields, who were responsible for drafting dispatches and position papers.[33] The only exception to this sharp bifurcation was the Geheime Haus- Hof- und Staatsarchiv, the director of which was to report directly to the minister, a precaution taken no doubt both against leaks and against ambitious directors who might attempt to make the archives a separate entity, as Baron Hormayr had tried to do before he was disgraced for his role in the patriotic conspiracy of 1813.[34] Indeed, centralized control was probably the pervading purpose throughout the plan, for separating external and internal business so completely would not necessarily have resulted in greater efficiency but it would certainly have necessitated the channeling of communications between the branches through the minister himself.

The new plan was among the documents that Metternich carried with him on 14 August, when he made the journey to Persenbeug to confer directly with the emperor. Although Francis promptly approved the project in principle and instructed the prince to submit names for the two *Staatsrat* positions, he suspected his minister of padding the roster and tailoring the positions to the personal qualities and financial needs of his friends. Hence he asked Metternich to write up job descriptions in objective terms as befitted a permanent bureaucratic system and to recommend "only those individuals who fit the ideal of a chancellery official that you exhaustively describe in your report,"[35] a sarcastic and not unworthy rejoinder to the minister's homily about the foreign service. What was worse, only one appointment was approved, that of Count Andreas Florimund von Mercy, who became a court councilor. Baron Friedrich von Binder, whom Metternich especially wanted for assistance in German affairs,[36] was refused the high-sounding title of imperial councilor, which Metternich had invented for him, and remained in the service simply as a counselor of legation.

[33] Mett. to Francis, 12 Aug. 1814, HHSA, StK., Vorträge, Cart, 195, pp. 119–121.

[34] Mayr, *Staatskanzlei*, 74–76; Kraehe, I, 165.

[35] Francis's notation of 16 Aug. 1814 on Mett. to Francis cited above, n. 30.

[36] Hudelist to Mett., 30 July 1814 and Mett's. marginalia of 1 Aug. 1814, HHSA, StK., Interiora, Fasc. 78.

Returning to Baden, Metternich hastily prepared a new plan, which he submitted on 20 August. Neither it nor a reminder to the emperor in November brought any results. In May, 1815, he tried again, only to be told that the plan still lacked system and information about the perquisites of existing personnel and must be put aside until peace was restored.[37]

It is doubtless true that Metternich, whose own emoluments, including the spacious living quarters in the chancellery building, were arrived at ad hominem, continued to recommend higher salaries than those in other departments and to adjust them to the persons proposed rather than to the intrinsic demands of the positions. Though claiming to be short-handed, he usually made promotion of existing personnel his first priority.[38] Francis, however, with his Josephinist instinct for order wanted standardized scales and economy. Still, neither the haphazardness of the one man nor the parsimony of the other can account for a full year of bickering during a time of crisis. It was more a struggle of principle. Metternich, who was already the only department head with true ministerial responsibility, was seeking to run the State Chancellery as he saw fit, as was the system in Prussia. The emperor, on the other hand, in repeatedly demanding a table of organization dissociated from personalities, was reminding his guest on the Ballhausplatz that even he might someday be replaced.

In the meantime Metternich had to do the best he could with the band of trusted officials already on the chancellery staff, as well as temporary personnel borrowed from other agencies or hired for specific purposes. Perhaps the man he saw most was Josef von Pilat, his personal secretary and, as editor of the *Osterreichischer Beobachter*, generally in charge of public relations. Pilat as well took clippings from other newspapers and maintained liaison with Gentz.[39] Of particular importance in this operation were the noted romantic writers, Adam Müller and Friedrich Schlegel, the latter assigned to the preparation of news releases for a Hamburg newspaper in order to spread the Austrian word in North Germany. He was also occupied with the German constitutional question, especially as it concerned the Catholic Church, though with more ultramontanist zeal than Metternich required of him.[40] Another private secretary was Baron Nikolaus von Krufft, who did the stenographic work on classified documents and,

[37] Mett. to Francis, 11 May 1815 with emperor's notation of 31 July, HHSA, StK., Vorträge, Cart. 198, pp. 87–90.

[38] *Ibid.*

[39] Mayr, *Staatskanzlei*, 145.

[40] Friedrich Schlegel, *Kritische Friedrich-Schlegel-Ausgabe*, ed. Ernst Behler, VII (Munich, Paderborn, and Vienna, 1966), xciv. Cf. Karl Völker, "Metternichs Kirchenpolitik," *Zeitschrift für Kirchengeschichte*, XLIX (1930), 222–246.

when necessary, was in charge of Metternich's travel arrangements. Other important aides were Friedrich von Hoppé, who had briefed the minister during his travels on developments at home and now returned to manage the executive details of the first section; Nikolaus von Wacken, an experienced and versatile *Konzipist*; Baron Engelbert von Floret, a veteran of the mobile section and later an advisor on German affairs; and Count Mercy, who had various assignments during the congress and, despite his background as an émigré French general, was well versed in South German affairs.[41]

None of these, however, was so important to the operation of the chancellery as Baron Josef von Hudelist, the man who had been in charge during Metternich's long absence. He was all the more needed now, retaining his authority over all but the major political issues during this indeterminate transitional period. His meticulous and plodding ways and long working hours invited complaint and even ridicule, but Metternich, perhaps because his own habits were so different, considered him indispensable, an absolutely trustworthy servant as well as a personal friend, who was a frequent dinner guest in the minister's family circle. Indeed, in times of crisis he was preferable to the scintillating but nervous and self-centered Gentz, who tended to panic under pressure. Already a *Staatsrat* and for all practical purposes filling one of the posts authorized by the emperor, the faithful Hudelist had no higher ambition than to be able to retire somewhere in Italy, "that glorious land" as he called it, which Austria had just acquired.[42]

One other man commands attention here even though he was no longer employed in the State Chancellery, and that is Count Stadion. Stadion was not only able and experienced, but he also had a constituency, a following large enough indeed to make him a political force in his own right and a formidable rival if he chose to be one. On the face of things he had been right all along about the futility of dealing with Napoleon.[43] His strong stand on Saxony was conventional and popular, especially in the army. His antagonism to the South German courts, his idea of a corridor to the Breisgau, and the recollection of his war aims in 1809 endeared him to the aristocratic imperial party, which now that Napoleon was gone, was making a striking comeback. The Auerspergs, the Dietrichsteins, the Lobkowitzes, the Salms, the Colloredos, the Fürstenbergs, all rooted in the old Reich territories of Germany as well as the Austrian empire, saw Stadion as one of them

[41] Mayr, *Staatskanzlei*, 18 and 144–146.
[42] *Ibid.*, 29f.; and Hudelist to Mett., 6 Aug. 1815, HHSA, StK., Interiora, Fasc. 79, pp. 155f.
[43] Cf. Corti, *Frauen*, I, 428f. for Eleonore's jealousy of Stadion on this score.

and Metternich a virtual traitor to his class.[44] Stadion, moreover, had a deserved reputation for integrity, candor, and seriousness, qualities that mankind normally prefers in high places to craft, subtlety, and reserve, to say nothing of amatory passion. He had, as well, the inherent advantage of the critic, the freedom to consider each issue independently on its merits without the responsible statesman's need to integrate, trim, and adjust. The one thing he lacked was the complete esteem of the emperor, for Francis was not a man to tolerate losers or aristocratic cabals.

For all that, Stadion was a professional, and his relationship with Metternich was not so venomous as his followers supposed. His hostility to the Rheinbund sovereigns did not reflect the narrow partisanship of the average *Reichsgraf* but rather a species of *Realpolitik* aimed at strengthening Germany and in fact calling for further mediatizing on a large scale. Considering that the king of Württemberg continued to impound the revenue from his estates at Warthausen,[45] he must have been disgusted at times with the continuous wailing against lesser offenses and the extravagant restorative goals of the mediatized as a group. He knew as well as Metternich that there were good arguments on both sides of the things that divided them, and that is why the latter, while still in London, twice implored Stadion to serve as second plenipotentiary to the congress.[46] In refusing, Stadion cited his exclusion from so many negotiations already consummated, especially those with Bavaria, but denied that he blamed Metternich. Rather it was the emperor, he said, who seemed to bear him a grudge, and he listed the slights he had suffered, including orders to wind up details in Paris rather than accompany Metternich to London. Instead of a second plenipotentiary, he proposed a technical bureau composed of Solms, Wessenberg, and Franz von Rademacher, the last a respected expert on the Reich and the Rheinbund. "The glory of the signature should belong to you alone," he said, more in resignation than with irony, but added that he would always be available for informal consultation.[47] Humboldt, when he heard that Stadion would not participate, regretted the withdrawal of his firm character but not the absence of his "old Austrian conceptions." On balance his judgment was "that Prince Metternich is on a much more reasonable course . . . and that it is only through him that we can expect support in all our demands."[48]

Still determined, however, to make use of Stadion's talents, Metter-

[44] Srbik, *Metternich*, I, 186.

[45] Stad. to Mett., 19 Aug. 1814, in Prague, SUA, Prague, Acta Clementina, Corr. pol., Cart. 6, folder 62–A, pp. 204f.

[46] Stad. to Mett., 8 and 17 June 1814 in *ibid.*, 62–A, pp. 194–199.

[47] *Ibid.*

[48] Humb. to Hard. 13 Aug. 1814 (intercept), in Fournier, *Geheimpolizei*, 110.

nich next proposed him to the emperor as minister of finance. Technically no such post existed inasmuch as the Court Chamber, which dealt with money matters, was one of the many departments run by a collegiate board under the chairmanship of a president. Metternich, however, argued that only a true minister, with complete control of his department, yet spared from administrative details, could cope with the colossal financial problems of the monarchy. The emperor resisted, perhaps because it seemed another case of trying to fit the post to the man. Stadion himself was reluctant, holding out at first for a super-ministry of interior of which finance would be only a part. Metternich, however, insisted that such an arrangement must await a final decision on the provincial structure of the monarchy, about which his views were more federalistic than those of either Francis or Stadion.[49] In the end, he had his way, at least in substance: officially Stadion would be merely president of the Court Chamber but with all the authority of a minister, thus bringing his functions into line with the title he had kept from his foreign-office days as a minister of state. If that was confusing, it was in the best native tradition of devising expedients, and Francis gave his final approval on 15 September, barely in time to make the arrangement serviceable to Metternich as the congress opened.[50]

The foreign minister's role in this episode was more than an act of friendship; it was part of a larger goal, that of overhauling the central administrative machinery of the monarchy, which had emerged from the wars in even greater disarray than the State Chancellery. Metternich's interest in domestic reform was natural enough. Anything that fixed responsibility, expedited decisions, and strengthened the monarchy also strengthened his hand in dealings abroad. Ever since his embassy in Paris he had yearned to impart to the Austrian machinery of state some measure of the efficiency he had observed in France. The emperor, moreover, consulted him on such matters, so that on arriving home in triumph it occurred to him that his reward might be the title of chancellor, which if it did not give him all the power over internal and external affairs that Kaunitz had enjoyed, would at least have made him clearly preeminent among the ministers. The honor was deferred for some years, and most observers laid the delay to the

---

[49] Mett. to Francis, 5 Aug. 1814. Text in Friedrich Walter, ed., *Die österreichische Zentralverwaltung*, Part II, Vol. 5 (Vienna, 1956), 217. The contention of Hellmuth Rössler, *Graf Johann Philipp Stadion, Napoleons deutscher Gegenspieler*, 2 vols. (Vienna and Munich, 1966), II, 133, that Metternich feared a rival if the post were too powerful is gratuitous and strictly conjectural.

[50] Rössler, *Stadion*, II, 182f.; Arneth, *Wessenberg*, I, 215. Rössler erroneously gives date of 18 Sept. Cf. Stad. to Francis, n.d., in SUA, Prague, Acta Clementina, Corr. pol., 62–A.

machinations of the officials entrenched in the existing internal agencies: notably Baron Anton Baldacci, president of the general accounting office; Count Josef Wallis, a leading member of the Council of State; and Count Alois Ugarte, who, much as Stadion aspired to do, managed both internal and financial affairs, the latter, however, only on an interim basis. Whether or not the influence of these men was decisive in denying Metternich the chancellorship, it is a fact that they were rivals of long standing and unavoidably targets of his reform program. This enterprise he pursued during the Baden days with a vigor that was not possible in foreign affairs, which had a tempo all their own, for the most part beyond his control.[51]

The traditional branches of administration in Vienna were the variously named *Hofstellen* or departments. Three were functional for the whole monarchy: the State Chancellery for foreign affairs, the Court War Council for defense, and the Court Chamber for finance. The rest administered particular areas: a chancellery for Transylvania, another for Hungary, and a combined chancellery for Bohemia, Galicia, and the Austrian hereditary lands. As previously indicated, all but the State Chancellery were headed by collegiate boards presided over by a president. As matters stood at the end of the war the only organ of centralism, apart from the emperor himself, was the Council of State, composed of councilors and some department heads and competent to advise the emperor in all fields except military and foreign affairs, the interests of Hungary, however, being represented by a special delegate who spoke to those affairs only. Theoretically, the function of the Council was purely advisory, for which purpose it met with some regularity under the chairmanship of Francis or, more often, his deputy, Archduke Rainer. In practice, however, it often meddled capriciously in the departmental operations, partly because of overlapping personnel, partly because departments headed by committees could not put up effective resistance and often in their bickering invited intrusion. On the other hand, the Council of State could not provide direction or coordination, especially as it rarely convened as a whole and was excluded from the foreign and military spheres completely. To cope with this problem there was on paper what was called a ministerial conference, but its proceedings were almost entirely in writing and it never met as a whole, with the result that it merely added to the confusion.[52]

[51] Lamb to Castle., 25 June 1814, in *Castle. Corr.*, x, 57–60; Humboldt's memorial of 27 Aug. 1814, in *Gesammelte Schriften*, xi, 34–38; and Count Ernst Hardenberg to Münster, 8 Sept. 1814, in Maurice-Henri Weil, ed., *Les Dessous du Congrès de Vienne*, 2 vols. (Paris, 1917), i, 69f.

[52] Cf. C. A. Macartney, *The Habsburg Empire 1790–1918* (London, 1968), 165–186.

Francis himself, recognizing the need for change, in February, 1814, approved a plan drawn up by Baldacci.[53] Under it a State Conference of department heads was authorized on a continuing basis as a review board for disputes arising within the Council of State or between the Council and the departments, and beyond that for any matters the emperor chose to refer to it. On the surface this seemed to create a unified, orderly system in which reports would be sent up from the departments, acted on by a body with broad imperial perspective, working in the modern mode "not by provinces but according to subject," and finally reviewed by a central committee of department heads. In fact, however, neither body met as a whole and meetings of the Conference were open to members of the Council as well. The result was not harmony but a system of checks and balances tending toward paralysis. Count Wallis, who was made director of the Council and charged with putting the plan into operation, did so with modifications and delaying tactics that embittered Baldacci.[54]

Such was the rancorous situation that Metternich found on his return home, and before long Francis, dismayed at the strife the plan had caused, called for his opinion. This he rendered in several reports as familiar in their didactic tone as they were uncharacteristic in their vehemence.[55] Baldacci he disparaged for asking the wrong questions and treating merely the symptoms of disease; Wallis he accused of ambitions to make the Council of State a giant ministry of interior with himself as prime minister, a terrifying prospect! Lecturing the emperor on the necessity for the separation of powers—not to achieve checks and balances but their opposite, the elimination of friction—he ridiculed Baldacci's plan because it lumped everything together. As advisory bodies to the crown the Council and the Conference would both exercise a legislative function and as supervisory bodies over the departments executive authority as well. If one or the other emerged supreme, its president would be a de facto prime minister without responsibility. If neither did, paralysis would set in, and the departments, reduced to mere "information bureaus," could hardly do their work.

Metternich's solution, adumbrated as early as 1811 and now fully elaborated, was the exact opposite: a complete separation of Council and Conference, the former becoming exclusively a private advisory body to the emperor, the latter a cabinet of true ministers, by which

[53] Text in Walter, *Zentralverwaltung*, Part II, Vol. 5, 207f.

[54] Walter, *Zentralverwaltung*, Part II, Vol. 1, No. 2, Part 2, pp. 123–127; and Egon Radvany, *Metternich's Projects for Reform in Austria* (The Hague, 1971), 31.

[55] This and following from texts of Metternich's two reports of 5 Aug. 1814 in Walter, *Zentralverwaltung*, Part II, Vol. 5, 212–221.

he meant department heads relieved of administrative detail and free to concentrate on policy, regardless of what they were called. In both bodies oral discussion would replace the hushed exchange of written opinions customary to that time. He proposed that the Council be divided into four sections, including at last one for defense (but not for foreign affairs) and normally meeting separately; each was to be headed, where possible, by a man with ministerial experience and staffed with officials who could be trained for advancement in time to the Council itself.[56] Though removed from the executive process,[57] this council would nevertheless constitute the reservoir of experience and technical expertise, which alone could produce the consistent advice that should be "the emperor's conscience." The Conference of Ministers, meanwhile, would be left as the fulcrum of government, its members able by mutual support to protect their departments from outside interference, to iron out differences between departments, and to present a united front to the emperor and his advisors. This was the long-range plan. Only the Court Chamber under Stadion and the Court War Council under Schwarzenberg needed to be converted immediately into genuine ministeries; a centralized ministry of interior must await the provincial reorganization that would follow the peace congress.

The devastating attack on Baldacci was unfair in a way, for as a means of expediting royal absolutism his plan made some sense. What Metternich was groping for, however, was something else, a modified system of bureaucratic absolutism; and if he expressly repudiated the Prussian model, it was only to the extent that he preferred a group of equal ministers to one supreme minister like Hardenberg, who dominated the rest. He could hardly have missed the point that the Prussian foreign minister, Count August Friedrich Ferdinand von der Goltz, counted for so little that until now we have had no occasion to mention him. In fact, Hardenberg at that very time was taking over the post himself.

Given these implications, Francis's reception of the plan was surprisingly cordial. When it was discussed during Metternich's visit to Persenbeug, the main issues were the permissible degree of interlocking personnel and the emperor's right to invite whom he pleased to

[56] This was proposed later, on 12 Sept. 1814. See Walter, *Zentralverwaltung*, Part II, Vol. 1, No. 2, Part 2, p. 133; and Radvany, *Metternich's Projects*, 34. This way of training future council members was probably an idea that Metternich derived from the so-called "auditors" on Napoleon's Council of State.

[57] Metternich did make one trivial exception. To be sure that the Council of State was informed of what action was taken on its advice, he proposed that orders to departments in such matters be channeled through that body for information only. Mett. to Francis, 26 Sept. 1814, HHSA, StK., Vorträge, Cart. 196, pp. 175–178.

sessions of the Council. Francis knew from long experience that people count more than tables of organization and that dual office-holding was one way to break down compartmentalization. Such blurring of responsibilities may seem untidy to the administrative mind, but many a statesman has found in jurisdictional disputes and tangled lines of authority the best assurance that his subordinates will let him know what is going on below. In any case, the amendments that Metternich had to accept were modest in scope and affected the Council more than his beloved Conference. Count Karl Zichy, his nominee for president of the latter, was given as well a place on the Council. Department heads might be called into plenary sessions of the Council; and foreign affairs, for which there was no section, were to be represented on the Council by either of the two councilors of state whom the emperor was just then awarding to the State Chancellery.[58]

Returning to Baden, Metternich made the necessary changes and submitted the new proposals. These the emperor approved on 27 August and along with them the appointments of the Council section chiefs: Wallis for internal administration, Zichy for finance, Field Marshall Count Franz Colloredo for defense, and Anton von Pfleger for legislation and justice. At the same time Francis ordered Wallis to join Metternich and the section chiefs in drafting a detailed set of rules for the Council preparatory to its early convening. In this endeavor Metternich had to continue the struggle till mid-November, particularly against the ingrained habits of written procedures and endless opportunities for submitting minority reports. The emperor too delayed things by breaking in from time to time with sudden inspirations, but on all major issues he stood with Metternich, even when the prince collided with such favorites as Wallis and Colloredo's deputy, General Peter von Duka, the main advocates of written communication. As a result the new Council of State was able to enter into its functions on 1 December.[59]

Metternich's victory was impressive, but like so many other hopeful beginnings in Austrian history, it did not in the long run produce the changes it promised. If the Council was "the emperor's conscience," it was a troubled conscience whose imperatives he often ignored, preferring the comfortable advice of confidants in his household. Plenary sessions with opportunity for debate were rare, and despite all criticisms of it, written procedure gradually came back, generating ever

[58] Mett. to Francis, 22 Aug. 1814; and Francis to Wallis and Francis to Zichy, both drafted by Mett. and signed by Francis, 27 Aug. 1814. All texts in Walter, *Zentralverwaltung*, Part II, Vol. 5, 221–227.

[59] *Ibid.*, 227–240; and Vol. 1, No. 2, Part 2, pp. 132–134; "Instruktion für den Staatsrath," 1 Dec. 1814, in HHSA, Kaiser Franz Archiv, Fasc. 196. Also Radvany, *Metternich's Projects*, 34f.

more exquisite examples of that abstruse and convoluted official style known among those condemned to grapple with it as *Kanzleideutsch*.[60] The State Conference fared no better. Apart from Stadion, who was officially named minister of finance in 1816, no department chiefs became ministers, not even Schwarzenberg, who remained president of the Court War Council until his death in 1820. Without full powers to act, department heads were averse to risking the compromises that meeting with each other might entail, and imperial summonses were rare. Metternich himself did not suffer from this failure, for his independence was all the greater, his policies seldom, if ever, reviewed by other departments or by the Council. Among the losers are historians, who at many critical points miss the records that would ordinarily show the course of controversy. Private discussion there was in abundance, but the records of it, if any, were likewise private and subject to the fate which that most prolific of jotters, Friedrich Gentz, prepared for most of his: he burned them, leaving us only a tantalizing log in the form of a diary.[61] The official contacts of the State Chancellery with other departments were maintained by exchanges of notes and confined in the main to administrative details. As Hudelist observed in 1815, "in the Conference there is little or nothing to do, in the Council much but nothing of consequence."[62] Only after Francis's death in 1835 and the ascension of the ailing Ferdinand did the conference of ministers come into its own as a regularly constituted body.[63]

So much for the disappointing future of reform. For present purposes the true significance of Metternich's victory was the stunning rout of his opponents. He may not have gained the chancellorship, but after the conversations at Persenbeug, where Francis turned on Wallis and Baldacci in a matter that concerned them more than the foreign minister, who could deny that Metternich was the emperor's choice to set the trim for taking the monarchy through the treacherous currents of the peace congress? Even in small talk Francis displayed an unaccustomed intimacy, asking about Sagan and waggishly calling her "one of the most necessary ingredients of the congress."[64]

Bearing sheaves of imperial orders and authorizations, Metternich returned to Baden on 17 August, ready to start affairs moving again. In the next few days the revised plans for the State Chancellery and the Council of State were drafted, and on the 18th Koller finally set out for Franzensbrunn and Petersburg. Meanwhile reports from Mer-

---

[60] Cf. Walter, *Zentralverwaltung*, Part II, Vol. 1, No. 2, Part 2, p. 34.

[61] Gentz, *Tagebücher*, I, 276.

[62] Hudelist to Mett., 15 Oct. 1815, HHSA, StK., Interiora, Fasc. 79, p. 289.

[63] Eduard Wertheimer, "Fürst Metternich und die Staatskonferenz," *Oester-reichische Rundschau*, X (1907), 41–54 and 111–128.

[64] Mett. to Sagan, Persenbeug, 14 Aug. 1814, in Ullrichová, ed., *Briefwechsel*, 260f.

veldt in London had arrived that pointed to a joint British and French action against Murat in Naples and, from the French side at any rate, the hope for an exclusive Anglo-French mediation at the congress.[65] To counteract these ideas and, as well, to maintain a steady influence on opinion in London after Castlereagh's departure, Metternich chose for a special mission the same General Laval Nugent who had initiated the rapprochement with England in 1812; he too departed on the 18th.[66]

By this time the anxiously awaited report from Zichy had also arrived containing Hardenberg's response to the overtures of 1 August. It was not encouraging. In a long interview with the Austrian ambassador Hardenberg seemed a trifle irritated at Metternich's platitudes, which, he said, only repeated what they had discussed many times before.[67] If Metternich really valued Austro-Prussian collaboration, why did he constantly encourage the aggrandizement of Bavaria and Württemberg, whose intrigues would cause untold difficulty? "I shall not be surprised to see that Russia, even if she does not abet them, will at least derive a secret pleasure from them," Hardenberg said, observing that Winzingerode had recently passed through Berlin headed for Petersburg. A federal fortress at Mainz was a possibility, however abhorrent, but a partitioning of Saxony, or anything less than total annexation, was out of the question. Regarding Poland the chancellor eschewed on the one hand Metternich's optimism about a retreat by the tsar and on the other his diplomatic combinations and declarations against the tsar. An independent Poland as the strategy of last resort he did not mention at all; but unless Austria was prepared to fight, he warned, Metternich would be well advised to confine his efforts to peaceful persuasion as Prussia was prepared to do. "We were both very wrong," Hardenberg added, cuttingly reminding the Austrian of his indifference to Prussia's travail before Kalisch, "we were *both* very wrong not to make our conditions with Russia on this subject before entering into the coalition with her."[68] The only way to repair the damage now was to build a powerful Germany.

Against these arguments Metternich had little leverage, only his gifts of persuasion. These were no mean assets, however, and he next used

[65] Merveldt to Mett., 2 and 15 Aug. 1814, extr. in Dupuis, *Talleyrand*, II, 278f. Cf. Sir Charles Stewart to Castle., Paris, 1 Aug. 1814, in Wellington, *Supplementary Despatches*, IX, 180f.

[66] Kraehe, I, 147; and Humb. to Fred. Wm., 20 Aug. 1814, in *Gesammelte Schriften*, XI, 148.

[67] This and following from Zichy to Mett., 12 Aug. 1814, in Fournier, "Zur Vorgeschichte," 319–323.

[68] *Ibid.*, 322.

them with Humboldt, whose timely appearance in Baden on 18 August[69] provided the minister with another channel to Berlin and an opportunity to dispel misunderstandings. Tactical considerations aside, Hardenberg's objections boiled down to Metternich's hedging on Saxony and his too bellicose tone toward Russia. The Austrian now retreated slightly, convincing Humboldt that he viewed the matter "in its true aspect" and in the end would be able to bring the emperor along with him.[70] Some ambiguity remained, though, since he still opposed transferring the king of Saxony to the papal legations. Metternich's principal concern, however, was persuading the Prussians of his peaceful intentions. If Austria maintained 375,000 men on a virtual war footing, he explained, it was only because he was certain that a show of force, backed by Prussia and Britain, would cause Alexander to yield. He begged the ambassador to reiterate to Berlin that Prussia's interest was no less involved than Austria's. This Humboldt did, and with a ringing endorsement of Metternich's analysis.[71]

For all his eloquence, however, and for all his profound understanding of the threat, Metternich could not remove the basic flaw in his argument. He spoke of peace; he spoke of firmness; but he could not tell Hardenberg what would happen if Alexander stood his ground. He could only pit his guess that the maneuver would succeed against Hardenberg's doubts. Actually pacifism in Vienna had its dark side too: the possibility that Prussia might be left to face the tsar's revenge alone. Consequently Humboldt's optimism lost something in translation to Berlin. True, Hardenberg on 26 August ordered his chargé d'affaires in St. Petersburg, Colonel Reinhold Otto von Schoeler, to impress on the tsar the danger to Europe inherent in his plans, but this pressure was applied as much to effect the immediate transfer of Saxony to Prussian occupation as to change Alexander's mind about Poland.[72] Writing to Castlereagh a day later (27 August), the chancellor questioned Metternich's optimism about the Bruchsal interview, criticized his pampering of Württemberg and Bavaria, and insisted that the main purpose of tripartite solidarity was a strong German league closely linked to Holland. He also denounced any idea of sharing Saxony with Austria, further evidence that he did not take Metternich's

[69] Gentz, *Tagebücher*, I, 295. Humboldt had been in Vienna since 8 Aug.
[70] Humb. to Fred. Wm., 20 Aug. 1814, in *Gesammelte Schriften*, XI, 145–159.
[71] *Ibid.*, 159.
[72] Hard. to Schoeler, 26 Aug. 1814, ZSTA, Merseburg, 2.4.1.I, No. 992, pp. 1–4. Cf. Heinrich von Treitschke, *Treitschke's History of Germany in the Nineteenth Century*, trans. Eden and Cedar Paul, 7 vols. (New York, 1915–1919), I, 681–685, who believes that Hardenberg acted so vigorously because he was misled by Metternich's lies and Humboldt's gullible optimism. The letter to Castlereagh however (see below, n. 73) shows that he remained as circumspect as ever. In any case, he never opposed unilateral pleading with the tsar, only concerted demonstrations.

intimations on this point as full capitulation.[73] The essentials of his policy were now clear: no concerted demonstrations against Alexander, only individual appeals; if these failed and Poland was lost, all the more reason for making Germany strong.

Given the chancellor's priorities, it is difficult to say whether Metternich or Humboldt was the more puzzled that he had not yet dispatched his finished plan for the German constitution. On their departure from London the understanding had been that he would send his draft by 1 August or so to Vienna, where Metternich and Humboldt could then come to terms before drawing in the representatives of Hanover, Bavaria, and Württemberg. Humboldt, as it happened, arrived late in the capital (8 August) and did not see Metternich until the latter's return from Persenbeug, but it did not matter: the only word from Berlin was Zichy's report of 12 August, which stated that Hardenberg would send the plan at once. Despite that, on the 20th Humboldt could still report merely that as far as Metternich had any fixed ideas on the matter, they seemed to be in line with Hardenberg's thinking. The Austrian minister in the next few days began to groom Baron Friedrich Binder as his assistant in German affairs, but what passed between then is not known, a truly unfortunate gap in the record.[74]

Binder and Humboldt, as they returned from Baden to Vienna on 26 August, no doubt attributed Hardenberg's delay to procrastination and summertime inertia. For the historian, however, there is a deeper mystery, and the matter is important enough to warrant an extended digression here. After leaving Metternich in Paris on 7 July, Hardenberg went on to Frankfurt and there attempted to reconcile the Austrian position to his own. The result was the plan in forty-one articles mentioned earlier, which he then, between 15 and 17 July, submitted to the scrutiny of Stein, just returned from Bruchsal, and Solms-Laubach. The plan under review,[75] provided for a division of Germany into nine Kreise, each headed by a director or in several cases two directors; a council of the eight Kreis-directing states with a rotating chairmanship; and a federal diet (*Bundesversammlung*) containing seats for all the sovereign princes, including the Kreis chiefs, as well as representatives of the mediatized Standesherren, that is to say, those

---

[73] Hard. to Castle., 27 Aug. 1814. Text in Griewank, "Preussen und die Neuordnung," 276–279. Cf. Webster, *Castlereagh*, I, 320.

[74] Humb. to Fred. Wm., 20 Aug. 1814, in *Gesammelte Schriften*, XI, 152; Gentz, *Tagebücher*, I, 298f.; Hoff, *Die Medistisiertenfrage*, 64f.; and H. Baumgarten, "Verhandlungen über die deutsche Bundesverfassung im Sommer 1814," *Im neuen Reich*, IX, pt. 2 (1879), 556f.

[75] "Entwurf der Grundlagen der deutschen Bundesverfassung." Text in Griewank, "Pruessen und die Neuordnung," 269–276, and in Stein, *Briefe*, V, 841–852.

houses which had formerly held seats in the old Reichstag. In the council the voting system was weighted in favor of Austria and Prussia, in the diet in favor of the Kreis directors. The main function of the Kreis directors was to enforce federal law, organize the Kreis military resources under federal supervision, and provide appellate courts with jurisdiction over the entire Kreis. Only states with territory outside the Bund might wage war independently of the Bund, and when they did so, they would have no special claim on federal support. The rights, duties, and status of the mediatized houses were to be defined later and guaranteed by the Bund, the federal diet in this connection acting as a federal court. As noted earlier, the Standesherren were not to be autonomous Kreis estates but only the first estate in the states to which they belonged. Federal norms, including provision for estates-type constitutions (*landständische Verfassungen*) in each state, were to define and regulate the rights of all other subjects. Similarly, standardized law codes, coinage, tariffs, postal service, and other "generally utilitiarian projects" were to be encouraged. The federal constitution as a whole was to be placed under the guarantee of the great powers, expressly including Russia and Great Britain.

On a scale running from a loose system of alliances at one end to a literal restoration of the hierarchies of the Reich at the other Hardenberg's project must be adjudged moderate, and while one could not truly call it Metternich's plan, it was certainly Hardenberg's version of a compromise between them. Stein and Solms, however, represented a different constituency. The council of Kreis chiefs was too large, Stein argued, and a rotating presidency too cumbersome; better an executive directory of only four or five with Austria the honorary president and Prussia a kind of chancellor actually managing affairs. If one must speak of sovereignty, one must also state explicitly that it was to be limited and make it clear, among other things, that attempted withdrawal from the Bund would be met by placing the offender under ban. It was not enough to guarantee *landständische Verfassungen* in the several states (he called them "provinces"); one must expressly guarantee to the Landtage the powers to make laws, approve taxes, and represent the constitution. One must specify then and there that the estates included, besides elected members, an hereditary order of mediatized family heads; that this order not be restricted to Standesherren but include the imperial knights, at least those with annual income of at least 6,000 guilders; and that they be permitted as under the Reich to organize corporations for mutual aid.[76] Their rights should include

[76] This and following from Stein's marginalia and observations in Stein, *Briefe*, v, 67-71. Cf. Gerhard Ritter, *Stein*, 2 vols. (1931; rev. ed. in 1 vol., Stuttgart, 1958), II, 274–277, and Griewank, "Preussen und die Neuordnung," 246–248. Corpora-

exemption from conscription and from the jurisdiction of the sovereign's courts, family autonomy (i.e., the right of entail, concluding family compacts to keep property intact), and recourse to the Bund for redress of grievances, for which purpose a special federal court should be established as Humboldt had so often advised. Hardenberg had included in a list of civil rights freedom of movement and freedom of state service and university attendance anywhere in Germany. To these Stein would add the right of emigration, *habeus corpus*, protection against extraordinary tribunals and indictments for ex post facto crimes, and the security of both material and literary property.

Finally, conspicuous by its absence was any suggestion of making the mediatized houses autonomous *Kreisstände*. On the contrary, ever resentful of favors not shared by the imperial knights, Stein thought it better to keep the Standesherren with the knights as privileged *Landstände*, where under strong federal protection they could more effectively check the ruling prince. Nowhere was this issue more acute than in his home state of Nassau, where the Standesherren ignored his pleas to attend a constitutional convention of notables and clamored for complete severance from the state instead. It was partly to meet this threat that the government, mainly at Stein's urging, on 1 September promulgated its own *landständische* but relatively centralistic constitution.[77]

This is not the place to praise Stein for the liberal elements in his thinking or chide him for his aristocratic bias, which always impelled him to cram too much detail into his constitutional drafts. He himself did not believe that Austria and Prussia would ever consent to reform their own domestic institutions to accommodate his program; the sketchiness of Hardenberg's draft was proof of that. Here was the central problem, and the solution Stein found was astonishingly simple: namely, to include in the Bund only the Prussian provinces west of the Elbe and the Austrian provinces west of Styria, that is to say the territories which for the most part had once had special affinities with the rest of the Reich, had shared the disruptive experiences of belonging to the Rheinbund or the French Empire, and were either joining Austria or Prussia for the first time or returning from a "Babylonian captivity," as Stein liked to say. The rationale he gave was that the remainder of the Habsburg and Hohenzollern monarchies

---

tions were an institution of former times that permitted very small *Ritter* to pool their population totals in order to retain the right to courts and other functions of local government. Corporations were also formed to manage the details of casting curial votes in the Reichstag.

[77] Stein to Münster, 20 Oct. 1814, Stein, *Briefe*, v, 171f. Hans Sarholz, "Das Herzogtum Nassau 1813–1815. Ein Beitrag zur Geschichte des Rheinbundes und der Befreiungskriege," *Nassauische Annalen*, LVII (1937), 80f.

constituted integrated wholes of long duration and enjoying benevolent rule; actually his aim was to avoid dragging the *Landstände* of the Bund down to the level of the captive estates to the east. At any rate, with scant regard for the forces of centralism in Berlin and Vienna, he maintained that since the new provinces required reorganization anyway, no one could object to using his models there, especially as one could cite Solms's argument that in regard to the definition of sovereignty and the rights of the mediatized houses, the Rheinbund Act itself was a friendly and serviceable instrument if strictly enforced. "Only the powers that destroyed the Rheinbund," Solms contended, "can make constitutional determinations concernings its victims."[78] With only Voralberg, Tyrol, Salzburg, and Berchtesgaden in the Bund Stein did not consider it an exaggeration to say that Austria's internal conditions would not be disturbed.

The notion of a narrower Bund no doubt expressed Stein's true convictions, recalling as it did the tripartite arrangement he had proposed just a year before as well as the persistent tradition that the Reich somehow had a life of its own apart from the affairs of the two powers.[79] But there were tactical considerations as well. Given his superficial grasp of international politics, Stein probably believed that in providing the new Bund a boundary hardly different from that of the old, he had eliminated the only possible objection that Metternich or Hardenberg could have to granting the Bund extensive powers over the internal affairs of its members. Invoking the Rheinbund Act in this connection could also be expected to have appeal for Metternich or anybody else who took the Rheinbund and the accession treaties of 1813 as his starting point. In this way did two distinguished scions of the old imperial nobility join forces at Frankfurt to provide Hardenberg with both a solution to a difficult problem and an ingenious foundation for it in international treaty.

The conferences adjourned on 17 July, Hardenberg promising that he would rewrite his plan and suggesting that Solms should join the preliminary conferences in Vienna.[80] He then proceeded to Leipzig and completed the new draft, also in forty-one articles.[81] From Solms

---

[78] Solms to Stein, 13 Aug. 1814, in Stein, *Briefe*, v, 112. Also see above, p. 26.

[79] Georg Heinrich Pertz, *Das Leben des Ministers Freiherr vom Stein*, 6 vols., 2nd ed. (Berlin, 1850–1854), IV, 49.

[80] Baumgarten, "Verhandlungen über die Bundesverfassung," 549.

[81] Of this revised draft there are several versions differing only in minor ways. These discrepancies, however, are helpful in establishing the sequence of events. The earliest is in the Stein papers and published in Pertz, *Leben von Stein*, IV, 49–65, and in Stein, *Briefe*, v, 841–852, where it is conveniently matched against the original Forty-one Articles before revision. The second, never published as such, is discussed in Schmidt, *Verfassungsfrage*, 170–171, with certain discrepancies noted and is probably the one in the Prussian State Archives noted by Griewank, *Wiener*

he adopted the mediatized houses' demand for the restoration of all revenues except the *Kontribution*. Stein's proposals pertaining to a federal court, civil rights, and the rights of the estates he incorporated almost verbatim, even to rewarding the Standesherren not by making them autonomous *Kreisstände*, which neither Stein nor Metternich had accepted, but by granting them greater representation at the federal level: two more curial votes and even several whole votes in the lower chamber.[82] Only a footnote suggesting that in an ideal world the mediatized *deserved* parity with sovereigns remained of the radical Kreis plan contemplated in the London articles, though as we shall see, the idea was far from dead. Even so, the additional seats were more than tokens: from a total of approximately thirty-four votes, ten would now be cast by the mediatized houses themselves and a majority of the rest by states uninterested in the problems of those that had mediatized subjects.

Hardenberg likewise heeded the demand for a "more concentrated direction," but instead of diminishing the council of Kreis chiefs and simply making Austria the permanent chairman as Stein had proposed, he sought the same result by assigning Austria and Prussia together a majority of the votes (six out of eleven) and constituting them as a separate directory over and yet within the council. In the terminology of the time this probably meant their exclusive right to appoint administrative staff, to keep and have access to records, and even to

---

Kongress, 132, n. 96. The text Schmidt does publish, calling it "definitive," is, however, indistinguishable from that in the Stein papers. The third, the one officially submitted to Metternich and likewise never published—in fact, never even noticed till now—is in HHSA, StK., Diplomatische Korrespondenz, Preussen, Fasc. 95, pp. 29–36. A fourth version is a working copy given to Baron Peter von Frank for intramural use and may be found in the Frank papers in HHSA, StK., Kongressakten, Cart. 6. Still another version was published by Johann Ludwig Klüber, ed., *Acten des Wiener Congresses in den Jahren 1814 und 1815*, 9 vols. (Erlangen, 1815–1835), Vol. I, pt. 1, 45–56, in the mistaken belief (shared by Schmidt) that it was the official copy conveyed to Metternich. In all probability it was rather Solms's copy containing reference to the minor revisions of 26 July. Unfortunately, despite its inaccuracies, it is the most widely known and copied. Cf. Aretin, *Bayerns Weg*, 136, who as recently as 1976, misled by a typographical error, believed that Hardenberg and Stein wanted to confine the *Stände* to hereditary nobility as implied in the Klüber version, whereas the authentic versions make clear their intent to include elected deputies.

[82] The first plan contained a complicated system of curial votes based mostly on family relationships and giving a majority to the Kreis-chief members. The new plan assigned one full vote to all houses, whether sovereign or mediatized, that had over 50,000 inhabitants, and curial votes for the rest, including six curiae for the lesser Standesherren. The practical effect of this would have been to give one full vote each to Hamburg, Bremen, Lübeck, and Frankfurt as Stein had proposed, as well as to the mediatized houses of Hohenlohe, Leiningen, Fürstenberg, and Oettingen. This conclusion based on population figures given in a list appended to Solms's memorial of 5 May 1814, HHSA, StK., Kongressakten, Cart 6. Cf. Jean Engelbert d'Arenberg, *Les Princes du St. Empire* (Louvain, 1951), 132–136.

introduce bills, the so-called *jus proponendum*. One aim was to leave no doubt about Prussian parity even though Austria would preside at the meetings, but the directory served another purpose as well. In his first version of the Forty-one Articles Hardenberg had lumped the Kreis chiefs together with all other princes in a unicameral legislature, counting on weighted votes to keep the former in control. In his new plan he made the council of Kreis chiefs a separate upper house of the diet, leaving the other princes, together with the two directing monarchs, to form a lower chamber called the council of princes and estates. Although still jointly called the federal diet, the two councils were to meet and vote separately and in case of a deadlock, the directory was to decide. Since in the one council Austria and Prussia would have the majority, the outcome could hardly be in doubt. As Hardenberg explained it to Solms, "the entire system requires as its foundation that Austria and Prussia are and remain united, that they decide and the rest are actually placed in a consultative relationship."[83] That was perhaps more concentration than Stein had bargained for,[84] and partly because of it, Hardenberg, after some hesitation, decided not to drop Baden and Hesse-Cassel from the council of Kreis chiefs as his friends has urged. Under the directory, he explained, they were now "harmless," and as former electors of the Reich, even though latecomers, they had as much right to a seat there as Württemberg. This was very likely the same argument Metternich had used in proposing their inclusion in the first place.[85]

The heart of the matter, however, was the question of the federal boundary, and here too Hardenberg adopted Stein's solution. Actually, in his first draft he had never explicitly defined the boundary; it had to be inferred from the list of nine Kreise, which included Bohemia, "Austria," and Brandenburg, appropriately delineated.[86] In the new plan Bohemia and Brandenburg were dropped altogether and Austria, renamed Vorderösterreich, was expressly confined to Salzburg, Berch-

[83] Hard. to Solms, 23 July 1814, in Baumgarten, "Verhandlungen über die Bundesverfassung," 549f.

[84] See his later critique of Article XXVI, wherein he proposed that in case the two councils disagreed, the matter should be deferred to the next session. Stein, *Briefe*, v, 141–145.

[85] Hardenberg's note to Art. XVII of the revised Forty-one Articles; Hard. to Solms, as per n. 79 above.

[86] It is commonly believed on the basis of later versions that Metternich was the originator of following the boundary of the old Reich (e.g., Brigitte Winkler-Seraphim, "Das Verhältnis der preussischen Ostprovinzen insbesondere Ostpreussens, zum Deutschen Bund im 19. Jahrhundert," *Zeitschrift für Ostforschung*, IV [1955], 330–331). He may indeed have been, but only because of his influence on the first version of the Forty-one Articles. Otherwise, Hardenberg must get the credit. Neither, however, mentioned the Reich; that was a later innovation demanded by Bavaria for the sake of exactness. See below p. 369.

tesgaden, Tyrol, and Vorarlberg. The chancellor was no doubt as gratified as he expected Metternich to be at this clean removal of the old core provinces from federal controls; the trouble was that the same device also removed them from the protective military system of the Bund. Some remedy was already available in the fact that the two powers were to have an absolute majority on the council of Kreis chiefs, which included in its functions exclusive control over war, peace, and foreign affairs in general.[87] On the other hand, Article XXXVII of the original plan emphatically disclaimed any responsibility of the Bund for nonfederal territories of its members and especially so if they were the aggressors. Hardenberg met the situation by first positing an "indissoluble alliance" between the Bund and Austria and Prussia as great powers and then making the council of Kreis chiefs the sole judge of how and when to apply its terms.

Although Hardenberg left no doubt about the role of Prussia and Austria as guarantors of the Bund, both its territorial integrity and its constitution, he was vague about obligations in the other direction. Federal support of manifestly aggressive wars seemed excluded unless the Kreis chiefs decided otherwise, but anything else would depend on the terms eventually written into the treaty of alliance.[88] Hardenberg probably did not intend a comprehensive defensive pact for the entire territory of all partners but did not categorically exclude the possibility. We are already approaching the quandaries of Felix Schwarzenberg's "Reich of 70,000,000."

The problem of defense, of course, also required the organization of a federal army, ostensibly the main objective of the Kreis system. Each state was to contribute men and money to the Kreis military establishment in proportion to its population. If a regiment or more, the unit would retain its identity and in peacetime stand at the disposal of its sovereign prince; rulers of the smaller states would simply contribute a prorated number of recruits to the army of the Kreis chief. In wartime the Kreis chief was to command all the Kreis forces, in peacetime maintain its uniformity of pay and equipment, supervise the federal fortresses in his area, and see that federally prescribed standards of proficiency prevailed. Significantly, nothing was said about the supreme command, the issue most likely to set the two directing powers against each other.

The revised plan called for seven Kreise. One was to be Vorderösterreich as previously noted. If, as Hardenberg evidently still expected, Austria took territory on the Upper Rhine, it would be associated with Baden in a separate Kreis under the codirection of those

[87] Article XXII.
[88] See Arts. II and XXXVIII.

two states. Similarly in the north Prussia was to be a codirector, along
with Hesse-Cassel, of an Upper Saxon-Thuringian Kreis and the sole
director of the Lower Rhine-Westphalian Kreis. Since the latter was
to include the German lands of the Dutch king, Hardenberg had originally intended to make him a codirector but later thought better of
it as he had never been an elector.[89] On the other hand, if the king,
as Hardenberg hoped, should place all his provinces within the Bund
he was to have a new Kreis, Burgundy, all his own.[90] This eventuality
aside, the chancellor visualized three more Kreise. Bavaria and Württemberg were each to constitute a Kreis in its own right and of its own
territory, while Hanover was to be the chief of a grouping that included
Holstein, Oldenburg, Brunswick, several small states, and the free cities
of Bremen, Hamburg, and Lübeck. Thus while the two South German
kingdoms would have no chance to use Kreis institutions to extend
their influence beyond their borders, Count Münster and his friends
would have the opposite problem: constant embroilment in the rivalries
of Russia, Denmark, and Britain, and the alien tugs of world commerce.
One other point requires mention here because of future controversy:
namely, that despite its name, the Kreis Upper Saxony-Thuringia was
to encompass Hesse-Darmstadt and the free city of Frankfurt, thus
extending Prussian influence well south of the Main and Mosel, where
Metternich had repeatedly warned it must never come.

Taken as a whole, the Forty-one Articles as revised represented an
alliance between Prussian *Realpolitik* and the Stein wing of the restorative movement, with its emphasis on the central institutions of the
Bund rather than the Kreise. For those who yearned to do so, it was
possible to penetrate the new nomenclature and make out the dim
outlines of the old Reich. Directory, council of Kreis chiefs, federal
diet, federal court—what were these but Kaiser, electoral college,
Reichstag, and Imperial Chamber Court in disguise? This was not the
Prussia of the Silesian wars but the Prussia of Frederick's League of
Princes in 1785, which had upheld imperial institutions against the
onslaught of Joseph II. This at any rate was the impression Hardenberg
wished to give, and only time would tell if this association would give
him the leverage he was seeking.

On 23 July the chancellor, still in Leipzig, sent a copy of the new
plan to Solms, reiterating the hope that he would "soon proceed to
Vienna to participate in the preliminaries of this most important mat-

[89] See Hardenberg's note to Art. XVII.

[90] "An excellent idea," Hardenberg commented in a note to Art. XVII. Cf. Ritter,
Stein, II, 27; and Peter Gerrit Thielen, *Karl August von Hardenberg 1750–1822: Eine
Biographie* (Cologne and Berlin, 1967), 305. The Austrian Netherlands had consti-
tuted the Burgundian Kreis in the old Reich.

ter," and promising to inform Metternich of this invitation at once.[91] Three days later, back in Berlin, he forwarded to Solms a few minor corrections.[92] Thus as early as 26 July Hardenberg had not only a finished plan but an emissary to carry it to Vienna. Yet a month later neither the plan, nor Solms, nor even an announcement of his coming had arrived.[93] The puzzle is partly solved by understanding the true nature of Solms's mission. He was not a Prussian courier, chosen for his legal expertise both to convey and explain the plan to Humboldt and Metternich, as historians have hitherto assumed.[94] Rather, as the leader of the Association of Mediatized Houses, Hardenberg was inviting him to Vienna as an independent force. Nothing was said about conveying the plan to anybody except Stein; his function was to add the voice of the restorative movement to the proceedings, which otherwise would have found Prussia isolated in the face of Austria and the middle states.

Indeed, Solms did not relish the assignment. Evidently suspecting that he was being used for a cause not entirely his own, he proposed that Metternich join in extending the invitation and insisted that he stay behind in Frankfurt to finish his work for Stein (he was still employed by the Central Administrative Council) lest an appearance in Vienna before the opening of the congress be taken as a sign of intrigue or an insult to Metternich's own experts on the Reich constitution. "In all honesty," he told Hardenberg, "I cannot work with pleasure and delight in a role that looks dubious to me."[95] The chancellor scoffed at these scruples, insisting that informing Metternich was enough, but in the end Solms played it his way: if he considered himself responsible to anyone, it was to Stein. When he finally did reach Vienna, on 28 August, he expected to find negotiations between Metternich and Humboldt in full swing and was astonished to learn that they were not.[96]

[91] Hard. to Solms, 23 July 1814, in Baumgartner, "Verhandlungen über die Bundesverfassing," 549f.
[92] Humb. to Hard., 31 Aug. 1814, in *Gesammelte Schriften*, XI, 220f.
[93] On 21 Aug. 1814 Humboldt bitterly complained about this neglect to his wife. Humboldt, *Briefe*, IV, 381f.
[94] Cf. Pertz, *Leben von Stein*, IV, 49; Schmidt, *Verfassungsfrage*, 187; Hoff, *Mediatisiertenfrage*, 65; Baumgarten, "Verhandlungen über die Bundesverfassung," 555–558; Gebhardt, *Humboldt als Staatsmann*, II, 125; and most recently Mager, "Problem der landständischen Verfassungen," 304, all of whom regard Solms as an official agent of Prussia. A more careful reading of old and familiar sources could have prevented this mistake.
[95] Solms to Hard., 16 July 1814, ZSTA, Merseburg, 2.4.1.I, No. 1559, pp. 141–142.
[96] Hard. to Solms, 23 July and Solms to Hard., 31 July and 19 Aug. 1814, in *ibid.*, pp. 143, 183–184, and 195–197. Also Solms's retrospective account of 30 Sept. 1814, in Baumgarten, "Verhandlungen über die Bundesverfassung," 551.

Hardenberg's inaction is harder to explain.[97] In response to Zichy's inquiries in Berlin he replied that the project was not yet finished,[98] and it is true that he was still pondering revisions. A Burgundian Kreis under the prince of Orange, the addition of Denmark for all her mainland territory, and the incredibly snarled problem of the German Catholic Church were all very much on his mind during August. How to reconcile the Netherlands and Denmark to the Austro-Prussian diarchy would have given anyone pause, and yet in the end he made virtually no changes. More likely the chancellor's timing was intended to promote a propaganda campaign against the Habsburgs, the traditional champions of the Standesherren. By advertising the plan among them in advance, he could later explain the alterations that were bound to come as the diabolical work of the unreliable Metternich and the Austria-first Josephinists in Vienna. Stein was especially active after the Frankfurt talks, pressing his own sovereign, the duke of Nassau, to accelerate the installation of a constitution that would meet the criteria set forth in the Forty-one Articles and using the pages of the *Rheinische Merkur* to publicize his ideas about the German constitution. The editor, Joseph von Görres, wrote the copy, but Stein supplied the material.[99] The Solms mission itself, especially given the earlier timing that Hardenberg had preferred, would fit well as part of a synchronized propaganda campaign and as a way to test the reception the plan might receive whenever the chancellor chose to make it official. Significantly, when he did at length send the official draft, it was immediately after the news of Solms's arrival in Vienna should have reached him.[100]

Whatever his intentions, the chancellor succeeded in confounding his own camp more than the enemy. When Solms finally called on Humboldt on 29 August, they were both stunned to learn at last the true state of affairs. Personally embarrassed at his ignorance of the revised Forty-one Articles, Humboldt begged Solms not to let Metternich know who had brought them to Vienna.[101] Worse yet was the plan

[97] His own excuse was that he had been waiting for Schoeler to report from St. Petersburg, but this in itself need not have held up transmittal of the Forty-one Articles. Hard. to Mett., 3 Sept. 1814, HHSA, StK., Diplomatische Korrespondenz, Preussen, Fasc. 95, folder 3, pp. 27f.

[98] So Metternich explained to Humboldt. Humb. to Hard., 10 Sept. 1814, ZSTA, Merseburg, 2.4.1.I, No. 5985.

[99] Görres to Stein, 4 Aug. 1814, in Stein, *Briefe*, v, 95–97; Pertz, *Leben von Stein*, IV, 65–69; selections in *Joseph von Görres gesammelte Schriften*, ed. Marie Görres, 9 vols. (Munich, 1854–1874), II, Nos. 41, 45, and 49. Cf. Ritter, *Stein*, II, 273f., and Hans Joachim Schoeps, ed., *Aus den Jahren preussischer Not und Erneuerung* (Berlin, 1963), 123f.

[100] Solms's arrival on 28 Aug., dispatch of Prussian plan to Metternich, 3 Sept. 1814—but it was high time in any case.

[101] Solms's written account of 30 Aug. 1814, in Baumgartner, "Verhandlungen über die Bundesverfassung," 551.

itself; to cut off from Germany the centuries-old residence of her emperors, to transform the capital "that had spread more light and knowledge than any other into a mere Prussian town"—that, he insisted, would shock the public, degrade the Bund, and was in any case unnecessary. It took Humboldt two days to recover, and when he did, he took to his code book to protest to his chief and announce that despite the shortage of time, he would await direct orders before showing the plan to Metternich.[102] Solms tried to dissuade him but in vain. It was a disappointment; just the day before he had assured Stein that he would "do all that's in me to see that the plan is at least provisionally discussed with the cabinet here."[103] Nothing proves Solms's independence more than his next move: on 2 September he made the trip to Baden to see Metternich himself.

Probably by way of Humboldt Metternich already knew that Solms was privy to some degree to Hardenberg's plan, and this was in itself a good reason to accord his visitor the hospitality that one expected in Baden: dinner first, then a leisurely discussion of business. Yet the interview, as reported by Solms,[104] did not get down to fundamentals, on Solms's part no doubt out of consideration for Humboldt, on Metternich's for the usual reason that he was more concerned with strategy than with substance. There is no evidence that Solms used the occasion to hand over Hardenberg's plan or even to let Metternich know that he possessed a copy. Possibly on the assumption that they were talking about ideas exchanged in Paris, the minister insisted that he and the chancellor "walked hand in hand." Yet the plan as he knew it was too discursive. As he had frequently told Humboldt, only the broad principles of a constitution could be considered at a European congress, the details being left for another meeting "to be worked out and completed in Germany by Germans,"[105] a point worth noting not only for its tactical implications but also because nationalist historians have usually given Stein the credit for this patriotic inspiration. Solms complained that anything from a sturdy tower to a castle in the sky was possible in this way, but Metternich assured him that with skillful handling "the bases adopted must necessarily contain the entire organism." This sounded like evasiveness. Actually it was a simple statement of Metternich's method: first bracket the target with a general proposition that commanded assent, then argue the competing parties step by step to the goal itself. It was the way of the mediator, and if some deception

---

[102] Humb. to Hard., 31 Aug. 1814, in *Gesammelte Schriften*, XI, 220–223; cf. Gebhardt, *Humboldt als Staatsmann*, II, 125.

[103] Solms to Stein, 31 Aug. 1814, Stein, *Briefe*, V, 129.

[104] This and following from Solms's account of 3 Sept. 1814 in Baumgarten, "Verhandlungen über die Bundesverfassung," 555f.

[105] *Ibid.*, 555.

was employed in the process—well, a little casuistry never hurt anyone if it brought people together.

The strategy of postponement, however, cannot succeed indefinitely. If the interview with Solms did nothing else, it dramatized the growing influence of the Standesherren, their alignment with Prussia, and the likelihood of an early showdown. Only a day or two after the interview with Solms, the regular envoy of the mediatized houses, Baron Gärtner, likewise called on Metternich and officially submitted an exhaustive list of demands that he had carried with him since 16 May.[106] Lone amateurs were also active, bombarding the chancellery with advice on how to reconcile the language of the accession treaties with imperial restoration. In these projects "Reich" and "Confederation" were often used interchangeably, as had occasionally been the case in the previous century. Expressions like "Reichsbund" and "Bundesreich" began to appear. Sometimes "Reich" meant only the third Germany, while "Bund" denoted the combination of the Reich with Austria and Prussia. If a Kaiser was *verboten*, let him be a protector (*Schutz- und Schirmherr*). Naive these efforts no doubt were, but piled high on the sorting tables of the State Chancellery, they had a cumulative effect.[107] Arriving in Vienna about this time, the Württemberg plenipotentiary, Baron Franz Josef Ignaz von Linden, was dumbfounded by the atmosphere. "At every turn," he wrote, "the idea of returning to the antiquated order is present and so widespread that even the still living imperial prelates are working for the off chance."[108] The pressure was mounting. In view of the rebuff that Metternich had administered to Gärtner at allied headquarters in March and the frequent charge that Austria was indifferent to Germany, how could anybody believe that he really intended to build a tower once the congress had fabricated a castle in the sky? The time had come to mend fences, perhaps even to seize some of the initiative from Hardenberg.

Metternich would in any case have required at the congress the services of technical experts on German affairs, but there was nothing in his previous policy that would have presaged the choices he now made. On 8 September upon approval of the emperor he set up a special advisory committee consisting of Franz von Rademacher, then the director of the chancellery archives; Baron Peter von Frank, an official left over from the old imperial chancellery; and Baron Kaspar Philipp von Spiegel zum Diesenberg, who had once served with the archbishop of Salzburg and later with Stein's Central Administrative

---

[106] Hoff, *Mediatisiertenfrage*, 63.
[107] Samples galore in HHSA, StK., Kongressakten, Cart. 6.
[108] Linden to King Frederick, 11 Sept. 1814, in HSA, Stuttgart, E 70, Fasc. 12, pp. 28–30.

Council. Frank was known as "ponderously learned" in the ways of the old Reich, and Spiegel's name was synonymous with *Landstände*.[109] Spiegel and Rademacher, in fact, had once been proposed by Stein himself as worthy to sit with Solms and Humboldt on a German constitution commission.[110] "This action," Metternich explained to Francis, "will not be lost on the public and cannot help but have a very favorable affect on opinion in Germany . . . if only because people will see that we are at work on a *German* enterprise."[111]

So far so good, but what the Standesherren most wanted to hear about from Austrian sources were the prospects for an imperial restoration. Metternich did not himself discourse immediately on this delicate subject, but he allowed Binder to do so and referred Gärtner to him for enlightenment. "If only Franz were Kaiser again," Gärtner sighed at an audience on 8 September, whereupon Binder assured him that if one first attained the good, the better would follow in due course "even on this score." Three days later he gave similar advice to Solms, professing, however, to be undecided about which country should provide the emperor. "That is easily answered," Solms slyly replied: the power "least dependent on France and Russia. Clearly this power is Austria." So easy was it to pry loose Hardenberg's following if Austria but half tried![112]

In the meantime, while Metternich was trying to confine the German question to generalities, Humboldt took the opposite course, seeking to amplify Hardenberg's draft with precise detail. Determined to make what progress he could while awaiting word from his chief, he brought together for this purpose Solms, Count Ernst Hardenberg, the Hanoverian minister in Vienna, and his German expert, Georg Friedrich von Martens of Göttingen, the well-known authority on international law. Count Hardenberg was shocked at first, not only by the exclusion of so much Austrian and Prussian territory but also by the loaded votes and the two-power directory that had replaced the rotating chairmanship, which he assumed had been settled in the spring. Yet despite the directory, he observed, Austria, with less territory in Germany than Prussia or even Bavaria, stood to lose "her moral and material pre-

---

[109] Linden to King Frederick, 14 Sept. 1814, *ibid.*, pp. 40–42; extr. in Pfister, *Lager der Verbündeten*, 299. Linden also reported that old Franz Georg Metternich was boasting that the committee was his idea. The report was probably accurate but the facts not since the foreign minister had good reasons of his own. The father may have influenced the choice of personnel, however.

[110] Stein, *Briefe*, v, 614. On Spiegel see Walter Lipgens, *Ferdinand August Graf Spiegel und das Verhältniss von Kirche und Staat 1789–1835* (Münster, 1965), *passim*.

[111] Mett. to Francis, 8 Sept. 1814, HHSA, StK., Vorträge, Cart. 196, pp. 83f. Emphasis in original.

[112] Hoff, *Mediatisiertenfrage*, 64–65; and Baumgarten, "Verhandlungen über die Bundesverfassung," 556f.

ponderance, with consequences that are difficult to calculate." Hardenberg agreed, however, to a compromise whereby both the Prussian plan and a set of ideas drafted by Martens were placed on the agenda.[113]

At several meetings held on 5, 8, and 9 September[114] the articles on civil rights were expanded and more sharply defined and the composition and rights of the *Landstände* were elaborated along the lines previously suggested by Stein but allowing, at Humboldt's insistence, the inclusion of all free landowners, whether noble or not. On the basis of a plan submitted by Humboldt, the structure of a federal court was outlined, and the competence of the court was extended to many cases involving the mediatized houses that Hardenberg had left to state or Kreis courts. Remarkably enough a provision never questioned before was deleted entirely: Article VIII, which called for the national standardization of various utilitarian services. This was mainly Count Hardenberg's victory, reflecting the fear of the North German state that Prussia would one day exploit "the sham system of voting" to impose her own coinage, commercial codes, and the like even in Kreise outside her own.[115] Humboldt's ready acquiescence, however, was a significant portent of surprising things to come. Most at issue, however, were the federal boundary and Solms's thesis that the Rheinbund Act provided the best foundation for securing the rights of the mediatized. After defending the constricted federal area with the familiar arguments Solms proposed a compromise: Austria and Prussia to place their old German provinces in the Bund for military purposes but exempt them from federal interference in their internal affairs.[116] To Humboldt, however, this must have seemed an unworthy, artificial contrivance that would still do violence to the organic wholeness of the German lands and culture. On more pragmatic grounds the Hanoverians always saw in large-scale participation by the two powers the best guarantee that the latter would keep the federal authority weak. As a result, Solms's colleagues insisted on a simple return to Hardenberg's original plan, changing the article to read that Austria and Prussia would join with "all their German states" and specifying that these include "Austria," Bohemia, and Prussian territory on both sides of the Elbe.

[113] Hard. to Münster, 3 and 13 Aug. and 7 Sept. 1814, NSHSA, Cal. Br. 24/II, No. 5026. Intercept in Fournier, *Geheimpolizei*, 116f. somewhat garbled but serviceable.
[114] This and following from protocols printed in Schmidt, *Verfassungsfrage*, 195–197, and summarized further in Gebhardt, *Humboldt als Staatsmann*, II, 128–130. Cf. Willy Real, *Die deutsche Verfassungsfrage am Ausgang der napoleonischen Herrschaft bis zum Beginn des Wiener Kongresses* (Leipzig, 1935), 16–19.
[115] Martens's "Bemerkungen über einige Punkte," 11 Sept. 1814, NSHSA, Hanover, Des. 91, No. 25.
[116] Solms's memorial of 7 Sept. 1814. Text in Schmidt, *Verfassungsfrage*, 192–195, and Baumgarten, "Verhandlungen über die Bundesverfassung," 553f.

Solms's views of the Rheinbund Act were likewise rejected, most eloquently by Humboldt, who argued that neither it nor the legal order of the old Reich should be allowed to bind one's hands for the future. Lurking in the abstract dialogue was a concrete dispute of growing importance. Literal enforcement of the rights reserved in the former (Article XXVII) and perhaps expanded along the lines of Gärtner's note of 16 May would leave the Standesherren but a short step removed from the status of autonomous *Kreisstände*, whereas Humboldt, like Stein, preferred to make them true *Landstände*, asserting their influence in the states through strong central parliaments. In general the conferences were very generous but in the end they made the Standesherren territorial estates, which they had never really asked to be. In any case, Humboldt declaimed grandly, the restoration of rights was a matter of obvious justice, not of narrow contractural obligations, and besides, he added, the sovereign rulers were tacitly committed to this program anyway by the very nature of a Bund.[117] This last pronouncement required a bold leap of the imagination, but such was the difference between the philosopher and an imperial count with vested interests at stake.

There the informal discussions abruptly ceased, for on 9 September a Prussian courier at last appeared, bearing the official plan together with a private covering letter for Metternich, which for the first time mentioned the participation of Solms. Hardenberg also announced the appointment of Baron Ferdinand August von Spiegel, the former bishop of Münster and the brother of Kaspar Philipp on Metternich's committee, to advise on the relations of German Catholics with the papacy. The chancellor expected the greatest difficulty from the attempted subordination of Bavaria and Württemberg to the two powers, especially when it came to denying them independent military and foreign policies. "But that is as it should be," he concluded. "The strength of Germany, her unity under the decisive sway of Austria and Prussia, completely united between them—that is the real foundation of the future repose of Europe and the equilibrium toward which all our concerns are directed."[118]

Information about Metternich's reaction is scanty and indirect. We know that he held a meeting on the subject with members of his staff on 13 September at his residence in Baden, but who was there and

[117] Gebhardt, *Humboldt als Staatsmann*, II, 129f.; and Hoff, *Mediatisiertenfrage*, 57–61. It is true that in his plan of 5 May Solms included the mediatized houses in the *Landstände*, but he defined their relationship to their *Regenten* as "approximately, as in the old imperial bond, that of *Landeshoheit* to imperial sovereignty." (HHSA, StK., Kongressakten, Cart. 6, p. 202.) On this basis they would have been freer than in the Kreise of Hardenberg's London Articles.

[118] Hard. to Mett., 3 Sept. 1814, as per n. 97.

what was done are unknown except that the Prussian draft was referred to the Rademacher committee for study.[119] More knowledge can be gleaned from the interview of 11 September between Solms and Binder, mentioned above. Solms found Metternich's aide fully informed and in general well disposed toward the plan. Like Humboldt, he was distressed by the constriction of the federal area but for a profoundly different reason: not the alienation of sacred German soil but rather "the notion that the Bund was supposed to be a bulwark more against France than against Russia." The primacy of defense in Austrian thinking also explains why Binder showed, where Humboldt did not, a willingness to consider Solms's alternative plan of placing the disputed provinces in the Bund for military purposes only. Solms was also critical of the directory—not its powers but rather its split personality, which was uniquely Hardenberg's idea. "A constitution whose sole basis is the friendly relations of two powers stands on wobbly legs," the *Reichsgraf* remarked. There followed the dialogue discussed earlier about an Austrian *Kaisertum* as the solution, Binder agreeing that, given time and the right conditions, this was indeed a possibility.[120]

As internal consideration of the Forty-one Articles began, the plenipotentiaries of the powers were already arriving in Vienna. Gone now was any possibility of producing a constitutional draft endorsed by the five major German states before the opening of the congress. But if Metternich had lost the advantage of Hardenberg's absence, the very audacity of the Prussian program improved his strategic position. He could "walk hand in hand" a long distance with the chancellor and still appear by comparison as the friend of the ruling houses. The tsar was his only rival in that regard. Under the circumstances, cooperation with Hardenberg tended as well to restore the confidence of the mediatized houses in Austrian policy and encourage hopes for an imperial restoration. Solms had shown the way. Perhaps with adroit management this sentiment could be exploited and Hardenberg induced to convert the directory in some way into an actual Austrian primacy but with Prussia sharing the burdens. Whether to call the office *Kaisertum* or *Präsidium* could be decided according to circumstances. Metternich did not really believe as yet that a strong central authority would emerge, but if it did, the imperial title need not necessarily be the burden he had previously considered it, especially if the world could see that

[119] Notation by Frank on his copy of the Forty-one Articles from Frank papers, in HHSA, StK., Kongressakten, Cart. 6. Klüber, *Acten*, I, 45ff. evidently misread Frank's note as meaning that Hardenberg handed his project to Metternich at the conference. In fact, Hardenberg did not arrive in Vienna until 17 Sept. and never went to Baden. Griewank, *Wiener Kongress*, 105, n. 34.

[120] Solms's account in Baumgarten, "Verhandlungen über die Bundesverfassung," 556f.

Austria had not sought it. Although the day-to-day sequence of events cannot be traced with precision,[121] there is no doubt that reconsideration of this question in Vienna was associated with the presentation there of Hardenberg's Forty-one Articles.

In the whole two months of Metternich's sojourn in Baden the Prussian project was the only really new development, containing as it did so many departures from previous understandings. Otherwise, as the foreign minister prepared to leave, little seemed to have changed. Russian occupation armies remained in Saxony and Poland, and another, 60,000 strong, was still deployed in Holstein four months after its mission, the capture of Hamburg, had been accomplished and the king of Denmark was impatient to take over. No Russian notes had come in, and Koller's report from St. Petersburg could hardly be expected before 20 September. A letter from Castlereagh casually mentioned a detour through Paris "to see how the land lays [sic] there," but there was nothing significant in this, especially as he did not disclose Talleyrand's initiative in the matter.[122] Hardenberg still demanded the whole of Saxony, and apart from Schoeler's private remonstrations with the tsar, which the chancellor tried to represent as fulfillment of Metternich's request, he was as far as ever from joining an anti-Russian front to demand moderation in Poland.[123] On the contrary, the Russian option was still Hardenberg's best bargaining tool. Metternich in turn, though in his own mind probably ready to concede all Saxony, was still not authorized to offer more than a partitioning of the country between the two powers. Even to be able to concede this much, however, required that he keep control of the situation so that the country was his to deliver in whatever way conformed to Austrian interests and the final decision of the emperor. How much Metternich knew of the grand instruction that Talleyrand had prepared for himself shortly before[124] is a matter of conjecture; but he knew instinctively that short of entente with Russia, which fortunately still seemed remote, France's best course would be the traditional policy of supporting all the disaffected in Germany. One way to counter this was to stand fast on the

[121] E.g., we do not know how much Metternich learned at his interview with Solms on 2 Sept.

[122] Castle. to Mett., 22 Aug. 1814, quoted in Webster, *Castlereagh*, I, 323, n. 1. In reality, the stopover in Paris, as the next chapter will show, was rather more significant than either Castlereagh or Webster, *ibid.*, 321–323, indicated. Cf. Henry A. Kissinger, *A World Restored: Meternich, Castlereagh, and the Problems of Peace, 1812-1822* (London, 1957), 150, who mistakes Castlereagh's response to Talleyrand's feelers for a British initiative.

[123] Hard. to Humb., 3 Sept. 1814, extr. in Dupuis, *Talleyrand*, II, 318f.

[124] "Instructions for the King's Ambassadors at the Congress," August, 1814, in Talleyrand, *Memoirs*, II, 157–184.

Paris agreements, which denied France a voice in these matters. Another was to keep the king of Saxony attached to Austria.

In the past Metternich had skirted the edge of duplicity in dealing with the Saxons; now he crossed the line. In an audience with the Saxon envoy, Schulenburg, on 11 September and in orders to Zichy on the 12th he painted an optimistic picture, advising the king to trust Austria, to count on the integrity of the powers, to do nothing on his own, and above all to avoid "any arrangement that might be proposed by other courts."[125] This advice must be called deceptive because its true aim was not necessarily to save the king but to tie him up until Austria was assured of receiving the fruits of the sacrifice. Had the aim been the salvation of Saxony, the assistance of other powers, even France, should not have made much difference.

Schulenburg, who had been one of Metternich's first callers in Baden, was one of the last. On 15 September Metternich departed for Vienna, careful as always to leave a message for Sagan, who had conferred both "happiness and misery" on him that summer. "At one of the most difficult times of my life," he wrote, "I very much needed to recover my strength. My head is completely full, my friend. I am like a general who deploys his army and chooses his terrain for a decisive battle. My friend will not abandon me now."[126] On to Vienna and immortality!

[125] Mett. to Zichy, 12 Sept. 1814, HHSA, StK., Diplomatische Korr., Preussen, Fasc. 95, p. 21. Cf. Kohlschmidt, *Sächsische Frage*, 62.
[126] 15 Sept. 1814, in Ullrichová, ed., *Briefwechsel*, 263.

CHAPTER V

ALL EUROPE IN MY ANTEROOM

A S HIS carriage clattered through the Kärtner Gate and into the heart of the capital, the forty-one year old minister of state and conference was perhaps reminded of his entry into Frankfurt only ten months before. Here again was a city of noise and crowded streets, the milling of adventurers, drifters, and curiosity-seekers, the sight of hundreds of stalls hastily erected to extract the last guilder from a captive market. Vienna, with a normal population of about 250,000, suddenly in the month of September alone attracted 16,000 visitors, all scrambling for lodging, bidding for scarce goods, and pressing a cause.[1] Waiting for him, Metternich well knew, would be the same "swarming envoys and deputies, all soliciting," who had badgered him before.[2]

The congress eventually recognized nineteen plenipotentiaries of the eight powers signatory to the Treaty of Paris, twenty-six more who represented other sovereigns (including the pope), another forty-two representing the states of Germany, and the envoys of countless mediatized houses. Of the Standesherren in this group many belonged to the association founded by Solms-Laubach and were represented collectively by Baron Gärtner, whose calling card, bearing the title "Plenipotentiary Extraordinary of 42 Princes and Counts," naturally enough invited ridicule from the nervous envoys of the middle states.[3] Other Standesherren appointed envoys of their own, one of whom was Franz Georg Metternich, representing not himself—he belonged to the Gärtner group—but the house of Stadion, a fellow sufferer at the hands of the king of Württemberg. The numerous members of the *Reichsritterschaft*, meanwhile, taking their cue from Baron Stein, had regrouped roughly into their old circles of Swabia, Franconia, and Rhine, and formed another across the Rhine; each of these likewise maintained an agent at the congress carrying instructions drafted by Stein himself.[4]

Another fifty or so plenipotentiaries acted for a variety of constituencies: the cities of Danzig and Bad Kreuznach, for example; the Jewish communities of Frankfurt and the Hanseatic towns; the Cath-

[1] Dispatch of 18 Sept. 1814 from Vienna, in [Augsburger] *Allegemeine Zeitung*, 1814, p. 1076.
[2] Kraehe, I, 237.
[3] Weil, *Les Dessous*, I, 84; Cf. Glaser, "Die badische Politik," 283.
[4] D'Angeberg, *Congrès*, I, 255f. and II, 257–263; list of mediatized properties in HHSA, StK., Kongressakten, Cart. 6, pp. 233–234; Pertz, *Stein*, IV, 69f.

olics of Frankfurt; the city of Mainz and its chamber of commerce, which was represented separately; the Teutonic Order and the Knights of St. John of Jerusalem; the German book trade; and in one anomalous case, the subjects of the count of Solms-Braunfels. Perhaps most important of this group was the German Catholic Church, which though hardly more than a memory, was represented by four plenipotentiaries, including the eminent general vicar, Baron Ignaz Heinrich von Wessenberg, one of those sanguine imperial prelates who had startled Linden so much.[5]

The above were only those officially recognized; dozens more were informal observers or disappointed petitioners who never had a hearing. Nor does the list include the numerous envoys of less than plenipotentiary standing, many of whom, such as Count Ioannes Capodistrias, Czartoryski, and Baron Stein (who usually counted in the tsar's entourage) were more important than, say, Count Andreas Razumovsky or Count Gustav von Stackelberg, who along with Nesselrode were the official Russian envoys.

Participants and posterity have described the grand congress a thousand times, but nobody has done so better than Gentz, who wrote to the hospodar, Janko Karadja, even before it began:

> All eyes are turned on the congress, and everybody expects of it the redress of his grievances, the fulfillment of his desires, and the triumph of his projects. For the most part all these expectations are unfounded and illusory; anybody who has a glimpse of the situation knows in advance that at most the congress will lay the foundations of Germany's future order without going into the details and that most of the ideas flitting about publicly are only daydreams that no one has either the will or the power to realize.[6]

Indeed, it is in the very nature of gatherings of sovereign states that they betray dreams and hopes; lacking as they do both the power of arms and the force of law, they can only look forward to compromise, and if in the end these are impossible and war the result, that too is a betrayal of ideals.

Metternich encountered his own first disappointment at the outset. To avoid the atmosphere of Vienna he had hoped to hold the opening conferences with his three allies in the seclusion of Baden, where their private discussions would not be so conspicuous; with luck it might still be possible to have a general accord before the congress convened. On arrival in the city, however, he found Castlereagh opposed to such secretiveness and Nesselrode anxious to stay by his pregnant wife, who

[5] *Ibid.*, II, 263f.
[6] Gentz to Karadja, 5 Sept. 1814, in Klinkowström, *Oesterreichs Theilnahme*, 404.

feared to travel; Hardenberg had not yet arrived.[7] As a result the first meeting was scheduled for the following afternoon in the chancellery.

Meanwhile Count Münster had also arrived and was immediately briefed by Ernst Hardenberg on the Forty-one Articles and the conferences with Solms and Humboldt, which, Hardenberg charged, were even worse than Humboldt's biased protocols indicated.[8] Incensed, the Hanoverian urgently requested an audience with Metternich, who received him on the 16th, shortly before the meeting of Castlereagh and Nesselrode.[9] Münster, who had assumed that the matter of a chairmanship alternating among five or more equals had been settled in Paris, found only the articles on the rights of the estates and a federal court to resemble previous understandings; for the rest of the plan seemed nothing but an assortment of devices to annul the influence of the other Kreis chiefs and to "raise Austria and Prussia to the rank of true sovereigns over Germany." Then to add insult to injury, he charged, "the only reason that might appear to justify this demand" was eliminated by removing most of their territory from the Bund. Worse yet, the directory of the two would never work: "their first rift would lead to the dissolution of the Bund," leaving Austria on the fringes and Prussia in control of North Germany.[10]

Metternich, who doubtless expected an outburst of this kind, was pleased to welcome an ally, one indeed who might take the brunt of challenging the Prussians. Not only did he assure his visitor that "he absolutely rejects the plan," but he gave the strongest hints yet of his belated interest in the imperial dignity. "Metternich does not hide it from me," Münster reported and was troubled by the thought that the artful minister, having missed his chance earlier, would recklessly use the Prussian monstrosity to frighten everyone else into begging Austria to take the crown, in the meantime risking chaos in Germany.[11] Such speculation was too simple, focused only on the reaction of the German states, not on European realities. Talleyrand, for one, had often inveighed against conferring the crown of Germany on any great power, once when he tried to write a prohibition of this into the Treaty of Paris and again when drafting his instructions for the congress,[12] and France could be ignored at best only if cooperation was forthcoming

[7] McGuigan, *Duchess*, 325f.

[8] Hardenberg to cabinet in Hanover, 28 Sept. 1814, NSHSA, Cal. Br. 24, Vol. IV.

[9] Mett. to Münster, 15 Sept. 1814, *ibid.*, Hanover, Dep. 110, No. 5a, Vol. 1.

[10] Münster to Prince Regent, 17 Sept. 1814, in Münster, *Political Sketches*, 185–187, and additional postscripts in Dupuis, *Talleyrand*, II, 325–329. Cf. Brandes, *Münster und die Wiedererstehung*, 101f.

[11] Postscript as per Dupuis in n. 10 above.

[12] Talleyrand, *Memoirs*, II, 179.

from Prussia, whose opposition to a German crown was a matter of still longer record. Circumstances could change, but for the moment Metternich's sincerity in this regard, like Binder's hints to Solms and Gärtner, was completely Platonic, to use Dupuis's ingenious phrase. In the meantime it was good to know that Münster could be trusted to mount an attack on the directory, the constricted federal area, and the two-power domination of the federal diet.

Sometime later in the day Castlereagh and Nesselrode came to the chancellery along with Baron Binder, who was to keep the protocol; Hardenberg was still absent. Although the German negotiation was a good month behind schedule, this first conference on the congress in general was less than a week late, so that one might still hope for a four-power accord before the opening on 1 October. The prospect was short-lived. Although Castlereagh was not averse to private talks among the allies, he now insisted that any select group of ministers must have the sanction of the congress and proposed that it be convened at once.[13] The formal accreditation of plenipotentiaries necessary to this end seemed only a routine matter of accepting everybody who appeared. When he realized, however, that Nesselrode could not recognize Schulenburg or he himself the emissary of Murat, and that Gärtner must be anathema to any German sovereign, it was clear that his plan would trigger the substantive conflicts before the steering committee itself was confirmed. In the end, at least for that day, the three ministers accepted a compromise: the steering committee would be its own raison d'être and begin its work even while engaged in verifying the credentials of the other envoys. Invitations to submit plenary powers would go only to representatives of "all the powers recognized by the totality of Europe"; later, however, the envoys of Naples, Saxony, and other controversial entities would be received with the title of petitioners.[14]

Castlereagh's casual treatment of the credentials problem was probably a simple miscalculation. His next move, though likewise designed to diminish schisms, was a blow of a different order: France and Spain, he said, must be added to the steering committee. In truth, Castlereagh's brief visit to Paris had proved more significant than he had indicated in his nonchalant letter to Metternich. Although he had rejected Talleyrand's bid for a joint Anglo-French mediation of the Polish question, he was nonetheless eager to attach the seapowers to Britain

[13] Castle. to Liverp., 24 Sept. 1814, Webster, *BD*, 194. Although Castlereagh does not single himself out as the instigator of this plan, it could hardly have been Metternich or Nesselrode.

[14] Binder's minutes of the meeting of 16 Sept. in HHSA, StK., Kongressakten, Cart. 1, pp. 71–72.

and to overthrow Austria's ally in Naples, Joachim Murat, in favor of a Bourbon regime that would be less a threat to the sea lanes of the Mediterranean.

Metternich was hardly prepared for this blunt challenge to his expectations. In regard to Murat, about whom he had misgivings in any case, he backed down entirely, insisting only that Austria be spared any initiative in the matter so that as Murat's ally she could advise him not to resist the overwhelming sentiment of the European powers. Coupled with this was a resolution calling as soon as possible for the removal of Napoleon himself from Italian climes either to a Spanish or Portuguese island or, "what would be infinitely more preferable," to an island in America. Nesselrode for one was impressed: Metternich, he said, had fooled all those who thought that he was only biding his time to bring Napoleon back.[15]

On the larger issue of organizing the congress the Austrian minister, who still intended to consolidate the European center without the advice of the flanking powers, fell back on the secret articles of the Treaty of Paris, demanding that however much France and Spain were to be consulted, the four allies must reach agreement first. Then, to be sure that at least Germany was discussed with a minimum of outside interference, he proposed that the business of the congress be divided between two committees, European affairs going to the main committee of the six powers, German affairs, both the federal constitution and the territorial settlement, to a commission composed of Austria, Prussia, Bavaria, Hanover, and Württemberg as he and Humboldt had previously planned. All the German states (including Saxony as a petitioner) were to be assembled for consultation, but the final word would remain with the committee of six, which would then incorporate into its treaty drafts "those dispositions which shall be of European interest," thus placing the future confederation under international guarantee. Yet, here too Castlereagh intervened to twist earlier assumptions, proposing that the committees begin their work with hearings open to all others concerned, both recognized sovereigns and "suspended, suppressed, or mediatized states and corporations," and end it by laying their proposals before the general congress for deliberation. What he intended by "deliberation" is not clear, but we may be sure that Metternich was the one responsible for the formula tentatively adopted: namely, that after consulting the general assembly the six powers would return to that body with a treaty draft, declare

[15] Webster, *Castlereagh*, I, 321–323; separate notation by Binder, HHSA, StK., Kongressakten, Cart. 1, p. 75; and Münster to Prince Regent, 17 Sept. 1814, Münster, *Political Sketches*, 186.

it "universally adopted," and invite the other states to sign as accessories.[16]

There was nothing binding about these points. Binder, in fact, drafted two versions of the meeting, neither signed, one of which, probably prepared for submission to Hardenberg, omitted many points seemingly settled in the other. Still, it was clear that for Austrian purposes Castlereagh's thinking brought both France and the congress into the process too much and too soon; that he still offered no solution for the problem of credentials; and that it was not clear to anybody exactly how German affairs were to be divided between the two committees. In view of these ambiguities Castlereagh agreed to submit his views in writing a few days hence, and Metternich decided to do the same.[17]

Yet on one point there was general agreement, the more striking for having been arrived at spontaneously, almost as a natural consequence of the habits formed in the past year. This was the use of "the English style of conducting business," by which was meant oral deliberation in committee without distinction as to the rank of the members. The written depositions and the endless ceremonials of past peace conferences regarding precedence were rejected. "The deputy from Frankfurt must be heard equally with any other," Metternich explained to Linden of Württemberg, who had waited patiently in the corridors for the meeting to end. Of course he did not really mean this literally, but the example was disturbing to Linden all the same; if Frankfurt, why not the *Reichsritterschaft*, he asked himself afterwards as he imagined the congress degenerating into a "stormy London-style parliament" of subjects pitted against their lawful sovereigns.[18]

The crowd in the State Chancellery, of which Linden was a part, convinced Metternich more than ever that the deliberations should move to Baden, but as the others had declined the invitation, he returned alone the following day, the 17th, to pack up his papers and to spend a few hours with Sagan.[19] That evening he also sat down to draft a project that would steer the discussion back to the proper course. Agreement among the four must clearly come first, not only on procedure but on the territorial settlement itself. Next should come consultation with France and Spain, and only when there was an informal consensus among the six should they constitute themselves a committee to present the results to the other states. The latter would

[16] Binder's minutes, HHSA, StK., Kongressakten, Cart. 1, pp. 73f.; and Castle. to Liverp. as in n. 13 above.

[17] Binder's minutes, HHSA, StK., Kongressakten, pp. 68 and 71; and Castle. to Liverp., 24 Sept. 1814, Webster, *BD*, 194.

[18] Linden to King Frederick, 20 Sept. 1814, HSA, Stuttgart, E 70, Fasc. 12, pp. 50–52.

[19] Mett. to Sagan, 15 Sept. 1814, Ullrichová, ed., *Briefwechsel*, 262.

thus be heard at the end of the negotiations rather than the beginning. Metternich likewise altered the treatment of the German question, shifting the territorial settlement to the province of the powers, and articulating his long-held view that the German committee should draft merely those essentials of a federal constitution pertinent to the European order and leave the details to the future *Bundestag* (his word). Consultation with the smaller German states he did not mention, perhaps intending that the federal diet be the forum for that purpose.[20]

This project was the last product of the interlude in Baden, where despite the continuing fine weather the chestnut trees were just beginning to drop diplomatic hints of things to come. The next day, a Sunday, Metternich placed the project in his dispatch case and returned once more to Vienna. Passing through the great iron gate of the chancellery building, he mounted the marble steps to his own living quarters and prepared to meet the world of affairs. "I found all Europe gathered in my anteroom," he reported to the faithful Eleonore, who had stayed behind. "I am faced with all these interminable chores, and if there's something good in the situation, there's certainly nothing good for me. I will have four to six weeks of hell."[21] To the not so faithful Sagan he was more specific: Marshal Wrede and Prince Hardenberg were there as were four envoys from Malta, fifteen or so German deputies, "all wretched senators," three old women, and a pretty girl saying she would do *anything* for a passport to Paris.[22] Hardenberg, the state chancellor, was of course the really important one at this juncture. He had arrived the day before with General Knesebeck and the counselor of legation, Johann Ludwig Jordan, and taken temporary lodgings in the Graben; later, when the king arrived, he was to move into the Hofburg. "He has to be fitted out like a daughter who is to be married," grumbled Humboldt, who had been hard put to find even these modest accommodations for his chief.[23] No matter. After all the speculation about the delays he was here at last; work could begin.

Accordingly the first official meeting of the four took place that night, and like most others to come, in Metternich's offices in the Ballhausplatz. Because of the chancellor's advanced deafness, Hum-

<hr/>

[20] Undated and untitled draft in Metternich's hand, HHSA, StK., Kongressakten, Cart. 1, p. 74. Cf. Mett. to Sagan, 19 Sept. 1814, Ullrichová, ed., *Briefwechsel*, 264, wherein he mentions the conference of the 18th at which "my work of the night before was accepted."

[21] Mett. to Eleonore, 19 Sept. 1814, quoted by Corti, *Frauen*, I, 471.

[22] Mett. to Sagan, 29 Sept. 1814, Ullrichová, ed., *Briefwechsel*, 263f. His exact words: "A pretty young person who came to offer me what is not worth a sou or what all the treasures of the world could not buy."

[23] Humb. to Caroline, 9 and 21 Sept. 1814, *Briefe*, IV, 385; Weil, *Les Dessous*, I, 93.

boldt was also allowed to attend, taking over Binder's secretarial function as well. As promised, Castlereagh had written down his ideas.[24] To gain some form of European mandate without precipitating the battle over credentials, he now proposed an informal convocation of all envoys present in Vienna who claimed to represent a sovereign state, the invitation to take the quaint form of an announcement in the *Wiener Hofzeitung*. At the meeting Metternich, as the representative of the host government, could then explain the need for the committee of six and, aided by previous lobbying, gain the approval of the group to this procedure, thus painlessly obtaining voluntary consent to what otherwise the six would have to assert as their right. France and Spain would then be told that though the allies must naturally have some preliminary understandings, they would confer regularly with the other two, particularly on matters of form and agenda. The aim was the laudable one of composing differences by minimizing distinctions, and Castlereagh probably believed that France would be more manageable as a member of the club than as an outsider free to agitate among the lesser states.

Yet this position could really be taken only by the power with general, not particular interests at stake. It must have shocked Hardenberg, if he heard correctly, to have to contemplate the appearance of Schulenburg at the meeting and the possibility that France might review the settlement in Saxony or suggest which German states should inherit the Rhineland. And Spain? What right had she to participate? For Prussia the problem was not how to gloss over French inferiority but to expose it and define it in unmistakeable terms, a task that Humboldt undertook for the next meeting. In the meantime, there was Metternich's counterproject, with its explicit grounding in the secret articles of Paris, its unequivocal distinction between the four and the six, and its relegation of the congress to the end of the process. Indeed, as was increasingly his custom, he did not refer to the "congress" at all but only to "the other powers." Even this was not sufficiently foolproof for the Prussians, but as far as it went, it satisfied them as it did Nesselrode. The Metternich articles were then combined with the earlier agreements to divide the work between two committees, and Castlereagh was modestly accommodated with a clause that gave France and Spain an equal voice in the modalities attending the eventual convening of the congress. Humboldt, finally, wrote up the agreements in a protocol designed for presentation to Talleyrand and the Spanish envoy, Don

---

[24] Text in Webster, *Congress of Vienna*, Appendix III. Though undated, the memorandum belongs here by virtue of the context.

Pedro-Gomez Labrador.[25] Something, however, blocked the final sign-ing at this point,[26] in all probability an argument between Castlereagh and the Prussians over the admission of Spain and the need for ad-ditional safeguards against French participation. Still, Metternich had all he wanted, for unlike Hardenberg he wished only to close the door to France, not to lock it. Besides, after five hours it was time to join the soirée that Princess Katherine Bagration was giving at the Palais Palm across the way.[27]

So far in the deliberations Nesselrode's role had been somewhat passive. He clearly opposed Castlereagh's proposals, perhaps sensing that the campaign to raise the voice of Europe against Murat could be turned on the tsar as well. He questioned the inclusion of Spain but only by way of suggesting that his master might in the event insist on admitting Sweden too. He might have demanded a voice for Russia on the German committee, which some of the tsar's advisers considered her right;[28] instead he followed Stein's advice that Russian influence in Germany was a fact of life and that her conspicuous absence from the committee would be the best way to keep France out too.[29] His instructions from the tsar, moreover, said nothing about the German constitution but rather focused on the territorial distribution, which was the business of the six. All in all, in the matter of organizing the congress, he seems to have followed Metternich's lead.[30]

Nevertheless, he realized as well as anyone that the ultimate cause of the sparring over procedure was doubt about the tsar's intentions in Poland. "It would be difficult to make the least progress," he re-ported to his master, "before the three courts were completely in-formed about the views of your majesty." When he notified his col-leagues that he had the information they had vainly sought for over

[25] The protocol, finally signed on 22 September, in Martens, *Traités par la Russie*, III, 174–177 (not to be confused with a separate protocol of the same day cited ambiguously by Webster, *Congress of Vienna*, 168 and in Webster, *BD*, 194). Articles III, IV, V, and VII duplicate Metternich's language almost verbatim. Astonishingly enough, Griewank, *Wiener Kongress*, 106, believes the protocol was Castlereagh's victory.

[26] Griewank, *Wiener Kongress*, 106, n. 37.

[27] Mett. to Sagan, 19 Sept. 1814, Ullrichová, ed., *Briefwechsel*, 264.

[28] Notably La Harpe and Pozzo di Borgo. See their joint memorandum of 7 July 1814 in Nikolai Karlovich Schilder, *Imperator Aleksandr Pervyi, ego zhizn' i tsarstvovanie*, 4 vols., 2nd ed. (St. Petersburg, 1904–1905), III, 534–537.

[29] Stein's memorandum for Nesselrode of 17 Sept. 1814 and diary entry of same period in Stein, *Briefe*, v, 148–150 and 316f. The date suggests that Nesselrode, after the meeting of the 16th, asked Stein's opinion. The latter, however, was certainly wrong to claim credit for the idea of keeping foreign powers out of the German question; obviously the notion had long been held by Metternich and Humboldt. Cf. Ritter, *Stein*, II, 282, who takes Stein at his word.

[30] Text of instructions of 12 Aug. 1814 in Schilder, *Imperator Aleksandr*, III, 537–540. Brief précis in *VPR*, VIII, 87f.

a year, they made it, rather than the still unsigned protocol, the subject of their next meeting, on 19 September. Now it was official: to Prussia Kulm on the lower Vistula and Posen with the line of the Prosna; to Austria a mere token, the salt mines at Wieliczka; to Russia all the rest of the duchy, including the strong points of Thorn and Cracow. Nesselrode defended this lopsidedness on grounds of the tsar's single-handed conquest and the right of the Russian people to "a military frontier that would preserve them forever from the calamity of a new invasion."[31]

From Metternich came the familiar points of rebuttal: Schwarzenberg's armistice, which had made the conquest possible; the mortal danger to Vienna from a Russian base at Cracow; and the outflanking of Galicia if Zamość were in Russian hands. Still worse would be the revival of the name of Poland, and he demanded reassurances. Following instructions, Nesselrode lamely replied that the tsar was no more obligated to discuss this purely internal matter than Austria was to say how she intended to govern her provinces in Italy. Hardenberg, too, stressed the danger in reviving Poland, while Castlereagh, though he personally thought Metternich foolish to continue sounding this mournful note, insisted that he would support the Austrian and Prussian position even if he incurred unpopularity at home.[32]

In spite of all, there must have been something reassuring in Nesselrode's manner or in his private remarks afterwards, for both Castlereagh and Metternich construed the tsar's refusal to have the constitutional issue discussed as a face-saving gesture covering a retreat or at least betraying indecision.[33] Further evidence to this effect arrived about this same time in the lines of Koller's long-awaited report from St. Petersburg. "The Russians of all classes are universally and unanimously against the restoration of the kingdom," the marshal said, and even the Poles would have preferred that Alexander stand aside and allow them to do the job themselves, and this is what Koller expected them to do if it came to war. The tsar told Koller nothing specific about his plans, contenting himself with a personal diatribe against Metternich for "setting the English on my neck" and seducing the Prussians from the side of their recent savior. "We must admit," Alexander continued, "that he is the first minister in Europe; Russia would be fortunate to have his like, but all the more dangerous is he for his hatred of the Russians." This was damning with strong praise, and it

---

[31] Nessel. to Alex., 25 Sept. 1814, *VPR*, VIII, 103.

[32] *Ibid.*, VIII, 104f., and Castle. to Liverp., 24 Sept. 1814, Webster, *BD*, 195.

[33] Webster, *BD*, 195.

probably swelled Metternich's ego and his confidence that he would prevail in the end.[34]

Since any sign of Russian weakening diminished the potential need for French participation, the effect of Nesselrode's démarche on the general proceedings, if any, was probably to nudge Metternich a step closer to the Prussians. When the next meeting took place three days later, it was much clearer what was troubling them: it was the fear that a general congress, standing on what in many quarters was called "the public law of Europe," would in the end refuse to countenance the expropriation of the king of Saxony; or that Austria and England, while formally respecting the Metternich articles, would nonetheless consult France on the side and thus bring her influence to bear in the councils of the four after all. Typically Humboldt met the situation with a convoluted memorandum that touched on every conceivable contingency.[35] There could be no question of great-power usurpation, he wrote for Castlereagh's benefit, for the Congress of Vienna was neither a peace conference nor a deliberative assembly; it was merely the site of many individual negotiations conducted mainly by the four in ad hoc consultation with other states as necessary. In certain issues of collective European interest such as the slave trade, river navigation, diplomatic protocol, and Napoleon's status, France and Spain should have parity, but their voice in the territorial settlement must be confined simply to judging whether allied decisions conformed to the Treaty of Paris.

Still more restrictive were his prescriptions for Germany. Concern for the European balance gave the four powers an interest in certain general questions such as the fate of Saxony, the organization of the Rhineland, the membership of the Netherlands in the Bund, and the extent to which the mediatized houses should remain under their existing sovereigns. All other matters, Humboldt advised, should be left to the German princes themselves, even certain territorial awards because of their close connection with the demarcation of Kreis boundaries. In short, where Prussia perhaps needed outside support, as in liberating the Standesherren, the allied powers had rights; where she could manage better alone, they did not. The congress was not to be excluded altogether, for when all issues had been privately settled, Humboldt still wanted a European guarantee of the results. Thus the

---

[34] Koller to Mett., 8 Sept. 1814, in Fournier, "Zur Vorgeschichte," 323–327. It is uncertain exactly when the report reached Vienna, but if dispatched on the 8th, it should have arrived by the 20th or 21st. Koller himself arrived on the 25th, but internal evidence indicates that he sent it ahead. On Metternich's optimism see Gentz to Karadja, 27 Sept. 1814, Klinkowström, *Oesterreichs Theilnahme*, 440.

[35] This and following from text in Humboldt, *Gesammelte Schriften*, xi, 163–172. Cruder version in Webster, *Congress of Vienna*, Appendix iv.

"old" legitimacy would not save the Saxon state, but the "new" legitimacy would sanction Prussia's retention of it.

The severity of the Prussian statement could only have exacerbated existing differences, but with Talleyrand's arrival imminent, the pressure for compromise was greater yet. Besides, the ministers here assembled were old hands by now; remembering past projects, with their articles sine qua non for France in tandem with secret understandings among themselves, they found it only natural to divide their problem in two. Accordingly, with a few modifications they adopted the existing draft containing the original Metternich articles; this would be presented to the French and the Spanish. They then instructed Humboldt to draft a separate protocol containing the safeguards demanded by Prussia for adoption among themselves. "Great progress," Gentz exclaimed when Metternich told him about it the next morning,[36] yet how little had things changed since Reichenbach and Teplitz and Châtillon!

The following night, 23 September, the four met again to read Humboldt's work. As he put it, the Treaty of Paris, in referring to allied agreements among themselves, meant final, definitive decision, not mere bases for discussion, and further that the reference was to all conquered territory, not just to the specific items enumerated in the secret articles. Therefore, the allies should agree that none of them would consult with the two others until they had reached "a perfect accord" on Warsaw, Germany, and Italy, but that the time required for achieving this end could be used to deal with general European issues, in relation to which the six were equal. Since France now had a legitimate government, she deserved some right of comment but only on general themes and only where her own security was involved. Otherwise the two were not to sit with the four, even as observers.[37]

The document had a harsh ring, not unlike Germany's summons to Versailles a century later, and Metternich might not have signed had he not optimistically put Prussia ahead of France in his calculations of the moment. There were too many serious differences with Hardenberg to warrant challenging him over nuances of phraseology. Castlereagh on the other hand did refuse to sign, issuing instead another separate document, a declaration that though he acknowledged the prerogatives of the four, their arrangements should be "open to free and liberal discussions with the other two powers as friendly and not hostile parties," and that while he would do his best to maintain four-power solidarity, he would not be bound by the majority. "Seen and

---

[36] Gentz, *Tagebücher*, I, 309.
[37] "Protocole séparé d'une conférence tenue le 22 septembre . . . ," d'Angeberg, *Congrès*, I, 249–251.

approved" was the laconic endorsement given by the three others.[38] Metternich could hardly have welcomed the assertion of such independence by the man he counted on most, but perhaps it was just as well that somebody was free to introduce France to the others if the need arose. As if by way of compensation, moreover, he scored a point for Austria. After another futile debate on the problem of credentials, the group at least agreed that a declaration of some sort was necessary and appointed Gentz to draft it. That same night some eight blocks away, Talleyrand arrived at his quarters in the Palais Kaunitz.[39]

The day after, a Saturday, was relatively quiet in Vienna, affording Metternich time with the family, interrupted only by a visit from the Danish foreign minister, Niels Rosenkrantz, who complained of the protracted presence of the 60,000 Russian troops in Holstein.[40] The next day was different. Shortly after daybreak Metternich was awakened by cannon fire in the distance, the signal that Tsar Alexander and Frederick William, who had joined forces at Wolkersdorf about twenty-five kilometers to the north, were leaving there and would be in Vienna in a matter of hours. Such ostentatious advance notice was hardly necessary, Metternich grumbled, but he shared the excitement of the whole city over the event that, more than any mere declaration could do, signaled the beginning of the congress. Shortly after midday they arrived—Prince Esterhazy in brilliant Hungarian uniform at the head of the guard troops, then Francis, who had crossed the Danube to meet his guests, at his right the king of Prussia, at his left the tsar of all the Russias, who was placed there contrary to normal protocol in deference to his bad left ear. Even the cynical Talleyrand, no stranger to grand parades, called it "a fine sight." The monarchs paraded through the Prater, on to the Rotenturm Gate, and thence to the spacious inner court of the Hofburg, where Metternich was waiting in the company of many dignitaries, including two monarchs: Frederick VI of Denmark and Frederick I of Württemberg. Of the six monarchs who eventually came to the congress only Maximilian Joseph of Bavaria was still absent.[41]

Significantly the tsar's first move, after luncheon with his fellow mon-

[38] Text in *ibid.*, I, 251.

[39] Text in Webster, *Congress of Vienna*, Appendices v and vi. See also Gentz, *Tagebücher*, I, 309.

[40] Niels Rosenkrantz, *Journal du congrès de Vienne, 1814–1815* (Copenhagen, 1953), 23; Bourgoing, *Wiener Kongress*, 62; Gentz, *Tagebücher*, I, 310; and Mett. to Sagan, 25 Sept. 1814, Ullrichová, ed., *Briefwechsel*, 265.

[41] Talley. to Louis XVIII, 25 Sept. 1814, Charles M. de Talleyrand-Perigord, *Correspondence*, ed. M. G. Pallain (New York, 1881), 4; McGuigan, *Duchess*, 330f.; Bourgoing, *Wiener Kongress*, 62f.; Mett. to Sagan, 25 Sept. 1814, Ullrichová, ed., *Briefwechsel*, 265. Metternich mistakenly had the tsar at Brünn, seventy kilometers from Vienna, an impossibility which says something about his nerves at the time.

archs, was to send for Metternich. ". . . I have had my first skirmish with the emperor," the latter wrote to Sagan as soon as it was over. "He sent for me and I saw that he wanted to reconnoiter the terrain . . . and the result of the emperor's attempt is that he knows nothing of what I want but I see clearly everything that he wants. I have chosen my outposts—my main guards are in position, and I can sleep easily— the army corps will not be taken by surprise."[42] This grandiloquent assertion of mastery no doubt made good copy for the eyes of one's beloved but it did not hold up in the conference room. Three days later, in the evening of 28 September, Metternich had a more serious audience with his imperial adversary, and if he was not taken entirely by surprise, he was rudely shaken from his lingering optimism. For three hours the tsar expounded his plans. Far from wavering on the constitutional question, he solemnly stated that he would not only establish a constitutional kingdom of Poland, by that name and under his sovereignty, but he would join to it his own Polish provinces derived from the earlier partitions. Thus the first official word from the lips of the tsar himself confirmed the worst of his fears: a Polish kingdom leaving few Poles to be redeemed except those in Galicia and Posen. As Castlereagh had put it in similar interviews with the tsar and Nesselrode a few days earlier, in military terms alone this arrangement would add ten million loyal Poles to Russia and leave five million disaffected ones to Austria and Prussia—all this without providing "the semblance of a military frontier" that would enable the central powers to stand up to "one colossal military power" as overpowering as Napoleonic France had been.[43] Gentz, learning of Metternich's interview "from a private and very reliable channel," hastened to correct the cheerful estimate he had sent the Wallachian hospodar just the day before.[44]

The gloom was not confined to Austria. Hardenberg, who had heard all about the tsar's recalcitrance from Castlereagh, spent the day of the 28th planning strategy with Stein, Humboldt, and General Knesebeck. All regarded the defense line offered by the tsar as intolerable, the general insisting that the Vistula between the San and the Bug was the maximum safe extension of Russian power and proposing alliances with Turkey and Persia to provide pressure on another front.[45] In the midst of these discussions Colonel Schoeler arrived, bringing an ac-

[42] To Sagan, 25 Sept. 1814, 3:30 p.m., Ullrichová, ed., *Briefwechsel*, 265.
[43] Castle. to Liverp., 2 Oct. 1814, Webster, *BD*, 198–200.
[44] To Karadja, 28 Sept. 1814, *Dépêches inédites*, I, 105. Indeed, Gentz is our main source for the interview, and the "reliable channel" was no doubt Metternich himself. Cf. a somewhat different version of this report in Weil, *Les Dessous*, I, 177f.
[45] From several memorials of Knesebeck dated 28 Sept. 1814. Texts in Pertz, *Leben von Stein*, IV, 649–654.

count of his mission to St. Petersburg. To Koller the tsar had at least been civil; Schoeler, however, representing the impudent ally, could only report a diatribe so brutal that he had dropped the matter and beat an embarrassed retreat, stunned at his tormentor's threats to seize East Prussia and Danzig. On balance the colonel's sober assessment was that the Vistula line was unattainable, but that with solidarity and determination in the West, Russia might be held at the Warta.[46] Everybody, then, talked common front, but there was one difficulty—the king. Nothing that Hardenberg had been able to tell his master in Berlin or in Vienna could match the warm and comradely embrace at Wolkersdorf; Frederick William was as loyal to the tsar as ever, a continuing source of frustration to almost all his ministers and advisers. "Pusillan. regis" was how Hardenberg recorded his feelings in his log book that day.[47]

The covert insult to the crown was unfair in one respect and perhaps even unrealistic, inasmuch as it was precisely Frederick William's attitude that made possible the one cheerful development of the day: Russia agreed at last to hand over the provisional administration of Saxony and to do so with the express intent "to prepare the minds of the inhabitants . . . for their destiny and to allow them to pass more easily under Prussian domination." There were conditions, to be sure. The merger of Prussia and Saxony must be confined to a personal union through the crown, Saxony retaining her integrity and her identity as a kingdom. Any provincial rights subsequently conferred by the future confederation would apply, but until then the existing constitution must remain intact. Sometime during the day Nesselrode arrived at Hardenberg's quarters to join Stein and Humboldt in drafting a formal declaration embodying these terms. Despite a certain tentativeness of expression Hardenberg now had a written assurance and with it a new sense of independence from the tsar—if only the "pusillanimous king" would allow him to exploit it.[48]

Alexander had come to Vienna obviously resolved to seize the initiative, perhaps deliberately to intimidate the opposition before it could coalesce. In just four days he had "reconnoitered" Metternich, summoned Castlereagh to hear his complete Polish program, summoned Metternich again for the same purpose, and virtually committed him-

[46] Schoeler to Hard., 10 Sept. 1814 and Schoeler's "Memoire über Russlands Forderungen," Sept., 1814, ZSTA, Merseburg, 2.4.1.I, No. 992, pp. 7–23.

[47] "Tagebücher des Staatskanzlers Hardenberg," p. 34, ZSTA, Merseburg, Rep. 92, Hardenberg, L37. (Hereafter cited as Hardenberg, "Tagebücher," with only the page number given.)

[48] "Protocole concernant la Saxe," 28 Sept. 1814, in Martens, *Traités par la Russie*, VII, 158f.; Stein "Tagebuch," in *Briefe*, V, 318; and Hardenberg, "Tagebücher," p. 34.

self on Saxony, meanwhile using Nesselrode to assess the effects of his blasts.[49] It is now possible to analyze his grand policy as he himself formulated it, not merely as a matter of speculation among his adversaries.

Despite the sense of betrayal that the Russian opponents of his Polish policy felt, there can be no doubt that the tsar's first concern was the security of the Russian homeland, a security that the pre-Napoleonic order in Poland and Central Europe had so tragically failed to provide. Part of the answer this time was military: Russia must now command the strong points of Thorn and Cracow, between which an invading force from the West would almost have to come. But to take so much of Poland raised the question of effective control. The explosive potentiality of Polish nationalism had governed Alexander's relations with Napoleon at Tilsit in 1807; now that he was master he could either try to suppress this force, a feat made more difficult by the vaster expanse of Polish territory he held, or try to appease it by political means. Either choice held risks. The former had failed before; but the latter was experimental, posing as many riddles as answers: what kind of constitution, what kind of connection with Russia, and how many of his own Polish lands to include. It was answers to these questions that he sought on his trip to St. Petersburg and back. In his instructions for Nesselrode, signed on 12 August, he was noncommittal on all but the frontier of the Prosna.[50] Then enroute to Vienna he exulted in the adulation of the Lithuanians at Vilna and held long conferences with a secret committee at Pulaway, Czartoryski's ancestral home near Lublin. There he promised to transfer twelve million of his existing subjects to the new Poland but hedged on the constitution apart from offering himself as king. "Put together a good constitution," he advised his friends, "organize a strong army, then we shall see."[51]

In Vienna the tsar's opponents were inclined to trace his actions to an exalted spirit of philanthropy, to religious fanaticism, to the spells cast by liberal advisers, or simply to the rashness of his promises to the Poles. Actually there was much logic in the tsar's plans. It was certainly no innovation in Europe to shower special favors on strategically crucial provinces: the Tyrol or the Croatian Military Border, to take the Habsburg experience as example. A constitution was not intended primarily to bring liberty, equality, and fraternity to the Poles but to provide them some assurance that Alexander's kingship would not compel the country to serve exclusively Russian interests. But beyond that, Alex-

[49] Castle. to Liverp., 2 Oct. 1814, Webster, *BD*, 198f.
[50] See n. 30 above.
[51] Quoted by Schiemann, *Geschichte Russlands*, I, 113. Cf. Kukiel, *Czartoryski*, 119f., and Waliszewski, *Russie il y a cents ans*, II, 266–270.

ander seems really to have believed that the explosion in the west that eventually propelled Napoleon into Moscow had been caused by mismanaged centralized despotism—whether of a Louis XVI, a Joseph II, or Napoleon himself—a despotism that had eradicated existing institutions, upset old balances and broken the organic ties between monarchs and their subjects. This was no democratic doctrine, not even a parliamentary one in the modern sense, but the philosophy of conserving or restoring old bonds, of preventing "arbitrary" acts by central governments against the traditional local elites. In their thinking the group around Czartoryski resembled the mediatized Standesherren of Germany.

Similar reasoning Alexander applied to Saxony, once the staging area of the Grand Army. To Charles Augustus of Weimar, who as head of the related Ernestine line sought the Saxon crown for himself, the tsar advanced not the Treaty of Kalisch as he could easily have done, but military necessity as the reason for awarding the kingdom to Prussia. Saxony alone, he explained, was too weak; the gap in the approaches to Poland, the gap, that is, between Prussia and Austria, could best be closed by making Prussia as strong as possible and for good measure awarding her the fortress town of Erfurt, which Goethe's famous patron also coveted.[52] Yet fearing that Prussian rule would meet resistance in the country, Alexander, as we have seen, made the award contingent on changing traditional institutions as little as possible and following the personal-union formula which he himself intended to use in Poland. Although Hardenberg had earlier stigmatized such conditions as "a real tragedy for this country . . . agreeable only to the oligarchs,"[53] the protocol itself described the terms as embodying "wise institutions" and "liberal maxims" designed to promote "the general tranquility."

In Alexander's grand design Austria, like Prussia, was to function as a buffer against the west. The difference was that whereas the latter, given the vulnerability of her eastern provinces, was virtually doomed to satellite status, Austria was not only more independent but was in fact a rival. Whether the tsar's Polish policy was deliberately calculated to provide cover for his flank while marching on the Porte is hard to say, but the idea did not escape La Harpe and Pozzo di Borgo, who advised him in July, 1814, that such a frontier would "give him the power, if he wants to use it, to go on and sing the *Te Deum* in Con-

[52] Charles Augustus to Duchess Louise, 28 May 1814, in Carl August of Weimar, *Politischer Briefwechsel des Herzogs und Grossherzogs Carl August von Weimar*, ed. Willy Andreas und Hans Tümmler, 3 vols. (Göttingen, 1954–1973), II, 248f.

[53] Hard. to Schoeler, 26 Aug. 1814, ZSTA, Merseburg, 2.4.1.I, No. 992, p. 3. One reason Hardenberg objected to such restraints was that the influential elites in the main wanted Charles Augustus as king.

stantinople."[54] In this connection, it should be recalled that the original partition of Poland had been the backlash of a Russo-Turkish war. It should be noted as well that throughout the Congress of Vienna Metternich had to contend with the agitation of Russian agents in Italy and the Balkans, and it was in part because of them that Gentz maintained his private newsletter for the hospodar of Wallachia.

If Austria and Prussia, in physical contact, constituted the bulwark of Alexander's fortress, the rest of Germany was to be the glacis, not in itself capable of offensive action but organized sufficiently for defense against France and accessible to at least indirect Russian influence. Alexander was one of the first to advocate that Mainz become a fortress of the German league, taking its place as the outermost bastion of a defensive triangle based on Thorn and Cracow. In seeking the means to maintain an influence in German affairs, the tsar, like Metternich, had to take a position somewhere between the existing governments and the restorative movement. As a group, the mediatized houses, if they did not seek Alexander as emperor, saw him as a protector and rained on him the same appeals for justice and the same documentary proofs of their legal rights that they conveyed to Emperor Francis. The foreign-ministry archives, we are told,[55] "contain cartons full of papers of this kind." Stein himself hoped to get along with a minimum of Russian help, but aristocrats from other lands backed these demands. We have already noted Golovkin's memorandum of 3 July in this regard. A few days later La Harpe and Pozzo advised that not only military factors but "the fair distribution of rights in regard to internal policy" should be the tsar's concern. In that case, they held, "Your Majesty will virtually be the head and guarantor of this federation."[56]

The tsar, however, had as few illusions as Metternich in this regard. Despite reports of "a great fermentation" said to stem from princely abuses, his instructions to Nesselrode dealt only with the reigning houses and the territorial settlement. Rejecting Hardenberg's plan of 29 April as creating "too much upheaval," he preferred to "adhere to simpler principles and unsettle things as little as possible." Not surprisingly Oldenburg was to be enlarged if possible and Württemberg, Baden, and Hesse-Darmstadt were to be favored. Saxe-Weimar and Saxe-Coburg were to receive small portions of Saxony not necessary to the Prussian defense system. These of course were all related houses, but the tsar also expressed solicitude for Prince Eugene and the former

---

[54] Joint memorial of La Harpe and Pozzo di Borgo, 7 July 1814, Schilder, *Imperator Aleksandr*, III, 534–537.

[55] By the great authority, F. Feodor Martens, in *Traités par a Russie*, III, 222.

[56] See n. 54 above.

Queen Catherine of Westphalia, wife of Jerome Bonaparte. The German constitution and the rights of the mediatized houses were not mentioned at all.[57]

To say that there was more rationality than mysticism, more *Realpolitik* than ideology in Alexander's planning does not mean that it was inherently reasonable or in line with the *juste équilibre* referred to in the treaties. At best it was a classic example of the maxim that the absolute security of one power means absolute insecurity for the rest. At worst, it was a formula for achieving continental hegemony the better to counter the supreme rival, England. For Alexander was no implacable foe of France, whose existing regime he expected to be short-lived, nor did he absolutely foreclose the possibility of allowing her a voice in the Polish settlement.[58] It was in Italy, the Balkans, and Holland that his agents were most disruptive. How do you achieve an equilibrium, Capodistria was asking about this time, "when one single power is mistress of all the seas? Is there any other maritime power than England? Can one be created? No. So good-bye equilibrium."[59]

For Metternich there could be little consolation in any knowledge that Austria was not the ultimate rival; it could only heighten the tsar's determination to press her into his service. One could argue, as Castlereagh did, that the Polish constitution was not the danger Metternich believed it to be or simply that it was none of his business. For the rest, however, the danger was real. The very comprehensiveness of the program compounded the dangers for Austria. The tsar wanted a Germany preoccupied with the western defenses, Metternich a Germany secure against the east as well, against both "the devouring powers," as he was beginning to call them. The tsar might speak of Cracow as a purely defensive point, but what would a Russian army based there do if Austria moved to defend her interests in the Balkans? (Even without Cracow the Russians in 1914, commanding the heights on Conrad's flank, compelled him to slacken his campaign in Serbia.) The tsar wanted a strong Prussia, but as the Austrians saw it, a Prussia bereft of defenses to the east would have to function militarily as an extension of Russia herself. The defense line "against the torrent pouring out of the north" would, as Wessenberg put it several weeks later,

<hr/>

[57] Instructions for Nesselrode, 12 Aug. 1814, as per n. 30 above.

[58] E.g., in his instructions for Nesselrode he quoted the Teplitz passage, "amicable arrangements among the three courts on the future of the duchy of Warsaw without any influence or intervention by the French government," but struck out the last phrase. Martens, *Traités par la Russie*, III, 172. Significantly Talleyrand made a similar emendation in his own instructions. In the original version "neither Poland as a whole nor the duchy of Warsaw [was to] fall to the sovereignty of Russia." In the final version room was left to allow Russia the duchy of Warsaw, Griewank, *Wiener Kongress*, 163, n. 39.

[59] Quoted by police agent to Hager, 12 Oct. 1814, Weil, *Les Dessous*, I, 276.

simply be moved from the Niemen to the Elbe. This more than any other was the argument of those who deplored Metternich's conciliatory talk about Saxony. Why surrender the friendly defiles of the Erzgebirge when Prussia could not be a loyal ally if she wanted to be?[60]

Notwithstanding these grim assessments, the four allied ministers carried on as before. The day following Metternich's audience with the tsar, they met to put the finishing touches on the declaration that Gentz had labored over for almost a week. Graced with elegantly phrased assurances that everyone would be consulted, the text that was finally adopted explained why the congress could not convene until the two working committees could present draft settlements for "the sanction of the congress." Surprisingly, the declaration purported to reflect the views, indeed the duties, of the eight signatories of the Treaty of Paris, but this was last-minute window dressing,[61] no doubt designed to bring to the fore the allied prerogatives contained in the secret articles without necessarily placing Portugal and Sweden on the preparatory committee. That is why no committee members were actually named, and also why, when Metternich invited Talleyrand and Labrador to join the four the next day, the Portuguese plenipotentiary, Don Pedro Count Palmella, was merely informed of the meeting.[62] Sweden presented no complications as her plenipotentiary had not yet arrived. Back of this somewhat puzzling strategy one senses a growing conviction—and this would be Metternich's view most of all—that a strong stand on the Treaty of Paris was more important than the size of the preparatory committee.

The first meeting of the six took place on 30 September in the quiet seclusion of Metternich's villa on the Rennweg. As intimated in the invitations, the four were already in session when Talleyrand and Labrador arrived about two in the afternoon. Curiously Castlereagh began by reading a letter of protest from Palmella, almost as if inviting Talleyrand and Labrador to insist on the full equality of the eight, which they promptly did. Metternich next presented the main protocol of 22 September with its emphasis on the allies' reserved rights. There is no need to repeat here Talleyrand's biting rebuttal, which, he maintained in a famous and self-serving report to his king, caused Metternich to

[60] Text of Wessenberg memorial of 27 Oct. 1814, in HHSA, StK., Kongressakten, Cart. 7, pp. 563–571.

[61] The reference to the signatories appears in the "Projet de déclaration," in d'Angeberg, *Congrès*, I, 252, but not in the version in Great Britain, Foreign Office, *British and Foreign State Papers*, vols. I-III (London, 1838–1841), II, 557f., which leaves a blank space as if for selectively adding names later. (This well-known collection will hereafter be rendered as *British Papers*.) For the four-power discussion of the declaration see Gentz, *Tagebücher*, I, 311f.

[62] Talley. to Louis XVIII, 4 Oct. 1814, Talleyrand, *Corr.*, 12.

retract the document in embarrassment and defeat.[63] One need only note that since the protocol was meant solely as information for Talleyrand's benefit, it hardly required any further attention.

More relevant was Talleyrand's repudiation of the Gentz declaration on the grounds that it proposed to finish where he thought they should all begin: with the immediate convening of the congress by the committee of eight. There ensued a scene that Gentz said he would never forget, but at length tempers cooled, Talleyrand asked for time to study the text, and the meeting was adjourned for two days. Metternich, who had probably expected the French minister to seek parity by unctuous cooperation and boring from within, was surprised at this act of defiance, but not so despondent as Gentz, who lamented after the meeting that "these two people have savagely upset our plans and torn them to shreds." It was not as bad as that, Metternich explained to the disappointed author and proceeded to show him the garden, where works were already being erected for the grand fête to honor the first anniversary of Leipzig.[64]

So far Talleyrand had been merely defiant; what he did next amounted to a breach of faith. Instead of waiting for the scheduled meeting, he delivered a note that repeated his previous views and advanced the proposition that if the congress had the right to sanction, it also had the right to initiate, even if certain modalities required the prior action of the eight signatories.[65] On this basis, he went on, not only should all eight have a hand in proposing the number and composition of the working committees but the congress as a whole should have to approve. Applied to Germany, this procedure would have eliminated the four allies' monopoly of the territorial settlement and undoubtedly led to a broadening of the German-constitution committee, for which in fact sentiment was daily growing. Given the historical background, this imputation of virtual sovereignty to the congress was an outright perversion. What angered the allied ministers most, however, was the form of the note: it was signed and official, intended for publication, and since it also contained allusions to the allies' plans, everything was now in the open. Thus on the very date the congress was supposed to open the only one demanding that it do so was Talleyrand, like the losing poker player who continually calls for the deal.

As the sponsor of France in the councils of the four Castlereagh was the most incensed at Talleyrand's conduct and promptly the following morning called to tell him so, insisting that he had "rather excited apprehension in both the Austrian and Prussian ministers than in-

[63] *Ibid.*, 12–20.
[64] *Ibid.*, 12–26; Gentz, *Tagebücher*, I, 312.
[65] Text in d'Angeberg, *Congrès*, IV, 1962–1964.

spired them with any confidence in his views."[66] The dressing-down expressed the disappointment of one who still hoped that by compromise on Saxony a four-power bloc against Russia might yet come into being. Metternich saw things differently. Though surprised at Talleyrand's tactics, he could be gratified that the French minister still rejected the more dangerous course of bargaining with Alexander, indeed had told the tsar to his face where he stood, this at a time when Pozzo di Borgo, the Russian ambassador in Paris, was on his way to Vienna to urge upon his master an entente with France crowned by a dynastic marriage bond.[67] Barring the unlikely success of such schemes, Metternich could hold his French option in reserve for the time being and use the three weeks remaining before the congress opened to pursue the great experiment of creating a three-power front against Russia. Experiment is the word rather than desperate gamble because even if the prospects for success were small, so were the risks, involving as they did mainly factors that Metternich could keep in his control: namely, the concessions to be made to Prussia. If in the end Hardenberg or the king asked too much, what would be lost other than time, time during which even the tsar might be worn down and induced to relent a little? Patience, as the Austrian minister once told Schulenburg, was one of his trustiest weapons.

Now faced with a propaganda war, Metternich and his allies caucused again on 2 October to prepare a counterattack. Since one could best answer abstract logic with concrete facts, the strategy devised was to fling the Treaty of Paris back at Talleyrand, on the one hand conceding that the signatories should indeed constitute the steering committee but on the other hand disclosing in the declaration those secret articles which did in fact charge the allies to draft a preliminary settlement. Until such a settlement was at hand the congress must be postponed. It was a fitting riposte, considering that Talleyrand had been the one to insist on keeping secret the more humiliating provisions of the treaty. On this basis Gentz drafted a new declaration, which was adopted at an evening session on 3 October. To heighten the effect of the rebuke it was represented to Talleyrand as Castlereagh's proposal, but it was Metternich who delivered it to him immediately after the meeting, typically enough at a soirée given by Wilhelmina von Sagan.[68]

[66] Castle. to Liverp., 9 Oct. 1814, *BD*, 202.

[67] Nessel. to Pozzo, 27 Sept. 1814, in Russian Imperial Historical Society, *Sbornik*, 148 vols. (Leningrad, 1867–1916), CXII, 96.

[68] The attribution to Castlereagh, the most pro-French of the four, heightened the rebuke but it does not prove his authorship, nor does the English text in *British Papers* II, 560f., which is obviously a translation of the French text in d'Angeberg, *Congrès*, I, 254f. even though dated a day earlier. Hints in Gentz, *Tagebücher*, I, 313f.

Castlereagh was undoubtedly right in charging that "the object of the French minister was to sow dissension in Germany and put himself at the head of the discontented states," though the latter hardly needed his encouragement. Even before his unexpected démarche, a number of envoys from the small states had begun to organize a protest movement of their own against their exclusion from the German committee.[69] On Bavaria and Württemberg, however, Talleyrand's action had an effect that he could hardly have desired. The government in Munich, as we have seen, tended to think of Bavaria as a European state on a par with Sardinia, Denmark, or Holland. None of these questioned the propriety of a six-power committee, but the addition of Portugal and Sweden seemed to make an invidious distinction, the more so as their signatures on the Paris pact had never been publicly divulged. Though all grumbled, only King Maximilian Joseph of Bavaria decided to act, persuading Frederick of Württemberg to join him in demanding that they too be admitted to the main committee. Frederick, with a rare appreciation of his limitations, wisely left the initiative to the Bavarians, asserting his rights not in order to place Württemberg on the committee, but to have Sweden and Portugal removed. He did, however, agree to support a Bavarian compromise that called for assembling the envoys of all states of royal rank or better and electing the steering committee from their midst.[70]

Considering the source, this advice on how to run the congress made Talleyrand's own presumption seem mild, but when Metternich received Marshal Wrede on the morning of 5 October, he was polite and, though explaining the difficulties, promised to bring the proposal before a ministerial conference scheduled for that afternoon.[71] Whether he did so is not known, but as his major purpose that day was to force Talleyrand to withdraw his note, he would hardly have missed an opportunity to exhibit evidence of the mischief it was causing. Talleyrand as it happened did not retract and thus plunged the group into another, for Gentz, "very tumultuous and very memorable" debate.[72]

suggest the primacy of Metternich in the matter, but nothing is certain. For the rest see Talley. to Louis XVIII, 4 and 9 Oct. 1814, Talleyrand, *Corr.*, 24f. and 30; Talleyrand, *Memoirs*, II, 238–241; and Josef K. Mayr, "Aufbau und Arbeitsweise des Wiener Kongresses," *Archivalische Zeitschrift*, XLV (1939), 74f. Cf. Webster, *Congress of Vienna*, 85f., who erroneously states that Metternich's communication was only oral.

[69] Castle. to Liverp., 9 Oct. 1814, Webster, *BD*, 203; and police councilor Goehausen to police minister, Baron Franz von Hager, 28 Sept. 1814, Weil, *Les Dessous*, I, 157f.

[70] Linden to King Frederick, 4 and 5 Oct. 1814, HSA, Stuttgart, E 70, Fasc. 12, pp. 90–95; Frederick to Linden, 5 October 1814, *ibid.*, E 70b, Fasc. 45, no. 1.

[71] *Ibid.*, 92–95.

[72] Gentz, *Tagebücher*, I, 314.

When he flatly rejected the Gentz declaration of 3 October, Metternich threatened to announce that there would be no congress at all. That was extreme talk, but it worked. The French minister at length agreed to a postponement of several weeks on condition that the announcement set a definite date for opening the congress and state the rules of admission. His notion of the latter he hastily scribbled on a piece of paper: only those states should be admitted which had been independent before the war and were still independent; likewise any prince should be seated who, regardless of physical possession, enjoyed a sovereignty that he had never relinquished. Posterity has emphasized in this statement the famous principle of legitimacy; the men who passed the paper from hand to hand that day saw mainly a device for seating the king of Saxony while keeping the king of Naples out. No wonder the meeting, instead of adjourning, simply dissolved, the participants muttering and drifting away one by one. At a ball that evening Metternich had a rare experience: a compliment from the tsar on his firmness.[73]

The following day Gentz once again made the rounds of the ministers, hoping to find through private consultations the formula that eluded them in conference. Talleyrand in his turn sent Metternich a draft plan for opening the congress, but as it still contained the provision for legitimacy, it was useless. Metternich now used every occasion to insist that Talleyrand must be trying to precipitate a war either by goading Murat to desperate acts in Italy or by challenging the Russians and the Prussians in the east. When Baron Linden called at the chancellery on 7 October to promote Wrede's plan, he found Metternich uncharacteristically grim, every inch "the representative of his monarch," waving Talleyrand's project and insisting that Wrede's scheme was no better: one would still have to choose between rival factions, and that meant war. Rebuffed by the congress, he warned, Murat would join his army of 80,000 to Napoleon's 20,000, and together they would reconquer Italy. It was a risk that Austria could take only if in the meantime the Bund had taken shape in Germany with a federal army of 200,000. That Talleyrand offered a Franco-Spanish force against Murat and an army of 200,000 for duty in Warsaw only made matters worse. "We must keep the French out of the game," he told his shaken visitor. Later that afternoon Metternich gave similar treatment to Wrede himself, asking what help Bavaria was prepared to give

[73] Reports of Castle., Talley., Talley.'s subordinates, and Gentz to be found respectively in Webster, *BD*, 202f.; Talleyrand, *Corr.* 31–34; Talleyrand, *Memoirs*, II, 239; and Gentz, *Dépêches inédites*, I, 110f., the dates ranging from 6 to 9 Oct. 1814. See also Webster, *Congress of Vienna*, 85–87; and Stein, "Tagebuch," in *Briefe*, v, 320.

in Italy. Was such talk the histrionics of diplomacy or genuine concern? We do not know, but Gentz believed that his chief's fears, even if excessive, were real.[74]

After two days of private consultations Gentz finally produced a simple declaration stating that the signatories to the Paris treaty could best carry out their responsibilities by entering into "free and confidential communications" with all states on an informal basis before convening the congress, which was then to open on 1 November. Nothing was said of sanctions, secret articles, rules of admission, or even committees.[75] On 8 October, proceeding in his usual piecemeal fashion, Metternich first sent Gentz to clear the draft with Hardenberg, the most sensitive of the allies on this issue; then at a meeting in the afternoon he obtained the approval of the four; and finally, late though it was, he summoned the remaining signatories to a full meeting that night, taking care to invite Talleyrand an hour earlier. The preliminary tête-à-tête, which began in Rennweg promptly at seven o'clock, recalls the many exchanges with Napoleon the year before, on Talleyrand's side the expression of incredulity that Austria "could contemplate placing Russia like a girdle around Hungary and Bohemia," on Metternich's side the hints at allied disunity, the assurance that Austria no less than France wished to hold Russia behind the Vistula, to keep Prussia out of Luxemburg and Mainz, and to preserve at least a part of Saxony. In short, what opportunities Talleyrand would have if he ceased his obstruction![76]

That was the carrot; there was also a stick. When the other plenipotentiaries had arrived, Metternich opened the meeting not by soliciting commentary on the Gentz project but by quickly reading both it and the last Talleyrand proposal, after which he promptly called for a vote. The Swedish envoy, Gustavus von Löwenhjelm, was in attendance for the first time, and since he was the protégé of the Russians (in fact, he was normally the Swedish minister in St. Petersburg) the outcome was never in doubt. It is not even certain that Labrador and Palmella supported the French position. The total effect was to demonstrate to Talleyrand that if there was any chance of winning Austria, he would have to play the game Metternich's way. He thereupon capitulated, but ever the parsimonious diplomat, he tried to salvage what

---

[74] Gentz, *Tagebücher*, I, 315; Talley. to Louis XVIII, 9 Oct. 1814, in Talleyrand, *Memoirs*, II, 345; Linden to King Frederick, 7 and 9 Oct. 1814, HSA, Stuttgart, E 70, Fasc. 12, pp. 98–108; Wrede to Mett., 8 Oct. and Max Joseph to Wrede, 6 Oct. 1814, both in HHSA, StK., Kongressakten, Cart. 8, pp. 3ff. Cf. Heilmann, *Fürst Wrede*, 401f.

[75] Text as amended at the meeting in d'Angeberg, *Congrès*, II, 272f.

[76] Gentz, *Tagebücher*, I, 316; Talley. to Louis XVIII, 9 Oct. 1814, Talleyrand, *Corr.*, 36–39.

he could, seeking Castlereagh's support for the Bourbons in Naples and proposing a statement in the declaration that the peace to be offered to the congress would rest "on principles of public law." At this Metternich, thinking to duplicate his first success, proposed another vote, but Hardenberg, shouting and pounding the table, was as adamant as Castlereagh was conciliatory. Gentz, who had enjoyed the attentions of Talleyrand in recent days, advised his chief to agree. In the end the phrase was inserted but in such a way that it expressed no obligation but merely a desired outcome. The meeting adjourned at eleven amidst great sighs of relief. Talleyrand, covering his defeat, prided himself on his public-law gambit while Metternich retired to his bedroom to read poetry and recall great moments with Sagan. "This evening, gentlemen, belongs to the history of the congress," exclaimed Gentz, much moved by his presence at the summit.[77]

[77] Talleyrand, *Corr.*, 39–44 with n. 10; Mett. to Sagan, 9 Oct. 1814, Ullrichová, ed., *Briefwechsel*, 267; and Arneth, *Wessenberg*, 218f.

CHAPTER VI

FROM FORTY-ONE ARTICLES

TO TWELVE

UNFORTUNATELY our knowledge of grand policy during the three weeks of procedural wrangling is not matched by the information available on the German question itself. As a result a day-to-day narrative of the soundings, arguments, and decisions is not possible. We know that Metternich spent much of his time with Hardenberg and considerably less time with Marshal Wrede, serving as mediator between the two states most important to his strategy. Wrede of course was eager for information about the Forty-one Articles, but Metternich, who had no desire to cope with Bavarian particularism before everything was arranged with Hardenberg and Münster, smothered the query with ridicule. The plan, he said, was "so bizarre" that he "rejected it on the spot" and hence saw no need to communicate it. The guileless marshal took him at his word, and the matter did not arise privately between them for another month.[1]

The territorial question was another matter. Metternich, as we have seen, had already done his part by forgoing an Austrian corridor to the Breisgau, thereby giving up an imposing total of 440,000 in population, which could be used to accommodate the South German states. Accordingly Hardenberg had discarded his idea of filling the trans-Rhine territory with a cluster of small buffer states and came to Vienna with a bold new plan in which Prussia and Austria would divide the whole area between them, roughly along the Mosel but with Austria receiving the province of Luxemburg beyond the Mosel.[2] In this way the strategically vital area would be stoutly guarded in a manner befitting the dualistic protectorate envisioned in the Forty-one Articles, and the unreliable middle states (including even Nassau-Usingen and Weilburg previously slated to adjoin Holland), would be confined to the right bank of the Rhine, Prussia still avoiding a common frontier with France.

The plan had been partially foreshadowed in the delineation of occupation zones, which assigned the area south of the Mosel to Austria

[1] Wrede to King Max Joseph, 22 Sept. 1814 in Geheimes Staatsarchiv, Munich (hereafter GSA, Munich), MA 1028, pp. 44–46.

[2] Hard. to Castle., 27 Aug. 1814, Griewank, "Preussen und die Neuordnung," 277, and *ibid.*, 239–240; and Hard. to Humb., 3 Sept. 1814, extr. in Dupuis, *Talleyrand*, II, 319.

and Bavaria jointly. As between the two, however, Metternich intended Bavaria to have the territory and in the Paris convention of the previous June had promised his offices to obtain as much of it as possible. It must therefore be recorded as a major victory for him that after a week, presumably filled with acrimony, Hardenberg, in a stunning reversal, discarded one of his deepest prejudices and proposed to Castlereagh that Bavaria have all the territory in question, Luxemburg included. In return, however, she must accept the limits of the Main, strictly interpreted to include the renunciation of Mainz and the restoration of Ansbach and Bayreuth. Among the advantages cited for the plan, both by Knesebeck, who drafted the details on 28 September, and by Castlereagh, who welcomed "so highly military a power as Bavaria on the left bank," was that of giving this Francophile court a vital stake in resisting reconquest by France, an argument suspiciously Metternichian in flavor.[3]

The new Prussian plan, as it happened, resembled Wrede's own instructions, which required him to demand the entire triangle formed by the Rhine, the Mosel, and the French frontier. There was a difference, however, for the Bavarians wanted the territory merely as trading material, the better to place their neighbors in the exposed position vis-à-vis France, much as Hardenberg had originally proposed, even to placing Baden almost completely on the left bank. As for gains north of the Main, those projected in the Austro-Bavarian accord included mainly Mainz and the remains of the grand duchy of Frankfurt as far north as Wetzlar on the Lahn. To these Montgelas now gratuitously added the department of Fulda, which Metternich had pointedly omitted from the accord. Considering that Fulda extended even further north than Wetzlar, which itself lay deep in the area that Prussia claimed for her Upper Saxon-Thuringian Kreis, it is perhaps understandable why Montgelas, contrary to the expectations even of the king, preferred to manipulate from behind the lines and allow the blunt and outspoken Wrede to face the fire in Vienna.[4]

Wrede apparently sprang this surprise on Metternich at that same interview of 5 October, where he also demanded a seat on the main

---

[3] Knesebeck memorandum of 28 Sept. 1814, in Wellington, *Supplementary Despatches*, IX, 307–312. The plan is further explained in Castle. to Wellington, 1 Oct. 1814, in *Castle. Corr.*, X, 142–145. In contrast to Castlereagh, Wellington opposed the plan. See Wellington to Castle., 17 Oct. 1814 in *ibid.*, X, 166–167. Cf. Wolf D. Gruner, "Europäischer Friede als nationales Interesse," *Bohemia, Jahrbuch des Collegium Carolinum*, XVIII (1977), 102, who assumes, merely on the basis of Castlereagh's dispatch, that he was the originator of the plan.

[4] Sahrmann, *Pfalz oder Salzburg?* 42-44; Real, *Deutsche Verfassungsfrage*, 29-32; Winter, *Wrede als Berater*, 219; and Karl Otmar Freiherr von Aretin, "Die deutsche Politik Bayerns in der Zeit der staatlichen Entwicklung des deutschen Bundes, 1814–1820 (Ph.D. diss., University of Munich, 1952), 4–6.

committee of the congress. Presenting two imperious demands at once no doubt contributed to Metternich's low opinion of the marshal's diplomatic talents, but it is only fair to consider that interviews at the chancellery did not come easily; one had to make the most of them. Indeed, pending an understanding with Prussia, Metternich had only one reason for dealing with the Bavarians at all: to try to induce them to turn over Salzburg and the Inn and Hausrück districts even before equivalents could be given. Under pressure from Emperor Francis in this regard, he went behind Wrede's back to appeal directly to King Max Joseph, advising him as delicately as possible that his plans "would be difficult to execute."[5] The king, however, only bristled the more and ordered his soldier-envoy to resume the attack on both fronts. In another interview on 7 October Metternich withstood the assault, relying on the imminent great-power declaration to answer the bid for Bavarian parity and reminding the marshal that Austria's treaty obligations were confined to her good offices. On the other hand, far from inducing the Bavarians to evacuate additional territory ahead of schedule, he only drove them to make difficulties even in regard to the still incomplete transfer of authority in Vorarlberg and the Tyrol. As a result he had to assign Wessenberg to negotiate on a ministerial level what should have been routine problems for technical commissions.[6]

Metternich's dealings with Hardenberg meanwhile, the key to everything else, were more intense and scrutable, at least so far as the meager record permits us to say. Saxony was incessantly discussed, at first to little avail. The ministers themselves were probably ready to strike a bargain, but Francis continued to demand a share of Saxony and Frederick William, after his arrival in Vienna on 25 September, ordered Hardenberg not to oppose Alexander's demands in Poland.[7] Then came the protocol of 28 September, which pledged the Russians to yield the occupation of Saxony to Prussia. Technically the transfer required the approval of all the four powers, but with Castlereagh pressing relentlessly for an accommodation, a refusal by Austria would have left her isolated and powerless to prevent the deed. Besides, Metternich, in line with his long established priorities, saw positive gain in any operation that moved the Russians out.[8] For these reasons, on or about 1 October he assured Hardenberg of his personal willingness

---

[5] Max Joseph to Wrede, 6 Oct. 1814, GSA, Munich, MA 1028, p. 67.

[6] Winter, *Wrede als Berater*, 219f.; Linden to King Frederick, 7 Oct. 1814, HSA, Stuttgart, E 70, Fasc. 2, pp. 90–91; and Note from State Chancellery to Count Lazansky, President of the Organisierungs- Hofkommission, 17 Oct. 1814, HHSA, StK., Noten an die Hofkanzlei, Fasc. 26.

[7] Hardenberg, "Tagebücher," p. 34: "Idées du Roi en contradiction avec mes plans."

[8] Mett. to Schulenberg, in Kohlschmidt, *Sächsische Frage*, 63.

to acquiesce, adding that he would try to bring the emperor around as well. Whether he joined to this promise allusions to a permanent possession is less certain, but what affirmative evidence there is also makes clear that he attached the usual conditions concerning Poland and the Bavarian claims, thus leaving the next move up to Hardenberg.[9]

In desperation the chancellor was now willing to lavish souls on Bavaria in almost any number if only they did not inhabit the coveted areas of Mainz and Fulda. The aforementioned plan of extending her boundary to Luxemburg was evidence of this as was a variant advanced on 9 October, which substituted Ansbach-Bayreuth for Luxemburg but still projected for her an increment of 241,000 souls above her existing population, a tenfold increase over the surplus envisioned in the master plan of April.[10] Where was the supplement to be found? Not at Prussia's expense certainly, for in addition to Mainz and Fulda Hardenberg now insisted on having the major share of the trans-Rhine territories, including a strip on the right bank of the Mosel, which had hitherto been recognized as part of the Austro-Bavarian sphere. Instead, the sacrifices were to be made by the princes with the more equivocal treaty guarantees, to which end the chancellor revived the principle he had never really abandoned: namely, that where the accession treaties required sacrifices as necessary for the independence of Germany, the territorial settlement should be based on the Imperial Recess of 1803, "the last legitimate act," he said, "in which all Germany concurred."[11] This language was bound to strike responsive chords with such as Solms, Gärtner, Stein, and even Münster, but more to the point, it would remove the mediatized houses from the control of Baden, Hesse-Darmstadt, Nassau, and others without compensation, thereby providing some 500,000 souls for easing the problem of redistributing territory among the larger states, that is to say, the Kreis chiefs.

In these projections the leading victim by far was Baden: she was to cede to Austria 140,000 in the Breisgau as well as another 203,000 in mediatized lands, Bavaria meanwhile receiving the whole Main-Tauber district in the north plus mediatized territories of unspecified extent. Altogether Hardenberg's plan for Baden envisioned a reduction from 973,000 souls to 510,000 or almost 48 percent. By comparison Hesse-Darmstadt and Nassau were scheduled to lose about 20 percent, all in

[9] Stein, "Tagebücher," *Briefe*, v, 319; Castle. to Liverp., 9 Oct. 1814, Webster, *BD*, 202.

[10] "Esquisse du plan prussien pour quelques arrangements de territoire," annexed to Hard. to Mett., 9 Oct. 1814, d'Angeberg, *Congrès*, IV, 1936–1939.

[11] *Ibid.*, 1938.

mediatized lands.[12] It would not be unfair to conclude that Baden, already burdened by an ailing ruler and an impending crisis over the Zähringen inheritance, was being prepared for eventual extinction. But even if the state survived as little more than the original margraviate, the question arises: how could such a dwarf function as the codirector of a Kreis, the role assigned to it and Hesse-Cassel in Hardenberg's Forty-one Articles? Again the territorial and the constitutional questions converge, and again the surviving documentation is disappointingly sparse.

As mentioned earlier, upon his return from the waters of Baden, Metternich's first discussion of the Prussian constitutional draft took place with Count Münster the day before Hardenberg arrived in Vienna. Henceforth he knew he could count on the Hanoverian to lead the attack on the dualistic directory and the narrowly conceived federal territory that provided military cover to so little Austrian soil. In the next few days Münster did in fact obtain supportive opinions from Castlereagh and Nesselrode, and from Hardenberg himself a promise that he would not insist on either the narrow limits or the directory.[13] Considering that the latter was neither Stein's nor Humboldt's idea but the chancellor's own, his capitulation was obtained with surprising ease, suggesting that he had considered the plan only a trial balloon.

But what would replace the dualistic directory: an honorary Austrian presidency with Prussia as a chancellor, as Stein had proposed in Frankfurt; an Austrian imperium with which Metternich himself had beguiled Münster shortly before; or a chairmanship rotating among the Kreis chiefs, the solution advanced in many earlier plans? Since the first two were anathema to Hardenberg, it is most likely that in their early discussions the two ministers were primarily concerned with finding a way to return the directorial powers to the council of Kreis chiefs without, at least on Hardenberg's side, conceding too much power to the middle states. It is also plausible to suppose that as the price for renouncing the directory Hardenberg insisted that any substitute at least be confined to no more than the five states visualized in his original proposals in London. As noted above, there was already good reason to drop a diminished Baden from the council, and Hesse-Cassel, when fully restored, would be by Hardenberg's calculations of similar size: 497,000. Such reasoning would also be consistent with the chancellor's later contention that only Kreis chiefs might possess mediatized subjects.[14]

---

[12] *Ibid.*, 1937–1939.

[13] Münster to Prince Regent, 17 Sept. 1814, extr. in Dupuis, *Talleyrand*, II, 325–329; Baumgarten, "Verhandlungen über die Bundesverfassung," 557; and Linden to King Frederick, 20 Sept. 1814, HSA, Stuttgart, E 70, Fasc. 12, pp. 50–60.

[14] See below, p. 152.

Metternich probably continued, as in London and Paris, to defend the larger directory, but there are also signs that he was beginning to toy with alternatives. However unwelcome, the dropping of Baden and Hesse-Cassel from the first council at least had the advantage of adding their weight to the council of princes and estates, in which case one could proceed in every possible way to strengthen this body as a counterweight to the Kreis chiefs and the whole Kreis system. Or, forced to it, one could take the opposite tack, conceding preponderance to the first council but increasing its membership and perhaps the number of Kreise so as to minimize Prussia's indirect acquisitions. All we know with any degree of certitude comes from Gentz; as of 27 September it was his understanding that "the direction of joint affairs [would] be entrusted to five or seven or nine of the leading members of the Confederation assembled in a permanent diet."[15] Five here would reflect Hardenberg's current position, seven the provisions of the Forty-one Articles, and nine the addition of Denmark and the Netherlands as previously broached, or less likely two other states such as Hesse-Darmstadt and Nassau. A seat for Saxony was apparently never mentioned, further evidence that Metternich no longer fought to save the kingdom but only to assure Austria a portion of it.

At this stage of the dialogue Metternich was suddenly assailed by King Frederick of Württemberg, who had finally obtained a copy of the Forty-one Articles and demanded an explanation. At about eleven in the morning on 30 September Frederick moved his bulk the short distance from the Hofburg to the chancellery for an interview that provides our best glimpse of the progress made to that time. From Frederick's summary of it[16] we learn that Metternich in the last few days (the days of his stormy audience with the tsar and the protocol regarding the Prussian occupation of Saxony) has acquiesced in the smaller council of five Kreis chiefs, Austria and Prussia each heading two Kreise and casting two votes. As a quid pro quo he evidently did not hold out for the lower house, the establishment of which, he told the king, was still undecided. If there was a trade, it more likely consisted of a new delineation of the Kreis boundaries. The seven Kreise that he listed for the king by name were Bohemia, Austria, Brandenburg, Westphalia, Hanover, Bavaria, and—no longer Upper Rhine under joint Austro-Baden direction, but a Swabian Kreis in which Württemberg as the sole chief would lord it over Baden, the two Hohenzollern principalities, and perhaps part of Hesse-Darmstadt and command a military contingent of 30,000 men. It was a dazzling prospect since in the king's mind this figure implied a Kreis population of 3 million, well above that of all these lands combined. "That the

[15] Gentz to Karadja, 27 Sept. 1814, in *Dépêches inédites*, I, 104.
[16] HSA, Stuttgart, E 70, Fasc. 12, pp. 83–87. Full text in Appendix B.

final hour has struck for the petty sovereigns pervades the spirit of the entire system," were Linden's rapturous words when the king told him about it a few days later.[17]

Metternich likewise assured the king that he would have all the executive powers, both in the Kreis at large and within Württemberg itself, necessary to maintain an effective military system. On the other hand, he said nothing about the judicial and administrative powers of Kreis chiefs, still spoke of the subordinate Kreis members as sovereign, and was surprisingly candid about the necessity of uniform *landständische Verfassungen* and guaranteeing the privileges of the mediatized houses, excluding, however, their representation in the federal diet. Equally surprisingly King Frederick professed these reforms to be in line with his domestic plans and did not protest. What worried him more were Hardenberg's references to a federal court and the Austro-Prussian majority on the directory. On these matters as well Metternich made light of the Forty-one Articles. Disputes among the Kreis chiefs, he explained, would be settled by arbitration, those between a Kreis chief and another member of his Kreis by the directory, and complaints of the estates, if admitted at all, likewise by the directory. In short, judgments would be largely political; they would not be judicial verdicts based on imperial antecedents. As for Austro-Prussian preponderance, that, Metternich added, was an illusion since Austria would find her majorities more often with Bavaria and Württemberg than with Prussia.[18]

The two great powers, moreover, would not have a claim to automatic assistance in defending their nonfederal provinces, even though they in turn would be pledged to defend the Bund regardless of distractions on other fronts. Regarding foreign policy in general Metternich likewise sought to minimize distinctions, indicating that in matters involving Germany as a whole vis-à-vis foreign powers the directory would act as a unit, but that "all other diplomatic affairs [would] remain exactly as they were [*unabänderlich bestehen*]," language that strongly implied some measure of freedom for the middle-state Kreis chiefs after all.[19]

Even though Metternich's first concern in the interview was obviously to dispel fears and soften the king for constructive participation on the German constitution committee, his words have the ring of sincerity, at least so far as his own views are concerned. How well these

---

[17] Linden to King Frederick, 4 Oct. 1814, HSA, Stuttgart, E 70, Fasc. 12, pp. 76–81. See especially the annex, called "Flüchtige Gedanken über das Resultat der Unterredung . . . mit Metternich . . . den 30. Sept. 1814."

[18] King's account as in n. 16 above.

[19] *Ibid.*

reflected prior agreement with Hardenberg is more problematical. The chancellor had certainly not abandoned a federal monopoly over all foreign and warmaking powers or his ideas about a federal court, although the latter was more important to Humboldt than to him. And what of that glorious Swabian Kreis, which Linden described a few days later as clearing the way "to establish sovereignty over the Kreis territories without attracting undue attention"? Did the chancellor understand the situation that way? We do not know, but it seems unlikely. There is no doubt, however, that Linden and his king assumed that an undiminished Baden would fall to their Kreis and even so wondered where the rest of their 3 million was to come from. Their disillusionment was to have profound consequences later on.[20]

A few hours after the interview with King Frederick Metternich found himself back in the Rennweg for that memorable meeting of six where Talleyrand dropped the bombshell that diverted attention from everything but the opening of the congress. That same day Count Münster broke some ribs in a carriage accident, placing still another obstacle in the way of the German negotiation. Metternich, as usual taking one step at a time, wanted no meeting of the full constitution committee until Austria, Prussia, and Hanover, as a majority, were agreed on a compressed version of the Hardenberg plan. Not until 7 October was a three-power conference held, Count Ernst Hardenberg representing Münster and Humboldt keeping the protocol. The incapacitation of Münster was doubly unfortunate in that his deputy carried on a feud with Humboldt going back to the years (1809–1813) when both were accredited to the Austrian court and the Prussian chancellor had consulted his Hanoverian cousin more confidentially than he had his ambassador. In letters to his wife Humboldt avoided confusion between them by calling Count Ernst "the perfidious one," as opposed to "our" Hardenberg.[21]

Under such auspices the review began of the Forty-one Articles as tentatively amended in the preliminary conferences with Solms-Laubach almost a month before.[22] Although Metternich gained his point that the main goal was agreement on a skeleton plan, the procedure adopted was a systematic reading of the articles one by one, which in fact favored Humboldt's propensity for further elaboration and refinement of the original. Still, a good beginning was made. The way prepared by the earlier discussions, the federal territory was now once

[20] Linden to King Frederick as in n. 17 above.
[21] Humb. to Caroline, 1 Oct. 1814, in Humboldt, *Briefe*, IV, 391–393; Brandes, *Münster und die Wiederestehung*, 98; Gebhardt, *Humboldt als Staatsmann*, I, 371–374.
[22] This and following from text of protocol of 7 Oct. 1814, in Schmidt, *Verfassungsfrage*, 200–202.

and for all defined, as Metternich, Münster, and Humboldt had desired all along, to take in "all the German provinces of Austria and Prussia." Metternich's hand, though not his alone necessarily, can also be seen in the rejection of ostracism as the punishment for violating federal law, the ill-tempered suggestion of Stein which the tactless chancellor had placed menacingly in his very first article. In similar fashion Metternich questioned the wisdom of imputing to the member states mere *Landeshoheit*, the old imperial term implying some subordination to a supreme authority, whereas all the accession treaties guaranteed sovereignty. Metternich no doubt preferred the latter term, which he had induced Hardenberg to use in the first version of the Forty-one Articles. Now, however, he accepted a compromise devoid of all allusions to the past, a vague reference to "governmental rights" (*Regierungsrechte*); these the states would continue to exercise within the limits imposed by the federal constitution.[23]

Somewhat fortuitously, owing to the reordering of topics in the second version of the Forty-one Articles, the status of the mediatized houses came up next. The debate, revolving around curial votes in the future diet and federal guarantees of the rights listed in Article IV, soon narrowed down to the question whether these estates, exclusive of the *Reichsritterschaft*, "should be *Bundesstände* or *Landstände* or in a certain sense both at the same time." At this point Hardenberg dumbfounded everyone, possibly even Humboldt, by reviving the plan originally advanced in the Ten Articles of London: namely, that Kreis chiefs alone might possess mediatized subjects; only this time he went further, holding that they should allow even their existing Standesherren to function within the framework of the Kreis rather than as mere *Landstände*. For Bavaria and Württemberg the result would be further disruption, for Prussia further consolidation as the grateful Standesherren would inevitably constitute in the Kreis assemblies the chief's party against the opposition of the demoted sovereigns.[24] This

[23] Cf. Aretin, *Bayerns Weg*, 132; and Wolfgang Quint, *Souveränitätsbegriff und Souveränitätspolitik in Bayern* (Berlin, 1971), 288–294, both of whom argue unconvincingly that Metternich preferred *Regierungsrechte* not as a compromise but because it was even more constraining than *Landeshoheit*. Humboldt in his April Memorandum used *Souveränität*, Hardenberg in his Ten Points of London *Regierungsrechte*, Stein always *Landeshoheit*. The issue is minor because whatever the expression used, the powers implied were always to be limited in accordance with the constitution. Later Metternich obtained general agreement on the German Committee to the statement that the expression *Regierungsrechte* meant the same as *Souveränitätsrechte*. Protocol of 22 Oct. 1814, Klüber, *Acten*, II, 109.

[24] Protocol of 7 Oct. 1814, Schmidt, *Verfassungsfrage*, 201. Further evidence comes from Gärtner, who reported that if Hardenberg prevailed, "unjust distinctions" would disappear and every imperial estate would make equal sacrifices. See Hoff, *Mediatisiertenfrage*, 67, who, still thinking in terms of the Forty-one Articles, could only conclude that Gärtner must have been mistaken.

was no mere abridgement of the Forty-one Articles but a fundamental revision undoubtedly linked with the abandonment of the directory. As will become clearer as we move along, once Hardenberg could no longer anticipate an equal partnership with Austria in the domination of the whole Bund, he had less incentive to strengthen its central apparatus and every reason to shift power back to the strong Kreise of his original London plan. In them at any rate Prussia could be sure of her gains whatever happened in the rest of Germany.

The plan, not really so new as Humboldt sarcastically termed it in his minutes, evidently disturbed the previous calm. Since it implied the yardstick of the Imperial Recess, it opened up the territorial question again and with it the problem of drawing the Kreis boundaries, which was certain to precipitate an Austro-Prussian confrontation over the assignment of Hesse-Darmstadt. As a result Metternich, who had once before defeated the plan, now at least induced the chancellor to withdraw it until he could combine it with a concrete project naming provinces and counting souls.[25] Stein was the main loser, for both sides could agree that, whatever the fate of the Standesherren, the imperial knights would be equated not with them but with the territorial nobility (*Landesadel*). "It seems to me," the tenacious baron complained to Münster a few weeks later, "that too much importance is attached to the fate of the mediatized and too little to the nation." The former, he explained, would exchange real influence in a medium-sized state for a position of servility under a powerful Kreis chief, to the detriment of themselves and of their people.[26]

The ministers next debated Articles VI and VII of the Prussian draft, those pertaining to civil rights and the powers of the estates. Freedom of movement Metternich accepted with the proviso that federal norms be devised to prevent evasion of military service. He also endorsed a copyright law favorable to German publications. *Habeas corpus*, on the other hand, he rejected as impracticable but agreed that some other form of personal protection should be found. Regarding the taxing powers of the future Landtage, he found the opposition more intense, for the one issue on which Count Hardenberg and Humboldt had agreed during the preliminary conferences was the need to strengthen these bodies, most importantly by granting them a veto over taxes, a proposal that the Hanoverian now renewed. Metternich would have opposed the motion in any case, but with the decision having just been made to restore Bohemia and all the Austrian crownlands to the Bund as well as Brandenburg, Silesia, and Pomerania, even Chancellor Hardenberg had to demur. Between them they agreed to require only the

[25] Schmidt, *Verfassungsfrage*, 201.
[26] Stein to Münster, 20 Oct. 1814, Stein, *Briefe*, v, 171f.

right of consultation, but when Münster's deputy insisted on recording his government's intent to grant the veto on its own, it was plain that the controversy was not over. By this time it was also obvious that the practice of reading the articles one at a time and admitting memoranda from the preliminary conferences, far from abridging the Forty-one Articles, was adding to them. As a result Humboldt was charged to compose a skeleton plan of his own for the next meeting, probably at Metternich's instigation.[27]

Meanwhile Metternich's own committee of three had likewise dissected the Prussian project and submitted its report on the day of the above conference but not in time to be of use there. In truth the procedures of the committee reflected the leisurely pace of imperial days and the lingering preference for written over oral communication. Not until 5 October did the court councilors, Frank, Rademacher, and Spiegel, hold a meeting, and even then they drafted no single report but simply read their separate opinions aloud. They then agreed that old Rademacher should deliver these to Metternich and press upon him their unanimous view that the Prussian draft was "full of dangers," which could only be overcome by replacing the dualistic directory with a single protector, alias Kaiser.[28] Rademacher, as it happened, could never find Metternich in, and growing weary of "climbing the stairs so often with my bad limbs," finally on 7 October did what came more naturally and sent the material upstairs with a covering letter.[29] If this sounds like the quaint rigmarole of a Mozart opera, it is only fair to say that Metternich on his side seems neither to have sent for advice, nor to have provided vital information about territorial exchanges, the destiny of the mediatized, or the schedule of deliberations.[30]

Although the papers of Spiegel and Frank—Rademacher did not submit his own—were broadly restorative in spirit, they were neither dogmatic nor unrealistic, nor lacking in shrewd insights that had considerable influence on Metternich.[31] They generally endorsed the treatment of the mediatized houses, the articles on civil rights and *landständische Verfassungen*, and with some modifications, the idea of a federal court. On the other hand, they preferred the use of "sovereignty" to

[27] Schmidt, *Verfassungsfrage*, 202.
[28] Frank's notation on his copy of the Forty-one Articles, HHSA, StK., Kongressakten, Cart. 6; and Rademacher to Mett., 7 Oct. 1814, HHSA, StK., Deutsche Akten, Fasc. 100, pp. 1f.
[29] Rademacher to Mett., 7 Oct. 1814, HHSA, StK., Deutsche Akten, Fasc. 100, p. 2.
[30] *Ibid.*, 1f.
[31] This and following from "Betrachtungen über den preussischen Entwurf der deutschen Bundesverhältnisse des Herrn Baron von Frank," and "Bemerkungen sammt Gegen-Entwurf des Herrn Baron von Spiegel," HHSA, StK., Deutsche Akten, Fasc. 100, pp. 3–53.

that of *Landeshoheit*, emphasized that indemnification rather than restoration was the most the mediatized could expect, and held that though Germany was not ready for French-style "representative" constitutions, elements of these might well be instituted wherever practical and conducive to the general welfare. In this same vein and going far beyond Hardenberg and even Stein, they argued for incorporating individual rights into a common German, as opposed to state citizenship, on the same plane with the projected common law codes, standardized coinage, weights and measures, and a customs union, which provisions in the Prussian plan Spiegel praised as having been "drawn from the very soul of every German man."

Yet at another level, they held, it was precisely this stress on German unity that was missing in the plan. Since the dualistic directory would not likely survive repeated clashes between the codirectors, the danger was that Germany would dissolve into her constituent Kreise. "The Kreis chiefs are the *Lieblingskinder* of the plan," Frank wrote; "they are given greater power than the purposes of the Bund require." To remedy this, he insisted that all Kreis powers must derive from the Bund itself and not be "delegated to the so-called Kreis chiefs in such a way that they acquire in the process special rights of their own."[32] Spiegel was more concrete, proposing that the Kreise be nothing but federal administrative districts whose offices and personnel would constitute a federal field staff responsible to a Kreis board of directors, which in turn would report to the council of Kreis chiefs as a whole. Similarly Kreis military affairs should be in the hands of federal officers responsible to the same council.[33] For all practical purposes the Kreis chiefs (or directors as Spiegel preferred to call them) would function not as autonomous bosses but only as members of the collective council. Even in this capacity Spiegel and Frank recommended that they share their powers over war and peace with the rest of the federal diet. In his memoirs Metternich ridiculed the efforts of the three antiquarian councilors, but the truth is that no one had yet produced such a penetrating analysis of Hardenberg's course, and this even without knowledge of his most recent statements regarding the Kreise.[34]

Naturally the centrifugal dangers of the system could be considerably diminished by installing Austria as the single hereditary directing head. While desiring to call the supreme office Kaiser rather than protector, neither Spiegel nor Frank intended to restore a true monarchical system; they merely wanted to invoke past glories to lift the "Reichsbund"

[32] Frank, "Betrachtungen," as per note above.
[33] Spiegel, "Bemerkungen," as per n. 31.
[34] *Ibid.*; Metternich, *NP*, I, 207f.; Griewank, "Preussen und die Neuordnung," 248f., who takes Metternich at his word.

above those parvenu leagues in Switzerland and America. Even so, Frank was pessimistic, regarding this solution as necessary to counter the Prussian grasp for domination but fearing that others would see Austria in the same light. Like Metternich himself, Frank distrusted a nominal supremacy devoid of real power, advising that if necessary Austria reject any confederation "that is incompatible with her honor and does not conform to the desires of her peoples," and rely instead on her own strength and the balance of power. It would be Metternich's greatest glory to arrange a European order in which Austria would be the rallying point for all the weak.[35]

The day after receiving the report, 8 October, Metternich was completely absorbed in the climactic negotiations leading to the declaration that postponed the congress and gave him three weeks to settle with his allies. On the 9th, however, he again sat down with the Prussians and Count Hardenberg, almost certainly to consider ten articles that Humboldt, as directed, had fashioned from the original forty-one.[36] One issue that had been settled by now was the establishment of a lower house for the lesser princes and the free cities, among which Humboldt, following the Forty-one Articles, included "Frankfurt as the seat of the federal assembly." Metternich, who still backed Bavaria's claim to the city, objected and proposed Regensburg or Nüremberg instead, probably on the advice of Frank and Spiegel. The Prussians, however, who still visualized the rich city as part of their Kreis system, insisted on its free status, and so in the final wording Humboldt named no cities and no capital at all.[37]

The long smoldering issue of a federal court, always a top priority with Humboldt, also flared up. In Hardenberg's original Ten Articles of London only a Kreis judiciary had been mentioned; and in the first version of the Forty-one Articles, the draft strongly influenced by Metternich, the federal diet itself had been designated to act as a court in disputes between member states. Only with the final date of the Forty-one Articles had the idea of an independent federal court come into its own, not as a court of appeals for ordinary civil and criminal law but as a special tribunal to adjudicate interstate disputes and hear grievances filed by individuals and estates against their government where violations of federal law were charged. This provision would have combined elements of the old Imperial Chamber Court and the Aulic Council and represented the greatest single invasion of states' rights by the federal, as opposed to the Kreis powers. From Harden-

---

[35] Frank, "Betrachtungen."
[36] Hardenberg, "Tagebücher," 35; Mett. to Sagan, 9 Oct. 1814, Ullrichová, ed., *Briefwechsel*, 267; Schmidt, *Verfassungsfrage*, 204.
[37] Schmidt, *Verfassungsfrage*, 206f. from a note of Humboldt.

berg's point of view, moreover, it fitted particularly well with the directory of the great powers and the exclusion of most of their provinces from the Bund. In his condensed sketch Humboldt not only retained this provision but in a sense strengthened it by omitting various exceptions and qualifications found in the original. Yet just nine days before Metternich had assured the king of Württemberg that interstate disputes would be settled by the council of Kreis chiefs or by arbitration and that if complaints from the estates reached the federal level at all, they too would be decided by the council.

Before Humboldt he maintained this same position save for including in the process the lower house, the creation of which had been in doubt on the former occasion. This change seems small enough, a mere technical adaptation to altered circumstances; in reality, however, it provides a clue to a larger endeavor. Having acquiesced in a council of only five Kreis chiefs, he was now determined at every opportunity to strengthen the lower house as a counterweight to the centrifugal tendencies of the Kreise, much as Bismarck used the Reichstag against the particularism of the states. With the court issue his success was small, however. Humboldt had always favored arbitration as a first step in settling interstate disputes, but that failing, he insisted that a joint tribunal drawn from the federal court and the upper house alone should decide the case. Regarding the grievances of subjects he stood his ground completely, arguing that "only the awe inspired by a court can keep the princes in check," a display of confidence in the rule of law that came all too naturally to this scholarly advocate of the *Rechtsstaat*.[38]

Why did Metternich yield on a point that was bound to be anathema to almost all the sovereign princes? Partly for that reason perhaps, partly as well because, for all its faults, a federal court, like the lower house, would be a force for centralism and, as we shall see, if properly constituted, might even be made to serve the interests of the lesser sovereigns. Besides, in the two following articles Humboldt returned to the more Metternichian language of the first version of the Forty-one Articles, saying merely that an explicit listing of the rights of individuals and the minimum powers of the estates would come later, in the definitive federal charter. Then, to remove complications from the side of the two great powers Humboldt added, as a substitute for the idea of a narrower Bund already rescinded, a final paragraph incorporating the Solms-Laubach formula he had earlier opposed: the proviso that nothing in those two articles would be binding on Austria

[38] *Ibid.*, 207.

or Prussia.[39] Other considerations might influence Metternich and Hardenberg in defining rights and powers but not a concern for their internal legislation or the fear of being summoned before a high tribunal at Frankfurt (or Regensburg) for offenses committed in Bohemia or Brandenburg.

Up to this point the meeting in all likelihood had been a dialogue between Metternich and Humboldt, Prince Hardenberg hearing very little, Count Hardenberg hearing little to dispute; the Hanoverians had always favored strong guarantees of estates' rights. But that final paragraph: what a mockery of the principle of equality! The Stein plan would have placed at least some Austrian and Prussian provinces under federal regulation. Now all would be exempt and at the same time still enjoy the military protection of the Bund. But discrimination did not stop there. Article VII of Humboldt's sketch gave only the two great powers the right to wage independent wars; all the rest must wait for a federal summons. We do not know in fact if Count Hardenberg argued this way then, but he had before and Münster himself was to do so at the next meeting. In any case, Metternich is our witness to a heated argument from which he stood aside, retiring to a corner to write Sagan. "I want to let them rough each other up," he told her, "before I get into it myself."[40]

Several hours later Metternich found himself circulating in the grand halls of the Spanish Riding School doing the emperor's honors at the most splendid ball yet given at the congress.[41] The Prussian chancellor, meanwhile, was free to spend the evening alone in his quarters pondering weightier matters.[42] At the European level his was the same old problem of attaining his goals before the voice of France was restored to great-power councils three weeks hence. At the German level Metternich had just told him (7 October) that the status of the mediatized lands and their distribution among the Kreis chiefs depended upon a comprehensive territorial settlement, which in turn hinged on Saxony. On his own behalf Metternich was tantalizingly encouraging, but in the name of the emperor he could not speak. Only a formal demand could force the Austrians into action, and the chancellor set to work.

The note that resulted was relatively brief and contained no surprises.[43] Prussia must have Saxony in its entirety, the Wettins could be

---

[39] Above from last two of the later Twelve Articles, which Humboldt himself said were identical to the last two of his ten. See *ibid.*, 207f. and 212.

[40] Mett. to Sagan, 9 Oct. 1814, Ullrichová, ed., *Briefwechsel*, 267. He also sent her tickets for a ball that night, a fact that helps us establish the time of the conference.

[41] Bourgoing, *Wiener Kongress*, 112f.

[42] Hardenberg, "Tagebücher," 35.

[43] Text in d'Angeberg, *Congrès*, IV, 1934–1936. Original in Hardenberg's own hand in HHSA, StK., Kongressakten, Cart. 7, pp. 93–96.

transferred to the legations in Italy, and Mainz must come under Prussian control, if necessary, as a fortress of the confederation. If Metternich could promise these concessions "in the name of the emperor," then he, Hardenberg, would join the common front against Russia; specifically, "I will enter with you into the most perfect accord on Poland." The note has long been known and certainly marked a decisive point in the negotiations. Yet of still greater interest for our discussion is an annex, likewise long in print,[44] which showed in detail how the acquisition of Saxony could be reconciled with the overall territorial settlement in Germany. This was the plan alluded to earlier,[45] which would have expanded Bavaria by 241,000 souls, kept Württemberg essentially unchanged, and reduced the other South German states and Nassau to about the level of 1803 by stripping them of their mediatized lands. Hardenberg was again very careful to list the population of mediatized lands separately both in "attaching" (his word) 203,000 to Austria and 186,000 to Bavaria, and in stripping some 163,000 souls from Hesse-Darmstadt and Nassau. In other words, only Kreis chiefs were to possess mediatized properties.

If one counts souls as carefully as Hardenberg did, one must conclude that in addition to yielding on Saxony and Mainz Metternich was being asked to accept the "new system" discussed on 7 October, if not necessarily particular Kreis boundaries, at least the principle of creating Kreis estates out of the mediatized and lesser sovereign houses. In language borrowed from his London articles Hardenberg eloquently declaimed that "the sovereigns of Baden and Darmstadt and all the others who were aggrandized by suppressing their former co-estates cannot complain if the mediatized are now removed from them."[46]

Rereading the note the next morning, the chancellor scribbled a personal message for Metternich. "Believe me," he implored, "believe me, only in union and very intimate understanding between us is there any salvation . . . but I pray you, get on with the concert between us."[47] A little later Gentz arrived, possibly already expecting a note of this kind, and hastened back to Metternich with it. In the afternoon the two Austrians joined Hardenberg and Humboldt at dinner as the guests of Count Schulenburg, the still unofficial envoy of Saxony.[48] A strained occasion it must have been, even by the standards of the congress, where encounters of that kind were daily fare. A pity that Gentz wrote no more about it.

[44] In d'Angeberg, *Congrès*, IV, 1936–1939.
[45] See above, n. 10.
[46] *Ibid.*
[47] Hard. to Mett., 10 Oct. 1814, HHSA, StK., Kongressakten, Cart. 7, p. 94.
[48] Gentz, *Tagebücher*, I, 316f.

That evening the Austrians and the Prussians met among themselves to discuss German affairs, this time being joined by Wessenberg, who had recently replaced Binder as Metternich's deputy in this field.[49] The absence of Ernst Hardenberg suggests that a common strategy to meet Hanoverian objections to the lopsided advantages of the two powers was discussed. Although Saxony and Mainz were uppermost in every mind, the presence of Gentz and Wessenberg, both adamant foes of giving in, likely precluded any constructive discussion of those subjects; besides, only the pledge of the emperor could interest the Prussians now. But if the territorial issues were stalemated, Hardenberg's sketch of that morning, though hardly the final word on the distribution of the mediatized lands, at least left room for resuming negotiation on the institutional issues. All signs point to a final showdown that night before bringing the Hanoverians into the proceedings again. A revised draft in eleven articles which Humboldt produced the next day (or at the latest, a day after) tells the story.[50] Metternich has at last acquiesced in the tight organization of the Kreise, and Hardenberg has conceded Austria a watered-down directorship of the Bund as a whole.

For the first time since the Ten Articles of London Kreis estates and Kreis diets are mentioned; once more there appears the invidious distinction between states with more and states with less than 100,000 in population, not only as regards seats in the federal diet but also as to their rights and duties in the Kreise.[51] To be sure, the language was less explicit than before, affirming vaguely that the relationship of the Kreis chief to his Kreis estates would "vary according to the greater or lesser importance of the latter," and suggesting that the essential distinction was to be made between states with whole votes in the federal diet and those with fractional votes, a formula that drew the line at the population level of 100,000 except in a few cases where allowance was to be made for antiquity of lineage. No more was said, but for

[49] *Ibid.*, 317.

[50] There are two copies, neither of them known to previous writers. One is in ZSTA, Merseburg, 2.4.1.I, No. 1559, pp. 274–277, the other is NSHSA, Hanover, Des. 91, No. 24. The latter has the added advantage that it shows the revisions that converted it into the famous Twelve Articles of 14 October 1814 published by Klüber, *Acten*, I, 57–61, and by Schmidt, *Verfassungsfrage*, 209–212. No date is given, but since the Twelve Articles were initialed on the 12th, Humboldt must have drafted the eleven after the meeting of the 10th and in time for the conference held at Münster's bedside on the night of the 11th.

[51] Arts. V and VII of the Eleven Articles (VI and VIII of the Twelve), and it is to be noted that Klüber's reference to 200,000 in Art. VII/VIII is an error. A more serious discrepancy also occurs in this article; where Schmidt's version (see n. 50) has the Kreis chiefs directing the *Kreisverhandlungen*, the others speak of *Kreisversammlungen*. Either term could mean Kreis diets, but the latter is unequivocal and, in the context, undoubtedly correct. To even the score, on a lesser point in this article the Hanoverian copy corroborates Schmidt's use of *Bundesvertrag* against Klüber's *Bundesvertretung* as the thing the Kreis chiefs are to enforce.

Hardenberg it remained in the future only to fill in the details of the London articles, which aimed at depriving the smaller states of their armies, most of their taxing powers, and all but the most local police and judicial authority. Clearly, given his concurrent statements about the mediatized, these passages summarized his original ideas and not the Forty-one Articles at all.

The clue to the quid pro quo is given in the sixth of the eleven articles;[52] Austria alone was to be in charge of a "federal business directory," not as a director standing above the two houses but simply as the permanent chairman of each, the first among equals. As Metternich explained it a few days later before the full German committee, no real directory was intended but only a *Präsidium*, which would neither infringe the right of the other Kreis chiefs to introduce bills, nor deny them access to federal records, nor monopolize administrative appointments.[53] But why not call the office *Präsidium* if that is what it was? Evidently the reasoning was that while Austria would indeed exercise directorial powers, she would do so in public view, at the seat of the diet, always as the faithful servant of her peers, not as in the old days operating from the musty chambers that housed the supreme imperial offices in far-off Vienna. In the meantime, actual executive power would remain in the council of Kreis chiefs, where Prussia was the equal of Austria and together with her could, as the Hanoverians bitterly complained, still dominate the others, thus saving the essence of dualism after all. Indeed, Metternich assured the committee that the Prussians themselves had pressed this largely ceremonial office upon his country.[54]

If this was a reference to the Forty-one Articles, which had given

---

[52] I.e., Art. VII of the Twelve. Using some casual notes of Humboldt, Schmidt, *Verfassungsfrage*, 204f., convincingly demonstrates that one of the two articles eventually added to the original ten had to be either Art. VII or Art. VIII of the Twelve. To decide between the two he then scanned the Twelve Articles, seeking one that had no antecedent in the Forty-one Articles and concluded that Art. VII regarding the Austrian directorship was the one. This could indeed be the case, and if so, the argument for the last-minute capitulation by Hardenberg would be stronger. Schmidt, however, on the one hand passes over the Austrian chairmanship contained in Art. XX of the Forty-one Articles as a possible antecedent and on the other ignores in Art. VIII of the Twelve the elements (Kreis estates, etc.) which definitely differed from the content of the Forty-one. One should note, moreover, that *both* Art. VII and Art. VIII deal with the status and prerogatives of the Kreis chiefs. Art. VII: "The Kreis chiefs are completely equal in all their rights. Austria, to be sure, is in charge of directing business. . . ." Art. VIII then lists the duties of the Kreis chiefs, including that of "directing the Kreis assemblies and referring to the difference between the larger and the smaller states. My guess, therefore, is that the two articles were originally one and that the issues within them were in varying combinations linked from the beginning. In no case can we flatly assume that one or the other was missing in its entirety until the final draft.

[53] Protocol of 16 Oct. 1814, in Klüber, *Acten*, II, 82.

[54] *Ibid.*

Austria presidential honors within the two-power directory, the statement was technically true though in the altered context highly disingenuous. Hardenberg's reward in any case was the tight Kreis system, which in combination with a weak central authority gave him what he had sought all along except for his brief flirtation with Stein. Metternich's gain was less tangible. Only time would tell if the directory would prove to be as innocuous as it seemed or the forerunner of that glittering imperium for which Frank, Spiegel, and even Münster in his way yearned. But in the meantime Austria was on top again and Metternich more than ever in the central position. On the German Committee he could mediate between Prussia and the other kingdoms; for the small sovereigns, who dreaded the Kreise, there was now a visible rallying point; if the demand for imperial restoration became irresistible, Austria could answer it. *Präsidium, Direktorium,* or *Kaisertum*: Metternich could move in any direction as circumstances dictated, always assuming of course that the territorial impasse could be overcome.

With this question mark hovering silently overhead the meeting adjourned, Metternich hurrying off to his own quarters to serve as host at a supper for no fewer than 250 guests. At eleven o'clock the king of Prussia himself arrived and to the amazement of all began to waltz to melodies struck from a pianoforte by Princess Marie, the adored daughter of the foreign minister. If only *papa* could play his piece as well![55]

At the end of a long day the guests at length departed and Metternich trudged to his room. Even then he did not sleep; instead he penned an anguished note to Sagan, who, it seems, was completing a none-too-diplomatic transition to Prince Alfred Windischgrätz.[56] Still, as earlier observed, outpourings of this kind often marked the minister's confrontation with hard decisions in grand policy. With a tolerable federal arrangement in prospect he now neared the moment of decision. He must soon resolve in his own mind the fate of Saxony and convince the emperor. First, however, he decided to take one more look at his French alternative. Could France be counted upon if the break should come? Conversely, would Talleyrand understand if, for the time being, Austria approved Prussia's occupation of Saxony? At the same time he must do nothing that would jeopardize his first choice, the entente with Hardenberg.

Overcoming a state of exhaustion so consuming that observers were beginning to comment on his haggard appearance, he managed to receive Gentz promptly at nine the next morning and sent him, not to Talleyrand, but to Marshal Wrede, who could be counted upon to

[55] Gentz to Karadja, 11 Oct. 1814, Klinkowström, *Oesterreichs Theilnahme,* 450.
[56] McGuigen, *Duchess,* 357.

share his information with his friends from Paris.[57] Officially, in the name of his chief, Gentz sounded out the marshal on the prospects of an Austro-Bavarian alliance with France, at the same time strongly urging approval of the provisional transfer of the occupation to show "the entire universe" where the blame for a rupture would belong. Wrede, as it happened, was somewhat cool, fearing French designs on Bavarian left-bank territory, but this did not keep him from pouring out a full account to Talleyrand shortly thereafter.[58] In similar fashion, another aide of Metternich, probably Floret, soon appeared before the second-ranking French envoy, Duke Emmerich Joseph de Dalberg, to protest the aspersions that Talleyrand had been casting on Metternich's fortitude. On the contrary, the Austrian agent insisted, "you appear to us like the dogs who growl cleverly but do not bite, and we shall not bite alone."[59] Metternich thus kept his distance, but the two missions had a telling effect on Talleyrand, as we shall see.

Sometime after dispatching Gentz, Metternich received the plenipotentiary of Mecklenburg-Schwerin, Baron Leopold von Plessen. Although the arrangement of the audience was probably fortuitous, it was timely nonetheless, for Plessen represented one of the small states most affected by the decisions of the night just past. By the last days of September the content of the Forty-one Articles had become common knowledge, and in their consternation the envoys of the small states began to meet informally at luncheon, at cards, and in drawing rooms to commiserate and to grope their way to a common course. Their principal concerns were their exclusion from the German Committee, the threats to their internal legislation, and Prussia's towering position both as a codirector of the Bund and as chief of the Kreise to which most of them would fall. Unlike the mediatized houses, the lesser sovereigns did not favor a literal restoration, but they did see their salvation, much as the Rademacher committee did, in an Austrian imperium over a league strong enough to defend Germany and to preserve the literal equality of all its members without any Kreise at all.[60] Such were the worries that Plessen conveyed to Metternich from the well-worn sofa in the inner office.

Like most of us, Metternich was at his best when he had all the facts and his listener did not. On all counts he was amiably reassuring. While advising Plessen's constituents to refrain from formal protests against

[57] Gentz, *Tagebücher*, I, 317.
[58] Wrede to Montgelas, 12 Oct. 1814, GSA, Munich, MA 1028, pp. 72–77; and king's ministers to Jacourt, 16 Oct. 1814, Talleyrand, *Memoirs*, II, 255f.
[59] Talleyrand, *Memoirs*, II, 256.
[60] Police spy Goehausen to Police Chief Hager, 28 Sept. 1814, Weil, *Les Dessous*, I, 157f. A typical case is explained in Erich Keerl, *Herzog Ernst I von Sachsen-Coburg zwischen Napoleon und Metternich* (Erlangen, 1973), 158–167.

their exclusion, he dismissed the so-called German Committee as a purely private forum for exchanging views and preparing a working draft for submission in due course to an assembly of all the German states, a step, we should observe, that had not been mentioned since the first informal conference of 16 September, which the Prussians did not attend. In any case, Metternich continued, no state would be subordinate to any other, the "equality of rights of all princes as members of the Bund" would be scrupulously observed, and the prospects for preserving their "internal independence" were excellent.[61] Given the understanding with Prussia not yet a day old, these assurances at first glance seem little more than outright lies. Still, the language had more a predictive than a promissory quality, and allowing for certain eccentricities of interpretation, of which Metternich was always capable, it accurately described the course that he was following. In any case, Plessen was much relieved, whether justifiably or not.[62]

Later in the day Humboldt burst into Metternich's crowded anteroom and was promptly shown inside ahead of all the other suppliants.[63] We do not know the reason, but if it was to deliver the freshly drawn eleven articles, Metternich was evidently satisfied and agreeable to consulting the Hanoverians again, preferably Count Münster himself if the project was to be speedily concluded. The latter having partially recovered from his injuries, the conference took place that night at his bedside.[64]

Since Münster had expected Count Hardenberg to represent him as before, he had put his objections down on paper, and these he proceeded to read. Granting that the so-called "wholly German" states could not have the same freedom of war and alliance as Austria and Prussia, he nevertheless insisted that if either of the latter became involved in a non-German war, the lesser states must at least be free to ally with each other or even with the power at war; otherwise, caught in the middle, they could well be overrun while waiting patiently for a federal summons that never came, never came because the majority were not similarly threatened.[65] Correctly he foresaw that Bavaria and the others would never endorse the article as it stood. Turning to the exemption of the two powers from any federal regulation of their

---

[61] Plessen's report of 14 Oct. 1814 as quoted by Fritz Apian-Bennewitz, *Leopold von Plessen und die Verfassungspolitik der deutschen Kleinstaaten auf dem Wiener Kongress 1814/15* (Rostock, 1930), 30f.

[62] *Ibid.*, 30.

[63] McGuigen, *Duchess*, 358.

[64] Hardenberg, "Tagebücher," 35.

[65] Statement by Münster read in conference of 11 Oct. 1814, NSHSA, Hanover, Des. 91, No. 23, pp. 14f. Cf. Ritter, *Stein*, II, 283, who assumes without evidence that owing to the connection with England, freedom of foreign policy meant nothing to Hanover.

internal affairs, he pointed out that Denmark or Holland or even Hanover as a constituent of the British crown could claim the same right. With aches in his bones and bitterness in his heart Münster testily suggested that if only for the sake of appearance, Austria and Prussia might at least place whatever rights they did allow their subjects, "however paltry these might be," under the sanction of the Bund, where they would not be subject to arbitrary change by the sovereign.[66] The sarcasm was to no avail. Metternich and Hardenberg stood firm; and this may be the reason why Hanover was not among the sponsors of the project when it came before the German Committee several days later.[67]

In the meantime Metternich himself had had some second thoughts, reinforced, if not actually inspired by his interview with Plessen. Humboldt's draft still centered too much on the Kreise to the detriment of equality on the one hand and the central mechanism of the Bund on the other. To achieve a better balance Metternich succeeded in adding two new paragraphs. In Article II Humboldt had defined the purpose of the Bund as "the preservation of external peace and independence and the securing of the internal constitutional rights of every class of the nation," adding (probably at Metternich's insistence)[68] the rather mild condition that "in the federal covenant only this purpose shall limit the governmental rights of the several states."[69] Metternich now wanted something more positive and explicit, in the manner of a lawyer with potential will-breakers in mind. As a result, Humboldt's sentence was changed to read that in joining the Bund the states, "each and every one, retain the full and free enjoyment of their governmental rights insofar as these are not limited by the purpose stipulated in the above article and the said limitations are not expressly set forth in the federal covenant." For still greater emphasis the new passage was inserted as a separate article, number three in a draft that now ran to twelve.[70] Although Metternich probably justified the revision as a simple matter of tact in dealing with the lesser states, there was actually

[66] *Votum* originally drafted for Count Hardenberg to present on 11 Oct. 1814, NSHSA, Hanover, Des. 91, No. 23, pp. 11–13. Cf. Brandes, *Münster und die Wiedererstehung*, 102, who implies that Münster was satisfied with this arrangement.

[67] Klüber, *Acten*, I, 57, to the contrary notwithstanding.

[68] Humboldt's plans of December, 1813, and April, 1814, contained the first part almost verbatim but not the addition given here. Humboldt, *Gesammelte Schriften*, XI, 102 and 212.

[69] This and the following from "12 Deliberationspunkte," NSHSA, Hanover, Des. 91, No. 24, which shows the revisions made in converting the Eleven Articles into the Twelve. Cf. n. 50. That the revisions were Metternich's work cannot be documented, but they could not have come from any other party involved.

[70] Schmidt, *Verfassungsfrage*, 204–208, who did not know about the Eleven Articles, mistakenly deduced that the additional article resulted from dividing Art. I of Humboldt's original ten.

a change in substance: henceforth a Kreis chief could not take it upon himself to decide what was in keeping with the purpose of the Bund.[71]

Metternich's next proposal is traceable to an idea that Frank and Spiegel had urged upon him a few days before: the insistence that Kreis chiefs derive their powers from the Bund and not from any superior status of their own. The paragraph finally adopted to this effect, as a rider to Article VIII[72] regarding the functions of Kreis chiefs, deserves quotation in full:

> All rights which according to the federal covenant belong to the Kreis chiefs are exercised by the same not by virtue of an inherent power connected with their capacity as rulers [*Landesherren*]—since in this respect all other German states have equal rights with them— but rather as agents of the Bund and by virtue of the office entrusted to them by the Bund.

One's first reaction to these lines is shock at Metternich's grotesque concept of equal rights, and indeed it is likely that he represented the amendment to the Prussians mainly as one more farfetched device for reconciling the Kreis system with the accession treaties. Yet the true significance lay elsewhere.

For one thing, it was now theoretically possible to impeach a transgressing Kreis chief and replace him by another, the king of Württemberg by the grand duke of Baden for example. But more to the point, recalling that these articles were intended for eventual sanction by the great powers and the congress, the powers of the chiefs over their Kreis territories were now to be recognized as contingent on the continued existence of the Bund and their membership in it. In other words, if a Kreis chief should secede from the Bund or pursue reckless policies leading to its collapse, he would forfeit his tutelary rights over the other members of his Kreis. The measure struck equally at the Russophiles in Stuttgart, the Francophiles in Munich, and the persistent Prussian aspirants to an exclusive hegemony over North Germany. Only within the Bund as a whole would the Hohenzollerns have title to dominate the Hessian, Mecklenburg, and Thuringian duchies and all the mediatized lands raised to the level of Kreis estates. Austria, of course, was not affected since her two Kreise, at least in Metternich's

[71] Since the new version also offered Münster some protection against efforts to expand the role of the Bund in uniform legislation of utilitarian value (which Ernst Hardenberg had resisted in the preliminary conferences) it is possible that he was the instigator of the new article. I choose Metternich, however, partly because the Hanoverian documents do not include the issue among their grievances here, partly because the style suggests Wessenberg as the drafter, and finally because Art. VI, dealing with legislation, would have been a better place to head off the threat.

[72] I.e., in the new and final numbering of the Twelve Articles.

thinking, would encompass nothing but her own crown lands and Bohemia. A minor revision pointed in the same direction. In Article V the clause, "the council of Kreis chiefs is made up of Austria, Prussia" et cetera was now changed to read: "in the council of Kreis chiefs there appear Austria, Prussia," et cetera as if the organ existed juridically prior to the appointment of its members.

Thus Metternich had deftly turned the tables: in the public law of Europe the Kreise were to owe their existence to the Bund, not the other way around. The insight probably originated with the councilors on the Rademacher committee, but the political twist that Metternich gave it was eminently his own, the more ingenious in that Hardenberg, even if he perceived the implications, could not object without exposing his own hegemonial ambitions for Prussia. Humboldt, who had once warned against the danger of large masses, may even have welcomed the stipulation.[73]

The meeting in Münster's rooms were continued the next day, 12 October, to approve the final wording of the amendments (probably the work of Wessenberg rather than Humboldt) and possibly to settle a related issue: the anomalous status of Hanover on the German Committee and the council of Kreis chiefs. Politically, of course, her favored status resulted from the English tie, but in the framework of German values she was still technically an electorate and the only member of either body not of royal rank, at least since the decision to drop Baden (a grand duchy) and Hesse-Cassel (also still an electorate) from the projected council. To give their program a more convincing rationale, especially in the atmosphere created by Talleyrand's intrigues among the lesser states, Metternich and Hardenberg had been urging Münster to declare Hanover a kingdom. He had hesitated, however, partly because he still hoped for an imperial restoration that would revalidate the electoral title and partly because within this category Hanover had obvious precedence over Württemberg, which had acquired the electorate only in 1803, followed by the kingship in 1806. In the context of the Twelve Articles, however, the title of kingdom was clearly more appropriate; and so with their tentative adoption on 12 October Münster on the same day released a circular dispatch declaring Hanover's claim to that rank, as justification arguing that "kingdom" was merely a modern name for electorate and explicitly contrasting the antiquity of Hanover with the parvenu character of Württemberg. "What a grand title for such a small and poor land" was Stein's peevish comment.[74]

[73] I.e., in his plan of December, 1813. See above, chap. III, pp. 68f.

[74] Brandes, *Münster und die Wiedererstehung*, 75–76; text of declaration of 12 Oct. 1814 in d'Angeberg, *Congrès*, II, 279; Stein, "Tagebücher," *Briefe*, v, 322. The royal patent promulgated on 26 Oct. 1814, which ratified the declaration, was even more

It is now time to review the Twelve Articles, trying to determine as best we can the authorship of the various passages. Article I, which restored the broader definition of federal territory and forbade the secession of any member, represented the new consensus among all concerned. Article II, stating the purpose of the Bund as quoted above was pure Humboldt, now that the statement regarding reserved rights had been strengthened and made into Article III, almost certainly at Metternich's bidding. Article IV read that the functions of the Bund were to be carried out a) by a federal assembly consisting of the council of Kreis chiefs and a council of princes and estates, and "b) by the influence over the estates of his Kreis conferred on each Kreis chief," this to be exerted "as prescribed in the federal covenant and under the supervision of the federal assembly." The reference to federal assembly was probably Metternich's contribution, in line with his emphasis on the whole diet as opposed to the upper house alone, which the Forty-one Articles spoke of in this connection. On the other hand, assigning the Kreise equal standing with the central organs of the Bund sounds definitely Prussian in tone.

Article V named the five Kreis chiefs, Austria and Prussia having two Kreise (not delineated) and two votes as in the September agreement between Metternich and Hardenberg. As a council they were to exercise all federal executive power, make war and peace, represent the Bund in foreign affairs where it functioned as a collective whole, and share legislative power with the lower council. Aside from the restrictive reference to a collective whole, which reflected Metternich's language with the king of Württemberg and left open some freedom for the separate states, these powers were much the same as those set forth in the Forty-one Articles.

The sixth article dealt with the lower house, the name of which was changed at the last minute to the council of princes and *cities* (rather than estates) probably for the sake of accuracy as well as to eliminate the implied distinction between sovereign and mediatized houses, which the Prussians in particular no longer desired. The article echoed Humboldt's idea, broached in his April memoir, of including the Kreis chiefs individually in the membership and Hardenberg's distinction (originally made in the London plan) between states above and below 100,000 in population, the former casting whole votes, the latter sharing a vote with others. Since the Forty-one Articles had drawn this line at 50,000, the effect was to reduce the representation of small sovereigns at the federal level and to set the standard (alluded to in Article VIII) for differential treatment at the Kreis level as well, a change fully in line

explicit in asserting precedence over Württemberg. Text in Klüber, *Acten*, Vol. I, Part 1, 65–67.

with Hardenberg's aim of downgrading the lower house. This aim was further reflected, again as in the London phraseology, in a vague and perfunctory statement of the council's legislative function, which was to be shared with the upper council despite the fact that the Kreis chiefs had seats in the former as well. The power to promote common law codes, uniform coinage, weights, and measures, and the regulation of commerce, expressly set forth in the Forty-one Articles, was deleted and in future was to appear again only in the *Austrian* projects! The Standesherren were neither awarded nor denied seats, presumably for tactical reasons since future plans did include them. Otherwise the article was Prussian through and through.

There followed Articles VII and VIII, the one awarding the directory to Austria, the other enumerating the powers of the Kreis chiefs and reviving the provision for Kreis assemblies and Kreis estates, the latter as previously explained, to be treated differently according to size and in a few cases antiquity of lineage. Article VIII ended then with the Metternich proviso that Kreis chiefs were to function solely as officers of the Bund.

In Article IX the Austrians and Prussians alike ignored Münster's objections and, strictly following the Hardenberg articles, banned all independent wars and extra-German alliances by the wholly German states while reserving complete freedom of action for themselves. Whether the Bund should join in great-power wars was to be decided by "the Bund" itself on the motion of the belligerent member. Since Hardenberg had pointedly, in one of the amendments sent to Solms on 26 July, assigned such decisions to the upper council alone, we may surmise that Metternich, again on the advice of the Rademacher committee, had succeeded in enlarging the role of the lower house.[75] Oddly enough, the principle that an attack on any federal territory was an attack on the whole Bund, though generally assumed, was not mentioned.

The remaining three articles have already been discussed: Article X, with its provisions for adjudicating disputes with the aid of a federal court; Article XI, which called for *landständische Verfassungen* and the later drafting of a bill of minimum estates' rights—with the Metternichian proviso that local conditions be taken into account; and Article XII alluding to a similar bill of individual rights and positing the all-important exemption of Austria and Prussia from any of the above. The last paragraph, ultimately traceable to Solms-Laubach as we have seen, certainly won Metternich's approval quickly enough, but its ap-

[75] See Note to Art. XXXVI in Klüber, *Acten*, Vol. I, Part 1, 55.

pearance in Humboldt's first draft in ten articles suggests that it suited Hardenberg equally well, though probably not Humboldt himself.

Traditionally the Twelve Articles have been measured against the liberalism and national unity thought to be imbedded in the Forty-one Articles; almost all accounts speak of "retrogression" or "watering down," some blaming Metternich for a work of demolition, others acknowledging his collaboration but imputing to him ulterior motives or duress.[76] This view is understandable but misguided. Apart from changing a directory of two into a modified directory of one (if that really represented a weakening), Metternich's amendments were either tactical in nature (e.g., deferring the wrangling over rights to a more propitious time) or actually in the direction of centralism (favoring the lower house and its legislative powers and making Kreis chiefs federal officials). Hardenberg's direction, on the other hand, was toward a number of large masses only loosely joined at the top, his revival of Kreis diets and Kreis estates, to which the mediatized houses would be elevated, being the greatest single departure from the Forty-one Articles and the influence of Baron Stein. Indeed, the ease with which he abandoned essential features of his long draft and returned not to the bland first version influenced by Metternich but to the severe Ten Articles of London raises doubts about the earnestness of his dealings with Stein and debases the one document that has always been taken as the authentic statement of Hardenberg's German policy.

Conversely, Metternich's general spirit of cooperation should occasion no surprise. Aside from the imperatives of grand policy, which dictated accommodation with Hardenberg at almost any price, the Twelve Articles cost Austria little and gained her much: broad military protection from the side of the Bund without interference in her internal affairs, and a privileged position as business director, which Metternich could use to influence the matters set aside for future negotiation. The test of his own earnestness was still to come.

An entirely different opinion of the Twelve Articles was forthcoming the next morning when Metternich summoned Rademacher upstairs, complimented him on his critique of the Forty-one Articles, and as-

[76] E.g., Gebhardt, *Humboldt als Staatsmann*, II, 135f., and Huber, *Verfassungsgeschichte*, I, 545f., both of whom call the Twelve Articles "retrograde" but capable of development; and Aretin, *Bayerns Weg*, 156, who believes that the article on estates constitutions was now so loose that "even representative constitutions fashioned after the French model" could be accommodated. More positive are Hans-Joachim Hartmann, *Das Schicksal der preussisch-österreichischen Verfassungsvorschläge insbesondere des Entwurf vom 14. Oktober 1814 auf dem Wiener Kongress* (Göttingen, 1964), 31, who believes the project, if realized, could have created a *Bundesstaat*; and Griewank, "Preussen und die Neuordnung," 249, who believes that Metternich's defense of the Twelve Points was sincere. Cf. Real, *Deutsche Verfassungsfrage*, 24, and Srbik, *Metternich*, I, 200.

sured him that he had "succeeded in bringing the Prussians to abandon this project completely."[77] He then sent the councilor to fetch the latest version from Wessenberg, who wanted an opinion that same day, in time to discuss it with Metternich at dinner. Hastily convening, the commissioners immediately focused their attention on the removal of Baden and Hesse-Cassel from the council of Kreis chiefs, seeing in the change nothing less than a plot by "perfidious Prussia" to line up Bavaria and Württemberg to promote their treasonous schemes of aggrandizement against an Austria crippled by the loss of the imperial crown. Austria, they agreed, would do better to bring all the other states into the deliberations at once. "It is scarcely believeable," Frank said, "how strong the sentiment for Austria is," and considered resigning if the procedure was not changed, just to protect his reputation. Rademacher was more modest, requesting only a chance to sit down with Humboldt and work things out.

The good commissioners could not know, of course, that Metternich in his own way did in fact keep the lesser states very much in mind, but it must have been sheer anger that blinded them to the influence they had already exerted in making the Kreis chiefs federal officials. In any case, true to his charge, Rademacher, who took time for his midday meal and left none for copying the articles, returned them to Wessenberg at four in the afternoon, acidly suggesting that if Metternich felt reassured by them, he must not have read them. As it turned out, the haste was not necessary; since the emperor had not yet returned his copy of the articles, the first full meeting of the German Committee, which had been scheduled for that night, was postponed till the next day.[78] As a result the Twelve Articles were not officially adopted as the Austro-Prussian plan until 14 October, but even so, only a week had passed—it may seem longer to the weary reader of these events—since the first formal conference on the 7th.

Obviously such progress was possible because both Metternich and Hardenberg, each on the string of a balky monarch, dared not let go of each other. And all the while the pressure continued to mount. After the chancellor's official demand for Saxony had gone out on 10 October, Castlereagh was prompt to throw all his weight behind it, arguing that a strong Prussia was essential "for the security of North

[77] This and the following from Rademacher's "Registratur über das, was in Absicht auf die Verhandlungen wegen der deutschen Foederations-Verhältnisse vorgekommen ist," 16 Oct. 1814, HHSA, StK., Kongressakten, Cart. 6, pp. 76–77; and Frank's "Einige flüchtige Betrachtungen über das neuere preussische Projekt," 15 Oct. 1814, HHSA, StK., Deutsche Akten, Fasc. 106, pp. 55–58.

[78] Wessenberg to Hard., 13 Oct. 1814, ZSTA, Merseburg, 2.4.1.I., No. 1559, p. 299; and Wessenberg to Münster, 13 Oct. 1814, NSHSA, Hanover, Des. 91, No. 23.

Germany against the greatest dangers that threaten it." He insisted only that Prussia must regard the acquisition not as compensation for a poor frontier in Poland but as her reward for insisting on a strong one. In the former case, he could hold out little "hope that Great Britain would consent to such an arrangement in the face of Europe." In this way he made clear on the one hand that British support did not apply to Alexander's plan of compensation and on the other reassured Hardenberg that gains in Poland would not be counted against him in regard to Saxony.[79] In a second, less formal note Castlereagh even made the case for the deed, emphasizing less the legal technicalities of treaties than the king of Saxony's total commitment to Napoleon. If Russia must be compensated at the expense of her Prussian ally, he asked, why was it wrong for Prussia to be compensated at the expense of an enemy? Compensation elsewhere could only be at the cost of somebody less guilty.[80] So much for legitimacy.

The argument was neither new nor, in Hardenberg's case, necessary. Its true target was Metternich, who received copies of both notes on 11 October, so quickly in fact that the second was still in the original English as was a private covering letter. "If there are any *Tender Consciences* [sic] on the part of Saxony," Castlereagh wrote with unaccustomed cynicism, "the enclosed memorandum appears to me to contain more than Enough of argument to reconcile them." Begging for a formal commitment as soon as possible, he went on to chide Metternich for "the excessive delays which are interposed in Congress Subjects."[81]

At their regular morning conference on the 12th Metternich gave the English memorandum to Gentz for translation and that evening, after the completion of the Twelve Articles during the day, once more discussed the situation with him and Wessenberg. He found little sympathy. Mounting anger had accompanied Gentz's efforts at the translation; emboldened by Wessenberg's presence, he turned on his chief "the most energetic language he has ever heard from me,"[82] and sneered at the logic of the British argument that what seemed vital to North Germany if Prussia was strong in the east, apparently ceased to be so

[79] Castle. to Hard., 11 Oct. 1814, d'Angeberg, *Congrès*, II, 274–276. Griewank, *Wiener Kongress*, 165f., comments that the language is unclear since greater Prussian gains in Poland would diminish her claims to Saxony, but it was precisely against this reasoning that Castlereagh wished to reassure Hardenberg.

[80] Castle. to Hard., *Note verbale*, Oct. 1814, d'Angeberg, *Congrès*, II, 276–278.

[81] English version of *note verbale* and Castle. to Mett., private letter of "Monday night" in HHSA, StK., Kongressakten, Cart. 7. An archivist evidently assumed that Monday the 17th was meant and penciled 18 Oct. on the English memorandum, but the overwhelming evidence points to Monday the 10th. Cf. Webster, *Castlereagh*, I, 344. A copy sent to Wellington in Paris is dated the 17th, to be sure, but that only shows that the memorandum was used several times over.

[82] Gentz, *Tagebücher*, I, 318.

if she was weak. It was in any case folly, he went on, to concede the provisional occupation until it was clear which of the two options Prussia would choose.[83]

Metternich was unmoved. As often before Gentz's analysis was rooted in an intellectual's love of abstraction, which confused the coherence of ideas with the logic of politics. In Metternich's more concrete calculations Prussia's retention of Saxony would depend in the long run on combinations that would take form one way or another long before her provisional control became entrenched, and in the meantime was it not better to have Prussian forces installed there than Russian? To challenge Hardenberg at this time on the lesser issue would risk everything. When Gentz returned the finished translation the next morning, he glumly advised that if Saxony must be sacrificed after all, Austria should at least base the "pernicious undertaking" on sheer duress and expressly disclaim for it any foundation in law or justice. "I have translated this note with a feeling of shame," he wrote. "It is hard to conceive how men with reputations to lose can lend their names to such drivel."[84] Two days later Metternich officially announced that the emperor Francis approved the Prussian occupation.[85]

[83] "Projet de response à quelques passages du memorandum de lord Castlereagh sur la Saxe," Gentz, *Briefe von und an*, III, 304, n. 1.

[84] Gentz to Mett., 13 Oct. 1814, *ibid.*, 303f.

[85] Hard. to Stein, 15 Oct. 1814, Stein, *Briefe*, v, 166; Hardenberg, "Tagebücher," 35.

CHAPTER VII

THE ROAD TO DECISION

EXCEPT for the weather, which held uniformly fine from 15 September till late October, the Congress of Vienna, still unofficial, seemed to have a rhythm all its own, apart from any individual will and indifferent to daylight or dark, Sunday or weekday. Each day had a distinctive character. On some business came to a halt for festivities like those attending the entry of the tsar into the city. Other days seemed, as if by common consent, set aside for plotting strategy, digesting the results of conferences, and drafting papers for negotiations to come. Then there were times when everybody seemed to be in conference at once. Such a day was 14 October, when all the major parties to the German-constitution question were in concerted action: the would-be Kreis chiefs, the smaller states consigned to the lower house, the mediatized houses, and almost a committee of one, Baron Stein, upholding, with growing acerbity toward all the rest, the pretensions of the *Ritterschaft*.

Technically, of course, the plenipotentiaries of the Kreis chiefs were as yet only the constituent members of the committee on the German constitution, the body that Metternich at 1:00 p.m. called to order for the first time. The meeting took place in Prince Wrede's quarters overlooking the Kärntner Gate, in part to remove the deliberations from the anxious glances of the small-state envoys, who thronged the chancellery, partly as well to flatter the marshal and reinforce the notion that all participants were equal. Even the seating showed a random order that carried no suggestion of rank and precedence. On one side of the long narrow table sat Metternich, Hardenberg and Humboldt (the Prussians were always together), Ernst Hardenberg, and Martens, who served as secretary. Across from them were Wrede, Linden, Münster, and Wessenberg. Only after the meeting did Metternich take Linden aside to inform him as delicately as possible of Hanover's new title and claim to precedence over Württemberg.[1] Wrede and Linden as the newcomers to the discussion were at a disadvantage: outnumbered, generally ignorant of the Twelve Articles, and, despite their many informal discussions together, uncertain whether they were allies or rivals.

As mentioned earlier, the Bavarians would have preferred no Bund at all, but if there must be one, so Montgelas had ordered, its purpose

---

[1] Linden to King Frederick, 14 Oct. 1814, extr. in Pfister, *Lage der Verbündeten*, 327.

had to be expressly limited to "guaranteeing the full and absolute sovereignty" of its members. To this end there might be a diet restricted to the states of kingdom rank and operating under an alternating presidency, its power limited to arbitrating interstate disputes, declaring war, and electing a commander-in-chief in time of war. In no case, however, must the individual members' right of war and alliance be infringed; nor could Bavaria tolerate interference with the new constitution then being prepared by a commission in Munich. On the other hand, Montgelas favored the extensive absorption of the smaller states by the greater; and although he probably had conventional mediatization in mind, it is obvious that the Kreis system set forth in the Twelve Articles would have comparable appeal. This was the lure that kept Wrede from boycotting the proceedings or even demanding that the territorial question come first as he had originally intended, and as Montgelas, in fact, ordered after it was too late.[2]

Linden's position was essentially the same except for variations in tactics, Wrede's orders stressing the importance of "leaning on the favor of the French embassy," whereas Linden was directed to cling unswervingly to Russia. Like Wrede, he put the territorial question first, ironically, however, because the kind of Bund Württemberg could accept depended most on her position vis-à-vis Bavaria. If dwarfed or enveloped by her rival, effective federal protection would be needed; if more nearly equal—Linden's instructions called for doubling the population to about 2.5 million—Stuttgart could collaborate with Munich in undertaking to keep the Bund weak, their bridges to France and Russia intact. King Frederick's hope for such aggrandizement had originally been predicated upon vigorous support from the tsar, who was thought to desire a large mass against France. Both Winzingerode's reports from St. Petersburg, however, and Frederick's own experience with the tsar in Vienna were disappointing in this regard. By contrast, it was Metternich who emphasized the need for strength on the Rhine and dangled before the king the enticing Swabian Kreis as an alternative to direct annexations. To keep this prospect alive, Linden had to participate in the deliberations, but as we shall see, always with fingers crossed.[3]

The meeting went smoothly enough, largely because the business was confined to establishing the competence of the committee, which none of those present had any reason to doubt. Even Wrede and

[2] Winter, *Wrede als Berater*, 161–165; Real, *Deutsche Verfassungsfrage*, 26–32; Aretin, "Deutsche Politik Bayerns," 5–8; *idem., Bayerns Weg*, 147–149; and Michael Doeberl, *Entwicklungsgeschichte Bayerns*, 3 vols. (Munich, 1908–1931), II, 549.

[3] Real, *Deutsche Verfassungsfrage*, 36–41; Pfister, *Lage der Verbündeten*, 302–304; Hölzle, *Württemberg im Zeitalter*, 167.

Linden, however, were amazed at the reasoning used, for they were encountering for the first time Hardenberg's thesis that all the other states' treaties of accession pledged them to accept in advance the power's idea of "whatever definitive order of things was required to preserve the independence of Germany."[4] "General laughter," King Frederick was told, greeted this latest twisting of the accession treaties— "to the disgrace of the politics of our times," he added, perhaps uneasy about what this meant for his own guarantees.[5] To explain to the outcasts that the committee was obligated by the sanctity of treaties to exclude them presented a delicate problem, and Martens was directed to solve it by drafting a declaration glazing this argument with reassurances that no constitution would take effect before the other states had seen it. It was also his task to draw up the protocol to be read at the next meeting, an English innovation that departed from the continental practice of approving minutes while those present could still insert extended statements. At least the Hanoverians could no longer complain of Humboldt's biased reporting.[6]

It may seem incongruous that Metternich, hitherto a strict constructionist, now seemed to endorse Hardenberg's tortured interpretation of the treaties, which did not specify who should make the decisions about German security. Still, given the need to proceed with a small group, a basis in treaty was better than an appeal to sheer power and convenience, which were also adduced at the meeting. In the end, moreover, the true test of whether the treaties were observed or not would be the kind of settlement that was eventually enforced. It was one thing to argue that key points like Mainz must be in strong hands or that military efficiency required large, unitary masses like the Kreise; it was quite another to impose the territorial scale of 1803 or confer judicial, administrative, and executive powers on the Kreis chiefs as if these, too, were indispensable to the independence of Germany. Unlike Hardenberg, Metternich really intended to consult the excluded states, in the meantime doing what he could for them without breaking step with the Prussian chancellor or disillusioning the king of Württemberg. As always before, a consensus among all concerned was more important than any particular facet of the German constitution.

In the meantime, the uninvited envoys of the lesser states were holding a meeting of their own. Originally they had thought to challenge the legality of the committee and demand representation on it. At a meeting on 12 October, however, Plessen of Mecklenburg-Schwerin,

---

[4] For this and following, protocol of 14 Oct. 1814, in Klüber, *Acten*, II, 70–74.

[5] Frederick to Mandelsloh, 17 Oct. 1814, HSA, Stuttgart, E 1, Fasc. 45.

[6] Klüber, *Acten*, II, 74n.; *idem.*, *Uebersicht der diplomatischen Verhandlungen des Wiener Congresses*, 3 vols. (Frankfurt, 1816), I, 44.

recounting his interview with Metternich and another with Humboldt, persuaded them to concentrate instead on undermining the Forty-one Articles. At this point Hans Christoph von Gagern entered the picture, a plenipotentiary for both Duke Frederick William of Nassau and Prince William of Orange-Nassau. An urbane man with broad European experience, he had proceeded cautiously, awaiting signals from Stein and Münster before offering his leadership, his sumptuous rooms in the Bräunerstrasse, and his celebrated wine cellar, all financed by a generous expense account from the Netherlands. It was at his invitation that the small-state envoys gathered for dinner and business on the 14th.[7]

Driven by an intense fear of Prussia, Gagern hoped to combine Nassau, the two Hesses, and Brunswick into a bloc closely tied to the Netherlands and functioning, along with Hanover, as a counterweight to Prussia in an empire effectively headed by Austria. As the price of empire he believed that the lesser states must do something for the mediatized, and *landständische Verfassungen* were obviously a lesser evil than the assimilation of small sovereigns and Standesherren in the dreaded Kreise. His primary concern, however, was the equality of all states under the benevolent protection of an Austrian emperor and with a minimum of federal interference in their internal affairs.[8] The second plenipotentiary of Nassau, Baron Ernst von Marschall von Bieberstein, shared the house in the Bräunerstrasse. No friend of provincial estates, he nonetheless had spent the summer fashioning a constitution for Nassau along the lines suggested in the Forty-one Articles, partly to forestall federal action, partly to humor Baron Stein, who was by far the most influential son of Nassau and occupied the floor above Gagern's apartment. Marschall, a brusque and short-tempered man, was still jousting with Stein over the proper powers of the estates—among other things he wished to deny them a legislative function—and he frequently collided with Gagern, who had Dutch interests to defend as well. With varying degrees of enthusiasm, then, the household stood for Austrian imperium, the equality of all states, and at least as an unavoidable political necessity, estates-style constitutions. Metternich could get along with people like that.[9]

---

[7] Apian-Bennewitz, *Plessen und die Verfassungspolitik*, 31–34; Agent Goehausen to Hager, 15 Oct. 1814, in Weil, *Les Dessous*, I, 306f.; and Hellmuth Rössler, *Zwischen Revolution und Reaktion. Ein Lebensbild des Reichsfreiherrn Hans Christoph von Gagern, 1766–1852* (Göttingen, Berlin, and Frankfurt, 1958), 162f.

[8] *Ibid.*, 163–165.

[9] Apian-Bennewitz, *Plessen und die Verfassungsfrage*, 134; Hans Sarholz, "Das Herzogtum Nassau 1813–1815. Ein Beitrag zur Geschichte des Rheinbundes und der Befreiungskriege," *Nassauische Annalen*, LVII (1937), 8of. and 92f.; Stein to Marschall, 10 Aug. 1814, Stein, *Briefe*, v, 106f.; and Marschall to Stein, 10 Aug. 1814, *ibid.*, v, 107–109.

The same was true, by and large, of the smaller states represented at the meeting. Plessen was under orders from Grand Duke Frederick to accept any central authority however strong, provided that the federal powers were vested in an assembly in which all states were represented as equals: in other words, no Kreise and no directing committee. His colleague from Mecklenburg-Strelitz, Baron August von Oertzen, had similar orders, except that if necessary, he might accept Kreise provided that they were confined to military affairs, did not include the east-Elbian territories (where Strelitz was located), and that the Kreis chiefs had no more votes than the smaller states. Similar views were held by—to take only the more distinguished—Günther Heinrich von Berg, a law professor representing Waldeck and Schaumburg-Lippe, Wilhelm von Schmidt-Phiseldeck of Brunswick, Johann Smidt of Bremen, and Johann Michael Gries from Hamburg, who spent his free hours at the congress translating Calderón.[10]

What all their states had in common were modest size, few territorial problems, remoteness from France, close proximity to Prussia, little interest in independent military and foreign policies, and practically no mediatized subjects. They had, as a result, little to fear from traditional estates constitutions, a federal court, or a military system to which they would merely deliver recruits. What they needed most was protection from Prussia and her Kreise, and this, they believed, would be more certain if Austria reacquired the grandeur of the imperial office and with it supervision of the federal army. Otherwise they made little distinction between the terms Bund and Reich.

For the larger states in the group, the true middle states, the issues were complicated by pending territorial exchanges, an abomination of estates assemblies, and an ambivalent attitude toward the Kreis system. Having been excluded from the German Committee, they had to assume that they would not be chiefs, but the more Metternich depreciated the significance of the committee, the more one could hope, and for a Kreis chief the Twelve Articles had their attractions, for which constitutions might be an acceptable price to pay.

One of the aspirants was Charles Augustus of Saxe-Weimar, ably represented in Gagern's group by Baron Ernst August von Gersdorff. Goethe said of his patron: "Narrow and small is his land / Circumscribed what he can do." And it was true: with a population of about 110,000, Saxe-Weimar was not a true middle state. But if the duke could acquire Erfurt, Fulda, and part of Saxony, which he especially

<hr />

[10] Apian-Bennewitz, *Plessen und die Verfassungsfrage*, 30–33; Real, *Deutsche Verfassungsfrage*, 55–63; and Jacob Grimm to Wilhelm Grimm, 2 Nov. 1814, in Jacob and Wilhelm Grimm, *Briefwechsel . . . aus der Jugendzeit*, ed. Hermann Grimm and Gustav Hinrichs, 2nd ed., ed. Wilhelm Schoof (Weimar, 1963), 368.

coveted, and if backed by the tsar, who had already promised to nom-
inate him for elevation to grand ducal rank, who could tell? As head
of the Ernestine line, he instructed Gersdorff, he would have first claim
to lead a Thuringian Kreis, should one be created from the five Saxon
duchies and other petty states in the area. Or, if a combined Thurin-
gian-Upper Saxon Kreis materialized, he should at least be a codirector.
In the meantime, prudence dictated solidarity with the small states,
whose interests in other respects were about the same as Weimar's, so
long as provincial estates were kept under the tight control of the ruling
prince.[11] Hence, when the Twelve Articles became known, with their
provision for only five Kreis chiefs, nobody worked harder than Gersdorff and his master to defeat them. Blaming "that miserable China-
man, von Humboldt," the duke insisted that he was "in open warfare
with the Prussians and [would] never set foot near them." For the
foreseeable future his hopes centered on Austria.[12]

As a prospective Kreis chief Charles Augustus was obviously a long
shot. Less remote appeared the chances of the two rulers originally
named codirectors in the Forty-one Articles: Charles of Baden and
Elector William of Cassel. Charles in fact feared that association with
the smaller states would compromise his chances and ordered his envoy, Baron Karl von Hacke, to keep clear of the Gagern group. Hacke,
as a result, did not attend the meeting but dealt directly with Humboldt
and Wessenberg, still hoping for a place on the German Committee.
Seeing the futility of this, he advised collaboration with the other outcasts after all, but Charles preferred to play a lone hand, confident
that he could always turn for support to his brother-in-law the tsar.[13]

William's situation was different. Just recently restored, his electoral
title still intact, he did not fear an imperial restoration, at least of the
kind that the small states were promoting. On the contrary, only on
the basis of imperial concepts could he use the title to advantage,
asserting precedence over his cousin in Darmstadt, whose position
depended on Rheinbund antecedents. He even dreamed of reuniting
the two states under a Greater Hessian crown that would alternate
between the two lines and command parity with the other kingdoms.
For this goal he was willing, if necessary, to pay the price of granting
an estates constitution. Taking his stand on imperial precedents, then,
he saw the small states as valuable allies to be solicited by his able

[11] Charles August's instructions for Gersdorff, 22 Sept. 1814, in Carl August,
Politischer Briefwechsel, III, 256-259. Also Hermann von Egloffstein, *Carl August auf
dem Wiener Kongress* (Jena, 1915), 27–32.
[12] Charles August to Duchess Louise, 17 Nov. 1814, in Carl August, *Politischer
Briefwechsel*, III, 262f.; and Egloffstein, *Carl August*, 32–36.
[13] Glaser, "Die badische Politik," 285–291; Real, *Deutsche Verfassungsfrage*, 41–45;
and Mager, "Problem der landständischen Verfassungen," 307f., n. 34.

plenipotentiary, Count Dorotheus Ludwig Keller, who carried unusual weight in that company because he had once represented Prussia in Vienna and was cultivated by Metternich's more imperial-minded enemies at home. He was assisted by a deputy, Georg Ferdinand von Lepel, and a young counselor of legation named Jacob Grimm, who used his free hours for the pursuit of German folklore.[14]

Almost of necessity but also by conviction one of Keller's closest collaborators in the group was Baron Johann von Türckheim, representing Grand Duke Louis of Hesse-Darmstadt, which, whether joined to Cassel or not, was certain to create difficulties when it came to drawing Kreis boundaries. An imperial knight with estates in the old province of the Ortenau, Türckheim was a patriot of the old school and had close personal ties with the Rademacher committee. For him, estates constitutions were a matter of principle, not mere diplomatic prudence. "My hair stands on end," he said, "when I hear talk about the sovereignty of the German princes."[15] Only his strong, even blind, Austrian sympathies and considerable diplomatic talents kept him his post; for, as one could readily guess, his master was as fanatical in the other direction, refusing to be panicked into granting a constitution as the other South German rulers were doing and viewing the future German league as essentially a new Rheinbund under Austrian protection. His instructions for Türckheim, to be sure, left room for a federal army under Austrian command, provided that he, Louis, became a Kreis chief, either in his own right or alternating in the post with his relatives in Cassel. Either way, it was imperative that Türckheim assert the precedence of a grand duchy over an electorate. Louis did not flatly forbid Türckheim to fraternize with the Gagern group but only because it provided a refuge should his bid for a Kreis directorate fail.[16]

The tension between the headstrong plenipotentiary and this most obdurate of all Rheinbund sovereigns, who both cultivated the tsar and was ready to switch to Napoleon again were he to make a comeback in France, persisted throughout the congress, imparting to the policies of Hesse-Darmstadt an erratic quality, which was aggravated by Louis's decision to remain at home. Metternich had little direct contact with Türckheim but in the end chose him alone of the entire group to receive one of Austria's most coveted decorations, the Order of St. Stephen, "for exhibiting the greatest accommodation and attachment

---

[14] Dietrich, "Hessen-Darmstadt auf dem Wiener Kongress," 183; Philipp Losch, *Geschichte des Kurfürstentums Hessen 1803 bis 1866* (1922; reprint ed. Cassel, 1972), 88–100; and Police agent to Hager, 15 Oct. 1814, Weil, *Les Dessous*, I, 296.

[15] Quoted by Dietrich, "Hessen-Darmstadt auf dem Wiener Kongress," 170.

[16] *Ibid.*, 150–180; and Real, *Deutsche Verfassungsfrage*, 45–54.

to the all highest court." The others, he said, had done nothing worthy of notice.[17]

Such were the opinions, the calculations, the *arrières pensées*, and the sometimes tortured interpretation of instructions lodged in the heads that came together in the Bräunerstrasse on 14 October. The immediate issues were representation on the German Committee and the fate of the imperial restoration that all preferred in some form. Opening the meeting, Gagern proposed a strong statement of expectations on both counts. Recalling Metternich's advice, however, Plessen advised doing nothing until Austria's intentions were clearer, especially as the news was out (probably by a leak from Baron Frank) that the Rademacher committee strongly favored a supreme head, whatever he was called. Accordingly Plessen proposed another discreet mission to Metternich, this time by Count Keller, who carried the prestige of an electorate as well as his own experience in the Austrian court. This was the course adopted, but more from a feeling of helplessness than from conviction.[18]

Meanwhile, in the salon of the widowed Princess Elisabeth of Fürstenberg, where the bona fide Reich-restorers were assembled at that same time, a gathering momentum was in evidence.[19] True, the Forty-one Articles fell short of an imperial restoration, but the obvious imprint of Solms and Stein was a pleasant surprise. As late as 5 September, when officially presented to Metternich, the program of the mediatized houses was still that contained in Gärtner's note of 16 May, which comprehensively listed their rights and privileges but dared not mention Reich, *Landstände*, or *Kreisstände* as the means of securing them or demand a voice in these determinations. Then came Gärtner's and Solms's encouraging interview with Binder, the appointment of the Rademacher committee, and the restorative course of the September preliminary conferences in which Solms himself figured prominently. Estates constitutions, federal court, and representation in a federal diet now seemed realistic aspirations; but even better was Hardenberg's recent turn toward equality within the Kreise. If the chancellor prevailed, Gärtner reported gleefully, "all unjust distinctions" would disappear and every imperial estate would make equal sacrifices.[20]

Solms himself grew bolder, daring at last to abandon the pretense of working for reform. Both his memorial of 5 May and the conclusions of the preliminary conferences with Humboldt had favored the inclu-

---

[17] See the list of honors in Mett. and Stadion to Francis, 26 May 1815, HHSA, StK., Vorträge, Cart. 198.
[18] Apian-Bennewitz, *Plessen und die Verfassungsfrage*, 36–38.
[19] Goehausen to Hager, 15 Oct. 1814, Weil, *Les Dessous*, I, 307f.; Hoff, *Mediatisiertenfrage*, 66.
[20] *Ibid.*, 67.

sion of a peasant estate in the Landtage. In a new memorial addressed to Hardenberg and Münster on 29 September (as if deliberately to bypass Humboldt in the matter) he argued in the patronizing way of aristocracy that peasants would only "fall into the clutches of mischief-making lawyers." The peasant, he insisted, "will be well represented if his manorial lord is there to protect the interests of landowners in general." The same was true of towns: only those not subject to a manorial lord should be represented on their own. The German constitution, he held, must be "the work of time and experience," not the result "of metaphysical inquiries by theorizing political dabblers."[21] At the federal level, too, Solms projected a favored position for his peers. To Münster, who had always opposed seats for the mediatized in a federal diet side by side with their sovereigns, he directed a poignant request to reconsider. It was not, he pleaded, as if they demanded reparations for their financial losses, which he estimated at 50 percent in the capital value of their estates as a result of mediatization; surely then the sovereigns in their "love of fair play" should not mind this harmless reminder that the Standesherren were by rights autonomous and equal to the sovereigns: *reichsunmittelbar*, to use the term usually applied to their former standing in the Reich.[22]

Meanwhile, on the manors themselves this image of the all-wise, benevolent, and patriotic lord was gaining new credibility. In the ex-Rheinbund states, taxes continued at wartime levels and conscription went on apace, giving the Standesherren ample opportunity to fan resentment and challenge the authority of state officials, whose morale and effectiveness diminished each day that passed without a territorial settlement. In Bavaria a royal high treasurer, Prince Fugger von Babenhausen, who was also a mediatized subject, created a scandal by publishing a tract against the "excesses" of the Rheinbund and demanding the full restoration of the Standesherren. The furor raged through the month of October, causing the king to demote him though not dismissing him outright as Wrede recommended.[23] In Hesse-Darmstadt, where Solms's own estates were located, many nobles refused to pay taxes, hoping that they would soon have a voice in determining them. As the anniversary of the battle of Leipzig approached and the Standesherren, abetted by genuine radicals at the University of Giessen, incited their subjects to stage rousing celebrations, Grand Duke Louis, who had been on the other side at Leipzig, had to choose

---

[21] Solms's memorial, "Teutsche landständische Verfassung," n.d., NSHSA, Hanover, Des. 91, pp. 28–33. Another copy with covering letter to Prince Hardenberg of 29 Sept. 1814, in ZSTA, Merseburg, 2.4.1.I., No. 1559.

[22] Solms to Münster, 12 Oct. 1814, NSHSA, Hanover, Des. 91, No. 20.

[23] Winter, *Wrede als Berater*, 186f.

between them and his own army officers, many of whom held the Legion of Honor. Compromising, he allowed the populace to do what it wished but held no state celebration.[24] And so, reactionary though they were, the Standesherren found themselves at the head of a restless populace, the local symbols of authority raising loud voices for the breakup of the Rheinbund regimes and the introduction of national institutions to bring back the old order, all accompanied by denunciations of France and her vile works.

Thus it was that nationalism, popular unrest, and denunciation of "tyranny" came to be combined at the time less with individual rights and equality than with corporate rights, social hierarchy, and manorial governance. Add to this chorus frequent appeals to revive the Order of Teutonic Knights and give it a raison d'être by making it a true military order, possibly with headquarters at Mainz,[25] and it is easy to see why nineteenth-century historians and many even today have confused the tumult with a people's clamoring for liberty. At the time, however it was seen differently, and one observer worth listening to is Talleyrand. As he reported it,

> The revolutionary ferment has spread all over Germany. Jacobinism is reigning there, not as it did five and twenty years ago in France in the middle and lower classes, but among the highest and wealthiest nobility. . . . [They] bear impatiently a state of things that turns personages whose equals they were or believed themselves into their masters, and they aspire to the reversal of conditions that hurt their pride and to the replacement of all the governments of this country by one only. The men of the universities and young men imbued with their theories conspire with these malcontents. . . . The unity of the German land is their cry, their dogma; it is a religion carried to the height of fanaticism, and this fanaticism has infected even the reigning princes.[26]

Talleyrand was no disinterested witness when it came to German unity; clearly he exaggerated and oversimplified and to some extent twisted his own doctrine of legitimacy, which should have declared the acts of mediatization invalid.[27]

[24] Dietrich, "Hessen-Darmstadt auf dem Wiener Kongress," 198, 220, and 253; and Heinrich Ulmann, "Zur Entstehung der Kaisernote der 29 Kleinstaaten vom 16. November 1814," *Historische Zeitschrift*, CXVI (1916), 480.

[25] Dietrich, "Hessen-Darmstadt auf dem Wiener Kongress," 240; also Note of Hesse-Darmstadt, the Saxon Duchies, and Nassau to Austria and Prussia, 25 Oct. 1814, Klüber, *Acten*, Vol. I, Part 2, pp. 45–57.

[26] Talleyrand to Louis XVIII, 17 Oct. 1814, Talleyrand, *Corr.*, 62. The last reference was probably to the Gagern group.

[27] Talleyrand himself recognized the problem, pointing out to Keller of Hesse-

But if Talleyrand's testimony seems eccentric, we should recall that Metternich, even if only for dramatic effect, often called Stein a Jacobin. Or let us listen to the archconservative *Reichsfürst*, Wilhelm Ludwig von Sayn-Wittgenstein, one of those who found state employment, in this case, as the Prussian minister of police. "The mood in Germany is already serious," he warned Hardenberg a few months later, and "it will become more so if the German princes, not powerful in material strength, nevertheless, out of bitterness at their subjugation, sway the Germans by their venerable names and trust and place themselves at the head of the unruly and the dissidents."[28] Samples of this kind do not, of course, prove that genuine radicalism did not exist, only that the hyperbolic verbal environment of the congress provides a false measure of what motivated the statesmen there. An ironic inversion of labels has dogged German history, the reactionaries of Metternich's time being taken for radicals, the radicals of the Nazi era being often enough mistaken for reactionaries. What was common to both, however, was the fanaticism of the dispossessed and the déclassés.

Needless to say, it was not such long-range issues that brought the mediatized houses together on 14 October. Their immediate concern was the evidence that the sovereign princes were rushing to introduce constitutions of their own, instruments that would save centralized administration and undercut the Standesherren by providing a measure of equality and civil rights for the citizenry as a whole. In Bavaria Wrede, taking to heart Metternich's pleas to make his state a model for the treatment of the mediatized houses, had pressed for constitutional amendments to this end, but the commission appointed by Montgelas in September moved rather toward an elected parliament with a franchise that included peasant leaseholders and urban artisans—hardly Solms's idea of *landständische Verfassungen*.[29] A similar course was ordered on 3 October by King Frederick of Württemberg, who concluded from Metternich's comments three days before that some kind of constitution would merit preferred treatment by the

Cassel that the Rheinbund Act and the interallied accession treaties were legitimate, despite the acts of mediatization, and would have to be taken into account at the congress. Police agent to Hager, n.d., in Weil, *Les Dessous*, I, 262ff. The instructions that he drafted for himself also weighed against the mediatized houses on the grounds that they had never been sovereign but only vassals who in 1806 had been transferred from the emperor to the Rheinbund sovereigns. Such were the fine distinctions necessary to the selective application of the doctrine of legitimacy. Talleyrand, *Memoirs*, II, 161.

[28] Wittgenstein to Hard., early April, 1815, in Hans Branig, ed., *Briefwechsel des Fürsten Karl August von Hardenberg mit dem Fürsten Wilhelm Ludwig von Sayn-Wittgenstein 1806–1822* (Cologne and Berlin, 1972), 212.

[29] Eberhard Weis, "Zur Entstehungsgeschichte der bayerischen Verfassung von 1818," *Zeitschrift für bayerische Landesgeschichte*, XXXIX (1976), 413ff.; and Hruby to Mett., 12 Sept. 1814, in Chroust, *Berichte der österreichischen Gesandten*, I, 29f.

allies.[30] Even in Nassau, where at Stein's prodding Duke Frederick William and Marschall had rushed to completion a quite different, estates-style constitution based on the English model, the mediatized princes, full of "hate and distrust," believed they could do still better by waiting for federal models and guarantees to be imposed; otherwise their rights might appear as flowing from the immediate sovereign rather than the federal/imperial authority. No less a figure than Hans von Gagern, himself a mediatized count, denounced "the Anglomania" reflected in the Nassau constitution and refused to take his seat in the Landtag.[31] But regardless of the particular character of such constitutions and whatever they were called, Count Solms was determined that the guidelines be drafted not by those who wanted to freeze the order established in 1806, but by the allied powers, who, he hoped, would revive the conditions of 1803. "The right of blessing Germany with a constitution is one of the most important conquests of the monarchs," he had told Hardenberg a few weeks earlier.[32]

Accordingly, the main purpose of the meeting was to appoint a delegation to talk in this sense directly with Francis, Alexander, and Frederick William and request a voice in the proceedings. The delegates named were Gärtner's master, the prince of Wied-Neuwied, the count of Erbach-Erbach, the landgrave of Fürstenberg, and the princess of Fürstenberg herself. Old Franz Georg Metternich was enlisted in the cause to draft a formal petition, and somebody, probably Solms, was assigned to draft the revised statement of mediatized claims mentioned above. The audience with Francis took place on 22 October, the princess of Fürstenberg doing the talking and pleading that Francis take back the imperial office. As usual, he hedged, pledging his interest in the German crown "if this consummation can be reconciled with the interests of my own lands." Franz Georg's petition rather inaccurately based the restoration of rights on allied pledges "to secure the independence and *autonomy[!]* of Germany" and demanded a voice in the proceedings. Similar audiences with Frederick William and Alexander never materialized, but the predilection of the Standesherren for a Habsburg emperor remained as of old, however much they welcomed as well the material backing of Prussia.[33]

[30] King Frederick to Mandelsloh, 3 Oct. 1814, HSA, Stuttgart, E 1, Fasc. 45. Cf. Bernd Wunder, "Landstände und Rechtsstaat. Zur Entstehung und Verwirklichung des Art. 13 DBA," *Zeitschrift für historische Forschung*, v (1978), 139–153.
[31] Count Waldboth-Bassenheim to Stein, 21 Aug. 1814, Stein, *Briefe*, v, 122f.; Rössler, *Revolution und Reaktion*, 176.
[32] Solms to Hard., 19 Aug. 1814, ZSTA, Merseburg, 2.4.1.I, No. 1559, 195–197.
[33] Hoff, *Mediatisiertenfrage*, 66–68. Princess of Fürstenberg's address, Francis's reply, and F. G. Metternich's petition in Klüber, *Acten*, Vol. I, Part 2, 37–41. Cf. Hager to Francis, 10 Oct. 1814, Weil, *Les Dessous*, I, 250, regarding La Harpe's "pretty promises."

Another group active at this time, though not literally in conference on 14 October, consisted of the numerous spokesmen for the Roman church in Germany, by far the principal victim of the Rheinbund period even in comparison with the mediatized houses. For the ecclesiastical estates had not been simply mediatized but expropriated, the properties and revenues of their cathedral chapters, their monasteries, their abbeys, and other foundations awarded to the several secular states, their financial support henceforth made dependent on governmental appropriations. The failure of all parties to this process of secularization, moreover, to reach agreement on the redrawing of diocesan boundaries and appointments to clerical offices had left many sees subject to the jurisdiction of several states and increasingly devoid of leadership as vacancies in church offices went unfilled.[34]

In his heart almost every Catholic cleric, including Pope Pius VII, would have favored an imperial restoration that went beyond the Recess of 1803 to reinstate the *Landeshoheit* once enjoyed by the imperial prince bishops. About the practical prospects of achieving this goal opinions varied, but the instructions of all clerical envoys to the congress pointed in this direction.

Perhaps the most sanguine was a group called "the orators," consisting of Baron Franz von Wamboldt, dean of the cathedral at Worms, Joseph Helfferich, a prebendary from Speyer, and Carl Schies, a lawyer from Mannheim. They represented about eighty German clerics who formed the core of the ultramontane movement, which sought a restoration in close collaboration with Rome and minimal concessions to secular authorities, especially in regard to tax exemptions and the pope's exclusive right to appoint bishops. As a practical matter they favored but did not insist upon a general concordat between Rome and all the German states collectively under the auspices of a German central authority, whether Bund or Reich.

In some opposition to them stood the general vicar of Constance, Baron Ignaz Heinrich von Wessenberg, who represented Karl Theodor von Dalberg, the former prince primate of Mainz and a leading champion of a German national church under a new primate, preferably himself. Wessenberg, a partisan of the reform movement called Febronianism, was not a doctrinaire anti-papist, but he believed that without a central authority in Germany the German bishops would be unable to resist the incessant secular attacks made by each of the state

---

[34] For this and the following see Erwin Ruck, *Die römische Kurie und die deutsche Kirchenfrage auf dem Wiener Kongress* (Basel, 1917), 10–58; Huber, *Verfassungsgeschichte*, I, 400–412; Lipgens, *Graf Spiegel*, I, 188–195; Srbik, *Metternich*, I, 204–206; and assorted memoranda and petitions in Klüber, *Acten*, Vol. I, Part 2, p. 26 and IV, 299 and 304.

governments. Even more than the orators, therefore, he pressed the cause of a collective concordat that would provide a uniform constitution valid in all the states—an ecclesiastical counterpart, as it were, to uniform *landständische Verfassungen*, whose assemblies, incidentally, should in Wessenberg's view contain seats for the clergy.[35] As the brother of Metternich's deputy, Johann Philipp Wessenberg, and a cousin of the foreign minister himself, Ignaz Heinrich was a powerful figure at the congress, leading many, including Prince Hardenberg's Catholic advisor, Count Ferdinand August Spiegel mentioned earlier, in a national direction.

The ablest diplomat among the Catholic spokesmen was the papal envoy, Ercole Cardinal Consalvi. His instructions assigned the highest priority to the secular interests of the church, above all the recovery of the Papal States in Italy, but beyond that any degree of restoration obtainable in Germany was to the good, with one limitation: he was not to jeopardize the possibility of negotiating concordats with each of the German states separately, in particular with Württemberg, which was already in touch with Rome on this subject. Such orders, drafted by the archconservative papal secretary Bartolomeo Cardinal Pacca, reflected the primacy of political interests, the fear of a German national church (Pacca vainly ordered Dalberg to dismiss Wessenberg), and the belief that separate concordats, negotiated in Rome rather than Vienna, would both forestall a German-style Gallicanism and produce better results than a necessarily more generalized collective concordat. Indeed, Consalvi at first held the latter to be impossible.

No one profited more than Metternich from the divisions among the Catholic churchmen, whom he could use against each other as he pursued an intermediate course. For reasons of grand strategy in Italy he was determined to end thirty-five years of Austro-papal antagonism ushered in by the extreme anti-clerical policies of Joseph II. Yet he had at his back an Austrian church still dominated by Josephinists. In the long run he did his best to combat this hierarchy, but in the near term, as in the matter of estates constitutions, there was value in preventing separate settlements in Germany that would make Austria appear unreasonable by comparison. On the other hand, he did not favor a German national church that might eventually force a *kleindeutsch-grossdeutsch* choice in the ecclesiastical realm, that is to say, a choice between an isolated Austrian church and one associated with an overall German settlement. A collective concordat acceptable to Rome, even if rather general in nature, was the answer.

During the fall of 1814 Metternich was in steady contact with Con-

[35] Wessenberg memorial of 28 Oct. 1814, HHSA, StK., Deutsche Akten, Fasc. 96 (old series).

salvi and Wessenberg and even gave several audiences to the orators, whom he beguiled with promises of support even though he privately considered their restorative ambitions "harebrained."[36] On Consalvi, who appreciated his pro-papal views, Metternich had a powerful influence, persuading him that a collective concordat was possible and need not lead to an autonomous national church. He added, however, that the most the congress could do would be to make the issue part of the obligatory agenda for the future federal assembly. It was perhaps Metternich's greatest victory in this matter that he was soon able to extract from the papal envoy the promise that he would negotiate no separate concordats without consulting Austria.

Another pressure group trying to bring order to its German-wide affairs was a delegation representing eighty-one publishers and book dealers throughout Germany. Aiming at the widest possible market, they desired a uniform copyright law associated with a federal guarantee of freedom of the press, or at least a uniform press code eliminating prior censorship and liberally defining the area of freedom. Though citing cultural benefits and the value to governments of diverse sources of information, they based their case mainly on the contention that without interstate protection against plagiarism and against prosecution under diverse and arbitrary state laws, publishing would be carried on only for a local market or confined to ephermeral works not worth copying. Less was said about freedom as a natural right, but this was not necessarily the best argument to direct at the ministers of absolutist states.[37]

Of six deputies appointed to plead this case in Vienna only two actually appeared: Friedrich Justin Bertuch of Weimar and Johann Georg Cotta of Stuttgart, publisher of the prestigious *Allgemeine Zeitung*. On the whole the cause won sympathy. Book pirating was generally deplored, and within states, though each government protected itself against criticism, neighboring states were regarded as fair game. Uniformity and reciprocity were clearly indicated. In Prussia Hardenberg, though demanding strict policing of newspapers and periodicals, favored repression of offensive materials under a licensing system rather than by preventive censorship. Humboldt's constitutional draft of April, 1814, spoke of freedom of the press "limited only by just and reasonable censorship," and the Forty-one Articles provided for "press free-

[36] Mett. to Francis, 5 Apr. 1816, Metternich, *NP*, III, 3.

[37] This and following based on various petitions and memoranda in Klüber, *Acten*, IV, 1–36; police reports in Fournier, *Geheimpolizei*, 60, 136, 160, 171, 180f., 329, 336, 378, 381, and 390; Carl Bertuch, *Carl Bertuchs Tagebuch vom Wiener Kongress*, ed. Hermann von Egloffstein (Berlin, 1916), *passim*; report of the Committee on Freedom of the Press, German Confederation, *Protokolle der deutschen Bundesversammlung*, 50 vols. (Frankfurt am Main, 1816–1866), III, 635ff.

dom on the basis of modifications still to be determined." The Twelve Articles omitted the topic entirely.

On this issue Metternich was at a disadvantage. As with the problem of the church, so here he had at home to cope with the legacy of Josephinism, which on its darker side had spawned a ubiquitous police system, perhaps the most severe censorship in Germany, and an un-limited right to plagiarize, the last on the notion that the traffic in royalty-free products benefited the economy. Nevertheless, when Met-ternich granted Cotta and Bertuch an audience (coincidentally, on that busy day of 14 October) he listened sympathetically as they explained why publishers, unless they knew that a given book could be sold everywhere, would soon publish nothing but prayerbooks and song-books. Their cause was timely, and he fully supported it, he assured them.[38] Was he in earnest? Regarding copyright most certainly; throughout the year he carried on a running battle with Baldacci, the president of the general accounting office, who defended the tax-paying Austrian book pirates. On the other hand, freedom of the press, as usually understood, he opposed, certainly more than the Prussians did, but he recognized the need for interstate regulation, as we shall see, even if it entailed Austrian concessions.

On one further issue of German-wide import the Austrian minister was more liberal, perhaps exceeding the Prussians in this respect. It was the status of the Jews, and as often happens with this perennial problem, it tended to invert normal patterns. For the mission of the Jewish deputies who came to Vienna was not the restorative one so familiar to us by now—even the book dealers preferred the lackadais-ical practices of the old Reich to the zealous censors of the Rheinbund—but that of preserving the gains of the Napoleonic era. These varied, to be sure, from the enjoyment of full equality of civil and political rights in Westphalia, Berg, Frankfurt, and the regions once part of France to the plethora of traditional disabilities that continued in Sax-ony; everywhere else the pattern was at least that of gradual amelio-ration. The most threatened were the Jews of Frankfurt, Lübeck, Ham-burg, and Bremen, whose magistrates, with the blessing of Baron Stein, were impatient to rescind French statutes lest the future Bund guar-antee them. The Jews formerly of Westphalia also faced trouble: from the restoration of a traditional *Ständestaat* in Hanover.[39]

[38] Police agent to Hager, 15 October 1815, Fournier, *Geheimpolizei*, 180f.

[39] This and the next two paragraphs based mainly on the monograph by Salo Baron, *Die Judenfrage auf dem Wiener Kongress* (Vienna and Berlin, 1920), 13–100, which despite its age, is still the standard work on the subject. See also Hans Liebe-schütz and Arnold Paucker, eds., *Das Judentum in der deutschen Umwelt 1800–1850* (Tübingen, 1977), especially the articles by Liebeschütz, 1–54, and Jacob Toury, 139–242.

On the Jewish issue Metternich's position was not burdened by the regime he represented. On the contrary, Joseph II had been a pioneer of emancipation, and although some discrimination survived (synagogues, for example, might not face the street), Austria ranked with Prussia as one of the most enlightened states in this regard. Metternich's personal inclinations matched. Tolerant, even if in the manner of those who are above the strife, scornful of superstition, and appreciative of the value to the state of Jewish industry and Jewish capital, he had every reason, personal and practical, to befriend Jews. Unlike Gentz, however, he took no gratuities for his services. His closest associate was the Viennese banker, Leopold Edler von Herz, a wizard at raising money for the Habsburgs and expediting British subsidies, but he was also on good terms with the other rich Viennese Jewish families such as the Arnsteins and the Eskeles. The same was true of Hardenberg and Humboldt and indeed all the great-power envoys, believing as they did that at a time of potential financial catastrophe for many states, the Jews were indispensable sources of credit, just as the territorial estates were vital sources of collateral. It may seem incongruous to link traditional estates with emancipated Jews, but many a state loan then outstanding had been obtained only with the endorsement of a Landtag that thus pledged the assets of its province. It was no accident that *landständische Verfassungen* and Jewish emancipation both attracted support at the congress disproportionately to the intrinsic strength of their constituencies.

The Jewish deputies at the congress were J. J. Gumprecht and Jakob Baruch of Frankfurt and Carl August Buchholz, a Christian from Lübeck, who represented the Jewish communities of the three Hanseatic cities. Metternich's first encounter with them occurred when the Frankfurt deputies were about to be expelled by the Austrian police for representing themselves as ordinary merchants. The charge was valid, as the two wished to avoid the appearance of challenging their city's own deputies, but Metternich, who had met Baruch at the coronation of Francis in 1792, intervened, recognized the propriety of their mission, and obtained diplomatic visas for them. Several months later (January, 1815) he made strong representations to the Hanseatic cities to desist from revising their French-style constitutions to the disadvantage of the Jews. The recriminations extended into the spring, but the pressure eventually succeeded. It is true that Hardenberg was several weeks ahead of his Austrian rival with similar protestations, but supporting dissident minorities was standard Prussian policy whereas Metternich's actions constituted a rare departure from his practice of supporting established governments, especially among the small states.

The affairs of the Catholic church, the German bookmen, and the

Jews presented legislative or regulatory issues complementary to the Bund but not integral to its structure. Even the petitioners, therefore, did not expect the German Committee to make their claims the first order of business. Returning to the deliberations of that body, let us recall that its principal decisions on 14 October were to confine the deliberations to its five members and to charge Martens of Hanover with drafting a declaration of reassurance to the excluded states. Metternich had hoped that this action would forestall formal complaints. The very next day, however, Baron Hacke upset the calculation by submitting Baden's official demand not only for eventual consultation but for immediate appointment to the German Committee, the main grounds being her electoral standing in the Reich and the contention that she was larger than Hanover, a most sanguine assumption considering the "onerous sacrifice" that Hardenberg expected of her.[40] At noon of the same day Metternich received Count Keller, who proposed that the small states might at least appoint a few delegates from their own ranks to serve on the committee. He also begged for an immediate declaration establishing a supreme head (*Oberhaupt*) for Germany, preferably Emperor Francis. A few days earlier Metternich had handled Plessen by making light of the committee. Now that the committee had actually met, however, he had to take a different tack, arguing that it was a real achievement but vulnerable at any time to foreign intrusion if more states were taken in. "The first aim in and for Germany," he declaimed with all the fervor of a patriot, "must be unity and a genuine *Deutschheit*; that is the only kind of Germany there must be." The argument bore particularly on the matter of the *Oberhaupt*, he added; for foreign states did in fact have a valid interest in Germany's relationship to the rest of Europe and might easily adduce the federal-bond clause in the Paris treaty as precluding a supreme head, whatever its name. Later one might announce such a goal, but for the moment prudence demanded silence.[41]

As far as it went, Metternich's argument was veracious enough. Talleyrand had frequently warned against a German crown associated with a great power; and even worse, Alexander might counter by proclaiming his own kingship in Poland. Moreover, to have separated the German constitution from general European affairs and kept Russia and France off the committee were no mean achievements, and arguments could be raised even yet against the procedure, especially

---

[40] Text in Klüber, *Acten*, Vol. I, Part 2, 58f.

[41] Keller's report of 16 Oct. 1814. Text in Fournier, *Geheimpolizei*, 212–214. Cf. Apian-Bennewitz, *Plessen und die Verfassungspolitik*, 38; and Heinrich Ulmann, "Zur Entstehung der Kaisernote," 468f. Ulmann, taking Metternich's later denials at face value, believes Keller misunderstood the reference to a future declaration.

where Kreis boundaries and territorial questions became entwined. What Metternich did not tell Keller was why the other German states were excluded, and the answer to that was the now familiar thesis that their accession treaties placed them at the mercy of the powers.[42] Metternich had his reservations about this contention, but obviously he could not take Keller into his confidence. He did, however, promise that all states would eventually be consulted and all would be equal, exactly the assurrance he had given Plessen.

After Keller's departure it was back to grand affairs again. At 2:00 p.m. Castlereagh, Hardenberg, and Humboldt arrived, full of compliments on Austria's consent to the Prussian occupation of Saxony, which Gentz had conveyed to them that morning, but reminding Metternich that he had not yet answered Hardenberg's demand for permanent possession. Castlereagh then recounted a stormy and depressing interview a few days before at which he had presented the tsar with a formal letter and a memorandum arguing the legal case for repartitioning the duchy of Warsaw.[43] The latter, the work of his chief aide and confidant, Edward Cooke, was now discussed by the three allies and found Metternich's endorsement, this despite a glaring fallacy that he must have recognized.[44] The central issue was whether the Teplitz treaty of 9 September 1813, with its provision for settling the Polish question by "an amicable arrangement among the three courts" merely elaborated upon or actually superseded the Reichenbach accord of 27 June 1813, which called for "the dissolution of the duchy of Warsaw and the division of the provinces forming it among Russia, Prussia, and Austria." Obviously the former wording, which left the matter entirely open, was preferred by the Russians. Cooke, however, argued that it was a gratuitous embellishment, merely a polite reaffirmation of what Russia had already conceded at Reichenbach, and many historians have agreed with him.[45]

The reasoning, however, was completely false. Actually, the Reichenbach phrasing was part of an offer to Napoleon, which, if refused, would have no further relevance. Indeed, in that event, the real event

---

[42] His statement to German Committee, protocol of 16 Oct. 1814, Klüber, *Acten*, II, 77f.

[43] Gentz, *Tagebücher*, I, 319; Hardenberg, "Tagebücher," 35; Castle. to Liverp., 14 and 20 Oct. 1814, Webster, *BD*, 208–211; and Humb. to Hard. (wrongly dated 3 Nov. 1814) Humboldt, *Gesammelte Schriften*, XI, 188f. On the wrong date see Griewank, *Wiener Kongress*, 168, n. 52.

[44] Full text in Wellington, *Supplementary Despatches*, IX, 332–336, and d'Angeberg, *Congrès*, II, 265–270. Précis in Webster, *BD*, 209.

[45] For the binding force of Reichenbach: Max Lehmann, ed., Tagebuch des Freiherrn vom Stein während des Wiener Kongresses," *Historische Zeitschrift*, LX (1888), 458f. Against: Hans Delbrück, "Friedrich Wilhelm III. und Hardenberg auf dem Wiener Kongress," *ibid.*, LXIII (1889), 244.

as it turned out, the war aims were to be those earlier proposed by Prussia and Russia, which in turn read that "the duchy of Warsaw expires with respect to name and the form of its constitution." If anything, this wording was almost an invitation to Alexander to revive the dreaded name of Poland. Since the British were not parties to the Reichenbach pact, Cooke probably believed what he said. Metternich, however, as a principal author, should have known above all others that the case was specious. Nevertheless, he allowed it, as we shall see, to become an integral part of the strategy against the tsar. If it came to an appeal to the whole congress, some foundation in treaty must be found, and Cooke's case had a certain plausibility that might withstand the scrutiny of the uninitiated.[46]

The afternoon conference yielded no decisions, only increased the pressure on Metternich to reach one of his own. Significantly the reports from all sides in those days complained of his "shallow frivolity" (Stein), his aversion to "such manly measures as are becoming the Minister of a great state" (Stewart), levity mistaken for "superior genius" (Talleyrand), "without any fixed plan" (Castlereagh), "guided by a timid and uncertain policy" (Dalberg)—not to mention the vicious opposition at home, which damned him for either having or not having imperial plans and almost unanimously denounced his spinelessness in regard to Saxony.[47] But such is the way a waiting game will always appear to those who must delay their own moves because of it. Ironically Metternich expected of Castlereagh, or alternatively, Talleyrand, what he himself had not been able to give Hardenberg during the summer: an unequivocal answer to what would happen if they threw down the gauntlet and Alexander refused to break. Now Hardenberg was willing to take the chance, but nowhere can be found a flat British guarantee of military support in event of war, only admonitions to hold the Austrian war hawks in check. Talleyrand was more understanding; he had taken seriously Metternich's soundings through Wrede and Dalberg. Having in the afternoon deflected the blows aimed at Saxony's destruction, Metternich that evening faced the fire of her now principal defender. After a dinner at Sagan's Talleyrand made one last effort. Drawing Metternich and Gentz aside, he pleaded for firmness and painted an optimistic picture of the military superiority Aus-

[46] Kraehe, I, 176, 179, 200–205; text of Reichenbach treaty in Martens, *Traités par la Russie*, III, 101–111, Article VI giving the reference to the previous program of 16 May. Text of latter in Wilhelm Oncken, *Oesterreich und Preussen im Befreiungskriege*, 2 vols. (Berlin, 1876–1879), II, 318. Oddly enough neither previous writers nor Czartoryski, who drafted the official Russian rebuttal, cited Art. VI, which is the proof.

[47] Stein, *Briefe*, v, 17; Webster, *Castlereagh*, I, 345; Talleyrand, *Corr.*, 9; Webster, *BD*, 202; Talleyrand, *Memoirs*, II, 256; Weil, *Les Dessous*, I, 225, 296, and 310.

tria, Bavaria, and other German allies would enjoy. The Austrian reaction cannot be documented, but Metternich must have remained
noncommittal and reiterated his skepticism about French fortitude.
The next day Talleyrand requested from Paris full and precise powers
for making war should the Austrians ask it.[48]

Metternich's thoughts the next day were far from war, far from
Talleyrand. Continuing the common march with Hardenberg, he prepared himself for the next meeting of the German Committee, now
concluding that the aroused feelings among the outcasts made a formal
explanation of their exclusion inadvisable. On opening the meeting,
however, he encountered a different dispute, not in itself important
but drawing after it the central reality of the age: the collision between
the imperial legacy and the existing Rheinbund order. Martens's protocol of the previous meeting listed Hanover ahead of Württemberg,
and Linden refused to sign, observing that a royal title dating from
1806 took precedence over one just four days old and not yet widely
recognized.[49] Münster objected, insisting that the dates of the electoral
titles (Hanover 1692, Württemberg 1803) governed the situation, and
the Prussians agreed. Metternich, anxious to proceed, suggested that
the order of signing this or any other protocol was fortuitous and had
nothing to do with rank as all states were equal. This too Linden
rejected, but being without instructions, he allowed the meeting to
proceed. It was the only way to obtain the Swabian Kreis.[50]

Metternich now produced the note from Baden as evidence of the
resistance mounting outside the committee and recommended that
explanations, though citing the accession treaties, be confined to private
exchanges. Significantly, however, his version of the argument, like his
remarks to Keller, focused on defense and the Bund's future relations
with Europe, thus staying within the original meaning of the treaties.
In any case, the motion was quickly adopted, with the understanding
that Austria and Prussia would reply orally to the note from Baden
and in their names only. It was further agreed that henceforth all
proceedings were to be confidential. In this way Metternich prevented
Hardenberg's interpretation of the treaties from becoming the official
position of the committee and the exclusion of the other states from
becoming irrevocable.[51]

Meanwhile the Twelve Articles themselves had been kept so secret
that no copies were available for distribution. Wrede had been told

---

[48] Gentz, *Tagebücher*, I, 318; McGuigan, *Duchess*, 364; Kings Ambassadors to Blacas,
16 Oct. 1814, and Talley. to Louis, 17 Oct. 1814, Talleyrand, *Memoirs*, II, 255–264.
[49] And not ratified even by the prince regent of England until 26 October 1814.
D'Angeberg, *Congrès*, II, 337.
[50] Protocol of 16 Oct. 1814, Klüber, *Acten*, II, 75f.
[51] *Ibid.*, II, 77–79.

nothing,[52] and Linden knew only the bowdlerized version that Metternich had put before the king two weeks before. As Metternich proceeded to read the articles aloud, nervousness set in, of the kind that often causes important negotiations to begin with peripheral and symbolic issues. Wrede, with Frankfurt in mind, objected to the expression "princes and free cities" in Article I on grounds that no such cities were yet recognized. Humboldt's substitute term, "estates," he rejected on same grounds. In the end "states" was adopted to cover both princes and all others, but the issue was far from dead. Similarly, Linden wanted in Article III to replace the neutral reference to "governmental rights" with unequivocal "sovereignty," but when all the others professed scorn for such "foreign words," he acquiesced for the time being, insisting that all decisions were provisional in any case. Throughout this meeting and the others to come Wrede and Linden, though not always on same points, maintained a dogged campaign to purge the articles of the imperial nomenclature so cherished by Humboldt and Münster; few of the particular cases, however, are worth our attention. As a result, Metternich, who always believed in trading words for substance, had ample scope for applying his verbal gifts and celebrated sense of nuance to the composing of differences.

Not that all issues could be settled by dexterous wordplay. As anticipated, Wrede, even in this opening round, challenged the double votes of the two powers and demanded more precise definitions of their territory and the scope of the Austrian presidency. In unison Metternich and Hardenberg explained that their "German provinces" meant all their territory except Italy, Hungary, "Prussia proper," and Poland, that is to say, more than was offered in the Forty-one Articles but still vaguely enough defined to permit hedging. Regarding the votes Metternich had his own reservations but for the moment joined Hardenberg in explaining that in matters of war and peace they must, if in agreement, have their way and if not, Wrede's fears would be groundless. As for the presidency, as noted earlier, Metternich pictured it as a pure formality, an office that Austria assumed only at Prussia's insistence.[53]

Pleasure's inroads on business at the Congress of Vienna have been greatly exaggerated in the legend, but one bona fide instance was now at hand. When the German Committee adjourned on the 16th, it scheduled the next meeting a full three days later, allowing time, it is true, for Wrede and Linden to study the Twelve Articles in detail, but also to permit proper observance of the great event that was upon them all: the anniversary of the battle of Leipzig, the key to their presence

[52] Aretin, "Deutsche Politik Bayerns," 9.
[53] See n. 50.

there. On the morning of the 17th Gentz found Metternich absorbed in preparations for his grand ball the next day and trudged off to brood with Wessenberg about the doom of Saxony and probably as well to wonder about their chief, whose thoughts were either on his beloved fête or on Sagan's betrayal, "which appears," wrote the avid diarist, "to interest him more than all the world's affairs."[54]

But perhaps Metternich's obsession with the ball transcended vanity. A celebration of peace, without soldiers, without guns, had been on his mind ever since June. "My soirée must breathe 20 years of peace," he had written Eleonore in regard to the preparations.[55] It must have cost him much effort to preempt this day for himself, for only at the last minute did the Hofburg decide to fill the daylight hours of the 18th with a military pageant. Marshal Schwarzenberg, the organizer and instigator of the plan, thus saw to it that the soldiers too would have their day. In public view the entire Vienna garrison of 16,000 men marched to the Prater, where they attended mass and received, each of them, a medallion struck from melted-down cannon captured during the war, the entire scene punctuated by artillery fire, drum rolls, and martial music. It was also Schwarzenberg's day, and none was more determined to make it so than the tsar, who pulled him from the crowd and shouted for all to hear: "Next to God, it is to you that we owe our success." The day spangled the memories of those who were there.[56]

Metternich's fête was just as glittering in a different way, featuring the tableaux in celebration of peace. No medals here; just let the darkness of war be banished! Was the whole affair designed to catch the conscience of the tsar, to impress upon him the laurels to be won by magnanimity, to wrap about him the sentiment of war-wearied Europe? Alexander suspected as much. The fête was splendid, he told Princess Maria Theresa Esterhazy, "but after that of this morning one should not give another. . . . There is always diplomacy in such things, and I do not like what is deceitful."[57] And to Metternich himself he burst out in front of Archduke John: "You diplomats make decisions, and then we soldiers have to let ourselves be shot up into cripples for you." Conceivably the tsar was too sensitive. Perhaps Metternich was only displaying the frivolity for which he was known, while Alexander was

[54] Gentz, *Tagebücher*, I, 319f.

[55] Quoted by McGuigan, *Duchess*, 365.

[56] Schwarzenberg to wife, 15 Oct. 1814, Fürst Karl zu Schwarzenberg, *Briefe des Feldmarschalls Fürsten Schwarzenberg an seine Frau, 1799–1816*, ed. Johann Friedrich Novak (Vienna, 1913), 408; and Karl Fürst Schwarzenberg, *Feldmarschall Fürst Schwarzenberg. Der Sieger von Leipzig* (Vienna and Munich, 1964), 360.

[57] Agent's report to Hager, 20 Oct. 1814, Weil, *Les Dessous*, I, 339. Cf. McGuigan, *Duchess*, 367.

deliberately courting the soldiers, who far more than the foreign minister stood in his way. "I don't trust any man who has never been a soldier," he maliciously told Metternich's mother that night, employing once more the dubious technique he had perfected in London: flattery toward the outs, insults to the ins.[58] Metternich had his revenge the next day, though the tsar had no way of knowing it: the emperor's permission to abandon Saxony was his at last.[59] "Constellation very black," Gentz wailed, but could not prevent it.[60]

While Metternich pondered how best to play this golden ace, the German Committee convened again on the 20th, a day behind schedule. Linden, evidently reprimanded by King Frederick for letting slip the opportunity to proclaim officially the broad interpretation of the accession treaties that could deliver Baden into Württemberg's Kreis, called for a formal declaration to the excluded states after all. The motion failed. Next he and Wrede read the statements they had prepared in consultation with their monarchs. Frederick had at first intended to reject the entire project, but in the end instructed Linden to go ahead, article by article, if Wrede did, with the understanding, however, that everything was provisional, pending agreement on the system as a whole, including a precise delineation of Kreis boundaries.[61]

Otherwise the statements were similar. Both demanded that all Kreis chiefs preside over equal populations and have equal votes in the upper council, the chairmanship rotating annually among the five. Both regarded the Bund essentially as a union of the Kreis chiefs, Bavaria repudiating a lower house entirely, Württemberg admitting one provided it was powerless. Holding that the only legitimate purpose of the Bund was the common defense, they denounced a federal court, a federal bill of rights, and federal guidelines for state constitutions. In fact, said Wrede acidly, the exemption of Austria and Prussia from such regulation was so appropriate that Bavaria claimed it as well.

[58] McGuigan, *Duchess*, 367; Fournier, *Geheimpolizei*, 39; and Frederick Freksa, comp., *A Peace Congress of Intrigue (Vienna, 1815)*, trans. Harry Hansen (New York, 1919), 235, which contains excerpts from Archduke John's diary.

[59] The evidence is indirect: a police report of 20 Oct. pinpointing the 19th as the day of decision, Weil, *Les Dessous*, I, 342; Humb. to the Prince of Orange, 19 Oct. 1814, revealing that "England and Austria . . . realize the necessity of giving Saxony to Prussia . . ."; and Castle. to Liverp., 20 Oct., Webster, *BD*, 211, saying that "Metternich has, as I learned, made up his mind and received the emperor's authority . . .": One would prefer to have a *Vortrag* with Francis's cryptic authorization in the margin, but as Metternich did officially make the offer to Hardenberg in writing three days later, the 19th is certainly close to the mark. The Humboldt letter is quoted by Paul R. Sweet, *Wilhelm von Humboldt: A Biography*, 2 vols. (Columbus, Ohio, 1978–1980), II, 186.

[60] Gentz, *Tagebücher*, I, 321.

[61] Memorandum für . . . Linden, 20 Oct. 1814, in HSA, Stuttgart, E 70b, Fasc. 45, No. 1.

Similarly in foreign affairs both demanded all the freedom of war and alliance claimed by the two powers as well as a more explicit statement relieving the Bund of responsibility for their non-Bund provinces.[62]

Though hardly unexpected, the strong stand on this last issue was especially alarming to Metternich, believing as he did that Austria must have a Central European defense league, for immediate leverage in the campaign against Russia if possible, regardless of what embellishments could be added later. Wrede's attack (Article IX was at issue) plunged the meeting into an angry debate. As Münster had predicted, the marshal argued that in a war, say, in Italy between France and Austria Bavaria might have vital interests in joining the latter even though the Bund itself decided to stay neutral. The principle extended to remote as well as immediate interests, to alliances as well as subsidy treaties. Bavaria did not intend the Bund to remove her from the European chessboard. Against this Metternich and Hardenberg painted a black picture of chaos: foreign powers, as in centuries past, intriguing with German states, Germans fighting Germans, the great intermediate buffer collapsing in ruin. Münster piously announced that despite her obvious obligation in a war between England and a continental power, Hanover would renounce the free choice of alliance for the good of Germany—as if this was not Britain's best way of protecting her exposed continental appendage. But it was Metternich who led the attack. As the fiercely partisan king of Württemberg reported it, "the animus of this fool against Russia goes so far that in yesterday's session he forgot himself so much that he stamped France and Russia with the name, 'the devouring powers,' and flatly declared security against them as the purpose of the Deutscher Bund." Wrede, however, persisted, strengthened by his knowledge that Metternich, despite his ringing oratory, was all the while considering alliance with France and Bavaria. Only when asked to draft proposals of his own did he break off the attack for the day.[63]

Though secondary in his calculations, Metternich defended federal regulation of subjects' rights as "categorically necessary" and proceeded to ridicule some of the Rheinbund regulations: residence requirements, for example, which he himself could not meet, possessing as he did properties in five different states. "We will not place Germany under five despots," he insisted; "we will allow the rights of the others to continue as well." Compared to these emphatic words Hardenberg's comment that estates constitutions were "salutary" and "often useful"

---

[62] Protocol of 20 Oct. 1814, Klüber, *Acten*, II, 83–89.

[63] *Ibid.*, II, 85–88, and 123f.; and King Frederick to Mandelsloh, 21 Oct. 1814, HSA, Stuttgart, E 1, Fasc. 45. The diversionary busywork assigned to Wrede included drafting an agenda to be studied by a technical military commission.

sounds halfhearted, but perhaps at this critical juncture the two ministers were speaking mainly to impress each other.[64]

Now that the hard opposition was in the open, new understandings with Prussia were in order. After the meeting Metternich drew Humboldt aside to discuss the possibility of giving up their double votes. The latter, clinging to the last vestige of a dualistic directory, refused, but agreed that private talks were necessary and set them for the following evening. Late that night, just back from a ball at Count Stackelberg's, Metternich felt a familiar urge, "a need that I shall not attempt to define. . . . You have compromised my existence," he reproached Sagan, "at a time when my life's destiny is joined to all the questions that will decide the fate of generations—mon amie, I forgive you everything." That was at 4:00 a.m. At 10:00 he was back at work discussing strategy with Gentz, Wessenberg, and General Friedrich Karl von Langenau, Schwarzenberg's trusted aide, probably to decide on how to cope with Wrede, whom the latter three visited later in the day.[65]

In the meantime Count Münster had developed reasons of his own for holding another private meeting. All along he and Stein had keenly felt the lack of a statement of minimum estates' rights in the Twelve Articles. Stein's conception was that of relatively centralized government but with the estates, mainly landowners and including the Standesherren, having the preponderance of influence by means of a strong parliament. The mediatized houses, on the other hand, attached more importance to the preservation of their autonomy against all central government and some had, as we have seen, specifically repudiated the Stein-Marschall constitution for Nassau. Münster stood somewhere in the middle, arguing that Germany was not ready for such English things as houses of peers and parliamentary debate, which would only encourage "demagogues." At length, however, they agreed that the minimal rights should be 1) veto power over taxes, 2) a voice in legislation, 3) sharing in the supervision of expenditures, and 4) the right to prosecute public officials for malfeasance. While Stein insisted that it was this program or nothing, Münster was willing to negotiate, but whether he meant that concessions should consist of diluting the rights or exempting more states from their imposition is not clear.[66]

Humboldt, meanwhile, had stumbled into this unpleasant dilemma on his own. In an effort to meet the opposition halfway he had pre-

[64] Klüber, Acten, II, 88f.; and Linden's "Bemerkungen" to the protocol of 20 Oct. 1814, HSA, Stuttgart, E 70, Fasc. 12.
[65] Humb. to Hard., 21 Oct. 1814, ZSTA, Merseburg, 2.4.1.I, No. 1559, p. 85; Mett. to Sagan, 21 Oct. 1814, Ullrichová, ed., Briefwechsel, 207ff.; Gentz, Tagebücher, I, 322.
[66] Münster to Stein, 19 Oct. 1814, Stein, Briefe, v, 167–169.

pared an elaboration of Article XI that restricted the estates to the rights of consultation and lodging grievances. But his heart was not in it; he wanted them to have the veto power. A marginal note to Hardenberg betrayed his anguish:

> I have been in a quandary about how I should conceive and suitably limit this right. Austria and Prussia cannot very well grant it to their estates, and if they do not, Bavaria and Württemberg ... will not put up with it either, at least not promise it in the federal act; the only thing left would be to impose this obligation solely on the princes of the 2nd council—but it seemed to me there was not sufficient reason for this exception.[67]

Although Humboldt thus preferred the combination of milder content and broader coverage, the reverse possibility had been broached.

On 21 October Metternich met as planned with the Prussians and Hanoverians, his hand at peak strength owing to both the stark reality of the South German opposition and the power that was now his to offer or withhold Saxony. That afternoon, in fact, Hardenberg had begged him for an answer, anxious to settle things before the 24th, when the monarchs were due to leave for a week's visit in Buda.[68] We have no protocol of the conclave, only the text of a secret agreement that emerged from it, but Metternich's impact is obvious. The three powers were still pledged "categorically" to permit every estate to bring grievances before the Bund—specifically, however, to the federal diet as Metternich had proposed several times before and not to a federal court. Similarly, they would insist on double votes for Austria and Prussia but concede that in case the two powers stood against the other three, Baden and Hesse-Cassel would be called in to cast votes as well. Though ostensibly designed to meet middle-state objections, the device also represented a step back toward the larger council that Metternich had always preferred. The modification also lessened the chances that Austria and Prussia could vote the Bund into a war for their non-German interests, but as a further concession it was agreed to add an explicit disclaimer of a right to federal aid even if their German provinces became involved.[69]

Regarding the rights of the estates, the strong four points devised by Stein and Münster were adopted but with the stipulation, so repugnant to Humboldt, that they would not necessarily apply to any of

---

[67] "Entwicklung des 11. Paragraphen," n.d., quoted in Mager, "Das Problem der Verfassungen," 327f., n. 70.

[68] Hard. to Mett., 21 Oct. 1814 (private), HHSA, StK., Kongressakten, Fasc. 7, p. 154.

[69] Text of convention in Humboldt's hand in Schmidt, *Verfassungsfrage*, 231f.

the Kreis chiefs. An attempt evidently would still be made to *persuade* Bavaria and Württemberg to accept the points, and since Austria and Prussia as great powers at the same time reaffirmed their own exemption, the strategy adopted was to have Münster take the lead, arguing that if Hanover was willing, even proud, to grant these ancient rights, why should Bavaria and Württemberg refuse? To this end he was commissioned to draft a motion for official presentation to the committee with the endorsement of the two powers.[70]

A strong stand was taken, probably with little controversy, in favor of the Austrian directory and the retention of the lower council with the existing list of members. The true measure of Metternich's leverage, however, is that he dared to challenge the Kreis system. The one thing that might affect the composition of the lower house, he argued, would be the possibility of *"giving up this [Kreis] division"*[71] and fashioning another, consisting of districts limited to military and judicial functions. If he actually tried to push this amendment through, he failed; but in the final agreement such a revision was expressly held forth as a later possibility "in the event that the Kreis system encountered too many difficulties or concern should arise that the Kreis chiefs were arrogating too much power to themselves." First Baden and Hesse-Cassel, then who knew how many others, were on their way to equality with the big five. There was one other possibility: in the event that Bavaria and Württemberg persisted in their obstruction, it would be better to remove them from the council of Kreis chiefs and bring in others "than to make a constitution that would only disappoint the just expectations of Germany." In spirit that, of course, was pure Humboldt, but any attempt to carry out such a threat would probably have led to abandoning Kreise altogether.[72]

When the German Committee reconvened the following afternoon, a second plenipotentiary appeared for Württemberg, the seasoned Count Winzingerode, King Frederick having decided that "the good Linden . . . has too little stamina to keep pace" and required reinforce-

---

[70] Text of Hanover's *Votum* to German Committee in Klüber, *Acten*, Vol. I, pt. 1, 68–71. So deeply ingrained is the habit of seeing modern liberalism in such clauses that in our own times Hans Mauersberg calls it "an irony of history" that "these classical liberal ideas" were later repudiated by Münster, who established nothing but a system of *Adelsoligarchie*—precisely what the articles called for. See his "Rekonstruktionsprojekte deutscher Staaten auf dem Wiener Kongress . . . ," in Wilhelm Abel et al., eds., *Wirtschaft, Geschichte und Wirtschaftsgeschichte. Festschrift zum 65. Geburtstag von Friedrich Lütge* (Stuttgart, 1966), 272.

[71] Emphasis in the original. Schmidt, *Verfassungsfrage*, 231, point 5.

[72] *Ibid.*, 232, point 10. Hartmann, *Das Schicksal der Verfassungsvorschläge*, 43f., to the contrary, believes the convention proves Metternich's basic loyalty to the Twelve Articles.

ment.[73] To Wrede's renewed demand for equality in external affairs Metternich responded with the plan agreed to the night before, that is to say the powers' renunciation of all claim to federal assistance in wars waged as European powers even if their German provinces should become involved.[74] These assurances may have afforded Bavaria some protection against an obligation to fight on the Nieman or the Po, but what Wrede wanted above all was the right to *make* war, without which Bavaria's traditional means of defense, the manipulation of the European balance, would be lost. Winzingerode, on the other hand, who had no such aspirations, announced that the new proposal was constructive and required new instructions. Hardenberg, perhaps fearing that his colleagues would try to redraft the article on the spot, proposed tabling it until the two powers could agree on the language. This was done, and Wrede was left to concentrate his complaints on the inclusion of Carinthia and the South Tyrol in the Bund, well realizing that Austria's pious self-denials could not easily survive, say, a Sardinian attack on German federal territory itself. Yet, once again left without support by Winzingerode, he agreed provisionally to the existing vague terminology pending a precise definition later. Still worse from the point of view of his superiors in Munich, he gave conditional consent to a federal court with a narrowly defined jurisdiction.[75]

From then on it was the Württembergers who were isolated. When they protested the reference in Article II to "the constitutional rights of every class in the nation," Münster produced the paper authorized the day before, which eloquently espoused the four-point minimum for the estates "even in the event that Austria, Prussia, Bavaria, and Württemberg, either because of their special circumstances or on the basis of treaties in hand, should exclude themselves therefrom."[76] Pending clarification of a few points, Wrede was completely won over, but there is a riddle. His endorsement is inconceivable unless he took Bavaria's exemption for guaranteed. Yet Winzingerode did not see it that way, nor did the minister-president in Stuttgart, Count Ulrich von Mandelsloh, when he received a copy of Münster's motion some time later. These ideas, he advised the king, "belong to the archaic reveries of theorists. . . . We would be going backwards by half a century."[77] Even granting that Bavaria's top priority was freedom in external affairs and considering as well that Metternich had promised Wrede that

[73] Frederick to Mandelsloh, 21 Oct. 1814, HSA, Stuttgart, E 1, Fasc. 45.
[74] Protocol of 22 Oct. 1814, Klüber, *Acten*, II, 103–110.
[75] *Ibid.*; and Aretin, *Bayerns Weg*, 166.
[76] Klüber, *Acten*, Vol. I, Part 1, 68–71.
[77] Mandelsloh to Frederick, 9 Nov. 1814, extr. in Mager, "Das Problem der Verfassungen," 333, n. 79.

same day the entire triangle between the Rhine and the Mosel, Wrede's conciliatory stand on this issue is baffling.[78]

Winzingerode, in any case, pursued his assigned tasks, objecting to "governmental rights" and insisting that the only members of the Bund were the five states there present. Metternich used the occasion to underscore once more the primacy of the council over the individual Kreis chiefs and warn against partitioning Germany into "five large states," which could only violate the rights and status of the other houses. As a compromise between "states" and "estates" the phrase "members of the Bund" was adopted, Winzingerode abstaining. At this point the meeting was adjourned until the next day, leaving Metternich at least with the satisfaction of having split the opposition.[79]

It was now 4:00 p.m., and he at last received poor Keller, who had been waiting in the chancellery since 3:00. At a conference the day before the moderates among the small-state envoys had beaten down a motion by Türckheim and Gagern to threaten resort to "other measures" unless the disorder and uncertainty in Germany was terminated. Instead they voted to send Keller a second time to express their dismay that they had still received no word from the German Committee.[80] Metternich repeated his previous excuses, avoiding reference to the accession treaties. He also tried to set at rest their fears about the Kreis system (or as Keller called it, "the oligarchy"), insisting that whatever they had heard about the present plan, in the end "the rights of the ruling princes inside their respective boundaries would be preserved." He even took modest credit for having got a statement to that effect entered into that day's protocol, the reference no doubt being to his warning against "five large states."[81] Regarding the imperial title, he again stressed the difficulties but invited the small states themselves to make suggestions, thereby smoothing the way for a voluntary presentation of the crown that Austria did not seek for herself; and even if she then declined the offer, it would still reinforce her claim to the presidency and provide a rallying point for all the foes of the Kreis system.[82]

With Keller's departure Metternich knew that all was in place that ever would be. The small states were mobilizing against the Kreis sys-

---

[78] Sahrmann, *Pfalz oder Salzburg?* 44; Klüber, *Acten*, II, 103–110; and Münster to Prince Regent, 25 Oct. 1814, NSHSA, Hanover, Des. 92, XLI, No. 112, vol. I, pp. 29–32.

[79] *Ibid.* Cf. Aretin, *Bayerns Weg*, 165, who blames Wrede's ineptness for the split.

[80] Apian-Bennewitz, *Plessen und die Verfassungspolitik*, 39; Agent's report to Hager, 22 Oct. 1814 in Fournier, *Geheimpolizei*, 197f.

[81] Fournier, *Geheimpolizei*, 216, n. 1, found no such reference in the protocol, but he had not completely learned how to read these documents.

[82] Text of Keller's report of 22 Oct. 1814 in *ibid.*, 214–216.

tem. The Prussians had conceded much toward Austria's leadership of a league of equals. Bavaria and Württemberg, though resisting stubbornly, were fascinated by the Kreise yet beginning to drift apart on particular issues. Hardenberg was ready to defy the tsar, and Castlereagh was daily increasing his pressure. The monarchs were soon to depart for Buda, where Emperor Francis would face in isolation the concerted blandishments of Alexander and Frederick William. The official offer of Saxony could be delayed no more.

CHAPTER VIII

THE FRONT AGAINST RUSSIA

AT DINNER shortly after Keller's departure Metternich told Gentz much about Sagan, nothing about the note that was on its way to Hardenberg officially conveying the emperor's consent to the Prussian annexation of Saxony.[1] It was a grudging offer, to be sure, dwelling on the bitterness the deed would bring, the one-sided risks to Austrian security, and urging the Prussians to leave an independent nucleus that would obviate the need for finding an indemnity for the king of Saxony.[2] In return for the sacrifice the emperor expected "the reciprocal support and absolute uniformity of policy between the two courts in the Polish question." What the substance of the common course should be Metternich did not say, referring simply to Castlereagh's note of 11 October, the one that expressly made Saxony the reward for demanding a strong frontier in Poland, not compensation for accepting a weak one. The fate of the duchy of Warsaw, Metternich emphasized, was in itself too important to be confused with any other issue.

In contrast to these brief and allusive formulations, the Austrian conditions regarding Germany, though awkwardly expressed, were concrete and given at length. Much as the emperor deplored a division of the country and believed it could become a viable whole, Metternich wrote, he insisted that a genuine equality between the two powers required separate, nonoverlapping defense systems divided by the Mosel and the Main. The former was to be the literal line of demarcation necessary to complete the South German territorial settlement; the latter was more loosely conceived, by implication at least, to include enough territory on both sides to place it securely in the southern defense system protecting the northern approaches to the Danube The exact status of Mainz was to be determined later but in no case in a manner contrary to Austro-Bavarian understandings or prejudicial to an overall settlement, for which Metternich would make recom-

---

[1] Gentz, *Tagebücher*, I, 322.

[2] The note poses another textual problem. The standard texts in d'Angeberg, *Congrès*, II, 316–320, and Klüber, *Acten*, VII, 19–26, are identical, but contain a garbled passage (paragraph 3, sentence 3) conveying the erroneous impression that Austria was claiming leadership (*l'initiative*) in the Confederation. The authentic text, based on the copy in the HHSA and published in Bourgoing, *Vom Wiener Kongress*, 362–365, makes it clear that Metternich was only taking credit for the idea of a confederation that recognized Prussia as an equal.

mendations later. The measures taken in this regard, moreover, were to be "directly linked to the conclusion of the federal compact and to the means that will be concerted for the defense of the Confederation." In other words, Mainz must go to Bavaria, probably as a federal fortress; Hesse-Darmstadt, at least in its existing form, could never be joined to a Prussian Kreis; if Austria wished Württemberg to lead a Swabian Kreis, that was her affair; and if a confederation for Germany as a whole failed to materialize, all other arrangements would be void. As earlier with Prussia's Kreis territories so now with Saxony, title depended on the founding of a whole-German Bund and the outlines of the entire Central European settlement. "His Imperial Majesty," the note concluded, "combines all these questions into a single body of negotiations."

A copy of the note was dispatched to Castlereagh with a covering letter explicitly endorsing the language used in the note of 11 October, which made Saxony the reward for demanding a strong frontier in Poland, not compensation for a weak one.[3] The point deserves emphasis here partly because of its intrinsic importance but also because it tends to refute the charge, repeated frequently ever since, that Metternich made the offer slyly expecting that once Prussia was rewarded in Poland, the conscience of Europe, nurtured by those earnest legitimists in Paris and Munich, could be counted upon to snatch Saxony back again.[4] Hypothetically the possibility existed. The duke of Coburg had already made formal protest of any sequestration, and Talleyrand was even then telling the Russians that Poland was, after all, not so important as Saxony.[5] Yet it was precisely reassurance against this eventuality that Metternich and Castlereagh meant to convey, and though some uncertainty remained, no deception was involved. Humboldt instantly perceived the risk, tracing it, however, not to dishonest motives but to the grudging nature of Metternich's offer, its tone of "reluctance" and "condescension." If it came to war, he wanted to know,

---

[3] Text in d'Angeberg, *Congrès*, IV, pp. 1939f.

[4] Citing Metternich's own testimony to this effect, Kohlschmidt, *Sächsische Frage*, 63–65, takes his words at face value despite the fact that they were directed to the Saxon envoy, Schulenberg, at a time (end of October) when the Saxon negotiation was not complete. More puzzling is Kissinger, *World Restored*, 158, who argues that Metternich was building a moral case in Poland that would be applicable to Saxony as well and adduces as evidence a "reservation" in Metternich's note to Castlereagh against "disproportionate aggrandizement." In context, however, the passage forbids Prussia to acquiesce in *Russia's* unjust and dangerous aggrandizement. Cf. further Delbrück, "Friedrich Wilhelm III und Hardenberg," 242–265, who agrees that Metternich's offer was deceptive but that Hardenberg and Humboldt knew what they were getting into, a point that Castlereagh himself later made. Castle. to Liverp., 25 Dec. 1814, Webster, *BD*, 272.

[5] Talley. to Louis XVIII, 25 Oct. 1814, Talleyrand, *Corr.*, 83–85.

would Austria fight for Prussian possession? Further negotiation, he advised, must obtain a binding commitment on this point.[6]

Hardenberg, meanwhile, received his copy of the note later the same night, too late for comment then but in time to alert Humboldt, who was ready with a critique the next day.[7] Mainz in South German hands, he reasoned, would be dangerous to Prussia only in the event of an intra-German confrontation, and since there was no way to get it and Saxony both, prudence required acquiescence, the absolute condition, however, being that Bavaria would loyally join the Bund and surrender all her independent war-making powers. Humboldt also challenged Metternich's complaints that the baleful sacrifice of Saxony was made solely for the sake of appeasing Prussia; on the contrary, he held, it was the European equilibrium that required it and would require it even more if the common strategy failed in Poland. "Neither the success nor the nonsuccess of the démarches for Poland," he argued, "nor the cession of a few more districts can change anything regarding the question of Saxony." It was over this issue, so shrewdly perceived before the fact, that Hardenberg and Metternich were to fall out in the end.

In the meantime Hardenberg had excitedly scribbled Metternich a request to find a pretext for postponing the meeting of the German Committee scheduled for the 23rd.[8] That accomplished, the two German ministers met with Castlereagh in the latter's quarters on the Minoritenplatz, all determined to concert a diplomatic offensive before the monarchs departed for Buda the next day. Hardenberg dismissed the idea of leaving a kernel of Saxony and reiterated his objections to placing Mainz in Bavarian hands, but agreed to proceed in the Polish question "without awaiting the result of the negotiations on Germany," to use Metternich's later rendering of the bargain.[9] There followed discussion of a plan of campaign which Castlereagh was afterwards charged with putting into writing. According to it, the tsar should be told at once that if on his return to Vienna five days hence direct negotiations again failed, his allies would lay their case before the full congress, proposing "other and more extended terms." What to demand of the tsar directly as a minimum Castlereagh left entirely to Hardenberg and Metternich, but for the case the congress was brought in, he proposed a three-stage sequence of offers harking back to the London discussions in June: first an independent Poland with the frontiers of 1772; next, the same with the frontiers of 1791; and these

[6] "Sur le mémoire de Lord Castlereagh concernant l'affaire de la Pologne," 25 Oct. 1814, Humboldt, *Gesammelte Schriften*, XI, 187.

[7] Text dated 23 Oct. 1814, Humboldt, *Gesammelte Schriften*, XI, 174–178.

[8] Hard. to Mett., 22 Oct. 1814, HHSA, StK., Kongressakten, Cart. 7, p. 155.

[9] Metternich's later resumé, "Serie de la négotiation entre la Prusse et l'Autriche," HHSA, StK., Kongressakten, Cart. 7, p. 454.

being refused, full repartition, the Russian frontier following the line of the Vistula up to its confluence with the San. In the last case the treaty of Reichenbach and the convention of 1797, which forbade the revival of the name of Poland, would be cited and the entire case laid before the congress, which would "declare to the Emperor of Russia to what extent and upon what conditions Europe in congress can or cannot admit His Imperial Majesty's pretensions to an aggrandizement in Poland."[10]

Castlereagh's memorial, in which this *modus operandi* was proposed, is often said to document a powerful British initiative that forced the Prussians to drop their customary dread of the congress and compelled the vacillating Metternich to demand more in Poland than he had ever before considered.[11] The thesis is untenable. The style was certainly English: namely the use of formal written memoranda to argue the technicalities of treaties. "If once the Emperor of Russia can be brought to a *guerre de plume,*" advised Cooke, all could be peaceably settled.[12] The worst possible course, said Gentz afterwards, in the cynical way of the continent. "Lord Castlereagh was wrong to undertake it; we were wrong to consent to it," because nothing could be denied later.[13] An appeal to the congress was also Castlereagh's idea, as it had been from the start, but it was never tolerable to the Prussians and only in an eccentric way was it acceptable to Metternich, who still hoped to proceed without France. The line of the Vistula, on the other hand, could not have been essential to Castlereagh; otherwise, for the direct negotiations to be attempted first he would not have removed himself from the drafting of the minimum. Austro-Prussian solidarity, not the exact frontier in Poland, was his primary concern. The appearance of the Vistula frontier in the program for the congress was probably due to Metternich, who knew that the Austrian military demanded as much. As to the grandiose proposals for Polish independence, these, reserved for the public forum that the congress would provide, were aimed at British public opinion, as Liverpool had recently requested,[14] and also

[10] Castle. to Liverp., 24 Oct. 1814, with enclosed memorandum on "The Best Method of Handling the Polish Question," Webster, *BD*, 212–215.
[11] Most recently Kissinger, *World Restored*, 159, who assumes full agreement on Castlereagh's plan; Griewank, *Wiener Kongress*, 168f., who says his radical démarche drastically altered the situation; and Wolf D. Gruner, "Die Interaktion von Deutschland- und Europapolitik," in *Grossbritannien und Deutschland*, ed. O. Kuhn (Munich, 1974), 112, who implies Castlereagh already had carte blanche to speak for Austria and Prussia and masterminded the maneuver. Bourgoing, *Vom Wiener Kongress*, 133f., is more perceptive in regard to the degree of understanding but still makes Castlereagh the driving force.
[12] Cooke to Liverp., 25 Oct. 1814, Wellington, *Supplementary Despatches*, IX, 374f.
[13] Memorandum of 12 Feb. 1815, Metternich, *NP*, II, 484.
[14] Liverp. to Castle., 14 Oct. 1814, Webster, *BD*, 210f.

at the Poles themselves, who should prefer a genuine restoration to Alexander's facsimile. Castlereagh's memorandum, though the product of mutual consultation and basic accord, was as yet only a British proposal, binding on no one.

Despite the loose ends that remained, a common front had been formed, and less than twenty-four hours remained in which to confront the tsar. It is further evidence of Metternich's leadership at this point that he undertook the mission himself. On the following day, at any rate, shortly after Francis and Frederick William had left for Buda, he had a two-hour audience with Alexander, an encounter so ferocious that it quickly became one of the great scandals of the congress. Our sources concerning it are mostly secondhand, but they all point to a courageous, almost rash, determination to tell the tsar bluntly where the matters stood. The latter in turn responded with a personal lambasting that, according to Talleyrand, "would have been thought extraordinary even toward one of one's own servants."[15]

The chief offense was Metternich's assertion that his side, too, was capable of restoring Poland, an utterance, said the tsar, so insolent that no one else in Austria could have made it. If there was any doubt, he screamed, Metternich had only to send someone to inspect the 200,000 men at his disposal in Poland. A mere minister could not reply to talk of this kind from one who was both a sovereign *and* a minister, was Metternich's biting reply. Whether he also threatened resort to the congress is less certain in view of his own reluctance, but he probably did. Both Münster and Hardenberg of Hanover, always well informed, so reported,[16] and Alexander himself began to refer to "the conspiracy of 23 October," which by itself could account for his fury.[17] In any case, taken in conjunction with the recent dressing-down at the Leipzig anniversary ball and concurrent efforts by the tsar to set Sagan to spreading tales of his imminent dismissal, this latest tirade suggests a deliberate campaign to sap his rival's credibility while he himself was dealing directly with his fellow monarchs at Buda.[18] Tantrums too have their place in the armory of politics, as Bismarck and Hitler understood only too well.

Shaken by the experience—he had trouble finding the door as he

---

[15] Talley. to Louis XVIII, 31 Oct. 1814, Talleyrand, *Memoirs*, II, 288–290; Swedish chargé d'affaires, Hegardt, to Stockholm, 12 Nov. 1814, Fournier, *Geheimpolizei*, 280f.; Archduke John's diary in Freksa, *Congress of Intrigue*, 369f. Cf. Bourgoing, *Vom Wiener Kongress*, 138–140; Stein, "Tagebuch," 24 Oct. 1814, in Stein, *Briefe*, v, 328f.; and Gentz's memorandum of 12 Feb. 1815, in Metternich, *NP*, II, 483.

[16] Hardenberg to the Prince Regent, 25 Oct. 1814, NSHSA, Cal. Br. 24, No. 5896; and Griewank, *Wiener Kongress*, 175.

[17] Bourgoing, *Vom Wiener Kongress*, 134.

[18] Cf. Police report to Hager, 28 oct. 1814, Fournier, *Geheimpolizei*, 422; and Corti, *Frauen*, I, 476.

backed out of the room—and alarmed that he, the minister, not Alexander, the monarch, was being eliminated from the negotiation, Metternich hastened to warn Francis of the tsar's mood. "The totality of nonsense that he advanced at the conference" was reminiscent, said Metternich, of his previous encounters with Napoleon. "In the entire monarchy I alone appear to be the antagonist." In his sober and stubborn Habsburg way Francis, though immersed in the monarchical fellowship at Buda, stood by his man, rejecting the tsar's repeated proposals to bypass their ministers and replying to Metternich's report that "even though we are away from each other, Emperor Alexander will find us talking in unison."[19]

Thus protected against unpleasant surprises when the monarchs returned, Metternich now pressed to have plans in readiness for that occasion, which was expected on 29 October. Since the award of Saxony was henceforth dependent on the formation of a German Confederation, the German Committee now took on a new importance and Metternich's role in it a new vigor as he prepared to play the cards he had wrested from the Prussians in the secret convention of 21 October. Before the capitulation on Saxony the pressure had been on him to accommodate to Prussian plans. Now it was Hardenberg who must take care that nothing jeopardize the negotiations; and he could in fact be more flexible because with Saxony in hand Prussia's preponderance in North Germany would not depend as heavily on the Kreis system.

Shortly after beating his humiliating retreat from the tsar Metternich returned to the chancellery, where the German Committee was already in session under the chairmanship of Wessenberg.[20] At issue was still Article IX, to which the Bavarians and the Austrians continued to give top priority, the former to preserve their right to make war, the latter to establish the defensive arrangements that to them were the central purpose of the Bund. If agreement could be reached on this one article, it might go into effect at once, establishing an alliance that could be thrown into the balance in the current struggle with Russia. Wessenberg and Humboldt had drafted a new version, which fell back on the secret accord. It still forbade independent wars by the wholly German states but bound Austria and Prussia not only to abstain from alliances against any other member states but also, in any wars they waged solely as great powers, to renounce all claim to federal assistance, even for their German provinces should they become involved. In the latter case the Bund, by procedures not specified, could decide for itself whether to participate or not. One wonders what would have happened

[19] Mett. to Francis, 24 Oct. 1814 with latter's reply. Extr. in Corti, *Frauen*, I, 477f.
[20] This and following, unless otherwise indicated, from protocol of the German Committee session of 24 Oct. 1814, in Klüber, *Acten*, II, 116–124.

in 1866 if the federal constitution had so provided. On political grounds the Bund would no doubt have joined the war anyway since, among other reasons, member states were invaded. With Saxony eliminated, however, an Austro-Prussian war without federal participation, though unlikely, would have been geographically feasible and, with the Wessenberg-Humboldt proposal, constitutionally permissible. In this situation, moreover, France would undoubtedly have offered herself once again as the protector of German neutrality.

It is a credit to Marshal Wrede's vision in military matters that he had already pondered such eventualities: not only an Austro-Prussian war but other combinations, in which Austria and/or Prussia might be at war with France or Russia or Turkey or even Sweden. In all these cases, he insisted, the Bavarian interest would in varying degrees probably require her participation, if only to protect her own soil, regardless of what the rest of the Bund decided. These were reasonable concerns, especially if Bavaria should acquire common frontiers with both the German powers, but when Wrede added to his examples that of a distant war in Spain, where Bavarian interests would be slight and indirect, he was defending not merely her territory but her standing as a European power as well. At bottom that is what divided him from Winzingerode on the most basic of issues. As an equal partner with the two powers Bavaria could concede much to the Bund; otherwise it was better that there be no Bund at all.

Metternich and Hardenberg, on the other hand, though differing on the measure of control they should have over the federal forces, agreed that as a minimum the Bund should be neutral in European affairs. "In any war with France and Russia," wrote Metternich four years later, when these matters were still in flux, in such a war

> Austria and Prussia must be covered by the Bund in the rear and on the flanks. . . . That [the states' contingents] take their places in the line and that the federal army fights for Austria and Prussia— and at the very least could never fight against Austria and Prussia— this is our great, our true and honestly expressed aim, firmly and cogently stated.[21]

From the shrill talk about "the devouring powers" in the previous session of the German Committee to these turgid lines of future years the rhetoric might change, but the central theme of Metternich's German policy remained constant.

In the meantime Count Münster, who during these same years was to become the leading expert on the function of the Bund in the

[21] Mett. to Zichy, 21 May 1818 (copy), HHSA, StK., Frankfurt Weisungen, Fasc. 2.

European balance of power, was even more incensed at the Bavarian stand. Only by relinquishing the right of private wars conferred by the Treaty of Westphalia could the German states justify the duty of the Bund to defend them; and only in this way could Hanover overcome her peculiar vulnerability as Britain's exposed continental beachhead.[22] Yet Austria and Prussia too must make adjustments, he held. Mindful that as matters stood then the decision of "the Bund" about participation in an Austro-Prussian war really belonged to the Kreis chiefs, Münster insisted that in such a war the two powers must abstain, leaving the decision to the three others. From here, however, it was but a short step to allowing each Kreis chief to do what he pleased, and Wrede and Winzingerode so proposed, naturally assuming that each chief would have the right to carry the entire Kreis with him—and in the process rend Germany into the five masses that Metternich so decried. As a result Wrede was asked to redraft Article IX himself.[23]

For the time being, such a graphic demonstration of the absurdities to which the Kreis system could lead only played into Austrian hands. When Wrede later in the meeting renewed his attack on the double votes assigned to the two powers, Metternich defended them not on grounds of size alone, but more fundamentally for the reason that in any federal war the total armed forces of the two powers, not just their federal contingents, would be at the disposal of the Bund. A commitment of such magnitude would have affected the entire European balance, and though it never became an article of federal law, Metternich always believed that regardless of constitutional obligations, any less an effort, should the Rhine again be crossed, would merely duplicate the disastrous half-measures of the past. It was also a one-sided offer, as the Austrian generals later complained, since Wrede and Linden were seeing to it that the Bund made no reciprocal commitments to the non-Bund lands of the empire.[24]

Although Münster enjoyed referring to England as Hanover's non-German territory, which should entitle her to parity with the two powers, he supported them on the issue all the same. Wrede and Linden, however, persisted in opposition, enabling Metternich to propose the compromise previously concerted with Prussia: namely, that any vote aligning the two powers against the other three be declared a tie, which could then be broken by calling in Baden and Hesse-Cassel. This solution, to be sure, offered protection against the powers, but it would also have diluted the exclusiveness of the club; each of the two middle

[22] Münster to Prince Regent, 25 Oct. 1814, NSHSA, Hanover, Des. 92, XLI, No. 112, vol. I, pp. 29–32.
[23] Protocol of 24 Oct. 1814, Klüber, *Acten*, II, 118.
[24] *Ibid.*

states wanted one vote out of five, not one out of nine. Since they professed to need new instructions, the matter rested there, setting the stage for Metternich's next and boldest démarche.

Just before his arrival at the meeting the committee had taken the positive step of adopting in principle the establishment of Kreise, Kreis chiefs, and a federal assembly. Now it was wrangling over issues that exposed the inherent difficulties of the system. None was keen about even the occasional presence of two lesser states in the Council of Kreis Chiefs, but if votes were to be tied to Kreise, how was the permanent majority of the two powers to be avoided? Perhaps, Metternich volunteered artfully, the time had come to consider if Kreise were necessary at all, whether the same purpose could be achieved in some other way: specifically "by the establishment of a Directorial Council and by the formation of at most military and judiciary districts without bringing these units into administration." Here was the genesis of what later became the corps areas and appellate court system of the Bund, and Metternich reserved the right to submit a plan later. Under this system executive orders would go from the council directly to the several states without the mediation of a Kreis chief. District military commands and judiciary areas would still have value but they would be no substitutes for revenue-producing Kreis estates.

However that may be, the suggestion for the moment produced consternation. Though probably surprised by the timing, Hardenberg and Humboldt were bound by previous concession to remain silent, but the outcry from the others, even the faithful Münster, was deafening: all extolled the virtues of the Kreise, Wrede adding—"most emphatically" according to the official record—that there must be no more than five and that the Hanoverian Kreis, "so enlarged as to produce a more equitable relationship," must encompass most of the small states in the north.[25] In this atmosphere the meeting was abruptly adjourned, leaving the earlier action on the Kreis system intact. Still distressed, however, Wrede concluded that the doubt cast on the Kreise made direct territorial annexations all the more vital. That night he renewed to Metternich his demand for a seat on the Committee of Eight and pressed him again on their particular territorial difficulties. For these Metternich proposed direct talks between Francis and Max Joseph, but the king refused.[26]

The following day, 25 October, Metternich again met privately with

[25] Klüber, *Acten*, II, 121f. Also Münster to Prince Regent, 25 Oct. 1814, as per n. 22 above.
[26] Wrede to Mett., 24 Oct. 1814, HHSA, StK., Kongressakten, Cart. 7, pp. 83f.; and Max Joseph to Wrede, 26 Oct. 1814, cited in Winter, *Wrede als Berater*, 220.

the Prussians and Hanoverians,[27] but what happened can only be inferred from the debates in the German Committee on the 26th. Metternich opened the meeting with debate on Bavaria's new version of Article IX.[28] This began with the broad assertion that "every member of the Bund" had the right to conclude alliances independently but then proceeded to list exceptions that in fact approximated what Metternich and Hardenberg had already conceded, the main difference being greater emphasis on self-help where federal action was deemed inadequate. The plan also allowed each state to determine for itself whether a given alliance was dangerous to the Bund. Reminding the marshal that the right to private wars was the hallmark of the old Reich, which Bavaria in every other respect found so repugnant, Metternich contended that the Bavarian interest was best served by collective security, which was possible only "if Germany emerges as a single dynamic state against all foreign powers." With this ringing oratory the issue was dropped for that meeting. Believing, however, that Wrede was mainly striving to rescue a principle, Metternich later took him aside and proposed the simplest phrasing yet: "Every state has the right of alliances so long as they do not conflict with the *nexus foederis*." This, he informed Humboldt in a hastily scrawled note, Bavaria would accept.[29]

Meanwhile, attention had turned to the regulations governing the Council of Kreis Chiefs and focused immediately on the voting procedure. Metternich now made two motions that suggest a prior bargain with Hardenberg. To the opponents of adding outside votes to break deadlocks he now held out the prospect that simple tabling should be permitted if both sides so preferred. On the other hand, he moved that when extra states were called in, the deliberations should begin anew with all nine voices participating and no one committed to previous positions. This procedure could be justified as common sense, but more important in Metternich's strategy, it also enhanced the status of Baden and Hesse-Cassel; when they took their turns on the council, they would participate as equals almost as if they were Kreis chiefs too. What a skillful presidium could do with this situation can easily be imagined. Prompt seconding by Hardenberg and Münster without comment is further evidence of a private understanding in the matter. Wrede and Winzingerode, as expected, repeated their demand for five

[27] Hardenberg, "Tagebücher," 35.
[28] Text in Klüber, *Acten*, II, 130f. Following from *ibid.*, 124–131, protocol of 26 Oct. 1814.
[29] Mett. to Humboldt, n.d., ZSTA, Merseberg, 2.4.1.I, No. 1456, p. 11. Schmidt, *Verfassungsfrage*, 244, puts this note either here or at the next session, but since the subject did not come up on the latter occasion, the meeting of the 26th is almost certainly correct.

equal votes, which of course would have been the simplest way to prevent deadlocks.[30]

More basic to Metternich's campaign in behalf of the lesser states was the character to be given the lower house or Council of Princes and Estates, as it was still called. This was the subject of Article VI, which came up next, and given the Bavarian-Württemberg view that the Bund was to be only a union of Kreis chiefs, Metternich could expect fierce resistance. As it happened, Wrede and Winzingerode did question the need for a second chamber, yet judging from the official protocol, eventually accepted it in principle with surprisingly good grace, preferring apparently to avoid a direct assault and concentrate on rendering the body harmless. Wrede, always mindful of Frankfurt, was reluctant to admit the so-called free cities as provided in the Twelve Articles, insisting that the very concept of such cities had been terminated by the dissolution of the Reich. True, replied Metternich, hastily improvising, but it had been revalidated in the treaties of alliance, at least for Hamburg, Bremen, and Lübeck. Wrede seemed satisfied with this explanation but reserved further comment. Winzingerode did likewise.[31]

Metternich's facile assurance had ominous overtones, however, for who could tell what these same esoteric treaties might have to say about the mediatized houses, which owing largely to Metternich's earlier efforts had not been mentioned in Article VI? Since there is no evidence that the Prussians forced the issue—indeed, Wessenberg later advised Humboldt that the sooner "this admittedly unpleasant motion" was introduced, the better[32]—the middle states must have broached the question spontaneously. Otherwise the protocol of the meeting would not have emphasized, where Article VI did not, that the current discussion was confined to those princes "who are still in possession of their governmental rights," i.e., sovereignty.[33] On this basis it was unanimously agreed to assign whole votes to princely houses (including Kreis chiefs) with populations above 100,000 and further, Württemberg abstaining, to allow smaller houses, if dynastically related, to share a vote. Wrede, who evidently considered the issue of whole and curial votes now settled except for the free cities, jubilantly reported that the session had finally subjugated the mediatized houses to the sovereignty

[30] Klüber, Acten, II, 127f. Cf. Martens's later summary of the issue in "Parallele zwischen den vorgeschlagenen und den bisher angenommenen Artikel," 21 Nov. 1814, NSHSA, Hanover, Des. 91, No. 25, pp. 2–18.

[31] Klüber, Acten, II, 129.

[32] Marginal commentary on parallel development of Art. VI by Wessenberg and Humboldt, n.d., ZSTA, Merseberg, 2.4.1.I, No. 1456.

[33] Klüber, Acten, II, 128, where this phrase is given emphasis in the type.

of the individual princes.[34] Metternich and Hardenberg, on the other hand, viewed the action as awarding seats for the present to the one class of princes but without prejudicing later motions in regard to others.

For Metternich, of course, the above issue was peripheral, provided that the mediatized houses acquired no more than token representation, just enough to assure their equality of birth with the sovereign princes. When it came to the competence of the lower house, however, the heart of his strategy was at stake, since any independent legislative power that this chamber acquired would be subtracted both from that of the higher body and from the powers of the individual Kreis assemblies. On this issue, therefore, the Austrians and Prussians were openly at odds. Hardenberg was willing to grant the lower house a certain initiative in the legislative process but insisted that in the end all bills must be ratified by the Council of Kreis Chiefs. Wrede and Winzingerode were still more grudging, holding that the higher body should draft bills, vote on them en bloc when they came before the lower house, and finally sanction the finished product.[35] Both proposals thus aimed at limiting the lesser states to a purely consultative role. The result, however, would probably not have been an unbridled tyranny of the Council of Kreis Chiefs but rather a severe stunting of the federal legislative power itself, as each chief jealously guarded the legislation of his Kreis.

Metternich's plan aimed at the opposite effect. To be sure, he viewed the Council of Kreis Chiefs, which would be in permanent session, as the logical organ to gather material over the year and make recommendations, but once these were sent down, the lower house, he insisted, should be free to make amendments, originate new bills, and enact binding laws by a majority vote, in which each Kreis chief acted only for himself. "To grant a formal veto to the first council," Wessenberg later said in criticism of Humboldt, "seems to me very ominous for the freedom of the German estates." Besides, he added, as if to depreciate the significance of the issue, "the influence of the more powerful estates will in any case provide a veto of sorts."[36] However that might be, Metternich's Council of Princes and Estates was to be a true legislature, passing laws for Germany as a whole; and operating by majority rule, it would have been a more effective body than the federal diet that did in the end materialize.

This arrangement should not be confused with democracy, however;

[34] Winter, *Wrede als Berater*, 172f., who does not say that seats for the mediatized houses was the issue, but this was the only topic in that session that affected them.
[35] Klüber, *Acten*, II, 129–132.
[36] Parallel development of Art. VI, as per n. 32.

it was rather Metternich's way of using the Kreis estates collectively at the federal level to outflank the individual Kreis chiefs, just as Hardenberg wanted seats for the mediatized houses to exert pressure on their sovereigns from above. As chairman, moreover, and with no Kreis estates of her own to sow distrust, Austria would appear to rise above the petty concerns of the other Kreis chiefs and shine as the patron of the lesser states. The lower council would be a peculiarly Austrian forum. The effect would have been greater German unity even though this was not in itself Metternich's principal concern. Whether he and Hardenberg had tried to reconcile their differences the night before we do not know, but never had they so openly disagreed in committee session. Perhaps that is why Wrede reported after the meeting that Austria's support of Prussia's plans for the Bund was only illusory.[37]

When these discussions resumed on 29 October, Metternich again arrived late and so was not on hand to defend himself when Wrede, calling his bluff about the status of the free cities, now demanded official notification that their freedom was in fact confirmed by treaty.[38] The Prussians, however, rose to the challenge, eager to exploit this opportunity to place their interpretation of the treaties into the committee records. Well no, Humboldt had to admit, the turbulence of war had prevented such niceties as formal treaties, but it was simply understood that the victims of French conquests, whether the Hanseatic towns or Brunswick or Hesse-Cassel, should be restored because their *Länder* constitutions continued in effect (as Münster had always insisted). If Wrede wanted a basis in law, Hardenberg interjected, the only order that Prussia recognized was the one inaugurated by the Imperial Recess of 1803. Thus the field marshal's obsession with Frankfurt had caused him, on this unfamiliar civilian terrain, to expose the flank on which the very existence of royal Bavaria rested.[39] Still, it was not the soldier but the perhaps more perceptive Winzingerode who blanched; in some panic he pleaded that whatever the case for others, those states which had been compelled under duress to sign treaties with Napoleon must be allowed to stand on them. Wessenberg, meanwhile, performing Metternich's duties as the practical-minded broker, had offered a compromise to the effect that the three cities should simply notify other governments officially that they were back in business. This was adopted.

Wrede's unexpected move was followed by another. When the com-

---

[37] Wrede to Montgelas, 26 Oct. 1814, in Heilmann, *Fürst Wrede*, 123. Cf. Winter, *Wrede als Berater*, 175, who believes this session inaugurated an Austro-Bavarian rapprochement.
[38] This and following from protocol of 29 Oct. 1814, Klüber, *Acten*, II, 135–144.
[39] Cf. Aretin, *Bayerns Weg*, 168.

mittee resumed debate on the organization of the Council of Kreis
Chiefs, Humboldt suddenly moved to change its name to the Council
of Kings, the same august title accorded to the upper house of the
Rheinbund, this from the man who normally steeped his proposals in
the language of the old Reich. There can be only one explanation: it
was his way of blunting Metternich's attacks on the exclusiveness of
the council. Baden and Hesse-Cassel might on their occasional ap-
pearances function as equals, but as grand duchies among kingdoms
they would always be seen as adjuncts, and no amount of tinkering by
Metternich could alter this distinction.[40] Five Kreis chiefs were enough.
If Wessenberg detected this implication, he considered it unimportant
and joined the delighted middle-state envoys in supporting the measure. Metternich, however, when he finally arrived on the scene, took
the matter seriously, rescinding the Austrian vote, reserving further
statements, and requesting that in the meantime everybody refer simply to "the first council." The request was granted, but it was only the
first step, as we shall see, in removing invidious distinctions between
the two councils. As if in revenge, however, the committee in turn
struck the name of Austria from the presidency of the council and
henceforth referred merely to "the presiding plenipotentiary," the middle
states hoping for a system of rotation, Metternich no doubt confident
that his understanding with Hardenberg would save Austrian primacy
in the end.

After this flurry the committee proceeded to fill in the attributes of
the First Council, vesting it with all executive power, certain judicial
functions, and authority to make war and peace and conduct foreign
policy for the Bund as a whole. Although the Kreis chiefs were to be
the agents of executive power, the council was made responsible for
seeing that they fulfilled but did not overstep their federal duties. In
the latter case the council might deputize one or more chiefs to use
force against the violator. Each chief's power, finally, was to be limited
to his Kreis, an understandable precaution if one recalls the interminable wrangling among Bavaria, Württemberg, and Austria over the
fragmented estates of Swabia in years gone by.[41]

All these provisions were as Humboldt had drafted them. Several
others, however, in the form of footnotes, which suggest that they were
later modifications, have all the marks of Metternich's deft strokes.
The council's judicial powers Humboldt had originally treated as something to be decided later, and in the specific case of a Kreis member's
complaint against a chief the council was merely to receive the case,

[40] Under the Rheinbund grand dukes were equated with kings to the extent that
they also sat in the College of Kings, but their rank otherwise was inferior.
[41] Protocol of 29 October 1814, Klüber, *Acten*, II, 139–142.

presumably for referral to the federal court for decision. In the version adopted by the committee the power of adjudication was given to the council itself as Metternich had often proposed and certainly as the middle states preferred. Another provision probably due to Metternich would have significantly diluted each of the Kreis chief's executive powers. Humboldt's draft said simply that the executive power of the council was to be carried out by the Kreis chiefs; a footnote, however, explained that "the *governments* execute federal decrees" and limited the Kreis chiefs to issuing a warning to those that balked; moreover, he was explicitly restrained from using force, this resort presumably requiring authorization by the council. Although the amendment did not remove the Kreis chiefs from administration as Metternich wished to do, it certainly made their function more supervisory than active, giving the Kreis more a confederate than a federal internal organization and protecting the "governmental rights" of its members.[42]

As the reading of Humboldt's draft progressed, the envoys from Württemberg grew more and more uneasy over approving one article at a time without knowing precisely what points had already been approved and by whom, how many reservations had been attached, or how each article in the end would relate to the whole German constitution. The concern is understandable considering that Metternich's conduct of the meetings deliberately allowed issues to hang in midair rather than cause needless confrontations before a consensus had emerged. Accordingly Winzingerode attached a blanket reservation to all the points without, however, necessarily disapproving.[43] Such agonizing caution was especially irritating to the Prussians, who were in no position to exercise patience. The return of the monarchs from Buda that evening promised an early showdown on the Saxon-Polish question, which would require the broadest possible understandings with Metternich if an effective stand was to be made against the tsar. But even victory in the Polish question could have its problems if in the meantime there was no progress toward a German Bund. At worst Metternich might consider his terms unmet and withdraw his consent to the annexation of Saxony; at best he could use Saxony as leverage for creating the kind of Bund he wanted. If the Bavarians preferred

[42] Despite the correspondence between these points and Metternich's known views, we could not necessarily attribute them to him save for some substantive discrepancies between the text of Humboldt's detailed development and the footnotes (Klüber, *Acten*, II, 132–135), which indicate last-minute insertions made without time to reconcile the original text with them. Whether the amendments were made in the three-power meeting of the 28th or at the committee meeting of the 29th is uncertain, though in regard to judicial powers the appearance of the term "the First Council" in both the note and the article adopted by the committee strongly indicate the later date for at least this amendment.

[43] Klüber, *Acten*, II, 141.

no Bund to any, Hardenberg now had to realize that for Prussia any Bund was better than none.

These considerations gradually brought friends of the Kreise closer together. When Württemberg objected to a Prussian proposal for accrediting foreign envoys to the Bund, Humboldt readily agreed that the idea had "many drawbacks" and offered to restrict accreditation to extraordinary missions. To accelerate the proceedings he then invited the middle states to cease their defensive tactics and submit any proposals of their own "that could appear necessary for the completion of the whole." The need now was for a finished draft that "could be placed before the other princes."[44]

What Gentz always referred to as grand affairs dominated the last days of October and probably had a part in delaying the next meeting of the German Committee till 3 November. In the interval, however, the sense of urgency about the Bund intensified and drove private negotiations forward. A day or so after Humboldt's invitation Winzingerode circulated a complete draft constitution,[45] designed not only to show the interdependence of all the parts but to test his understanding of what had been agreed to so far, at least provisionally.[46] Accordingly, the piece repeated much that we have already been through. For present purposes the core of it was the voting system of five equal voices operating by majority rule and a division into Kreise, each encompassing contiguous territory and a population of between 3 and 4 million, the closest any one had yet come to facing the ultimate truth: the actual delineation of boundaries. The powers of the First Council as a whole were similar to those recently adopted but diluted somewhat in favor of the individual chiefs. The latter, for example, would not be "instructed" but "requested" to enforce given measures; complaints by a Kreis estate to the council would not be "adjudicated" by the council but "mediated" with his Kreis chief. Within each Kreis the chief was to enforce federal and Kreis law, using force if necessary. He was to maintain and command the military system, with authority to impose assessments on the other Kreis estates. He was to convene the estates at his pleasure, preside at their meetings, draft the bills, lead the debate, and if dissatisfied, veto the results. With such powers the king of Württemberg as Kreis chief would have controlled the Hohenzollern principalities, Baden, and perhaps Hesse-Darmstadt as fully as he ruled his Standesherren at home, and that may explain why he was willing

---

[44] *Ibid.*, 139.

[45] Schmidt, *Verfassungsfrage*, 236, estimates the date as 2 November, but this does not allow time for the drafting of two other papers based on it. See below, pp. 222–224.

[46] Protocol of 3 Nov. 1814, Klüber, *Acten*, II, 146f. and 165f. The following is based on the text of the draft constitution in *ibid.*, 148–156.

to require *landständische Verfassungen*—to be sure, adapted to local conditions.[47]

Metternich meanwhile had been busy with grand affairs, but on Tuesday night, 1 November, he and Wessenberg received the Prussians at the chancellery to resume private discussions.[48] Applying our usual hypothesis that the subject matter of an informal Austro-Prussian parley devoid of records can be roughly inferred from the contents of the next meeting of the German Committee, we see a remarkable scene unfolding. The Prussians, in redrafting Articles IV and V about the First Council and the Kreis chiefs, have followed the Württemberg text almost verbatim, adopting not only the language but accepting Kreise of roughly equal population and, at last, the system of five equal voices. The only significant deviation was the insistence that Prussia, like Austria, have two Kreise whereas Winzingerode had assigned her only one. With the capitulation on the question of votes, the last vestige of the Austro-Prussian diarchy disappeared. It would now be possible for the middle states to prevail against the great powers.[49]

The king of Württemberg, who must have had prior indications of the Prussian démarche and may even have seen Humboldt's revisions before the Austrians did, was overjoyed. "The Council of Kings," he boasted to Mandelsloh, "concentrates more power than the Roman emperor ever had; it has an exclusive veto in all matters brought before the Council of Princes and alone decides on war and peace." The lower house, he believed, was only "a *simulacre*," the restrictions on the Kreis chiefs mere formalities "to console the injured parties." His confidence regarding the scope of the Kreis is still more striking, worthy of quoting as he rambled on:

> It is no longer a question of the mediatized; and of those still remaining, the Hohenzollerns, Isenburg, and probably Reuss as well have already been butchered. We pay no attention to the noise that the smaller ones make, which tends to turn into threats. I must, however, except Baden, which behaves more quietly and awaits its fate. The Swabian Kreis will be retained with a population of 3,500,000.[50]

The king, to be sure, realized that these points were only "tacitly agreed upon," but he had every reason to believe that Hardenberg now endorsed them, and Metternich's hand was too well concealed to reveal

[47] *Ibid.*, 152–156.
[48] Hardenberg, "Tagebücher," 36.
[49] "Vorschläge des Herrn Staatskanzlers Fürsten Hardenberg," annexed to protocol of 3 Nov. 1814, Klübe. *Acten*, II, 156–160.
[50] Frederick to Mandelsloh, 31 Oct. 1814, HSA, Stuttgart, E 1, Fasc. 45.

that he did not. In any case, his enthusiasm was far removed from his mood of only a few days earlier, when he had denounced Prussia for parading a reactionary program as liberalism, seeking to lure the mediatized "from their lawful rulers," and hanging out *landständische Verfassungen* "as signboards of liberalism."[51]

If the Prussian démarche and King Frederick's optimism were unexpected, Metternich's reaction was no less so. Since the time he himself had first proposed the abandonment of the double votes, his substitute remedy for great-power preponderance, the addition of Baden and Hesse-Cassel, had become an end in itself, demanding ever more sedulous cultivation if it was to be the indirect means of enlarging the council. Another consideration was the course of the deliberations, which strongly suggested that the normal alignment might not always be the three South German votes (plus Hanover in many cases) against Prussia, but rather the Kreis-oriented states against Austria. In the crucial matter of war and peace, moreover, who could tell whether the Prussians and the equally ambitious Bavarians might not some day lure Württemberg to join them in voting the Bund into a war of perhaps dubious defensive character, especially as Humboldt's development of Article V pointedly excluded the lower council from a voice in such matters? Connoisseurs of Freudian slips might also find it significant that the same document included a procedure for dividing the booty should the Bund happily *gain* territory after a war. The idea would never have occurred to the Austrians, but perhaps it signified nothing more than routine Prussian thoroughness.[52]

Whether Metternich challenged the Prussian stand in its entirety is not clear, since the records are contradictory.[53] On such a solemn issue as war and peace, however, he had no intention of allowing Austria to be dragged into war by a fortuitous combination of three votes that she could not control. In this sphere at least he at length induced the Prussians to withdraw the Humboldt articles in favor of a substitute project prepared by Wessenberg. The latter envisioned a complicated system in which the First Council, in a crisis, deliberated with the envoys of Baden and Hesse-Cassel, who would then meet with three elected members of the Second Council. This committee of five would then decide by majority vote how Baden's and Hesse-Cassel's votes were to be cast when they returned to the deliberations of the higher body,

[51] Same to same, 25 Oct. 1814, *ibid.*
[52] Klüber, *Acten*, II, 143f.
[53] E.g., the Hardenberg "Vorschläge" with the blanket provision for five equal votes "in all cases proper to the council" were submitted to the German Committee on 3 Nov. together with a joint Austro-Prussian proposition which retained the double votes in decisions on peace and war. Klüber, *Acten*, II, 156–164.

where the final decision would be reached by a majority, Austria and Prussia casting two votes each in a total of nine.[54]

Thus the two powers, if united, would need to find only one supporter in order to prevail; if not, the power favoring war would be hard pressed to persuade three others, and Austria would have the advantage because of her influence in the lower chamber. Apart from the substantive issue, however, the plan marked another step toward institutional equality. The Second Council would now have an organic link with the First, a positive voice equal to that of either of the powers in a question of grave importance, as the Rademacher committee had once recommended. The participation of Baden and Hesse-Cassel, moreover, would be obligatory, not contingent upon a deadlock, and the precedent would be created for extending the procedure to other cases.

Ostensibly the Wessenberg amendments were offered at this time because they affected the powers of the Kreis chiefs, the main concern to most of the committee. Metternich, however, whose immediate goal was the establishment of a defense league, in his own hand incorporated into the substitute proposition the Austrian position on all the issues raised by Articles IX and X of the Twelve Articles. Thus the duty of mutual assistance against attack from abroad was explicitly stated for the first time, so emphatically in fact that the clause seemed to make no exception for wars of the great powers, which by another article, the Bund would not have to join unless the majority so decreed.[55] The "Bavarian" clause permitting individual states to render aid independently was also retained. Members of the Second Council were barred from all foreign wars, the Kreis chiefs, however, only from wars that endangered the Bund or one of its members. As for the conclusion of peace, only the prorated sharing of losses was mentioned, the reason presumably being that a defense league had no business to contemplate gains.[56]

The Prussian endorsement of the Wessenberg articles on the one hand and much of the Württemberg draft on the other brought the Austrians and Prussians closer than ever before on the question of the Bund. "I get on well with Metternich," Humboldt wrote the day afterwards. "He could not bypass me in any case; still he also feels the

[54] *Ibid.*, 162.

[55] Wessenberg draft, Art. II: "Dagegen verpflichten sich sämmtliche Bundesglieder ebenfalls *ohne Ausnahme* einander gegen auswärtige Gewalt mit allen ihren Kräften und Mitteln nach den hier folgenden Bestimmungen beizustehen" (emphasis mine). This ambiguity found its way into the Federal Act and was not remedied until the Vienna Final Act of 1820.

[56] *Klüber, Acten*, II, 162–164; and Metternich's note, n.d., ZSTA, Merseburg, 2.4.1.I, No. 1559, p. 288.

need to make sure of my opinion, and so he works with me frequently and with a good attitude."[57] When all the papers were presented to the full committee on 3 November, final action was deferred, but no protests were forthcoming. Winzingerode, to be sure, reiterated the tentativeness of his position on all counts but only pending the compilation of a detailed collation comparing previous actions with his twelve articles.[58]

Metternich seems to have taken these reservations as technicalities, however. Conveying to the emperor the next day the protocols of the first seven sessions, he added the cheerful assurance that

> The progress of affairs improves daily, and I can especially say this of the eighth session, the protocol of which has not yet been drafted. *So far I have remained true to the principle of protecting the less powerful against the stronger.* The role that will fall to Your Majesty has such a protective character that with a little adroitness and a precisely correct course, the preeminence of Austria will rest on a far more secure and solid foundation than it had before the overthrow of the last imperial constitution.[59]

At last we have it from the master himself: in his own words the unifying theme of his labyrinthine maneuvers, proof that our artful constructs, our labored inferences, our obsession with detail have headed us right after all. The patient chipping away at the privileges of the Kreis chiefs, the gradual shift of influence from the First to the Second Council, the promotion of equality for all are no longer merely suggested in vague promises to Plessen and Keller but are now affirmed in an accounting to the emperor.[60]

As the German negotiation mounted to a climax Metternich could not forget that, intricate and time-consuming as it was, it was still an adjunct to grand affairs. In this sphere, moreover, he was peculiarly alone. The enormous chorus raised against his German policy—by the old councilors in the chancellery, by the coterie of mediatized noblemen

[57] Humb. to Caroline, 2 Nov. 1814, Humboldt, *Briefe*, IV, 399.

[58] Klüber, *Acten*, II, 145–147 and 165f.

[59] Mett. to Francis, 4 Nov. 1814, HHSA, StK., Vorträge, Cart. 196, XI, p. 40 (emphasis mine).

[60] Cf. Griewank, *Wiener Kongress*, 182, and Mager, "Das Problem der Verfassungen," 319f., n. 57, both of whom, imputing to Metternich and Hardenberg equally restorative intentions, assume that the "less powerful" Metternich referred to were the mediatized houses. That would be true coming from Hardenberg, but here it is inherently improbable. More conclusive, however, is the context. Metternich is explaining the content of the protocols he is transmitting, in which the mediatized houses so far are hardly mentioned. Griewank's account is further garbled by giving as the date 20 Nov., which is when Francis returned the *Vortrag* to Metternich and, more important, is also after a decisive turn in the Saxon-Polish question and the suspension of the German negotiation.

around Stadion and Starhemberg, and by the scions of "new" princely houses who blamed him for Prussia's designs on them[61]—all this could be dismissed as the whining of disappointed suppliants. On Saxony and Poland, however, reasonable men could differ with him objectively, and most did. Wessenberg, his gifted collaborator on the German Committee, never accepted the capitulation on Saxony and warned that "the federative system in Germany would be only a chimera" if he went through with it.[62] Gentz was more reticent, but his views were well known, his talents therefore best utilized in maintaining a continuous backdoor contact with the French and Bavarians should the first, preferred combination fail. The formidable prestige of Schwarzenberg was seldom on the foreign minister's side. Valuing strong dependable frontiers above fluctuating diplomatic alignments, he was skeptical of a German Bund and opposed to concessions in either Saxony or Poland. In the chancellery itself such old favorites as Krufft, Hoppé, and Hudelist complained behind their chief's back, jealous as they were of foreigners like Count Mercy and Baron Paul Handel, who along with Binder remained the most faithful.[63]

Towering over all these, however, was the immovable figure of Kaiser Franz, who in the end was the only one who counted. He backed his minister partly because he had a striking record of success, partly because old Baron Franz von Thugut, Francis's first foreign minister, advised him that the incumbent was superior to Stadion, the favorite candidate of Metternich's detractors. Nor did it damage Metternich's cause that the tsar reviled him and tried so crudely to have him replaced; for in the final reckoning the basic factor was Francis's agreement with Metternich's policy.[64] The bond between the frivolous minister and the dour, plodding emperor seems absurd on the surface, but underneath what was Metternich's way if not steadiness, patience, and perseverance—the soul of Habsburg statecraft through the ages, spiced now with imagination? Even the great démarche on Saxony, when it came, seemed inevitable, like the climax of a logical development. In comparison Hardenberg's transitions—the abandonment of the Forty-one Articles, for example, the sudden lavish territorial offers to Bavaria, or the capitulation on the double vote—seemed always abrupt, frenetic, without preparation.

But now the emperor was in Buda, and the minister had to act without the benefit of their daily conferences. On the other hand, Alexander and Frederick William were also out of the way as he had

---

[61] Weil, *Les Dessous*, I, 225, 296, 310, 384f., and 427f.
[62] Memorial of 27 Oct. 1814, HHSA, StK., Kongressakten, Cart. 7, pp. 563–571.
[63] Fournier, *Geheimpolizei*, 77, 252.
[64] *Ibid.*, 77.

intended in scheduling the preliminary negotiations before the congress. Hardenberg was the key, for Metternich could not reply to the Castlereagh plan of attack until the Prussians responded in detail to his note of the 22nd. The chancellor meanwhile, as always resisting the resurgence of France, ruled out both an appeal to the congress and a stand on the treaties. Reichenbach, as Humboldt correctly pointed out, was no longer relevant and the Convention of 1797, which forbade the revival of the name of Poland, could prejudice the Treaty of Kalisch, which was for Prussia what the Treaty of Ried was for Bavaria, a license for sweet dreams. The Prussians likewise held that it was idle to begin the bargaining with more than the boundaries of 1791. That offer failing, they were willing to demand repartition: on the Warta-Nida line, however, anchored by Thorn and Cracow, not on the line of the Vistula, as leverage offering the tsar a free hand in regard to a constitution and a merger of his old and new Polish provinces. A Polish constitution might endanger Austrian Galicia, Humboldt argued, but enlightened administration would contain the situation in Prussia. Conversely the greatest danger for Prussia was immediate, the tsar's 200,000 troops in Poland and 60,000 in Holstein; for Austria it lay in the future and depended on the settlement in Poland. Castlereagh's maneuver, therefore, must allow Prussia to remain in the background. There were, finally, all those nagging doubts about Metternich and Saxony: promises were not enough; now there must be guarantees and undertakings by Britain and Austria to assure that acquiescence of Europe which was not likely to spring spontaneously from the congress.[65]

On 27 November Hardenberg laid these ideas before Metternich and Castlereagh in a long memorandum,[66] affirming that he was ready to cooperate in an inconspicuous way but not to the point of rupturing the four-power alliance. Similarly, if Russia should refuse the Warta-Nida line, he would insist only on Cracow for Austria, Thorn for Prussia, precisely the sine qua non that Metternich himself had broached in the August correspondence with Berlin, but neither he then nor Hardenberg now knew what to advise if the tsar still stood firm. It was a timid program compared to a reach for the Vistula, but considering the chancellor's previous refusal to participate in a concerted demonstration of any kind, it was a major advance, and Metternich promised a counterproject of his own when the emperor returned two days hence.

[65] "Denkschrift Steins für Hardenberg," 26 Oct. 1814, Stein, *Briefe*, v, 176f.; Humboldt's memorandum "Ueber das Memorandum Castlereaghs," 25 Oct. 1814, in Humboldt, *Gesammelte Schriften*, XI, 179–188; "Hardenbergs Notizen," text in Klothilde von Olshausen, *Die Stellung der Grossmächte zur sächsischen Frage auf dem Wiener Kongress* (Munich, 1933), 146–151.
[66] "Hardenbergs Notizen," 149–151.

In the meantime the negotiation was threatened from another direction. Regardless of anybody's strategy, the congress was scheduled to open on 1 November, and even Hardenberg, concerned about the restlessness of the small German states, advised against another postponement, provided that the agenda was confined to general issues.[67] Metternich, on the other hand, doubted that such constraint could survive in a forum that gave Talleyrand full voice without exacting anything from him in return. Once again procrastination seemed the best policy. On 29 October, he and Gentz devised a plan to turn the bickering over credentials to advantage. The Committee of Eight should invite all plenipotentiaries to deposit their credentials in the chancellery building with a commission that would then proceed to verify them while the eight powers were devising procedures for the congress and declaring their determination to complete the preliminaries. An ingenious formula for producing activity without action, it was adopted later in the day at a private meeting of the four powers. Gentz was a better prophet than he knew in boasting that he had "killed the idea of the congress."[68]

That was not Talleyrand's view of it, however. On the 30th the full Committee of Eight held its first official meeting, some eighteen people altogether, counting secretaries and deputies, seated at a great round table covered with a cloth of green felt. Talleyrand intoned the familiar refrain, demanding that the congress convene first and verify credentials later. To conduct its business he proposed that all states of imperial or royal rank form a general commission and three subcommittees for German, Italian, and Swiss affairs, each reporting to the general commission and ultimately to the entire congress. As a courtesy to Metternich, or perhaps to tie his hands, Talleyrand proposed him as permanent president. By this time, however, the purpose of the French stratagems was so obvious that the four powers, despite their differences, successfully resisted and, supported by Portugal and Sweden, won adoption of the Metternich plan, with the additional proviso that the commission on verification be chosen by lot. The choice then fell on Britain, Russia and Prussia; and Metternich was unanimously elected president of the Committee of Eight. Action on Talleyrand's three-tiered committee plan was put off for a day and further deferred when Nesselrode on the 31st requested more time to prepare.[69]

---

[67] *Ibid.*, 150.

[68] "Projet de declaration" presented by Metternich to the Committee of Eight, 30 Oct. 1814, d'Angeberg, *Congrès*, II, 361; Talley. to Louis XVIII, 31 Oct. 1814, Talleyrand, *Corr.*, 107f.; and Gentz, *Tagebücher*, 324.

[69] Protocols of 30 and 31 Oct. 1814 with annexes, in d'Angeberg, *Congrès*, II, 358–362; Gentz to Karadja, 1 Nov. 1814, Klinkowström, *Oesterreichs Theilnahme*, 456f. Cf. Webster, *Congress of Vienna*, 88–90; and Griewank, *Wiener Kongress*, 160.

However inconvenient, the opening of the congress had been a fore-seeable problem. But now another complication arose that was less anticipated, for contrary to at least Castlereagh's expectations, the tsar had actually investigated Cooke's interpretation of the treaties and deigned to submit a formal written rebuttal.[70] Composed by no less a team than Czartoryski and Baron Johann von Anstett, the Russian negotiator at the Congress of Prague, it was not as incisive as Humboldt's analysis, but it touched the main points about the contingent nature of the Reichenbach pact and reminded Castlereagh that the latter treaty in any case awarded to Austria no more than the Illyrian Provinces. If it had a fault, it was the tedious emphasis on Alexander's good intentions, which Cooke easily refuted in his rejoinder, expounding the truism that "the liberties and security of States cannot be built upon the personal confidence or upon the life of an individual."[71] Nevertheless, the tsar's riposte gave promise that Cooke's lighthearted *guerre de plume* would be fought with more sophisticated weapons than Castlereagh had imagined.

Despite the defects in the treaties, Metternich decided to press forward along the course mapped out by Castlereagh, taking his stand on the treaties and differing only "on the character to be given to the appeal to the congress."[72] The British plan required that "the several Powers of Europe should be invited to support the said overture," almost as if to participate in a parliamentary roll call. Metternich, however, intended only to declare to a captive audience of individual envoys that Austria would never recognize the tsar's title to the duchy of Warsaw because it violated solemn engagements. Why have a debate on the flimsy evidence of the treaties when opinions would be formed by interests in any case? Why have a public demonstration when opposition could be marshaled privately with fewer risks, an operation that Austrian diplomacy was already conducting in European capitals?[73]

The foreign minister's immediate concern meanwhile was hostile opinion at home, where the absence of the emperor opened all stops on the cries for Metternich's resignation. When Francis returned to

[70] Text annexed to Alex. to Castle., 30 Oct. 1814, d'Angeberg, *Congrès*, II, 350–358; and Webster, *BD*, 224f.

[71] Memorandum of 4 Nov. 1814, Webster, *BD*, 226.

[72] This and following from Metternich's draft reply regarding the Castlereagh plan, n.d., HHSA, StK., Kongressakten, Cart. 7, 53–56. Cf. Griewank, *Wiener Kongress*, 170.

[73] See the Russian complaints about Merveldt's intrigues in London. Lieven to Nessel., 18 Oct. 1814, *VPR*, VIII, 115f. Also Mett. to Genotte (Austrian minister in Spain), 27 Oct. 1814, extr. in Dupuis, *Talleyrand*, II, 267 and 305f. Metternich also maintained secret contacts with the French foreign minister, Blacas, behind Talleyrand's back. *Ibid.*, II, 201–204.

the Hofburg on the 29th, Metternich, in an effort to broaden the base of his support, requested him to summon a state conference—"basically only to hang the bell around our necks," according to Schwarzenberg.[74] Francis so ordered, and the council met on the 31st, General Duka representing the emperor, Schwarzenberg the Court War Council, and Stadion the treasury department. Wessenberg, who kept the protocol, was the only friend, and even he opposed his chief on this issue. Metternich himself arrived with a draft program that served as the basis of discussion.[75] Combining the British and the Prussian ideas, he endorsed the three-step approach to the tsar, with Castlereagh as the intermediary and beginning with the perfunctory offer of a full Polish restoration. If Alexander should accept the Poland of 1791, however, Austria would make a sacrifice too, throwing "into the balance of the arrangements the major part of the circle of Zamość, and she would renounce the 400,000 souls" in the Tarnopol circle ceded to Russia in 1809. The third and most serious offer was not the Warta-Nida line, even though Metternich knew it to be Prussia's maximum demand, but the line of the Vistula, plus Warsaw on the left bank provided Prussia received Thorn.

On this basis Austria would give the tsar a free hand in his own domains; she would not even oppose

> his giving to his new territorial acquisitions separately or in combination with his other Polish provinces the name Kingdom of North or East Poland, His majesty the Austrian Emperor in this case reserving the right to apply the title Kingdom of South Poland . . . under whatever constitutional form he likewise found useful and convenient.[76]

Here was a new twist: if Alexander must have his Kingdom of Poland, perhaps the poison could be neutralized by creating several Polish kingdoms. Actually the idea had originated with Czartoryski, but Metternich's use of it was more than a matter of currying favor with him. Given his strong belief in a federalistic reorganization of the monarchy, he no doubt believed that under the name of South Poland Galicia, with an estates-style constitution, could become a showcase of Habsburg moderation competing on favorable terms with Russian constitutionalism and Prussia's "enlightened administration."

The trouble was that the Prussians refused to cross the Warta-Nida line, and so Metternich added one more proposal for Castlereagh to

[74] Schwarzenberg to wife, 2 Nov. 1814, Schwarzenberg, *Briefe an seine Frau*, 410.
[75] This and following from Metternich's draft cited in n. 72 above and protocol of state conference, 31 Oct. 1814, HHSA, StK., Kongressakten, Cart. 7, pp. 456f.
[76] Metternich's draft cited in n. 2.

make, though not in the name of Austria: namely, that if Alexander declined the title of king and reaffirmed the treaty of 1797, he could have the Warta-Nida line. This strategy has been cited as proof that forestalling a Polish constitution was still Metternich's first priority;[77] but if that had been so, would he not have reversed the order of the options? Is it conceivable that, given a choice, he would have preferred the immensely less favorable frontier once he had devised a political antidote to Alexander's Poland? The final offer, which he dared not make in Austria's name, was a desperate effort to convince his skeptical colleagues that retreating to the shorter line, which he knew to be the Prussian maximum, could have a compensating advantage.[78]

Regardless of circumlocutions, Metternich's primary aim at the conference was to gain acceptance of the Prussian limits, and in this he failed. His colleagues preferred the tangibles of territory to the abstractions of terminology; to lose the Vistula on top of Saxony was too much to ask for the sake of a diplomatic campaign so full of uncertainties. Metternich thus yielded, rescinding the contingent sacrifices of Zamość and Tarnopol and accepting the line of the Vistula as the final offer that Castlereagh was to make before listening to Russian counterproposals.[79] Caught between the Vistula and the Warta, he now had to hope either that Alexander, beguiled by the royal title, would accept the Vistula frontier, or that the Prussians, seeing the true state of Austrian opinion, would increase their demands accordingly. Conversely, if the tsar should accept the Warta frontier to accommodate the Prussians, Metternich could then return to the emperor with the overpowering argument that Austria would face isolation if she refused a solution backed by Britain and virtually all of the continent. The future was uncertain but not necessarily forlorn.

Now that the Austrian course was set, pending authorization by the emperor, it was all the more urgent that the congress, when convened, be merely a sounding board, not a parliament of Europe. Within hours of the state conference Metternich met with the Committee of Eight again, accepted its presidency, and aided by Nesselrode, who asked for more time, again managed to delay consideration of Talleyrand's tiered committee system. Delay, however, was no permanent solution. Metternich could count on the Prussians, and since "the conspiracy of

[77] Griewank, *Wiener Kongress*, 171.

[78] Cf. Gentz to Karadja, 28 Oct. 1814, Klinkowström, *Oesterreichs Theilnahme*, 454, which shows that Metternich had devised the choice for Alexander at least by 28 October, that is, the day after the private conference with Castlereagh and Hardenberg on the 27th. Whether it had been discussed there is not known.

[79] Protocol of 31 Oct. 1814 cited in n. 75 above. Cf. Castle. to Liverp., 11 Nov. 1814, Webster, *BD*, 229f.

23 October" the Russians had no reason to make the congress the arbiter of affairs. But Talleyrand had Labrador with him and the sympathy even of Löwenhjelm, who found the idea of a congress preposterous if it could make no decisions.[80] Castlereagh, meanwhile, though incensed at Talleyrand's tentative overtures to the Russians, obviously viewed an appeal to the congress as imputing positive powers of decision to the body. Portugal was uncertain. Hence the need for another four-power caucus, which took place on 1 November in Humboldt's quarters.[81]

This conclave, together with private talks with Gentz, must have brought Castlereagh around. His primary concerns were consensus and, at this juncture, harmony with Metternich at all costs. When the eight again convened on 2 November, the four were unanimous in pronouncing that the sanction of the congress meant only that it should note the arrangements arrived at privately without binding all states in all particulars but merely conferring an extra solemnity on the settlement as a whole. They were back to Metternich's original view that the gathering in Vienna should be for signing, not negotiating. The congress, he now repeated, was no corporate entity but a convenient mechanism for conducting multilateral negotiations; committees were not committees but "opportunities for negotiation"; the congress in essence was "Europe without distances." The French sneeringly reported on Metternich's "marvelous command of words that are vague and devoid of meaning," but he made his point, Castlereagh moving deferral of all theory till the end in order to get on with the establishment of regional committees.[82] No decision was actually made at the time, but when such committees were eventually created, the action was taken on this pragmatic basis. Henceforth, moreover, assemblies of the great powers, whether four, five, or eight, were scrupulously referred to in the official documents as conferences of the powers, not committee meetings, a fine point that posterity has tended to ignore.

[80] Löwenhjelm to Engeström, 5 Nov. 1814 (intercept), Fournier, *Geheimpolizei*, 277–279.

[81] Hardenberg, "Tagebücher," 36; Gentz, *Tagebücher*, I, 325.

[82] Two committees already existed, Castlereagh contended, one on Germany, the other on Poland, by which he no doubt had in mind the Anglo-Austrian-Prussian combine, which of course had no official status. This probably accounts for the fact that the protocol in *British Papers*, II, 563–565, had Talleyrand including a committee on Poland, whereas the French version in d'Angeberg, *Congrès*, II, 358–360, mentions committees only for Germany, Switzerland, and Italy. Webster, *Congress of Vienna*, 89; Griewank, *Wiener Kongress*, 110; and Mayr, "Aufbau," 77, all accept the notion of four, but a committee on Poland seems very unlikely to me partly because "Poland" could not be isolated from other issues. The Danish envoy, Niels Rosenkrantz, not an eyewitness to be sure, also understood that Talleyrand proposed three committees. Rosenkrantz, *Journal*, 61.

To spare Talleyrand the embarrassment of a public defeat, however, no protocol of the meeting was kept.[83]

Metternich now had some leeway; if appeal to the congress must be made, he could give it whatever character seemed suitable at the time. But meanwhile even better things were in the offing. The tsar, having failed in Buda to separate the emperor from his minister, now tried to lure the minister from the emperor, making overtures the exact nature of which we do not know. As Metternich reported it to Francis, however,

> I must inform your All Highest without delay of the various moves the Russian emperor has made in the course of the day to win me over by any means. I am fully convinced that Your Majesty's forceful stand in Buda not only completely reinforced my last vehement declaration, but I am certain that we are nearing a development in Polish affairs that we could hardly have contemplated and that would never have occurred and still would not occur without a display of strength.[84]

An appeal to the congress, it now appeared, would not only be less hazardous, it was also less likely to be needed. "I am no longer astonished at anything," Metternich told Sagan, whose aid Alexander enlisted in the attempted rapprochement, "especially when it comes to that man."[85]

The tsar's overtures, according to Metternich, were made in the course of 2 November, the day that ended with the rout of Talleyrand and the scuttling of the congress. That same day he prepared for the emperor's approval a formal note to Prussia that invited Hardenberg to join him in requesting Castlereagh to proceed with his mission. The following day the credentials committee was installed in the chancellery, and the German Committee held the meeting that prompted Metternich's exuberant report to the emperor that "the preeminence of Austria" would be greater than under the Reich. Everything was rushing to maturity at once, favorably to be sure but at a breathtaking and exhausting pace. "I am completely ill," the minister cried out to

[83] Löwenhjelm to Lars Engeström, Swedish foreign minister, 5 Nov. 1814 (intercept), Fournier, *Geheimpolizei*, 277–279; Gentz to Karadja, 7 Nov. 1814, Klinkowström, *Oesterreichs Theilnahme*, 457; report to Jacourt, 6 Nov. 1814, Talleyrand, *Memoirs*, II, 295, which incorrectly gives date of 1 Nov. for meeting. Cf. Mayr, "Aufbau," 77–79; and Bourgoing, *Vom Wiener Kongress*, 150f. Because the protocol of the meeting was not published (see d'Angeberg, *Congrès*, II, 424f.), Fournier and Mayr, "Aufbau," 84, evidently took Engeström's allusions to "the last session" to mean that of 31 October.

[84] Mett. to Francis, 2 Nov. 1814, HHSA, StK., Vorträge, Cart. 196, XI, p. 10. Cf. Gebhardt, *Humboldt als Staatsmann*, II, 99.

[85] Mett. to Sagan, 1 Nov. 1814, Ullrichová, ed., *Briefwechsel*, 270.

Sagan, "my body is wracked, my soul has not protected it for a long time. I am still needed for a few weeks more; they will finish the most painful year of my life, and if they finish my life, the world will lose nothing but the sad remains of an existence that I deserved to lose."[86] Into this tormented existence now fell the last missing piece: the imperial order to proceed with the offensive in Poland. In the note for Hardenberg Francis made only one change, substituting "administrative" for "constitutional" in referring to the structure of a future kingdom of South Poland. "With God's help and steadfastness," he concluded, "I hope to see the matter brought to a good end."[87]

[86] *Ibid.*
[87] Francis's marginalis of 3 Nov. 1814 on Metternich's *Vortrag* as in n. 4.

CHAPTER IX

THE FRONT COLLAPSES

WITH the dispatch of another note to Hardenberg Metternich had again reached a resting point whence the next move was up to others. Since the congress was "Europe without distances," the pause was brief this time, but into it fell two unexpected events that began a process of unraveling all that he had patiently basted together. The first was the British reply to the Russian memorandum of 30 October. As mentioned earlier, Castlereagh, who had not expected a response from the tsar himself, now unwittingly found himself in a direct confrontation with the sovereign. He thereupon had Cooke prepare a rejoinder, using the opportunity to indicate to Alexander in an accompanying letter that his points were aimed not at him but solely at the ministers responsible for drafting the memorandum. Not surprisingly this lame explanation only made things worse. Cooke's brief did finally acknowledge the contingent nature of the treaty of Reichenbach, but otherwise it fell back on purely speculative statements about what the parties to it must have intended.[1] Worse, since the letter had to be addressed to the tsar, it in fact continued the direct relationship that Castlereagh wished to terminate. Nor did it help that he chose "as the most respectful and least formal channel of conveyance" his half brother, Lord Charles Stewart, known for his drunken escapades and at the time unfairly held by some to be "slightly insane."[2] Clumsiest of all was the timing. Just when the British secretary was preparing to act as mediator between Russia and the German powers, he was advertising in advance a wholly partisan position and needlessly reminding the tsar of "the conspiracy of 23 October." As the Russians acidly replied in their turn, the duty of a mediator was "to bring spirits together"; otherwise "it is better to let the parties concerned take care of debating their differences."[3] In this same spirit Hardenberg a few days later proposed and Metternich agreed that because of "the direct démarches [of Lord Castlereagh] the British cabinet will hereafter be more useful to us as a point of support than as a mediator."[4]

Such an abrupt change of tactics, however could hardly have oc-

---

[1] Text in Wellington, *Supplementary Despatches*, IX, 410–416.

[2] Castle. to Liverp., 5 Nov. 1814, Webster, *BD*, 223; Rosenkrantz, *Journal*, entry of 5 Nov. 1814, p. 64.

[3] Text of Second Russian Memorandum, 21 Nov. 1814, again with covering letter by the tsar, in Wellington, *Supplementary Despatches*, IX, 441–446.

[4] Hard. to Mett., 9 Nov. 1814, HHSA, *StK., Kongressakten*, Cart. 7, p. 295; Mett. to Hard., 12 Nov. 1814, d'Angeberg, *Congrès*, II, 418. The quotation is from the latter.

curred without a more serious development: another virtuoso exercise
in browbeating by the tsar, this time inflicted upon Hardenberg in the
presence of his master, Frederick William. The initiative was the tsar's
and with it he succeeded in breaking up the three-power front before
it had fairly taken form. On 5 November the chancellor answered an
imperial summons and used the occasion to press all the usual arguments for the Warta-Nida line. By way of an answer the tsar then
dragged him off to see the king, and the brutal dressing-down took
place, accompanied by a seductive lie.[5] Metternich, he swore, had offered to yield Poland in return for Russian support in the preservation
of Saxony. Whether the king believed this or not, he turned to his
chancellor with the peremptory order not to conspire against his Russian ally. In desolation Hardenberg reeled away to brood over the
results. "Russia," he confided to his diary, "Russia, supported by the
king on all points, is wrong. But what to do?" One thing was to try to
stop Castlereagh's letter, now seen as more provocative than ever, but
he was too late.[6]

The humiliation of Hardenberg naturally became a *cause célèbre* of
the congress and ever after a favorite topic of historical speculation.
On a personal level it is hard to say which was most inglorious: the
tsar's bullying, the king's disloyalty to his chancellor, or Hardenberg's
failure to resign over the affront. On another plane the episode is
often considered a point of no return, some writers blaming the king
for a spinelessness that lost the only chance to gain the whole of Saxony,
others holding that Alexander was a more certain support than the
treacherous Metternich and—to add a more objective point in the
king's defense—more capable of destroying Prussia on the spot. The
Russian army in Holstein was viewed with particular concern. Still, the
actual lines were not so starkly drawn. Metternich and Hardenberg
were not yet agreed on a minimum program in Poland, and the chancellor himself had always said he would never carry things to the point
of rupture. Nor were Britain and Austria as yet pledged to defend
with arms Prussia's survival, let alone her possession of Saxony in the
face of a disapproving Europe. Granted, then, the king's singular qualities—his infinite gratitude for salvation in 1807, his steadfast loyalty
to the tsar, and his admittedly cautious nature—there were still sound
reasons for his stand and corresponding weaknesses in Hardenberg's
position. It was really the same old riddle: what happens if we challenge
the tsar and he does not yield? Austria could always retreat into the
arms of France, Prussia only into the Baltic.

[5] Hardenberg, "Tagebücher," 36; Hardenberg's memorandum to Castle., 7 Nov.
1814, d'Angeberg, *Congrès*, ii, 406–408.
[6] Hardenberg, "Tagebücher," 36; Stein, "Tagebuch," *Briefe*, v, 331f.

The consequences of the dramatic encounter were profound all the same. The tsar, who could have considered Hardenberg's intrigues grounds for repudiating his pledges, instead felt an enhanced obligation to the king and became for a time the main advocate of delivering Saxony to him as a territorial and constitutional whole. The Prussians, on the other hand, were left in disarray, the king meekly subservient to Alexander, Humboldt the more determined to save "the cause of Europe" by seeking ironclad guarantees from Britain and Austria that would meet the king's obsession with immediate security,[7] and Hardenberg beginning to sense that only Austria could save Prussian independence now. Picking up the pieces, he asked Knesebeck and the able state councilor, Johann Gottfried Hoffmann, to work out a plan leaving the king of Saxony his capital and enough territory to sustain him at grand-ducal rank. In this way what Saxon provinces did not come to Prussia directly would at least remain in a Prussian Kreis without Frederick Augustus's becoming a Kreis chief himself. To be sure, this was the course of last resort, and Hoffmann himself chafed at the assignment, but at last the unspeakable had been spoken.[8]

We are witness here not so much to a rift between Hardenberg and Humboldt, rumors of which made the rounds of the salons and embassies for the next month, as to the exposure, under pressure, of slightly different priorities. For in the abstract both men sincerely favored the Anglo-Austrian option over the Russian, both coveted the whole of Saxony, and both generally endorsed the Twelve Articles. The necessity for hard decisions, however, gradually forced underlying differences to the surface. From this point on Hardenberg was more inclined to yield at least the kernel of Saxony that Metternich had pleaded for even in the famous note of 22 October, but that was all the more reason to stand firm on the Kreis system, which would presumably keep even the kernel under Prussian control, more control possibly than under the tsar's plan of placing all Saxony in mere personal union with Prussia. Prussia's escape, Hardenberg began to sense, now required him to act as mediator between Austria and Russia, if necessary giving a little on Saxony in order to finesse them into an accommodation in Poland.

Humboldt, by contrast, continued to believe that all the advantages for Prussia, whether if war or if peace, still lay in collaboration with

---

[7] Humboldt's memorandum of 9 Nov. 1814, Humboldt, *Gesammelte Schriften*, IX, 185–197; précis in Delbrück, "Friedrich Wilhelm III. und Hardenberg," 260–263; Humb. to Caroline, 13 Nov. 1814, Humboldt, *Briefe*, IV, 418f.

[8] Griewank, *Wiener Kongress*, 177f. Hoffmann on 12 Nov. submitted a plan leaving a mere 360,000 population to Saxony, hardly up to grand-duchy standards. Hardenberg also indicated to Wrede that he might be satisfied with part of Saxony. Olshausen, *Stellung der Grossmächte*, 73.

the West, in being "placed rather on the European side than the Russian."[9] If Austria and Britain could be brought to give unconditional military guarantees, in their own names and those of France and Bavaria should they join in, guarantees of Prussia's security, her territorial claims in Germany, Saxony above all, and her minimum in Poland, then the main fears of the king might be overcome. On the other hand, with Saxony firmly in hand and Mainz a federal fortress there would be less reason to insist on the Kreis system, to which opposition steadily mounted, increasingly convincing Humboldt that its political costs were too high. That much can be documented as we shall see; whether Humboldt deserved the reputation he acquired in the next month as the foremost intransigent regarding Saxony, however, remains conjectural, an allegation incessantly repeated, by Humboldt indignantly denied, and by the historian seriously doubted. It would nevertheless be fair to say that if something had to give, Humboldt preferred weaker Kreise, Hardenberg less of Saxony. The question fundamentally was how best to appease Metternich.[10]

Like everyone else at the congress, the Austrian foreign minister learned of Hardenberg's humiliation almost at once, but he did not immediately see it as the end of the great experiment. At first he actually felt himself to be on the defensive because of the tsar's slurs against him and rushed to restore his credibility. "I not only deny the fact," he wrote to Hardenberg is great agitation, "but I am ready to maintain the contrary in the presence of the emperor himself." It was an obvious attempt to divide and conquer, he went on, adding: "You know what we think about Saxony. You will find everything there is between us in my letter of 20 October [sic]."[11] The bond even survived an arrogant action from the Russian side the next day, when Prince Repnin, in transferring his powers to the Prussians, spoke of the "former" king and the "future" king, proclaimed the step as preparatory to permanent union with Prussia, and implied that Britain and Austria endorsed such a settlement. Metternich, to be sure, joined Castlereagh in protesting this crude presumption (in reality traceable to a directive penned by Stein) but did not explicitly disavow the possibility of such an outcome.[12]

[9] Humboldt's memorandum of 9 Nov. 1814 as in n. 7. Cf. Humb. to Caroline, 13 Nov. 1814, Humboldt, *Briefe*, IV, 418–419: "If we must really choose between standing with Russia or with Austria and England in this affair, I am so decisively of the latter persuasion that I will stake everything on it."

[10] Fournier, *Geheimpolizei*, 72–76; Humb. to Caroline, 4, 8, and 11 Dec. 1814, Humboldt, *Briefe*, IV, 427–429; Castle. to Liverp., 25 Dec. 1814, Webster, *BD*, 272.

[11] Mett. to Hard. (private), 7 Nov. 1814, ZSTA, Merseburg, 2.4.1.I, No. 1649, p. 43.

[12] See Stein to Repnin, 21 Oct. 1814, in Stein, *Briefe*, V, 172f. Text of his circular (which Talleyrand gleefully had published in the *Moniteur*) in Talleyrand, *Memoirs*,

Meanwhile, on 7 November, the German Committee met again, and except for the absence of Hardenberg, seemed unaffected by the uproar in grand affairs. Under Metternich's direction debate proceeded on the Austro-Prussian plan for the First Council, specifically its role in adjudicating interstate disputes, if necessary with the assistance of a federal court.[13] The mere mention of a court, however, diverted the discussion, Winzingerode rejecting a tribunal for any purpose, Humboldt on his favorite subject straying from the issue at hand to proclaim the court's competence not only over interstate disputes but over grievances of individuals and estates against their sovereigns as well. Instead of pulling the discussion back onto course, however, Metternich entered the fray himself, reversing all previous positions on the issue to declare that much as he defended the sovereignty of states, "even those of the second and third rank," they should not forget that they were once again German and that "a German Bund and a great German political body" were impossible if "the political existence of an individual" could be infringed and his "Germanic rights" threatened. Even Switzerland and the United States of America had courts to rule on violations of the federal constitution, he added in a display of erudition that problably contained more guesswork than a knowledge of *Marbury vs. Madison*. On the surface this seemed a solid endorsement of the Prussian position, but much would depend on how the court was constituted and what kinds of cases it could receive. Metternich, hitherto indifferent, was beginning to realize that with proper management a court could serve his cause as well. We shall come back to this question later. For now the most important result of the debate was the conversion of Marshal Wrede. As long as the court dealt only with violations of the federal constitution, as opposed to state constitutions, he announced his approval in principle.

In other action the terms First Council and Second Council were officially adopted, and all but Winzingerode approved the Wessenberg plan for giving an elected committee from the latter a voice in decisions on peace and war. The specific naming of Baden and Hesse-Cassel as the delegates to sit with the Kreis chiefs, however, was dropped for the time being to placate Wrede and Winzingerode, who argued that there were older and more deserving lines, by which they no doubt meant houses that belonged to any Kreis other than their own. In regard to the right of alliance Wrede and Humboldt continued the old dispute over the Bund's right to determine if a given treaty con-

---

II, 327, n. 2, and Klüber, *Acten*, Vol. 1, Part 2, pp. 6f. Cf. Gebhardt, *Humboldt als Staatsmann*, II, 102, and Olshausen, *Stellung der Grossmächte*, 70, both of whom exaggerate the impact of the episode on Metternich's relations with Hardenberg.

[13] This and following from protocol of 7 Nov. 1814, Klüber, *Acten*, II, 166–176; and "Bemerkungen zum Protokoll," HSA, Stuttgart, E 70, Fasc. 13, pp. 352–358.

stituted a danger, the former insisting on the exclusion of subsidy agreements from this category. Metternich, on the whole siding with the Bavarian, argued that since the federal act could not anticipate every contingency, each case should be decided on its merits so long as all treaties were at least reported to the Bund. Münster agreed, but Humboldt, in Hardenberg's absence, insisted on tabling the matter. All in all, the Austro-Prussian plan as drafted by Wessenberg fared well, even Winzingerode's opposition on most items being pro forma.

Yet hanging over the proceedings was still the unsettling Württemberg draft constitution of the previous session with its demand for Kreise of equal size, which meant in the language of the protocol "the enlargement of the Kreise of southern Germany" and bringing the territorial settlement before the wrong forum at the wrong time. Metternich accordingly ruled the proposal out of order and, supported by Münster and Humboldt, directed that in the further reading of the Württemberg draft the articles must be discussed in their numerical order and comment confined to each point as it arose. Thus the clash between King Frederick's and Hardenberg's conceptions of the Swabian Kreis was averted for the time being, and Metternich used the occasion once more to expose the difficulties of the Kreis system itself, again reserving the right to propose an alternative, something that would retain "closer regional combinations of individual parts" and at the same time "remove the objections present in the division into Kreise." Thereupon all issues related to this subject were deferred, and the committee went on to a less explosive issue, acceding to Winzingerode's wishes that Kreis chiefs should be "requested," not "directed," to enforce federal decrees.

It is possible that Metternich deliberately cast his criticism of the Kreise and his defense of "the political existence of individuals" in patriotic rhetoric for the sake of the official record, the confidentiality of which had been severely compromised. The offenders were mainly, though probably not exclusively, the Prussians, who regularly consulted Stein but could not, even if they had so wished, discipline him as one of their own. With regular access to the protocols the headstrong imperial baron increasingly saw it as his duty to mobilize support outside the committee against the greed and obstructionism of the two South German courts. To forestall Bavarian possession of Mainz, which seemed implicit in Metternich's conditions of 22 October, he incited the envoys of Hesse, Nassau, and the Saxon duchies to demand the base for themselves, the Bund providing the funds and the Order of Teutonic Knights the local administration.[14] At the same time he supplied to his friend Görres details from the protocols that provided fuel

[14] Note of 25 Oct. 1814 in d'Angeberg, *Congrès*, II, 336f. Cf. Stein, "Tagebuch," *Briefe*, v, 326.

for a scathing article in the *Rheinische Merkur* denouncing Wrede and Winzingerode by name, thus serving up another titillating distraction for the onlookers at the congress and later causing dispute on the German Committee.[15]

Such interference was annoying to Metternich but hardly dangerous. More threatening was Stein's determination to bring the power of Russia into the negotiations, this time by a formal note from the tsar asserting his backing for the Twelve Articles, upbraiding the South German courts for "maintaining the usurpations made in a former era," and most significantly, adducing the Rheinbund Act as the basis of the claims of the Standesherren. Fortunately Alexander, whose only objection to the two middle states derived from the momentary priority he gave to his relations with Prussia, called Stein's language "too rambling and bitter" and asked Nesselrode to soften it. The latter thereupon consulted Metternich, who convinced him that German affairs were actually going very well and required no additional stimulants. Then Stein took it upon himself to modify the note, avoiding direct criticism of Bavaria and Württemberg and, when Nesselrode still refused, dropping the reference to the Rheinbund entirely. He also enlisted the services of La Harpe, who expressed to the tsar his dismay that the protocols made no more mention of Russia "than if she were on the moon"—this despite the obvious right of "a prince from the house of Holstein" to have his own seat on the committee.[16] Nesselrode finally yielded, but the formal note he addressed to Metternich and Hardenberg on 14 November was an innocuous piece that did not threaten Russian intervention but merely offered support if it was asked for. Technically it put the tsar's name behind the Twelve Articles, especially in regard to *landständische Verfassungen*, but being confidential, it left the two recipients free to use it as they wished.[17]

Stein was also engaged in organizing the lesser states to protest against the obduracy of the South Germans. When his colleague Marschall on 4 November convened the group, the protocols of the German Committee created all the sensation that Stein had desired, but for different reasons. What shocked the inquisitive envoys was not so much the perversity of Bavaria and Württemberg as the enormity of the Kreis

[15] Ritter, *Stein*, 500.
[16] La Harpe to Alex., 12 Nov. 1814, *VPR*, VIII, 129–130.
[17] Stein's drafts of 5, 7, and 11 Nov. 1814, Stein, *Briefe*, v, Nos. 198, 202, and 203. Notes of 14 Nov. 1814 to Mett. and Hard. in HHSA, StK., Kongressakten, Cart. 6, pp. 307f.; and Schmidt, *Verfassungsfrage*, 252–254; Metternich's reply to Nesselrode, 22 Nov. 1814, HHSA, StK., Kongressakten, Cart. 6, p. 337. Cf. Apian-Bennewitz, *Plessen und die Verfassungsfrage*, 46; and Ritter, *Stein*, 500f., who along with many others (including d'Angeberg, *Congrès*, II, 417f.) assumed that Stein's draft of 11 Nov. was the final and official one.

system, which threatened to devour them all—"a Napoleon in five parts," Türckheim called it, and without waiting for group action immediately sent notes of his own to Metternich, Hardenberg, and Münster, protesting the work of the committee, denouncing Kreise, and pleading instead for "military districts" that would place Hesse-Darmstadt with similar states in her region, not in a Swabian Kreis under Württemberg.[18] This assault on the committee as such was not what Stein had intended, contradicting, as it did, his concurrent efforts with the tsar; but he accepted it, partly because of his own ambivalence toward the Kreise but even more because the small states were willing to include endorsement of estates constitutions in a note of protest that Marschall and Stein drafted in the next few days. In return the note also spoke of the "illegal actions" of the German Committee. It did not, however, call for an emperor as most of that group would have preferred.[19]

Metternich's major concern, meanwhile, was how to cope with the defection of Prussia. He now had to recognize "the impossibility of supporting the present system," but he was not yet prepared to appeal to France. "We must think twice before calling on her," he told Rosenkranz of Denmark, "because once in motion, she could not be stopped at will, and she would demand at least the frontier of the Rhine."[20] A half step toward Talleyrand, however, was always possible through Wrede, to whom Metternich now extended unprecedented confidences. On 8 November he divulged to the marshal the contents of his correspondence with Hardenberg, emphasizing that Prussia's territorial proposals were based on Kreis plans that would give her, not Bavaria, control of Frankfurt, Mainz, and Wetzlar. Shortly thereafter Schwarzenberg and General Josef Radetzky initiated the field marshal into the secrets of their military operations: the bulk of Austria's army of some 370,000 moving into Hungary and Galicia to strike across the Vistula and a lesser force stationed in Bohemia. The latter, Metternich explained, could be supplemented by 25,000 Bavarians and the combined army placed under Wrede's command for a strike at the Prussians in Saxony.[21]

On 9 November Metternich at last heard from Hardenberg himself, but what at one time was to have been either an endorsement of the

[18] To Hard. 5 Nov. 1814, text in Schmidt, *Verfassungsfrage*, 245–247; to Münster, 6 Nov. 1814, in Klüber, *Acten*, IV, 45–48; to Mett., 7 Nov. 1814, HHSA, StK., Kongressakten, Cart. 6, pp. 306f.—each with variations appropriate to the recipient. See also Ulmann, "Zur Entstehung der Kaisernote," 476f.

[19] Schmidt, *Verfassungsfrage*, 245; Apian-Bennewitz, *Plessen und die Verfassungsfrage*, 53–55.

[20] Gentz, *Tagebücher*, I, 328; Rosenkrantz, *Journal*, 71.

[21] Heilmann, *Wrede*, 411, n. 14; Winter, *Wrede als Berater*, 175, 188, and 201.

Austrian program or a formal counterproject was, under the new circumstances, only an informal letter exuding good will and proposing confidential talks to devise a new strategy without using Castlereagh as mediator.[22] To it the chancellor attached a memorandum describing his audience with the tsar and arguing that to obtain even the Warta-Nida line, one must allow Alexander his Polish crown. In the long run, however, the disadvantage would be his: so many rebellious subjects and the Russian army withdrawn from Europe; two years later conditions for rolling Russia back to the east would be far better. For similar reasons he believed that three Polish kingdoms would only reinforce the sentiment for independence from every foreign government.[23]

In this ambiguous situation the German Committee met on 10 November, incapable of rising above the trivia necessary merely to keep the discussions going. On those rare occasions when a foreign envoy should arrive at the seat of the Bund, should he deal with the president alone or the entire First Council or a committee? If the Bund should ever send a Hanoverian as an ambassador, what would prevent the rest of the council from issuing decrees in his absence, Münster wanted to know. And who would pay for the mission, Wrede asked. Of more significance was renewed debate on the role of the Second Council in deciding questions of peace and war. Winzingerode continued his opposition to any role, since at bottom his government wanted no lower house at all. Wrede, on the other hand, possibly feeling himself now an equal partner of Metternich and bringing a soldier's sense of honor to bear, insisted that if the smaller states were expected to shed their citizens' blood, they had a right to be consulted as in the Wessenberg plan discussed at the previous session. Metternich closed the meeting with his familiar argument that the Second Council was only window dressing to let the lesser princes feel important too.[24] The Württembergers, however, were no longer so gullible. Originally, complained King Frederick to Mandelsloh, these matters as well as the initiative in legislation were to be left exclusively to the First Council. Now the new project was so far removed from the first "by which we were hoodwinked into the negotiations, that it would be foolish any longer to enter into piecemeal voting." That was an intramural observation; soon it would become a public declaration.[25]

Hardenberg, meanwhile, had been in touch with Castlereagh, who

[22] Hard. to Mett., 9 Nov. 1814, HHSA, StK., Kongressakten, Cart. 7, p. 295; Extract in Oncken, *Zeitalter*, II, 852.
[23] Text of memorandum of 7 Nov. 1814, d'Angeberg, *Congrès*, II, 406–408.
[24] Protocol of 10 Nov. 1814, Klüber, *Acten*, II, 176–181; "Bemerkungen zum Protokoll," HSA, Stuttgart, E 70, Fasc. 13, pp. 368–373.
[25] Frederick to Mandelsloh, 11 Nov. 1814, HSA, Stuttgart, E 1, Fasc. 45.

agreed that he was no longer a useful mediator and proposed that the chancellor himself assume this role, since the real impasse regarding Poland was between Austria and Russia. Believing that this would give him the pivotal position, Hardenberg agreed, and the next day Metternich accepted his services. In doing so he took a first soft step toward separating the Saxon and Polish questions, which previously he had labored methodically to unite; that is to say, he was now in a position to let Hardenberg negotiate the best settlement he could in Poland and then to decide how much Austria could yield in Germany. No Austrian minister, he told the chancellor, could give way on Poland, Saxony, and Mainz at once. For a start he suggested preserving a kernel of Saxony with Dresden and a population of 500,000 and making Mainz a federal fortress, as the Prussians wanted, but with an Austro-Bavarian garrison as he wanted. Hardenberg of course refused, but henceforth, whenever the Austrians talked partition, he assumed that they meant a territory of this same small size. Significantly, in a tactical error, neither he nor Stein complained at the time that Metternich was reneging his earlier offer.[26]

A day later, 12 November, Metternich, after another conference with Schwarzenberg, informed the Prussians "that His Imperial Majesty sees with much regret that the point of view of the Prussian cabinet differs in several ways from its own." Later he was to cite this passage as a repudiation of his offer of 22 October regarding Saxony; for the time being, however, he had no intention of abandoning collaboration. Austria, he continued, was not ready to offer more than the previous alternatives, but she was still interested in hearing Russia's counter-proposals. Specifically Hardenberg was to ask the tsar what frontiers he had in mind, what limits he would set on Russian influence in a constitutional Poland under his scepter, and how he proposed to guarantee the security and repose of Austria's Polish provinces.[27] Even before hearing the answers, however, Metternich in later conversations with the chancellor made a major concession of his own, acquiescing in *both* a Polish constitution and the Warta-Nida line rather than the Vistula,[28] a concession now deemed acceptable if the Dresden nucleus

[26] Hardenberg, "Tagebücher," 36; Stein, "Tagebuch," *Briefe*, v, 335. Cf. Bourgoing, *Vom Wiener Kongress*, 160.

[27] Mett. to Hard., 12 Nov. 1814, extract in d'Angeberg, *Congrès*, II. 418–419; complete text with sharp criticism of Prussian policy in HHSA, StK., Kongressakten, Cart. 7, pp. 319–324.

[28] Hard. to Mett., 2 Dec. 1814, HHSA, StK., Kongressakten, Cart. 7, pp. 333–340; Castle. to Liverp., 25 Nov. 1814, No. 24, Great Britain, Public Records Office, Foreign Office, 92/8, pp. 194f. (Hereafter abbreviated PRO, F.O.). Also Stein, "Tagebuch," *Briefe*, v, 338. When Metternich made the concession is not known, but conferences between him and Hardenberg on 13, 18, and 20 Nov. are the most likely occasions. Hardenberg, "Tagebücher," 36.

could be preserved, as he continued to urge, promising in this case that "everything would be done" to obtain the sanction of Europe, France and the German states in particular, for Prussia's title to the rest.[29]

Hardenberg, meanwhile, eager to muster maximum support from the tsar's own advisers and to minimize possible damage in regard to Saxony, moved slowly. As a result almost two weeks went by before he could report, affording additional proof, if any were still needed, that Metternich's frivolous ways were not the only cause of delay at the congress. In the interval Metternich on 13 November assembled the Committee of Eight once more and at last obtained an indefinite postponement of the congress. Thereafter committees on Switzerland and various Italian problems (Metternich insisted that there was no Italian problem as such) began work, but the major developments concerned German affairs.[30]

On 11 November the small states met to examine the draft protest that Stein and Marschall had prepared. They strengthened it, first by demanding representation on the German Committee as a right grounded in the treaties, and next by adopting a motion powerfully pressed by Türckheim to call for a "common supreme head" furnished with executive, administrative, and judicial powers as well as the command of the federal army, essentially the same powers that the Twelve Articles reserved for the Kreis chiefs. Yet with or without a supreme head, the essential thing was the equality of rights and equality of representation for all states.[31] On 15 November the envoys of some twenty-nine states signed the note, which the next day was officially dispatched to Metternich and Hardenberg. The two Hohenzollern principalities acceded eight days later, but two others, Baden and Oldenburg, abstained entirely, still placing their primary trust in their protector, the tsar. Baden however, issued a separate protest, mainly against "the inconceivable notion" that five princes should take it upon themselves to say "that the independence of the German fatherland should consist in the dependence of the others."

The note represented fundamental changes from Stein's original

[29] Hardenberg's memorandum for the tsar, 23 Nov. 1814, ZSTA, Merseburg, 2.4.1.I, No. 1650. Précis of same in Delbrück, "Friedrich Wilhelm III. und Hardenberg," 259–260; extract in Obermann, "Wiener Kongress," 484f.

[30] Protocol of 13 Nov. 1814, d'Angeberg, *Congrès*, II, 424–427. Cf. Mayr, "Aufbau," 80 and 82.

[31] This and following from Apian-Bennewitz, *Plessen und die Verfassungsfrage*, 55–64; Ulmann, "Zur Entstehung der Kaisernote," 477; Rössler, *Zwischen Revolution und Reaktion*, 166; Ritter, *Stein*, 501; Schmidt, *Verfassungsfrage*, 258–279; Goerdeler, "Reichsidee in den Bundesplänen," 107–111; Humb. to Caroline, 9 Nov. 1814, *Briefe*, IV, 411–414. Text of note of 16 Nov. 1814 in Klüber, *Acten*, I, 72–76; Baden note of same date, *ibid.*, 97–99.

plan but not necessarily from views that he had previously asserted on occasion. What was most important to him moreover, was retained: the endorsement of estates constitutions and Münster's minimum four-point program of estates' rights. Still, coming just two days after Nesselrode's note in support of the Twelve Articles, it betrayed a basic inconsistency and an ironic inability to control events. Humboldt foresaw trouble from these "popular assemblies," as he derisively called such meetings and advised the few envoys who consulted him to sign nothing. For Metternich, however, the action could be only gratifying, one of Türckheim's greatest services, for regardless of the fate of an actual imperial title, the document posited a strong bond between Austria and the lesser states, whose weight he endeavored to throw into the balance against the Kreise.

On the German Committee itself Metternich no longer bothered to disguise or explain away his defense of the excluded states. When Winzingerode on 12 November attacked the legislative competence of the Second Council, especially where the execution of treaties was involved, Metternich defiantly replied that

> we proceed . . . on the principle that it [the Bund] is to consist not only of the five powers assembled here but of all the German princes. . . . Accordingly Austria views herself on the same plane as others, taking nothing from it ahead of anybody else and attributes to Nassau and Hohenzollern, for example, and the others the same rights of sovereignty as she claims herself.[32]

Wrede, Münster, and Humboldt seconded these remarks, the first no doubt because of his recent disillusionment with the Kreis system, the last because in private discussion over the past week or so he had already lost the battle to Wessenberg.

These talks concerned the expansion of Article VI of the Twelve Articles, which dealt with the Second Council. Throughout Humboldt maintained his grudging attitude toward the body. Though willing to concede the council the right of legislative initiative and helpful in devising procedures that permitted amendments to be made by either council, he insisted to the end that no bill could become law without the approval of the First. Even his language accented the negative. The competence of the council, he maintained, should be "limited to only those matters which could provide the basis for a general law valid throughout Germany" and further was expressly not to encroach on the legislative powers of the *Landstände* or the Kreis assemblies or the executive powers of the First Council. Wessenberg chided him for his

[32] "Bemerkungen zum Protokoll vom 12. Nov. 1814," HSA, Stuttgart, E 70, Fasc. 13, p. 394.

heavy-handedness, proposing language that "extended" the council's competence to "all subjects" suited to general German legislation. "The expression 'extended to' " he explained, "will ring better in the ears of the small princes than that of 'restricted to.' "[33]

More seriously he rejected, as noted earlier, a veto right for the First Council and, almost predicably by now, proposed that disagreements between the two councils could most appropriately be resolved by a conference committee consisting of the Kreis chiefs and the same five-member committee of the Second Council that had already been agreed upon for deciding war and peace and for breaking tie votes among the Kreis chiefs. This same procedure he advanced for settling disputes as to whether a given subject fell within the competence of the lower chamber or not. Furthermore, he added, since this committee was now assuming such importance, its members, like the Kreis chiefs themselves, should be in permanent residence throughout the year at the seat of the Bund.[34]

Given the demoralized state of the Prussians and Humboldt's determination to stay on Austria's side in the contest with Russia, it is understandable why Wessenberg was able to prevail. Hence it was essentially an Austrian program that came before the German Committee on 12 November as another jointly sponsored proposition. Besides the above points there were other traces of Austrian influence. Without Austria's being named, the chairman was to be "the first in rank" and the same who presided over the First Council. The precedence of state and Kreis legislation was no longer mentioned. Election to the five-member committee was to be open only to states with whole votes, thereby shutting out the mediatized houses. Without implying differences in rank the order of voting was to follow that of the Reich, assuring that Austria's position would always be announced first as a guide to others. Finally a single chancellery and a single archive were to serve and their personnel to be chosen by both houses, again making for equality between them and giving the eventual Austrian president the strategic position in both. (Humboldt had wished to put the First Council in charge of these services.)[35]

How much Metternich personally contributed to the project is uncertain, but in view of the importance he attached to the second house, it is unlikely that he would have stood aside. His intercession is suggested by the fact that several of the stipulations, including that re-

[33] Parallel development of Wessenberg's and Humboldt's versions of Art. VI, n.d., ZSTA, Merseburg, 2.4.1.I., No. 1456.

[34] *Ibid.*, and Wessenberg's personal notations of several days earlier, *ibid.*

[35] Oestereichisch-preussischer Vorschlag zur Redaktion des sechsten Artikels, 12 Nov. 1814, Klüber, *Acten*, II, 188–190.

garding the conference committee, appeared as amendments to articles that Wessenberg had previously approved. Beyond that it must be left to the reader to decide what the minister had in mind when he told Sagan on 9 November that he had interrupted a conference to send her tickets to a carousel. "I am going to regain the time," he explained, "by doing a good article for the German constitution, something very useful but not too much connected with life's happiness."[36] Whether the conference was with his own staff or another private consultation with Humboldt, the timing suggests Article VI as the subject more than any other.

Debate on the proposition began 14 November but not before Marshal Wrede unburdened himself in regard to the article inspired by Stein in the *Rheinische Merkur*. His personal vanity wounded by Görres's insults, and getting no satisfaction from direct appeals to Prussia, he now demanded that the committee itself issue a protest. Seconded by Winzingerode, he denounced even more vehemently the dastardly leaks of the protocols on which the article was based. The main target, of course, was Prussia, inasmuch as the newspaper was published at Coblenz, in her zone of occupation. Humboldt made light of the matter and, virtually confessing his guilt, maintained that the confidentiality earlier agreed to did not extend to the protocols, which he lamely tried to represent as public property. That simply was not the truth. Although it was customary to distinguish between informal remarks and those read into the protocols, the secrecy agreed to at the second meeting emphatically applied to both. In any case, Metternich, impatient to proceed with his beloved Second Council, agreed with Wrede that since libel was involved, the committee had a right to investigate but as a practical matter should simply request Hardenberg to do so. After further acrimonious exchanges, exacerbated by the enhanced sense of crisis and the dread induced by the movement of troops into Bohemia and Poland—Wrede himself the next day requested Montgelas to mobilize the army—Metternich's compromise was adopted and the issue buried forever.[37]

Now it was Winzingerode who delayed the proceedings, pleading that the king had scarcely seen the new draft of Article VI, had not received the protocol of the previous session, and again demanded a recapitulation. Thereupon Metternich and Humboldt promised prompt action, and the debate on the expanded Article VI began. In the course of it two points stood out. The first was Humboldt's mendacity in telling

---

[36] Mett. to Sagan, 9 Nov. 1814, Ullrichová, ed., *Briefwechsel*, 270.

[37] Protocol of 14 Nov. 1814, Klüber, *Acten*, ii, 190–192; "Bemerkungen zum Protokoll," HSA, Stuttgart, E 70, Fasc. 13, pp. 409–413; Winter, *Wrede als Berater*, 201f.

Wrede that curial votes were meant "in general" only for the free cities and "small princes still in possession of their sovereignty."[38] The second was Wrede's refusal to extend the legislative power of the council beyond questions relating to military defense. If the Bund was to deal with such things as coinage, tariffs, or the mails, he insisted, these formulations should be inserted into the federal act as organic provisions that could be meticulously defined. To burden the constitution with details prejudicial to the future would be absurd, Metternich retorted, and adjourned the meeting.[39] When debate resumed on 16 November, Wrede was more conciliatory, endorsing the proposed structure of the body, even the idea of a permanent committee to consult with the Kreis chiefs. Regarding its legislative competence Münster suggested that Wrede's complaints could best be met by stating in the federal act that the guidelines should be those of the old imperial constitution, in which the *jura singulorum* were adequately protected. This proposal eventually did in fact become federal law.[40]

And then it happened: Württemberg, declared Winzingerode, would no longer comment on particular parts of particular articles; she must now insist on seeing a comprehensive plan incorporating all "the various points to be included in the federal act." The complaint was nothing new, but this time it was trumpeted in a formal note of protest filed separately for publication and not merely as an obscure allusion in the protocol. This time as well it was made explicit that such a plan must include the territorial distribution and the delineation of Kreise. The note thus was an attack not merely on Metternich's day-to-day stewardship or on his gradual undermining of the Kreise but on his fundamental strategy going back to the original division of the constitutional and territorial issues between two committees.

"Scarcely had the deliberations over the first draft begun," Württemberg's complaint ran," "when there was introduced in its place in the form of *detailed developments* something far removed from it and

[38] This is clear from the candid "Bemerkungen" but not from the protocol. See previous note.

[39] Protocol of 14 Nov. 1814, Klüber, *Acten*, II, 194f.

[40] Protocol of 16 Nov. 1814, Klüber, *Acten*, II, 195–197. *Jura singulorum* in the German conception were rights that an individual did not surrender by virtue of belonging to a particular political body. They were defined as restrictions on the body, limiting its authority to measures relevant to its purpose. In practice other measures might be taken under certain conditions but could not be binding on individual members who objected. Thus, to take an example from Wrede's concerns, unless the regulation of coinage was expressly made a function of the Bund, Bavaria would never have to submit in this respect, regardless of what a majority of other members might decide. See Philipp Anton Guido von Meyer, ed., *Corpus Juris Confoederationis Germanicae*, 3 vols. 3rd ed. (1859–1861; reprint ed., Aalen, 1978), II, 86–87; and Carl von Rotteck and Carl Welcker, *Staats-Lexikon oder Encyklopädie der Staatswissenschaften*, VIII (Altona, 1839), 698–705.

then again something else and so on." And every time the most important thing of all was missing: an overview of the whole.

> Neither the members of the Bund, nor the extent of their possessions, nor the physical and political boundaries of the Bund, on which alone its military forces can be calculated are known with certainty, and yet in these demands, advanced bit by bit, are embedded the assumption of obligations and the renunciation and abandonment of undisputed rights, for which nothing is offered in return but the well-worn platitude about compensating advantages to be gained.[41]

In this volatile atmosphere Humboldt and Metternich rushed to give assurances about accelerating action on everything from the German Catholic Church to the federal postal service, but after less than an hour the committee adjourned and never met again.

Opinion regarding the breakdown has traditionally been divided between those who regard Württemberg's démarche as a boycott of the committee and those who blame the international crisis, which was dissolving that Austro-Prussian amity without which the committee deliberations could be nothing but a farce.[42] It was, however, another of the false climaxes of the congress. True, Metternich's dealings with Hardenberg now had to be more tentative, but at this particular juncture no break had occurred. Rather, Hardenberg was just beginning his mission as mediator to which Metternich had given his consent and, according to the disapproving Gentz, was "still thinking of a hundred feeble palliatives to avoid a separation—I say separation, not break— from Prussia."[43] Not until mid-December was tension between Austria and Prussia severe enough to have alone prevented meetings of the committee.

Similarly, King Frederick in his own mind was merely demanding a new approach and fully expected Humboldt to produce the promised digest of past progress at the next meeting, which was in fact scheduled for 19 November.[44] Despite his rant that "Metternich has lost his head and does not know what he is doing," his concern basically derived from the import of the other notes of that same period. His Russophile sentiments notwithstanding, he construed the Nesselrode note of the

---

[41] "Note der königlich-wirtembergischen Bevollmächtigten an die übrigen Mitglieder der Comité für die teutschen Angelegenheiten," 16 Nov. 1814, text in Klüber, *Acten*, Vol. I, Part 1, pp. 101–104. Emphasis in original.

[42] Most recently Huber, *Verfassungsgeschichte*, I, 551, argues the first, Aretin, *Bayerns Weg*, 169f. the second.

[43] Gentz of Schwarzenberg, 21 Nov. 1814, quoted by Founier, *Geheimpolizei* 73, n. 3.

[44] This and following from Frederick to Mandelsloh, 20 Nov. 1814, HSA, Stuttgart, E 1, Fasc. 45.

14th "merely as the first step" toward a Russian intervention that would, in the existing international situation, be mostly in Prussia's favor. Still more threatening was the note of the twenty-nine small states with its call for an emperor, *landständische Verfassungen*, and representation on the German Committee. This outrage would never have been perpetrated, Frederick maintained, but for "the ridiculous refusal of Prince Metternich" to declare, as agreed at the first meeting, that the accession treaties bound their signatories to accept the decisions of the committee. "Now," he lamented, "we have a situation in which the five allied monarchs will no longer give a constitution to the other German states but the latter will prescribe one for us." Thus, Frederick, far from boycotting the committee, intended to accelerate the deliberations before external forces could be brought to bear. Nor was he alone. Ernst Hardenberg also believed that the time had come to stop pretending that the territorial and the constitutional questions could be completely separated.[45]

Frederick's action was disruptive all the same, for in demanding the linking of the territorial and constitutional questions, or rather the priority of the first, he was asking for something that could be accommodated only after the Saxon-Polish controversy had been settled, delaying the formation of the Bund till the end of the congress, as the Austrian reply of 22 November pointed out. Logically, Metternich went on in the note, the whole should precede the parts and a strong Bund would provide such security for all states that boundary lines would lose their strategic significance, an argument that ignored the importance of Kreis boundaries as Württemberg's own rejoinder of the 24th pointed out.[46]

The notes that worried Frederick also posed problems for Metternich. The Russian note was easily disposed of since Nesselrode had virtually invited him to confine his reply, as he did, to the assurance that he would file it away till such time as it would "produce the best effect" on his colleagues.[47] The note from the small states was more difficult, calling for assurances about their participation and Austria's stand on the imperial crown, either of which would have split him and Münster from the other three on the German Committee. As often before, he avoided a written reply, meanwhile expressing appreciation in private and asking for trust and patience.[48] His handling of the note

[45] *Ibid.*; and Count Hard. to Hanoverian ministry, 4 Dec. 1814, NSHSA, Cal. Br. 24, IV.

[46] Metternich's "Gegennote," 22 Nov. 1814 and Württemberg's "Erwiderungs-note," 24 Nov. 1814, Klüber, *Acten*, I, 104–113.

[47] Mett. to Nessel., 22 Nov. 1814, HHSA, StK., Kongressakten, Cart. 6, p. 337.

[48] Apian-Bennewitz, *Plessen und die Verfassungsfrage*, 64; Ulmann, "Entstehung der Kaisernote," 479.

from Baden was more complicated. At first he and Hardenberg requested Münster to draft a response, but when this was delivered and accepted by the Prussians, Metternich refused to have it sent. The Münster version to be sure, gratuitously rambled on at length about the internal misdeeds of Grand Duke Charles's regime and Baden's extraordinary aggrandizement under Napoleon, but its main offense was reviving Hardenberg's argument that Baden's accession treaty obliged her to acquiesce in anything the committee proposed. Earlier Metternich had prevented this from becoming official doctrine by eschewing a formal note, as King Frederick complained, and that was probably his purpose now. Since no other argument was any better, no reply was made; and it could be argued that as long as the German Committee, the principal source of jealousy, did not meet, no reply was needed.[49]

Thus, the situation after 16 November was really more mundane than the flurry of notes made it appear. To continue regular meetings before a comprehensive plan was available would only have conspicuously prolonged the impasse while needlessly exacerbating relations with the lesser states. This then was the main reason why Metternich neither declared the committee dissolved nor called it to order. As with the congress as a whole, it was better to take each day at a time, hoping on the one hand for the success of Hardenberg's mediation regarding Poland and on the other for progress on the constitutional question by means of private bilateral negotiations, which in fact had paralleled the committee meetings all along and now continued regardless of what the official record implied.

The most urgent project was the synthesis of past actions by the committee. Although Humboldt was not ready by 19 November as originally hoped, Martens by the 21st had prepared a paper which Humboldt then submitted in his own name to Winzingerode and Linden, who returned a voluminous commentary on 28 November. Among other things they defended the veto power of the First Council on the grounds that collectively it represented more population than all the other states combined. They also complained that the voting order of the old Reich, if adopted, would place Württemberg behind the Saxon duchies and Mecklenburg, gravely imperiling her dignity as a Kreis chief. Whatever Humboldt thought of these views, he reserved comment until the still expected next meeting of the German Committee,

---

[49] Münster to Prince Regent, Promemorium II, 28 Nov. 1814, NSHSA, Hanover, Des. 92, XLI, No. 112, vol. I, pp. 71–74. Cf. Schmidt, *Verfassungsfrage*, 289–291. Münster also drafted Metternich's reply to Württemberg. Cf. Hardenberg, "Tagebücher," 36; and Mett. to Hard., 20 Nov. 1814, ZSTA, Merseburg, 2.4.1. I, No. 1649, p. 98.

in the meantime using the material in the eventual preparation of a comprehensive draft for a German constitution.[50]

At the same time Wessenberg continued a dialogue with him regarding the further development of the Twelve Articles. King Frederick's demands and the fact that the reading had reached Articles VII and VIII combined to place the Kreis system next on the agenda. The time had come for Metternich to lay his alternative on the table. All that exists in this regard, however, is a memorandum by Wessenberg which merely argued that since the federal executive powers were to be vested in the First Council and since the military establishment could be managed in another way, Kreise would be redundant. Judiciary districts he did not mention at all, even though Metternich often had.[51] Wessenberg did not elaborate on the military establishment, but Metternich continued to talk about "military divisions," which probably meant clusters of medium and small states pooling their resources cooperatively under federal supervision instead of the direct orders of one prince. In this way Austria and Prussia would both be confined to divisions in their own territory as was later the case with the Bund, which limited Austria, Prussia, and Bavaria to corps areas on their own soil and distributed the rest of the states among three composite federal corps. Unlike the Kreise, then, divisions would not only be restricted to the military realm but they could not be the instruments of indirectly aggrandizing one dominant member of the group.

The status of the mediatized houses was another subject that called for Austro-Prussian consultation, but whatever Metternich's contribution, our knowledge rests on evidence that can at best be described as tantalizing. For some months, as we have seen, he had favored the Bavarian ordinance of 1807 as a model, and the Bavarians themselves insisted that this was their limit. Beyond that we know only that when the Prussian privy councilor, Johann Emmanuel von Küster, was assigned to the problem by Humboldt, he based his work mainly on the Bavarian ordinance and the several memorials of Solms-Laubach. Whether this was the result of Austrian pressure, however, can only be conjectured.[52]

---

[50] "Parallele zwischen den vorgeschlagenen und den bisher angenommenen Artikeln," 21 Nov. 1814, in Martens's hand, NSHSA, Hanover, Des. 91, No. 25, pp. 2–11; identical work submitted by Humboldt in HSA, Stuttgart, E 70, Fasc. 13, pp. 484–491; and "Bemerkungen über die Königliche Preussische Zusammenstellung . . . ," ibid., pp. 513–528. Cf. Humb. to Winz., 2 Dec. 1814, ibid., pp. 555f. (copy).

[51] "Betrachtungen über die Eintheilung Teutschlands in Kreise," n.d., HHSA, StK., Deutsche Akten, Fasc. 100, pp. 444–446. Partly because filed with material from Wessenberg's activities in spring, 1815, this and other important memoranda have hitherto been overlooked. The context, however, leaves no doubt that these undated pieces belong here.

[52] "Bemerkungen zu der vorgeschlagenen Bestimmungen der Rechte der Me-

The ordinance was long and complex, but its general concept was to permit the former Strandesherren considerable latitude in continuing their patrimonial functions, administering schools, churches, forests, mines, local government, and administering justice at the local level and in some cases at the first appellate level. All these activities, however, were conducted under state supervision and within the framework of state law, which was given precedence. Domain revenues were not taxable but most other things were subject to state taxes and applied to all subjects alike. Privileges, family compacts, and laws of inheritance remained intact but required re-confirmation by the state. Titles and coats of arms were retained except for the deletion of all references to the former Reich. Private armies, of course, were outlawed. Prayers in local churches were to be said first for the king, then the local lord. No oath of personal fealty was required, but a written recognition of the king's sovereignty had to be filed with the government. All in all, Montgelas and the king of Bavaria were less interested in interfering with traditional ways than with asserting royal sovereignty and preventing secessionist rebellions.[53]

Since the basic premise of the system was the reduction of the Standesherren to the status of territorial nobility, it is difficult to see how it could have been applied to the Kreis estates that Hardenberg, probably with Küster's strong encouragement, had in mind. The answer is that Humboldt, still backing away from monolithic Kreise, now visualized two classes of mediatized: those who remained with their existing sovereigns would continue to be treated as *Landstände*; those who had been liberated, so to speak, by the dissolution of such states as Berg and the grand duchy of Frankfurt or who were eventually separated by the territorial settlement from their existing sovereigns would "belong not to the *Landstände* but continue to exist on their own as true *Kreisstände*." The former pertained mainly to Bavaria and Württemberg, the latter mainly to Prussia.[54] The device was obviously a concession, but whether Metternich had a hand in it is unknown—apart, that is, from his pressing the Bavarian ordinance as a standard.

Regarding the federal court, Austrian intentions are better docu-

diatisierten," n.d., ZSTA, Merseburg 2.4.1.I, No. 1456, pp. 56–57; Aretin," Deutsche Politik Bayerns," 11. Küster had been the Prussian envoy to Bavaria and Württemberg, and his arrival in Vienna was widely held to signify Hardenberg's challenge to Humboldt in regard to the Kreis system.

53 "Königlich Bayerische Declaration von 19. März 1807 . . . ," text in Meyer, *Corpus Juris Confoederationis Germanicae*, II, 8–14.

54 Humboldt's "Entwurf einer Verfassung . . . mit Eintheilung der Bundesstaaten in Kreise," Dec. 1814, Art. LXX. Klüber, *Acten*, II, 49; Humb. to Hard., 11 Dec. 1814, Schmidt, *Verfassungsfrage*, 317. On Küster see Linden to King Frederick, 2 Dec. 1814. HSA, Stuttgart, E 70, Fasc. 13, pp. 546–550; and Hoff, p. 57, n. 1 and p. 72, n. 1.

mented and reveal a remarkable development of Metternich's surprisingly strong and positive statements before the German Committee on 7 November. Wessenberg's negotiations with Humboldt on this subject took place in the course of developing Article X, probably sometime before 22 November. As usual, a draft by Humboldt provided the basis of discussion.[55] It visualized a body of seven justices chosen, one from each Kreis, from two nominees, one proposed by the Kreis chief, the other by the Kreis estates. Thus Austria and Prussia would have the same advantage as in the First Council itself. Regarding interstate disputes the court would hear any case not previously settled by arbitration or by the First Council. The court's other area of competence was to be complaints of the mediatized houses, *Landstände*, and individuals against abuses by their sovereigns so far as these pertained to rights incorporated in state constitutions as guaranteed by the Federal Act. No other class of grievances was mentioned, and even within the latter category cases involving mainly procedural errors were, once the court had pointed out the errors, to be remanded to the supreme court of the Kreis chief for final decision. "Never and in no manner may the federal court invade the jurisdiction of a strictly civil-law court," Humboldt insisted with surprising emphasis. In these and numerous minor ways the plan was unexpectedly narrow, especially considering that in all other spheres of state law the final court of appeal, that is a court of third instance, was to be in most cases the supreme court of the Kreis chief. Only those some nine states with populations of over 300,000 were to be permitted their own supreme tribunals.

Now compare this plan to Wessenberg's counterproject. In it the court was to be larger, the justices being appointed by both councils in a manner related to the number of whole and curial votes rather than the number of Kreise.[56] Surprisingly, in light of the history of this project, the Austrian would have preferred to dispense with the arbitration of interstate disputes altogether and have the adversaries proceed directly to the federal court. To accommodate Humboldt, however, he accepted arbitration as an optional first step but provided incentives to the litigants to choose the court instead. In either case the First Council was not to intervene at all, but the instance thus eliminated was to be restored within the court itself by means of a special senate or bench to hear appeals from the verdicts of the senate of original jurisdiction. Thus the process was to be more judicial in

[55] This and following from "Entwicklung des 10ten [Artikels] in Absicht des Bundesgerichts (Preussischer Vorschlag)," n.d., HHSA, StK., Deutsche Akten, Fasc. 100, pp. 473–477.
[56] This and following from Wessenberg's "Entwicklung des 10. [Artikels] in Absicht des Bundesgerichts," n.d., *ibid.*, 456–461.

character and more centralized in structure than in Humboldt's plan, almost the opposite of Metternich's original views.

Similarly, in regard to federally guaranteed rights Wessenberg enlarged on the Prussian project. Nor merely the rights of subjects within states but *all* rights inscribed in the Federal Act as well as those conferred in other state treaties could be the basis for filing federal suits. In other words, not only might the lesser sovereigns sue a Kreis chief (in a court friendlier to them than the one the Prussians had in mind), but they might invoke the guarantees of the accession treaties in doing so. Wessenberg went even further, adding to the court's jurisdiction two classes of suits not mentioned by Humboldt at all. One consisted of certain cases pending in imperial courts at the time of the dissolution and never nullified by subsequent legislation during the Rheinbund period, a restorative provision that may have reflected nothing more than Wessenberg's Breisgau origins. The other class went to the heart of the plan and explains why his critique of the Kreis system did not mention judiciary districts.

As noted above, Humboldt made it a cardinal function of the Kreis chief to provide a court of third instance for all states in his Kreis with a population of under 300,000. Wessenberg now proposed that this function be transferred to the federal court, once again bypassing both the individual chiefs and the First Council, too. Moreover, "the federal court, as the supreme court for the territories [was to] exercise over all the courts of the states in question a right of oversight that represent[ed] a continuation of the sovereign's supervisory power." Cases of this kind might also be appealed to a higher bench of the court, providing still a fourth instance or review. When it is further considered that the complete range of the law, civil and criminal, customary and statutory, was so encompassed, the boldness of the Austrian position appears truly astonishing. Viewed in strictly political terms, Humboldt's federal court was to be mainly the protector of the mediatized houses and *Landstände*, Wessenberg's the guardian of the lesser sovereigns without being a threat to the larger states, which would provide the third instance themselves. Though not necessarily intending it, the Austrians were headed toward a degree of federal unity never visualized in Berlin.

Faced with the challenge, Humboldt made a few concessions. While insisting on a judicial function for the First Council, he grudgingly proposed that this might be exercised conjointly with the permanent committee of the Second. He also admitted state treaties other than the Federal Act as valid sources of rights and acknowledged the possibility of dividing the court into several senates, though the latter he did not pursue in his subsequent formulations. On all else he was adamant, proving that his original position was strongly held or, more likely, imposed on him by Hardenberg.[57] Wessenberg too stood his ground and drafted a précis of the points of difference between them as Metternich prepared to deal with Hardenberg and Münster on this subject on 22 November. What the conference produced and whether under the pressure of regular meetings of the German Committee they could have closed the gaps to present another Austro-Prussian development, the existing records do not disclose.[58]

Without a major change in international affairs, the probability is that Austria and Prussia had gone as far as they could, for Humboldt's court plan throughout presupposed strong internally concentrated Kreise whereas Wessenberg's just as pointedly assumed their absence. As noted earlier, there was some discussion of Metternich's military divisions, and perhaps Humboldt was even converted, but regardless of his personal views, his pen was still guided by the orders of the chancellor. Hence, the development of Article VIII, which dealt with the internal organization of the Kreise, was an exercise for him alone, though he tried, even within the Kreis system, to steer a middle course between the egalitarian position of the Austrians and the autocratic Kreis chiefs visualized by Württemberg. At one stage his elaboration reached more than sixty-six paragraphs, many of which favored the Kreis estates as against the chief.[59] With or without Kreise, he later advised Hardenberg, it was "uncommonly important that Prussia appear to the lesser princes not as a threat but as a refuge." Why try so hard to acquire by institutional means influence that Prussia as the stronger state would have in any case, when with "a little more effort" she could earn it and keep it?[60]

The negotiations between Wessenberg and Humboldt increasingly resembled a card game between opposing soldiers in no man's land, each listening uneasily to artillery shells arching overhead and wondering when the real battle would be joined. As the days passed and Hardenberg had nothing to report on his assignment, which he had accepted on 11 November, Metternich too began to wonder. The illness of the tsar shortly thereafter was part of the problem though it did not prevent him from flashing words of encouragement to the Aus-

[57] Text of Humboldt's second development in *ibid.*, 449–456 and in ZSTA, Merseburg, 2.4.1.I, No. 1559, pp. 267–273.

[58] Hardenberg, "Tagebücher," 36; Wessenberg's "Wesentliche Abweichungen des Preussischen Vorschlags von den meinigen," HHSA, StK., Deutsche Akten, Fasc. 100, pp. 447–448.

[59] E.g., when functioning as the supreme court of the Kreis, the chief's court was now to be enlarged to include associate justices from the other Kreis estates. ZSTA, Merseburg, 2.4.1.I, No. 1456, pp. 34–56.

[60] Humb. to Hard., 11 Dec. 1814, Schmidt, *Verfassungsfrage*, 315.

trians. Finally, by 20 November Metternich could contain himself no longer. "I pray you, my dear chancellor," he wrote on that date, "go as soon as possible to the tsar, first because he's in a good mood now and second because he's made me all kinds of hints while avoiding any commitments."[61] Similar optimistic advice Hardenberg received from Baron Stein, who was rapidly becoming the key figure, having just recently persuaded the tsar to remove the pro-Austrian Nesselrode from the Polish negotiation and bring in his henchmen, Czartoryski and Capodistria.[62]

The twenty-third of November was Metternich's name day, and he celebrated at a luncheon given for the family by Count Karl Zichy. It was also the occasion for a grand carousel held in the evening in the Spanish Riding School. By all accounts this exercise in medieval tournament play and intricate cavalry figures was a highlight of the congress, but not for the serious-minded. Gentz did not attend, nor did Humboldt and Stadion. The tsar, for whom in large measure the spectacle had been planned, was likewise absent, still confined to his rooms though receiving visitors.[63] One of these was Hardenberg, who arrived at 7:00 p.m. to state the mediator's terms: for Austria the Nida line with Cracow and Zamość, for Prussia the line of the Warta with Thorn, the latter permanently demilitarized if the tsar wished. Austria's acquiescence in a Polish constitution was included, but linkage with Saxony and Mainz was not—except so far as Hardenberg recited all the tempting offers being made from the other side.[64] The tsar promised an answer in a few days, and the chancellor, departed, spirits uplifted for a change. After the carousel Metternich also called on the Russian ruler, probably at the latter's request. Not wishing to interfere with Hardenberg's mission, however, he kept his distance from Alexander's cross-examination, but in general found him conciliatory. As Castlereagh said later, for the first time the tsar was at least "willing to consider the question as a matter of regular negotiation."[65]

In groping for a decision Alexander again consulted Stein and Czartoryski, who along with Humboldt were appalled at Hardenberg's apparent willingness to leave the king of Saxony his Dresden nucleus. Accordingly, they begged the tsar not only to link the German and

[61] Mett. to Hard., 20 [Nov. 1814], ZSTA, Merseberg, 2.4.1.I, No. 1649, p. 98.
[62] Hardenberg, "Tagebücher," 36; Stein, "Tagebuch," *Briefe*, v, 336–338.
[63] Gentz, *Tagebücher*, I, 333; McGuigan, *Duchess*, 407–410.
[64] Hardenberg's memorial for the tsar, 23 Nov. 1814, cited in n. 29; Castle. to Liverp., 25 Nov. 1814, PRO, F.O., 92/8; same to same 5 Dec. 1814, Webster, *BD*, 248, Stein, "Tagebuch," *Briefe*, v, 338.
[65] Hard. to Mett., 24 Nov. 1814 (private), HHSA, StK., Kongressakten, Cart. 7, p. 330; Mett. to Hard., 25 Nov. 1814, ZSTA, Merseburg, 2.4.1.I, No. 1649, p. 104. Cf. Castle. to Liverp. 25 Nov. 1814, No. 24, PRO, F.O., 92/8, pp. 194–197.

Polish issues in a single negotiation but to insist on the whole of Saxony for Prussia and the exclusion of Bavaria from Mainz. In return they requested of him only that Thorn and Cracow become free cities neutralized under the guarantee of the allied powers. Because of his own interest in a strong Prussia, united with a strong Saxony, Alexander at length agreed and put his signature to a declaration that Stein had previously prepared. When Hardenberg saw it on 27 November, he was disappointed, realizing that this program represented for Metternich precisely the retreat on all fronts that he vowed he would never make. For Prussia, moreover, it meant the end of evenhanded mediation and her final attachment to Russia.[66]

The following day, almost three weeks after he had accepted the mission, Hardenberg finally made his report to Metternich, putting the best face he could on the situation. Acknowledging the paltriness of the concessions but emphasizing the futility of expecting more, he waited till the end of their conversation to mention the necessary linkage with the German issues and even then treated it as an obvious Prussian interest, not necessarily as a condition insisted upon from the Russian side.[67] This intimation was correct, of course, so far as the proviso had entered the Russian declaration in the custody of Baron Stein. After the long wait and for all the maneuvering behind the scenes, the only result of the mediation, then, was a neutral Cracow and no concessions at all from the Prussian side. It remained for Hardenberg to convey these terms in writing, but Metternich already knew that a second offensive had failed.

And still he refused to set France in motion, despite enormous pressure from the panicky and the stolid alike. Schwarzenberg was still moving troops toward the Polish frontier and now spoke of calling on the French for another 100,000 to check Prussia in Franconia and on the Lower Rhine.[68] Münster feared that any delay would drive Talleyrand into the Russian camp, reviving the dread Tilisit alignment, delivering Belgium and the Rhine frontier to France, and compensating Prussia with Hanover itself. To prevent this, he pleaded with Metternich to drop Murat in Italy and close ranks with Talleyrand at once. The Austrian minister, with the kind of coolness that others often mistook for procrastination, preferred to keep Murat in reserve as a means for creating upheavals in Bourbon France if things should come to that.[69] With France internally paralyzed and with military support

[66] Stein, "Tagebuch," *Briefe*, v, 336–340; Stein's draft declaration for Alexander, 27, Nov. 1814, *ibid*, v, 209f. Cf. Ritter, *Stein*, 505–507.

[67] Mett. to Francis, 2 Dec. 1814, HHSA, StK., Vorträge, Cart. 196.

[68] Talley. to Louis, 25 Nov. 1814, Talleyrand, *Corr.*, 167f.

[69] Münster to Prince Regent, 30 Nov. 1814, text in Webster, *Castlereagh*, I, 557–559.

from England, the forces of Denmark and the larger German states could suffice, he was advised, to make a stand against a Russo-Prussian alliance.[70] This hope was considerably dimmed, however, when Castlereagh responded to his demand for a military guarantee simply that he had no instructions.[71] Even worse, the instructions that did arrive shortly thereafter emphatically stated "the impossibility of His Royal Highness consenting to involve this country in hostilities at this time for any of the objects which have been hitherto under dicussion in Vienna."[72]

Before succumbing to the panic that had engulfed Münster, however, Metternich decided to try still a third combination, the very one the tsar had already accused him of: a deal with Russia at Prussia's expense. After his depressing talk with Hardenberg on the 28th he spent two hours with the tsar.[73] What passed between them is unknown, but if Emperor Francis's meeting with Alexander the following day is any clue, the latter professed a desire to stay out of the Saxon affair, referring Francis to the king of Prussia instead. That would not help, the emperor replied, because Hardenberg and Humboldt gave conflicting advice and in this case the latter prevailed. Humboldt was a scoundrel, Alexander said, and dropped the subject.[74]

Even the tsar, however, much as he relished conducting affairs by himself, would never have changed course in a face-to-face meeting with another sovereign. Accordingly, Metternich was still more encouraged when he learned that the day after the meeting of the two emperors Czartoryski and Nesselrode were dispatched almost simultaneously, the former to Talleyrand, the latter to Wrede, to announce that their master wished to extricate himself from his obligations to Prussia. Further trouble for Prussia Metternich suspected from Hardenberg's slowness to follow up their conversation with a formal project. "It seems to me" he reported to the emperor, "that the Prussians do not quite know how they should begin if they are to keep their affair *pari passu* with the Polish."[75]

[70] This sanguine view was pressed by General Steigentesch, an expert on Denmark. See his memorial "Idées politiques et militaires de Steigentesch en partant de la supposition d'une alliance entre la Russie et la Prusse," 26 Nov. 1814, HHSA, StK., Kriegsakten, Fasc. 497, pp. 484–487.

[71] Rosenkrantz, Danish foreign minister, quoting Francis, entry of 1 Dec. 1814, Rosenkrantz, *Journal*, 96.

[72] Bathurst to Castle., 27 Nov. 1814, Webster, *BD*, 448.

[73] Mett. to Sagan, 28 Nov. 1814, Ullrichová, *Briefwechsel*, 273.

[74] As told by Francis to King Frederick of Denmark, who informed Rosenkrantz. Entry of 30 Nov. 1814, Rosenkrantz, *Journal*, 93f. A tougher stand by the tsar was reported by the Württemberg embassy, but its information did not come from Francis himself. Linden to King Frederick, 2 Dec. 1814, HSA, Stuttgart, E 70, Fasc. 13, pp. 546–550.

[75] Mett. to Francis, 1 Dec. 1814, HHSA, StK., Vorträge, Cart. 196.

When the chancellor's *note verbale* finally arrived on 2 December,[76] it contained several new embellishments indicating he had won some points from the extremists. As a gesture to the cause of legitimacy the king of Saxony could be transferred to a territory in Münster and Paderborn with a population of 350,000 and the royal title for the rest of his life. Prussia would pledge herself never to make Dresden a military base and would cede to Austria parts of Upper Silesia to improve her frontier. Mainz and Luxemburg must both have Austro-Prussian garrisons, but Bavaria might participate if she chose, and actual ownership of the site at Mainz could go to Hesse-Darmstadt. An accompanying table contained the customary juggling of souls, including the proviso for distributing the mediatized properties among the Kreis chiefs. "It is evident," Hardenberg said in closing, "that Prussia less than any other power thinks about wanting to expand."

More striking to Metternich than these substantive refinements was the chancellor's transparent effort to manipulate the international situation to advantage. As if nothing had happened since 22 October, he took his stand "on the consent already given by Austria and England and on their assistance."[77] Four days earlier he had spoken of a combined negotiation as a Prussian interest; now he held that this was the tsar's condition, the sine qua non for his concessions in Poland. "Today he has changed his language," Metternich reported to Francis and continued:

> The more advantageous he considers this linkage between the objects of negotiation to be, the more emphatically must we separate them. Now we must seek to rescue the Saxon question, if possible even with the help of Russia, seeing that all attempts to modify the Polish [affair] with the cooperation of Prussia have been in vain. I have already too often had the honor to perceive the views of Your Majesty to return to the latter conception of things.[78]

Whether this last sentence was simple etiquette or evidence that Francis had favored a direct approach to the tsar all along, Metternich was now ready to move and received authorization to proceed as follows: the tsar to cede Cracow and environs to Austria, to adopt a constitution that would limit Russian influence in Poland, to guarantee in treaty the permanent separation of Austria's Polish lands from his own, and finally to promise his good offices to dissuade the king of Prussia from seeking the whole of Saxony or at least to remain neutral in the matter.[79]

[76] Text with charts in d'Angeberg, *Congrès*, iv, pp. 1941–1952.
[77] *Ibid.*, iv, p. 1945.
[78] Mett. to Francis, 2 Dec. 1814, HHSA, StK., Vorträge, Cart. 196.
[79] *Ibid.*

Under the circumstances Metternich's meeting with Hardenberg that same day would have been rancorous even if he had not just risen from a sick bed. "Posterity will never forgive us," the Austrian complained, "for having missed the opportunity, when we had all Europe with us, to confine Russia within reasonable boundaries." Angrily the chancellor, who was himself recovering from a cold, rejected the charge and the next day continued the recriminations in writing, complaining that Austria had never been positive enough in her demands and must now find the means to deliver Prussia from her pitiable position. With genuine, if self-centered, emotion he cast off the shackles of officialese and launched into verse to remind Metternich of the lofty aspirations that had once bound them together:

> Away discord, vanish from our folk.
> Give way, thou monster with the snaky hair!
> A single perch atop a giant oak
> The double eagle and the black one share.

> From this time forth in all the German Reich
> One word, one thought, is uttered by this pair,
> And where the lutes sound out in German tongue
> There blooms one Reich so mighty and so fair.[80]

The bathos and desperation evident in Hardenberg's letter were amply justified. Metternich, of course, could not give a formal answer at once for there was still the tsar to sound out, but there were other ways to prepare the ground. Through Czartoryski and Gentz he insisted that "the king of Saxony must be accommodated with a part of his land," adding, somewhat portentously, that this would meet the objections of France and satisfy public opinion in Vienna. Further intransigence, he warned, "would dissolve the alliance with Austria," which was another way of saying she would at last ally with France.[81] On 5 December he submitted to the tsar himself the new Austrian terms, declaring that the emperor would never yield on the Saxon point, a vow that Francis personally repeated to Alexander at a banquet later that night. Though calm and affable, the latter still resisted, arguing that the people of Saxony prized their unity above all else. Even if true, Francis replied, the statement expressed nothing less than the doctrine of popular self-determination, which no sovereign could endorse.[82]

[80] Hard. to Mett., 3 Dec. 1814 (private), HHSA, StK., Kongressakten, Cart. 7, pp. 343 and 346. Translation mine.
[81] Stein, "Tagebuch," *Briefe*, v, 340f., especially n. 141; Gentz, *Tagebücher*, I, 337.
[82] Talley. to Louis, 7 Dec. 1814, Talleyrand, *Memoirs*, II, 345–346; Castle. to Liverp., 7 Dec. 1814, Webster, *BD*, 257; Rosenkrantz, *Journal*, entry of 6 Dec. 1814, p. 103.

At this juncture Metternich turned back to the man who had once scoffed at "tender consciences," who had drafted the moral indictment of King Frederick Augustus, the man who had sought to build his anti-Russian bloc on the corpse of Saxony. Castlereagh too had changed, but even if he had not, new orders from Lord Liverpool had just arrived, and these demanded the preservation of the king's throne. Promptly, on 6 December he sought out Hardenberg, handing him Liverpool's dispatch, citing the hostile opinion of Europe, and explicitly withdrawing his offer of 11 October, which he now declared obsolete. Later in the day he boasted to Metternich that he had prepared the chancellor "for a negative from Austria" but suggested that the Austrian reply should include an alternative settlement that would still meet Prussia's "just views."[83]

With Castlereagh's conversion Metternich had recaptured the pivotal position. When he delivered his reply to Hardenberg, the tsar would finally have to choose between his two German allies. If Austria, France could still be kept in isolation; if Prussia, at least an alliance with France, Bavaria, Britain and a number of lesser states, would pose a formidable counterforce. There remained in the meantime one piece of unfinished business that Metternich was resolved to settle if he could: the fate of the Kreis system, which would determine whether the surviving part of Saxony would be truly free or not. How else can we account for the fact that at this decisive moment in grand affairs, in the morning of 7 December, another meeting of the Austrians, Prussians, and Hanoverians was held to discuss the German constitution?

Just before the meeting Metternich had a private session with Count Münster. As once with Wrede, so now he dilated on the evils of the Kreise, showing his guest in secrecy the territorial distribution proposed by Hardenberg and the counterproject to be advanced by Austria. Münster was aghast to see that Prussia claimed not only Saxony but much of Hesse-Darmstadt as well; moreover that by means of Kreise she would dominate all of Hesse, Thuringia, and North Germany and envelope the lands assigned to the Hanoverian Kreis. "This prospect," he hastened to report to the prince regent, "would be so menacing that I must agree with the opinion of Prince Metternich, who seeks to parry the blow by repudiating the Kreise entirely and granting no more than military divisions."[84]

Thus reinforced, Metternich faced the Prussians. This conference,

---

[83] Liverp. to Castle., 18 Nov. 1814, Webster, *BD*, 235f.; and Castle. to Liverp., 7 Dec. 1814, PRO, F.O. 92/8 which contains a valuable introductory paragraph omitted in Webster, *BD*, 255–257. Cf. Webster, *Castlereagh*, 360–364.

[84] Münster to Prince Regent, 7 Dec. 1814, text in Webster, *Castlereagh*, 560. Cf. Dietrich, *Hessen-Darmstadt auf dem Wiener Kongress*, 242f.

like many another before it, has left few traces in the record. It is probable, however, that Metternich made headway to the extent that the Kreis system, the core of the Twelve Articles, was now recognized as negotiable. At least we know that Humboldt at the meeting was charged with drafting not one but two constitutions, one with Kreise, the other without. A sense of urgency, moreover, attended the project; for three days he labored at top speed, leaving his rooms only to dine with Hardenberg and complain again of Metternich's "coolness, negligence, and procrastination." Had Metternich suggested that the destruction of Saxony would appear less menacing to the other German states if they were not to be subordinated to Kreis chiefs? Did the Prussians believe that without the Kreise Metternich would concede the whole of Saxony after all or, conversely, that he would accept the Kreise provided that a nucleus of Saxony was spared, possibly to be joined to the Bohemian Kreis? On 10 December they had their answer.[85]

[85] Hardenberg, "Tagebücher," 36; Humb. to Caroline, 8 Dec. 1814, *Briefe*, IV, 234f.

CHAPTER X

THE CRISIS OVER SAXONY

METTERNICH'S note, which reached Hardenberg on Saturday night, 10 December, ignited one of the great diplomatic explosions of the century. Not until Alexander Izvolsky's impassioned accusations against Alois von Aehrenthal in 1908 was there to be such an outburst as Hardenberg's frenzied charges of betrayal when he saw Metternich's counteroffer: not the whole of Saxony, not even the major share, but one-fifth, a mere 432,000 souls from a total of about 2,200,000! "Loathsome times," he wrote that night. "Metternich's reply totally unexpected." The notion of devouring Saxony had become so familiar, observed Gentz, that "all the Prussians and all their supporters cried murder."[1]

Superficially the controversy revolved around the nature of Metternich's note of 22 October, specifically whether Hardenberg had or had not met the Austrian conditions or at least had not yet failed to do so. At the time the Prussians insisted that they had faithfully maintained the "uniformity of policy" asked of them and that it was not their fault that the efforts had failed. Hardenberg, moreover, in dealing with the tsar, had a special interest in declaring the Austrian terms fully met: namely, to be able to represent Metternich's action as Prussia's punishment for loyally standing by her Russian ally, whose support was now more vital than ever.[2] It is impossible to believe, however, that the Prussians had been oblivious to conditions that Humboldt had analyzed in a least two memorials and Castlereagh had again pointed out only a few days before.

And yet the chancellor was obviously shaken. Why? Not because of the note as such, but because of Metternich's own strained efforts of the past month to keep the collaboration alive, the "hundred feeble palliatives" that so irritated Gentz. Not once in the innumerable conversations dating back to the days in London and Paris or even in Freiburg, where the first offer of Saxony had been made, not once had Metternich set his minimum at more than a small nucleus, at first to be annexed to Austria herself, later to be preserved for King Frederick Augustus. It was this point that Hardenberg stressed in his angry reply to Metternich on 11 December. "These ideas," he fumed, coldly

---

[1] Mett. to Hard., 10 Dec. 1814, d'Angeberg, *Congrès*, ii, 505–510; Metternich, *NP*, ii, 503–509; Bourgoing, *Wiener Kongress* 370–373; Hardenberg, "Tagebücher," 37; and Gentz's memorial of 14 Feb. 1815, in Metternich, *NP*, ii, 490f.

[2] Castle. to Liverp., 17 Dec. 1814, Webster, *BD*, 258.

addressing him as "Your Highness" rather than with his customary, "my dear prince," "are exactly the opposite of the suggestions that you indicated to me right up to the last minute and which went only so far as leaving a kernel of Saxony to its former sovereign."[3] Such was his reward for having defended Metternich's moderation against Stein, Czartoryski, and Humboldt and for consenting to study a constitutional draft without Kreise.

Hardenberg's expectations, then, were not really based on the technicalities of a diplomatic note but on the course of man-to-man conversations over a period of many months. This is not to say, however, that he was right. As a Prussian statesman he could never understand why it should matter to the Austrians (or the English too, for that matter) where the Russo-Prussian boundary was drawn or why the question should affect the status of Saxony, so long as Austria and Prussia were united to direct the defenses of the German Confederation. The Austrians, on the other hand, perhaps with excessive anxiety, always viewed a Prussia without the Warta frontier as a captive surrogate for Russia, a strong frontier vis-à-vis Prussia therefore as part of their eastern defenses even while they were nominally in alliance with Berlin. Metternich's note actually made this point, albeit obliquely: If Germany was to form a political body and defend the peace of Europe, "the frontiers of the great intermediate powers must not remain uncertain." More incisive, if overly dramatic, was his explanation to Türckheim a month later. The dream of an Austro-Prussian defense of the center against the flanking powers, he told the Darmstadt envoy, he had regretfully abandoned only "when he realized that Prussia, instead of concentrating her forces to defend the north and west, reverted to her old habits and wanted to train her batteries solely on Austria and the German Confederation."[4]

With this obligatory nod to an issue that once scorched the pages of Prussian historiography let us turn to other aspects of the note, which were equally unsettling to the chancellor. First of all, as objects of negotiation it separated the two questions that the Prussians were trying so hard to combine. The duchy of Warsaw, Metternich curtly advised, was no longer an issue; Austria still demanded Cracow and regarded a Polish constitution as a legitimate point of contention, but these were matters that she would negotiate directly with the tsar. In other words, Hardenberg had failed as mediator and was no longer needed. In the second place, Metternich went on, though Austrian interests required Prussia to be strong, the treaties nowhere singled out Saxony to serve

---

[3] Hard. to Mett., 11 Dec. 1814, HHSA, StK., Kongressakten, Cart. 7, p. 375.
[4] Türckheim's report of 14 Jan. 1815, quoted by Ulmann, "Entstehung der Kaisernote," 460.

this purpose; what had appeared to the partners of Kalisch in 1813 as clever reticence about Saxony Metternich was now exploiting against them. A table prepared by Wessenberg[5] showed that the scale of 1805 could be met by taking only the 432,000 from Saxony, by extending Prussia's eastern frontier to the Warta, by absorbing a number of mediatized properties in the old Westphalian Kreis, and by taking more on the left bank of the Rhine than the mere strip along the river hitherto claimed. The Rhenish awards, though extensive, were still to be confined to the north of the Mosel and included Luxemburg, possession of which was increasingly equated with an assignment to bell the French cat. Though subject to negotiation, he went on, a viable Saxony must be preserved: first, because Austrian interests and traditions demanded it; second, because "the principal German powers" demanded it; and third, because France demanded it. The spectacle of the two protective powers conspiring to devour one of their wards would inevitably drive the German states into the arms of France and pose "an insurmountable obstacle to the conclusion of the German federal pact."

Thus Metternich had not merely diminished the Hohenzollern share of Saxony; he was pressing on Prussia the mission of defending Germany against both the flanking powers and, moreover, using the latter to strengthen his hand. To obtain fulfillment of the treaties let Hardenberg speak to the tsar, to Castlereagh, to the prince of Orange. Metternich even provided an incentive: the more Prussia could wrest from the tsar in Poland, he said, the more Austria would reduce her own claims there. Here too was the first real bid to France, for the proposed one-fifth of Saxony was almost exactly what Talleyrand himself had always made his maximum concession. And the principal German powers? Here Metternich exaggerated. To be sure, any sovereign who dreaded the Kreis system must oppose outright despoliation anywhere, but when Talleyrand attempted to rally the German states behind a formal protest, Alexander, with some assistance from his uncle in Württemberg and of course the Prussians, intimidated enough governments to stifle the project. Only the Bavarians and the duke of Coburg braved tsarist wrath, and Bavaria issued a manifesto of her own. However that may be, it is clear that Metternich's famous note of 10 December was the call for a new system, the opening salvo in a campaign to isolate Prussia.[6]

In this campaign England was to play a pivotal role. Although she was now as committed as any other power to the preservation of a

[5] Text in d'Angeberg, *Congrès*, II, 509–510.
[6] Talley. to Louis, 7 and 15 Dec. 1814, Talleyrand, *Memoirs*, II, 355 and 363–364; and Dietrich, "Hessen-Darmstadt auf dem Wiener Kongress," 207f.

Saxon state, Metternich, in the note, did not mention her as such. Rather, in a separate note to Castlereagh, in which he justified his action, he asked the foreign secretary to act a second time as mediator, specifically to use his offices to bring Frederick William and Frederick Augustus to terms on the basis of a divided Saxony, and to join Austria in an effort to gain Europe's approval of the results. In the interest of Europe, Metternich vaunted, he had been willing to make the odious sacrifice, but with Poland lost, it would now have no redeeming value. In the "unfortunate case," however, that Prussia, with Russian support, refused, what was Britain herself prepared to do? There was always that rude question, it seemed.[7]

Metternich's first inkling of the uproar his note had produced was provided by Hardenberg's private letter, mentioned above, which was hastily dispatched in the morning of 11 December. Besides the charge of treachery, treachery so gross that he could continue negotiations only "at the express order of His Majesty," Hardenberg requested Metternich to send a spokesman to discuss with Hoffmann serious errors found in Wessenberg's tables. He also asked for a copy of Castlereagh's letter of 11 October, the one enthusiastically endorsing the complete annexation of Saxony. Routinely Metternich complied, little realizing that he was actually abetting Hardenberg's revenge. Whether on his own initiative or at the prodding of his advisors, the usual coterie of Stein, Czartoryski, Knesebeck, and Humboldt, with whom he had met earlier in the day, the chancellor, under immense emotional stress, had decided to justify himself by laying portions of his private correspondence before the tsar, a "very incorrect act," according to Castlereagh and, as it turned out, a very imprudent one.[8]

Alexander was especially incensed by Metternich's private letter of 7 November in which he denied the tsar's accusations of duplicity and implied he was a liar. Going immediately to Francis, the tsar resumed his tirades against the minister and even threatened to challenge him to a duel. Francis as usual stood firm and admonished his visitor to hear Metternich's side before resorting to an act of personal violence in the midst of a peace conference. This Alexander at length agreed to do.[9]

Francis thereupon informed his foreign minister, who scribbled a

---

[7] *Note officiel*, Mett. to Castle., 10 Dec. 1814, HHSA, StK., Kongressakten, Cart. 7, pp. 363–374.

[8] Hard. to Mett., 11 Dec. 1814 (private) and Mett. to Hard. same date, HHSA, StK., Kongressakten, Cart. 7, pp. 375 and 377; Stein, "Tagebuch," *Briefe*, v, 345–346; Hardenberg, "Tagebücher," 37; Castle. to Liverp., 17 Dec. 1814, Webster, *BD*, 258.

[9] Mett. to Francis, 12 Dec. 1814, HHSA, StK., Kongressakten, Cart. 7, p. 381; Metternich's "Portrait of Alexander," in Metternich, *NP*, 1, 326f.

note to Hardenberg expressing his dismay at the allegations and his hope that they were false. That was at 9:00 p.m. Later that night Wessenberg returned from his discussions with Hoffmann bearing with him Hardenberg's reply: not only did the chancellor admit the disclosure; he maintained it was necessary because Metternich himself had abandoned "the confidential way."[10] Baffled by this allusion, Metternich made a search of his own files, extracting a passage from Hardenberg's note of 9 October that on the face showed the chancellor himself to be the instigator of all that followed. With this and other damaging material he sought out Castlereagh, whose note of 11 October, it was now plain, could be involved as well. Rather than expose Hardenberg, however, they decided to use the documents as leverage with him and have Metternich show the tsar only his own remaining documents, which were innocuous by comparison. "We have nothing to gain," he explained to the emperor at 2:00 a.m. "by breaking the state chancellor's neck. He would only be replaced by someone worse." Francis, who had in the meantime learned from his brother, the Palatine Archduke Joseph, the full magnitude of Hardenberg's revelations (the tsar had read the pieces aloud to him) approved this strategy and passed the new information on to his minister.[11]

Despite the rigors of the day, Metternich arose before 8:00 a.m. on the 12th to arrange a meeting with Hardenberg. This took place later in the morning, and contrary to the earlier plan, Castlereagh did not attend. It speaks poorly for Hardenberg's memory or his judgment at this trying time that when Metternich announced his intention to exhibit to the tsar all the papers he himself had written and invited Hardenberg to do the same, the latter emphatically agreed. Whether he followed through is doubtful, but Metternich was henceforth free to be less considerate of the chancellor's neck. Conversely, it may be that Castlereagh remained away precisely in order to avoid having to display his own papers, two of which, the harsh indictment of Frederick Augustus and the memorandum of 23 October outlining the three-power strategy against the tsar, would now be as embarrassing as anything Hardenberg had written. The chancellor evidently decided against undermining the man whose support he still hoped for, but the possibility worried Metternich all the same. By contrast, Archduke John, with whom he spoke later in the day, urged him to reveal everything and have it out with Prussia once for all, by war if necessary. It was

[10] Hardenberg's marginalis on Metternich's letter of 9:00 p.m., ZSTA, Merseburg, 2.4.1.I, No. 1649, p. 130.
[11] Mett. to Francis, 12 Dec. 1814, HHSA, StK., Kongressakten, Cart. 7, p. 381; extract in Bourgoing, *Wiener Kongress*, 218f.

not so simple, was the minister's reply; Austria's own weaknesses would be exposed.[12]

Although Alexander avoided a ball given by Metternich that night, he did arrange an audience with the minister the following morning as he had promised Francis he would. Unlike the encounter of 24 October, which had been largely a calculated exercise in intimidation and quickly became a scandal, this one saw an outburst of honest emotion, the product of insult keenly felt, and was not widely discussed, even among Austria's secret agents. The tsar was "cold, dry, and stern," Metternich reported, entirely obsessed with the accusation of lying and certain that the Austrian minister had put foolish notions into Hardenberg's head. In self-defense Metternich produced the chancellor's memorandum to Castlereagh of 7 November, wherein he had argued that one should give in for the time being and await more favorable opportunities for rolling back Russian power in Europe. Confessing that he did not know which minister to trust any more, the Russian autocrat terminated the session by declaring that he would get the truth from the emperor Francis and henceforth deal only with him. Thereupon Metternich strode out, face flushed and muttering to an aide as he passed by that the heat in the imperial chamber was too much to bear.[13]

His schedule that day next took him to a conference with Hardenberg, where he endeavored to impress upon the chancellor that his proposal for Saxony was not the final word but a negotiating position and for that reason alone should have been treated as confidential. Recriminations behind them, they turned to the results of Wessenberg's discussions with Hoffmann. The Prussians generally accepted the Austrian figures in themselves, which were based on the year 1810, but they argued that war and other upheavals had since reduced the population of the provinces concerned by some 700,000. In that case, Wessenberg replied, the solution depended more on Russia than on Austria. Another Prussian objection was Wessenberg's counting the population of mediatized lands on a par with any others. Hardenberg, as we have seen, had always listed such properties separately on the grounds that the bulk of their revenues would remain with the local proprietor under the protection of *landständische Verfassungen*, and still

---

[12] Mett. to Hard., 12 Dec. 1814, HHSA, StK., Kongressakten, Cart. 7, p. 379; Hardenberg, "Tagebücher," 37; Talley. to Louis, 15 Dec. 1814, Talleyrand, *Memoirs*, II, 366; Diary of Archduke John in Freksa, *Congress of Intrigue*, 252–253. Talleyrand gives the impression that Castlereagh's papers were disclosed, but I find no corroboration in other sources and some contrary indications.

[13] Talley. to Louis, 15 Dec. 1814, Talleyrand, *Memoirs*, II, 366–367; Castle. to Liverp., 17 Dec. 1814, Webster, *BD*, 258–259; Stein, "Tagebuch," *Briefe*, v, 345–346; and McGuigan, *Duchess*, 416f.

more so if they were "attached to Prussia" only as Kreis estates. Either way, he was unwilling to have any such awards charged against Prussia's indemnification. In all, he insisted that the Austrian tables were 1,200,000 short. Wessenberg, a newcomer to such sophisticated demographic calculus, was stunned. "This method of aggrandizement," he charged, "has until now never been asserted by any power.[14] Now, in the meeting with Hardenberg, Metternich was ready with one of his pragmatic compromises, offering to apply a one-third discount to such lands, that is (to use the jargon that soon became standard at the congress) counting each inhabitant as two-thirds of a soul. To apply the formula in particular cases and to settle all disputes over conflicting figures he proposed the establishment of an impartial statistical commission. The latter Hardenberg accepted, the two-thirds rule he did not.[15]

Metternich's next stop was at the Palais Kaunitz, ostensibly to recount to Talleyrand the results of his previous two interviews, at least so far as he wished to divulge them. The visit was also another step toward an alignment with France. According to Talleyrand, when the Austrian invited him to be still another reader of the by now much perused note to Hardenberg, he declined, proposing instead that since France was mentioned in it, an official communication would be more appropriate. Metternich so promised, and Talleyrand jubilantly reported to Paris that this meant "the rupture of the coalition." Whether Metternich would have reported the meeting in this way is of course open to question, but there is no doubt that he too, he who had done more than any other to hold the coalition together, now recognized that Talleyrand was right. When conveying the note three days later, he expressly requested that it be sent directly to King Louis in Paris as a pledge of Austria's solidarity with France. This note, he told Talleyrand privately, would be "the last sent by the coalition."[16]

The closer Metternich and Talleyrand drew together the more anxious Alexander became lest they were already secretly allied. To obtain assurances on this point he sent Czartoryski to see the plenipotentiary in person, at the same time reviving the project of a dynastic marriage between Anne and the duke of Berry and insinuating his willingness to leave as much as half of Saxony for the legitimate king.[17] Meanwhile, the wrath he had directed at Metternich on 13 December turned to

[14] Wessenberg's "Bemerkungen über die Hoffmannschen Tabellen," extr. in Arneth, *Wessenberg*, 235–236, and Bourgoing, *Wiener Kongress*, 213f.

[15] Bourgoing, *Wiener Kongress*, 213f.; Hardenberg, *Tagebücher*, 37; Talley. to Louis, 15 Dec. 1814, Talleyrand, *Memoirs*, II, 367; Münster to Prince Regent, 17 Dec. 1814, Münster; *Political Sketches*, 305; Stein, "Tagebuch," *Briefe*, V, 345.

[16] Talley. to Louis, 15 and 20 Dec. 1814, Talleyrand, *Memoirs*, II, 367 and 371, official note of conveyance in d'Angeberg, *Congrès*, IV, 1961.

[17] Talley. to Louis, 15 Dec. 1814, Talleyrand, *Memoirs*, II, 365f.

warm congeniality in dealing directly with Francis the day after. Actually apologizing for his rigid stand regarding Cracow—the burial place of the Polish kings, he explained—he offered Tarnopol instead, the province he had taken from Austria in 1809. This proposal held little military advantage for Austria, but the cession of 400,000 souls was by far the most benevolent gesture he had yet made, especially as he hinted that he did not expect capitulation on Saxony as a quid pro quo. On the other hand, still indulging what Cooke called "his dirty views of overturning Metternich," he rejected Francis's earnest pleas that he resume normal intercourse and return negotiations to the ministerial level.[18]

In the face of coalescing opposition the tsar now began to press the Prussians to develop a plan that France and England might find tolerable. After a series of meetings with Knesebeck, Stein, Humboldt, Czartoryski, and Capodistria, who by now functioned as an informal cabinet, Hardenberg finally decided to offer his opponents a choice: either leave the king of Saxony the province of Upper Lusatia, which had a separate constitution anyway, or establish him on the left bank of the Rhine with a territory twice as large as Münster-Paderborn (the previous offer), a large Rhenish city as his capital, the fortress of Luxemburg, and *a seat on the First Council of the Bund*! In a demonstration of Hardenberg's loosening grip on affairs Stein later managed to persuade the tsar that since partition of Saxony would be no less pernicious as an option than as a demand, only the second plan should be advanced. Hardenberg then prepared a paper to this effect, adding for the sake of the record that Prussia's claim was based on Metternich's "promise" of 22 October. Instead of sending it to Austria as a formal note, however, he cast it in the form of a memorandum to the tsar, who was then to communicate it informally to Francis while another copy was being routed to Metternich via Castlereagh with the hope that he too would endorse it. In this way the weight of England and Russia might be directly brought to bear, Hardenberg could avoid responding to a note that he considered an insult, and the tsar could carry out his threat to shun Metternich and deal directly with the emperor. Although this "ministerial report," as Castlereagh called it, was ready by 16 December and Hardenberg discussed it informally with Metternich while strolling on the city wall on the 18th, the many hands through which it had to pass delayed delivery till the 20th.[19]

[18] Castle. to Liverp., 17 Dec. 1814, Webster, *BD*, 259; Stein, "Tagebuch," *Briefe*, v, 346; Münster to Prince Regent, 17 Dec. 1814, Münster, *Political Sketches*, 204, who got his information from Metternich himself; and Cooke to Liverp., 24 Dec. 1814, Wellington, *Supplementary Despatches* IX, 502.

[19] Stein, "Tagebuch," *Briefe* v, 346–347; Hardenberg, "Tagebücher," 37; Hard. note to Alexander, d'Angeberg, *Congrès*, II, 531–535; slightly different text of same

As the crisis mounted to its climax, while armies marched into position and insiders and onlookers alike believed themselves at the threshold of war, the tactical struggle focused on winning allies in Germany. Nobody realized better than Metternich that few things in life are all gain and no loss, and so it was with his new territorial plan. When he had to tell Wrede that Mainz must involve the Prussians in some way, the marshal testily replied that Bavaria in that case would keep Salzburg and the Inn District.[20] Similarly, when the loyal Baron Türckheim learned that Wessenberg had assigned Grand Duke Louis's favorite province, Westphalia, to Prussia, held forth a federal solution for Mainz, and allowed Prussia to expand into lands deemed vital to Darmstadt's compensations, he was aghast, and Louis himself felt betrayed. Lamely Metternich explained to Türckheim as he had to Hardenberg that the plan was only "an *aperçu* of possible alternatives," while Humboldt, to whom Türckheim also complained, at last had something to smile about: "the idea was entirely Austrian," he smugly pointed out. On 25 December the aggrieved envoy submitted a formal protest, but Metternich never answered it.[21]

Still, there was no chance that Bavaria, the only state that had officially condemned the seizure of Saxony, could be moved to desert Metternich on this issue. When Humboldt tried, threatening to revive Prussia's claim to Ansbach and Bayreuth, Wrede surprised the free-thinking humanist by naming divine providence as his ally. Even Grand Duke Louis believed that after the war, which he considered inevitable, Austria would remain his best hope for holding on to Westphalia. His confidence in war was so great that unlike his counterparts in Nassau, Württemberg, Bavaria, and Baden, he still rejected the notion of introducing a constitution merely to appease the powers and forestall federal regulation. And so it was that Bavaria and Hesse-Darmstadt, along with Hanover, continued to provide the foundations of Metternich's German policy.[22]

Metternich's relations with Saxe-Weimar, on the other hand, took almost the opposite turn. As a Wettin supporting the preservation of Saxony in the family and dreading Hardenberg's Kreis plans, Charles Augustus, as we have seen, had all along favored Austria over Prussia, counting on Tsar Alexander to obtain aggrandizement and a grand-ducal title for him. When the project for a small-state declaration in

---

prepared for Metternich in *ibid.* IV, 1952–1956; Münster to Prince Regent, 18 Dec. 1814, in Münster, *Political Sketches*, 207–208; and Castle. to Liverp., 24 Dec. 1814, PRO, F.O., 92, Vol. 9, No. 37.

[20] Winter, *Wrede als Berater*, 220.

[21] Dietrich, "Hessen-Darmstadt auf dem Wiener Kongress," 241–247.

[22] Winter, *Wrede als Berater*, 203f., n. 6; Olshausen, *Stellung der Grossmächte*, 90; Dietrich, "Hessen-Darmstadt auf dem Wiener Kongress," 194 and 247.

favor of Saxony arose, however, Hardenberg warned that Weimar's participation would jeopardize its rewards, whereupon the envoy Gersdorff, rather than desert the group, persuaded his colleagues not to take sides in grand affairs. Although it was the envoy and not the duke, as Talleyrand supposed, who initiated this course, Hardenberg and the tsar were grateful all the same. Then came Metternich's démarche: if Prussia received only a fifth of Saxony and had to be accommodated elsewhere, it was difficult to see where Weimar's share, some 100,000 souls that Hardenberg had offered from Prussia's gains, could be found. From this point on, about 7 December, Charles Augustus managed to suppress his legitimist sentiments and his small-state desire for neutrality to march with his powerful northern neighbors.[23]

This bond, as it happened, was strengthened in another way, also on Gersdorff's initiative. In private talks with Humboldt he had learned of the plan for a committee of five on certain occasions to represent the Second Council on the First. From here it was but a short step to suggest involving the committee permanently in all the affairs of the First Council, precisely as Metternich himself intended. Gersdorff's plan called for dividing the lower chamber into four regional units, each with an elective director who would sit on the First Council. In this way Charles Augustus, though not a true Kreis chief, would have a chance to function at their level.[24] Although Humboldt did not endorse this particular scheme, he used it to show Hardenberg that some such extension of the existing committee plan was imperative to appease the small states at this time of crisis. Relations with Gersdorff thereafter continued to be close, and Metternich could not compete.[25]

The same was true of Hesse-Cassel, a more critical state. Despite the desire of some of the elector's officials to break free of Prussian domination, William himself remained a Prussophile and recognized that he was in any case trapped by his geographical position. In early December he declared his readiness to enter a Prussian Kreis provided that a union with Hesse-Darmstadt was decreed.[26] By this he probably meant more than membership of both states in the same Kreis, but even this much association would help pull Darmstadt into the Prussian system. Another sovereign that Humboldt expected to drift into the Prussian camp was Grand Duke Charles of Baden, embittered as he was at Austria's designs on the Breisgau and her backing of Bavaria's bid for the Main-Tauber district. Charles, however, wisely looked be-

[23] Egloffstein, *Carl August*, 40–67; Talley. to Louis, 15 Dec. 1814, Talleyrand, *Memoirs*, II, 202–212. Text of note never sent, *ibid.*, 213–215.
[24] Schmidt, *Verfassungsfrage*, 303–307.
[25] Humboldt's memorial on his double draft, 9 Dec. 1814, text in *ibid.*, 306–315.
[26] Losch, *Geschichte des Kurfürstentums*, 99.

yond Germany for his support, at last joining the Association of Small States to please Talleyrand and officially declaring his intent to introduce an estates constitution to impress the tsar.[27]

At the same time he attempted to fend off the Kreis system by seizing the initiative with a German-constitution plan of his own, one that was to have such an impact on the issue that it deserves brief treatment here. Drafted and circul ted by the minister of state, Baron Karl Wilhelm Marschall von Bieberstein, with advice from his brother, Ernst Ludwig Marschall of N: ~u, it featured a basically unicameral assembly that for legislative purp :es would afford each state at least one vote but in executive matters would group the smaller states into curiae, the net result being an executive committee with nine seats. Another striking article not only required *landständische Verfassungen* but specified that they must balance an upper house of mediatized and territorial nobility against a lower house reserved entirely for elected deputies of the urban bourgeoisie and property-owning peasants, another instance of the strategy of utilizing popular forces to outflank the Standesherren. Significantly Marschall's draft was also the first to make the Bund responsible for preserving order and tranquillity within member states, this by deputizing neighboring states to render assistance against disturbances. This provision obviously foreshadowed the Carlsbad Decrees of 1819, but given Nassau's recent experience, its target was more likely the obstreperous Standesherren than the students of Heidelberg and Freiburg. In most other respects Marschall's proposals were strongly particularistic, in military affairs and freedom of alliance, for example, resembling the Bavarian position. Humboldt, who discussed the plan with Gersdorff on 11 December, dismissed it as feeble, but this did not prevent his borrowing from it later.[28]

Then there was Württemberg, as usual following a serpentine course peculiarly her own. During the crisis she was generally regarded as pro-Prussian, partly because Crown Prince William was so inclined, partly because King Frederick, like Charles Augustus, threw his weight against the projected declaration to save Saxony.[29] Another bond, as we have seen, was the Kreis system, which Frederick believed to be imperiled by the clamor of the lesser states for admission to the negotiations. On 23 December, just before departing the congress, he left instructions for Winzingerode to inform him at once if Metternich at last submitted his plan for military districts but in the meantime to

[27] Baden's note to Mett. and Hard., 1 Dec. 1814, Klüber, *Acten*, I, 100. Also new list of members in the association, *ibid.*, 96.

[28] Glaser, "Die badische Politik," 294–299. Text of "Artikel welche der künftigen Verfassung Deutschlands zu Grunde zu legen seyn möchten," in Pertz, *Leben von Stein*, IV, 673–682.

[29] Talley. to Louis, 15 Dec. 1814, Talleyrand, *Corr.*, 202–205.

hold out for the Kreise at all costs. He and Hardenberg were now virtually the only die-hards left in this regard. To placate the smaller states in an innocuous way he was even ready to withdraw his abstentions and vote for the participation of the committee from the Second Council in the matters previously discussed: that is, in breaking tie votes, deciding on peace and war, determining when the Second Council should be consulted, and sending and receiving extraordinary envoys—anything to put the lower classes at ease as long as "the unity and concentrated strength of the Bund are not impaired." His opposition to a federal court and federally dictated *landständische Verfassungen*, however, remained as fierce as ever.[30]

And yet the true object of Frederick's attentions was not Prussia, and the true aim of his policy was neutrality. This much he boasted of to Metternich in a farewell audience on 26 December. What he did not mention was his candidate for guaranteeing that neutrality. Using Grand Duchess Catherine as his emissary, he conjured up for the tsar the specter of an Austro-French-Bavarian alliance that would surround Württemberg and leave him no choice unless Russia protected him, or better yet, joined in a mutual security pact with Württemberg and other German sovereigns as well.[31] He was in fact trying to revive the project of July, 1814, for a Russo-German Union, the essence of which was a neutral league under Russian protection. Such a body, he instructed Winzingerode, would be "the natural ally of the Russian Empire" and offer an escape route from the Austro-Prussian war that could break out at any time.[32] On this basis Winzingerode and Capodistrias conferred shortly after Christmas, and without waiting for an imperial decision Winzingerode in early January began to line up Baden, Nassau, Hesse-Darmstadt, and the Saxon duchies for the plan; the crisis, however, passed before the project could be completed.[33] Capodistrias' belated reply of 31 January, another of those Russian notes to which Stein gave so much of himself, stressed that Russia's pledge to bring about a *corps germanique* meant all Germany and not the establishment of several competing systems. Besides, he insinuated, the Württemberg plan was singularly silent about the rights of all classes of the nation.[34]

[30] "Weitere Instruktion" to Winzingerode, 23 Dec. 1814, HSA, Stuttgart, E 70, Fasc. 13, pp. 562–569.
[31] Fred. to Alex., 16 Dec. 1814, HSA, Stuttgart, E 70; Alexander's reply, 18 Dec. 1814, *VPR*, VIII, No. 61, p. 136; Winz. to Fred., 24 Dec. 1814, HSA, Stuttgart, E 70b, Fasc. 46, No. 1.
[32] "Instruction secrète pour . . . Winzingerode," 25 Dec. 1814, HSA, Stuttgart, E 70b, Fasc. 46, No. 1.
[33] Glaser, "Die badische Politik," 299; Winz. to Fred., 8 Jan. 1815 (postscript in cipher), HSA, Stuttgart, E 70, Fasc. 14.
[34] Capodistrias to Winz., 31 Jan. 1814, d'Angeberg, *Congrès*, II, 688.

Meanwhile, in the transition from collaboration to open rivalry between Austria and Prussia Humboldt's work on parallel drafts of a German constitution occupied an intermediate position, performed as it was during the tense days between 7 and 9 December but before Metternich's devastating note, which Humboldt learned about on the 11th. Most of the draft's 120 articles conscientiously reflected agreements reached, partly reached, or proposed in the deliberations of the German Committee. Even the version without Kreise[35] required, in his expert hands, surprisingly few modifications. In it the First Council as a whole was to issue executive orders directly to the member states instead of through the agency of Kreis chiefs, but the details regarding procedures otherwise remained much the same. Some twenty articles relating to the internal affairs of the Kreise, mainly those concerning relations between the chiefs and the Kreis assemblies, were simply deleted. Somewhat more tinkering was required to devise a substitute for the process of judicial appeals, which in the Kreise, as we have seen, was to terminate in the Kreis chiefs' supreme courts. With the elimination of Kreise Humboldt had the signal opportunity to adopt the Wessenberg plan of assigning to the federal court the final appeal or third instance in cases originating in states with fewer than 300,000 inhabitants. Instead he proposed that a number of such states pool their resources to create a regional supreme court for the group, an arrangement much like Metternich's military districts. Their procedures, norms, and personnel policies, moreover, were to be filed with and approved by both councils of the federal diet, not by the federal court itself. All in all, it was a most deliberate rebuff of the Austrian plan, giving every appearance of being a calculated appeal to the small states in a sphere where Metternich's ideas seemed to be more centralistic.[36]

Because Humboldt's double draft, as the work is usually called, was not officially circulated, even to Metternich, till early February,[37] after the resolution of the Saxon crisis, the only features relevant at this point are those that reflect his tactical thinking at the time. The court plan described above is one example. It is also striking that he used every opportunity, especially in the opening articles, to follow, wher-

---

[35] The standard text of both versions in Klüber, *Acten*, II, that with Kreise in 120 articles, pp. 18–55, that without Kreise in 106 articles, pp. 55–64. Technically these texts are dated February, 1815, but are with negligible exceptions identical to those of December. See Schmidt, *Verfassungsfrage*, 321–327, who gives some of the slight variations.

[36] Draft without Kreise, Arts. XXXIII–XXXVII, Klüber, *Acten*, II, 59f.

[37] A text of the Kreis version only was received on 14 Dec. 1814 at the Austrian State Chancellery and may well have affected a later project drafted by Wessenberg. HHSA, StK., Deutsche Akten, Fasc. 100, pp. 113–143.

ever the substance permitted, the wording preferred by Württemberg, the main exceptions being the restoration of the double votes for Austria and Prussia on the First Council and the elimination of the First Council's legislative veto. A second important concession to the South German states was the differential treatment of the mediatized houses alluded to earlier, whereby existing subjects of this rank, numerous in the South, would remain *Landstände* with little role in Kreis affairs except curial votes in the Kreis assemblies. By contrast, newly acquired Standesherren, as would be the overwhelming majority to be joined to Prussia, were to be "true *Kreisstände*"; yet, contrary to Hardenberg's earlier plan, this status did not mean genuine independence from a sovereign, only exclusion from the Landtag. In comparison to their kind in South Germany, they were to find their rewards rather in greater autonomy, more tax exemptions, the retention of honor guards, and the rights both to sit in the Kreis assembly and to name associate justices to the Kreis supreme court.[38]

In the version without Kreise, of course, the last functions were not available, and Stein later wondered why the Standesherren themselves in this eventuality should deem it an advantage not to be *Landstände*, without a voice in legislation, taxes, and justice, all of which would still affect them. Humboldt's answer, based on his dealings with Solms and Gärtner, was that they feared complete assimilation if they once involved themselves in affairs of state. Their tax privileges, moreover, especially the right to retain the direct taxes collected from their subjects, were to be so considerable that Humboldt himself wondered if the state's share of revenue would even meet the costs of maintaining the troops recruited in such lands. All in all, he replied to Stein, it would be better to wait until they requested admittance to the *Landstände*. In the meantime, these technicalities could be cited to a skeptical Europe to explain why Bavaria and Württemberg must count their mediatized lands in their population totals whereas Prussia need not.[39]

However self-serving, it is obvious that Humboldt's maneuvering was to accommodate the South German sovereigns while demonstrating to the Standesherren themselves Prussia's superior liberality. To reinforce this impression consideration was given to the immediate

[38] On the mediatized, Arts. LV-LXXIX in version with Kreise, Arts. XLI-LXIV in that without. Regarding taxes the first group was to be subject to both direct and indirect state taxes, the second group only to the latter.

[39] Stein's critique of the draft without Kreise, 25/26 Dec. 1814 and Humboldt's rejoinders in Stein, *Briefe*, v, 226–231. See also Humb. to Hard., 10 Jan. 1815, Schmidt, *Verfassungsfrage*, 399, and Humb. to Caroline, 12 Feb. 1815, *Briefe*, IV, 470. Cf. the remonstrance of the houses of Solms and Wied, 27 Dec. 1814 that "they neither can nor will become *Landstände* of the prince of Nassau. . . ." Klüber, *Acten*, Vol I., Part 2, pp. 41–44.

introduction of the articles as Prussian state law, but it was finally decided to await the action of the congress in that regard. The important thing, Humboldt advised his chief, was "to show that Prussia stands out before all princes in her concern about the perpetration of this injustice, since the small states make no mention of it and Austria espouses the cause with lofty coolness. . . ."[40]

Such words, directed to Hardenberg of all people, do not sound like genuine advice but rather an affirmation of loyalty at a time when Humboldt was coming to see that Metternich's concentration on the sovereign princes was winning the game after all. This, too, he pointed out in words that came close to declaring the bankruptcy of Hardenberg's policy. Austria, he maintained,

> as Your Highness has also certainly observed, has willingly and not without design thrust us out in front in the German constitutional affairs and readily yielded to us in everything because she preferred that it was we who should appear offensive and dangerous . . . to the princes who find all the fetters of constitution so burdensome.

Lately, Humboldt, continued, Austria had gone ahead and yielded to their demands even without consulting Prussia. If those states, moreover, should be admitted to the deliberations, Austria's opportunities would be still greater and Prussia's choice limited either "to giving in or placing ourselves in conflict with the majority of the princes."[41]

As a description of Metternich's goals this account is fair enough; the implication of deliberate deception, however, is not. Had Humboldt forgotten the ringing pleas for making Germany "a single dynamic state," or the rousing defense of estates-style constitutions, or the impassioned warnings against dividing Germany into a few large masses? True, the campaign against the Kreise and for the equality of the lesser states had proceeded gradually and with great subtlety, but hardly with an ulterior intent to expose. On the contrary, through Wessenberg's private talks with Humboldt the Austrians usually tried to associate Prussia openly with their moderate propositions. Consensus was always Metternich's goal, and that included Prussia, too. Again, Humboldt's insinuations, made privately to the chancellor, sound more like veiled criticism of Hardenberg's relentless *Kreispolitik* than righteous indignation at Metternich.

To undo the damage, to steal a march on the Austrians, Humboldt advised that Prussia take the initiative in giving the states of the Second Council a larger role. Specifically he proposed that since the five-mem-

---

[40] Hoff, *Mediatisiertenfrage*, 85; Humboldt's covering letter to Hard. of 11 Dec. 1814, in Schmidt, *Verfassungsfrage*, 317.
[41] Schmidt, *Verfassungsfrage*, 316.

ber committee was already to serve ad hoc in so many capacities, the time had come to merge it permanently with the First Council to form an integral whole. Without increasing the number of Kreise Baden and Hesse-Cassel could, as previously suggested, become codirectors, the result being a council of seven permanent members and three members elected each year from the Second Council, in all a body of ten representing the great majority of the German population.[42]

The double draft as well as the supplementary recommendations were all written before Humboldt knew of Metternich's reversal on Saxony, but when he conveyed the material to the chancellor on 12 December the bomb had fallen. "I am truly sorry," he apologized, this time with genuine compassion, "to send you such a bulky piece of work at a time like this," but he believed the matter had lost none of its urgency, and even under those circumstances he was impatient to resume deliberations with Metternich, perhaps to propose the next step in the evolution of the committee before the Austrians themselves did.[43] If so, it was another case of being too late with too little: Metternich had already moved beyond him.

Though not officially submitted, a copy of Humboldt's draft, at least the version with Kreise, reached the Austrian State Chancellery on 14 December.[44] On the morning of the 16th Metternich launched his counterattack, inviting Count Münster to join a league based "on the liberal principles on which we had wrought" and featuring a single chamber of equal states with Austria as president, first among equals. For the time being Prussia and Württemberg were to be excluded, pending settlement of the Saxon question, but could join later if they so chose. "I saw distinctly," Münster reported to London, "that his conception was to form an alliance of all Germany against Prussia in case she should wish to assume Saxony de facto." Münster's own preference was the reverse: to invite Prussia at once, hoping for a peaceful solution, and reserve the anti-Prussian cast of the league for the event of actual hostilities.[45]

At the time of the interview it is doubtful that Metternich had a written draft in hand; Wessenberg, however, in the next few days produced the first complete plan to emanate from Austrian sources.[46] Throughout it reflected Metternich's quest for consensus. In a unicameral diet, so often proposed by Plessen and his colleagues, the lesser

---

[42] Humboldt's memorial on double draft, 9 Dec. 1814, *ibid.*, 312–315.

[43] Humb. to Hard. 12 Dec. 1814, ending with: "I embrace you with all my heart." *Ibid.*, 318.

[44] See above, note 37.

[45] Münster to Prince Regent, 17 Dec. 1814, Münster, *Political Sketches*, 210f.

[46] Text in Klüber, *Acten*, II, 1–5, which incorporates several variations made later as will be explained below.

states would find the equality they sought, modified only by the fact that the smallest must share curial votes, by an Austrian directory, which those same states had always regarded as their best protection, and by a permanent committee consisting of the director and two elected members solely for the purpose of conducting foreign affairs. The whole diet, however, was to act on war and peace, the conclusion of alliances, and the maintenance of a military establishment, decisions being made by a simple majority. Military and financial levies were to be proportional to size (this was almost universally taken for granted by now), but small states clustered in the same curia might negotiate to place their contingents at the disposal of the largest among them, thus creating military districts on a voluntary basis. Members were to retain their freedom of alliance with the same restrictions that Wessenberg, with Bavaria in mind, had previously formulated: namely, that neither the Bund nor any member be threatened.

Although Wessenberg's draft contained more than most previous plans about the military system, his Bund was to be more than a simple defensive alliance, as is usually maintained.[47] In fact, it had to be if it was to impress the Hanoverians. A federal court was included, though only for adjudicating interstate disputes.[48] An article on the rights of the mediatized houses, though more concise than Humboldt's detailed formulations, coincided in general with the latter's provisions (in turn based on the Bavarian ordinance) for those Standesherren who did not change sovereigns. Indeed, many phrases were identical, suggesting either that Wessenberg had collaborated with Humboldt on the topic after all or that he actually drew on the Prussian plan that found its way to the state chancellery.

More surprising even than the possible influence of Humboldt's work is the impact of Baron Marschall's constitutional plan.[49] Here there is no doubt about the connection. The first three articles of each are identical in wording and substance, the solitary exception being Wessenberg's omission of the maintenance of internal order and tranquillity as a function of the Bund. Other articles copied almost verbatim from Marschall's work expressly prohibited the subordination of one

[47] In recent times even by specialists on the subject: Hartmann, *Das Schicksal der Verfassungsvorschläge*, 61; and Quint, *Souveränitätsbegriff in Bayern*, 310–313.

[48] Klüber's text (note 46 above) makes no provision for a federal court, but as the Bavarian critique of the plan expressly rejected one, its presence in the original must be inferred. See Aretin, "Deutsche Politik Bayerns," 23, and Quint, *Souveränitätsbegriff in Bayern*, 318, neither of whom, however, notes the discrepancy. The Württemberg envoy in Vienna, who eventually obtained accurate information about the plan, also mentioned the inclusion of a court. Winz. to Fred., 8 Jan. 1815, HSA, Stuttgart, E 70, Fasc. 14, pp. 57–64. To this evidence, of course, should be added Wessenberg's documented advocacy of a relatively strong federal court.

[49] See above, note 28.

state to another, required the abolition of serfdom against compensation to the lord, stated the right of all subjects to move freely and own property in member states without financial penalty, and called for freedom of trade, commerce, and river transit throughout Germany. Significantly, this last provision, which offered a distant glimpse of the Zollverein, had no counterpart in Humboldt's plan, an omission probably due to his general neglect of the federal, as opposed to the Kreis, legislative powers. Another Wessenberg innovation, unaccountably omitted by Humboldt but probably discussed with the Austrian, provided for the equal protection of civil rights among the Catholic, Evangelical, and Calvinist confessions and toleration of the Jews, the latter in response to a petition submitted a week earlier by the Jewish deputy, Buchholz. There remained the critical issue of *landständische Verfassungen*. The Twelve Articles, as we know, had expressly exempted Austria and Prussia from this obligation. Less obtrusively Humboldt, in the double draft just discussed, sought a similar result by allowing existing constitutions to remain as they were while requiring only new ones to grant the estates specific rights. Now Wessenberg, upholding the principle of equality, required *all* states (i.e., including the two powers) to grant their estates "special rights regarding taxes and state government in general." This language was ambiguous, to be sure, but, as Humboldt himself had once observed, the choice was always between generalities and exemptions. Metternich should rather be commended for extending the article to the powers than denounced for diluting it.

Although the Wessenberg plan was more than a propaganda piece and reflected many of his and Metternich's convictions, there is no doubt that its appearance at that time was a function of grand strategy. Contrary to Münster's conjecture, however, the Austrian minister did not intend to challenge Prussia with it; rather he desired to provide a common program among the states he was trying to align against her, but without destroying all possibility of a later reconciliation, for in the long run only by entangling Prussia in the nets of the Bund could she be even partially drawn away from an exclusive dependence on Russia. In the event of hostilities, of course, the plan could also serve as part of a program of war aims. For this reason Metternich proceeded with extreme caution, personally keeping his distance from the plan, parrying inquiries, or simply denying knowledge of it.[50] Even in the great source collection published by Johann Ludwig Klüber it is attributed vaguely to an unnamed Austrian minister as if it were hardly more than an intramural memorandum. Metternich in fact confided it only

[50] Winz. to Fred., 5 and 8 Jan. 1815, HSA, Stuttgart, E 70, Fasc. 14, 36–40 and 57–64.

to the states that figured in his alliance plans and in the order of their importance. Accordingly, when shortly before Christmas he proposed to Marshal Wrede a defensive alliance between their states, he also conveyed the Wessenberg articles and requested an immediate opinion from Munich.[51] Winzingerode, by contrast, was told only that Metternich knew of a plan he believed Württemberg would find suitable. Thus, Wrede was the first outsider to see the actual text and the Bavarian cabinet the first to study it, this at an emergency meeting that Montgelas called on Christmas day. So impressed were most of the ministers that one of them at first thought the plan reflected Wrede's triumph on the German Committee, which in a sense it did. Montgelas, to be sure, believed that a federal covenant was no place to talk about the rights of subjects but decided not to object "because these things have long been in force with us."[52] Despite cavils from those who opposed any Bund, the plan was endorsed with only two serious reservations: deletion of the federal court and all legislative power except that over matters of defense.[53]

Wrede received this information about 28 December and informed Metternich a few days later when accepting the offer of alliance, the latter with the proviso that Bavaria receive a share of the subsidies expected from England in case of war. Only then did Münster and, a few days later, Türckheim receive copies, but no one else did except by covert means. As Bavaria, Hanover, and Hesse-Darmstadt were also the only German states invited to accede to the triple alliance of 3 January, the linkage between German and European alignments in Metternich's strategy was complete.

Despite the secrecy surrounding the plan, a copy did reach the Prussians toward the end of December, but there is no evidence that they believed it to be aimed at them except as a new offensive in the propaganda war for the affection of the smaller states.[54] Once more compelled to match Metternich's bid, Humboldt at the height of the Saxon crisis likewise turned to Marschall of Baden for inspiration and produced a unicameral plan of his own.[55] In it all the German states were to be represented in a single diet that would meet in two different forms. As a legislative or constituent assembly it would allow each state to cast for itself one to five votes, depending on its population. Meeting for all other purposes, such as war and peace, foreign affairs, and enforcement of federal law, it would constitute itself as a smaller council

[51] Winter, *Wrede als Berater*, 205; Gentz, *Tagebücher*, I, 342.
[52] Quoted by Aretin, "Deutsche Politik Bayerns," 23.
[53] *Ibid.*, 24.
[54] Schmidt, *Verfassungsfrage*, 379–394.
[55] Text in Humboldt, *Gesammelte Schriften*, XI, 279–285.

in which the six largest states (by then including Saxony) would cast whole votes, the others fractional votes as members of a curia. Each of the five curiae would cast one vote as decided by the majority and reported by a director to be chosen from one of the two largest states in the curia on an alternating basis. On the smaller council Austria and Prussia together were to have but two votes out of eleven and in a plenary session only ten of fifty, "very far removed from the absolute majority that had been so earnestly demanded in the beginning," as the Hanoverian Martens observed some time later. Indeed, he went on, "the project hardly seems explicable unless perhaps the Prussians want to win enormous popularity on the assumption that the other powers will oppose these concessions."[56]

Actually, Humboldt's strategy was more subtle. Combining executive and legislative powers in the same body, he explained in a note for Metternich which was never sent,[57] would work because a league of states by its nature left little scope for legislation common to all; the smaller council would be the normal mode of operation. Humboldt did not mention a federal court, but in providing that the diet would have "a yet to be determined share in the judiciary," he left room for his previous plan for dividing these functions between the First Council and a federal court. Most revealing of all, as he explained it, "the Kreis system can exist in this plan just as well as in the previous one; for it is not at all necessary that the Kreis directors form a special college." In other words, although the small states would enjoy relative equality in the federal diet, they would still be subordinated to the same old overlords envisioned in the Twelve Articles. The king of Saxony, more-over, could have his seat on the First Council and still not be a chief himself, as Hardenberg's memorandum of 16 December already made clear. Even without actual Kreise, moreover, the subordination of the small states to a "military head" would be severe, as a plan drafted by Knesebeck a few days later provided.[58]

Meanwhile, in Austria the great reversal in Metternich's policy had the salutary effect of restoring a semblance of domestic harmony. Having been almost alone in his willingness to sacrifice Saxony for the greater goal of a formidable European center, he was now back in the mainstream of Austrian opinion; even the emperor, who had never withheld his support, felt more comfortable on the familiar terrain of Count Kaunitz and the great wars of the eighteenth century. A cor-

[56] Critique of the Humboldt plan in Marten's hand, NSHSA, Hanover, Des. 91, No. 28, p. 10.
[57] Text in Schmidt, *Verfassungsfrage*, 395–399.
[58] "Entwurf zur Einrichtung des deutschen Kriegswesens," 21 Jan. 1815, Stein, *Briefe*, v, 247–251.

ollary of that tradition was a pro-French orientation, and now Talleyrand, so long the mischief-maker among the lesser states, rose to the
occasion, extending a hand but at the same time allaying the fears that
had previously deterred Metternich, causing him to try almost any
combination that did not depend on France.

On 19 December Talleyrand, in perhaps his finest moment at the
congress, made formal reply to Metternich's official transmittal of his
note to Hardenberg. France, he wrote, had no territorial claims, no
particular interests of any kind in the existing situation but only the
general interests that all states should have in legitimacy and equilibrium, the two principles that uniquely converged on the issue of Saxony. He eloquently elaborated on these themes, but the diplomatic
message he meant to convey was simple: that alliance with France held
no risk for Belgium or the Rhineland; she would be satisfied to recover
her lost parity. In this regard, moreover, Saxony was not merely one
of the several German territorial problems, in which France was denied
a voice by the treaty of Paris, but, by embodying the principle of
legitimacy, a general European affair, like the slave trade or river
navigation, in regard to which the same treaty recognized French parity. By conceding, moreover, that the Polish question was already effectively settled, he could expect to diminish Russian fears as well.
Here, then, was the key to admitting France to the inner councils of
the congress. The restraint, the measured cadences of this note, constituted Talleyrand's greatest act of statesmanship at the congress and
gave Metternich renewed confidence as he awaited Hardenberg's reply
to his note of 10 December.[59]

As noted earlier, the reply came on 20 December in the form of a
memorandum conveyed to Francis by the tsar and to Metternich by
Castlereagh. Its central point was the transfer of Frederick Augustus
to a territory on the left bank of the Rhine with a population of 700,000
and carrying with it a seat on the First Council of the Bund. By providing the king a throne somewhere the plan to a degree met the
claims of legitimacy without requiring the partition of Saxony, which
was said to hold great peril for order and stability. Obviously, however,
these were hardly the main issues, and the opposition was intense.
Apart from the issue of Saxony itself, the English and Austrians alike
knew that Frederick Augustus in the Rhineland could hardly avoid
becoming a French client, whereas Talleyrand, paradoxically, for the
same reason feared that a future seizure of the left bank would be
more awkward with him there than the Prussians.[60] Both of these

[59] Talley. to Mett., 19 Dec. 1814, d'Angeberg, *Congrès*, II, 540–544; Bourgoing,
Wiener Kongress, 228.
[60] Griewank, *Wiener Kongress*, 192.

contrary concerns, of course, assumed the rejection of the Kreis system, which would have given Prussia a strong military presence in any case.

Fortunately the novel mode of communication employed obviated the need for a response, and Metternich took no official notice of the plan; indeed, according to Gentz, he left it unread for half a day while correcting the proofs of satirical pieces to be recited at the next fête. If the remark was true, Hardenberg was well advised to write him privately the next day begging him "in the name of the friendship that so very specially binds us" to take the plan seriously and to keep in view the great system "on which we have never ceased to work and which you always considered crucial, the most intimate union between our respective courts." Their common boundary, he concluded, was already so snug that a further extension would hardly matter.[61] Castlereagh, meanwhile, was the object of similar entreaties, coupled with a request to mediate. Since he already had a like invitation from Metternich, he agreed, candidly insisting, however, that, given the attitude of Austria and France, he would never endorse the principle of removing the king from his ancestral home. In a two-hour conference with Hardenberg and his circle of advisors he repeated the suggestion originally made by Metternich that before any new projects were advanced, a statistical commission should be appointed to verify facts and figures so that Prussia could be told with some precision what she would receive in return for giving up part of Saxony. This was agreeable to all.[62]

In undertaking the mediation between Austria and Prussia Castlereagh hoped to bring France into the negotiation, not as an ally but as an advocate of Saxony to balance Russia's support for Prussia. Who first perceived that the statistical commission offered an unobtrusive means to ease open the door the records do not make clear, but certain it is that Metternich, Castlereagh, and Talleyrand himself favored a seat for France on this body. Naturally the Prussians objected at first, but under pressure, evidently deciding that a mere fact-finding body was not the place to make a pugnacious stand on principle, reluctantly acquiesced. Metternich, meanwhile, the true author of the plan, undertook to draft the charge to the commission. It should, he advised, investigate all territory conquered from Napoleon without regard to its ultimate destination. Talleyrand tells us that the Austrian minister originally intended to count all souls equally; if so, it was probably with

[61] Castle. to Liverp., 24 Dec. 1814, PRO, F.O. 92/9; Rosenkrantz, *Journal*, 113, entry of 21 Dec. 1814; Hard. to Mett., 21 Dec. 1814, HHSA, StK., Kongressakten, Cart. 7, p. 402.

[62] Castle. to Liverp., 24 Dec., Webster, *BD*, 270; Webster, *Congress of Vienna*, 92; King's ambassadors to Blacas, 27 Dec. 1814, Talleyrand, *Memoirs*, II, 375; and Stein, "Tagebuch," *Briefe*, v, 348f.

the aim of countering the Prussian thesis that the value of mediatized properties should be discounted by some undetermined amount. Apart from this consideration, however, as Talleyrand pointed out, there remained very real differences between the productivity of the Polish provinces Prussia would cede and the more highly capitalized districts of the Rhineland that she would acquire. Metternich, who stood to gain the most from any credible formula that would limit Prussia's compensations, readily agreed and added to the charge that the commission should consider the type and productivity of provinces as well as raw population. The political status of properties, whether dominical or mediatized, he did not mention.[63]

The commission began its deliberations on 24 December, Wessenberg and the court councilor, Nikolas Wacken, representing Austria, Hoffmann and Jordan Prussia, and Dalberg France. Münster was smuggled aboard as one of the British members (Clancarty was the other), and the Russians at first sent no one, believing their interests well enough served by the Prussians—as indeed they were because everybody recognized the preeminence of Hoffmann in this field and agreed that he should draft the preliminary reports, an assignment that gave him leverage for mostly ignoring qualitative factors after all and limiting statistics mainly to the simple counting of souls that benefited Prussia.[64]

On one issue, however, of a more political nature, he blundered, at least in the eyes of his chief. Count Münster questioned the designation of the defunct kingdom of Westphalia as conquered territory on the good legitimist grounds that as Hanover had never ceded her part of it, she was entitled to that part as a matter of course just as the elector of Hesse-Cassel was automatically restored to his former lands. In this way he sought to keep all of old Hanover out of the reach of the covetous Prussians before the bargaining began. At the first meeting the commissioners, Hoffmann included, declared Westphalia within their jurisdiction but expressly without prejudice to the principle that Münster adduced. This action was nothing less than the first general endorsement of Talleyrand's theory of legitimacy and no less applicable to Saxony than to Hanover. Hence, when the commission convened on 28 December, Hoffmann arrived with a reinforcement in the person of a Russian representative, Baron Anstett, and orders to repudiate the previous decision. He filed a written protest, to which Münster issued a rebuttal. It is perhaps indicative of growing congress fatigue that the commission, possibly at Wessenberg's instigation, simply noted

[63] Castle. to Liverp., 24 Dec. 1814. Webster, *BD*, 269–271; Talley. to Louis, 28 Dec. 1814, Talleyrand, *Memoirs*, II, 379; text of Metternich's proposed charge in d'Angeberg, *Congrès*, II, 561f.
[64] *Procès-verbal* of 24 Dec. 1814, d'Angeberg, *Congrès*, II, 562–566.

without further action both statements of principle and proceeded with its business, which was concluded on 19 January after a total of six sessions. On the whole the victory belonged to Hoffmann inasmuch as the final reports were based almost entirely on raw population, partly because of his efforts, partly because the determination of qualitative factors was too subjective and time-consuming to be practical.[65]

A more serious setback for Metternich occurred on another front. In the note of 10 December he had condescendingly informed Hardenberg that the Polish question was now a matter for Austria and Russia to settle separately on their own. With Nesselrode in charge that tactic might have been possible at once, but the tsar, who frequently kept his foreign minister in reserve to redirect policies that were going awry, placed the negotiation in the hands of Razumovsky and Capodistria. Stein, who incorrectly saw in the move the demise of Nesselrode, probably took too much credit for it, but the policy adopted was pro-Prussian all the same, as the tsar no doubt ordered. Informed of the appointment by the emperor Francis—Alexander was still avoiding personal contacts with Metternich—the latter on 26 December invited Razumovsky to begin *bilateral* negotiations with him or, in his absence, with Wessenberg. Clearly he still imagined the possibility that he could be tied up with Castlereagh and Hardenberg in the Saxon affair while Wessenberg dealt separately with the Russian envoy in regard to Poland.[66]

It was not to be. Accepting the invitation the following day, Razumovsky also reported his master's "firm resolution not to separate . . . the interests of his empire from those of his allies" and proposed the addition of Hardenberg and Castlereagh to the discussions "in order that the questions be treated and decided in common accord." A parallel letter from Hardenberg repeated this message, adding that written communication should be abandoned in favor of direct talks, the surest way to keep the negotiations interlocked. Convinced (for the first time, according to Francis) that he had failed to divide his opponents, Metternich saw no alternative but to accept these arrangements. It was another defeat and removed the last lingering doubts about the necessity of bringing France into the negotiations.[67]

The first explicit overture to this end was made by Castlereagh in a

[65] *Ibid.*; *procès-verbal* of 28 Dec. 1814 with annexes, *ibid.*, II, 573–578. Cf. Arneth, *Wessenberg*, I, 234–235; Griewank, *Wiener Kongress*, 194–196; and Schmidt, *Verfassungsfrage*, 386f.

[66] Stein, "Tagebuch," *Briefe*, v, 349; Mett. to Razumovsky, 26 Dec. 1814, HHSA, StK., Kongressakten, Cart. 7, 539f.

[67] Razumovsky to Mett., 27 Dec. 1814, d'Angeberg, *Congrès*, IV, p. 1861; Hard. to Mett. same date, *ibid.*, 1863; Mett. to Hard., 28 Dec. 1814, *ibid.*, 1863; Rosenkrantz, *Journal*, 119, entry of 28 Dec. 1814, relating Francis's remarks to the king of Denmark.

private conference with Hardenberg and Razumovsky on 28 December. Naturally they refused, agreeing, however, to include the matter at the four-power conference that had been arranged for the 29th, the first formal such conference among them.[68] After many false starts the climax of the congress was at hand, like the championship round of a tournament in which only players of world class remain.

Opening the meeting, Metternich first allowed Razumovsky an introductory statement designed to make the tsar appear as the patron of the group. He then proposed, and the others agreed, that to accelerate the deliberations the protocols should be confined to written declarations and propositions, leaving actual debate open and uninhibited. In this way the arguments advanced for the admittance of France might escape the close scrutiny that the written word would have provided.[69] On this basis, in any case, Hardenberg read his long-awaited official reply to the Austrian note of some twenty days earlier. Generally it duplicated the original memorial of the 16th but was more specific about the king of Saxony's establishment on the left bank: namely, Luxemburg; most of the old archbishopric of Trier with Cologne, Bonn, and other towns; Stablo and Malmedy, a total of 700,000 in population. Luxemburg was to be a federal fortress, and the king was to sit on the First Council of the Bund. Beyond that Hardenberg's paper contained the familiar litany of complaints: Prussia's ill-treatment, the king of Saxony's crimes, the impertinence of Bavaria, which stood to lose Ansbach and Bayreuth if Prussia did not acquire Saxony, and above all, the utter irrelevance of France, whose acquiescence "the king of Prussia counts on his High Allies and especially the support of Austria herself to obtain."[70]

Instantly Metternich took up the challenge. Drawing on Talleyrand's arguments but without mentioning legitimacy as such, he distinguished between the Polish question, which concerned only the three neighboring powers and was in any case now reduced to the technicality of fixing boundaries, and the Saxon question, which was European in character because France and Britain had expressed their interests in it. An agreement on Saxony between Austria and Prussia alone, he added, without explanation in his increasingly cocksure way, would

[68] Stein, "Tagebuch," *Briefe*, v, 352; Castle. to Liverp., 1 Jan. 1815, Webster, *BD*, 276.

[69] Fortunately an informal *discussion verbale* for this and the following meeting of 30 December was kept, at least by the Austrians, and this is copiously summarized in Arneth, *Wessenberg*, i, 264–265, and Bourgoing, *Wiener Kongress*, 231–236. The somewhat bland official protocols with various depositions are in d'Angeberg, *Congrès*, iv, 1858–1874.

[70] Hard. to Mett. 29 Dec. 1814, d'Angeberg, *Congrès*, iv, 1863–1869.

violate the Treaty of Paris![71] This was nonsense, and Metternich knew it. As pointed out in Chapter II of this study, one could argue whether the Treaty of Paris excluded France from all questions affecting the European equilibrium or only from the territorial problems directly on her borders, and Metternich at the time had taken the broader view of French exclusion. The one argument that could not be made was that Poland and Saxony differed in this respect.[72] Actually, until early December he had argued the reverse: that Poland was the key to the European balance while Saxony was being disposed of in his private dealings with Hardenberg.

Still, he knew that on the highest plane of international politics, where no court existed to weigh competing briefs, so long as the mores of humanity were not flagrantly abused, all parties would be guided by interests, expecting legal arguments to provide only a veneer of civility to veil the strength of the victor and soften the blow to the ones who yielded. In this case, if Alexander tired before the Prussians did, as surely he must, his dignity would suffer less by acknowledging ostensibly superior logic and moral principles than by appearing to submit to force. At bottom Metternich's forced distinction merely extended the drive to separate the two issues even yet, to show the tsar that the weight of France would be thrown at Prussia, not against him.

Realizing as much, Hardenberg, still determined to maintain the negotiation whole, insisted that inasmuch as both issues emanated from the Treaty of Paris, they were equally European in character. What he probably intended was a warning to the Russians that if they permitted France to speak on Saxony, they must be prepared to hear her on Poland as well. The proposition, however, was as self-defeating politically as it was cogent intellectually. Talleyrand had long since reassured the tsar of his diminished interest in Poland, but even worse, the chancellor had inadvertently endorsed Metternich's argument that even if they were in accord, Austria and Prussia could not settle the fate of Saxony by themselves. Without intending it, his was an argument for giving France a perfunctory voice in Poland without denying her a decisive one in Saxony. No wonder Humboldt left the meeting "in a very foul mood about all grand affairs."[73]

Considering that the four-power conference had originated in Met-

[71] Bourgoing, *Wiener Kongress*, 233; Arneth, *Wessenberg*, I, 264.

[72] There was one difference, to be sure: Poland by the treaty of Teplitz was to be settled by "an amicable arrangement" among the three adjoining powers, whereas no treaty mentioned the fate of Saxony in so many words. These circumstances could exclude a French voice in Polish affairs, but they could hardly give her one on Saxony.

[73] Bourgoing, *Wiener Kongress*, 233; Humb. to Caroline, 29 Dec. 1814, Humboldt, *Briefe*, IV, 444.

ternich's proposals for bilateral talks with Razumovsky, it was natural enough that the next meeting, which opened at noon on the 30th, should begin with a reading of a Russian draft convention[74] ostensibly outlining her latest offers regarding Poland. These were hardly new: Wieliczka and Podgorze to Austria, roughly the line of the Prosna for Prussia, Thorn and Cracow to be neutral free cities, reciprocal guarantees of possessions, and the protection of native institutions in all Polish provinces. The memorial also provided a distant glimpse of the Holy Alliance, invoking as it did "the Christian religion common to all" as the only true basis of social and political order and exhorting "the sovereigns, united in brotherhood [to] purify their political conduct and guarantee the relations among peoples that Providence had confided to them." Historians have seen in this phraseology many things: the call for a united Europe in which Russian influence would preponderate, an attempt to rise above the widening schisms and restore on another plane the unity of the Quadruple Alliance, or simply the conversion of Alexander to religious mysticism. The diplomats of the time displayed no such concerns, taking the language to be only another example of the rhetorical flourishes to be expected from him. Besides, the matter was overshadowed in the document by a more insidiously political factor. Far from treating the Polish question in isolation, the project went on to tie in the Prussian demands of the previous session, including a German Confederation "to establish the respective rights of the mediatized and the nobility as well as those of the other classes," language that could only have come from Stein and Humboldt.

This new demonstration of Russo-Prussian solidarity brought to the fore once again the issue of France, and this time Castlereagh, who took the obdurate stand on Saxony as a personal affront to the mediator, now openly demanded Talleyrand's participation. Even so, he was, as usual, moderate and pragmatic. One might contest the *right* of France to be consulted, he admitted, but political wisdom, the importance of essentially satisfying all great powers, and even the ambiguities in the treaties all recommended a role for the most populous country west of Russia. Relieved that legitimacy had not been mentioned, the one principle that guaranteed Frederick Augustus's throne, Razumovsky and Hardenberg were surprisingly conciliatory, replying only that their instructions did not cover the situation.[75]

Then Castlereagh pressed his luck, adding that French participation was doubly important as her influence would be necessary to persuade the king of Saxony to accept whatever fate was decided for him. Now

[74] Text in d'Angeberg, *Congrès*, IV, 1869–1874.
[75] Bourgoing, *Wiener Kongress*, 234; Arneth, *Wessenberg*, I, 264.

Metternich, who for months (with honorable intentions, we can now see) had encouraged Schulenburg to remain firm, rendered Castlereagh's point explicit: not only France but the king of Saxony must freely acquiesce, and the latter should be moved from Berlin to somewhere nearer Vienna for that purpose. Whether he was deliberately goading Hardenberg to rash action of merely trying to clinch the argument for French participation is unknown, but the effect was the same. Hardenberg could take no more. He would sooner break up the congress, he shouted, than concede the king of Saxony such a right. Then casting aside all restraint, he blurted out that if the expenses of provisional occupation should make permanent possession of the country imperative, then Prussia and Russia would regard any refusal by the others "as tantamount to a declaration of war!" Metternich's reaction is unrecorded, but Castlereagh was shocked, protesting "in the loudest terms against this principle as a most alarming and unheard-of menace." At length, however, tempers cooled, and the mediator proposed a compromise: the assent of Saxony should be considered "desirable" but not so important as that of France. This formula was accepted, most particularly by Metternich, who doubtless realized that even if France was not actually admitted to the conference, she would now have the last word.[76]

Still, Hardenberg's threats had to be taken seriously all the same. Neither Metternich nor Castlereagh could have known that just before the conference he had, in the presence of Frederick William, asked the tsar for a military commitment, only to find that the latter was "not very pronounced" and confined himself to "ambiguous explanations" that may still have rankled as the chancellor entered the conference.[77] But even if they had been sure of the tsar's restraining influence in the abstract, there was always the chance, so Castlereagh at least believed, that precisely because of it, the desperate Prussians would gamble on a *coup de main* to force their ally into action, especially as there had so far been no sign in the conferences that he was backing away from the Prussian claims. On the contrary, Razumovsky had raised no objection to the fact that Hardenberg's threat was made in Russia's name as well. Besides, the impulsive Alexander was at least as unpredictable as the restless Prussian generals, whom Hardenberg consulted

[76] Bourgoing, *Wiener Kongress*, 235; Arneth, *Wessenberg*, I, 265; Castle. to Liverp., 1 Jan. 1815, Webster, *BD*, 277–278. Castlereagh places these bitter exchanges at a meeting on 31 December, but no other records show a four-power meeting on that day. He must have been in error, especially as the continuity of the dialogue on the 30th is obvious. Most writers, however, faithfully copy Castlereagh's date.

[77] Hardenberg, "Tagebücher," 37, entry of 30 Dec. 1814.

daily, poring over operational plans that General Karl Wilhelm Grolman had recently brought from Berlin.[78]

Scholarly opinion has generally discounted the likelihood of war, mainly on the grounds that all sides were exhausted and facing financial ruin.[79] Yet the desperate acts of the weak are as often the triggers of hostilities as the deliberate aggressiveness of the prepared and strong. While Castlereagh pondered these contingencies, weighing the need for a countervailing force and studying his instructions, which on the one hand urged him to save part of Saxony but on the other forbade military commitments, an impulse to action came almost as if from outer space: a message early on New Year's day that peace had been signed at Ghent between Britain and the United States. Suddenly the remote framework of the proceedings in Vienna had been modified, that is to say, the global rivalry between Britain and Russia that had always caused the tsar to support the lesser maritime powers and repeatedly to offer his mediation in the Anglo-American war. It is probably true, as Charles K. Webster has argued, that faced with Hardenberg's threats and the tsar's seeming toleration of them, Castlereagh now favored an alliance with Austria and France on its merits; what the treaty of Ghent imparted was the courage to proceed and the confidence that London would approve. And so the combination that Metternich had once tried to build with Napoleon's aid and Talleyrand himself had so often proposed was at hand.[80]

The triple alliance,[81] largely the work of Castlereagh, who submitted his draft to Metternich and Talleyrand on 1 January, pledged the signatories to render assistance in the event any of them was attacked. The *casus foederis*, however, mostly at Castlereagh's instance, was limited strictly to hostile actions arising out of the joint efforts to enforce and complete the Treaty of Paris. In this way Talleyrand's earlier assurances about the Low Countries, the Rhineland, or territory in Italy were officially reaffirmed, and the French voice in the settlement could, if necessary, be confined to Saxony. The military aid specified followed past practice, in which each power was to contribute 150,000 men, Britain, however, retaining the option of discharging her obligation in subsidies for foreign levies at the by now customary rate of twenty

[78] *Ibid.*, 37, entries of 28 Dec. 1814 and 2 Jan. 1815.

[79] E.g., Griewank, *Wiener Kongress*, 198–199; and Olshausen, *Stellung der Grossmächte*, 117–120. Opinion is not unanimous, however, many writers wisely avoiding a clear and unambiguous judgment. Webster, *Congress of Vienna*, 128, by contrast, considers the threat real—probably because Castlereagh did.

[80] Castle. to Liverp., 1 Jan. 1815, Nos. 44 and 45, Webster, *BD*, 278–279; Talley. to Louis, 4 Jan. 1815, Talleyrand, *Memoirs*, II, 285–289; and Webster, *Castlereagh*, I, 369–372.

[81] Text in Neumann, *Traités par l'Autriche*, II, 497; also in English translation in Talleyrand, *Memoirs*, II, 389–391.

pounds for a foot soldier and thirty for a cavalryman. In a separate article Holland, Hanover, and Bavaria were to be invited to accede under penalty of forfeiting their existing treaty guarantees if they refused. Further extensions of the treaty were not foreclosed; Hesse-Darmstadt was not mentioned, but Metternich was already in touch with Türckheim on the matter even before the treaty was signed, on 3 January.

For obvious and valid reasons historical attention to the treaty has focused on the reentry of France into the ranks of the powers. To Metternich, however, who since October had worried more about the price of French assistance than the availability of it, an even greater advantage was the British commitment, which at so many critical points he had sought in vain. Indeed, his prolonged resistance to an alliance of this kind, so often discussed in the abstract, had been due in part to the absence of a British guarantee that would both sustain Austria and restrain France. Now he had the protection of both powers and, moreover, in respect to an issue that was most of all a particular Austrian interest, regardless of the universal significance that Talleyrand grandly accorded to Saxony. Intensifying this euphoric atmosphere, moreover, was the psychological impact of the Treaty of Ghent, for now it was easy, as most did at the congress, to imagine the shift of countless English ships to European waters, the reinforcement of the Anglo-Dutch forces in the Netherlands, and the release of untold riches for disbursement on the continent. In the salons and conference rooms of Vienna Britain's credibility was now as solid as sterling itself.[82]

Although the signatories were pledged to secrecy, the existence of some such pact had been so long suspected that the reality hardly changed matters. Now slight movement could be noticed. The tsar's "ambiguous explanations" of 30 December were perhaps the beginning. On the next day Hardenberg and Humboldt, meeting with Stein and the Russians, agreed that at the next conference they would accept French participation provided that Saxony was settled in advance and the king's consent was not required. Regarding Saxony itself the concession was slight, since prior agreement among the four had been the understanding all along. Yet the mere presence of France, even in a limited capacity, would be a step toward the restoration of the European pentarchy, which, as argued earlier, was certain to diminish the weight of Prussia in international scales more than that of any other power.

On the same day, in a puzzling move still not completely clarified, Nesselrode returned to the scene, circulating a note identical to the

---

[82] Sources too numerous to mention since almost every contemporary observer recounted the sensation the treaty made.

project previously introduced except for the omission of all articles relating to Saxony.[83] Had the tsar, perhaps alarmed at Hardenberg's reckless language, changed his mind, bypassed Razumovsky, and decided to settle the Polish question independently after all? The records do not say, but henceforth Hardenberg and Razumovsky were noticeably subdued, and Metternich persisted in his course with new self-confidence. When the four again convened on 3 January, he genially approved the intent of Razumovsky's project and complained only that it contained too many disparate elements. In a display of verbal legerdemain unmatched since his earlier jousting with Talleyrand, "he found himself obliged impartially to separate the objects without however dividing the negotiation."[84] But there was more. Since all their efforts were now said to be aimed at completing the Treaty of Paris, the topics of negotiation should be divided up in the same way as in the treaty, due notice being taken of the fact that besides the common articles, each allied power had a few side agreements in its treaty with France. Reluctantly Hardenberg and Razumovsky acquiesced in this dubious rationale, insisting only that the separate negotiations proceed simultaneously so that the individual treaties that resulted could at least be signed in unison.

Thereupon, as the first application of this procedure Metternich produced a counterproject confined to Razumovsky's Polish articles, most of which, including at last free and neutral status for Thorn and Cracow, he accepted with only minor changes. Only the matter of guaranteeing each power's possessions aroused serious concern, and Metternich was authorized to redraft the article in more precise terms.[85] For all practical purposes the Polish problem was now settled, and since there was hardly anything more the tsar could desire, Hardenberg had nothing to offer anybody for support in Saxony. His only hope now was to reach a settlement before Talleyrand could be consulted, but when Metternich and Castlereagh declared "peremptorily" that they would negotiate no further without him, the chancellor and his Russian partner meekly moved adjournment in order to obtain new instructions, in all probability realizing that the issue had become mainly symbolic.[86]

Hardenberg's only recourse now was to contain the damage, for

[83] Text in d'Angeberg, *Congrès*, II, 579–582. Gentz, who like Stein believed that Nesselrode had been demoted, later reported his reinstatement, which by the end of March, he said, was complete. Gentz to Karadjo, 26 June 1815, *Dépêches inédites*, I, 160f.

[84] This and following from the protocol of 3 Jan. 1815, d'Angeberg, *Congrès*, IV, 1874f.

[85] Austrian counterproject in *ibid.*, 1875–1877.

[86] Castle. to Liverp., 3 Jan. 1815, Webster, *BD*, 280f.

which purpose he met with his advisors the next day, 4 January. They concluded that they could admit France on two conditions: first, that her role be limited to the issue of the reconstruction of Prussia, and second, that Castlereagh and Metternich officially declare for the protocol that the king of Saxony must accept the decision of the powers. They also decided to continue the efforts then in progress through the Russian ambassador, Maximilian von Alopeus, and Colonel Dietrich von Miltitz, who represented a pro-Prussian faction in Saxony, to persuade the king voluntarily to accept resettlement in the Rhineland. That evening Castlereagh agreed to make the declaration and later obtained Talleyrand's consent to it, but firmly warned the chancellor not to renew the transfer plan. This would not merely prolong the dispute but was the one solution that Castlereagh personally regarded as contrary to Britain's particular interests, which he had long believed required a strong Prussia in the area as the principal bulwark against France.[87]

The Wessenberg plan of 10 December eminently met that objective, but as it had already antagonized Hardenberg and had been considerably mauled on the statistical commission, Castlereagh decided to present a plan of his own, the product of Clancarty's and Münster's experience on the commission.[88] The result resembled Wessenberg's plan in substance but differed in proportions: less for Prussia in Poland (942,256 as against Wessenberg's 1,316,770), more in Saxony (695,235 versus the 432,400 that had so upset Hardenberg) and about the same on the left bank with the important exception that it pointedly excluded Luxemburg, which Castlereagh intended for the Netherlands, and instead, dismissing the Mosel as "not a good military line," included 200,000 souls to the south of it, in the region that Metternich so far had jealously guarded as an Austro-Bavarian monopoly. In all the plan would have yielded a surplus of 257,196 above the scale of 1805. Compensation for Hesse-Darmstadt, Saxe-Weimar, and, of course, Hanover were also identified. Most interesting, however, was the British endorsement of Hardenberg's interpretation of the accession treaties: if still more lands were necessary to reach a settlement, the note read, mediatized properties could be taken from those states obliged to make sacrifices "necessary for the maintenance of the independence of Germany"—that much-abused phrase again! Also adopted was the view that Rhenish souls were worth more than Polish. On the other

[87] *Ibid.*, 282–283; Stein, "Tagebuch," *Briefe*, v, 355; Olshausen, *Stellung der Grossmächte*, 118f.

[88] "Castlereagh's Plan for the Reconstruction of the Kingdom of Prussia," 5 Jan. 1815, HHSA, StK., Kongressakten, Cart. 7, pp. 549–555, for this and following. Despite its important role in the negotiations, Castlereagh seems not to have sent a copy home; it is not to be found with his correspondence in the PRO.

hand, the English drafters followed Wessenberg in counting the population of mediatized lands the same as any other; the commercial and military advantages and the administrative services of the proprietors, they held, were value enough.

Like Wessenberg, Castlereagh did not view his plan as definitive but rather as a demonstration that Prussia's just claims could be satisfied short of awarding her all Saxony. It was especially important that the tsar understand this since much of the sense of honor he felt to be involved in his personal pledges could be redeemed if at least the treaties were fulfilled. On the morning of 7 January Castlereagh had a chance to explain the plan to him, exaggerating perhaps the danger of dominoes falling across Europe if France should at a future date assist Frederick Augustus to return home, that is, from Bonn to Dresden. The tsar, who had probably never thought much about the complexities of mediatized lands, responded agreeably, promising that he would be satisfied with the plan if the king of Prussia was. Whether this conciliatory tone was due to or in spite of his knowledge of the triple alliance, which he broadly hinted at during the audience, is of course conjectural, but whatever the reason, it was now likely that Alexander would support any reasonable solution.[89]

Further progress came later in the day, when at the next conference of the four Razumovsky announced the tsar's approval of the Austrian counterproject on Poland and proposed the appointment of a technical commission to work out the details. The only sticking point left was that of drafting constitutions (or administrations, as the Austrians preferred to call them) for Thorn and Cracow, but even this problem was referred to the technical experts. And there was more. Calling upon Castlereagh to make his promised declaration, Razumovsky defined the issue as one of finding a way "to make the question of how Prussia was to be satisfied with a part of Saxony" dependent on the great powers and not the king of Saxony. It is inconceivable that language of this kind, which on the face of it ruled out the transfer of the king, could have been prompted by Stein and Humboldt. Taken in conjunction with Nesselrode's note and the passive acquiescence in Metternich's specious arguments, this turn adds still more evidence that the tsar himself, always his own minister, had intervened to change course. However that may be, Razumovsky's phrasing must have been a blow to Hardenberg.[90]

On the other hand, when Castlereagh volunteered to make his declaration at the next session, Metternich himself felt betrayed, ostensibly because deals of this kind had been previously ruled out of the official

[89] Castle. to Liverp., 8 Jan. 1815, Webster, *BD*, 282–285.
[90] Protocol of 7 Jan. 1815, d'Angeberg, *Congrès*, IV, 1877–1878.

record, but more to the point because, seeing the Russians waver, he believed the concession unnecessary. As pieces went in the game, Frederick Augustus, to be sure, could be rated as no more than a pawn, but in an atmosphere of general exhaustion, which found Hardenberg often in tears and falling asleep at his desk and Metternich complaining to Sagan that he "worked like a convict on a chain" and desperately needed sleep—in such an atmosphere the stubbornness of the king might have gained a few more souls, another salt mine, or a useful frontier adjustment. Indeed, that was to be the case anyway.[91]

Actually, the declaration, when Castlereagh finally submitted it to the conference on 9 January, reflected concessions to everybody.[92] For Talleyrand the first secret article of the treaty of Paris, hitherto the basis for France's exclusion, was now cited, precisely because it was binding on her, as the reason for including her. To satisfy Metternich the right of Frederick Augustus to refuse the powers' terms was acknowledged, but indefinite occupation of his country by Prussia was threatened if he did so, this with the express concurrence of France. Finally, there was the laconic definition of the five-power mission: namely, to determine "what proportion of the states of Saxony" should be incorporated into Prussia. First Razumovsky and now Castlereagh officially endorsed partition rather than resettlement as the basis of accommodation.

With both the mediator and the ally against him Hardenberg was checkmated, and the great European crisis was over. Metternich would have preferred to reach his goal without the use of France, but whatever the means employed, his strategy, in a remarkable recovery from the shambles of the first initiative, had at last succeeded. Gentz for a change was full of praise. "The firm and shrewd position that Prince Metternich took against all threats and unacceptable proposals," he wrote even before success was assured, "the direction he was able to give to England's actions, the uncommonly adroit way in which he used France as support against these projects by relying on her neither too much nor too little—all this did not fail to make an impact on the opposing party."[93] Even as propaganda aimed at Karadja, this is a fair assessment. Once Metternich had decided to have it out with Prussia, his campaign was not only "firm and shrewd" but plain vicious in its abruptness, range, and tenacity, leaving no avenue for retreat. On the

[91] *Ibid.*; Stein, "Tagebuch," *Briefe*, v, 356; Schmidt, *Verfassungsfrage*, 388–389; Humb. to Caroline, 5 Jan. 1815, Humboldt, *Briefe*, iv, 448–449; McGuigan, *Duchess*, 424.

[92] Text in d'Angeberg, *Congrès*, iv, 1882–1883, as annex to protocol of 9 Jan. 1815.

[93] Gentz to Karadja, 4 Jan. 1815, Klinkowström, *Oesterreichs Theilnahme*, 485.

other hand, the price was high: almost total capitulation in Poland and, as we shall see, a severe dislocation of his plans for the territorial settlement in Germany. Even the final shape of Saxony itself posed a battle still to be fought. The time to demobilize armies and dissolve alliances had not yet come.

CHAPTER XI

THE GERMAN QUESTION

BETWEEN CRISES

THE FIRST conference of the five powers took place on 12 January, Talleyrand attending for France and in the popular imagination appearing triumphantly as the man who has broken an insoluble deadlock and now takes charge of European affairs. This is a misconception. At the meeting he took special pains to be inconspicuous, and though his voice became louder in the coming months, in general he continued this prudent course, conspicuously silent now about the duty of the powers to convene the congress.[1] The Conference of Five deliberated, but it seldom voted on matters not well decided in advance. The storied alignment of the three allies of 3 January against the outmaneuvered minority is also an illusion. True, Metternich always tried to assure himself of Anglo-French support before submitting propositions to the formal conference, but this entailed tortuous private negotiations that in fact found Castlereagh occupying the middle ground and continuing his role as the mediator between Austria and France on the one side and the two eastern powers on the other. Thus France reentered the ranks of the powers as a counterweight, not as the holder of the balance.

Even the central issue that drew Castlereagh to the Austro-French side, the preservation of the king of Saxony in some part of his ancestral lands, was still not settled, at least in a technical sense. Despite his isolation on the issue, the plan that Hardenberg formally submitted to that first conference repeated the previous idea: a left-bank establishment with 704,000 inhabitants with Bonn as its capital.[2] In Berlin there persisted the desperate hope that the king even yet would listen to Colonel Miltitz and voluntarily choose this arrangement over all the uncertainties attached to the homeland. The day after the conference Humboldt still considered the matter open.[3] It was generally understood, however, that Hardenberg, in offering the resettlement plan, did so mainly to establish 700,000 as the proper size of the king's territory, wherever located, and probably as well to place on the record the principle, embodied in the concluding paragraph, that in Prussia's

[1] Protocol of 12 Jan. 1815, d'Angeberg, *Congrès*, IV, 1883f.; Rosenkrantz, *Journal*, 124f., entry of 12 Jan. 1815; And Mayr. "Aufbau," 85.
[2] "Plan pour la reconstruction de la Prusse," d'Angeberg, *Congrès*, IV, 602–604.
[3] Humb. To Caroline, 13 Jan. 1815, Humboldt, *Briefe*, IV 454.

compensations mediatized lands should not count. Privately, the chancellor assumed the partition of Saxony and began to concentrate his efforts on obtaining as compensation Ansbach and Bayreuth rather than a large responsibility on the Rhine. Even this proposal, which Castlereagh, as might have been expected, received coolly the next day, may have been little more than a ruse designed to win British support for greater gains in Saxony.[4]

With the formal submission of the Prussian note it was once again up to Metternich to produce a counterproject. But what to offer? For what it was worth, the principle of legitimacy had been saved, but the physical components of equilibrium could still be lost if Prussia acquired too many of the vital strong points ringing Bohemia or if the kernel of Saxony was too weak to survive.[5] These were quantitative matters on which judgments differed, and Metternich found himself, as before, caught in the middle of contending forces. On one side was Talleyrand urging him to demand much, complaining as usual of his weakness and "endless concessions," fearful that without stout frontiers Austria, much like Saxony herself, would have to maintain larger armies than her strength could bear. Castlereagh, on the other hand, warned that the triple alliance was no blank check, no license to press Prussia to the wall; he had saved a kernel of Saxony, and that was all his instructions required. The grandson-in-law of Count Kaunitz could hardly have been surprised: keeping *both* the central powers strong against the flanks was a British policy as old as the War of the Austrian Succession.

As before, Talleyrand's chief supporters were the Austrian military, eager, as Castlereagh feared, to make the most of the new strength that the alliance appeared to confer. "If we must strike, we can still find the arms; count on me"—thus Schwarzenberg's plea to Metternich on 9 January.[6] A week later he produced a long memorial outlining what today would be called the worst case.[7] Lamenting that Prussia's feckless Russian policy had destroyed the possibility of that noble dream, a united *Mitteleuropa* (his word) holding off the flanking powers, he undertook to explain how Austria must attempt to save herself. Prussia's bases in Silesia, even without Russian assistance, he maintained,

---

[4] Gentz's "Uebersicht der Verhandlungen . . . ," 12 Feb. 1815, in Klinkowström, *Oesterreichs Theilnahme*, 514; Castle. To Liverp., 11 Jan. 1815, Webster, *BD*, 286; Hardenberg, "Tagebücher," 38; and Griewank, *Wiener Kongress*, 187f.

[5] "Bases de Négotiation," n.d., in Metternich's hand, text in Griewank, *Wiener Kongress*, 311–313, where it is given the date of December. Its similarity to Metternich's counterproject of 28 Jan. 1815, however, suggests a considerably later dating.

[6] Schwarz. To Mett., 9 Jan. 1815, Klinkowström, *Oesterreichs Theilnahme*, 822.

[7] "Allgemeine Uebersicht der gegenwärtigen Verhältnisse der Oesterreichischen Monarchie," 16 Jan. 1815, HHSA, StK., Kongressakten, Cart. 8, pp. 54–62.

already threatened both the left flank of Austria's Galician army and the right flank of her Bohemian forces. If the line of the Oder were now extended in a great arc through Dresden, Torgau, and Erfurt to Mainz, all in Prussian hands, or to use his language, in the hands of Russia's allies, Austria would be hopelessly outflanked at the start. That was his broad continental concern, but there was also the regional problem of Saxony's survival. To be politically viable, the victor of Leipzig contended, Saxony must "categorically" retain, besides Dresden, Görlitz and Zittau on the Neisse, Bautzen on the Spree, Kamenz, Torgau, Leipzig, and numerous lesser points; and Erfurt, though not part of Saxony, must not be joined to the Prussian system. Converted into population totals, the frontiers he visualized for Saxony would approximate those in Wessenberg's plan, which had provided only 432,000 for Prussia.

This was indeed the worst case, and even General Duka, the confidant of the emperor, though in basic agreement, believed it farfetched to place distant Mainz and Erfurt on a par with Torgau and Dresden as direct threats to Austria. What Schwarzenberg regarded as a line of envelopment, he pointed out, could just as easily be called a legitimate line of defense. Either way, however, Prussia would command the heights, and so he too advised a strong stand, as did Stadion, who emphatically endorsed Schwarzenberg's ideas.[8]

Common to both Talleyrand, who relished it, and the Austrian generals, who were resigned to it, was the assumption that Austro-Prussian rivalry would continue. Metternich, by contrast, still believed in a Central European barrier based on collaboration with Prussia and hoped to avoid a settlement that would prevent reconciliation, antagonize the British, and perpetuate Austrian dependence on France. As always his central premise was that Austrian security depended more on diplomatic combinations, which the central power was in a position to manipulate, than on another military base here or there purchased at the price of permanent hatreds.

In this spirit he and Castlereagh had been busy with the extension of the triple alliance. The latter signed Holland and Hanover in due course, but Metternich's efforts with Bavaria were more complicated. Montgelas was not the war hawk that Wrede was, but when the official invitation was extended on 6 January, the minister's notoriously long nose scented an opportunity to overcome the inferiority so long associated with not being signatory to the Treaty of Paris. He thereupon proposed that Bavaria sign separate treaties with each of the three

---

[8] Duka's critique of 5 Feb. 1815 regarding the Schwarzenberg memorial cited in the foregoing note, *ibid.*, pp. 65–69; Münster to Prince Regent, 21 Jan. 1815, Münster, *Political Sketches*, 220–224.

powers, thereby avoiding the role of mere accessory and becoming a principal party entitled to participate at the highest level of negotiation. The consequences of such a development for the German constitution and Austria's territorial conflicts with her neighbor were so obvious that Metternich refused, demanding simple accession to the existing treaty as befitted a suppliant. Since the modalities were only marginal concerns of Talleyrand and Castlereagh, however, Montgelas persisted and finally accepted one of Metternich's ingenious expedients, on 13 January grudgingly signing with each of the powers separate acts of accession which gave Bavaria the appearance of an independent negotiator but still left her an accessory.[9] The separate instrument with Bavaria had the additional advantage for Metternich that it could potentially fit with similar treaties signed with other German states to form a bloc independent of Britain and France. It was such a pact that he concluded with Hesse-Darmstadt on 14 January, promising Austria's good offices in behalf of this strategically located client in return for assistance in war and for "attaching itself exclusively to the political system" of Austria and Bavaria; dealings with any other power the grand duke was obliged to clear with Vienna.[10]

Unfortunately for Metternich the strengthening of Austria's diplomatic position only whetted the appetite of the war party, forcing him against his better judgment to engage in ever harsher exchanges with Castlereagh. In the early discussions he undoubtedly made "the endless concessions" of which the French plenipotentiary complained. We may also believe Talleyrand's boast that it was he, not Metternich, who suggested that the Austrian generals attend these informal meetings. To Castlereagh's dismay, Metternich now began to show "a disposition to aim at objects which before he had considered unattainable."[11] Meanwhile, Münster, who was negotiating separately with Hardenberg about Hanoverian claims, reported that though Prussia was now ready to abandon the resettlement plan, she would leave the king no more than 840,000 subjects. For herself she demanded among other objects Leipzig and the whole of Upper Lusatia, which happened to include Görlitz, Zittau, and Bautzen. As at the Paris peace conference, now nine months past, population totals and military strong points stubbornly failed to mesh, and Hardenberg referred grimly to the 300,000 troops that Prussia and Russia could bring to bear, again speaking gratuitously for his less ardent ally. Since Metternich continued to press the de-

[9] Winter, *Wrede als Berater*, 205–207.

[10] Text in Neumann, *Traités par l'Autriche*, II, 499–501; Heinrich Ulmann, "Der Beitritt Hessen-Darmstadts zu dem Wiener Geheimvertrag vom 3. Januar 1815," *Archiv für hessische Geschichte und Altertumskunde*, n. s. XI (1915), 319; and Olshausen, *Stellung der Grossmächte*, 115.

[11] Castle. to Liverp., 22 Jan. 1815, Websters, *BD*, 292.

mands forced on him by the Schwarzenberg party, which had the ear of the emperor, the threat of war, once seemingly banished, now returned to haunt the congress again.

At this point the mediator stepped in with all the energy and resources he could muster, categorically laying it down to Metternich that the fortresses on the Elbe, Torgau and Erfurt, must go to Prussia. Against Prussia alone, he argued, Austria was in any case larger and more compact, and against Prussia and Russia together her only effective defense was alliance with other powers, not a few strong points in Saxony.[12] With the French he now played his trump card, insisting that England must defer any armed undertaking against Murat, which Talleyrand had been urging, till the Saxon affair was settled.[13] Reassessing his priorities, Talleyrand began to listen and sent Dalberg to collaborate with Münster and Clancarty on a new plan. The result was a compromise awarding Torgau, Erfurt, and Upper Lusatia to Prussia but allowing Saxony to retain the Lusatian fortresses with military roads connecting them to the main body of the country. In all, Prussia's share would come to 906,369 in population, and Hardenberg, though still demanding Leipzig and Bautzen, was on the whole receptive.[14]

Metternich, who had previously hesitated to bring Schwarzenberg into the deliberations, now evidently believed that a subdued Talleyrand would be a moderating influence and brought the two together on 24 January to hear an ingenious plan conceived by Gentz and Wessenberg to supplant the diminished support of France with the assistance of the impatient tsar: Austria would retrocede to Russia half of the Tarnopol Circle, Russia adding the equivalent to Prussia's share of Poland in return for concessions in Saxony. Schwarzenberg now retreated, conceding Erfurt, always the most dubious of his demands and even Torgau, provided its fortifications were razed. Grudgingly Francis too agreed, only to find that Castlereagh was still not satisfied: Prussia must have Torgau as a fortress; otherwise he would not try to save Leipzig. Metternich now had the disagreeable task of persuading the emperor, against all military advice, to retreat once more, and he succeeded.[15]

Meeting again on 26 January, the three allied ministers proceeded to complete what technically was an "Austrian" counterproject but in

---

[12] Castle. to Liverp., *ibid.*, 292–294.

[13] Same to same, 29 Jan. 1815 (private), *ibid.*, 198f.; Mett. to Count Ludwig Bombelles, Austrian ambassador to Paris, 13 Jan. 1815 (copy), PRO, F.O., 92/11, pp. 139–148.

[14] Münster to Prince Regent, 21 Jan. 1815, Münster, *Political Sketches*, 220–224; and Hardenberg, "Tagebücher," 38, entry of 23 Jan. 1815.

[15] Rosenkrantz, *Journal*, 129; Talley. to Louis, 25 Jan. 1815, Talleyrand, *Memoirs*, III, 21f.; Olshausen, *Stellung der Grossmächte*, 126.

reality had been virtually dictated by Castlereagh with the last-minute compliance of Talleyrand, likewise the victim of British pressure even though he had had more choice in the matter. The measure of Castlereagh's ascendancy is indicated by still another concession that Metternich was forced to make. For the first time he consented to a pattern of compensations on the left bank of the Rhine that moved the Prussian frontier from the Mosel to the Nahe and the Glan rivers as far south as Grumbach, but stopping short of the French boundary. He thus not only abandoned the line that he had hitherto called the boundary between the Austrian and Prussian military systems but also sacrificed substantial territory where he had hoped to find compensations for Bavaria and Hesse-Darmstadt. The main reason for his retreat was Castlereagh's determination, Prussia having refused Luxemburg, to obtain that province for the Netherlands, but it is also likely that Metternich found Schwarzenberg less censorious where an immediate buffer was not concerned. In any case, Prussia would now have for herself part of what she had previously sought through the Kreis system: a South German presence and close proximity to Mainz, while Bavaria would suffer the anxieties of a common frontier with France.[16]

On the bright side, Metternich was able to salvage more of Upper Lusatia, including Bautzen and Zittau, so that the awkward military corridors could be avoided. He also saw to it that Ansbach and Bayreuth were expressly reserved for Bavaria and obtained Castlereagh's promise to bring all his resources to bear on the Prussians and Russians to forgo Leipzig and give population to Prussia toward the Warta in measure as Austria renounced subjects in Tarnopol. Throughout the plan mediatized lands were equated with any others.[17] On balance, however, the outcome was disappointing, as Metternich admitted to Schwarzenberg in transmitting a copy of the project, but there was no help for it. "Every day," he said, "my conviction grows that in alliance with France and England we could have done anything, but two of us alone can risk nothing," and even France was a doubtful factor. "I have," he added, "wrangled more these last days than in all the rest of my life."[18]

On 28 January he placed the project before the Conference of Five, in a separate note complaining, even as Hardenberg was wont to do, about the shabby treatment Austria had received.[19] At the same time

[16] Castle. to Liverp., 29 Jan. 1815, Webster, *BD*, 296; same to same, 30 Jan. 1815, PRO, F.O., 92/11, pp. 211–218 with maps; text of Austrian counterproject, d'Angeberg, *Congrès*, II, 680–683.

[17] D'Angeberg, *Congrès*, II, 681–683; Castle. to Liverp., 24 Jan. 1815, Webster, *BD*, 296–298.

[18] Mett. to Schwarz., 27 Jan. 1815, Klinkowström, *Oesterreichs Theilnahme*, 823.

[19] Text in d'Angeberg, *Congrès*, II, 677–680.

Castlereagh submitted the Dutch claims on Prussia, offering the fragments on the right bank belonging to the house of Orange in exchange for Luxemburg and Liège and a favorable boundary well to the east of the Maas, the last in contrast to the occupation arrangements, which placed the line at the river itself.[20] Both projects Hardenberg resisted, and the meeting adjourned. Castlereagh, who expected at any time to be recalled home to face Parliament, now redoubled his efforts, immediately after the conference informing Hardenberg privately that Leipzig, Bautzen, and Zittau were not negotiable and urging the tsar to take up the Austrian offer involving Tarnopol. Alexander refused but indicated he would at least not obstruct a settlement. By contrast, Castlereagh's audience with Frederick William the next day was "the most painful in all respects that it has been my fate to undergo since I have been upon the continent." For the king Leipzig conjured up memories of the glorious victory, which dwarfed even the great riches and commercial value of the city. The audience, Castlereagh reported "terminated as unpleasantly as it had begun."[21]

Stung by the king's raving, Castlereagh turned again to the only man who could reason with Frederick William, and this time Alexander came through. Weariness and renewed threats of war uttered by Schwarzenberg and Francis played their part, but the decisive factor was almost certainly Castlereagh's offer, of that same time, to have Britain and Holland assume half of the Russian debt in Amsterdam.[22] Even without taking from Tarnopol the tsar agreed to cede Thorn as a substitute for Leipzig, no mean concession in view of its great military value. This the king resentfully accepted but demanded the Lusatian fortresses as well. Receiving negative responses from Metternich and Talleyrand, Castlereagh as a last resort threw in more of his own capital, inducing Münster to reduce his claims on Prussia by 50,000 souls and on his own initiative reducing the prince of Orange's expectations by a like amount. Together these concessions helped to close the gap caused by Hardenberg's persistent refusal to count as indemnities the population of mediatized lands. Metternich approved at once and Talleyrand after some hesitation did so too. Although Hardenberg revived the issue of Leipzig again, proposing a neutral status, he and his master at last yielded, moved as much by Castlereagh's example as the actual

[20] Castle. to Liverp., 30 Jan. 1815 with enclosures as cited in n. 16.

[21] Hardenberg, "Tagebücher," 38, entry of 31 Jan. 1815; Castle. to Liverp., 6 Feb. 1815, Webster, *BD*, 299f.; and Webster, *Castlereagh*, I, 383.

[22] At least a deal of this kind was Nesselrode's advice at the time. See his memorandum for the tsar, 1 Feb. 1815, *VPR*, VIII, 181; and Sherwig, *Guineas and Gunpowder*, 331, citing Castle. to Liverp., No. 69, 13 Feb. 1815.

population involved. On 6 February Castlereagh called on Hardenberg once more, and the bargain was sealed.[23]

Although the ordeal was over, there remained another week of frenzied negotiation.[24] When Hardenberg officially submitted his acceptance on 8 February, he gratuitously added one-half of Fulda to his conditions in order to facilitate exchanges with Hanover and Hesse-Cassel (the other half had already been lost at Russian insistence to Saxe-Weimar, now officially designated a grand duchy). In acknowledging the Prussian plan two days later Metternich protested this new incursion into the dwindling acreage available for his own protégés and, driven by "a furious oral declaration" by Wrede, succeeded in deferring the matter until all the territorial exchanges of the region could be considered. Similarly he turned back a Prussian grasp for Bingen, a town on the left bank of the Rhine but south of the Nahe, the agreed-upon boundary at that point. As a possible fortified site its status was to be worked out by the future possessor and the committee charged with the military organization of the Bund.

Another modest victory for Metternich concerned the Bund itself. Hardenberg, characteristically playing up to his constituency, attempted with Razumovsky's support to include an article for the first time committing all five powers to a confederation that would "fix and guarantee the respective rights of the princes, the mediatized, and all the classes of the nation." In the final action, however, this goal was imputed only to Austria and Prussia and was entered in the protocol as a statement of good intentions rather than a treaty commitment. In a related action Luxemburg and Mainz, and at the last minute Ehrenbreitstein on future Prussian soil and Philippsburg on Bavarian, were declared federal fortresses, the assumption at the time being that regardless of who furnished the garrison, the Bund would supply the funding.

In all these decisions Metternich was a direct participant. In a still more important side effect of the Saxon settlement he was only a bystander, but a beneficiary all the same. This was the settlement between Prussia and Hanover, now eased by Castlereagh's sacrifice of 50,000 souls, in which the latter managed to strengthen Hanover in two im-

---

[23] Castle. to Liverp., 6 Feb. 1815, Webster, *BD*, 301f.; Webster, *Castlereagh*, I, 384; and Rosenkrantz, *Journal*, 150, entry of 14 February 1815.

[24] The documentation for this and the following paragraph is too complicated to cite in individual pieces. Suffice it to say that it consists of the protocols of the Conferences of Five on 8, 10, 11, 12, and 13 February with attached declarations, reservations, and the articles provisionally drafted and amended by an editorial committee appointed on 8 February, on which Hudelist and Wacken served for Austria. All in d'Angeberg, *Congrès*, II, 706–724, 737, and 772–777; and IV, 1887–1892. See also Winter, *Wrede als Berater*, 223.

portant ways. The first was the acquisition of East Frisia, which gave his ward direct contact with the Netherlands and the North Sea, consolidating Britain's continental beachhead, one of his major goals at the congress. The other was the return of southern Hanover, the region around Göttingen, which provided contact with Hesse-Cassel and the other middle states to the south, without which Hanover would have been enveloped by Prussia with or without the Kreis system. Prussia was allowed two military roads to connect with her Westphalian lands, but coming on top of the disappointment in Saxony, this was hardly the consolidation that the generals had dreamed of since Kalisch. "We have now really two Prussias," wrote Humboldt, "but it will hardly remain that way for long. The unnatural soon rights itself." He was wrong: it took half a century for the "unnatural" to be righted and in the meantime it served Metternich and his successors well. Though not directly his work, it offered some consolation for the loss of the Elbe fortresses and the line of the Mosel. But all affairs, as his father was fond of saying at the congress, turn out one way or another: in 1866 the Prussian first army launched its drive from Görlitz while the army of the Elbe advanced from Torgau.[25]

One other collateral negotiation not involving Metternich directly deserves mention here because of its ominous implications for the German settlement in general. In taking over the former Orange territories on the right bank of the Rhine, Prussia, it was understood, was to negotiate exchanges with the duchy of Nassau to acquire the fortress of Ehrenbreitstein and to arrive at convenient frontiers for both states. From Nassau's viewpoint the bargaining was prejudiced from the outset by the attitude of the same defiant Standesherren who had protested the Stein-Marschall constitution of September, 1814, and in late December had declared that "they neither can nor will become *Landstände* of the prince of Nassau but consider themselves bound only by what will be decided about their fate" by the allied powers.[26] This manifesto, issued in the name of all branches of the houses of Solms and Wied, amounted to a declaration of independence and was almost certainly encouraged from Berlin. The head of the government, Ernst Ludwig Marschall, would have been only too happy to trade such troublemakers to the Prussians for otherwise less desirable proprietary properties. A plan that the minister submitted to the powers on 7 February

---

[25] Castle. to Liverp., 13 Feb. 1815 with annexes, PRO, F.O., 92/12, pts. 1 and 2, pp. 88f–98.; Webster, Castlereagh, I, 390f.; Brandes, *Münster und die Wiederestehung*, 81–86; Griewank, *Wiener Kongress*, 207–210; and Humb. to Caroline, 5 Feb. 1815, Humboldt, *Briefe*, IV, 465 and Günther Lange, "Die Rolle Englands bei der Wiederherstellung und Vergrösserung Hannovers 1813–1815," *Niedersächsisches Jahrbuch für Landesgeschichte*, XXVIII (1956), 144–163.

[26] Text in Klüber, *Acten*, Vol. I, Part 2, 41–44.

incorporated this principle and was favorably received, even by Hardenberg.[27]

Five days later, however, when Marschall began serious discussions with Humboldt, he learned the dismal truth: his figures meant nothing because Prussia refused to count in her totals some 64,000 souls belonging to the houses of Wied and Sayn-Wittgenstein. The Prussians, as we know, had taken this position all along when acquiring conquered lands, but to apply the principle to exchanges with another state implied taking without giving and came close to actually putting into practice Hardenberg's dictum that only kings had a right to mediatized subjects. Marschall was so taken aback at Prussia's "bad and deceitful faith" that he promptly broke off the negotiations for the remainder of the month. "What distinguishes us most," Humboldt reported to his wife, "is our protection of the mediatized, but that makes us few friends among the princes." That was putting it mildly.[28]

With the settlement of Saxony a sense of emptiness settled over the congress. The joy of breakthrough, of decisions made, of war averted had crested more than a month before, when it had appeared that the rest would be routine, hardly enough to intrude on the merrymaking of the *Fasching* season in Vienna. Instead, the capitulation of Hardenberg on 6 February came only two days before the beginning of Lent. Castlereagh departed Vienna on 15 February, leaving his embassy in the hands of Wellington, and many others prepared to follow. Wessenberg, Winzingerode, and Gentz were all ailing, and Metternich himself, according to Winzingerode, "is no longer gay, his color is grayish, that readiness of speech is gone, his habits have changed.[29] Humboldt, who usually considered Metternich the least of the Austrian evils, was now less kind, deploring what he considered his chaotic conduct of affairs, complaining of his inaccessibility, and ridiculing his opinion of himself as "the ablest and most adroit, yes, the one with whom none other can compare." Even when Metternich sought Humboldt out at social gatherings, he received no credit; these gestures only showed an "absolute lack of character, not even capable of hate." Such was the bitterness of the loser.[30]

Still, it was only by the barest of margins, if at all, that Metternich could be considered the victor. He still faced the task of regaining Salzburg, Berchtesgaden, and the Inn and Hausrück districts and finding compensations for Bavaria from a much depleted inventory of

[27] Sarholz, "Nassau 1813–1815," 98.
[28] *Ibid.*; Humb. to Caroline, 5 Feb. 1815, Humboldt, *Briefe*, IV, 466.
[29] To King Fred., 12 Feb. 1815, HSA, Stuttgart, E 70, Fasc. 19, pp. 26–32.
[30] McGuigan, *Duchess*, 434; Humb. to Caroline, 12 Feb. 1815, Humboldt, *Briefe*, IV, 470–472.

valuable objects. The Prussians, by contrast, though still skirmishing with Nassau and with Denmark and Sweden over Pomerania, could view the North German territorial order as set in its essentials and concentrate on installing the Kreis system to complete their hegemony.[31] Humboldt had already seen to the preliminaries, sending to Count Münster toward the end of January both the double draft of 9 December and the alternative unicameral plan of 10 January. The Hanoverians, who recognized the latter for the propaganda piece it was, easily persuaded the Prussians to proceed only with the double draft, which Hardenberg, too, preferred.[32] On the other hand, it was still necessary to court the small states as far as possible. Accordingly, when the latter, whose organization now counted thirty-two members, on 2 February formally petitioned for the reopening of the negotiations and representation on the German Committee, Humboldt and Hardenberg agreed to admit a small delegation, the more readily as this time the declaration did not explicitly call for an imperial restoration. This was a major retreat from their former insistence on dictating a constitution, but a delegation was better than the whole crowd that the association had in mind. On 4 February the Prussians proposed to Metternich the early convening of the committee on this basis. He, of course, was in full agreement and (after waiting a day till Hardenberg on the 8th accepted his final counterproject on Saxony) endorsed the proposal, smugly adding that he had always held it essential to the final result. What he did not say was that in accordance with Württemberg's incessant demands, the remaining German territorial problems must be settled first. As a result he did not answer the Prussian note that came the next day conveying the double draft, even though it manifested a flexibility scarcely imaginable earlier. Though arguing at length for the version with Kreise, it insisted, with an air of resignation, that everything was negotiable except "a powerful military force, a federal court, and *landständische Verfassungen* guaranteed by the federal compact."[33]

Explaining his difficulties about Bavaria to the emperor Francis later in the year, Metternich blamed Hardenberg and Castlereagh almost equally. "The struggle to salvage a part of Saxony," he reported, "has

[31] Hard. to Gneisenau, 10 Feb. 1815: "The Saxon dukes as well as all the smaller North German princes come into our military system, except for a few, who will be joined to Hanover." Pertz and Delbrück, *Leben des Feldmarschalls Gneisenau*, IV, 319f.

[32] Schmidt, *Verfassungsfrage*, 400; Martens's critique of the plan of 10 January, NSHSA, Hanover, Des. 91, No. 28, p. 10. As between the two plans in the double draft Münster preferred the one without Kreise. Hartmann, *Schicksal der Verfassungvorschläge*, 67f.

[33] Correspondence in d'Angeberg, *Congrès*, II, 689–691; 703–704; and 736f.; and Hard. and Humb. to Mett., 10 Feb. 1815, Klüber, *Acten*, II, 6–12.

entailed the greatest of sacrifices and resulted in ceding the provinces on the Mosel to Prussia. It also happened that the English, in order to establish their new Dutch empire [*sic*] laid claim to more than 3 million people in the former Austrian Netherlands and the lands on the Maas. . . ."[34] The charge against England is clear, but what was the other point? Would not the preservation of *all* Saxony have compounded the problems in the west? Or was the minister arguing that perhaps it would have been better to sacrifice the entire state of Saxony after all? Considering the part of Schwarzenberg in the outcome, the latter possibility cannot be lightly dismissed, but there is one other possible explanation: namely, that the sacrifice of which he spoke consisted not merely of the 200,000 souls on the right bank of the Mosel but also of allowing Prussia not to count the mediatized lands, properties that contained some 600,000. But for that extraordinary concession, all the Mosel provinces could have been at Metternich's disposal and more besides.

The first creditor to complain of Metternich's shrinking assets was, not surprisingly, King Max Joseph of Bavaria. On seeing the protocol of 28 January, which contained the outlines of the final settlement, he was dumbfounded. "This villainous wretch of a liar has kept me from closing my eyes tonight," he told Wrede, and ordered the marshal to protest. It was not merely the cession of the Mosel lands, Wrede then told Metternich, but the fact that the deed was done behind his back, in violation, he maintained, of the confidences pledged in the Austro-Bavarian alliance of 12 January and contrary to the "promises" of the notorious note of 22 October. What a commentary on the foreign minister's plight that both the Prussians and the Bavarians should cite the same document as proof of his treachery! Bavaria, moreover, had all the leverage, still occupying, as she did, Salzburg and the Inn and Hausrück districts, lands that she actually preferred, as the king himself reminded Metternich a few days later in laying out what he called "the unvarnished truth."[35]

In the meantime the other interested parties would not sit still while Austria and Bavaria worked out their problems. When the award of Westphalia to Prussia was made final and Hesse-Darmstadt became a competing legatee on the left bank, Baron Türckheim returned to the fray, issuing protests to all the powers and arguing that the precariousness of left-bank holdings justified more than a one-to-one ex-

[34] Mett. To Francis, 21 Sept. 1815, HHSA, StK., Vorträge, Cart. 199, pp. 76–85.
[35] Max Joseph to Wrede, 31 Jan. 1815, quoted in Winter, *Wrede als Berater*, 222, n. 4; Wrede to Mett., 31 Jan. 1815, and Max Joseph to Francis, 2 Feb. 1815, HHSA, StK., Kongressakten, Cart. 8, pp. 9–17; and Adalbert, Prinz von Bayern, *Max I. Joseph von Bayern* (Munich, 1957), 705.

change of souls. The arrangement was Austria's idea, Humboldt again reminded the envoy, and advised him to see Metternich about it.[36] Other suppliants with unsatisfied claims that hinged on the Austro-Bavarian settlement were Baden, Württemberg, Saxe-Weimar, Saxe-Coburg, Oldenburg, and even Eugene Beauharnais, all of whom had been named in Nesselrode's instructions of August, 1814, as deserving special favors. To Metternich's discomfiture the tsar continued to give them his support, on 9 February ordering his plenipotentiaries to accommodate Weimar and Prussia by keeping Fulda from Bavarian hands, to force Max Joseph to honor the promises impulsively made by the tsar himself to Prince Eugene, and, astonishingly, to establish the prince royal of Württemberg at Mainz as commander of the forces of the German Confederation! The notion of placing his future brother-in-law at the head of the federal troops was surely a passing fancy, but it demonstrated once again the tsar's postulate that the organization of Germany was essentially a matter of arranging Russia's forward defenses for her convenience.[37]

In the week following the Saxon settlement Alexander, eager to leave Vienna but "not before having exercised his influence on this question" of Bavaria,[38] began to press for bringing it before the Conference of Five. Metternich knew that the powers would have to ratify in the end, but he preferred to reach agreement with the Bavarians first. Turning to Talleyrand and Wellington for assistance, he found the former unwilling to choose between two close allies while the latter contented himself with privately disapproving the king's avarice.[39] Direct talks with Wrede were hampered by the illness of Wessenberg, Austria's own expert juggler of souls. When Razumovsky, however, on 18 February expressly called for action by the powers, Metternich decided to make one more attempt with Wrede; if they could agree, the dispute would cease to be between Austria and Bavaria and become the responsibility of others. To this end he and the speedily recovered Wessenberg fabricated a proposal they knew would never satisfy the powers but would discharge the Austrian obligation under the convention of June, 1814, to use their good offices for Bavaria. Specifically, for her cessions to Austria Bavaria was to obtain Mainz with environs, Frankfurt, half of Fulda (to be exchanged for Hanau), and portions of Baden, Württemberg, and Hesse-Darmstadt. All in all she would have gained 110,000 more population than she released. The first three were "points

---

[36] Dietrich, "Hessen-Darmstadt auf dem Wiener Kongress," 250–252.

[37] Instructions for the Russian delegation, 9 Feb. 1815, VPR, VIII, 185–187.

[38] Rosenkrantz, Journal, 156, entry of 19/20 Feb. 1815.

[39] Talley. to Louis, 15 Feb. 1815, Talleyrand, Memoirs, III, 42; Well. to Castle., 18 Feb. 1815, Wellington, Supplementary Dispatches, IX, 569–572.

which he knows he cannot dispose," Wellington commented when he was told about it. The purpose, Metternich admitted, was to force Wrede to produce an alternative.[40]

It is scarcely imaginable that Metternich would deliberately have offered a plan that neither the powers nor the Bavarians would accept, but that is what happened. When he and Wessenberg met with Wrede on the 19th, the marshal announced that the unanticipated proximity of Prussian holdings along the Mosel removed all the allure of Mainz, especially as the territory to go with the fortress would not support more than a fourth of its upkeep. Not only that, but reenacting Hardenberg's scene of two months earlier, he insisted that the Austrians erred in equating the population of mediatized lands with any other. It was now plain that the evil legacy of "victory" in Saxony was not only Prussia's own peculiar profit but also the precedent she had established for the rest. Her menacing presence astride the Mosel, moreover, was frightening others away.[41] The marshal could hardly have dealt a harder blow, for Mainz was not just an object of Bavarian compensation but the key to Metternich's policy of using his neighbor to block the advance of Prussia. If Munich refused this role, then, given the outspoken desire of Britain and Russia to award the fortress to one of the powers, either the mighty base would fall to Prussia after all—or Austria must claim it for herself, giving up the concept of a Bavarian surrogate. Wrede, to be sure, left some room for maneuver by proposing a partition of Salzburg, but whether an Austrian sacrifice there could create an Austrian right to Mainz, or whether such a course was even advisable, were questions barely perceived as yet, let alone answered.

This latest demonstration of Bavarian intransigence came in the midst of other troubles that had been dammed up by the Saxon crisis. One immediate consequence of the settlement was the virtual disappearance of the *casus foederis* that had given meaning to the triple alliance. With Austria for practical purposes once more alone, Metternich and Talleyrand, who had similar concerns, considered expanding the coverage of the pact only to find Castlereagh opposed, fearing that this arrangement would alienate the tsar, who at the same time was proposing the renewal of the alliance of Chaumont. To avoid the emergence of rival blocs Castlereagh proposed that the eight signatories to the Treaty of Paris all pledge themselves in a formal dec-

[40] Razumovsky to Mett., 18 Feb. 1815; HHSA, StK., Kongressakten, Cart. 6, pp. 453–456; Landauer, "Die Einverleibung Salzburgs," 5; Sahrmann, *Pfalz oder Salzburg?*, 45; Well. to Castle., 21 Feb. 1815, Wellington, *Supplementary Despatches*, IX, 574.
[41] Sahrmann, *Pfalz oder Salzburg?*, 45f.; and Winter, *Wrede als Berater*, 223f.

laration to guarantee the settlement, with arms if necessary. Metternich, who from the beginning had taken it for granted that the results of private negotiations would eventually be sanctioned by the congress, quickly agreed, as did Talleyrand and the tsar. The Austrians would have preferred incorporating the guarantee into the treaty itself, but a separate declaration, depending on the wording, could serve as well, and Gentz, who was charged with drafting the instrument, saw to it that the signatories were indeed bound to employ all means, including arms, "to stifle at birth any undertaking that threatened to overthrow the established order and to provoke anew the disorders and calamities of war."[42]

Until a settlement was reached, of course, Gentz's project could only be filed away—a pity for a document so moving, according to its author, that it brought the tsar to tears. In the meantime Metternich, who from the beginning of the congress had promised the Porte that the Ottoman Empire would be included in the future guarantee, found Castlereagh and Talleyrand in agreement. The tsar, however, made his participation conditional on an undertaking by the other three powers first to mediate his disputes with the Turks. The Austrian and British ministers pressed the latter to consent, but they refused, and the project lapsed till near the end of the congress.[43] Nevertheless, Metternich, who had once, in Napoleon's time, endeavored to place the Rheinbund under international guarantee, remained no less determined to gain this protection for whatever Bund emerged from the Congress of Vienna.

Another issue that suddenly came to life as peace settled on Austria's northern frontier was the fate of Murat. As long as war threatened over Saxony Metternich could reasonably resist Talleyrand's demands for action in Italy, and Castlereagh, as we have seen, backed him in this. No more. As a result, the second half of February found the Austrian minister in complicated negotiations aimed at gaining French support for Austrian and papal plans in Central Italy in return for a military expedition to overthrow the last of the Bonaparte sovereigns. In a related negotiation he was locked in battle with Talleyrand and the tsar over the valleys of the Valteline, a district situated on the edge of Switzerland and incessantly demanded by Schwarzenberg for its vital military route to Italy. Metternich was also doing what he could to back Denmark's territorial claims and took every opportunity to

---

[42] Webster, *Castlereagh*, 1 428f.; Gentz to Karadja, 25 Feb. 1815, *Dépêches inédites*, I, 144; Griewank, *Wiener Kongress*, 241ff.; and "Projet de Déclaration," in Gentz, *Tagebücher*, I, 443–446. I disagree with Griewank's contention that a mere declaration would have given Britain the right but not the duty to intervene on the continent.
[43] Webster, *Castlereagh*, I, 429; Griewank, *Wiener Kongress*, 243.

urge King Frederick VI to join the Bund. It was the only way, he told
Rosenkrantz, by which Austria could extend her protection into the
Baltic region and keep Prussia in check for the sake of them both.
Meanwhile, all the parties interested in the German constitution—
besides the familiar ones, the Jewish community of the free cities, book
publishers in Leipzig, envoys of the *Reichsritterschaft* on the left bank
of the Rhine, deputies of cathedral chapters interested in safeguarding
their traditional revenues, powerful prelates like Ignaz von Wessenberg speaking for the German Catholic Church, and the house of
Thurn und Taxis, anxious to recover its imperial postal monopoly—
these and many others, seeing that the congress was ready to march
again, bombarded the chancellery with petitions and begged its chief
for interviews. When the Austrian minister wearily asked Count Münster not to bother him about the Bund just yet, Ernst Hardenberg, like
many others full of advice as to what Metternich should have done
earlier to prevent the problem with Bavaria, sadly reflected that the
affair now absorbed him almost as much as Saxony had the month
before.[44]

But facts were facts, and they had to be faced. After vainly trying
to interest Wrede in seeking British mediation Metternich finally concluded that direct negotiations having failed, only the intervention of
the powers could force the marshal to yield. He doubted, however,
that his scarcely disinterested counterparts would deny Bavaria Mainz,
Fulda, and Frankfurt without asking Austria herself to make up part
of the difference, especially as she was already some 300,000 souls
above the scale of 1805, all of them dues-paying subjects not eligible
for discount. Accordingly he decided to volunteer a sacrifice by accepting Wrede's offer to divide Salzburg, thereby proving Austria's
benevolence and leaving it to the powers collectively to disappoint
Munich on other fronts. Meeting with Schwarzenberg and Stadion on
25 February, the foreign minister, in a stark revelation of his ultimate
priorities, asked them to weigh the military value of the entire province
against the certain alienation of a pivotal ally. Obviously, the veteran
soldier replied, communications between Styria and the Tyrol would
be more secure with the whole province, and there would never be a
better opportunity to obtain it. Stadion agreed: Salzburg, he said, was
permanent, friendship with Bavaria fleeting. In that case, Metternich
advised wryly, before going to the powers he would have to try to
obtain preliminary understandings with their ministers separately to

---

[44] Alan J. Reinerman, *Austria and the Papacy in the Age of Metternich* (Washington,
D.C., 1979), 16f.; Rosenkrantz, *Journal*, 162–165, entries of 27 and 28 Feb. 1815;
Hardenberg to Hanoverian ministry, 17 Feb. 1815, NSHSA, Hanover, Cal. Br. 24,
No. 5027.

prevent the affair from "degenerating into a suit that could still be lost to Bavaria." It was a classic confrontation between the complex calculations of the man attuned to the remote consequences of decisions, and the more static mind-set of those who, not necessarily mistakenly, prefer a concrete certainty regardless of context. The next day the emperor's orders to Metternich added another dimension: moral indignation, which, soaring high above arid calculation, thundered that there was an end to the sacrifices that Austria could make for Europe, that the powers whose greed had created the situation should provide Bavaria's just rewards, that Metternich must under no circumstances yield any ground in Salzburg! This was strong language, no doubt influenced by a recent decision, personally disappointing to Francis, to renounce the Breisgau and advance indemnification for it as another argument for Salzburg. Such was the price Metternich was willing to pay for harmony with neighboring states.[45]

What happened next cannot be completely verified from the records, but all signs point to another typical Metternichian maneuver. Following his own advice, he made informal soundings with each of the powers except France[46] but also continued confidential negotiations with Wrede, who was anxious to forestall the intervention of the other powers. In these talks Metternich ignored the emperor's orders and accepted the partition of Salzburg, at least for himself, and reached agreement on a complete plan that omitted Mainz from the previous project but still included Hanau, Frankfurt, a few bailiwicks in Fulda, and very substantial parts of Baden, Württemberg, and Hesse-Darmstadt. An establishment for Prince Eugene at Speyer was the only trans-Rhine territory involved. Wrede was jubilant in reporting his success on 1 March.[47]

That same day Metternich brought Wellington, Hardenberg, and

[45] Protocol of the conference and Metternich's memorial "Ueber die gegenwärtige Verhältnise zwischen Österreich und Bayern," n.d., in HHSA, StK., Kongressakten, Cart. 8, pp. 19–32; Francis to Mett., 26 Feb. 1815, extract in Landauer, "Die Einverleibung Salzburgs," 5f. When the important and controversial decision about the Breisgau was made is not known, but the elusive evidence for it dates from about this time, Wessenberg alluding to it in a paper of 1 March 1815 as an argument for Austria's right to Salzburg (HHSA, StK., Kongressakten, Cart. 8, pp. 35–38), Humboldt using it to denigrate Austria's interest in Germany and thereby discredit Stein's plan for giving her the German crown. "Gegen Stein's Denkschrift über die deutsche Kaiserwürde," 18–23 Feb. 1815, Humboldt, *Gesammelte Schriften*, XI, 299. Gentz and Binder also discussed the Breisgau on 9 March. Gentz, *Tagebücher*, I, 363.

[46] Talleyrand never figured in his mediation plans, technically because France was not a party to the accession treaties, but one must surmise as well that Metternich considered him pro-Bavarian. He was later present, however, when the preliminary agreements on this matter, as with all other territorial problems, was ratified by the Conference of Five.

[47] Sahrmann, *Pfalz oder Salzburg?*, 46f.; Winter, *Wrede als Berater*, 225.

Nesselrode together and submitted the plan to them, representing it as Marshal Wrede's, which in essence it was. At the same time he read a statement drafted by Wessenberg blaming the Saxon settlement for the situation and insisting that Salzburg in its entirety was no less vital to Austrian security than the powers had deemed Torgau and Wittenberg to be for Prussian. As expected, the group dissallowed Frankfurt and took the stand that Prince Eugene's establishment should be under Bavarian sovereignty and counted to some extent against his father-in-law's compensations. As for Salzburg, Metternich's maneuver was successful, his colleagues agreeing that Austria should have the entire province. With these revisions, Wellington reported, "the principle of this project was generally admitted to be reasonable and fit to be adopted." Even Hardenberg, who was gratified by a plan that finally confined Bavaria to the right bank and forced Baden to bear the brunt of the sacrifices, considered Austria's claims reasonable. "It is only fair to support her in her demand," he penned in the margin of his copy.[48]

Although the meeting was informal and binding on no one, Wellington, who is our only source, believed that the tsar would temper Württemberg's resistance and would also accept the conclusion already reached by the others that Baden must yield more than she could be recompensed. Hardenberg, however, balked at forcing Hesse-Cassel to renounce Hanau, probably because he still hoped to annex other Hessian lands that would provide the only direct contact between "the two Prussias," to use Humboldt's jaundiced expression.[49] The evidence is strong, moreover, that the chancellor was trying to use the situation to demonstrate the advantages of the scheme that Metternich had so often rebuffed before. How simple it would be to solve all problems by stripping Baden, Hesse-Darmstadt, Nassau, and the Hohenzollern principalities of the approximately 381,000 souls on their mediatized domains! The only task then would be to distribute them in a manner that best served German security in the region of the Rhine-Main confluence, especially to provide a secure hinterland for the support of Mainz as the Prussian generals had always urged. The solution, moreover, might revive the fading prospects of the Kreis system and slash through the difficulties that Marschall was making in Nassau. No wonder Hardenberg considered Austria's demands so reasonable.

This rendition of the chancellor's thinking cannot be conclusively

---

[48] Hardenberg, "Tagebücher," 39; Wessenberg, "Premier projet . . . ," 1 Mar. 1815, HHSA, StK., Kongressakten, Cart. 8, pp. 35–38; Well. to Castle., 4 Mar. 1815, with Wrede's plan enclosed PRO, F.O. 92/14. Griewank, *Wiener Kongress*, 215, n. 30. Wellington himself believed that military considerations favored Austrian possession of Salzburg with Bavaria powerfully situated on the left bank of the Rhine.

[49] Well. to Castle., 4 Mar. 1815, Wellington, *Supplementary Despatches*, IX, 585; Hardenberg, "Tagebücher," 39.

documented, but it is more than mere hypothesis. We know that Wessenberg met privately with him on 2 March and again on the 4th, this time with General Grolman present. Both meetings concerned Bavaria, as did another between Metternich and Hardenberg on the 5th.[50] At one of these the Austrians submitted a memorial obviously aimed at refuting arguments previously made. If Bavaria had received Mainz, Wessenberg maintained, she would have accepted connecting military roads on the Prussian model rather than insist on the contiguity promised her in the treaties, and in that case all the states in the area could have been kept reasonably intact. Now the least disruptive arrangement would be the award of Hanau to Bavaria, the only equivalent for Salzburg short of resorting to massive exchanges that would undermine stability throughout the region. The problem, he added, was exacerbated because Bavaria, influenced by the Prussian example, now insisted on discounting the value of the mediatized lands by at least two-thirds. "As to the principle *put forward in one of the last conferences*," he continued, "the principle of removing the mediatized houses from sovereign princes who are not endowed with the rank of royalty, this will be very difficult to carry out literally either in regard to geographical location or because their number is too large to permit transferring them without an indemnity of some kind." A middle way was needed, Wessenberg concluded, "between the interests of the powers and justice to the small states of whom one expects sacrifices." Apart from indicating where Hardenberg stood, Wessenberg's words leave no doubt about Metternich's policy: to minimize shocks to existing states, to count mediatized lands as much as possible the same as others, and to pay a decent respect to the obligations incurred in the treaties. It is not too much to say that for the sake of larger issues he refused the easy way out.[51]

Hardenberg's position at this point was all the more important as it registered a new stage in the evolving alliance between Prussia and the Standesherren, a topic of such importance that it warrants extended reconnoitering in the camp of Metternich's opponents. As noted earlier, Humboldt was concerned that the tax exemptions that Hardenberg insisted on granting the mediatized assigned to Prussia almost eliminated any financial advantages normally expected from annexed territory. If further studies showed this to be the case, he advised the chancellor on 10 January, "then it would be preferable to make all the

[50] Hardenberg, "Tagebücher," 39.

[51] Wessenberg memorial "Sur l'indemnisation de la Bavière," 4 Mar. 1815, HHSA, StK., Kongressakten, Cart. 8, pp. 22–26. Emphasis mine. Stein spoke in similar language at the time. Memorandum for the Russian Cabinet, 5 Mar. 1815; Stein to Hard., 8 March 1815, Stein, *Briefe*, v, 280–282. "The wrenching of the mediatized from the *Länder*," he advised the chancellor, "will cause much screaming."

mediatized equal, even if they are certain to be dissatisfied." Prussia must never relinquish sovereignty over them, he insisted, and intimated that the double draft in other ways as well conceded them too much.[52] In the next few weeks he argued the matter with Solms and Gärtner, stressing (as Stein himself had done) the advantages of being members of the territorial estates. They, however, continued to demand the status of autonomous enclaves mostly outside the machinery of state government, as the double draft already provided. For the princes transferred from one sovereign to another Gärtner by mid-February considered that the draft left "almost nothing more to be desired," and similar treatment was possible for the others, Humboldt told him, if only Austria could be won over. "You would not believe," he wrote his wife, "how much popularity we have won, not among the princes of the Rheinbund to be sure, but among the others and all the oppressed."[53]

In blaming Austria Humboldt only wished to remind his friends that the source of their protection in imperial times was no more. Solms and Gärtner, however, took him literally and apparently believed there was a chance to regain Austrian support. A gesture in this direction they made in early February when they induced the Association of Mediatized Houses to create a steering committee with Franz Georg Metternich as president, an elder statesman among the Standesherren, as we know, and presumably not without influence at the State Chancellery or the family dining table. Their main hope, however, was that the Austrians, despite their coyness in times past, could be won to their cause by offering Francis the imperial dignity, the crowning glory of a restored Reich. If this hope strikes us as not merely naive but recklessly entailing a slap at their more eager protector, we can only speculate that they considered previous difficulties washed away by the end of the Saxon crisis and that everything depended on what particular institutions were devised for the Reich. They had, at any rate, strong advice to this effect from an informed and experienced insider: Baron Stein.[54]

The doughty *Reichsfreiherr*, who had endorsed a Reich in November, was sorely troubled by developments since. Though the immediate crisis was past, he could not believe that there was sufficient harmony between the archrivals to sustain through the vagaries of all future

[52] Humb. to Hard., 10 Jan. 1815. Text in Schmidt, *Verfassungsfrage*, 399.

[53] Hoff, *Mediatisiertenfrage*, 91–98; Humb. to Caroline, 12 Feb. 1815, Humboldt, *Briefe*, IV, 470. About the only fault Gärtner found in Humboldt's draft was the omission of an article recognizing the right of the Standesherren to represent their subjects in the Landtag, a right that would have precluded some minor nobility from sitting there.

[54] Hoff, *Mediatisiertenfrage*, 89–91.

time a system based on a five-power directory, especially if the natural cleavages among the directors were widened by delegating so many of the federal powers to them individually as Kreis chiefs. Austria, he believed, should possess the crown not because of close ties to Germany, but precisely in order to tighten the relationship. With or without Kreise, moreover, what influence could the imperial knights exert as *Landstände* if they lacked reinforcement from the self-isolated Standesherren, who disdained parliamentary life as Hardenberg seemingly encouraged them to do? These and other considerations amply account for Stein's sudden initiatives in early February in renewing the struggle for an imperial restoration.[55]

What has puzzled most writers is the timing, for almost simultaneously he was urging the Russians to exert pressure on the German Committee in support of Humboldt's draft. There is nonetheless a simple answer: that he considered his imperial plan merely a variant of Humboldt's proposals, involving little more than the transfer of the functions of the First Council to a supreme head. Capodistrias, who was Stein's stalking horse in seeking Russian support, said as much in advancing a plan ostensibly on his own initiative. "The same federal system that has been under consideration is such as can accommodate a chief," he wrote on 9 February, the same day the instructions went out to the Russian delegation to consider the question of a supreme head.[56] Furthermore, when Stein himself on 17 February finally released his own memorandum "On the Reestablishment of the Imperial Dignity in Germany," it was confined to just that: an emperor who in varying degrees shared legislative, judicial, and military powers with a federal diet but would possess no more executive power than the First Council of Humboldt's plan without Kreise.[57]

And whose advice did he follow in proposing an emperor with these powers? None other than Count Solms, who had submitted his ideas four days earlier.[58] Stein's strategy, then, was to build a coalition of small states and mediatized princes against the exorbitant ambitions of Bavaria and Württemberg, a coalition whose offer of the crown Austria could not refuse and Prussia could not oppose. All sides, however, persisted in their previous attitudes. On 11 February discreetly raising the issue in the guise of Capodistrias' plan, Stein received a blunt refusal from Hardenberg; and later, when his own memorial was in the public domain, Humboldt called it "madness." Metternich

---

[55] Ritter, *Stein*, 509–512.

[56] "Considérations sur l'Empire Germanique par le Comte de Capo d'Istria," 9 Feb. 1815, Pertz, *Leben von Stein*, IV, 735–739.

[57] Text in Stein, *Briefe*, V, 274–276.

[58] Solms to Stein, 12 Feb. 1815, *ibid.*, V, 269f.

was less abrupt, as usual expressing personal sympathy but doubting that others would agree. He did, however, consent to hear Solms and Plessen on the subject. With the former he took the same noncommittal position, but Wessenberg, who received Plessen about the same time, was more encouraging. All in all, Humboldt was undoubtedly right in arguing that the power Stein intended for the emperor was too little to interest Austria and too much for Prussia and the large South German states to accept.[59]

The most obvious flaw, however, was the incompatibility between the small states, which included Baden, Hesse-Darmstadt, and Nassau, and the Standesherren, many of whom were trying to break away from these prison houses. The latter, indeed, encouraged by Hardenberg's proposals, grew bolder as their steering committee reassessed the situation and in March adopted a more ambitious program. At their low point a year earlier they had been content to argue that even the Rheinbund Act had left the old *Länder* constitutions and their patrimonial rights intact. Later Solms had argued that the dissolution of the Rheinbund had left the mediatized houses at the disposal of the conquering allies. Now the steering committee, in a memorial drafted by Gärtner,[60] adopted a new orthodoxy to the effect that the annulment of the Rheinbund Act automatically restored the legal order of 1805, leaving the lesser estates free, as in the days of the Reich, to enter into "a voluntary political-military protective union" with a larger state, surrendering to the protector only such powers as were once possessed by Reich and Kaiser, but as *Landesherren* retaining all others. The latter, described in great detail, duplicated to a large extent the note of 16 May 1814, and bore a remarkable resemblance to the provisions of Humboldt's double draft, with emphasis on Kreis estates rather than *landständische Verfassungen*. For the persons and families of the Standesherren the memorial went further, claiming the old imperial status, which would make them the equals of the sovereigns and their progeny eligible to marry at that level. Concluding, Gärtner paid his respects to Francis as the future emperor, but his deepest sentiments lay elsewhere. "Blessed then will everyone be," he exulted, "and doubly blessed those who in the future can honor Frederick William the Just as their special protector and share in the general affairs of a government distinguished by wisdom, harmony, and humanity."[61]

---

[59] Stein, "Tagebuch," *Briefe*, v, 362–364; Humb. to Caroline, 23 Feb. 1815, Humboldt, *Briefe*, IV, 485; Hoff, *Mediatisiertenfrage*, 95; Schmidt, *Verfassungsfrage*, 411f.; and Humboldt memoranda of 23 Feb. and 3 Mar. 1815, Humboldt, *Gesammelte Schriften*, XI, 295–306.

[60] Text, dated 15 Mar. 1815, in Klüber, *Acten*, Vol. I, Part 4, pp. 16–35.

[61] Cf. Hoff, *Mediatisiertenfrage*, 91–96. The argument for the legal order of 1805 was made more explicitly in a memorandum of Solms from the same period, but it was the premise of Gärtner's work as well.

Needless to say, the states with sizable mediatized domains were shocked at such developments and appalled that Metternich seemed to be unwilling to help. "The mediatized," reported Winzingerode, "are always in motion; Herr Humboldt openly protects them; Herr Metternich the Younger would like to but dares not take the lead." At an interview about 18 February Metternich succeeded in calming the Württemberg envoy at least to the extent of proving that he understood the situation: i.e., that Prussia was trying to seize the military forces of North Germany "by flattering the mediatized in these parts, to arouse those in the South against their sovereigns, and to nourish in them the hope of enjoying the protection of Prussia in preference to that of Austria." Winzingerode still feared that Metternich's "indolent vanity" would yet deliver him into the clutches of the "fanatical" Hardenberg, but the interview cheered him all the same.[62]

In the meantime, King Frederick, the sovereign over more mediatized than any other ruler—nineteen princes, twelve counts, and about 120 members of the *Reichsritterschaft*—was seeking his own salvation. In one operation Winzingerode continued his efforts, even without Russian support, to persuade the other middle states, especially Baden, Hesse-Darmstadt, and Nassau, to join Württemberg in a neutral league of their own. As these particular states had never felt completely comfortable with the smaller states and their imperial plans, their interest was considerable, and Marschall of Baden even drafted articles of confederation as the basis of discussion.[63] In the end, however, the project failed, partly because Talleyrand and Castlereagh, to whom they turned for external backing, discouraged it, partly because Winzingerode himself shied from a démarche that would compromise Württemberg's status as a member of the German Committee. Besides, if a Swabian Kreis materialized, Württemberg might have her separate league after all and under her domination.

Frederick's masterstroke, however, was to be delivered at home, the introduction of a new constitution designed to smother the Standesherren in a parliament that brought together in a single chamber all thirty-one of them with whole votes, nineteen members of the *Reichsritterschaft*, four delegates from the churches and the University of Tübingen, and seventy-one deputies elected by the population at large on the basis of a male franchise and relatively low property qualifications. Thus, even if all the traditional orders voted en bloc, the commoners would have the majority. Other modern, egalitarian fea-

---

[62] Winz. to Fred., 16 and 19 Feb. 1815, HSA, Stuttgart, E 70, Fasc. 19, pp. 28–31; Winz. report of 20 Feb. 1815 quoted in Mager, "Das Problem der Verfassungen," 342, n. 97.

[63] Winz. to Fred., 14 Jan. 1815, HSA, Stuttgart, E 70, Fasc. 14, pp. 85–96; and same to same, 17 Feb. 1815, *ibid.*, Fasc. 19, p. 29f.

tures included equality of all subjects before the law, freedom of occupation, equal access to government offices, *habeas corpus*, the addition, later, of seats for the Jews, and strict adherence to the separation of powers by excluding state officials from the Landtag and denying to the Landtag its traditional treasury and role in supervising administration. True, its legislative competence was to be limited to the approval of *new* laws and *new* taxes, but in their old-fashioned way, neither Münster's four-point minimum nor Humboldt's double draft called for more.[64]

Regardless of Frederick's ulterior motives and the retention of strong royal powers, the projected system would have laid the foundations for a modern society. What matters here, however, is the plight of the Standesherren, who were not only to be absorbed still further into the body of the state but forced to rub elbows with commoners, who, as the first elections turned out, included some of their own magistrates, notaries, and tax collectors.[65] Seen in this light, their revulsion at descending into the ranks of the *Landstände* is more understandable than it appeared to Stein, even if potentially self-defeating.

Frederick announced his intentions on 11 January, when setting 15 March as the date for the first Landtag elected in this manner. Significantly, the first response from the powers gathered in Vienna was favorable, Hardenberg, Metternich, and even Stein complimenting Winzingerode on the king's decision to introduce a constitution.[66] But as the Standesherren and the imperial knights directly concerned showered protests on the congress, opinions there changed, and Solms himself on 1 February condemned the work in an unusually long treatise in which he reemphasized that only the powers could determine the provisions of state constitutions.[67] Thus encouraged, two of the king's subjects, the princes of Hohenlohe-Langenburg and Hohenlohe-Jagtberg, repeated this refrain in protesting to the minister of the interior, Count von Reischach, adding that rather than take an oath to a constitution they had never seen, they would boycott the meeting.

Frederick's response, conveyed through Reischach, was characteristically harsh, informing the Hohenlohes that the purpose of the Land-

[64] Höltzle, *Württemberg im Zeitalter*, 189–193; Walter Grube, *Der Stuttgarter Landtag 1457–1957. Von den Landständen zum demokratischen Parlament* (Stuttgart, 1957), 449–491; Hoff, *Mediatisiertenfrage*, 98–100; Huber, *Deutsche Verfassungsgeschichte*, I, 331–333; and Dr. Friedrich Wintterlin, "Die württembergische Verfassung 1815–1819," *Württembergische Jahrbücher für Statistik und Landeskunde* (1912), 47–83.

[65] Grube, *Stuttgarter Landtag*, 492.

[66] Winz. to Fred., 20 Jan. 1815, HSA, Stuttgart, E 70, Fasc. 14, pp. 103–107; same to same, 21 Jan. 1815, *ibid.*, E 70, Fasc. 19, pp. 17–19.

[67] Text in Pertz, *Leben von Stein*, IV, 718–733.

tag was not to negotiate oaths of fealty but to receive a constitution promulgated by the crown, that they were free to absent themselves but "whoever stayed away would have to expect for himself and his family the inevitable consequences." Then lecturing the insolent lords on their false principles, he contended that the proceedings in Vienna had no bearing on the internal affairs of any state, that the Treaty of Paris, in speaking of a "federal bond among the sovereign states of Germany," clearly limited the German Committee to the regulation of external relations.[68] Although addressed to his subjects, these lines were quickly brought by Solms and Gärtner to the attention of the powers. Hardenberg, of course, had most cause to reject this thesis, but Münster was not far behind, and both urgently requested Metternich to join them in demanding that Württemberg desist until the German Committee had acted.[69]

In one way, ironically, Metternich was more intimately affected than they, or at least as the reigning prince of Ochsenhausen, his father was. Franz Georg, in fact, was not only the president of the mediatized houses' steering committee but in Württemberg itself a member of a group of would-be *frondeurs*, called the Spenzer corps, dedicated to promote resistance. Unlike most of his associates, however, he blamed Prussian agitation as much as Frederick for the confrontation and discreetly refrained from advising Prince Clemens what he should do.[70]

The latter, in his most private thoughts, must have considered the king's stand on the Treaty of Paris somewhat presumptuous but even so his concept of sovereignty closer to the truth than the remarkable views propounded by the friends of the mediatized. For this reason he had steadfastly, as we have seen, parried Hardenberg's efforts to have the committee officially endorse the Prussian view, which somehow always converted "the independence of Germany," the language of the treaties, into something like the internal "liberties of the German people."

Even if true, Winzingerode asked Hardenberg at this time, how could he equate the German people with the mediatized houses?—a question that bothered even the distinguished Prussian administrator, F.L.W. Vincke, who insisted that the Standesherren had "brutally mis-

[68] Notes of Reischach to the two princes Hohenlohe, 19 Mar. 1815, annexed to note of Gärtner to the allied powers, 5 Mar. 1815, in Klüber, *Acten*, Vol. I, Part 4, pp. 3–8. Note of *Reichsritterschaft* envoys, 24 Feb. 1815, summarized in Schmidt, *Verfassungsfrage*, 426.

[69] Gärtner notes of 27 Feb. and 5 Mar. 1815 in Klüber, *Acten*, Vol. I, Part 4, pp. 1–4; Hard. to Mett., 6 March 1815, and draft note proposed for submission to Württemberg by the German Committee, Schmidt, *Verfassungsfrage*, 428–433; Münster to Mett., 7 Mar. 1815, HHSA, StK., Kongressakten, Cart. 6, pp. 468–469.

[70] Franz Georg to Clemens, 4 Mar. 1815, HHSA, StK., Kongressakten, Cart. 6, pp. 457–458.

treated" their subjects.[71] But if leaning toward the middle-state conception of sovereignty as stated in the treaties, Metternich always believed that everybody ought voluntarily to do what was necessary for the common welfare. The true aim of the German Committee was consensus. He was therefore willing to follow Hardenberg in issuing a separate note requesting the king to postpone the meeting of the Landtag on the grounds that it was inconsistent to proceed unilaterally in a matter that his envoys were still negotiating on the German Committee. Hardenberg's note to this effect went out on 5 March, Metternich's the day after, the latter placing the emphasis on the desirability of "avoiding complications at the congress as much as possible." Metternich refused, however, to sign a more litigious note that Hardenberg intended as both a protest and a legal brief for the jurisdiction of the German Committee over its errant member. Thus, once again Metternich managed to prevent the theories of Hardenberg, Münster, and Solms from becoming the official doctrine of the committee. Frederick, for his part, proceeded with his plan, abandoning it only when the Landtag itself, including the elected deputies, most of whom yearned for the "good old law," indignantly refused to recognize a dictated constitution.[72]

The irony of the positions taken by Hardenberg, the bureaucratic centralist, and Metternich, a mediatized prince himself, has been thematic throughout our narrative but nowhere more strikingly than here, where the Metternich estates themselves were involved and Franz Georg was in the thick of the action. Less visible at this time was another irony, perhaps of even greater magnitude. In the midst of Frederick's campaign against the Standesherren the king learned of Humboldt's double draft and on 23 February, instructed Winzingerode anew to insist on the retention of the Kreis system, to oppose absolutely a supreme head "whatever his title may be," and to vote with the majority on Austria's and Prussia's double votes and all matters relating to the competence of the Second Council and the role of its permanent committee in the affairs of the First. He continued to reject a federal court and federal guidelines for state constitutions, but on the whole, considering that Bavaria and Hanover now opposed Kreise, King Fred-

---

[71] Höltzle, *Württemberg im Zeitalter*, 192; and Sweet, *Humboldt*, II, 200.

[72] Hard. to Winz., 5 Mar. 1815, Schmidt, *Verfassungsfrage*, 427; parallel but not identical note of Mett. to Winz. 6 Mar. 1815, HHSA, StK., Kongressakten, Cart. 6, pp. 459–461; Hardenberg's tendentious draft project of 7 Mar. 1815, *ibid.*, pp. 462–467. Metternich never answered the proposal, but the simple assumption of Schmidt, *Verfassungsfrage*, 430, and Hartmann, *Schicksal der Verfassungsvorschläge*, 71, that the sole cause was the news that same day of Napoleon's departure from Elba, overlooks the kind of arguments that Austria was being asked to endorse. The news, of course, provided an excellent cover for ignoring the proposal.

erick in all matters but the mediatized houses stood closer to Hardenberg than any other monarch. He was even inclined, despite
Winzingerode's reports to the contrary, to suspect that Talleyrand,
with Metternich in tow, was the principal agitator among the Standesherren.[73]

During the first week of March, while Frederick went ahead with
his plans to convene his Landtag and Max Joseph waited to hear what
the powers had to say about Salzburg and Hanau, an event occurred
that everyone had been waiting for: on 4 March Frederick Augustus
of Saxony arrived in nearby Pressburg to receive the powers' terms.
As noted earlier, he was not bound to accept them, but he faced continued occupation of his country until he did. Since tedious negotiations had preceded his journey, hope was high that the whole miserable
business would at last disappear from the agenda of the congress. To
decide on the modalities and make certain of a united front Metternich
on the night of 6 March assembled the plenipotentiaries of the five
powers in the chancellery. There it was decided to prepare an extract
from the protocol of the meeting and attach to it the pertinent articles
initialed almost a month earlier. Metternich was chosen to present the
document in Pressburg and in the name of the five powers to request
the king's endorsement.[74]

This much was routine. A more spirited debate that night concerned
the form of the settlement. The end seeming near, the five had to face
again the issue of guarantees and the closely related question of whether
to draft a single comprehensive treaty or be satisfied with a series of
separate agreements. As it happened, Gentz's draft declaration had in
the meantime been compromised by premature disclosure in the press
and an ensuing debate in the House of Commons that cast doubt on
Britain's willingness to assume permanent commitments on the continent. With or without a formal guarantee, however, a grand treaty,
which associated all parties to it with all its parts, would be a useful
instrument implying, if not decreeing a universal obligation to maintain
it. Wellington grasped at this solution, while Metternich and Hardenberg viewed it as an essential first step toward something more binding,
preferably an article of guarantee in the treaty itself. Talleyrand cautioned against anything that might delay a settlement but was in principle likewise positive. The Russians, on the other hand, persistently
favored separate treaties, for reasons not readily discernible inasmuch
as they continued to support a declaration of guarantee. Among their

[73] Fred. to Winz., 23 Feb. 1815, extract in Pfister, *Lage der Verbündeten*, 334f.
[74] Olshausen, *Stellung der Grossmächte*, 133f.; protocol of five-power conference of
6 Mar. 1815, d'Angeberg, *Congrès*, III, 896–899; Talley. to Louis, 7 March 1815,
Talleyrand, *Memoirs*, III, 68.

concerns were probably uncertainty about the Porte's relationship to the settlement, the possibility of external interference with a Polish constitution, and an uneasy feeling that Britain was seeking to freeze the European order only to enhance her freedom of action in the non-European world, which was peculiarly and overwhelmingly hers. (She had, in fact, recently concluded a mutual assistance pact with Persia.) However that may be, the concept of a comprehensive treaty at length carried, and the conference ended with the appointment of an editorial committee charged with pulling the bewildering array of articles, protocols, and conventions into a coherent whole. Gentz, Anstett, and J. B. de la Besnardière were the principal members.[75]

The meeting did not adjourn till 3:00 a.m.; only then could Metternich climb the stairs to his private quarters, thankful once more that his valet had standing orders not to disturb his sleep in the early morning hours. This time, however, the servant awakened him at 6:00 with an urgent dispatch. What could be so pressing about a message from the Austrian consul general in Livorno, he wondered, and closed his eyes again. Still, sleep, once interrupted, would not return, he wrote years later, and at 7:30 he reached for the dispatch on his night table. Napoleon, it said briefly, had disappeared from Elba and could not be found.[76]

[75] Protocol of 6 March 1815, d'Angeberg, *Congrès*, III, 896–899; Gentz to Karadja, 26 June 1815, *Dépêches inédites*, I, 161f.; Webster, *Castlereagh*, I, 431f.; and tsar's instructions for all Russian missions, 25 May 1815, text in Schilder, *Imperator Aleksandr*, III, 540–548.

[76] Metternich, "Autobiographische Denkschrift," *NP*, I, 209f. In this retrospective account Metternich mistakenly recalled Genoa as the point of origin.

CHAPTER XII

THE IMPACT OF THE

100 DAYS

CONTINUING his reminiscences, Metternich recalled how that morning he hastily dressed and dashed across the Ballhausplatz to inform the emperor, who then ordered him to convey the news to the tsar and the king of Prussia. It was then eight o'clock. In the next hour, striding through the corridors of the Hofburg, he carried out his mission, returned to the chancellery to meet Schwarzenberg at nine and the allied ministers at ten. By this time couriers were on their way in all directions to alert the commanders in the field. Francis, without consulting Schwarzenberg, personally ordered General Count Heinrich Bellegarde in Italy to use his force of 70,000 to destroy Napoleon with all dispatch should he land there. At the same time another Austrian army of 60,000, already headed for Italy to intimidate Murat, was ordered to step up the pace. Similarly, the Prussian general, Emil von Kleist, commander of a composite so-called federal corps at Coblenz, who had just begun to furlough his troops, was directed to bring them back. Comparable instructions went to the British troops in Belgium while the tsar ordered his army in Poland to head for Germany. In less than an hour, Metternich boasted, the decision for war had been made.[1]

This remark must not be taken literally. It was rather an exercise of retrospective license, honestly indulged, perhaps, but still compressing the events of weeks and wishfully emphasizing that he had never wavered in his determination to destroy the Corsican. The measures were precautionary and could be no more as long as Napoleon's intentions and even his whereabouts were unknown. Meanwhile, a British report corroborated the event, and in the midst of doubt the ministers deemed it unwise to alarm the congress. No announcement was made. Neither the *Wiener Zeitung* nor the *Oesterreichischer Beobachter* carried the news for another week. Even Gentz, who called on Metternich that morning, only received the news later from Humboldt. It was business as usual that day.[2]

As planned, Metternich convened the Conference of Five and re-

---

[1] Metternich, *NP*, I, 210; Schwarz. to Francis, 13 Mar. 1815, Klinkowström, *Oesterreichs Theilnahme*, 829–831; Talley. to Louis, 7 Mar. 1815, Talleyrand, *Memoirs*, III, 66–68; Hardenberg, "Tagebücher," 39.

[2] Bourgoing, *Vom Wiener Kongress*, 316; Gentz, *Tagebücher*, I, 363.

ported that Francis preferred to send a delegation, not his foreign minister alone, to cope with the king of Saxony in Pressburg. Accordingly Wellington and Talleyrand were appointed, restoring as a pressure group the partnership of 3 January and sparing Metternich a single-handed encounter with the king.[3] A grand fête, long planned by the court, likewise took place in the Redoutensaal, becoming a bourse for the exchange of facts and rumors. The pantomines went on but in front of long faces, loud whispering, and not a few outbursts of recriminations as to the blame for Napoleon's escape. It was the last significant fête of the congress, for Francis thereafter halted the court's festivities, and the nobility soberly followed the imperial example.[4]

In keeping with a common practice of those years, the delegation began the journey to Pressburg late the following night, arriving at its destination at 4:00 a.m. on 9 March. At noon Metternich presented the articles to Frederick Augustus, who passed them unopened to his first minister, Count Detlev von Einsiedel. Later the king received the envoys separately, insisting to each in turn that since he was no longer a prisoner, he was free to negotiate not merely the loose ends mentioned in the articles but the articles themselves. If he hoped in this way to divide his visitors, he failed. In further talks with Einsiedel the next day they unanimously declared that the terms were final and that the Prussian occupation would continue until they were accepted, Wellington maliciously adding a cautionary word against attaching any hope to Bonaparte. Another day passed, and as Metternich and his colleagues prepared to leave, Einsiedel arrived with the king's answer: a formal note repeating all the old arguments for his innocence and demanding that his plenipotentiary be admitted as an equal to renegotiate the settlement from the beginning. Dumbfounded by both the substance and the form, the envoys replied in kind, hastily drafting a note deploring the king's addiction "to hopes that can never be realized." A little after noon they departed for Vienna, Metternich perhaps ruminating along the way that it was easier to do business with the load-bearing members of the system than with the Max Josephs and Frederick Augustuses of this world. A few hours later they reached the city and learned that on 1 March Napoleon had landed on the coast of France.[5]

[3] Protocol of 7 March 1815, d'Angeberg, Congrès, III, 899; Talley. to Louis as per n. 1 above.

[4] Bourgoing, Vom Wiener Kongress, 338; Adalbert, Max. I Joseph, 708–710; and McGuigan, Duchess, 444–446, who summarizes the vast memoir literature.

[5] Mett. to Francis, 10 Mar. 1815, HHSA, StK., Vorträge, Cart. 197, pp. 325 and 327; Talley. to Louis, 12 Mar. 1815, Talleyrand, Memoirs, III, 70; Well. to Castle., 12 Mar. 1815, Wellington, Supplementary Despatches, IX, 588–590; texts of Einsiedel's

With the major uncertainty eliminated, planning could proceed. That same day, though before Wellington's return, Schwarzenberg had already met with Knesebeck and Wolkonsky to plan a deployment of armies to meet all contingencies, for no one knew if Napoleon would swiftly succeed or fail in France or plunge the country into protracted civil war. Because Murat was also an uncertain factor, the Austrian forces, now numbering about 150,000, were to remain in Italy. At the other end of the line Kleist's corps, the Austrian garrison at Mainz, and units of several small states were to join the British, Hanoverian, and Dutch units near Namur under Wellington's command. A third army under Schwarzenberg was to be formed on the Upper Rhine. Its eventual strength was to be 200,000, but because of Austria's distance from the scene, its initial size was calculated at half that number, consisting almost entirely of units from Bavaria, Württemberg, and Baden.[6] Later the arrival of Austrian troops reduced the disparity, but the Austrian complement, even when it reached 100,000, was never more than half. Thus, the effectiveness of this main force was from the outset heavily dependent on the South German states, whose political leverage was amplified accordingly. Their loyalty was not in doubt—Max Joseph, Frederick, and Grand Duke Charles were too terrified of Napoleon's vengeance to stray from the protection of the tsar—but they were now in a position to drive hard bargains when it came to subsidies, strength of contingents, and, as we shall see, the final constitution of the Bund.[7]

Alexander, meanwhile, provided an anxious moment when he offered himself as generalissimo of all allied forces, but Metternich and Wellington the day after their return from Pressburg talked him out of the notion and induced him to accept instead a supreme council of the tsar, the king of Prussia, and Schwarzenberg, as in the previous campaign. More serious was the problem of the Russian army itself. These troops were farther removed than Austria's, presenting the prospect that they would reach the Rhine in full vigor after all the others, Napoleon's included, had been battered by combat. When the generals assigned the Russian forces a reserve position in Württemberg, Metternich implored Francis at least to keep them off Austrian soil. In the end, the imperatives of military sense decreed differently, but the terms of their transit through Bohemia, negotiated some weeks later, re-

---

note of 11 Mar. 1815 and reply by Metternich et al. in d'Angeberg, Congrès, III, 908–910. Also Kohlschmidt, Sächsische Frage, 126f.

[6] Protocol of conference of 11 Mar. 1815, PRO, F.O. 92/14 (annexed to Well. to Castle., 18 Mar. 1815); Well. to Castle., 12 Mar. 1815, Webster, BD, 312.

[7] Max Joseph to Montgelas, 21 Mar. 1815, quoted in Adalbert, Max I. Joseph, 710; Münster to Duke of Cambridge, 19 Mar. 1815, NSHSA, Hanover, Cal. Br. 24, no. 5027; Hölzle, Württemberg im Zeitalter, 169f.

stricted their movement to a narrow corridor heavily patrolled by Austrian units, and subjected their provisioning to unusually severe regulation.[8]

The tsar's bid for the supreme command had been handily parried. More difficult for Metternich were the importunities of Talleyrand, who from the first had demanded that the congress declare Bonaparte an outlaw and offer Louis XVIII all help necessary to preserve his throne. Such a measure was obviously premature as long as Napoleon's destination was unknown, but when the news of the landing arrived, Talleyrand was ready with a draft, which under the circumstances was difficult to ignore without putting at risk all the progress the congress had made. The problem was how to support the king without condemning the man who was still the son-in-law of the Austrian emperor and by some in Vienna, including Gentz, considered an acceptable and perhaps a superior alternative to the Bourbons. By this standard the French draft, which virtually called Napoleon a wild beast and invited any peasant lad or manic to shoot him down at sight, was impossible.[9]

Compromising, Metternich on 12 March before the Committee of Eight agreed to a declaration, but had Gentz compose a new version for submission the next day. The latter made Napoleon out to be a mere disturber of the peace, toned down the emphasis on legitimacy, and centered mainly on the powers' determination at all events to uphold the Treaty of Paris. In two stormy sessions the next day, first of the five powers, then of the eight, the debate continued, Talleyrand still insisting on including what Wellington denounced as the right to murder for private sport, Wessenberg joining Gentz in repeated efforts to moderate the document and keep open as many options as possible. In the final text, adopted at midnight, twenty people shouting at once, according to Humboldt, Napoleon was said by his illegal actions to have "placed himself beyond the pale of civil and social relations" and "delivered himself up to public justice." This was still strong language, implying (as Metternich admitted to Marie Louise) that if captured in France, Napoleon might be tried and executed, but it did not put a bounty on his head. The Austrians, resorting to a strategem useful in the past, also managed to have the declaration published not as an independent manifesto but as part of the protocol, a less binding

[8] Well. to Castle., 12 Mar. 1815, Webster, *BD*, 312f.; Mett. to Francis, 12 Mar. 1815, cited by Arneth, *Wessenberg*, 273; text of transit convention of 23 May 1815 in Martens, *Traités par la Russie*, III, 194–206; Schwarzenberg, *Schwarzenberg*, 369f.; Münster to Prince Regent, 24 Apr. 1815, NSHSA, Hanover, Des. 92, XLI, No. 112, vol. II; and Mett. to Francis, HHSA, StK., Vorträge, Cart. 198, pp. 92–98.

[9] Gentz to Karadja, 24 Apr. 1815, "Vertrauliche Denkschrift," Klinkowström, *Oesterreichs Theilnahme*, 596f. This disptach, highly critical of Metternich, was not seen by the latter till years later, after Gentz's death.

expression of the powers' thinking at the time. So fine did the issue become that Talleyrand attached importance to drawing an inked line between the declaration and the rest of the protocol, and this was done. Several weeks later, when Louis had actually been ousted, there was general sentiment for a new declaration expressing the allies' willingness to accept any regime but Bonaparte, and Metternich at first agreed. The difficulty of drafting truly neutral language, however—Clancarty wanted to encourage the legitimitists, while the tsar and Talleyrand favored the so-called "Jacobins" around Fouché—caused him to resist any declaration, and in this he succeeded. As a result, the declaration of 13 March, with its noncommittal nod to the Bourbons, remained the last word and suited Metternich's tentative views well.[10]

For all the acrimony attending its drafting, the declaration for the time being cleared the air and promoted a new spirit of cooperation. At Francis's bidding the tsar ended his personal vendetta with Metternich—as a matter of Christian forgiveness, the ruler explained, still accepting no blame.[11] Hardenberg resumed negotiations with Marschall of Nassau and began to press Hesse-Cassel to surrender Hanau to facilitate the settlement with Bavaria. He also confessed to Gärtner, on the day the Württemberg diet was to convene, that apart from polite appeals to King Frederick, the powers were helpless to interfere.[12] Talleyrand too made a contribution, on 18 March allowing the Conference of Five to award the Valteline to Austria.[13] That same day, spurred by news that a royal regiment had deserted before Grenoble, Metternich, Wellington, Hardenberg, and Nesselrode agreed in principle to renew the Treaty of Chaumont, thus damping out the last dim embers of the combination of 3 January.[14]

It was easier to hail the treaty than to draft concrete articles adapting it to the situation at hand. Wellington wanted to include William of Orange (who took the title of king for the purpose on 16 March) as a principal signatory but yielded when Metternich explained the troubles there would be with Max Joseph and the other monarchs of second rank. The continental powers demanded subsidies, more even than

[10] *Ibid.*, 597; Talley. to Louis, 12 and 14 Mar. 1815, Talleyrand, *Memoirs*, III, 69–75; protocols of the Committee of Eight, 12 and 13 Mar. 1815 and text of declaration, d'Angeberg, *Congrès*, III, 910–913; Arneth, *Wessenberg*, 270; Humboldt to Caroline, 14 Mar. 1815, *Briefe*, IV, 494f.; G. de Bertier de Sauvigny, *Metternich et la France après le Congrès de Vienne*, 3 vols. (Paris, 1968–1971), I, 14f.

[11] Stein, "Tagebüch," *Briefe*, V, 374; Metternich, *NP*, I, 374.

[12] Well. to Castle., 18 Mar. 1815, Wellington, *Supplementary Despatches*, IX, 603; Hoff, *Mediatisiertenfrage*, 101.

[13] Protocol in d'Angeberg, *Congrès*, III, 930–932.

[14] Well. to Castle., 18 Mar. 1815, Arthur Wellesley, First Duke of Wellington, *The Dispatches of Field Marshal the Duke of Wellington* ... ed. Colonel Gurwood, 2nd ed. in 8 vols. (London, 1844–1847), VIII, 4–5.

the 5 million pounds they had received the year before, but Wellington had no authority to promise anything.[15] All could agree on upholding the integrity of the Treaty of Paris and the arrangements made at the Congress of Vienna, but did this formula include the maintenance of Louis XVIII, or if necessary, his restoration as implied in the declaration of 13 March? As before, Metternich opposed such a commitment simply because he had not yet decided what was best.[16] Until his secret soundings in France had produced more tangible information, he would go no further than language resembling that of the original Chaumont pact, which left open the question of the postwar government. In the end, however, the main obstacle to the conclusion of the treaty was not Metternich or even a matter of grand policy but a furious dispute over the command and deployment of the contingents of the German states.

At a military council held on 17 March in Wellington's quarters and attended by the tsar, Schwarzenberg won a crucial point for Austria by gaining consent to the addition of Hesse-Darmstadt's 8,000 troops to his army of the Upper Rhine, an important step toward keeping this pivotal state free of the Prussian system as Metternich had always tried to do. Only in this way can one account for his willingness then to assign all the North German states except Hanover to Prussian command, an arrangement that could become the foundation for permanent Kreise.[17] But Wellington protested and refused to sign the protocol. At first his objection was probably in the main to the meagerness of the reinforcements allotted to his command. Then Münster, putting the matter in historical perspective, convinced him that Prussia's true aim was "to procure for herself a military supremacy over Northern Germany," and Hardenberg virtually corroborated the point himself by offering reinforcements from the *Prussian* army if the small states went to Blücher,[18] a clear case of putting politics ahead of military efficiency. The matter was further complicated by the question of subsidies. It was already understood that in the treaty being drafted Britain might fulfill her manpower obligation in part with monies used to subsidize foreign troops, and Wellington's idea, traditionally British, was to hire mercenaries from the smaller states to fight with his army

[15] Sherwig, *Guineas and Gunpowder*, 334f.
[16] Bertier, *Metternich et al France*, I, 13–16.
[17] Protocol of military conference enclosed in Well. to Castle., 18 Mar. 1815, PRO, F.O. 92/14.
[18] Münster to Prince Regent, 25 Mar. 1815, Münster, *Political Sketches*, 231f. Cf. Humboldt's instruction for General Friedrich Wilhelm von Zastrow, 31 Mar. 1815: "Prussia's sights must be directed at tying the princes of North Germany to her not only as closely but also as exclusively as possible," to be sure, by persuasion. Humboldt, *Gesammelte Schriften*, XI, 325f.

in Flanders. Since the British deficit was calculated at about 100,000 men, he would in this fashion come into command of almost all the North German contingents, especially as most states dreaded subordination to Prussia and desired as well to be in direct contact with the source of the money. Indignantly Hardenberg countered with the familiar thesis that the German states, being bound by the accession treaties, were not free to flock to the highest bidder but must conform to whatever plan the allied powers concerted among themselves. Wellington, who feared that those states would be sullen and ineffective partners unless they were free to bargain, replied with the equally extreme contention that until the Bund was established, they were completely free, even to stay neutral if they chose. In this spirit he employed Münster to urge Hesse-Cassel and Brunswick to apply for union with British forces.[19]

Though only a bystander, Metternich, whatever he thought of the duke's argument, supported him on the issue. The states concerned were the ones that were to constitute his phalanx in the diet of the Bund, and he seems to have promised them his best efforts to save their contingents from the Prussians.[20] For once, however, we may reasonably prefer Hardenberg's interpretation of the treaties, for this time "the independence of Germany" really was involved. The chancellor, in any case, stood his gound, and Wellington, alarmed that the issue was impeding the conclusion of the treaty of alliance and his departure for the front, finally accepted a compromise. Instead of exporting their contingents to the British army as mercenaries, the several states were to accede to the coalition as allies, each undertaking to provide a stipulated number of troops in return for conventional subsidies provided by England but administered jointly by Austria, Prussia, and Russia. The distribution of the contingents was to be arranged by four-power agreement.[21]

Although this distribution and the amounts of subsidies, both for the small states and the continental powers, remained unfixed, it was now possible to proceed with the treaty of alliance, which was initialed on 25 March.[22] By its terms each of the four powers pledged 150,000 troops to enforce the settlements made at Paris and Vienna, to act in the sense of the declaration of 13 March, and to place Bonaparte "beyond all possibility" of exercising power in France. This delicate and allusive wording bound the allies to aid Louis XVIII as long as he

[19] *Ibid.*; Humboldt, *Gesammelte Scriften*, xi, 325f. Humboldt to Caroline, 18 and 30 Mar. 1815, *Briefe*, iv, 497f. and 515–517; Well. to Castle., 25 Mar. 1815, PRO, F.O. 92/14, pp. 234–236. Extract in Webster, *BD*, 316f.

[20] Rosenkrantz, *Journal*, 16 Apr. 1815, 227f.

[21] Well. to Castle., 25 Mar. 1815, PRO, F.O. 92/14, pp. 234–236.

[22] Text in d'Angeberg, *Congrès*, ii, 975f.

was in power but not necessarily to restore him afterwards, a point that both Metternich and Castlereagh later made explicit in declarations accompanying their ratifications. All the sovereigns of Europe were to be invited to accede, including Louis. As previously agreed, Britain was authorized to fulfill her obligation by subsidies, but at the request of the continental powers the provision was kept secret, presumably to prevent a stampede of the small states to attach their troops to the Anglo-Dutch army. Regarding subsidies to the powers themselves, Wellington could do no more than promise his best efforts in London. Disappointed, his allies, the same who a few weeks before had been threatening to fight each other with or without aid, now declared in a separate note that without proper assistance they could not fulfill their obligations under the treaty. As a stopgap, meanwhile, Metternich urged the emperor to raise money in Hungary, always an act of last resort in Habsburg statecraft, almost like dealing with Bavaria.[23]

Metternich seems to have joined the condemnation of Napoleon as a matter of course. Yet, given his patient and protracted backing the year before, the still unsevered marriage bond with Marie Louise, and an eloquent formulation by Gentz of a contrary point of view, the act reflected a deliberate and momentous decision all the same. According to Gentz, whatever justification there might have been to condemn Napoleon as long as he remained "a rebellious adventurer," was gone now that he was attracting responsible men to his cause, winning over the army, and obviously fulfilling "the secret desires of almost all the French people." (We have come to expect surprises at the congress, but with Gentz's espousal of self-determination we reach new heights of incredulity.) Britain, he went on, had her Netherlands buffer to defend and Prussia her ill-gotten gains in the Rhineland, but what did Austria have to lose if Napoleon accepted reasonable limits?[24] What Gentz forgot was that during Metternich's grand mediation of 1813, which offered Napoleon the Rhine frontier, Austria held the balance of military power. Now, given the weakness of France, even if momentary, there was no chance that Britain and Prussia would yield. War was certain, and even if Austria remained neutral, Napoleon was likely to lose and Austria herself to be ignored at the peace table. As it turned out, he did lose and without Austria and Russia being seriously engaged. Against all the hazards connected with this course of events, most particularly the effects on the former Rheinbund courts, Met-

[23] D'Angeberg, *Congrès*, III, 971; Hudelist to the State Conference, 24 Mar. 1815, HHSA, Kabinetsarchiv, Konferenz-Akten a. Cart. 1812–1815, no. 109.
[24] Gentz to Karadja, 24 Apr. 1815, "Vertrauliche Denkschrift," Klinkowström, *Oesterreichs Theilnahme*, 596–626.

ternich preferred to preserve the fruits of the Treaty of Paris and the Congress of Vienna, sour though some of them may have been.

Ironically, the first state to accede to the treaty was France, Talleyrand on 27 March chortling that she thereby joined the alliance of Chaumont. It was none too soon, for the next day the news arrived that Napoleon had triumphantly entered Paris. In the next few days the invitations of accession went out to the other states, separate ones to all the kingdoms, a collective one to the Association of Princes and Free Cities, the latter containing, in response to an earlier note from the association, assurances that deliberations on the German constitution would resume immediately, the small states participating and at least the bases being adopted before the congress adjourned. Similar assurances were extended to Baden and Hesse-Darmstadt, which, safely in the ranks of Schwarzenberg's army, did not wish to jeopardize their relative independence by continued association with the smaller states of the North.[25]

The treaty signed and the king of France retreating to the Belgian frontier, Wellington left Vienna on the 29th, entrusting political affairs to Clancarty, military matters to Lord William Shaw Cathcart. His departure, together with the sudden undercutting of Talleyrand's position, left Metternich more than ever preeminent in allied councils, the State Chancellery increasingly the center of activity. With war now a certainty and only its location in doubt, agreement on the deployment of armies was imperative. On 31 March another military council met in Schwarzenberg's office and included for the first time Marshal Wrede and Crown Prince William of Württemberg. Believing that the size of their contingents would govern the degree of their independence, Wrede offered a contingent of 60,000, William one of 25,000, both approximately double the normal quota of 1 percent of population. Besides his own contingent William was to command 8,000 Badenese and a small Austrian detachment, also of 8,000. By now 40,000 more Austrians were available, and after a futile attempt by Cathcart to transfer the Darmstadt contingent to Wellington, another 8,000 from this source.

Concerning the North German contingents, the Anglo-Prussian dispute continued in full fury, Cathcart pleading that British subsidies entitled Wellington to have his pick, Knesebeck insisting that only by serving with Prussia could the troops feel that they were fighting for Germany. He eventually yielded on Hanover, Brunswick, Oldenburg, and the Hanseatic cities, but regarding Nassau, Hesse-Cassel, and Sax-

[25] Texts of protocols of five-power conferences of 27 and 28 Mar. 1815, d'Angeberg, *Congrès*, III, 978–981; notes of invitation, 29 Mar. 1815, *ibid.*, III, 986f. and IV, 1895.

ony the argument was so fierce that the issue was passed on to the Conference of Five for political resolution. There on 1 April, it was finally settled, Prussia obtaining Hesse-Cassel, Wellington Nassau, part of whose troops were already serving with the Dutch under the occupation arrangements. The Saxon question as usual was more complex. Because Prussia still occupied the entire country and the Saxon army was already serving with Kleist's corps in the Rhineland, it seemed natural to continue this arrangement. On the other hand, the reliability of the unit was in question, because Frederick Augustus, in his sparring with the allies, refused to release any troops from their oath to him; if free to do so, he would have gladly assigned them all to Wellington. In the end, it was mainly because of this low morale that Hardenberg offered a compromise: despite Prussia's de facto control, the troops from royal Saxony would be released to Wellington and those from Prussian Saxony would go to Blücher. This solution Clancarty accepted, but mainly because he misunderstood the numbers involved. Wellington, when he heard the outcome, was disappointed, complaining that "Metternich has as usual left us in the lurch notwithstanding his promises." However that may be, the latter for his purposes could well be satisfied that Hardenberg was denied control of three contingents (i.e., Hesse-Darmstadt, Nassau, and royal Saxony) that he had always assigned to the Prussian Kreise, and for this reason Humboldt, at the end of the meeting, moved that the scheme "shall have no bearing on the German federation or prejudice anything in this regard." For Metternich that was fair enough, and the motion was adopted. Precedents are not necessarily eliminated by denying their existence.[26]

Among the powers almost everything was settled except subsidies. Their task now was to obtain the accession of all the other states to the alliance, and this entailed laborious negotiations regarding the size of contingents, the amounts of subsidies when available, and regulations governing supply and procurement in the states that had allied troops deployed on or in transit through their territory. To complicate the situation still more, the small states, as we have seen, made their accession contingent on the establishment of the Bund, at least in sufficient scope to assure their integrity and sovereignty, whereas the South German states, the prospective core of Schwarzenberg's army, refused to discuss the Bund until a territorial settlement had been reached.

[26] Protocol of 1 Apr. 1815, d'Angeberg, *Congrès*, III, 1000–1001; Cathcart to Well., 1 Apr. 1815 and to Castle. 1 Apr. 1815, Clancarty to Well., 1 Apr. 1815, and Well. to Clancarty, 9 Apr. 1815, all in Wellington, *Supplementary Despatches*, x, 11–14 and 48; and Julius von Pflugk-Harttung, "Die Gegensätze zwischen England and Preussen wegen der Bundestruppen 1815," *Forschungen zur brandenburgischen und preussischen Geschichte*, XXIV, no. 2 (1911), 125–179.

For Metternich everything hinged once more on Bavaria, and never had Wrede held a stronger hand.

As noted, the marshal was able to offer the coalition what amounted to a double contingent of 60,000 men. With such numbers he once more hoped to elbow his way into the ranks of the powers, avoiding the role of mere accessory by signing separate treaties of alliance with each of the four powers. He also hoped to obtain an independent command that would enable him to maneuver his corps to Bavarian advantage, even to seize by force, if necessary, the territories she claimed. As a start he proposed to Metternich that Bavaria should take over the garrisoning of Mainz. With such fantasies in his head he contemptuously refused even to read a new Austrian territorial plan because it still demanded all of Salzburg. That was on 19 March. On the 22nd, in the midst of the furor over the German contingents, Metternich decided to face again the rage of Schwarzenberg, Stadion, and the emperor by reviving the project to partition the province. Under existing circumstances, he pleaded, one could hardly expect the other powers to prolong this unsettling matter as long as they had already met Austria's treaty claims, and Wellington was now arguing that Bavaria was militarily more exposed than Austria in the Salzburg region. Francis reluctantly acquiesced, and Wessenberg returned to his charts to fill in the details.[27]

The result of these labors was a plan that offered Bavaria, besides two-thirds of Salzburg; Hanau; Isenburg; parts of Fulda; and a compact amalgam of territory taken from Württemberg, Hesse-Darmstadt, and Baden; most importantly much of Baden's Neckar circle, the rough equivalent of the old right-bank Palatinate. Because the plan offered no frontage on the Rhine, however, and counted mediatized souls at one-half rather than one-third, Wrede still balked, in hopes of adding Mannheim and Heidelberg to the booty. As additional leverage he refused, despite Metternich's pleas, to resume negotiations on the Bund until the territorial question was settled.[28]

This time the blunt marshal and his recalcitrant monarch overreached themselves. In their single-minded concentration on Bavaria they had forgotten that not Austria alone but all the powers were impatient to get on with the war, with the accession treaties, and with the Bund. Reluctantly Metternich now turned to them, reasonably confident that as they had been favorably disposed before, they would

[27] Landauer, "Die Einverleibung Salzburgs," 6; Wrede to Max Joseph, 19 Mar. 1815, cited in Quint, *Souveränitätsbegriff*, 336f.; Winter, *Wrede als Berater*, 225; Rosenkrantz, *Journal*, 205; Mett. to Francis, 22 Mar. 1815, HHSA, StK., Kongressakten, Cart. 8, pp. 40-42.
[28] Sahrmann, *Pfalz oder Salzburg?*, 48f.; Winter, *Wrede als Berater*, 226; Wrede to Mett., 1 Apr. 1815, HHSA, StK., Kongressakten, Cart. 6, p. 483.

be more so now in view of Austria's latest concession. On 3 April he formally laid the Wessenberg project before the Conference of Five, finally making the issue a European affair. Generally his expectations were justified but not without another grating concession: the city of Mainz was to be awarded to Hesse-Darmstadt, the fortress, however, becoming a federal base with a garrison drawn from Darmstadt, Hesse-Cassel, Nassau, and Prussia, the last appointing the governor as well. On the face of it this was more than a concession; it was the abandonment of a principle steadfastly held to through all the storms of the past year.[29]

Metternich himself later explained that the arrangement was now tolerable because the fortifications of Hanau "assured coverage to sourthern Germany and the line of the Main."[30] To this one might add Schwarzenberg's view that without left-bank territory Bavaria was not so vulnerable to intimidation from Mainz.[31] More importantly it could be argued that Prussian command of a mixed garrison on Hessian soil would not confer the same advantages as a Prussian garrison on Prussian soil, Hardenberg's original aim with or without federal status, which he had once described as a last resort. Finally, there is evidence that Metternich accepted the arrangement only because resistance at home, particularly from Schwarzenberg, for the time being prevented the solution that he now preferred: the acquisition of Mainz and the left-bank Palatinate by Austria! We shall return to this question.[32] In any case, for the duration of the war the Austro-Prussian garrison was to remain, Archduke Charles, after "very warm discussion," was appointed governor; and the base was to support the several contingents according to need and not the Prussian army alone as Knesebeck had demanded.[33] In a parallel action the conference resolved that the basis for raising contingents was to be the existing, not

[29] Protocol of 3 Apr. 1815, d'Angeberg, *Congrès*, III, 1012f.

[30] Mett. to Francis, 17 Nov. 1815, HHSA, StK., Vorträge, Cart. 200, pp. 67–76.

[31] Schwarzenberg's "Allgemeine Uebersicht der gegenwärtigen militärischen Gränzverhältnisse der . . . Monarchie," HHSA, StK., Kongressakten, Cart. 8, pp. 54–62.

[32] On Schwarzenberg the evidence is contradictory, for he always considered Mainz "the key to Germany," which must be kept from Prussia at all costs, and in the fall of 1815 urged that Austria take it over. In the spring of 1815, however, he considered the federal-fortress concept inherently unsound and Mainz too distant to be of use to Austria. (See his "Bemerkungen über Bundesfestungen und Bundes-Generäle," 13 Feb. 1815, HHSA, StK., Kongressakten, Cart. 6, pp. 448–452.) Moreover, when Metternich gained Prussian consent on 10 June to Austria's sole possession, he still had to make this contingent on an Austrian decision to take left-bank territory, proof that Metternich wanted it but others in Vienna did not. See below pp. 398f. in Chap. XIII.

[33] Protocol of 3 Apr. 1815, d'Angeberg, *Congrès*, III, 1012f.; Winter, *Wrede als Berater*, 226; Well. to Castle., 6 Apr. 1815, Wellington, *Supplementary Despatches*, x, 25f.

the future territorial order. For the time being at least Austria would control the right bank of the Mosel.[34]

In the next two days Metternich faced Wrede again and in the presence of the other allied ministers conveyed the terms. The marshal was still dissatisfied, reducing by 20,000 or so the population he would cede to Austria, valuing souls on the mediatized lands at one-third, and again demanding Mannheim and Heidelberg, as well as Ellwangen from Württemberg.[35] Now even the tsar was exasperated at the massive assault on his protégés and on 5 April lent his support to a compromise often whispered before but not really attractive to anyone. This was to limit Bavarian gains in the Palatinate for the present but provide for the reversion of the entire Palatinate on both sides of the Rhine upon the death of Grand Duke Charles, which would terminate the Zähringen line.[36] Although Max Joseph continued to haggle, the intervention of the tsar was the turning point, and Metternich felt confident enough at last to threaten Wrede with the forcible occupation of the lands he claimed in Salzburg and the Inn and Hausrück districts. On 10 April the Conference of Five adopted a new plan incorporating these adjustments and agreed that Wessenberg and Nesselrode should meet separately with Wrede to present it as an ultimatum of the powers. The following day the bargain was sealed—provisionally to be sure, pending the outcome of negotiations with the other states affected.

These talks were entrusted to Wessenberg, Nesselrode, and Humboldt, who spent the next week trying to complete the jigsaw puzzle only to conclude that there were not enought souls left to do justice to everybody, especially as mediatized lands had been discounted so heavily by Bavaria. Their final plan, much simplified, consisted of dividing the remaining left-bank territory between Baden and Hesse-Darmstadt, the latter, as observed above, obtaining the city of Mainz as compensation for Westphalia. The grand dukes, however, Charles and Louis, refused to accept the net losses involved as well as compensation on the increasingly precarious left bank and demanded that a settlement be postponed till after the war. Negotiations continued nonetheless, at least with Darmstadt, partly because Türckheim again ignored his orders, partly because Hardenberg was especially eager to wring final title to Westphalia from Louis as soon as possible and made Metternich, as the special advocate of Darmstadt, responsible. Meanwhile, rather than delay the Bavarian settlement, the powers, in a

[34] Well. to Castle., 6 Apr. 1815, Wellington, *Supplementary Despatches*, x, 25.

[35] Protocols of 4 and 5 Apr., 1815, d'Angeberg, *Congrès*, III, 1013–1016 and 1021–1023.

[36] Note, Nessel. to Wrede, 5 Apr. 1815, *VPR*, VIII, 264; Sahrmann, *Pfalz oder Salzburg?*, 49; Winter, *Wrede als Berater*, 226f.

convention signed on 23 April, affirmed the above awards for Bavaria but made the settlement provisional. Wrede was satisfied and departed the next day to take command of his corps, but neither his government nor any of the powers thought enough of the pact to ratify it. Whether Metternich had foreseen this result we do not know, but its effect was to leave open the possibility of a better settlement later, including, as we shall see, the acquisition of Mainz by Austria.[37]

Commenting on the Bavarian affair, Münster reported that "Austria shows in it a moderation which approaches feebleness and which has injured Prince Metternich in public opinion."[38] This was no doubt a common impression, for Wrede was personally unpopular, and the Bavarian claims, asserted so pugnaciously, touched many raw nerves. As we know, however, disappointing results must always be measured against the alternatives available. Under the circumstances Metternich had to choose between throwing Austrian capital into the solution and simply violating treaties, which, short of a unilateral act of force, could only be done with the firm support of the other powers. But what did he encounter in them? The tsar limited the despoliation of Baden and Württemberg; Hardenberg protected Hesse-Cassel, not to mention his own gains beyond the Mosel; Talleyrand had neither the influence nor the desire to take a stand; and Clancarty played a singularly passive role, not even signing the convention, though he approved it. If the powers had recognized the *justice* of the Austrian position as early as 1 March, not until the tsar's intervention of 5 April did they signal Wrede that he had gone far enough and Metternich that he might threaten force. Just as Castlereagh was the principal architect of the new Saxony so was Alexander the final arbiter of the Bavarian claims.[39]

A full appreciation of Wrede's bargaining power, however, requires an examination of the concurrent attempts to bring Bavaria into the alliance. When Metternich courteously informed him on 28 March that the invitations to accede had been prepared, the marshal blustered that Bavaria would only negotiate as a principal party and curtly asked him not to mention the word accession again; his official reply took the same position. Answering it, Metternich, who knew the difference between words and substance, asked him "to cooperate" with the allies, at the same time bluntly laying it down that the Bavarian corps would still be under Schwarzenberg's supreme command. Even so, Bavaria, several days later, was granted representation at Schwarzenberg's head-

[37] Protocol of 10 Apr. 1815, d'Angeberg, *Congrès*, III, 1054f.; Sahrmann, *Pfalz oder Salzburg?*, 49f.; Winter, *Wrede als Berater*, 227–230; Cf. Münster to Prince Regent, 13 Apr. 1815, Münster, *Political Sketches*, 244f.; Stein, "Tagebuch," *Briefe*, v, 384; and Dietrich, "Hessen-Darmstadt auf dem Wiener Kongress." 263–273.
[38] To the Prince Regent, 8 Apr. 1815, Münster, *Political Sketches*, 237.
[39] Cf. Clancarty to Castle., 8 Apr. 1815, PRO, F.O. 92/17, pp. 105–113.

quarters, the right to be consulted on strategy, and the use of Mainz as a supply depot. "A terrible period for Bavaria," Wrede reported in all seriousness.[40]

Nevertheless, when the marshal on 2 April came before the commission that had been appointed to process the accessions (Wessenberg, Cathcart, Nesselrode, and Humboldt), he arrived with a draft treaty that contained verbatim the articles of 25 March plus several more that included specified guarantees of Bavaria's territorial claims and her percentage of the British subsidies. This was no mere act of accession but a new treaty, which he meant to conclude separately with each of the powers.[41] Again the Conference of Five was called in. Metternich, who had earlier denied the Netherlands a similar right, now reversed himself, evidently concluding that he had more serious conflicts with Bavaria than a technicality that presented only abstract dangers. Clancarty disagreed, seeing endless wrangling ahead if each state was allowed to negotiate its way into the coalition—or, what he really meant, to practice blackmail with regard to subsidies. The dispute ended in compromise. Bavaria and all the other "kingly powers," as Clancarty called them, would join the alliance as principal parties with parallel treaties; all others would accede in the usual way. Wrede, however, was forced to drop the articles of special guarantee, receiving in their place official assurance that no secret engagments concerning Bavaria existed among the allies. On that basis he signed, significantly enough, with Russia on 6 April, the day after the tsar's intervention in the territorial question, and only on 15 April with the other three powers. The way cleared by Bavaria, the other kingdoms signed similar treaties in the next few weeks. Württemberg, eager not to be outclassed by her rival in the eyes of the tsar, likewise signed with Russia on 6 April but not until 30 May with Austria.[42]

Throughout the wrangling with Wrede Metternich was engaged in similarly frustrating negotiations with Schulenburg, who still represented the king of Saxony at the congress. Schulenburg himself was in poor health and considered the questionable advantages to be gained from stretching out the negotiations not worth the risk of antagonizing friendly powers. Frederick Augustus, however, the lonely, unyielding figure of the battlefield of Leipzig, was again determined to hold out as long as possible. Surrounded in Pressburg by optimists, buoyed up by an overwhelmingly anti-Prussian public opinion, and hopeful that

[40] Quint, *Souveränitätsbegriff*, 338f.; Bavarian convention with Austria, Prussia, and Russia, 2 Apr. 1815, text in Wellington, *Supplementary Despatches*, x, 109f.

[41] Clancarty to Castle., 3 Apr. 1815, PRO, F.O. 92/17, pp. 66–77.

[42] *Ibid.*, 66–77; three-power note to Bavaria, 6 Apr. 1815, *VPR*, VIII, 266; texts of accession treaties in Neumann, *Traités par l'Autriche*, II, 534–537.

rapidly unfolding events along the Rhine still might save his country, he doggedly refused to yield. Technically Metternich was involved only as a mediator, but more than the other allies he had an interest in ending the Prussian occupation and restraining the king from acts of defiance that might cost him his throne after all.[43]

The king, it must be said, conducted a skillful rear-guard action, exploiting to the full his power to refuse accession to the alliance and to release his lost subjects from their oaths. At length, however, the Conference of Five delivered an ultimatum, the penalty for refusal being the indefinite continuation of the occupation in the king's territory and the installation of normal civilian government in the Prussian share, a prospect that worried Metternich perhaps more than the king. Fortunately Frederick Augustus stopped short of that grim eventuality and on 1 May sent a special envoy, Fürchtegott von Globig, to assist with the negotiation. Wessenberg, Humboldt, and Capodistria were appointed as commissioners to represent the allies.[44]

In the meantime the embattled monarch had benefited from a flare-up of feuding between Hardenberg and Clancarty over the status of the Saxon army. Learning that the contingent assigned to Wellington was smaller and more demoralized than he had supposed, Clancarty on 23 April lodged a protest with the Conference of Five, insisting that the duke deserved better than "the picked and culled remains of the Royal Saxon corps."[45] As a remedy he proposed that all of the Saxons go to either Wellington or Blücher as a unit, and if the latter, that Britian would fill in with Portuguese and Danes, deducting the cost from Prussia's subsidies. Hardenberg proposed instead to transfer additional troops from ducal Saxony, and this was done. Tension was further eased by Blücher's willingness to draw his army closer to Wellington's, almost as if to make them a single force. Ironically, neither Saxon contingent ever saw action. Consciences troubled by the oath combined in early May with the pain of forced separation from old comrades to produce mutinies, and Blücher's firing squads finished off whatever fighting qualities were left.[46]

Sobered by this debacle and by the earlier ultimatum, Globig and Schulenburg settled down with the allied commissioners to complete

---

[43] Kohlschmidt, *Sächsische Frage*, 89 and 125–129.

[44] Protocols of 28 and 31 Mar., 1, 7, 13, 20, 27 Apr. and 1 May 1815, with supporting correspondence with Schulenberg, d'Angeberg, *Congrès*, III, 979–1131. Also Kohlschmidt, *Sächsische Frage*, 127–145; and Arneth, *Wessenberg*, I, 275.

[45] Clancarty to Well., 21 Apr. 1815, Wellington, *Supplementary Despatches*, X, 125–127; Clancarty's "observations," 23 Apr. 1815, d'Angeberg, *Congrès*, IV, 1898.

[46] Protocol of 23 Apr. 1815, d'Angeberg, *Congrès*, III, 1102; Hard. to Clancarty, 29 Apr. 1815, *ibid.*, IV, 1899f.; Clancarty to Well., 26 Apr. 1815, Wellington, *Supplementary Despatches*, X, 165; Pflugk-Harttung, "Gegensätze wegen der Bundestruppen," 149f.

the negotiation. On 18 May they at last signed the treaty that returned Frederick Augustus to his ancestral home, terminated his rights in ducal Saxony and Poland, and released his former subjects from their oaths. As for the army, enlisted men, if native Saxons, were to be posted according to their place of birth, officers and foreigners given a choice of service between the Saxon and Prussian armies. When the king joined the alliance on 27 May, he made the gesture of pledging 7,000 men, receiving in exchange a treaty almost identical to that accorded Bavaria.[47] To Metternich's satisfaction his troops soon replaced Prussia's on the Austrian frontier. He was once more truly a king, eligible by all standards observed so far to take a permanent seat on the First Council of the Bund.

As mentioned previously, the right of adhering to the alliance as a principal party was limited to the kingdoms of Europe, most of which signed treaties before Saxony did. Conscious of their inferiority, the lesser states were the more tenacious, hoping that the new accession treaties would guarantee sovereignty and integrity more forcibly than the old. To this end Baden and Hesse-Darmstadt, following the Bavarian example, rushed to offer contingents twice as large (16,000 and 8,000 respectively) as those in the previous campaign. Partly for this reason perhaps, their instruments of accession, signed in mid-May, guaranteed their political existence and a voice in those peace negotiations that concerned them, another burden heaped on Metternich's Bavarian problem.[48]

There remained the thirty some states belonging to the Association of Princes and Free Cities and representing a total force of 35,000 to 100,000, depending on the effort demanded. As they were required to sign a single collective treaty, no one state saw an advantage in fielding more than the 1 percent of population contributed in 1813. Since Hardenberg wished to impose the demanding Prussian standard of 3 percent, argument was lively until a compromise of 2 percent was adopted. Ideally the association would have preferred to deploy its contingents in one or two independent corps, but as we have seen, this matter was decided otherwise for them. The main concern of the small states, however, was the Bund, for only when they had ratified a constitution that guaranteed equality, integrity, and independence and recognized the sovereignty they thought they had received in the treaties of 1813—only then could they be sure that the projected deployment was not intended as their induction into permanent Kreise. On

[47] Texts of both treaties in d'Angeberg, *Congrès*, III, 1191–1200 and 1252f.
[48] Glaser, "Die badische Politik," 304–306; Dietrich, "Hessen-Darmstadt auf dem Wiener Kongress," 267–273. Texts of accession treaties in d'Angeberg, *Congrès*, III, 1178f. and 1220f.

24 April Metternich and Hardenberg issued an official declaration of their intention "to conclude the constitution of the German league" but this was not included in the treaty as one of the conditions of accession, nor was a guarantee given of political existence such as Baden and Darmstadt had obtained. With this exception the association's treaty, signed on 27 April, was almost identical to theirs.[49]

Now that the Bund was officially on the agenda, Metternich at last turned his attention back to this central problem. By now the files of the State Chancellery fairly bulged with petitions, memoranda, and declarations filed by the interested parties. There was the usual influx of appeals for the restoration of the Reich, including another, more constructive than most, from the ever hopeful Mecklenburg envoy, Leopold von Plessen.[50] The city council of Wetzlar, where the old imperial chamber court had once sat, filed a bid to locate the federal court there, citing as inducements the low cost of living, spacious buildings, fresh air, and devoted citizens. Among these last were former members of the court's legal staff, who were now eager to recover back pay and assure their pensions for the future. Another petitioner was Baron Alexander von Vrints-Berberich, the postal director of the princely house of Thurn und Taxis, once the official carrier of mails in the Reich. The larger German states now had their own postal systems, but Vrints-Berberich was determined to restore what franchises he could and protect the ones that were left, especially those in the free cities, whose magistrates were trying to wrest control for themselves, charging that the Thurn und Taxis rates were extortionate. Vrints also sought to reinstate a former contract to handle the German mail of Austria.[51]

The four deputies of the *Reichsritterschaft* were also prolific petitioners, but none more so than Count Edmund von Kesselstadt, representing the knights on the left bank of the Rhine. For them long years of French rule, which had converted fiefs into allodial estates held in fee simple and destroyed old deeds and charters, ruled out all prospects of restoration. Kesselstadt's constituents wanted the best of two worlds: to retain the advantages of freeholds but at the same time to obtain

---

[49] Assorted protocols and declarations in Klüber, *Acten*, IV, 390–438; Austro-Prussian declaration, *ibid.*, 425; text of treaty, d'Angeberg, *Congrès*, III, 1121–1125.

[50] "Allgemeine Betrachtungs-Punkte als Grundlagen des teutschen Staatenbundes," HHSA, StK., Deutsche Akten, Cart. 100, pp. 417–428, n.d. and no signature. Authorship derived from Stein to Plessen, 21 Mar. 1815, Stein, *Briefe*, v, 291.

[51] Memorials of 14 Jan. and 28 Mar. 1815, in Willy Real, "Von Bemühungen um die Errichtung eines Bundesgerichts zur Zeit des Wiener Kongresses," *Zeitschrift für die Geschichte des Oberrheins*, XLIX (1935), 222–225. Numerous petitions in HHSA, StK., Kongressakten, Cart. 8, "Postwesen," pp. 1–115. Also Josef K. Mayr, *Metternichs geheimer Briefdienst, Postlogen und Postkurse* (Vienna, 1935), 10–12 and 55f.

compensation for lost fees, dues, and services. At the time Metternich, with his eye on the left-bank Palatinate for Austria, might have been directly concerned, but as the province eventually went to Bavaria, it was mainly she and Prussia that later had to make invidious distinctions among their landholding subjects. This was one of the reasons why Humboldt stubbornly resisted Metternich's efforts to equate the imperial knights with the Standesherren.[52]

Immersed in grand affairs, Metternich probably did not read many such depositions. Still, he did not neglect them entirely, and continued to give audiences as time allowed. He was in steady contact with Consalvi, whom he assured in early February that the German Committee would indeed discuss church affairs on the basis of a collective concordat.[53] A month later he promised a delegation from the Frankfurt senate that the article on the Jews would satisfy everybody.[54] To a reminder from Friedrich Bertuch that the book dealers expected action on a federal copyright law recognizing the concept of literary property Metternich responded with an apology for the delays but promised early consideration of it.[55] Similar avowals he made to Buchholz regarding equality for the Jews and, as noted earlier, throughout the early months of 1815 he vigorously pressed their cause with the retrograde governments of the Hanseatic cities.[56] In all these encounters Metternich was veracious enough; it was not his fault if the suppliants mistook forecasts for promises or interpolated optimistic specifics from broad generalizations. As everyone knew, however, a federal structure of some sort had come first.

It had always been Metternich's aim, as we have seen, to confine the deliberations of the congress in this regard to the general bases of the Bund in order, on the one hand, to complete the new international order in Europe as soon as possible, and on the other, to remove the further negotiations from the direct influence of the non-German powers. His failure is a matter of record: from forty-one articles in September to 120 (or 106) in Humboldt's double draft of 10 February, most of them affecting the internal order of the member states. Enter Napoleon! Was it now possible to contemplate a paragraph-by-paragraph reading of such a tome? Hardenberg at first favored suspending

---

[52] Rudolf Vierhaus, "Eigentumsrecht und Mediatisierung," in *Eigentum und Verfassung*, ed. Rudolf Vierhaus (Göttingen, 1972), 254–256; memorials by Kesselstadt, 20 Jan., 6 and 28 Feb. 1815 in Klüber, *Acten*, VI, 475–505.

[53] Erwin Ruck, *Die römische Kurie und die deutsche Kirchenfrage auf dem Wiener Kongress* (Basel, 1917), 63.

[54] Baron, *Die Judenfrage*, 109.

[55] Mett. to Bertuch, 25 Apr. 1815, HHSA, StK., Kongressakten, Cart. 8, pp. 1–14.

[56] Baron, *Die Judenfrage*, 101–145.

all negotiations till after the war, believing that, as in the past, French defeat would enhance Prussia's role in Europe. Humboldt, however, with support from Stein and Münster, urged immediate action on the Bund, even if nothing more than a few general principles could be adopted. Hardenberg eventually agreed, but whether he was persuaded by the merits or by the pressure of the lesser sovereigns, who threatened not to march without the creation of a Bund, cannot be determined.[57]

It is, at any rate, significant that just three days after he and Metternich promised them an acceleration of the deliberations, Humboldt was ready with another plan, this one stripped of all but what he considered the fundamentals.[58] These included, in somewhat looser language than before, a federal court whose panels would reflect the general membership of the Bund; an executive council with some permanent and some rotating members; a legislative assembly with a voice in federal assessments and appropriations but no other legislative powers; an article on war and alliance along the lines of Wessenberg's proposals adopted in November; a relatively liberal bill of rights including "unabridged" religious freedom and freedom of the press under police supervision; and a military system requiring the smaller states to assign their forces "to the army of one of the military powers of Germany," an obvious repudiation of Metternich's military districts based on the voting curiae of the diet. Regarding *landständische Verfassungen*, Humboldt maintained the distinction he had made before, recognizing existing constitutions but requiring new ones to grant a strong program of rights, including that of approving new taxes. Some articles were entirely new, guaranteeing to the Catholic Church "the most uniform and cohesive constitution attainable," to the house of Thurn und Taxis compensation for the loss of its postal franchises, and to various pensioners of the old Reich a continuation of their income as derived from the toll system on the Rhine.

Significantly, he had relatively little to say about the mediatized houses, only a single sentence stating that they would be treated as generously as possible and placed under federal guarantee. The issue was too important to be put at risk at a time when compromises of all kinds would be required merely to get the Bund established. Later he was to handle the article on *landständische Verfassungen* in similar fashion. As the double draft had demonstrated, moreover, it was awkward to write a catalog of rights without knowing whether the Standesherren were to constitute autonomous Kreis estates or simply the highest of territorial estates; even at this late date Hardenberg had not given up

[57] Schmidt, *Verfassungsfrage*, 435f.
[58] Text, in Klüber, *Acten*, Vol. I, Part 4, 104–111, dated "beginning of April."

hope for the Kreise. Although all states were said to be equal, some of them might exercise special powers in the name of the Bund. Enforcement of federal law, according to article three, would be the responsibility of each state "unless the future organic laws establish Kreise and Kreis *chairmen*," as the chiefs were now to be called.

Such hopes explain why Humboldt omitted all specifics not compatible with Kreise (e.g., courts of third instance shared by several small states as in his February draft without Kreise) and also why the project, unlike its predecessors, was not itself called a constitution but merely a federal treaty pledging its signatories immediately to draft one. These hopes may also account for a glaring lacuna in Humboldt's plan: there was no mention of an Austrian presidency. Contemporaries and posterity alike have tended to see in this gap nothing less than a new drive for Austro-Prussian parity.[59] More likely the aim was different. Recalling that Hardenberg had originally conceded the presidency in exchange for the Kreis system, how could he now stand by and allow Metternich to repudiate the one without giving up the other? The omission was thus a tactic to provide the leverage for renegotiating the original bargain, if not in the preliminary treaty, at least by mutual support in the later negotiations at Frankfurt. One further departure from previous drafts was likewise tactical in import: the compact was not to be among the princes and free cities "of Germany" but among those "whose plenipotentiaries sign this treaty," an unmistakable threat to act without the South German states if necessary, in which case the constitution-making in Frankfurt would proceed in the absence of the most tenacious foes of the mediatized houses. It is likely that Hardenberg at least and increasingly as time went on even Humboldt would actually have welcomed such an eventuality.[60] What is plain in any case is the prospective limit to concessions, the drift of Prussian policy from whole-German experiments back to Hardenberg's original focus on a Prussia-led North Germany, leaving it to Bavaria and Württemberg to take their places as Kreis chiefs or not as they saw fit. Later in the month Humboldt said as much to Count Aloys Rechberg, Wrede's replacement as the Bavarian plenipotentiary, intimating that Austria endorsed the idea.[61]

Actually Metternich's position, as we know, was the reverse: a union of all the German states, even if only a defensive alliance, was better than a partial league with more concentrated powers. For the central

[59] E.g., Schmidt, *Verfassungsfrage*, 445; Hartmann, *Schicksal der Verfassungsvorschläge*, 77f. The latter provides the text of a report by Count Keller to the Elector of Hesse-Cassel insisting that in the absence of an emperor there must at least be an Austrian presidium.

[60] Cf. Humboldt to Caroline, 21 May 1815, *Briefe* IV, 558.

[61] Quint, *Souveränitätsbegriff*, 342.

purpose of the Bund was to fetter Prussia in Germany while forcing her into the service of Europe, and to this end the South German states were indispensable. Without them Austria's physical contact with the Bund would be limited to Saxony and Prussia, Hanover would be isolated, and Prussia's control of North Germany assured, especially under the circumstances of the moment, which found so many small contingents serving under Prussian command. Paradoxically it was easier for Metternich to contemplate a Bund without Prussia, as he had intimated to Münster in December, than one without Bavaria, whose lead Württemberg, Baden, and Hesse-Darmstadt would probably follow. Like it or not, it was idle to consider constitutional drafts that could not find approval in Munich. The task was to convince the Bavarians that their refusal to accept a reasonable plan for all Germany would deliver the North to Prussia by default, to the peril of all. Münster, who was on the verge of panic at the prospect of doing without the South Germans, joined the chorus demanding an immediate settlement. Without a Bund, he wailed, "we shall risk treachery in Germany."[62]

The situation called for a new strategy. During the fall of 1814 Metternich had first consulted the Prussians, then cleared with Münster, and finally brought their projects before the German Committee, counting on the Kreise to convert the men from Munich and Stuttgart. The next step, had matters progressed so far, would have been to modify the Kreise with the aid of the small states. Now he decided that while continuing confidential talks with the Prussians and Hanoverians, he would conduct parallel negotiations with Wrede, acting, so to speak, as a mediator incognito. Accordingly, on 31 March, while requesting Münster to join preliminary talks with him and the Prussians, and Winzingerode to return to the German Committee, he invited Wrede to have "preliminary and confidential" talks with him. In responding the next day the marshal not only agreed (pending completion of the territorial settlement), but also submitted his own version of a federal treaty, originally drafted in all probability as a counterproject to the Wessenberg plan of December. Winzingerode, on the other hand, who was then busy making soundings for a separate South German league, returned a belated and noncommittal reply and even so was rebuked by his king for not positively refusing.[63]

Like the Humboldt plan, the Bavarian project took the form of a

[62] To Prince Regent, 13 Apr. 1815, Münster, *Political Sketches*, 246; cf. Stein, "Tagebuch," *Briefe*, v, 384.

[63] Winz. to Fred., 21 and 23 Apr. 1815, HSA, Stuttgart, E 70, Fasc. 19, pp. 52–56; Münster and Ernst Hardenberg to Mett., 31 Mar. 1815, HHSA, StK., Kongressakten, Cart. 6, p. 470; Wrede to Mett. and Wessenberg, 1 Apr. 1815, *ibid.*, pp. 481–483, with text of Bavarian draft attached.

treaty of alliance directed toward the later drafting of a constitution. Its members were referred to as "allies," and four of its eleven articles provided for the mutual defense against foreign assault as well as assistance in case of internal rebellion. In guaranteeing territorial integrity, however, the Bund was to take due cognizance of the Frankfurt accession treaties, which, as we know, would favor Bavaria in her wrangling with her neighbors. A federal diet as such was not mentioned, but common deliberations were called for in which, curiously, voting strength was to be proportional to population; otherwise all states in their relationship to "the German *Gesamtstaat*" were to be absolutely equal. Neither was an army mentioned, only the obligation of each state to maintain a contingent of a certain size in a state of readiness. Encouragingly for Metternich Wrede included three provisions previously conceded by Bavaria to some extent: the prohibition of alliances harmful to the Bund, the *judicial* settlement of interstate disputes in a manner to be determined in the federal act, and *landständische Verfassungen* adapted to local conditions. Finally, and again as in the Humboldt plan, membership in the Bund was left open, as if to challenge Prussia to take it or leave it.

Metternich (who on the 1st was not above playing an April Fool's prank on Gentz) received both the Humboldt and the Wrede projects that day. All at once he had in his hands statements of the extreme positions that he must attempt to draw together. And yet the parallel negotiations did not move forward—because of Metternich's "indifference and indolence," according to the impatient Humboldt[64] but in reality because Marshal Wrede's attention until the 23rd was concentrated on the fruitless territorial negotiations with Bavaria's neighbors and his imminent departure to join the Bavarian corps. Until a semblance of order was restored among his quarreling protégés of the South, not to mention the termination of the tedious contest with Saxony, Metternich had little incentive to face the Prussians in a serious negotiation. As a result, the month of April marched to the cadences of territorial bickering, coalition-building, scrambling for subsidies, and the deployment of armies.

Even without fusillades from the Austrian camp the Humboldt plan drew fire enough "Its undulating expressions" met with little approval, according to Stein, who along with Plessen and Gersdorff urged Humboldt to cease his efforts to accommodate Bavaria. The clause on the Catholic Church was welcome to Consalvi as a gesture but disappointing because it implied, as he read it, the subordination of the church to the secular authority of the bund and said nothing about a con-

---

[64] To Caroline, 3 Apr. 1815, Humboldt, *Briefe*, IV, 517.

cordat. The Protestants, on the other hand, objected that they were not mentioned at all. There was also no reference to the Jews, and whether their deputies knew about the plan or not, it was Metternich who assured them that the omission would be remedied.[65]

The loudest moans, however, welled up from the ranks of the Standesherren. Humboldt's meager article in their behalf seemed a shocking comedown from the heady provisions of the double draft, which Gärtner had considered to be almost ideal, at least for the houses that changed sovereigns. Then in the course of March, there followed the favorable developments recounted in the previous chapter. Gärtner, who wanted immediate guarantees, not lessons in strategy, was now inconsolable. The work was full of "aphorisms," he complained, and branded it "the death sentence" of the mediatized. Prince Wilhelm von Sayn-Wittgenstein, who in December had declared his independence from the duke of Nassau, implored Hardenberg to reconsider, threatening that if the matter "turns out unjustly, it will grieve me forever and, more than you think, I shall never be able to suppress this feeling." Coming from the Prussian minister of police, these were strong words, and within a month he acted on them.[66]

Responding to these complaints, Humboldt on 22 April produced an enlarged version,[67] but Gärtner was still not satisfied. As a result, the indefatigable Prussian went to work again, on 30 April completing still another draft.[68] It listed many of the familiar rights and privileges, including the possibility of seats in the federal diet and Kreis assemblies, but only within limits compatible with the necessary governing and supervisory powers of the states. The Standesherren, as Stein and Humboldt had always urged, were unequivocally to be territorial estates rather than Kreis estates, and any titled subjects they might have were likewise to enjoy this status. The Landtage, moreover, were to be open "to all classes of citizens," which probably meant the creation of an estate of non-noble freeholders. Though vaguely drawn, the article came closer to the Bavarian ordinance of 1807 than the many memorials of Solms and Gärtner. As if to make amends, however, Humboldt once again made explicit the federal court's jurisdiction over states' violations of the Federal Act and their own constitutions. Other

---

[65] Stein, "Tagebuch," *Briefe*, v, 383f.; Ruck, *Römische Kurie*, 68; Baron, *Die Judenfrage*, 148f.

[66] Gärtner memorial, n.d., in HHSA, StK., Deutsche Akten, Fasc. 100, pp. 463–466; and Wittgenstein to Hard., early April, 1815, Branig, *Briefwechsel Hardenbergs mit Wittgenstein*, 213f. Though the Gärtner memorial is unsigned, his authorship is confirmed by comparing phrases quoted by Hoff, *Mediatisiertenfrage*, 108f.

[67] Hoff, *Mediatisiertenfrage*, 109f.; Schmidt, *Verfassungsfrage*, 449–451, who unaccountably does not mention the article on the mediatized in any of his summaries.

[68] Text in Klüber, *Acten*, ii, 298–308.

amendments to the draft of 1 April provided for the equality of the three Christian religions, federal guarantees of the rights of Protestants as set forth in past treaties, a more comprehensive guarantee of old Reich pensions, and the civil and political equality of the Jews so far as they assumed the duties of citizenship. Finally, the reference to the equality of all states was deleted, presumably to remove an argument against future Kreise.

Metternich received the new plan on 1 May along with a prefatory note and covering letter calling attention to "the still indeterminate Article III," which omitted the presidency, and reserving an exchange of views later.[69] Since the prefatory note advertised that the Prussians "remain, except for minor changes, true to the content of those earlier drafts,"[70] the conclusion is now inescapable that they were not trying at this late date to revive a dualistic directory but rather were again holding back the Austrian presidency as hostage to the Kreis system. The problem for Metternich, then, was how to avoid a repetition of the October debate, which had come about in part bacause he had accepted the Forty-one Articles as the sole basis of discussion. The strategy that he now adopted was to take the initiative, to meet Hardenberg head-on with a project of his own that would firmly assert the Austrian presidency and arrange the federal diet in a way that would preclude Kreise and, for that matter, an executive council. By insisting that both plans be made the basis of discussion he could frame the issues in such a way that it would be difficult for the Prussians to bring the Kreise into the bargaining.

Even before 1 May Wessenberg had been at work on such a plan, taking account not only of Humboldt's work and his own December articles but various other drafts voluntarily submitted, notably Marschall's December plan and Plessen's most recent work, which though aimed, as we have noted, toward a Kaiser, was realistic enough in other respects. The plan that he now completed was thus a synthesis reflecting Metternich's search for consensus.[71] The core of it was a unicameral diet representing all states, ten of them casting whole votes, the rest sharing six curial votes: one for all the Saxon duchies, another for the free cities, and so on. Another article provided for grouping small-state military contingents on this same pattern, further militating against Kreise. Most interesting perhaps was the bracketing of Nassau with Luxemburg (i.e., the Netherlands), a transparent effort to continue

[69] Hard. and Humboldt to Mett., 2 May 1815, text in Schmidt, *Verfassungsfrage*, 451f.

[70] Klüber, *Acten*, II, 298f.

[71] "Der sogenannte erste österreichische Entwurf von Wessenberg," HHSA, StK., Deutsche Akten, Fasc. 100, pp. 271–278.

the service of the Nassau contingent with the Dutch forces rather than with Prussia. Austria was to be the permanent president, with the only permanent seat on a small ad hoc committee on foreign affairs and the power to cast tie-breaking votes in the diet. On the other hand, federal administrative officers were to be appointed by the assembly and limited to personnel of German origin and German experience, and who can say whether this last was merely a cheap nod to national feeling or perhaps rather intended to prevent King Frederick or Max Joseph from slipping Napoleonic refugees into the federal apparatus?

The article on war and alliance in all plans had not varied much since the agreements on the German Committee in November, and Wessenberg's was no exception. In contrast, his statement about the federal court was weaker, deferring a definition of its competence for action by the federal diet but keeping open the possibility of making it the supreme court of the states under 300,000 in population.[72] His article on estates constitutions was even milder than the one in his December draft, combining Humboldt's scheme of recognizing any existing constitution with a vague definition of Landtag rights for new ones. Regarding the mediatized houses, he and Humboldt were closer together, but there was certainly no mention of Kreis assemblies or curial votes at the federal level. On the other hand, more than the Prussian he steadfastly refused to designate the great lords as *Landstände*, choosing instead to call them, somewhat evasively, "the first Standesherren in their states with the rank due them." Why? Subsequent developments suggest here a concern that the bare mention of *Landstände* in this connection might jeopardize the one right that Metternich as an imperial prince personally valued: recognition of their equality of birth to the sovereigns (*Ebenbürtigkeit*) with the right to marry at that level. But for this rare concession to his private interest, which at the time affected his sister Pauline's romance with Duke Ferdinand of Württemberg, he stayed within the limits of the Bavarian ordinance, which, we should remind ourselves, still left the Standesherren as a very privileged class, Gärtner's and Solms's laments notwithstanding.

In regard to other issues Wessenberg essentially endorsed Humboldt's views on guaranteed pensions, was more favorable to the house of Thurn und Taxis, was more emphatic about the equality and self-administration of religious confessions, and added provision for negotiating a federal concordat with Rome. To the Jews he at first guaranteed only existing rights, but when he saw Humboldt's statement granting full equality, he endorsed that too. Finally Wessenberg, as in

[72] I.e., indirectly by not including any article on the appellate system for small states.

his December plan, placed freedom of trade, commerce, navigation, and matters of "common interest" on the agenda of the first meeting of the federal diet. Again the contrast with Humboldt's silence on this topic is striking, reminiscent of the November debates in which the Prussian had resisted a strong legislature lest it encroach on the prerogatives of the Kreise. That was probably still the Prussian concern.

Though lucid and to the point, as Wessenberg's papers always were, the draft was perhaps too precise for Metternich's purposes, containing specifics that, for purposes of bargaining, might better be glossed over in a working draft. Presumably on his orders Wessenberg reduced the plan to shorter, more flexible propositions and made some small substantive changes as well.[73] The term "allies," borrowed from the Bavarians, was changed to the customary "members of the Bund." Restricting federal personnel to German natives was dropped in favor of making German the official language of the Bund.[74] The problems of Thurn und Taxis were not mentioned. And, most importantly, the two Hessian states, previously assigned one vote each, were now combined in a single curia, implying the future union of their troops and, as in the case of Nassau, greater independence from Prussia.

Metternich dispatched the plan to the Prussians on 7 May, the first such from the Austrians in all these months. Two days later he sent for the new Bavarian plenipotentiary, Count Rechberg, and confided to him his dread of the new Prussian draft, which aimed only at self-aggrandizement that would soon result, he predicted, in a Prussian "Reich stronger than anyone had ever expected."[75] Only the immediate founding of the Bund, however loose and provisional, could stop it, and Bavaria must help. A simpler man at this point might have produced the Austrian plan by way of comparison. Metternich, however, preferred to summarize it orally, virtually dictating the points so that Rechberg could write them down. Naturally these were still more general than in the original, but they were consistent with it and candidly included the provisions for *landständische Verfassungen*, based on certain federal guidelines. Metternich also admitted the possibility of a federal court but jocularly predicted that years and decades would go by before the diet, tangled in abstractions and hounded by learned publicists, reached any conclusions—one of his more accurate prophecies as it turned out. Rechberg remained skeptical all the same and departed,

---

[73] Text in Klüber, *Acten*, II, 308–314.

[74] Even though the provision was never adopted, it became the custom in diplomatic correspondence to use German in discussing federal affairs whereas European issues were usually dealt with in French.

[75] Rechberg to Montgelas, 9 May 1815, extr. in Quint, *Souveränitätsbegriff*, 349, n. 159.

doubting that "the written proposals will coincide with this conversation."[76]

The urgency expressed in Humboldt's note of 1 May implied that the Prussians would reply immediately to positive action by Metternich, and they did so, notwithstanding that the first week of May found them embroiled in a storm of untoward events that affected others, to be sure, but fell with a vengeance on them in particular, severely damaging their bargaining position and necessitating a word of explanation here. First of all, 2 May was the day the Saxon troops mutinied, forcing Blücher and Gneisenau to slip out their back doors and flee for their lives.[77] An embarrassment in itself, shattering the Prussians' image of themselves as popular liberators, the damage was soon compounded by Blücher's harsh measures to impose order on German soldiers.

This explosion, moreover, occurred in the midst of another imbroglio with lesser states. To supply the armies in an orderly way the allied military commission on 1 May divided Germany (exclusive of Austria and most of Prussia) into three zones, each the source of supplies to be purchased by the Austrian, Prussian, and Russian commissaries at fixed and uniform prices. There was grumbling enough the next day at the prices set and the exemption of Austria, but the main object of abuse was Prussia. Not only were most of her merchants spared selling at a loss, in a war that was mainly for the defense of the Rhineland, it was charged, but her procurement zone included Hanover, Brunswick, the Hanseatic cities, Oldenburg, and part of Nassau, all with troops assigned to Wellington. His support area was mainly the Netherlands, which with his permission sold only for cash and at market rates. The German states were thus faced with paying dear to supply their own troops while selling cheap to others and being, in Count Münster's words, "abandoned to the rapacity of a Prussian commissariat." It seemed almost a preview of life in a Prussian Kreis, and they demanded a hearing at the ministerial level.[78]

On 3 May Metternich placed the issue before the Conference of Five, Hermann von Boyen, the Prussian minister of war, attending as the military expert, and Count Münster representing the disaffected states. Everyone admitted the injustice but professed that in the absence of additional subsidies little could be done. The solution finally adopted was to allow the German contingents in the Netherlands to pay German prices, leaving it to the Dutch government to subsidize its vendors for

---

[76] *Ibid.*, 48–50 and n. 161; Lieselotte Klemmer, *Aloys von Rechberg als Bayerischer Politiker* (Munich, 1975), 50–52; Aretin, "Deutsche Politik Bayerns," 39–41.

[77] Humboldt to Caroline, 12 May 1815, *Briefe*, IV, 548f.

[78] Protocols of military commission, 1 and 2 May 1815, d'Angeberg, *Congrès*, III, pp. 1136–1138 and 1143; Pflugk-Harttung, "Gegensätz wegen der Bundestruppen," 136; and Münster to Prince Regent, 13 May 1815, Münster, *Political Sketches*, 259.

the difference. Until this arrangement could be negotiated with The Hague, however, the existing system would continue. Münster reluctantly acquiesced but announced that all Hanoverian sales would be made subject to the success of the negotiation, which in time came about.[79]

What happened next can well be described as the climax of the congress, if only for sheer melodrama. Metternich had brought to the meeting unopened letters from Napoleon to himself and Francis, which he ostentatiously proposed to open in the presence of the diplomats. Before doing so, however, he asked Humboldt to find a pretext for "politely easing" Boyen, who was not an envoy, out of the room. This done, somewhat clumsily evidently, Humboldt returned to witness the opening of the letters. These turned out, as Metternich no doubt had guessed, to offer peace to Austria on the basis of the Treaty of Paris, whereupon he dramatically announced that they would go unanswered. The performance was overly theatrical, serving only as a demonstration of loyalty, which the father-in-law of Napoleon felt obliged to make from time to time. The drama, alas, ended in farce. After the meeting, Humboldt, at Hardenberg's quarters for dinner, encountered Boyen, who, still fuming over his dismissal, challenged him to a duel. This had to be sandwiched in between conferences and out of public sight, but finally at 3:00 p.m. on 5 May—they chose a time when Hardenberg was out of town—they faced each other in a quiet grove on the Kahlenberg, both firing into the air. Such were the tensions and frayed nerves of those excruciating days. It was a bad week for the Prussian delegates.[80]

But there was worse. In the course of April the leading Standesherren of Nassau, various branches of the Solms, Wied, and Wittgenstein lines, though shocked at the curt treatment of their demands in Humboldt's draft of 1 April, took heart from the knowledge that the Prussian negotiator, Hoffmann, was exerting himself to bring them under Prussian sovereignty as part of the territorial settlement or, failing that, to pledge the duke of Nassau to treat his mediatized subjects as Prussia intended to treat hers. On 24 April, Hoffmann, frustrated by the leverage available to the small states at the time, accepted a settlement that did neither. In a desperate move, Prince Wilhelm of Sayn-Wittgenstein, venting his anger at Hardenberg, on 27 April appealed directly to the king of Prussia to take him as a subject, adducing

[79] Protocol of 3 May 1815, d'Angeberg, *Congrès*, IV, 1902–1905; Mayr, "Aufbau," 110; Pflugk-Harttung, "Gegensätze wegen der Bundestruppen," 136.

[80] Protocol of 3 May 1815, d'Angeberg, *Congrès*, IV, 1902–1905; Clancarty to Castle., 6 May 1815, Webster, *BD*, 331; Humboldt to Caroline, 5 May 1815, *Briefe*, IV, 541–546; Humboldt to Boyen, 5 May 1815, *Gesammelte Schriften*, XVII, 76; Mayr, "Aufbau," 111.

the now familiar doctrine that the legal order of 1805 prevailed. Encouraged by Gärtner, Prince August of Wied-Neuwied on 30 April did likewise. The day after, Frederick William astonishingly agreed and ordered Hardenberg forthwith to maintain this position at the congress, in glaring contradiction to the provisions of Humboldt's draft constitution being submitted to Metternich that very day. In the next week—the week of the mutinies, the supply controversy, the duel, and Metternich's counterdraft—similar declarations by the count of Bentheim-Rheda and the entire house of Solms spread the rebellion to Hanover and Hesse-Darmstadt.[81]

Even without these acts, however, the king of Prussia's endorsement of the legal order of 1805 threatened all the middle states, north and south, much of the territorial settlement so far completed, and the accession treaties themselves. Consternation swept through the congress and the German capitals. Whatever Hardenberg's responsibility for encouraging the mediatized, he could hardly have wished to scandalize Europe at this crucial time. Not since the terrible dressing-down on 5 November in front of the tsar had the king wrought such havoc with the chancellor's policy, and for a similar reason: personal loyalty, in this case to Wittgenstein, who was his confidant as well as minister of the Prussian police. Again there was talk of Hardenberg's resignation. Nesselrode, Metternich, and of course Marschall of Nassau demanded disavowals, to which Hardenberg replied, playing for time, only that he expected a satisfactory outcome.[82]

Wittgenstein's baleful influence on the king at this time hurt Hardenberg in another way. As an archconservative leader of absolutists and east-Elbian Junkers, who dreaded the sharing of their informal influence in Berlin with deputies from the new western provinces, he was gradually turning the king against the plan for a *landständische* constitution in Prussia, which Hardenberg, no less than Frederick of Württemberg and Montgelas in Bavaria, viewed as the best means of assimilating new provinces and tapping the estates' financial resources. A commission was at work on what Hardenberg, with some exaggeration, called a "national representation," and as recently as 10 April an interim assembly demanded action. In the accelerating contest for the king's mind it would be more important than ever to have a strong article in the federal constitution *requiring* Prussia to introduce an estates constitution. Indeed, Humboldt's recent distinction between existing constitutions and new ones with specified powers for the Landtag probably stemmed in large measure from the diverse conditions in her

[81] Sarholz, "Nassau 1813–1815," 100–103; Hoff, *Mediatisiertenfrage*, 104–106; texts of declarations and Frederick William's reply in Klüber, *Acten*, II, 236–254.
[82] Sarholz, "Nassau 1813–1815," 103f.; Hoff, *Mediatisiertenfrage*, 106f.

old and new lands, especially the various estates of her Saxon provinces.[83]

The disarray in the Prussian camp continued, Hoffmann insisting that the Standesherren did indeed have the right to choose their sovereigns,[84] Humboldt denying it. In a courageous memorial of 12 May the latter released the pent-up anger of months over this, pointing out that the treaties decreed the opposite, that if free to choose, some Standesherren might opt for sovereigns other than Frederick William or even accept no sovereign at all. Why, he asked, should they alone be free to choose and not their long-suffering subjects or for that matter the free cities, the *Reichsritter*, the bishoprics, and all the other corporations of the Reich? It was not "un-German," he insisted, to oppose the preferred treatment of one class or violent changes in the existing order; any change of sovereigns must be the result of conventional negotiation based on treaty, in which connection he could not resist openly denouncing at last "the principle mentioned *here and there* that the mediatized could be annexed only to courts of royal rank."[85] If long in coming, this was a severe indictment, possible perhaps only in Hardenberg's extremity. In any case, Humboldt's argument prevailed, and on 31 May the treaty with Nassau was signed as originally drafted. "The detestable Prussians," wrote Baron Marschall when the outcome was certain. "It is a race I am truly sorry for, that in victory knows as little how to behave as in the defeats of yesteryear."[86]

However that may be, the Prussians were compelled to resume the contest with Metternich at the height of their internal discord and the nadir of their prestige abroad. On 11 May the two sides met to consider equally the Prussian plan and Wessenberg's counterproject of the 7th. Metternich continued to reject language threatening any state with exclusion, to demand an explicit ban on subordinating any state to another (the anti-Kreis clause, we can call it), and to insist on a unicameral assembly with Austria presiding and empowered to break tie votes. He agreed, however, to enlarge the assembly from fifteen to twenty voices by giving whole votes to some smaller states of venerable lineage, thus, among other things, separating Darmstadt from Cassel and Nassau from Luxemburg and awarding two votes to the mostly pro-Prussian Saxon duchies. The Prussians, however, continued to insist on a separate executive council, now referred to as a *Bundesrat*.[87]

---

[83] Ernst Klein, *Von der Reform zur Restauration* (Berlin, 1965), 186–191; Huber, *Verfassungsgeschichte*, I, 302f.

[84] Hoff, *Mediatisiertenfrage*, 106f.

[85] "Ueber die Mediatisierten," 12 May 1815, in *Gesammelte Schriften*, XI, 306–314. Emphasis mine.

[86] Quoted in Sarholz, "Nassau 1813–1815," 104.

[87] This and following paragraph based on Schmidt, *Verfassungsfrage*, 454–461, as corrected in the light of later Wessenberg drafts. See n. 91 below.

Regarding *landständische Verfassungen*, the Austrians yielded a bit, adopting Humboldt's language about existing constitutions and conceding that they must be designed at least to protect property and personal freedom. The Prussians, however, still insisted on the minimum powers long ago put into the records by Count Münster. Completely irreconcilable were the rival positions on the federal court and the distribution of military contingents, Metternich taking the expedient way of leaving these projects to the future diet, the Prussians demanding immediate action. Less controversial were the articles on religious equality, Jewish rights, the postal rights of Thurn und Taxis, and the recognition of debt and pension claims based on the Rhine tolls and the imperial recess. Even so, on most of these points the Austrian position was stronger, providing, for example, full administrative autonomy to each religious denomination and guaranteeing without qualification all rights then enjoyed by the Jews. Ths last, Humboldt objected, would cause "opposition and even strife" in lands that had inherited French legislation. On the other hand, the rights of the Standesherren and of subjects generally remained, as before, more generously and precisely formulated by the Prussians—except for Metternich's continued refusal to speak of the mediatized as *Landstände*.

After two days of heated exchanges both sides agreed to bring Count Münster into the talks, Hardenberg no doubt because of the Hanoverian's strong advocacy of estates' rights, Metternich because of his obvious anxiety to create a Bund that the South Germans would be willing to join. On 13 May Münster and Ernst Hardenberg arrived at the chancellery to join the others. Metternich began by reading a proposed preamble explaining that the current emergency necessitated a swift conclusion if the independence of Germany was to come under guarantee "in the great assembly of European powers" and the Bund take its place in the European state system. Internal issues could then be dealt with later without foreign influence. Metternich, as we know, had struck this chord for almost a year, but now, as a preamble, it had a practical function: an official rationale for referring most difficult issues to the federal diet. The declaration also stated Austria's determination to conclude the pact "with all German-minded princes," an allusion that, given Metternich's true policy, must have been designed solely to reinforce Münster's fears, which in fact prompted him to declare at the meeting that if Bavaria and Württemberg did not join the Bund, neither would Hanover.[88]

The centerpiece of the meeting was a revised plan drafted by Wes-

[88] Text of preamble in HHSA, StK., Deutsche Akten, Fasc. 100, pp. 283–285; Münster to Prince Regent, 13 May 1815, Münster, *Political Sketches*, 260f.; Schmidt, *Verfassungsfrage*, 456.

senberg ostensibly to reconcile the Austrian and Prussian drafts; actually it was not very different from the previous plan, mostly reasserting the Austrian positions as set forth above.[89] And yet "our opinions varied very little," according to Münster,[90] indicating that Metternich was ready to abandon many positions he had upheld not as Austrian interests but solely for tactical advantage in courting the other German states. A point-by-point critique drafted by Humboldt afterwards and a new draft by Wessenberg in reponse to it record the progress.[91] Metternich has agreed expressly to describe the Bund as "permanent" and to delete reference to "sovereign" princes as well as the phrase prohibiting the subordination of one state to another. In exchange Humboldt admitted that all states were to be called equal. He demanded as well substantive articles on the military system and the federal court, and Wessenberg supplied them. The contingents and financial assessments for war were to be proportional to population and organized for maximum efficiency consistent with the rights of the "Bundesstände" [sic]. A federal court representative of the membership was to deal with disputes among members as directed by the federal diet "as well as with every other grievance constitutionally brought before the Bund"—language taken directly from Humboldt's more cryptic draft of 1 April. Similarly, Wessenberg, whose previous draft said nothing about appellate courts for small states, now endorsed Humboldt's plan, with one exception: states under 300,000 in population would not be *required* to establish joint supreme courts but *allowed* to, thus keeping alive a slight possibility of handing this function to the federal court. Regarding religion Wessenberg deleted the grants of administrative autonomy to the churches and existing rights to the Jews, adopting all of Humboldt's language except that he continued to hold out for a federal concordat. In matters of war, peace, and alliance, where Austria and Prussia had differed only about the amount of detail to place in the federal act, Wessenberg now decided to let the Prussians have it their way and did not supply an article of his own. In the same spirit he restored to the list of civil rights those of state service and university attendance anywhere in Germany and at least gave copyrights and freedom of the press a place on the first agenda of the federal diet. More and more, Austro-Prussian differences boiled

[89] Text in Schmidt, *Verfassungsfrage*, 456–461, who regards the document as "the decisive turning point." Cf. Hartmann, *Schicksal der Verfassungsvorschläge*, 77f., who correctly notes its similarity to the previous draft.

[90] Münster to Prince Regent as per n. 88 above.

[91] Humboldt critique, Schmidt, *Verfassungsfrage*, 461–464; Wessenberg, "Erster Entwurf a," HHSA, StK., Deutsche Akten, Fasc. 100, pp. 285–307. Schmidt, using only Prussian records, incorrectly places some of Wessenberg's revisions (without attribution to him) *before* the meeting of 13 May, but the consonance between them and Humboldt's critique, written after that meeting, leaves little doubt about the sequence offered here.

down to determining which issues to defer and which to act on in the federal convenant itself.[92]

Not all issues, of course, could be so handily disposed of. In response to Humboldt's specific complaints Wessenberg finally agreed to classify the mediatized houses as *Landstände*, placed their rights under federal guarantee, and specified comprehensively what these rights were. As before, however, all was subject to state supervision, the precedence of state legislation, and compatibility with "governmental rights." Similar equivocation attended his treatment of *landständische Verfassungen*. Copying Humboldt almost verbatim, he listed the approval of taxes, consultation on any legislation that affected property and personal rights, the filing of complaints against administrative abuses, and defending the constitution—not, however, as rights or powers of the Landtage but as topics to be addressed in devising constitutions. We are approaching the Delphic language of the Federal Act itself.[93]

The key to an Austro-Prussian accommodation, however, concerned the structure of the federal assembly. Humboldt complained that Wessenberg's plan did not make the body continuous and did not specify its competence, its powers, or the means of enforcing its resolutions. Metternich in turn protested the withholding of the Austrian presidency and refused to accept Kreise as the means to win it back. To bridge the gap he pulled from the files Humboldt's plan of January, the one that envisioned a single diet, meeting either as a smaller council or in plenary session, where each state had at least one whole vote and the agenda was limited to constitutional amendments, internal federal institutions, and German-wide legislation "insofar as this [last] is possible in a league of states." Wessenberg now made this plan his own, even to the gratuitous casting of doubt on the feasibility of legislation. An Austrian presidency was included but without the right to cast deciding votes. With a few insignificant changes in the makeup of the curiae, the structure of the smaller council was the same as Humboldt's: six integral votes and five curial votes, a designated director in each curia casting its vote as instructed by the majority.[94]

For the plenary sessions, however, Wessenberg rejected Humboldt's voting scheme, which made some allowance for differences in population, and proposed, with a few exceptions, one vote for each state, i.e., no more for Austria or Prussia than for Waldeck (population

---

[92] Cf. Humboldt to Caroline, 15 May 1815, *Briefe*, IV, 533; Münster to Prince Regent, 15 May 1815, Münster, *Political Sketches*, 253f.

[93] Humboldt critique and Wessenberg's "Erster Entwurf a," as n. 91.

[94] *Ibid.* Although the term "smaller council" (*engerer Rat*) was not officially mentioned till the Vienna Final Act of 1820, I shall use it here and throughout because of its familiarity and to keep our bearings through variations used in succeeding drafts. In the Federal Act of 1815 the reference was to the "smaller assembly," in Humboldt's January draft the "smaller committee."

50,000), thirty-one votes in all, including, as a token, one for the mediatized houses. Here was Metternich's doctrine of equality with a vengeance, a dramatic exercise of that "protective influence" he had always said Austria would provide for the small states. If Prussia must have some semblance of a bicameral diet, then let its members, as sovereigns, have equal votes. For all its demographic disproportions, however, the body, operating under simple majority rule, would have been more effective than the diet that was finally achieved. Besides, Wessenberg's mocking disparagement of legislation notwithstanding, he and Metternich persisted with their article on freedom of commerce and navigation and "other affairs of common interest," which Humboldt dismissed as too detailed and "not important enough" in comparison with the many things now discarded.[95]

The latest Wessenberg articles were subjected to debate at a series of private three-power conferences held from 14 to 17 May.[96] At these, Metternich withdrew two concessions previously made: a federal guarantee of the rights of the mediatized and the definition of their status as mere *Landstände*, the latter, as we have suggested, to protect their peerdom, their hereditary equality with the sovereign princes. Otherwise he accepted a relatively strong statement of rights and finally won the Prussians over to according the same to the imperial knights. The right to levy and collect direct taxes, the main gift that the Prussians had in mind for their own Standesherren, was no longer an issue. Regarding judicial appeals, the figure of 300,000 as the population needed to possess one's own supreme court was dropped and the task of drawing the line left to the future diet, presumably to forestall bickering over the sensitive but sterile issue of status. At the same time the article no longer referred to *several* composite courts but to *a* common court, which if Wessenberg's idea prevailed, could conceivably be the federal court itself, the competence of which, by another amendment, was also to be decided by the diet.

More bitterly disputed was the organization of the diet. Although Wessenberg's smaller council of six whole votes and five curial votes followed Humboldt's January plan, the Prussians now wished to broaden the body. As a result, the old princely houses of Baden, Electoral Hesse, and Darmstadt, as well as Denmark (for Holstein) and the Netherlands were assigned integral votes, leaving four curial votes, fifteen in all. The arrangement could be justified as giving rank its due, especially in the case of the two non-German powers, but it should also be ob-

---

[95] Humboldt critique and Wessenberg's "Erster Entwurf a," as n. 91.

[96] This and the following paragraphs based on Schmidt, *Verfassungsfrage*, 464–468 and text of the final draft "Zu der Grundlage der Verfassung des deutschen Bundes" submitted by Austria and Prussia to German Committee on 23 May 1815, Klüber, *Acten*, II, 314–323.

served that each of Wessenberg's five curiae lost its leading member, leaving to the four new groups only small states that could hardly combine their forces into effective independent military units. If this was in fact that Prussian intent we do not know, but it was the result, a potentially serious obstacle to Metternich's plan for basing military districts on the voting curiae.

Less speculative are several other points of conflict. According to Wessenberg's articles, bills dealing with the fundamental laws of the Bund were to originate in the smaller council and be acted on by majority vote in plenary session. If this system stood, most of the federal constitution in the early sessions of the diet would be virtually dictated by the small states, as King Frederick had once prophesied. On 14 May the Prussians evidently (here we must read between the lines) forced through an amendment allowing "the federal diet" to decide which form to assume in dealing with fundamental law and organic institutions. But in which forum was this determination to be made? The answer was preordained, perhaps inadvertently, by another amendment. After vehement debate over the distribution of votes in plenary sessions, a compromise emerged which adopted gradations in voting strength as a principle, but again left it to the diet to determine the actual distribution of the weighted votes. In this situation the diet would obviously have to begin its work with only the smaller council in existence and the future of the plenary body in doubt. This Metternich could not tolerate, and so another compromise emerged: the plenary body retained the express right to approve or reject various bills but "with the difference that in the adoption of fundamental laws no member can be bound by the majority."

Since this provision still did not clarify how the plenary body was to vote on the allocation of its own votes, it was probably meant as stopgap protection for all, even though the work would necessarily begin with the smaller council. The absurdities in the plan no doubt explain why the German Committee later prescibed a voting system in the Federal Act after all. It was the first explicit departure in any of the drafts of the past year from the principle of majority decision (so far as the Prussians and the Württembergers were willing to allow the old Second Council any power at all) but it was almost inevitable once it was clear that the diet would begin life as a constituent assembly. In any case, there was a vast difference between allowing dissenters not to be bound and requiring unanimity for any action at all as the small states later demanded.[97] Metternich's initiative in this development cannot be documented, but it can be reasonably inferred from his tactical concerns, even if Austria had most to gain from majority rule.

[97] Hartmann, *Schicksal der Verfassungsvorschläge*, 79, is wrong in taking the language to mean that unanimity was required for adoption of a measure.

In contrast to this muddle the long debate on *landständische Verfassungen* ended with a decisive Austrian victory. Metternich's latest effort to accommodate the Prussians consisted, as noted above, of admitting the four-point minimum, but as a future agenda rather than a binding commitment. He himself probably believed that with patience and skill expressions of intent in the Federal Act could eventually be translated into substance; "the bases adopted must necessarily contain the entire organism," he had told Solms as far back as September. Humboldt, however, must have seen here pure sophistry relegating the issue to dead storage. Wessenberg's previous formulations had at least decreed constitutions "based on the security of property and personal freedom" under federal guarantee, language resembling that intended for Prussia's own constitutional plans; and there is evidence that, with Münster's support, this version was briefly reconsidered.[98] In the end, however, Hardenberg and Humboldt decided that sham and half measures would be of little use to restrain either "the petty despots" in Germany or the foes of the constitution in Prussia; better an innocuous article that kept all roads open than a deceptive one that could lead to a federal guarantee of tyranny. Humboldt marked the surrender in pencil, crossing out his most cherished lines and inserting a simple substitute: "In all the German states there shall be an estates-style constitution." No minimum. No federal guarantee. No definition of estates.[99]

For domestic purposes and to evade responsibility in the eyes of Germany for these enigmatic words it was now necessary to commit the king to something more incisive at home, and that is doubtless why Hardenberg rushed him into issuing a public promise of a "representation of the people" consisting of delegates elected by the provincial estates and empowered to deliberate "on all legislative matters that concern the personal and property rights of citizens, including taxation."[100] This elastic phrasing was not very different from the Austrian proposals, but then the Prussians never intended for themselves the precision they desired for others. The proclamation was issued on 22 May, the day before the final Austro-Prussian draft constitution was announced.

For the past week, meanwhile, a plan purporting to be Austria's "General Outline" of a German constitution had been in quiet circulation, and Rechberg of Bavaria, angered at its deviation from Metternich's last oral assurances, demanded an explanation. On 17 May the master of the Ballhausplatz received him, again dwelling on the

---

[98] Wessenberg's "Erster Entwurf b," HHSA, StK., Deutsche Akten, Fasc. 100, pp. 309–330; Brandes, *Münster und die Wiedererstehung*, 112.

[99] Quint, *Souveränitätsbegriff*, 352–355; Klemmer, *Rechberg als Politiker*, 52–54; Aretin, "Deutsche Politik Bayerns," 41f.; and Schmidt, *Verfassungsfrage*, 468f.

[100] Text of proclamation in Huber, *Verfassungsgeschichte*, I, 303.

predatory plans of Prussia and her capacity to incite demagogues against the other states. Without a Bund and without federally circumscribed *landständische Verfassungen* there was no limit to the demands these fanatics would make. Gravely he spoke of "ferment" in the North; and even though he meant the machinations of the rebellious Standes-herren more than popular unrest, whatever the cause, it was the be-ginning of a long campaign to seek his ends by offering the Bund as a refuge for the nervous and the insecure. Wrede had already, in his draft of 1 April, singled out "the promotion of internal repose" as the purpose of constitutions and objected only to federal guarantees and guidelines. Rechberg's other worries concerned the federal court, the federal concordat with Rome, and seats in the diet for the mediatized. Metternich could truthfully say that, so far as he was concerned, apart from interstate disputes (which Bavaria already admitted) the court was meant only for the petty princes, who actually desired it. With equal veracity he could say that the single voice he intended for all the Standesherren together was a harmless concession to Prussia. Finally, a concordat, he assured his listener, would concern only the status of church property, not education or administration, and was really di-rected against Prussia's confiscatory policy in Silesia.[101]

The truth of this last statement is not so plain, but it hardly matters because shortly thereafter Metternich, seeing that both Bavaria and Prussia were against him, agreed to drop the clause. Was there a quid pro quo? We do not know, but if another guess is admissible, he could well have tried to delete the clause protecting Protestant rights, which Consalvi so resented, or failing that, to remove from the general bill of rights free choice of university attendance, which apprehensive Aus-trian authorities opposed lest their sons be exposed to Protestant ideas or the ferment at Giessen and Jena, which in their eyes amounted to the same thing. All we know in fact is that the final draft contained the Protestant clause but not the right to choose a university anywhere in the Bund.[102]

After dismissing Rechberg, somewhat curtly it would seem, it was back to the Prussians again to make the concession discussed above and probably to argue still about the distribution of votes in the diet. Paradoxically Hardenberg, who at one time had resisted even the ad-dition of Württemberg to the Council of Kreis Chiefs, now wanted to expand the smaller council to as many as thirty members with whole

[101] Quint, *Souveränitätsbegriff*, 352–355, and Klemmer, *Rechberg als Politiker*, 52–54, both of whom seem to believe that the draft of 7 May was at issue, but that one did not provide curial votes for the mediatized houses. Here and elsewhere I believe Quint exaggerates the importance of the word "sovereign." Cf. Aretin, "Deutsche Politik Bayerns," 41f.

[102] Text of 23 May 1815 in Klüber, *Acten*, II, 314–323.

votes, ostensibly to do justice to old houses such as Mecklenburg and Oldenburg. More likely, however, he feared the pro-Austrian bias of Metternich's gerrymandered curiae, and besides, the less suited the body was to be an executive organ, the better the argument for later appointing Kreis chiefs to enforce its resolutions. In the end Metternich prevailed with the fifteen votes previously noted, and the modalities of enforcement, once a high priority with Humboldt, were not mentioned at all. As Hardenberg explained to Rechberg, total silence was better than Metternich's glib generalities, which would only invite derision.[103]

In this spirit at one last meeting on 21 May the preliminary work ended, the Prussians seeking brevity, Metternich full of editorial tricks aimed at courting the other states, and Wessenberg, according to Humboldt, pontificating that if Prussia wanted more than a loose confederation, she should accept an emperor. Münster, once the stubborn foe of "dilution," dared not oppose it lest Bavaria and Württemberg refuse to join. Humboldt was disconsolate at the result and frustrated that Metternich left him no choice. It would have been better, he wrote his wife that evening, to have gone it alone with a few "well-disposed princes," but that course was not open. Münster, he explained, would have opposed and "Austria would have used all her influence to seduce the small states." The best to hope for now was that at the federal diet "the affair go to smash again and then perhaps a more rational even if smaller Bund will arise."[104] Even as the invitations went out the next day to the other states, Winzingerode was under orders to boycott the proceedings, and Rechberg had instructions as a last resort to join the separate South German league for which draft articles had existed since January. From Darmstadt orders were on their way to Türckheim to enter no Bund unless all the major states did so. Berstett of Baden, in the absence of instructions and even without accreditation to the congress as such, decided to attend only as an observer. Desperately and with astonishing naïveté the Württemberg envoy, who personally opposed a boycott, asked Metternich if the Kreis system would be kept. "For God's sake, no" he replied; "that would only be to Prussia's advantage." The single inducement that Württemberg had ever had was gone. The last phase of Metternich's struggle for German unity was about to begin.[105]

[103] Klemmer, *Rechberg als Politiker*, 54.
[104] Humboldt to Caroline, 21 May 1815, *Briefe*, IV, 556–558.
[105] Münster to Prince Regent, 15 May 1815, Münster, *Political Sketches*, 253f.; Montgelas and King Max Joseph's instruction for Rechberg, 14 May 1815, extracts in Klemmer, *Rechberg als Politiker*, 50; Winz. to Fred., 21 May 1815, and Fred. to Winz., 10 May 1815, extracts in Pfister, *Lager der Verbundeten*, 339f.; Dietrich, "Hessen-Darmstadt auf dem Wiener Kongress," 215–218.

CHAPTER XIII

THE FOUNDING OF

THE BUND

ON 23 May, in the morning, the Austrian foreign minister entered the familiar conference room with its large green table to find the other German envoys already assembled. Of the original committee of five the Prussians and Hanoverians were there, as well as the Bavarian envoy, Rechberg. Winzingerode, having failed to convert King Frederick, was absent.[1] The rest were attending their first conference of this kind. Schulenburg and Globig, who had signed peace for Saxony a bare five days before, now took their places alongside their peers from the other kingdoms. The Association of Princes and Free Cities was represented by five deputies, most notably, as one might expect, Plessen of Mecklenburg-Schwerin and Keller of Hesse-Cassel. Baden and Hesse-Darmstadt, having withdrawn from the association, were represented by Berstett and Türckheim respectively, the former, however, attending merely as an observer on the pretext that he was accredited only to allied headquarters. Finally there were Gagern for Luxemburg and Count Christian von Bernstorff for Holstein, whose presence was based on the royal standing of their non-German sovereigns.[2] Here, then, was Metternich's ensemble, previously rehearsed only a section at a time, waiting for the conductor to pass out the music and begin to play.

Explaining the long delay, Metternich now emphasized the urgency of a swift conclusion. The Bund, he pleaded, must be established before the war began; the armies were already on the march, and he himself must soon join them. He then read through the seventeen articles sponsored jointly by Austria and Prussia, asking that comment be reserved for the next meeting, which was set for 26 May. As they filed out some grumbled that there had been no debate, that copies of the plan were distributed only at the end of the meeting, and that the time for study was rather brief, considering that they had waited nine months only to see the project whipped through in haste. Plessen and Keller afterwards informed Metternich that although they could convey information, only the individual states could make commitments and must be admitted en masse to the deliberations. His reply is unrecorded

---

[1] Winz. to Fred., 23 May 1815, HSA, Stuttgart, E 70, Fasc. 19, p. 63.
[2] Protocol of 23 May 1815, Klüber, *Acten*, II, 339–341.

but probably contained the usual optimistic combination of asking for trust and counseling against reckless actions.[3]

That evening Metternich called together the Conference of Five to consider another matter crucial to his plans for the Bund. It should be recalled that the night before the news of Napoleon's escape reached Vienna, the five had made Gentz chairman of an editorial committee to combine the multitude of separate agreements into a comprehensive general treaty to serve as the vehicle for an international guarantee of the settlement. Since then, the impending hostilities had engendered second thoughts; why lend a false solemnity to a settlement that would disappoint many, was provisional in some of its parts, and would likely be outdated by the war? With more conquests in prospect in the west, Hardenberg was of this view, especially as the Saxon settlement was already guaranteed by the powers; and the Russians, though favoring a declaration of guarantee, had always resisted a general treaty. Talleyrand, by contrast, was eager to preserve in bronze the only settlement to which he was sure to be a party, and Clancarty, believing that he was carrying out Castlereagh's wishes, pressed for a general treaty containing an article of guarantee.

Because Metternich's goal was a guarantee regardless of means, he seems to have hesitated between the British and the Russian positions as the issue was debated throughout May. At the meeting of the 23rd, however, essentially siding with Talleyrand and Clancarty, he revived an idea he had put forward in the very first meeting on 16 September. There should indeed be a general instrument, consisting, however, of only those articles in the particular treaties and protocols that possessed a general European interest; the others would be attached as annexes but would have the same force and value. In his own thinking Metternich already set apart the first nine articles of the Austro-Prussian draft for inclusion in the main treaty. Gentz, despite his opposition to the plan, was again appointed along with Clancarty and Humboldt to draft the work. No decision was reached about an article or declaration of guarantee, but Metternich could now be sure that the settlement would have a unique grandeur that at least implied a certain obligation to maintain it.[4]

The initialing of the territorial settlement between Prussia and Nas-

---

[3] *Ibid.* and Apian-Bennewitz, *Plessen und die Verfassungspolitik*, 68.

[4] Gentz to Karadja, 26 June 1815, Klinkowström, *Oesterreichs Theilnahme*, 546–548; Talley. to Louis, 27 May 1815, Talleyrand, *Memoirs*, III, 126f.; Nesselrode's instructions to Russian missions, 25 May 1815, Schilder, *Imperator Aleksander*, III, 540–548; protocol of 23 May 1815, d'Angeberg, *Congrès*, III, 1218; Webster, *Castlereagh*, I, 430–434; and Nikolaus Dommermuth, *Das angebliche europäische Garantierecht über den deutschen Bund von 1815 bis 1866* (Ph.D. diss., University of Frankfurt, 1928), 38–42.

sau on 24 May left the Bund as the only major business of the congress. In the next two days Alexander, Frederick William, and Francis departed Vienna, bound for allied headquarters at Heidelberg. Metternich himself was making final preparations for closing down the congress, proposing to the emperor a list of foreigners who deserved decorations for their services to Austria, mostly commissioners dealing with boundaries and transit rights for the armies but also Baron Türckheim for "showing the greatest accommodation and attachement to the all highest court." To him went the Commander's Cross of the Order of St. Stephen, for which his greatest service was still to come. Nor did Metternich forget himself. Thankful as he was for two great fêtes at government expense, he wrote his master, there were some seventeen others that were no less official and deserving of at least partial reimbursement.[5]

A deeper concern, meanwhile, than 5,000 guilder more or less was the absence of Württemberg from the German conference, which could only encourage Berstett to maintain his unofficial status and leave Türckheim, the notorious friend of Reich, Standesherren, and estates, as the only South German support for Rechberg, who in turn would probably withdraw before acquiescing in any plan acceptable to Prussia. On 25 May Metternich appealed again to Winzingerode, agreeing that the prospects were bleak but that the attempt to found the Bund must be made now "lest Prussia create her own [einen bloss] North German Bund with the boundary of the Main," becoming as dangerous a neighbor as France. Winzingerode, whose orders were to avoid all contact with "Humboldt's monstrosity," had no choice but to reiterate his firm intention to stay away. To gloss over the rupture, however, he at least refrained from issuing defiant statements and to the next meeting merely sent word that he was indisposed and Linden had not yet returned from a jaunt in the country. There the matter rested till the end of the congress.[6]

When Metternich opened the next conference on 26 May, Winzingerode's absence was not the only disappointment. Berstett maintained his enigmatic demeanor, expressing a personal view that he desired a Bund but could say nothing more till his full powers arrived. The Saxons too pleaded no instructions, but in their case it was the simple truth. Thus Metternich had to proceed without key middle states that could either have brought pressure to bear on Bavaria or, by siding

[5] Mett. and Stadion to Francis, 26 May 1815, HHSA, StK., Vorträge, Cart. 198, pp. 92–98; Mett. to Francis, 25 May 1815, SUA, Prague, Acta Clementina, Corr. politique autriche, Cart. 6, folder 62-A, pp. 232f.

[6] Winz. to Fred., 25 May 1815, extr. in Pfister, Lage der Verbündeten, 340f.; Winz. note of 23 May 1815, Klüber, Acten, ii, 370.

with her, have demonstrated to the Prussians the necessity for compromise. As it happened, this latter role, surprisingly, was to fall to Türckheim. Rechberg, though genuinely without instructions, improvised for his government what amounted to a complete counterdraft, the same tactic Metternich had used against Hardenberg earlier in the month. In these articles he restored the attribution of sovereignty to the members and the anti-Kreis clause of Wessenberg's earlier drafts. Just as Wrede had once rejected a lower council altogether, Rechberg now insisted that the diet meet only in the narrower form and even then not necessarily in continuous session. Within this forum organic institutions and *jura singulorum* must be exempt from majority rule. Regarding war and alliances he again insisted on the right of the Bund to remain neutral in wars waged by Austria and Prussia as European powers and proposed that their "German" provinces be more precisely defined as those that had formerly belonged to the Reich. He also demanded an explicit affirmation of a state's right to conclude any alliance not directed against the Bund. Otherwise, Rechberg endorsed the Austro-Prussian recommendations on this basic subject as well as those on the appellate courts for the small states and the article on *landständische Verfassungen*, the last, however, with a small revision. Such constitutions, he proposed, "will come to be" not "shall exist." The fatefulness of this change, which was ultimately adopted, has been greatly exaggerated in the literature. For Bavaria the issue was not constitutions as such—Montgelas had often pointed out that his plans exceeded the federal norms usually advanced—but the appearance of federal dictation, which would constitute an infringement of sovereignty. As for the future history of the issue, the latitude allowed in this article was never cited by any ruler as the reason for not introducing a constitution.[7]

All these positions Türckheim either strongly seconded or proposed variants of that were not far removed. The same was true of the clauses on pensions derived from Rhine tolls, the rights of Thurn und Taxis, and religious equality, where the interests of Bavaria and Hesse-Darmstadt, though not identical, were similar. Concerning the rights of the mediatized houses Rechberg was more critical than Türckheim of the Austro-Prussian draft, but on the main point, seats in the federal diet, the two stood together in opposing them. They differed sharply on only two issues, Türckheim endorsing a federal court and, with unusual

---

[7] Protocol of 26 May 1815, Klüber, *Acten*, II, 342–400. Regarding *landständische Verfassungen*, although the protocol itself states that Bavaria endorsed the original language (p. 358), Rechberg's draft substituted *wird* for *soll*. Later *bestehen* was changed to *stattfinden* (p. 424) and both changes were adopted in the final draft of the Federal Act.

vigor, a federal concordat with Rome, Rechberg rejecting the latter completely and conceding in place of a court no more than ad hoc boards of arbitration for interstate disputes.[8]

This record of Bavarian-Hessian solidarity could easily be explained by the common interests of their monarchs, neither of whom desired a Bund at all while Grand Duke Louis spurned state constitutions as well. The problem is Türckheim, the man whose "hair stood on end" at the mention of sovereignty, who embraced estates constitutions as a principle, who even at this conference proposed that Standesherren and prince bishops have seats in the Landtage, and who at the end of the congress was once again to violate Louis's orders by signing the Federal Act. Why did he suddenly line up so staunchly for states' rights as propounded by Rechberg? And why were the only major exceptions, the federal court and the federal concordat, precisely objects that Metternich still pursued despite Bavaria and despite the fact that the concordat had been removed from the Austro-Prussian project? Why, further, was it Türckheim who at the same meeting moved the restoration of Austria's right to cast the decisive vote in case of ties, and in Article VII (pertaining to the first meeting of the diet) proposed language lifted verbatim from Wessenberg's December plan? To ask these questions is virtually to give the answer: Metternich was using the *Reichsfreiherr* from the old Austrian Ortenau to advance propositions that Austria, as the cosponsor of the current project, could not make herself without Prussia's consent. Münster, as we have seen, had often performed similar service for the two powers.

If Metternich's concern about the middle states was their possible withdrawal from the German conference, the small states meanwhile were clamoring for direct participation, as their deputies declared early in the meeting, adding that they were not empowered to accept any article in the name of their constituents. This stand, however, did not prevent their "raining on" the committee a "torrent" of tentative observations, to use the language of Prussian historians, who once believed that even if the accession treaties had not obligated the lesser states to accept quietly whatever the powers prepared for them, patriotism and right thinking did.

The deputies, to be sure, did have much to say, but most of it was reasonable and some of it constructive. Who could blame them at this point that, still smarting from Hardenberg's tortured reading of the accession treaties, they wished their sovereignty made clear by listing them all in the first article by name, that they wanted not only "the German states" to be preserved but "each and every one" as an indi-

[8] *Ibid.*

vidual entity, that they, no less than Bavaria and Hesse-Darmstadt, wanted the explicit anti-Kreis clause restored, and that they insisted on unanimity for the adoption of the Federal Act and subsequent constitutional amendments? Their version of the article on the structure of the diet, moreover, was actually an improvement over the original in both clarity and substance. Besides conducting the ordinary business of the Bund, the smaller council was to draft all fundamental law and submit it to the states, all of which must approve. For measures of general welfare, internal institutions, and procedural matters, however, a plenary session would be called in which each state had one vote and a *simple majority* would decide even in regard to erecting a federal court. The distinction between the diet as constituent assembly and year-to-year governing body was thus sharply drawn, as it should have been; the scope of majority decisions was broader than in the Bavarian plan and more like Wessenberg's first plenum. Similarly, the small states' criticism of the article on *landständische Verfassungen* was precisely that it omitted the four-point minimum that Münster and Humboldt had so cherished. On other points the deputation made numerous objections but mostly on matters pertaining to local conditions, the free cities, for example, objecting strongly to existing Jewish rights and Thurn und Taxis's postal franchises. These concerns, as well as the bickering over rank and status, made the small states appear more obstructive than they actually were in regard to the structure of the Bund.[9]

To the Prussians, however, who really believed that the lesser states had no right to any objections, the session seemed all chaos and scandal, a state of affairs bound to get worse if the conference was to be opened to all, as Humboldt admitted it must. And yet, he reminded Metternich in an official note the day after, if the Federal Act was not completed in time to become part of the general treaty, the two sponsoring courts would lose the only advantage for which they had already sacrificed so much, and one might just as well leave everything till Frankfurt. The only course now was an ultimatum, he insisted, proposing one more private parley with Münster to take account of as many objections as possible and presenting a revised draft at the next meeting. Austria and Prussia should there declare their adherence to it and call on the others to take it or leave it, advising them that amendments could always be made later.[10]

Metternich suspected that an ultimatum of this kind must come eventually, but for him it was imperative to make sure of Bavaria first.

[9] *Ibid.*

[10] Hard. and Humb. to Mett., 27 May 1815, text in Humboldt, *Gesammelte Schriften*, XI, 314–317.

His next move, therefore, was to summon Rechberg to the chancellery once again. There he chided the Bavarian for firing a broadside when he might easily have pleaded no instructions but admitted that Austria could endorse many of his suggestions. One must distinguish, he said, between the first nine articles, which were designed to establish a voluntary association on international principles, and the remaining eight, which outlined a program mostly for later action and left the door open to revision as Bavaria or other states should prefer. Seats for the mediatized, Metternich now conceded, were not necessary provided that the hereditary equality with the sovereigns symbolized by them could be salvaged in some other way, perhaps by a special clause to that effect. Rechberg, who was aware of Duke Ferdinand of Württemberg's interest in Princess Pauline Metternich, agreed that that was a possibility and later in the day advised his government to adopt this harmless way to humor the Austrian foreign minister in a matter involving a personal interest. An ultimatum, Metternich privately concluded, must at least await the arrival of a courier from Munich, and Rechberg departed, confident that he could prolong the deliberations a while longer.[11]

The rejection of an ultimatum, of course, only enhanced the importance of another conference of the three as Humboldt had proposed. This took place on 28 May and, except for easy agreement to invite all states, including Württemberg, to the next conference, was perhaps the most acrimonious in the long series going back to the memorable gathering at Münster's bedside on 12 October, where the Twelve Articles had been completed. At the German conference on 26 May Humboldt had virtually dared Rechberg to repudiate the Bund, threatening to stir up the mediatized houses against Bavaria.[12] With an ultimatum in view the Prussian had little reason to yield. Metternich, by contrast, still aiming at consensus, was now virtually the bargaining agent for Bavaria, fully aware that if she could be accommodated, an ultimatum would consolidate, not divide Germany. Although Münster now believed that Hanover was more secure with a Bund than without one, even if Bavaria did not join, he sided with Metternich.[13]

Against the overwhelming majority the Prussians still refused to admit "sovereignty" into the Federal Act or expressly forbid the supremacy of one state over another, and Metternich gave in, leaving it to the other states to force the issue.[14] He also gave ground on the

[11] Klemmer, *Rechberg als Politiker*, 59–61; Quint, *Souveränitätsbegriff*, 363, who incorrectly places the interview on 28 May.

[12] Aretin, "Deutsche Politik Bayerns," 44.

[13] Münster to Prince Regent, 3 June 1815, Münster, *Political Sketches*, 267–271.

[14] This and the following inferred from the revisions proposed at the next German conference on 29 May 1815. Protocol in Klüber, *Acten*, ii, 401–409.

organization of the diet, accepting an expansion of the smaller council from fifteen to seventeen or nineteen as the German conference should decide and, for plenary sessions, a scheme of weighted votes ranging from four each for all the kingdoms to one each for the smallest states. In return he regained for Austria the right to cast the deciding vote in case of deadlock. He also obtained a redrafting of the article on wars and alliances in the Bavarian sense, removing all restrictions on subsidy treaties and rephrasing the text with Rechberg's emphasis on "the right of alliances of all kinds" except those directed against the Bund or its members. If Bavaria accepted this one article, Metternich could be flexible on all the rest, but for good measure he also obtained Rechberg's proposed "will come to be" in place of "shall exist" in regard to *landständische Verfassungen.*

Concerning representation of the mediatized houses in the federal diet, he seems to have been more devious, agreeing to pursue it vigorously but gaining Prussia's permission for him to move on his own the explicit recognition of equality of birth as discussed with Rechberg. With this adopted, actual votes would have little additional value and if Bavaria insisted, could later be quietly dropped or referred to Frankfurt. Referral to Frankfurt was probably also Metternich's solution to the Jewish clause which, far from winning votes, had actually provoked laughter at the previous meeting. Hardenberg, however, was adamant, fearing that delay would allow time for the revocation of reform measures and result in flooding Prussia with refugees. Despite Münster's support, which must be presumed, Metternich, with encouragement from Gentz, yielded and agreed to press for an immediate decision in favor of the existing article, which had loopholes enough but still protected, by inference at least, the existing gains.[15]

Thus prepared, Metternich on the 29th opened the next German conference, facing for the first time the entire mass of German envoys, some thirty-seven in all, not counting the Württembergers, who still did not attend. The task was a complete reading of the Austro-Prussian articles as amended, a process that despite the chairman's whirlwind tactics required daily meetings through 3 June, most of them tumultuous and full of confusion. At one time, Wessenberg reported years later in taking credit for the final product, he had no fewer than forty-six different drafts on his desk. The pace at times was so fast, the level of noise so high, that Martens, who was hard of hearing, found it impossible to take more than cursory minutes that relied heavily on written declarations rather than the oratory of the crowded conference room. To avoid embroilment in this confusion ourselves, it is advisable

[15] Baron, *Die Judenfrage*, 160; Gentz, *Tagebücher*, 381; Humb. to Caroline, 4 June 1815, *Briefe*, IV, 565–567.

for once to abandon our day-to-day narrative and pursue each issue in turn through the vagaries of the several meetings.[16]

The bedlam began at once, precipitated, however, from an unexpected source. With everybody primed to deal with the central issue of article one, whether or not to refer to the members as sovereign, Reichsgraf Gagern quixotically interjected a motion to call the confederation "the Bund in the German Reich." After it was discreetly decided to refer the suggestion to Frankfurt, the real business began, and even though the sovereignty issue too was in part a verbal quibble, it continued to excite passions, generating a debate of almost an hour, mainly between Rechberg and Humboldt. To circumvent the problem Globig of Saxony revived the small-state proposal simply to list all members in this article with their titles, making it clear that they were the equals of the two powers and the superiors of the mediatized houses. Contrary to all previous orders from Munich, Rechberg obligingly accepted this solution only to find at the next meeting that when it came to the actual listing, all the old strife over rank and precedence broke out again, especially among the grand dukes, who opposed an hierarchical order derived from the former Reichstag. The problem was solved by agreeing to refer to the rulers of Baden and Darmstadt as "Their Royal Highnesses" and equating them with the elector of Hesse-Cassel.[17]

On this basis the article was adopted, but only for a while. On 1 June the Saxon envoys, at last provided with instructions, announced that they must insist on the term "sovereign" in addition to the listing of members. Bound by his pledges to Prussia not to yield, yet determined to forestall another diatribe by Hardenberg on the true meaning of the accession treaties, Metternich entered the debate himself, declaring that no one contested the principle of sovereignty, which every line of the document exuded, but that there was no need to state the obvious, especially in the very first sentence. Like all arguments based on trivialization, this one could cut both ways: if nothing more was involved than redundancy, why make an issue of it? In any case, as long as this interpretation was only in the protocol, not in the Federal Act itself, Humboldt did not challenge the Austrian view and the Saxons retreated, reserving the point for another session. Two days later, however, Rechberg and Schulenburg, with support from Nassau and the two Hesses, renewed the demand for sovereignty, and this time Metternich, breaking ranks with Hardenberg, supported the motion, provided that the listing of members, now an obvious redundancy, was

---

[16] Protocol of 29 May 1815, Klüber, *Acten*, II, 401f.; Arneth, *Wessenberg*, I, 276f., n. 2; Aretin, "Deutsche Politik Bayerns," 47.

[17] Protocol of 29 May 1815, Klüber, *Acten*, II, 402f. and 414f.; Quint, *Souveränitätsbegriff*, 365–367; Klemmer, *Rechberg als Politiker*, 61.

dropped. The article, redrafted on this basis, was now unanimously adopted, Hardenberg confining his hostility to the observation that Prussia still considered the mention of sovereignty superfluous. To balance the loss, however, he had in the meantime defeated repeated attempts to restore the anti-Kreis clause forbidding the supremacy of one state over another. Thus the final formulation of Article III read simply that as members of the Bund the states had equal rights and an equal obligation to uphold the Federal Act.[18]

The next four articles concerned the structure and organization of the federal diet. On 29 May Metternich, as by agreement with the Prussians, offered two alternative plans for the smaller council, one with nineteen votes, the other with seventeen, depending on whether Nassau, Brunswick, and Oldenburg had votes of their own or fractional ones. As all the other states (except Prussia, which now favored a larger body) naturally desired that their votes, whether integral or collective, constitute a larger fraction of the whole, the plan for seventeen was adopted, Nassau and Brunswick forming one curia, Oldenburg under protest joining the five houses of the Anhalt and Schwarzburg lines in another, thus receiving only one-sixth of a vote. The arrangement owed much to Marschall's efforts and no doubt pleased Metternich as well, for Nassau and Brunswick both had ties to the non-German world and were similar in size and equally exposed to Prussia. If the tsar had still been there, his uncle in Oldenburg might have fared better.[19]

The main achievement of 29 May was the decision to provide for plenary sessions to act on general laws, organic institutions, and constitutional amendments. Rechberg and Türckheim continued to register their disapproval of such a body but acquiesced in order to deny Humboldt the opportunity to charge sabotage and perhaps drive them from the conference. Metternich then presented the Prussian scheme of alloting one, three, or four votes to individual states, but in the course of the debate, which continued the next day, a class with two votes was established for Nassau, Mecklenburg-Schwerin, and Brunswick, each of which had a population slightly above 200,000. With this amendment the total number of votes came to sixty-nine, where it remained until Hesse-Homburg was added as a sovereign state in 1817.[20]

More controversial were the procedural questions. Rechberg, who feared that an assembly in permanent session would gradually develop into a true government, proposed that the diet must adjourn when

[18] Protocols of 30 May, 1 and 3 June, 1815, Klüber, *Acten*, ii, 420, 454, 493f.; Quint, *Souveränitätsbegriff*, 374–376.
[19] Sarholz, "Nassau 1813–1815," 95; protocol of 29 May 1815, Klüber, *Acten*, ii, 403–406.
[20] Klüber, *Acten*, ii, 406–409; Quint, *Souveränitätsbegriff*, 370.

the year's business was finished.[21] The compromise solution was to permit this while still retaining Humboldt's reference to a "continuous" body. Still more bitter was the dispute over majority decisions. On 29 May the conference adopted the rule of absolute majority for the smaller council, with the exception demanded by Rechberg that the *jura singulorum* of all members were to be honored. At the same time, on the motion of Türckheim Austria at last received her right to cast tie-breaking votes, at least in the smaller council. In a move to clarify the confused language of the Austro-Prussian draft, the power of decision on whether an issue must come before the plenum was given exclusively to the smaller council, voting by majority, in regard to both the completion of the constitution and all subsequent business.[22]

After the small states on 26 May had stated their willingness, with a few exceptions, to extend majority rule to plenary sessions, that issue appeared settled, but suddenly on 2 June, the same Saxon envoys who the day before had demanded both sovereignty and a roster of the members, now demanded that *all* bills must require unanimity, in which case the graduated voting system already adopted would be unnecessary. What the prospect of any general-welfare measure or constitutional amendment would be in that case was obvious to all and ignited heated debate. It was just as well that Hardenberg was not present that day to witness the latest outrage perpetrated by people who, if he had had it his way, would not have been there at all. Be that as it may, it was Münster who stepped in to restore order, proposing that a majority of two-thirds be the standard. As Metternich and Humboldt grasped at this expedient, and even Globig admitted that he personally favored it, it was tentatively adopted.[23]

Rechberg and most of the other middle-state envoys, however, continuing their campaign to protect internal legislation from federal interference, in the end succeeded in having the entire article redrafted to read that in both the smaller and plenary forums constitutional amendments, organic institutions, *jura singulorum*, and religious affairs were not amenable to majority decision of any kind. The language was not precise but seemed, in contrast to Wessenberg's earlier drafts, positively to require unanimity, not merely to exempt the minority from the application of a measure effective for the rest. The only remaining category subject to even the two-thirds rule was measures affecting the general welfare, though in its broadest interpretation this was potentially the equivalent of the legislative power itself.[24]

[21] Klemmer, *Rechberg als Politiker*, 62.
[22] Protocol of 29 May 1815, Klüber, *Acten*, II, 407–409.
[23] Protocol of 2 June 1815, Klüber, *Acten*, II, 466f.
[24] Protocol of 3 June 1815, Klüber, *Acten*, II, 497f.

Although Metternich, with his attention riveted upon the establishment of a whole-German defense league, willingly, perhaps cheerfully made these concessions, Austria lost more than Prussia did. In his most ambitious moments he had visualized himself presiding over an assembly of equals, certain that with the aid of his small clients he would command comfortable majorities against Prussia. The system that was in fact emerging was in future years to force him back to Berlin, for only the combined pressure of both powers, as the history of the Bund was to show, could produce the votes necessary to clear the hurdles to legislative action or institutional change. Only after 1848 and the shock of Josef Maria von Radowitz's Prussian Union plan did the middle states act on the danger and collaborate with the Austrians in projects to expand the federal legislative authority and the sway of majority resolutions as Metternich had intended in the beginning, but by then it was too late; Bismarck's skillful filibuster blocked the way, with the very tools that the middle states had made available.[25]

Metternich's principal concern, meanwhile, next to the articles founding the Bund, was Article IX, which defined the mutual defense obligations of the members that for him constituted the true meaning of the organization, whatever else could be achieved. Consensus had long prevailed that the members be pledged to abstain from the use of force against each other, to render military aid against foreign attack, to make no separate peace, and unilaterally to withdraw no troops from the common effort. Additionally Austria and Prussia now recognized, as noted above, "the right of alliances of all kinds" except those directed against the Bund or any of its members, and expressly removed their non-Bund lands from the federal protective umbrella. Yet the precise relationship of the Bund to these territories had never been defined. The Forty-one Articles of Stein and Hardenberg had projected a separate treaty between the Bund and the powers to regulate the matter. The Twelve Articles of 14 October had provided that in wars waged by Austria and Prussia as European powers the Bund, by means not specified, was to decide whether to enter or not. Then, in the October deliberations Marshal Wrede had demanded that in such wars or in any other European conflict not dangerous to Germany, each state should be free to join regardless of what the Bund as such decided to do. At the time Wessenberg and Humboldt had partially conceded this right, but upon more mature reflection, they evidently concluded that the probable outcome would be the breakup of the

[25] Cf. Enno E. Kraehe, "Austria and the Problem of Reform in the German Confederation, 1851–1863," *American Historical Review*, LVI (1950–1951), 276–294.

Bund as some states became belligerents and others did not.[26] In any case, the later drafts of Austria and Prussia simply omitted both issues, and that is why Rechberg in his counterproject of 26 May raised them again, in the same paragraph coupling the Bund's option to remain neutral with the individual members' right to all alliances not directed against the Bund.[27]

When the debate resumed on 30 May, the Danish envoys, Christian and Joachim von Bernstorff (brothers) added their weight to Rechberg's cause; for the king of Denmark the purpose of the Bund was to protect Holstein and the land approaches to his kingdom, not to drag Denmark into a war in Italy or the Balkans. But there was the rub. The Bund's *option* to remain neutral implied the right not to, and this raised the problem of determining when, under what circumstances, and by what procedures the Bund might render aid to Austria or Prussia, or for that matter to Denmark and the Netherlands. The issue was too complex and too fundamenal to the European equilibrium to solve in the existing atmosphere, which cast doubt on the very establishment of the Bund. Any solution that Metternich could have obtained then would have fallen short of his goal: a flexible system leaving Russia, say, uncertain about the response of the Bund in event of an attack on Hungary or East Prussia.[28] By omitting the issue now, he kept this option open even while granting, as the revised Austro-Prussian draft did, the right of all alliances not directed against the Bund.[29]

Somewhat incongruously Article IX contained another explosive issue: the federal court. Inasmuch as the members were enjoined from using force against each other, their disputes were to go to the diet, which was then to call in a federal court representative of the membership, its competence to be determined later in Frankfurt. Obviously this language opened the door to cases other than interstate disputes, and Rechberg, not risking a reprimand from Munich such as Wrede had received in November for wavering on this issue, was emphatic in his opposition. Hoping to expose Bavaria's isolation, Metternich called for a vote, which apart from abstentions by a few envoys without instructions had that result, and Rechberg, loath to cast the only negative

[26] E.g., in a Franco-Austrian war over Italy, the South German states might fear a French drive for the Danube and wish to join Austria, whereas the more numerous states of North Germany might vote to keep the Bund neutral.

[27] Bavarian *Votum*, 26 May 1815, Klüber, *Acten*, II, 383f.

[28] Cf. Enno E. Kraehe, "From Rheinbund to Deutscher Bund: The Road to European Equilibrium," *Proceedings of the Fourth Annual Consortium for Revolutionary Europe* (Tallahassee; Florida State University Press, 1977), 163–175. Russia was his main concern, but the case that actually occurred was the French assault on Lombardy in 1859 against which Austria appealed in vain for federal aid.

[29] Protocol of 30 May 1815, with annexes, Klüber, *Acten*, II, 423–432.

vote, reserved a further declaration regarding both the court and the neutrality of the Bund. As consolation, however, the conference proceeded immediately after to adopt, at least until something better could be devised, the Bavarian language regarding state constitutions. Although the small states, led by Gagern, continued to demand the four-point minimum, the article as finally adopted read: "In all German states there will be *landständische Verfassungen.*"[30]

On the following day, 31 May, Metternich opened debate on the fate of the mediatized houses, deviously insisting that the first question was whether they should have several curial votes or only one. Thereupon Keller of Hesse-Cassel, probably acting as a surrogate for Humboldt, proposed four seats reflecting, he said, the traditions of the Councils of Westphalia, Swabia, Franconia, and the Rhine in the old Reichstag. He also demanded an extension of the list of privileges and a narrower definition of governmental rights, the same demands that Gärtner was making at the time.[31] Türckheim then ventured an ingenious compromise: a small hereditary state with sovereignty vested in all the Standesherren collectively should be created with a seat in the diet, thereby separating their federal standing from their status as bona fide subjects within the several states. If Metternich had felt strongly, he might have seized on the expedient; instead he joined Humboldt, who objected in principle, to move that the issue *of the number of curial votes* be among the many now to be referred to Frankfurt. After the other points in the lengthy article had been read and more or less approved, Metternich at last came to his own interest, moving, with the aid of a statement by Gagern, that hereditary equality with the sovereigns was among the undisputed attributes of the mediatized. This point too was informally approved, Rechberg alone reserving a later statement. "Not a voice dared propose restrictions on their rights," he somberly reported, adding "that without the mediatized and the imperial nobility perhaps no one would ever have thought about a federal act." That was a half truth, partially applicable to the Prussian plans, perhaps, but not to Metternich's.[32]

As Franz Georg Metternich, Gärtner, Solms, and other agents of the mediatized houses assiduously made the rounds of the German delegations, Rechberg, still without instructions but resolved to avoid the stigma of obstructionism while playing for time, suddenly at the next conference offered the Bavarian ordinance of 1807 as a model and

[30] *Ibid.*, II, 423f.; Klemmer, *Rechberg als Politiker*, 68f; Quint, *Souveränitätsbegriff*, 370f.

[31] Hoff, *Mediatisiertenfrage*, 112. The tone of Keller's written proposal, Klüber, *Acten*, II, 445–447, reflects the hands of Solms and Gärtner.

[32] Protocol of 31 May 1815, Klüber, *Acten, ibid.*, II, 433–450; Rechberg's report of 31 May as quoted by Quint, *Souveränitätsbegriff*, 372.

proposed the appointment of a committee to study it. Whether Metternich had a hand in this démarche cannot be proved, but he supported it even though in a few respects it contradicted the action of the previous day. The committee chosen, moreover, could hardly have been more congenial: Rechberg himself and Türckheim; Münster, who at the time had the rebellious Count Bentheim-Rheda to cope with; Plessen, who had recently proposed that the whole problem be studied later by a committee drawn from states without mediatized subjects; and finally Gagern, the only strong advocate of the Standesherren in the group.[33]

Even recalling that Wessenberg and Humboldt had already borrowed much from the Bavarian ordinance, the degree of harmony attained is surprising. Ironically, the deliberations were helped along by Gärtner, whose testimony before the committee seems to have given the impression that his constituents accepted the Bavarian ordinance as a valid norm. Later, under a rain of protests from Franz Georg, Princess Elisabeth of Fürstenberg, and all the Solms lines, he retracted, but the damage was done. In the finished report, which Plessen as chairman submitted on 2 June, the ordinance was made the guideline for all details of implementation. Rechberg also obtained a stronger role for the state in supervising the patrimonial operations of the lords, the right of the state authorities to record and certify private family compacts, and the conversion of an explicit exemption from personal taxes to a bland statement that the lords were a privileged class "especially in regard to taxation." On the other hand, the Bavarian, as he had half-promised Metternich, conceded equality of birth and even added exemption from military service and a privileged position before the law, which had not been in the original article at all. The committee also wrestled with the problem, potentially a direct concern to Austria, of the imperial knights on the left bank, finally agreeing to permit differential treatment as circumstances there necessitated. The main obstacle, however, was not overcome. Most of the committee now conceded that the federal diet would decide "*whether* and to what extent" to grant curial votes to the Standesherren, but Rechberg and Türckheim refused to admit even the possibility and submitted a minority report. As a result, the issue was held over till 3 June, when the revised article was adopted, Bavaria and Hesse-Darmstadt still protesting.[34]

As the reading of the Austro-Prussian articles continued, attention

[33] Protocol of 1 June 1815, Klüber, *Acten*, II, 452f.; Hoff, *Mediatisiertenfrage*, 115f.; Quint, *Souveränitätsbegriff*, 373f. On Plessen see draft constitution in Chap. XII, n. 49.

[34] Protocol of 2 June 1815 and revised text of Article XI (now numbered 14), Klüber, *Acten*, II, 467–469 and 486–489; Hoff, *Mediatisiertenfrage*, 115–117; Quint, *Souveränitätsbegriff*, 376f.

turned to what can be called special interests as opposed to the structural components of the Bund. The article guaranteeing the continuation of pensions now included not only those paid from tolls collected on the Rhine but all pensions and other claims previously recognized in the imperial recess, payment to be made by the current sovereign where holdover funds did not suffice. With minor tinkering that extended the coverage to "subsidiary" claims and expressly included payments due members of the Order of Teutonic Knights, the article, completely restorative in spirit, was adopted on 3 June, Metternich taking no part. Regarding the claims of Thurn und Taxis the free cities continued to protest the imposition on them of the house's allegedly exorbitant postal rates, arguing that their sovereignty voided such bondage. On 31 May Humboldt offered to redraft the article, but the only change he and Metternich made was to avoid mentioning the cities by name. This version, which as well continued to require compensation for certain lost franchises, was adopted on 1 June, Metternich seeing in it mainly a political favor deserving future services to Austria.[35]

The free cities likewise led the attack on the article extending civil and political rights equally to all Christians and civil rights to the Jews, the latter at least to the extent that all members of the Bund were to declare their intent to remove any existing disabilities "so far as possible." Since the prevailing statutes in the free cities, the legacy of French rule, had eliminated virtually all discrimination, a pledge of this sort would amount to freezing the existing order, which, as we have seen, the cities bitterly resented, the more so perhaps as they also seemed to be singled out to bear the brunt of the claims of Thurn und Taxis. Their solution was to refer the issue to the future diet, hoping that in the interval, of indeterminate duration, they could quietly rescind the French legislation. The cities, of course, were not alone in their anti-Semitism; Globig of Saxony and Keller of Hesse-Cassel were especially hostile, but when Münster, another anti-Semite, declared that, as he read the article, each state was free to determine the pace of amelioration, most of the envoys were satisfied.[36]

Nevertheless, Metternich and Humboldt offered to present a revised version, and did so the next day, 1 June. The new text was, if anything, stronger than before, charging the federal diet to study ways to secure the civil rights of the Jews and expressly requiring that until then all rights thus far granted in the several states must be preserved. In this way the cities were given an incentive to accelerate federal action, and

[35] Protocols of 31 May and 1 June 1815, Klüber, *Acten*, II, 438 and 453.
[36] Protocol of 31 May 1815, Klüber, *Acten*, II, 439–441, and 456–457, 463–465; Baron, *Die Judenfrage*, 160–177.

Prussia was momentarily spared the prospect of an unwanted influx, at least from those quarters—or so it seemed. At that same session an editorial committee, consisting of Smidt of Bremen and Günther Heinrich von Berg of Schaumburg, was appointed to prepare a new draft of the entire Federal Act. Both were well-qualified professionals, but Smidt was also the leader of the opposition to the Jews and took it upon himself to change the clause preserving all rights "granted *in* the several states" to those granted *by* those states, thus exempting legislation inherited from the French period, as he candidly admitted at the next session. As Bavaria, Hesse-Darmstadt, and Saxony openly and several others tacitly questioned the propriety of the entire paragraph for inclusion in the Federal Act, its champions, Metternich included, acquiesced. Again, anything to establish the Bund; and, besides, he never believed that verbal tricks, much as he used them himself, changed political realities. In the end, the fate of the Jews would depend on the pressure Austria and Prussia could bring to bear, and that, despite his and Hardenberg's conscientious efforts in the federal diet, was to prove inadequate.[37]

No less impassioned were the debates, inside and outside the German conference, on the rights of the Catholic and Evangelical churches. In the article under consideration the Bund was to grant to the Catholic church a constitution guaranteeing its rights and appropriate funding and to the Lutherans the rights incorporated in state constitutions, peace treaties, and other covenants. Both clauses were repugnant to Consalvi, who feared the supremacy of the secular authority and resented that the Protestants would receive immediate protection, the Catholics merely promises. Without a concordat, moreover, the article served little purpose, the cardinal concluded, and along with the orators advised Metternich to delete it. As the latter knew by now how fiercely the Bavarians opposed it, he was easily persuaded. On 31 May, on his motion, the deed was done, Humboldt also feeling relieved perhaps to be rid of a dispute from which Prussia had little to gain.[38]

That was not the end of it, however. Ignaz von Wessenberg, shocked that the inchoate Federal Act said nothing about a German church, now concluded that a slight advantage for Protestants was better than no article at all. Marshaling all his resources—the Dalberg legions, his influence with the brothers Spiegel, and his intimate contacts at the highest level of the Austrian service—he obtained a new version, which on the model of the article on *landständische Verfassungen*, projected

[37] Protocols of 1 and 3 June 1815, Klüber, *Acten*, ii, 463–465 and 501f.; Baron, *Die Judenfrage*, 177–180; and Humboldt to Caroline, 4 June 1815; *Briefe*, iv, 565–567.
[38] Protocol of 31 May 1815, Klüber, *Acten*, ii, 441; Ruck, *Römische Kurie*, 70.

both Catholic and Protestant rights into the future and omitted a federal guarantee. On 3 June the article by a majority vote was tentatively
restored. Consalvi was reconciled somewhat but remained indifferent
as did Metternich, whose only interest, the possibility of a federal concordat, had long ago vanished.[39]

In comparison with the passions generated by religious issues, the
article on general rights met only perfunctory opposition, perhaps
because the preliminary conferences had already siphoned off the
ferments—*habeas corpus*, which Stein had long ago proposed, freedom
of university attendance, which Austrian authorities had struck down,
and a few guarantees of person and property contained in Humboldt's
earlier drafts. What remained was the freedom of movement, of property ownership, and of government service anywhere in the Bund
without penalty, subject, however, in the case of emigration to the
fulfillment of military obligations. Copyrights and freedom of the press
were referred to the federal diet, which was to draft "appropriate laws"
regarding them. On 26 May Rechberg tried in vain to make these
rights only the subject of friendly negotiations among the governments.
On 2 June the editorial committee, following a Bavarian proposal,
changed "rights" to "permission" and substituted "uniform dispositions" for "appropriate laws," an amendment revealing that, contrary
to popular belief later on, this was not a promise of freedom of the
press but an effort to institute standardized regulation throughout the
Bund. The records unfortunately do not pinpoint the instigator of the
change. Finally on 3 June, on a motion by Saxony, the committee added
a proviso charging the diet to establish uniform principles to determine
when military obligation had been fulfilled. With these amendments
general rights entered the Federal Act as Article XVIII.[40]

Still less controversy attended the final article of the draft, the one
charging the federal diet at its first meeting to enact appropriate measures for freedom of trade and commerce, freedom of navigation on
the basis of principles enacted by the congress, and all matters affecting
the general welfare. Next to the federal presidency and the common
defense, this was perhaps the most "Austrian" or at least the most
Metternichian article of all. Though not without antecedents in both
versions of the Forty-one Articles (when Hardenberg assumed Prussia's
full parity with Austria), the article thereafter was exclusively an Austrian project, coming to full bloom in Wessenberg's December plan
and later, with the exact wording given here, in his first counterproject

[39] Protocol of 2 June 1815; Klüber, *Acten*, II, 471 and 490; Orators' memorial,
ibid., IV, 295–299; Ruck, *Römische Kurie*, 71–73.

[40] Protocols of 26 May, 2 and 3 June 1815, Klüber, *Acten*, II, 369f., 491f., and
502.

of early May. Nothing like it ever appeared in the Humboldt plans; on the contrary, the latter as late as mid-May had advised deleting it as unimportant. Nevertheless, he allowed it to stand, and even Rechberg, in his counterproject of 26 May, did not rule it out though he did propose that any action taken under it should require unanimity. Aided by Humboldt's apathy, he succeeded on 2 June in diluting the text further, making the topics subjects of deliberation, not necessarily enactment, and deleting the reference to freedom.[41]

On the surface, it is hard to say which is more astonishing: the widespread support Metternich had in the matter or the indifference displayed by the predecessors of the founders of the Zollverein. Still, the latter attitude was consistent with Humboldt's continuing reluctance to strengthen the Second Council and expand the legislative activity of the Bund, which Wessenberg always sought to do. One purpose was certainly to reserve that sphere for the Kreis assemblies, but there was something else, perhaps lurking only in the subconscious. Apart from the elements of power politics, the Prussian articles reflected the old concept of the Reich as the protector of rights and status, not as an engine of government engaged in practical projects to improve the commonweal. Federal court, seats for the mediatized, even *landständische Verfassungen* (at least as seen by such as Solms and Gärtner)—these were instruments for protecting privilege, not for getting things done. Metternich's thinking, if not necessarily more liberal, was more modern in this regard, shaped, it is perhaps trite to say, by eighteenth-century rationalism and an admiration for Napoleonic models. For him, a Bund empowered to bring its members together to promote projects of mutual benefit was no threat to the multinational Austrian state, as his policies in the early years of the federal diet were to demonstrate. It was rather the emperor and his Josephinist minions who prevented him from collaborating constructively in such projects, and so the initiative eventually passed to Prussia.[42]

To be sure, there were elements of self-interest in the two positions. It was vital to Austria, for example, to keep the Rhine, the Elbe, and other rivers of the North open to her goods. The Prussian interest, even though her policies were fairly liberal, was not the same, and

---

[41] Protocols of 26 May and 2 June 1815, Klüber, *Acten*, II, 369f., 472f., and 492.

[42] See Adolf Beer, *Die Finanzen Österreichs im XIX, Jahrhundert* (Prague, 1877), 175–183 and now even more emphatically Eva Weiss, "The Vienna Conference of 1819–1820: Metternich and Article 19 of the Federal Act" (Ph.D. diss., McGill University, 1979), *passim*. Cynics might say that in measures of common interest Metternich was already thinking ahead to the Carlsbad Decrees, but apart from the lack of evidence for this conjecture, the repressive enactments of 1819 were based on Article II, concerning internal security, not the diet's power to legislate for the general welfare.

Humboldt had seen to it at the congress that the commission on river navigation blocked an effort by Clancarty to extend freedom of navigation and commerce on continental waterways to "all the nations." In the final formulation freedom was complete for riparian states but to others the ubiquitous qualifier "as favorable as possible" was applied. Humboldt, who was satisfied that Prussia had won the dominant position in regulating the Rhine, undoubtedly feared that the Wessenberg article could bring on federal regulation.[43] As in the 1850s, a Bund that Prussia did not dominate had better have, apart from measures of defense and repression, as little legislative power as possible.

On the whole Metternich seems to have been satisfied with the progress made. The draft was much improved, he reported to the emperor, now at Heidelberg, and almost all the princes followed Austria's lead, even Prussia, "who goes along *faute de mieux* while putting a good face on a sorry business." But the minister's reports to Francis were almost always cheerfully optimistic, the more so when they were distances apart. Hardly had he assured the latter that Baden would shortly join the Bund when Berstett on 1 June declared before the conference his government's blanket endorsement of all the Bavarian and Württembergian positions and walked out. After the meeting Metternich begged him "not to separate himself from the common cause," but in vain. Berstett never returned.[44]

That left Rechberg and Türckheim. Just before the conference of 3 June, when the third reading of the complete draft was to begin, Metternich again summoned the Bavarian to make one last offer. If he would only declare Bavaria's membership in the Bund, he, Metternich, would support him on all outstanding issues. Rechberg thanked him, but without orders from Munich, he said, he could not make a commitment of that magnitude, mentally noting, no doubt, that Metternich's support, though valuable, was no guarantee. Several times Metternich repeated his pleas, almost begging now and perhaps imagining that were the roles reversed, he would have gambled on his government's support. As it was, Rechberg merely repeated his certainty that his instructions, when they arrived, would demand as a minimum freedom of alliances, no representation for the mediatized, no court, and no interference in internal affairs. With that he departed, ever the faithful servant, not a free spirit like Türckheim.[45]

If Metternich had tried to force a commitment on Rechberg in return

---

[43] Relevant records of the commission in Klüber, *Acten*, III, especially pp. 21, 170f., and 258–260. Also, Griewank, *Wiener Kongress*, 230–232, and Gebhardt, *Humboldt als Staatsmann*, 164–167.

[44] Mett. to Francis, 31 May 1815, extract in Hartmann, *Schicksal der Vorschläge*, 86; Glaser, "Die badische Politik," 302.

[45] Quint, *Souveränitätsbegriff*, 377f.

for support but no guarantee of the outcome, he now faced a similar dilemma himself. A firm stand would probably drive Bavaria out, but weakening the federal constitution still more would not guarantee her participation. Typically he adopted a middle course. When the third reading began of a draft that now came to twenty articles, he at last deserted Hardenberg and, as noted earlier, succeeded, with broad support from the lesser states, in making the princes and free cities "sovereign." His next move is more problematic. After obtaining several minor changes desired by Rechberg in the article on defense, he faced the issue of the federal court again. Hitherto, although a few objections had been raised about its jurisdiction, Bavaria had stood alone in the conference in opposing its very existence. Now Türckheim announced that new orders required him to repudiate his stand of 26 May and endorse the Bavarian declaration, which called for boards of arbitration instead.[46] Since his last instruction from Darmstadt while at the congress came on 22 May, and since he personally favored the court, another influence must have been at work. Could it be that his reversal was really Metternich's, that the latter was now planting opposition to the court to justify his own démarche when Rechberg's instructions arrived, whose content on this point could not be in doubt? Could anyone expect him to persist with the court when all the South German states—we must count Württemberg and Baden—denounced it? In the absence of evidence to the contrary, we here take the view that Türckheim was still earning his Order of St. Stephen.

Türckheim's volte-face, made in the course of the third reading on 3 June, added a voice against the court but did not abrogate the provision. With the completion of the reading, the draft still provided for a federal court, the regulation of religious affairs, and seats for the mediatized, at least as part of the future agenda of the diet. On such terms was the document held over for further consideration at eight o'clock the following night, Metternich prayerfully hoping that Rechberg would have his instructions by then. The latter too was anxious, fearing that if the Federal Act was signed without him, he would have no chance to modify it and might forfeit concessions already made to Bavaria. Nervously writing Montgelas the next day, he pleaded that the battle had been won, that the Bund was, as Metternich said, only an alliance, a little more formal than most, with a few regulations demanded by public opinion. "The constitutionalists are furious about it," he maintained, "and the Prussians penitently lament that they have achieved neither of their goals: constitutional regimes and a situation

[46] Protocol of 3 June 1815, Klüber, *Acten*, II, 499f.

that would permit them to achieve their ends. . . . I await the courier as a Messiah."[47]

Further pressure meanwhile bore in from another quarter. On the few days when the German Committee was not in session, the Conference of Five was, and sometimes both met on the same day. In rapid order articles for the grand treaty were coming up from Gentz's editorial committee to be approved or modified, and the work was nearing completion. Once a finished draft was in hand, prompt signing was imperative to release the envoys of the eight powers for duty at allied headquarters. If the German articles were still missing, they could not easily be included later, and whatever guaranteeing force the treaty might have would not cover the Bund. Once more the Prussians demanded an ultimatum, and this time Metternich did not refuse. Although he obtained a postponement of the next German conference, to permit another strategy meeting with Hardenberg, Humboldt, and Münster, time was running out.[48]

At the three-state meeting, held in the morning of 4 June, Humboldt submitted for discussion a draft declaration stressing the urgency of inserting the German articles into the grand treaty. Nothing less was involved, he explained, than "the tranquillity and independence of the common fatherland and the political equilibrium of Europe." This much Metternich could easily accept, but when Humboldt maintained that there were no longer any genuine difficulties with the plan, merely "obstructive objections, and these only from a few quarters," the gratuitous challenge to Bavaria was all too obvious, and he would have none of it. He had to admit, however, Humboldt's premise that Bavaria would probably at best sign later. On this distressing assumption Metternich agreed that at the next conference, now rescheduled for the 5th, he would declare that Austria and Prussia endorsed the plan as it was, could admit no more amendments, and invited all states to sign.[49]

This he did, avoiding any criticism of the dissidents, however, and reminding the small states how incessantly they had importuned the two powers to create the Bund before the end of the congress. The ensuing roll call, however, was not what Humboldt had anticipated. Although all the states present except Bavaria and Saxony voted for the Federal Act, Luxemburg, Nassau, Hesse-Darmstadt, and even Hanover did so subject in varying degrees to the adherence of all the

[47] Rechberg to Montgelas, 4 June 1815, extracts in Klemmer, *Rechberg als Politiker*, 69, and Hartmann, *Schicksal der Vorschläge*, 87.

[48] Schmidt, *Verfassungsfrage*, 477f.

[49] Schmidt, *Verfassungsfrage*, 478f.; Münster to Prince Regent, 7 June 1815, Münster, *Political Sketches*, 271f.

German states. Thus a sizable minority of relatively large states was still in doubt. Had Metternich followed Humboldt's plan, he would have declared the twenty articles adopted for those states so voting, urging the others to sign as soon as possible. Given the size of the opposition, however, he could still play for time and hence requested all states with reservations to submit declarations to Secretary Martens by noon the next day, indicating whether their opposition was general or to particular points or merely due to want of instructions. A meeting of the German Committee would follow at 2:00 p.m. The Bavarian courier now had another twenty-four hours.[50]

After the declarations had been duly filed on 6 June, the situation was more precarious than ever. Saxony, which had been without instructions the day before, and Denmark, following Münster's example, now made their own adherence contingent on the participation of all, while Hesse-Cassel advised further amendments if necessary to bring this result about.[51] Was the long struggle to found the Bund to end in failure after all? Metternich at any rate had ample argument for canceling the scheduled meeting of the committee and that evening met privately once more with the Prussians and Hanoverians.

Münster was deeply troubled, tempted to declare for a truncated Bund and yet, as he reported it, finding it "impossible to enter unreservedly into a League from which a great part of Germany would be excluded." Metternich concurred, observing that even if Hanover did join, she, Austria, and Prussia would be the only states of importance to belong. From the Prussian point of view, that was by no means such a cheerless prospect, and Humboldt pressed once more for closing with those states that were willing. By allowing certain reservations, he believed that, Württemberg and Baden aside, all but Bavaria, Darmstadt, and Saxony would vote in the affirmative; with thirty-two against three, he pleaded, there was no need to surrender. He even toyed with the idea, later advanced by Radowitz, of forming a *Nationalbund*, as he called it, among "like-minded" states within a wider *Staatenbund*, evidently not comprehending that likemindedness existed only for states that were helpless before Prussia in any case. Except for delay, which could not go on much longer, Metternich's options now seemed to be either a partial league that included Austria or a still smaller one dominated by Prussia. The best he could hope for was that another demonstration of Austro-Prussian solidarity would bring Montgelas and Frederick and Charles and Louis to their senses. Yielding to Humboldt's entreaties, he agreed to a new ultimatum, his only compensation being a delay of one more day, ostensibly to handle the paper work

[50] Protocol of 5 June 1815, Klüber, *Acten*, II, 510–516.
[51] *Ibid.*, II, 517–529.

388

necessary to adjust the Federal Act to a smaller Bund. The decisive session was scheduled for the morning of the 8th.[52]

The 7th of June was a day of nervous waiting. Metternich attended a routine meeting of the Conference of Five and wrote Francis to prepare him for the partial Bund, assuring him as usual that in spite of all, his influence in Germany was greater than ever, but reminding him that the work would only be completed when the final act of the congress was signed, a triumph, he added, "that without my presence would never have come about."[53] One last interview with Rechberg in the evening yielded no results, only an opportunity to scold the Bavarians for their insensitivity to others' opinions. Afterwards a conversation with Gentz lasted till midnight.[54]

Sometime after eight o'clock the next morning, a few hours before the conference was to begin, the miracle occurred. A message from Rechberg reached the chancellery announcing that his orders had arrived during the night, that Bavaria was prepared to sign the Federal Act if amendments were made. These concerned mainly the nature of the federal compact, the federal court, the ecclesiastical regulations, and the article on general welfare measures—all negotiable as far as Metternich was concerned. Jubilantly he informed Hardenberg that only a few points now separated the two sides. Almost at the last minute the German conference was again postponed till that night in order to leave time for a preliminary understanding with Rechberg.[55]

First, however, came another stormy three-power conference. Metternich, to accommodate Bavaria, had earlier proposed that the first eleven articles, those with international implications, be included in the general treaty, the rest adopted among the German states only. Humboldt now desperately tried to convert the latter into a separate treaty uniting those states that were willing into the separate league mentioned above. Metternich refused, insisting that all articles must be adapted to the tastes of all states even though the distinction between international and German was maintained. For the rest the Austrians demanded capitulation on all counts, to be sure not without further negotiation with Rechberg. For Humboldt it was "really the last drop, the bitter cup running over," but Hardenberg, concentrating on grand

---

[52] Münster to Prince Regent, 7 June 1815, Münster, *Political Sketches*, 273–275; Humb. to Caroline, 9 June 1815, *Briefe*, IV, 568f.; and Mett. to Francis, 7 June 1815, HHSA, StK., Vorträge, Cart. 198, VI, 51–53, extracts in Hartmann, *Schicksal der Vorschläge*, 88, and in Arneth, *Wessenberg*, I, 291.

[53] Mett. to Francis, 7 June 1815, as in note preceding.

[54] Klemmer, *Rechberg als Politiker*, 71; Gentz, *Tagebücher*, 384.

[55] Rechberg to Mett., 8 June 1815, 8:00 a.m., Hartmann, *Schicksal der Vorschläge*, 88; Klemmer, *Rechberg als Politiker*, 70f.; Quint, *Souveränitätsbegriff*, 380.; Humb. to Caroline, 9 June 1815, *Briefe*, IV, 568f.

affairs and the coming cannon fire in Flanders, was resigned and, according to Wessenberg, very cooperative in these last days. Münster, of course, favored anything to bring the South Germans into the Bund.[56]

In the meeting with Rechberg immediately following, the federal court was dropped almost as a matter of course, for as Münster said, if its jurisdiction was to be limited to interstate disputes, what difference did it make that it was called "a well-regulated process of arbitration"?[57] The article pertaining to Catholic and Protestant affairs, having been deleted once before, was now dropped again without a murmur. The rights of the mediatized houses continued to give trouble, but at length Rechberg, without authorization from Munich, conceded equality of birth with the sovereigns, at least for the heads of the houses, and even a place on the diet's agenda for the issue of curial votes. To damp the effects, however, the latter clause was shifted from Article XIV, which listed the rights of the mediatized, to Article VI, where it appeared to be merely a technical issue attending the organization of the diet.[58]

The only article that Metternich defended with vigor was the one on "general-welfare measures." Here he succeeded in keeping trade, commerce, and navigation on the first agenda of the diet but agreed to drop the comprehensive expression. It was a small concession, however, as its equivalent was still included in the article on the functions of plenary sessions.[59] Even more, however, did Metternich exert himself over the form of the Federal Act. If Humboldt had tried to build a sub-Bund around the last nine articles, Rechberg proposed to make them nothing more than subjects of voluntary negotiated agreements. This formula, however, contained the double danger that the articles would either be nullifed completely or would lead in fact to the narrower Bund that Humboldt desired. It was the final victory for Metternich's whole-German concept that he succeeded in reducing the distinction to one between "general provisions" to be incorporated in the final act of the congress and "special provisions" which would have the same force and status.[60] To the extent that guarantees were implicit in the treaty Austria was thus protected against separate leagues of any kind, whether of the South German or North German variety.

That night Metternich was understandably in a jovial mood as he met Rechberg outside the conference hall and escorted him into the

[56] Humb. to Caroline as in preceding note; Münster to Prince Regent, 11 June 1815, Münster, *Political Sketches*, 79–83; Arneth, *Wessenberg*, I, 276f., n. 2.
[57] Münster to Prince Regent as per note above.
[58] Klemmer, *Rechberg als Politiker*, 71–75; Quint, *Souveränitätsbegriff*, 380–382.
[59] Deleted in Article XX: "auf die gemeinschaftliche Wohlfahrt Bezug habende Angelegenheiten." Retained in Article VI: "gemeinnützizige Anordnungen" requiring a two-thirds majority.
[60] Cf. Quint, *Souveränitätsbegriff*, 383.

meeting. It was perhaps his proudest moment at the congress, at least since 9 January, the night he had bent Hardenberg to his terms on Saxony. There was some unpleasantness, to be sure. At the outset he had to submit several protests from the ranks of the Standesherren, one from his own father which repudiated the Bavarian ordinance of 1807 as the norm for the mediatized. It was a poignant occasion, for without that norm Prince Clemens would probably not have presided over this kind of meeting. On the other hand, it was a fine setting in which to highlight once more his utterly selfless conduct in the matter.[61]

The rest of the meeting was routine. Backed by Austria and Prussia, sometimes with professions that they hoped for more, the articles as revised were adopted one after another with little more than editorial emendations and a few obiter dicta aimed at public opinion. (Gagern and Türckheim were especially unctuous in their praise of estates constitutions.) The deletion of the ecclesiastical article was matched by the addition of another calling for ratification in six weeks so that the total remained at twenty. At the end Metternich read a short preamble reiterating that the Bund was a permanent institution designed "for the security and independence of Germany and the repose and equilibrium of Europe"—an echo of the accession treaties which he had drafted some nineteen months before. The whole was initialed all around and the formal signing scheduled for noon of 10 June. It was almost midnight when Prince Clemens adjourned the meeting and went to his rooms to write his father the news. Shifting the issue of votes for the mediatized houses to Article VI was a marked improvement, he commented ambiguously.[62]

Afterwards Humboldt lamented that the result was sheer accident, and that is certainly true. If Rechberg's instructions had arrived a few hours later, the Federal Act in its previous form would have been adopted. Further delay was impossible, if for no other reason than the simultaneous completion of the general treaty, which was initialed the very next day, 9 June, at the first and only official meeting of the congress according to Gentz but more accurately at merely another session of the Committee of Eight. Even so, there was barely time to include the first eleven articles that established the Bund, as witness the footnotes in Klüber's collection, which point out numerous textual discrepancies in the various copies of the Federal Act. Another accident was also an irony. After the rush to found the Bund in time to place it under European guarantee, no guarantee was forthcoming, despite

[61] Quint, *Souveränitätsbegriff*, 380f.; protocol of 8 June 1815, Klüber, *Acten*, II, 530f.
[62] Klüber, *Acten*, II, 530–537; Mett. to Franz Georg, 8 June 1815 (actually 1:00 a.m. of the 9th), SUA, Prague, Acta Clementina, Corr. de famille, Cart, 49, vol. 5.

the fact that all powers desired one, Austria most of all. The reasons are not clear, but they included a misunderstanding between Clancarty and Nesselrode about the nature and scope of the project, perhaps the beginnings of the antithesis between the Holy Alliance and the Quadruple Alliance later in the year. As a result Metternich had to be satisfied with whatever awe was inspired by the grandeur of the Vienna Final Act, as the great treaty was called.[63]

Still another accident concerned King Frederick of Württemberg. In contrast to Montgelas's superb timing, which gave him maximum leverage, Frederick waited a little too long, his courier reaching Vienna on the 9th. That night Metternich informed Winzingerode that there was still time, as the formal signing was to take place the next day. The trouble was that Frederick wanted to endorse only the General Provisions and even those with reservations. These conditions Winzingerode revealed in a written declaration that otherwise exuded professions of loyalty and willingness to cooperate. No doubt savoring the last-minute squirming of his frequent tormentors, Metternich read the piece at the final conference on the 10th and proposed that as the Federal Act had already been closed, Württemberg must not only take it as it was but must also adhere in a separate act of accession. As most of the envoys were packed to leave Vienna, he also dictated an instrument of accession stating Württemberg's "unqualified and complete adherence" and had the conference presign an act of acceptance in the event that full capitulation was forthcoming. The treaty was an "absurdity," wrote Frederick a week later, "a fraudulent concoction of Metternich to show the world that at least something was achieved at this interminable congress." Nevertheless, Württemberg finally acceded on 1 September while Baden did so on 26 July. Despite that all the rest formally signed on 10 June, the official date of the Federal Act was set back to the 8th to legitimate its incorporation into the general treaty of the 9th—a quite unnecessary move actually since the latter was not formally signed until 19 June.[64]

And so the Bund was a reality at last, the fulcrum of the European order, a monument to Metternich's vision, persistence, and steadfast course. Despite the many twists and turns, traveling now with Prussia, now with Bavaria, first conceding, then withholding Saxony, again supporting Kreise to lure Max Joseph and Frederick into the Bund

[63] Humb. to Caroline, 9 June 1815, *Briefe*, IV, 568; text of Federal Act in Klüber, *Acten*, II, 590–615; protocol of 9 June 1815, d'Angeberg, *Congrès*, IV, 1915ff.; Nesselrode to Lieven, 17 June 1815, *VPR*, VIII, 376–378; Webster, *Castlereagh*, I, 433f.

[64] protocol of 10 June 1815 and annexed notes, Klüber, *Acten*, II, 558–577; Winz. to Fred., 11 June 1815 and Fred. to Winz., 17 June 1815, extracts in Pfister, *Lage der Verbündeten*, 340f. and 344; Mett. to Franz Georg, 10 June 1815, SUA, Prague, Acta Clementina, Corr. de famille, Cart. 49, vol. 5, p. 62.

only to undermine them bit by bit in expanding the powers of the lower chamber—through all these convoluted maneuvers, he arrived at last at his goal: a Central European defense community standing as a barrier to France and Russia, the keystone of the continental equilibrium, almost exactly as he had outlined it to Ernst Hardenberg in Prague on the eve of the battle of Leipzig.[65]

Nowhere is his contribution more striking than in the final negotiations over the Bund. Until then Humboldt, at least, the earliest foe of the narrow Bund conceived by Stein and an occasional critic of the Kreis system, had stood with Metternich and Münster for a whole-German Bund. In the end, however, other priorities won out: better a partial Bund with federal court, *landständische Verfassungen*, and a privileged class of mediatized houses than a mere defense league even if the latter did combine the resources of all the Rheinbund states and the two German powers. *How* small such a Bund would have been is a matter of speculation, since not all states that attached conditions to their membership could have acted on them. At a minimum, however, all the South German courts, including Darmstadt and possibly Nassau, would have defected, leaving Germany and Europe in the same uneasy limbo that followed the events of 1866; dreading incorporation into a North German Bund but unable to create a viable South German union among themselves, Stuttgart and Karlsruhe would have looked to St. Petersburg for support, Munich to Paris. Hanover, isolated in the northwest, would have done her utmost to increase Britain's commitment to her independence and draw closer to the Netherlands. Indeed, even in Metternich's Bund another five years were to be required to eradicate external influence, to convince the French and the Russians that the days to Teschen, Regensburg, and Tilsit were over. Only after 1820 did Metternich's Bund in fact provide that independent center of which he and Hardenberg had dreamed.

Nor was his concern for German unity confined to the definition of the federal area. In at least five ways his plans were more genuinely unifying than those of Hardenberg. First of all, a single Austrian presidency, however innocuous Metternich represented it to be, was inherently more unitary than either the dualistic directory of the Forty-one Articles or the rotating chairmanship of the Ten Articles of London, especially if it had incorporated the foreign-policy committee of three projected in Wessenberg's December plan. Secondly, whatever weakness was inherent in an assembly of more or less equal states, i.e., the Second Council of the November deliberations, its overall purpose was to check the centrifugal forces represented by tightly organized

---

[65] Kraehe, I, 213–218.

regional units directed by powerful Kreis chiefs. Even when the plans for the federal diet had evolved into the unicameral forms of the final deliberations, Metternich continued, against the thrust of all Prussian plans, to press for a broad legislative authority exercised under majority rule. This is hardly surprising, for given the political realities, the advantages were all with Austria, as Felix Schwarzenberg, Karl Buol-Schauenstein, and Ludwig von Biegeleben also realized some decades later. Thus, the erosion of this authority by restricting the scope of majority rule in the final stages was not Metternich's goal but rather his greatest sacrifice. A third project with unusual unitary implications was Wessenberg's plan to make the federal court the supreme appellate tribunal for all the lesser states. Here the contrast with the Prussian projects—apart from the Ten Articles of London, which omitted a federal court entirely—is not so sharp, both because Humboldt's projected court was unitary too, even if narrower in range, and because Metternich, correctly gauging the opposition, never defended the court as he did the legislative powers of the Bund. The point to be made here is simply that he was no doctrinaire foe of unitary projects that were politically feasible.

A comparison of Austrian and Prussian projects in the military realm is more tenuous yet because this thorny issue continued to be set aside for later resolution. Still, it is to be observed that the early Prussian projects described at length the powers of each chief over the military establishment of his Kreis but barely mentioned federal supervision of the whole by the Council of Kreis Chiefs. In the Forty-one Articles, for example, even federal fortresses were to be maintained and commanded by the chief of the Kreis in which each was located. This same spirit of regionalism informed the one detailed plan of the period, Knesebeck's memorandum of 21 January 1815, which was tailored to Humboldt's unicameral project. In it he spoke of "military districts," each under a "chairman" with far-reaching powers, but confined the federal role to the election of a supreme commander at the outbreak of war.[66] One can argue that some five military masses in coalition would have performed better than Metternich's army of fifteen or so smaller units based on the integral and curial votes of the smaller council, but the latter, which approximated the eventual federal army, necessitated, as the subsequent military constitution of 1821 was to bear out, a much larger federal role in the maintenance of the military establishment despite the considerable deficiencies in the system.[67]

Finally, though more a matter of uniformity than of unity, there is

[66] Text in Stein, *Briefe*, v, 247–251.
[67] Kriegsverfassung des deutschen Bundes . . . ," 9 Apr. 1821, Meyer, *Corpus juris*, II, 133–136.

the issue of *landständische Verfassungen*. It has been the common view that Metternich favored every dilution of this fiercely contested article because any extension of estates rights would have contradicted Austria's own domestic institutions. As we have seen, however, better solutions were available, most notably the Solms plan, incorporated into the Twelve Articles, for simply exempting the Austrian and Prussian provinces from all internal regulation by the Bund; on this basis Austria need not have maintained provincial diets of any kind. And yet it was the Austrians, in the Wessenberg plan of December, who first abandoned this exemption in favor of an article applicable to all. Admittedly the phrasing was vague, but it required estates representation of some sort with consultative powers regarding taxation and state government in general. This formula, to be sure, well suited the Austrian situation, where the struggle between the provincial diets and the Josephinists in Vienna was in full swing with indeterminate results,[68] but Metternich's primary concern was to remove the political handicaps attending the crassly self-serving treatment of the powers, which Münster had so eloquently denounced during the debate on the Twelve Articles, and which Wrede wished to extend to Bavaria. As finally adopted, article thirteen was looser yet, but it made no exceptions and had one merit hitherto overlooked: without a prescribed restorative program it was easily twisted by the South German states in the coming years to justify the more modern parliaments that they installed—though Metternich hardly intended that.[69]

Could more have been achieved if he had tried? Rechberg professed surprise at his complaisance in the final stages, causing some writers to conclude that Metternich, because of Austria's peculiar problems, really wanted no more.[70] This judgment ignores on the one hand the long history of the negotiation and on the other the balance of risks that Metternich faced at the end. What did the last-minute concessions, most of them deleting restorative provisions that benefited mainly the mediatized, amount to in comparison with the total collapse of the federal project or the emergence of a North German confederation? Even so, Metternich resisted Rechberg's attack on the general-welfare article, an issue potentially of far greater significance than the court or seats for the Standesherren for the development of the Bund.

If one must have a culprit, why not Hardenberg himself? One could

[68] Cf. Christine L. Mueller, "The Estates of Styria, 1740–1848: A Century of Transition" (Ph.D. diss., University of Virginia, 1980), 206–223.

[69] Enno E. Kraehe, "The Origins of the Carlsbad Decrees: Some Perspectives" (Paper read before the American Historical Association, New York, 28 December 1971).

[70] Quint, *Souveränitätsbegriff*, 385–392; and Aretin, "Deutsche Politik Bayerns," 54–57.

hardly imagine a better way to alienate the small states than to threaten them with tutelage to the Kreis chiefs, arguing all the while that this subjugation and the territorial scale of 1803 were quite in harmony with the sovereignty and integrity held out in the accession treaties. It was he who taught them to pay attention to the fine print in the treaties. It is at least conceivable that a more honest approach to them would have allayed their fears and induced a spirit of cooperation appropriate to the post-imperial commonwealth of equals that Metternich sought to build. As it was, their paranoia and feelings of insecurity persisted, causing them to see in the Bund nothing more than the instrument of their survival, a bulwark not only against Prussia but also against domestic radicalism and violence.

By any measure that takes account of the whole of Germany and the divisive regionalism inherent in the projected Kreise, Metternich must be counted the leading champion of German unity at the congress. He did not, of course, want a national Germany based on popular self-determination, but neither did his opponents there, whose patriotic outpourings, though often sincere, were predominantly expressions of yearning for the old world of the Reich. Stein's main concern was the "third Germany," Hardenberg's Prussian hegemony over the North, Württemberg's the Swabian Kreis, Bavaria's the status of an independent European power, Solms's the restoration of the Standesherren. Only Metternich, Humboldt, and Münster, though for different reasons, were concerned with keeping Germany whole, and in the end even Humboldt put other issues first. To make these points does not of course mean that Metternich deliberately pursued an ideal of German unity, only that it is erroneous to explain his policy as a struggle against it and that it is time to set the record straight.

If the bedrock of his German policy was the preservation of the former Rheinbund regimes, the reasons were rooted in considerations of foreign policy, in particular his belief that the weakening of existing regimes would create voids that only Prussia was in a position to fill. Beyond that, however, he was genuinely convinced that the true dangers to order were wholesale territorial upheavals, arbitrary interference with functioning bureaucratic systems, and, as an extreme, misguided efforts to return Germany to the status quo of 1803. In this respect he honestly differed from those who with equal conviction and no little nostalgia viewed the Rheinbund regimes as inept—not to say immoral—despotisms that would soon succumb to revolution unless forced to restore organic links with society, mainly by revitalizing the old estates, the presumed custodians of local order and the underwriters of state credit. To discuss these positions in ideological terms is almost irrelevant, but so far as there is point to it, the fact is obvious that Metternich in his pragmatic way was no more trying to restore the old regime than he was to stifle German unity. The restoration of a balance of power, yes, but that is inherent in international politics; it is not the mark of an age or a social order. Besides, the balance that he strove for was not the pre-1789 system of Kaunitz, based on the Franco-Austrian alliance, but the Austro-German system discussed in these pages.

Why did Metternich come out ahead? Obviously he was a skillful negotiator, a master at marshaling his assets, scattering his opponents, and always leaving open alternative courses. He also had in Wessenberg a deputy of comparable political talents, the man who bested Humboldt in the contest over the Second Council, who probably showed Metternich how to turn a strong federal court to Austrian advantage, and had the courage to stand up to his chief in the Saxon affair. Metternich for his part, despite his boastful ways, usually took criticism with good grace. His real secret, however, lay at the beginning, in his ability to determine in advance where the center of gravity was located in the interplay of forces. Whereas Hardenberg and Humboldt fixed their eyes on specific ambitious goals, the former for the sake of Prussian power, the latter with some admixture of genuine idealism, Metternich studied the terrain and from the outset spent his time probing what was possible. So long as a German defense league took its place in the European balance, his primary goal was the consensus necessary to sustain it, the broadest possible reconciliation of diverse interests. In the final analysis Hardenberg failed because his goals were narrow and blatantly self-serving, whereas Metternich's, though certainly in the Austrian interest, were also seen, at least by those capable of influencing events, to serve the interests of Europe and Germany.

One further reason why his plans for the Bund prevailed is the relative quiescence of Great Britain and Russia, neither of which had much interest in more than a defense league in Central Europe serving to contain France. Despite the repeated efforts of Stein, Czartoryski, and Capodistria to interest the tsar in varying degrees of imperial restoration, he remained surprisingly aloof, mainly because he calculated the political realities much as Metternich did, especially in regard to the South German states. With the territorial question, however, the opposite was true. Here Metternich had to operate under severe constraint and was seldom master of events. In Poland he came away almost empty-handed, at first because of Prussia's sudden defection from the three-power front, later because appeasement of the tsar was necessary to obtain his permission to partition Saxony. To be sure, in the maneuvering that led to Hardenberg's capitulation, Metternich played his hand with consummate skill, but the cards were dealt by Alexander and Castlereagh. The latter had British maritime hegemony to balance against Russia's destabilizing advance to the Prosna, Metternich only his gifts for "tacking, evading, and flattering." It was the beginning of the road to Troppau and Münchengrätz.

The partition of Saxony, moreover, though it preserved part of the buffer demanded by the military party in Vienna, had repercussions elsewhere that almost annulled the gains. For the generous awards to Prussia, in the end virtually dictated by the British, included the breaching of the Mosel line, which not only removed some 200,000 souls from Metternich's store of compensations for the South German states but also caused Bavaria to refuse the acquisition of Mainz. Since Bavaria was the least of the states to which the powers might have entrusted the fortress, Metternich either had to yield it to Prussia or claim it for Austria. For reasons suggested earlier, he was forced to accept the former arrangement, to be sure with federal supervision and a composite garrison drawn from the region.

It is a measure of Metternich's predicament that even as he signed the Federal Act on 10 June and was already four days overdue in his departure for Heidelberg, the issue of Mainz still dangled. Its award to Prussia on 3 April had been tied to the South German territorial settlement, in particular the award of Hanau, another fortress, to Bavaria. Since that settlement could not be immediately consummated, it was, on 23 April, declared provisional till after the war. Metternich now saw his chance to undo the damage. Taking advantage of Hardenberg's anxiety to annex Westphalia as soon as possible, he argued that all territory not definitively assigned be ceded forthwith to the occupying powers, which would later become responsible for negotiating exchanges as necessary. In this way Austria would acquire the Palatinate outright, and Metternich would gain time to make the case in Vienna for yielding Salzburg and keeping most of the left bank that Austria currently occupied. If he succeeded, the Prussian claim to Mainz would be voided by the annulment of the provisional settlement with Bavaria, while Austria, with a position forward of Mainz, would have an imposing argument for taking command of the fortress herself. Hardenberg's acquiescence was not certain, but all along he had hoped for Austrian rather than Bavarian help in the defense of the Rhine; perhaps Mainz was not too high a price to pay, especially as it was now outflanked by Prussian territory.

In the last days of the congress, as the general treaty took shape, Metternich, with strong backing from Nesselrode and Clancarty, worked out the main points with Hardenberg. The basis was the formal award of the Palatinate to Austria together with the right of reversion of the Breisgau and the right-bank Palatinate with the understanding that she was free to keep the territory or to exchange it for Salzburg and the other nearer provinces. In the latter case, or at least in the case that the provisional settlement became definitive, the powers would support Austria in her negotiations with Bavaria, and Mainz and environs would, as previously arranged, go to Hesse-Darmstadt and the fortress to the Bund, under Prussian command and with a garrison drawn from Darmstadt, Nassau, and Prussia—not a pleasant alternative to set before Schwarzenberg. Conversely, if Austria should accept her watch on the Rhine, *she* would command a similar garrison there and form with the same two middle states a sizable military bloc deep in a region once claimed by Hardenberg as part of a Prussian Kreis. In other arrangements Metternich assumed responsibility for providing from his left-bank total 140,000 souls for Darmstadt as compensation for Westphalia as well as 69,000 more to meet a variety of small claims on Prussia. The bargain was his last triumph at the congress, restricting Prussia's claim to Mainz to the literal execution of the provisional settlement while awarding the great fortress to Austria entirely at her option and with the remote possibility of gaining both it *and* Salzburg, depending on the outcome of the war. In the meantime, the joint Austro-Prussian garrison, installed there one year earlier, would continue under the governship of Archduke Charles.[71]

These last-minute negotiations lasted through 12 June, when Wessenberg and Humboldt at last signed a secret convention incorporating the above. Metternich was agreeable through it all, the latter reported in the first kind words for many weeks.[72] That evening there was one last meal with Gentz, and at one o'clock the next morning the weary foreign minister sped through the empty streets of the darkened city, bound for Heidelberg and the news of Waterloo. The Congress of Vienna was a *fête accomplie.*

[71] Text of Austro-Prussian convention in Griewank, *Wiener Kongress,* 313–315. See also Arneth, *Wessenberg,* I, 289f.; protocol of Conference of Five, 10 June 1815, d'Angeberg, *Congrès,* III, 1442f.; Münster to Prince Regent, 7 June 1815, Münster, *Political Sketches,* 273–275; and Mett. to Francis, 21 Sept. and 17 Nov. 1815, HHSA, StK. Vorträge, Cart. 199, pp. 76–85 and Cart. 200, pp. 67–76, respectively.
[72] To Hard., 12 June 1815, Humboldt, *Gesammelte Schriften,* VII, 79.

APPENDIX A

HARDENBERG'S TEN

ARTICLES OF LONDON[1]

1. Deutschland wird in 7 Kreise eingetheilt:
   a. Für Oestreich 2
   b. " Preussen 2
   c. " Bayern 1
   d. " Hannover 1
   e. " Würtemberg 1

2. Jedem Kreise wird ein Kreis Oberster vorgesetzt, also 5 Kreis Obersten.

3. Ihre Befugnisse und Verpflichtungen
   a. Oberbefehl über das ganze Kreis Militair, Aufsicht und Controlle auf die gesammte Kriegs Verfassung auch in Friedens Zeiten, auch auf die Festungen,—Musterung der Truppen, u.s.w.
   b. Oberaufsicht auf die allgemeine Polizey, Handhabung der öffentlichen Sicherheit, Vollstreckung der gerichtlichen Erkenntnisse im Kreise.
   c. Direction und Leitung der Kreis Versammlung.
   d. Aufrechthaltung des Bundes Vertrages und Befolgung der Bundes Beschlüsse

4. Rath der Kreis Obersten unter wechselndem Geschäfts Directorio nach einem Turno der 7.

5. Dessen Bestimmung
   a. Leitung und executive Gewalt des Bundes
   b. ausschliessliche Ausübung des Rechts des Kriegs und Friedens
   c. Mitberathung allgemeiner innerer Gegenstände der Bundes Staaten nach näher festzusetzenden Normen,

6. Rath der Fürsten und Stände.
   a. Viril Stimmen haben darin: alle diejenigen, die entweder für sich allein, oder mit ihren Gesammthäusern, Länder besitzen, die 100/m Seelen und darüber zählen.

[1] ZSTA, Merseburg, 2.4.1.I, No. 1559, pp. 77–79, in Hardenberg's own hand. Published by permission. Identical copy in NSHSA, Hanover, Des. 91, No. 23, pp. 21–24, which also gave permission.

b. Alle übrige nur, zweckmässig zu bildende Curiat Stimmen.

c. Ob die Stände mediatisiert sind oder nicht, macht hiebey keinen Unterschied.

Nach diesen Bestimmungen würde nur das Gesammthaus Hohenlohe welches 106,000 Einwohner hat, nämlich 103,000 unter Würtembergischer, 3,000 unter Bayerischer Hoheit, eine Viril Stimme bekommen, alle übrige mediatisierte eigneten sich nur zu Curiat Stimmen.

Die alten Deutschen Fürsten Häuser würden sämmtlich Viril Stimmen erhalten, wie auch Nassau und Schwarzburg.

Die Hansen Städte und Frankfurt könnten zusammen eine Viril Stimme führen oder zwey. Wegen des Verhältnisses von Hohenlohe zu Bayern und Würtemberg weiter unten.

d. Der Rath der Fürsten und Stände constituiert mit dem der Kreis Obersten die allgemeine Bundes Versammlung, welche sich mit allem beschäftigt was die Wohlfahrt desselben im Innern und ein allgemeines Interesse betrifft.

e. Sollen beide Räthe in einer Versammlung, oder getrennt berathschlagen?—Ich meyne getrennt und so dass in Jedem die Mehrheit entscheide—Sind beyde verschiedener Meinung; so würde, wie sonst bey den Re. und Correlationen eine Vereinigung versucht, wäre diese nicht zu bewirken, könnte ein näher zu bestimmender Ausschuss der beiden als Obmann entscheiden.

7. In jedem Kreise sind die dazu zu schlagenden Stände, Kreis Stände und bilden unter der Direction des Kreis Obersten die Kreis Versammlung, welche sich mit den inneren gemeinsamen Gegenständen der Kreise beschäftigt.

8. Zuerst gehören dazu: die Fürsten, welche entweder für sich allein, oder mit ihren Gesammthäusern 100/m Seelen und darüber in ihren Ländern zählen.

Diese sollen das Recht haben—die Hohenlohischen Häuser ausgenommen, welche nicht wohl von Würtemberg und Bayern in diesem-Maasse zu trennen sind:

a. Eigene Truppen zu halten. Ihre Anzahl, Waffenart u.s.w. ist genau zu bestimmen und ihre Verfassung der des Heers des Kreis Obersten gleich zu stellen.

b. Die Steuern von ihren Unterthanen behufs Erhaltung der Truppen und anderer Landes Anstalten zu erheben, nach Bestimmung der Kreis Versammlung

c. Die Gerichtsbarkeit in zwei Instanzen in ihrem Namen ausüben zu lassen.

   d. Desgleichen alle Regierungs Rechte, in sofern sie nicht durch die Bundes Acte beschränkt sind oder durch allgemeine Bundes oder Kreisschlüsse beschränkt werden.

9. Ferner würden zu den Kreisständen gehören: alle weltliche Fürsten und Stände ohne Ausnahme, die ehedem Sitz und Stimme auf dem deutschen Reichstage hatten, sie mögen mediatisiert seyn oder nicht, Viril Stimmen gehabt haben, oder Curiat Stimmen. Die Gerechtigkeit spricht laut für die Mediatisierten. Bei dem Länderbesitz, sollte man als Regel den Besitzstand annehmen, den der Reichsschluss von 1803, nach dem Lüneviller Frieden festsetzte, und nur da Ausnahmen machen, wo es das allgemeine Beste erfordert, oder diesem wenigstens nicht hinderlich ist. Baden, Darmstadt, Nassau, Siegmaringen, können sich nicht beschweren, wenn man ihnen die durch Verfügungen Napoleons zugetheilten Mediatisierten nimmt. Die ersteren drei behalten doch noch mehr als sie nach jenem Recess hatten, der letzte nicht weniger als dieses. Man theile also die Mediatisierten den Kreisen zu und schliesse sich dadurch den Staaten der Kreis Obersten an, so wie es die geographische Lage angibt. Hiedurch werden sie eo ipso den kleineren Staaten die zum Rhein Bunde gehörten gleich gesetzt und das ist billig und recht. Alles dieses ist auch den in Frankfurt geschlossenen Verträgen gar nicht zuwieder. Die Mediatisierten, welche Bayern und Würtemberg jetzt angehören, blieben bey ihnen, nur würden sie gleiche Rechte mit den übrigen erhalten müssen. Diese könnten in Folgendem bestehen:

   a. Truppen dürfte keiner dieser Stände halten, aber man könnte ihnen nach den Umständen gestatten Ehrenwachen zu haben. Ihre Unterthanen wären dem Militair Conscriptions System des Kreis Obersten unterworfen, und stellten danach Recruten zu dem Heere desselben.

   b. Ihre Unterthanen zahlten die Steuern, nach den Beschlüssen der Kreis Versammlung, bis auf den Theil der ihnen etwa zu anderen Zwecken der Regierung zur Disposition gelassen werden möchte, zur Kriegs Kasse des Kreis Obersten.

   c. Die Gerichtsbarkeit in erster Instanz, würde durch Gerichte ausgeübt welche unter der Oberaufsicht der Obergerichte des Kreis Obersten stünden und nach angestellter Prüfung der dazu bestimmten Personen. Unter gewissen Umständen könnte ihnen auch die zweite Instanz bewilligt werden.[2]

   d. Ihre Familien und persönlichen Rechte wären näher festzusetzen.

[2] A marginal notation to this clause reads: "Ist die Criminal Gerichtsbarkeit ganz oder zum Theil auszunehmen?"

e. Allgemeinen Verfügungen des Kreis Obersten in Landespolizeilicher Hinsicht, müssten sie sich unterwerfen, hätten aber überall die Ausführung durch ihre Behörden zu besorgen.

f. Man könnte ihnen einen Theil der Regalien überlassen.

g. Dass sie das Eigenthum aufs Vollständigste behalten versteht sich.

10. Die ehemalige Reichs Ritterschaft bleibt den Landesherren unterworfen. Sie hatte auch früher keine Reichsstandschaft. Man sichere ihr aber Vorrechte als Landstände und in persönlicher und Familien Rücksicht.

Die Militair Verfassung und Gerichts Verfassung des Bundes übergehe ich für jetzt.

APPENDIX B

KING FREDERICK'S PRÉCIS OF
CONVERSATION WITH METTERNICH
30 SEPTEMBER 1814[1]

Morgen wird durch Note an samtliche zum Kongress eingegangene
Gesandtschaften wegen Eröfnung des Kongresses die Einladung er-
gehen, worinn denselben eröfnet wird, dass zwischen den groessten
Maechten: Oestreich, Russland, England, u. Preussen die Einleitung
getroffen worden, das Geschäft in 2 Comités zu theilen. Zu ersterem
sind, ausser den 4 oben genannten, Frankreich u. Spanien eingeladen
worden;—in demselben sollen alle Objekte, die auf das allgemeine
Interesse von Europa Bezug haben, abgehandelt werden, dahin gehoeren: die polnischen Angelegenheiten, die sächsischen Angelegenheiten, die italienischen, u. übrige spanische u. portugiesische, so wie
auch die Vertheilung der noch nicht disponierten Laender, sie moegen
gelegen seyn, wo sie wollen.

Die teutsche Angelegenheiten im Allgemeinen werden in einem 2ⁿ
Comité abgehandelt, bestehend aus Oestreich, Preussen, Bayern,
Württemberg, und Hannover. (Lezteres wird bey dieser Gelegenheit
die Koenigswürde annehmen) Erst wenn die Hauptzüge des nach dem
Pariser Traktat zu errichtenden Foederationssystems entworfeⁿ seyn
werden, wird das Resultat dem ersten Comité überbracht um dessen
allgemeine europäische Garantie zu erhalten.

Die künftige Verfassung Teutschlands betreffend wird dasselbe in 7
Theile unter der Benennung Kreise getheilt, um die ältere Benennung
beyzubehalten.—
Zwey dieser Kreise: Oestreich u. Boehmen erhalten Oestreich zum
Directorium;
Preussen erhaelt den Brandenburgischen u. Westfälischen Kreis;
Bayern den bayerischen Kreis;
Württemberg den schwäbischen u. Hannover den hannoverschen Kreis.

Diese 5 Mächte bilden das Oberdirectorium von Teutschland; die Dé-
tails werden nicht zu Wien, sondern auf einem Bundestag vollends
ausgearbeitet.

[1] HSA, Stuttgart, E 70, Fasc. 12, pp. 83–87. Published by permission.

Hauptgrundzüge der politischen Verfassung sind: Alle nicht benannte teutsche Staaten gehoeren zu einem oder zum anderen Kreis;—Von dem schwäbischen wurde Baden bestimmt genannt;—Ob diesen Staaten eine unter dem Namen der 2ten Kammer, wie ehmalen das Fürsten Collegium am Reichstag, eine besondere Versammlung gestattet werden solle? ist noch der Diskussion unterworfen.—Den Kreisdirectoren wird ein moeglichst ausgedehntes pouvoir exécutif, besonders in militärischer Rücksicht, zugestanden, in so ferne solches ohne Verletzung der immediaten Souverainetaits Rechte thunlich ist;—in allen Staaten Teutschlands wird unter den Modifikationen, so die Lokalität erfordert, eine möglichst gleichfoermige staendische Verfassung eingeführt, wobey jedoch dem pouvoir exécutif so viele Latitude gegeben wird, als notwendig erforderlich ist, um das nicht aggressive,—aber äusserst starke defensiv-Militär-System Teutschlands auszuführen.

Ausser dem repräsentativen System der Verfassung sollen den Untertanen aller Staaten gleiche Rechte in dem einen wie in dem andern zugestanden werden.—Den Mediatisierten sollen ausser der Repräsentation alle mit der Einfoermigkeit der Staats Verfassung verträgliche Privilegien zugesichert werden.

Auf Meine erklärte Bereitwilligkeit, in diese Ideen einzugehen, welche von je her in meiner Absicht nach Beseitigung des bisherigen politischen Systems gelegen sind, machte ich folgende Fragen: Wenn zwischen den Mitgliedern des Directorii Uneinigkeit entstünde, wie würde sie geschlichtet werden?

Man antwortete Mir: Durch ein vom Comité und den Betheiligten niedergesetztes Austrägalgericht, über dessen Modalitäten aber das weitere nachgeholt werden sollte.

Wenn zwischen den Directoren und übrigen Souverains der Kreise Zwistigkeiten vorfielen, wie werden sie geschlichtet? Durch das Directorium, war die Antwort.

Wird es den ständischen Repräsentanten gestattet, gegen ihre Landesherrn Klage zu führen? Über diesen Punkt wollte man sich bey weitem nicht mit ja erklären, glaubte aber über diesen noch ganz nicht entschiedenen u. zur Sprache gebrachten Punkt weitere Diskussionen und Übereinkunft erwarten zu müssen.

Die Ideen des bayerischen Verfassungs Entwurfs:—die Steuern, deren Einzug u. deren Administration den Ständen zu überlassen, wollte man ganz verwerfen.—

Das Kontingent eines Kreises soll auf 30/m Mann bestimmt werden;—die Verbindlichkeiten gegen Oestreich u. Preussen gehen durchaus nur auf teutsche Kriege, so dass alle türkische, nordische, italienische, ausgeschlosen sind;—jedoch sind Oestreich u. Preussen verbunden, zur teutschen Macht das von ihnen schuldige Kontingent beständig marschfertig zu erhalten.

Die übrige diplomatische Verhaeltnisse bleiben unabaenderlich bestehen, jedoch werden bey dem Bundestag auswärtige Repraesentationen angenommen und das Directorium in politischer Rücksicht von Teutschland gegen alle auswärtige Mächte vertretten.

Auf Meine Bemerkung: dass durch die doppelte Stimmen von Oestreich u. Preussen diesen Mächten die beständige Majorität im Directorio gesichert scheine,—erwiederte der Fürst: dass in den teutschen Angelegenheiten wohl nichts unwahrscheinlicher angenommen werden könne als diese beyderseitige Zustimmung u. dass wohl nicht zu miskennen seye, dass Oestreich, Bayern u. Württemberg die Majorität behaupten würden.—
Wegen Vertheilung der noch disponibeln Eroberungen äusserte der Fürst: dass man hierinn zu Gunsten Württembergs thun würde, was man könne;—es würde leicht seyn, dasselbe bis an den Rhein zu bringen, wenn man einigen kleinen anderweitigen Wünschen und arrangements sich bereitwillig finden liesse.—Ich erklärte hierauf bestimmt, dass so angenehm natürlich jeder Zuwaches seyn müsse, Ich doch als ersten und Hauptgrundsatz die Integrität Meiner Staaten und ihre Unveränderlichkeit zu behaupten wünschte,—natürlich aber erwarte, dass man den Napoleonischen Anomalien in Beybehaltung der Duodez-Souveraine ein Ende mache. Hierauf äusserte Fürst Metternich: dass seine Meinung, mit der er nicht vorgreifen dürfe, ganz dahin gehe.

Über den Antheil, so Dänemark, Schweden, Neapel, Sardinien, Holland, Portugall, an allen diesen Negociationen nehmen sollen, ist bis jezt nichts bestimmt.

BIBLIOGRAPHY

I. UNPUBLISHED DOCUMENTS

Haus- Hof- und Staatsarchiv, Vienna

Staatskanzlei
    Kongressakten: Cartons 1, 6, 7, 8, 10, and 16.
    Vorträge: Cartons 195, 196, 197, 198, 199, and 200.
    Deutsche Akten: Fascicle 100.
    Interiora: Fascicles 78 and 79.
    Kriegsakten: Fascicles 489, 497, 498, 509, and 510.
    Noten an die Hofkanzlei: Fascicles 1, 26, and 27.
    Russland III
        Weisungen: Carton 41.
        Berichte: Cartons 17 and 18.
    Diplomatische Korrespondenz
        Baden: Fascicles 10, 11, and 12.
        Bayern: Fascicles 116 and 117.
        Hannover: Fascicle 12.
        Preussen: Fascicles 95, 96, and 97.
        Württemberg: Fascicles 20 and 21.
    Frankfurt Weisungen, Fascicle 2

Gesandtschaftsarchiv
    Berlin: Fascicles 43 and 44.
    Karlsruhe: Fascicles 4 and 5.

Kaiser Franz Archiv: Fascicle 196.

Kabinettsarchiv
    Konferenz-Akten a, Cartons for 1812–1815.

Státní Ústředný Archiv, Prague

Rodinný archiv Metternišsky: Acta Clementina.
    Correspondance royale (47/3), Carton 1, folio 1.
    Correspondance (47/5), Carton 3.
    Correspondance politique Autriche (47/4), Cartons 1, 3, and 6.
    Correspondance de famille, Carton 49, vol. 5.

Zentrales Staatsarchiv, Historische Abteilung II, Merseburg.

Auswärtiges Amt (= 2.4.1.I)
    No. 992 [Re Russia at the Congress of Vienna]
    No. 1436 [Re Austro-Russian convention of 12 June 1815]

No. 1454 [German constitution plans before the Congress of Vienna]

No. 1456 [Re the work of the Committee of Five on the German constitution]

No. 1559 [Hardenberg correspondence and draft constitutions]

No. 1564 [Miscellaneous petitions and notes]

No. 1566 [Humboldt-Hardenberg correspondence]

No. 1570 [Hardenberg's territorial plans before the Congress of Vienna]

No. 1649 [Negotiations re Saxony, Poland, and Mainz]

No. 1650 [Hardenberg drafts on above]

No. 5985 [Hardenberg-Humboldt correspondence before the Congress of Vienna]

Rep. 92, L 37 [Hardenberg's Tagebücher 1814–1815]

NIEDERSÄCHSISCHES HAUPTSTAATSARCHIV, HANOVER.

Dep. 110 A (Nachlass Ernst Herbert Münster)
III, Nos. 1, 2, 5a, 5b, 7, 8, 16, and 27.

Cal. Br. 24 (Aüssere Angelegenheiten)
Oesterreich II, Nos. 5026 and 5027.
III, Nos. 5398 and 5399.
IV, Nos. 5896, 5898, 5903, 5904, 5905, and 5918.

Des. 91, Nos. 20, 21, 22, and 23.

Des. 92, XLI, No. 112, vols. I and II.

HAUPTSTAATSARCHIV, STUTTGART

E 1, Fascicle 45.

E 70, Fascicles 12, 13, 14, 19, and 20.

E 70b. Fascicles 41, 42, 45, and 46.

GEHEIMES STAATSARCHIV, MUNICH

Ministerium des Äussern: MA 1028.

PUBLIC RECORD OFFICE, LONDON

F. O. 92, vols. 10–17.

II. PUBLISHED DOCUMENTS, LETTERS, DIARIES, AND MEMOIRS

Alexander I, Emperor of Russia. *Correspondance de l'empereur Alexandre Ier avec sa soeur la Grande-Duchesse Catherine, Princesse d'Oldenbourg, puis Reine de Wurtemberg 1805–1818*. Introduction by the Grand Duke Nicolas Mikhailovitch. St. Petersburg, 1910.

Angeberg, Comte d', ed. [pseud. for Chodzko, E.J.B.] *Le congrès de Vienne et les traités de 1815*. 4 vols. Paris, 1864.

Arndt, Ernst Moritz. *Briefe*. Edited by Albrecht Dühr. 3 vols. Texte zur Forschung, vols. 8–10. Darmstadt, 1972–1975.

Bertuch, Carl. *Carl Bertuchs Tagebuch vom Wiener Kongress*. Edited by Hermann von Egloffstein. Berlin. 1916.

Bosl, Karl, ed. *Dokumente zur Geschichte von Staat und Gesellschaft in Bayern*. III/2: *Die bayerische Staatlichkeit*. Munich, 1976.

Branig, Hans, ed. *Briefwechsel des Fürsten Karl August von Hardenberg mit dem Fürsten Wilhelm Ludwig von Sayn-Wittgenstein 1806–1822*. Veröffentlichungen aus den Archiven preussischer Kulturbesitz, vol. 9. Cologne and Berlin, 1972.

Campbell, Neil. *Napoleon at Fontainebleau and Elba; being a journal of occurances in 1814–1815, with notes of conversations by the late Major-General Sir Niel Campbell. . . .* London, 1869.

Carl August, Grand Duke of Saxe-Weimar-Eisenach. *Politischer Briefwechsel des Herzogs und Grossherzogs Carl August von Weimar*. Edited by Willy Andreas and Hans Tümmler. 3 vols. Göttingen, 1954–1973.

Chroust, Anton, ed. *Gsandtschaftsberichte aus München 1814–1848*. Part I: *Die Berichte der französischen Gesandten*. 6 vols. Schriftenreihe zur bayerischen Landesgeschichte, vols. 19–24. Munich, 1935–1937.

———. *Gesandtschaftsberichte aus München 1814–1848*. Part II: *Die Berichte der österreichischen Gesandten*. 4 vols. Schriftenreihe zur bayerischen Landesgeschichte, vols. 33–35 and 38. Munich, 1939–1943.

———. *Gesandtschaftsberichte aus München 1814–1848*. Part III: *Die Berichte der preussischen Gesandten*. 5 vols. Schriftenreihe zur bayerischen Landesgeschichte, vols. 39–43. Munich, 1949–1951.

Colenbrander, Herman Theodor, ed. *Gedenkstukken der algemeene Geschiedenis van Nederland van 1795 tot 1840*. 22 vols. The Hague, 1905–1922.

Czartoryski, Adam Herzy. *Memoirs of Prince Adam Czartoryski and His Correspondence with Alexander I*. Edited by Adam Gielgud. 2 vols. 2nd ed. London, 1888.

Demelitsch, Feodor von. *Actenstücke zur Geschichte der Coalition vom Jahre 1814*. Fontes Rerum Austricarum, 2nd ser., vol. 49, pt. 2. Vienna, 1899.

Fournier, August, ed. "Briefe vom Wiener Kongress." *Deutsche Rundschau*, CLXIV (1915), 67ff.

Fournier, August, ed. *Die Geheimpolizei auf dem Wiener Kongress.* Vienna and Leipzig, 1913.

———, ed. *Der Kongress von Châtillon. Die Politik im Kriege von 1814.* Vienna and Prague, 1900.

———, ed. "Londoner Präludien zum Wiener Kongress (Geheime Berichte Metternichs an Kaiser Franz)." *Deutsche Revue,* XLIII (1918), no. 1, 125–136 and 205–216; no. 2, 24–34.

———, ed. "Zur Vorgeschichte des Wiener Kongresses." In *Historische Studien und Skizzen,* Vienna and Leipzig, 1908.

Freksa, Frederick, comp. *A Peace Congress of Intrigue (Vienna, 1815): A Vivid, Intimate Account of the Congress of Vienna Composed of the Personal Memoirs of Its Important Participants.* Translated by Harry Hansen. New York, 1919.

Gentz, Friedrich von. *Aus der alten Registratur der Staatskanzlei. Briefe politischen Inhalts von und an Friedrich von Gentz aus den Jahren 1799–1827.* Edited by Alfons von Klinkowström. Vienna, 1870.

———. *Briefe von Friedrich Gentz on Pilat.* Edited by Karl Mendelsohn-Bartholdy. 2 vols. Leipzig, 1868.

———. *Briefe von und an Friedrich von Gentz.* Edited by Friedrich Carl Wittichen and Ernst Salzer. 3 vols. Munich and Berlin, 1910–1913.

———. *Dépêches inédites du chevalier de Gentz aux Hospodars de Valachie pour servir à l'histoire de la politique européenne (1813 à 1828).* Edited by Comte Anton Prokesch von Osten. 3 vols. Paris, 1876–1877.

———. *Gentz und Wessenberg. Briefe des ersten an den zweiten (1809–1832).* Edited by August Fournier. Vienna and Leipzig, 1907.

———. *Tagebücher von Friedrich von Gentz.* 4 vols. In *Aus dem Nachlasse Varnhagen's von Ense.* Leipzig, 1873.

German Confederation. Bundesversammlung. *Protokolle der deutschen Bundesversammlung,* 50 vols. Frankfurt am Main, 1816–1866.

Great Britain. Foreign Office. *British and Foreign State Papers,* vols. I–III. London, 1838–1841.

Grimm, Jacob and Wilhelm. *Briefwechsel zwischen Jacob und Wilhelm Grimm aus der Jugendzeit.* Edited by Hermann Grimm and Gustav Hinrichs. 2nd ed. edited by Wilhelm Schoof. Weimar, 1963.

Hansard, T. C., ed. *The Parliamentary Debates from the Year 1803 to the Present Time,* vol. XXVIII. London, 1814.

Huber, Ernst Rudolf. *Dokumente zur deutschen Verfassungsgeschichte.* 3 vols. Stuttgart, 1961–1966.

Humboldt, Wilhelm von. *Wilhelm und Caroline von Humboldt in ihren Briefen.* Edited by Anna von Sydow. 7 vols. 1907–1918. Reprint. Osnabrück, 1968.

———. *Wilhelm von Humboldts Gesammelte Schriften.* Edited by Albert

Leitzmann and others. 17 vols. 1903–1936. Reprint. Berlin, 1967–1968.

International Committee of Historical Sciences. *Repertorium der diplomatischen Vertreter aller Länder seit dem Westfälischen Frieden (1648)*. Edited by Ludwig Bittner, et al. 3 vols. Oldenburg, 1936–1965.

Karl, Archduke of Austria. *Ausgewählte Schriften, weiland seiner Kaiserlichen Hoheit des Erzherzogs Carl von Oesterreich*. Edited by F. X. Malcher. 7 vols. Vienna and Leipzig, 1893–1894.

Klinkowström, Alfons. *Oesterreichs Theilnahme an den Befreiungskriegen. Ein Beitrag zur Geschichte der Jahre 1813 bis 1815 nach Aufzeichnungen von Friedrich von Gentz nebst einen Anhang: "Briefwechsel zwischen den Fürsten Schwarzenberg und Metternich."* Vienna, 1887.

Klüber, Johann Ludwig, ed. *Acten des Wiener Congresses in den Jahren 1814 und 1815*. 9 vols. Erlangen, 1815–1835.

──────. *Öffentliches Recht des Teutschen Bundes und der Bundesstaaten*. Frankfurt am Main, 1840.

──────. *Uebersicht der diplomatischen Verhandlungen des Wiener Congresses überhaupt und insonderheit über wichtige Angelegenheiten des teutschen Bundes*. 3 vols. Frankfurt am Main, 1816.

LaGarde-Chambonas, Auguste Louis Charles, Comte de. *Souvenirs du Congrès de Vienne, 1814–1815*. Edited by Count Fleury. Paris, 1904.

La Harpe, Frédéric-César de, *Correspondance de Frédéric-César de la Harpe et Alexandre Ier*. Edited by Jean Charles Biaudet and Françoise Nicod. 2 vols. Neuchâtel, 1978–1979.

Lehmann, Max, ed. "Tagebuch des Freiherrn vom Stein während der Wiener Kongresses." *Historische Zeitschrift*, LX (1888), 385–467.

Londonderry, Robert Stewart, 2d marquess of. *Memoirs and correspondence of Visount Castlereagh, Second Marquess of Londonderry*. Edited by Charles Vane, 3d marquess of Londonderry. 12 vols. London, 1848–1853.

Martens, Fedor Fedorovitch, ed. *Recueil des traités et conventions conclus par la Russie avec les puissances étrangères*. 15 vols. St. Petersburg, 1874–1909.

Martens, Georges Frédéric de. *Recueil de traités d'alliance, de paix, de trêve, de neutralité de commerce, de limites, d'échange etc. et plusieurs autres actes servant à la connoissance des relations étrangères des puissances et états de l'Europe depuis 1761 jusqu'à présent*. 8 vols. Göttingen, 1817–1835.

──────. *Nouveau recueil de traités . . .* [Continuation of above]. 16 vols. Göttingen, 1817–1842.

──────. *Nouveau supplément au recueil de traités . . .* [Continuation of above]. 3 vols. Göttingen, 1839–1842.

Metternich-Winneburg, Clemens Lothar Wenzel von. *Aus Metternich's nachgelassenen Papieren.* Edited by Prince Richard Metternich. 8 vols. Vienna, 1880–1884. Published in English as *Memoirs of Prince Metternich.* 5 vols. New York, 1880–1882.

Meyer, Philipp Anton Guido von., ed. *Corpus Juris Confoederationis Germanicae.* 3 vols. 3rd ed. 1859–1861. Reprint. Aalen, 1978.

Müffling, Friedrich Karl von. *Passages from my Life together with Memoirs of the Campaign of 1813 and 1814.* Translated by Col. Philip Yorke. 2nd ed. London, 1853.

Müller, Adam. *Adam Müllers Lebenszeugnisse.* Edited by Jakob Baxa. 2 vols. Munich, Paderborn, and Vienna, 1966.

Münster, George Herbert, Count. *Political Sketches of the State of Europe from 1814–1867. Containing Count Ernst Münster's Despatches to the Prince Regent from the Congress of Vienna.* Edinburg, 1868.

Nesselrode, Charles Robert Comte de. *Lettres et papiers du chancelier comte de Nesselrode 1769–1850.* 11 vols. Paris, 1904–1912.

Neumann, Leopold, ed. *Recueil des traités et conventions conclus par l'Autriche avec les puissances étrangères, depuis 1763 jusqu'à nos jours.* 32 vols. Leipzig and Vienna, 1855–1912.

Oncken, Wilhelm, ed. *Oesterreich und Preussen im Befreiungskriege. Urkundliche Aufschlüsse über die politische Geschichte des Jahres 1813.* 2 vols. Berlin, 1876–1879.

Prussia. Laws and Statutes. *Gesetz-Sammlung für die königlichen preussischen Staaten 1815.* Berlin, 1815.

Rosenkrantz, Niels. *Journal du congrès de Vienne, 1814–1815.* Copenhagen, 1953.

Roveri, Alessandro, comp. *La Missione Consalvi e il Congresso di Vienna.* Fonti per la Storia d'Italia, vol. 115. Rome, 1971.

Russian Imperial Historical Society. *Sbornik.* 148 vols. Leningrad, 1867–1916.

Schoeps, Hans Joachim, ed. *Aus den Jahren preussischer Not und Erneuerung. Tagebücher und Briefe der Gebrüder Gerlach und ihres Kreises 1805–1820.* Berlin, 1963.

Schwarzenberg, Karl Philipp zu. *Briefe des Feldmarschalls Fürsten Schwarzenberg an seine Frau, 1799–1816.* Edited by Johann Friedrich Novak. Vienna, 1913.

Spiel, Hilde, ed. *The Congress of Vienna: An Eyewitness Account.* Translated by Richard H. Weber. Philadelphia, New York, and London, 1968.

Stein, Heinrich Friedrich Karl vom. *Freiherr vom Stein. Briefe und amtliche Schriften.* Edited by Erich Bozenhart and Walther Hubatsch. 10 vols. Stuttgart, 1957–1974.

Talleyrand-Perigord, Charles M. de. *The Correspondence of Prince Tal-*

leyrand and King Louis XVIII during the Congress of Vienna. Edited by M. G. Pallain. New York, 1881.

――――. *Memoirs of the Prince de Talleyrand.* Translated by Raphaël Ledos de Beaufort. 5 vols. New York, 1891–1892.

Ullrichová, Maria, ed. *Clemens Metternich—Wilhelmine von Sagan. Ein Briefwechsel 1813–1815.* Veröffentlichungen der Kommission für neuere Geschichte Österreichs, vol. 52. Graz and Cologne, 1966.

U.S.S.R., Ministry of Foreign Affairs. *Vnesniaia politika Rossii XIX i nachala XX veka. Dokumenty rossiiskogo Ministerstva inostrannykh del.* [Foreign policy of Russia in the XIXth and the beginning of the XXth century. Documents of the Russian Ministry of Foreign Affairs.] 1st ser., 8 vols. Moscow, 1960–1972.

Vitrolles, Eugène François Auguste d'Arnaud de. *Mémoires.* 2 vols. Paris, 1950–1951.

Walter, Friedrich, ed. *Die österreichische Zentralverwaltung. Part II Von der Vereinigung der österreichischen und böhmischen Hofkanzlei bis zur Einrichtung der Ministerialverfassung (1749–1848). Vol. 1, No. 2, Part 2 and Vol. 5: Die Zeit Franz' II. (I.) und Ferdinands I. (1792–1848).* Vienna, 1956.

Webster, Charles K., ed. *British Diplomacy 1813–1815: Select Documents Dealing with the Reconstruction of Europe.* London, 1921.

Weil, Maurice-Henri, ed. *Les Dessous du Congrès de Vienne. D'après les documents originaux des archives.* 2 vols. Paris, 1917.

Wellington, Arthur Wellesley, First Duke of. *The Dispatches of Field Marshal the Duke Wellington during His Various Campaigns in India, Portugal, Spain, the Low Countries, and France.* Edited by Colonel Gurwood. 2nd ed. in 8 vols. London, 1844–1847.

――――. *Supplementary Despatches and Memoranda of Field Marshal Arthur, Duke of Wellington, K.G.* 15 vols. London, 1858–1872.

Wolzogen, Ludwig von. *Memoiren des königl. preussischen Generals der Infanterie L. Freiherr von Wolzogen. Aus dessem Nachlass unter Beifügung officieller militärischen Denkschriften mitgetheilt von A. Fr. v. Wolzogen.* Leipzig, 1851.

Zöllner, Erich. "Aus unbekannten Diplomatenbriefen an dem Freiherr Franz Binder von Kriegelstein." In *Festschrift zur Feier des zweihundertjährigen Bestände des Haus- Hof- und Staatsarchivs.* Edited by Leo Santifaller. 2 vols. Vienna, 1949–1951.

III. NEWSPAPERS AND CONTEMPORARY TRACTS

Allgemeine Zeitung. Augsburg, 1814–1815.

Görres, Joseph von. *Joseph von Görres politische Schriften.* Edited by Marie Görres. 9 vols. Munich, 1854–1874.

Le moniteur universel. Paris, 1814–1815.

Pölitz, Karl Heinrich Ludwig. *Die Staatensysteme Europa's und Amerika's seit dem Jahre 1783.* 3 vols. Leipzig, 1826.

Rotteck, Karl Wenzeslaus Rodecker von, and Welcker, Karl Theodor. *Staats-Lexikon, oder Encyklopädie der Staatswissenschaften.* 15 vols. Altona, 1834–1843.

Vaterländische Blätter für den österreichischen Kaiserstaat. Vienna, 1814–1815.

Vollgraff, Karl Friedrich. *Die teutschen Standesherrn. Ein historisch-publicistischer Versuch.* Giessen, 1824.

IV. MONOGRAPHS AND GENERAL WORKS

Adalbert, Prinz von Bayern. *Max I. Joseph von Bayern. Pfalzgraf, Kurfürst, und König.* Munich, 1957.

Andreas, Willy. *Aufbau des Staates im Zusammenhang der allgemeinen Politik.* Leipzig, 1913.

Apian-Bennewitz, Fritz. *Leopold von Plessen und die Verfassungspolitik der deutschen Kleinstaaten auf dem Wiener Kongress 1814/15.* Ph.D. dissertation, University of Rostock, Eutin, 1930.

Arenberg, Jean Engelbert d'. *Les Princes du St. Empire.* Louvain, 1951.

Aretin, Karl Otmar Freiherr von. *Bayerns Weg zum souveränen Staat, Landstände und konstitutionelle Monarchie 1714–1818.* Munich, 1976.

———. "Die deutsche Politik Bayerns in der Zeit der staatlichen Entwicklung des deutschen Bundes 1814–1820." Ph.D. dissertation, University of Munich, 1952.

———. "Metternichs Verfassungspläne 1817/1818. Dargestellt an Hand des Briefwechsels des bayerischen Gesandten in Wien Frhr. von Steinlein mit dem bayerischen Aussenminister Aloys Rechberg." *Historisches Jahrbuch,* LXXIV (1955), 718–727.

———. *Vom deutschen Reich zum deutschen Bund.* Deutsche Geschichte, vol. 7. Göttingen, 1980.

Arneth, Alfred von. *Johann Freiherr von Wessenberg. Ein österreichischer Staatsmann des neunzehnten Jahrhunderts.* 2 vols. Vienna and Leipzig, 1898.

Baasch, E. *Hamburg und Oesterreich, 1814–1866.* Freiburg im Breisgau, 1930.

Baron, Salo. *Die Judenfrage auf dem Wiener Kongress, auf Grund von zum Teil ungedruckten Quellen dargestellt.* Vienna and Berlin, 1920.

Baumgarten, H. "Verhandlungen über die deutsche Bundesverfassung im Sommer 1814." *Im neuen Reich,* IX, pt. 2 (1879), 549–561.

Beer, Adolf. *Die Finanzen Österreichs im XIX. Jahrhundert.* Prague, 1877.

Benna, Anna Hedwig. "Organisierung und Personalstand der Polizeihofstelle (1793–1848)." *Mitteilungen des österreichischen Staatsarchivs*, VI (1953), 197–239.

Berney, A. "Reichstradition und Nationalstaatsgedanke 1789–1815." *Historische Zeitschrift*, CXL (1929), 57–86.

Bertier de Sauvigny, Guillaume de. *The Bourdon Restoration.* Translated by Lynn M. Case. Philadelphia, 1966.

———. *Metternich et la France après Congrès de Vienne.* 3 vols. Paris, 1968–1971.

———. "Sainte-Alliance et Alliance dans les conceptions de Metternich." *Revue historique*, CCXXIII (April-June 1960), 249–275.

Bibl, Viktor. *Metternich, der Dämon Österreichs.* Leipzig and Vienna, 1936.

———. *Der Zerfall Österreichs. I: Kaiser Franz und sein Erbe.* Vienna, Leipzig, Berlin, and Munich, 1922.

Binder, Wilhelm. *Fürst Clemens von Metternich und sein Zeitalter.* Ludwigsberg, 1836.

Bippen, Wilhelm von. *Johann Smidt, ein hanseatischer Staatsmann.* Berlin, 1921.

Bittner, Ludwig. *Chronologisches Verzeichnis der österreichischen Staatsverträge. Vol. II: Die österreichischen Staatsverträge von 1763 bis 1847.* Veröffentlichungen der Kommission für neuere Geschichte Österreichs, vol. 8. Vienna, 1909.

Boogman, J. C. *Nederland en de Duitse Bond 1815–1851.* 2 vols. Groningen and Djakarta, 1955.

Born, Karl Erich. "Hardenbergs Pläne und Versuche zur Neuordnung Europas und Deutschlands 1813–1815." *Geschichte in Wissenschaft und Unterricht*, VIII (1957), 550–565.

Bourgoing, Johann von. *Vom Wiener Kongress. Zeit- und Sittenbilder.* Brunn, Munich, and Vienna, 1943.

Bourquin, Maurice. *Histoire de la Sainte-Alliance.* Geneva, 1954.

Brandes, Karl Friedrich. *Graf Münster und die Wiedererstehung Hannovers 1809–1815.* Urach, Württemberg, 1938.

Brandt, Hartwig. *Landständische Repräsentationen im deutschen Vormärz. Politisches Denken im Einflussfeld des monarchischen Prinzips.* Neuwied and Berlin, 1968.

Branig, Hans. *Fürst Wittgenstein. Ein preussischer Staatsmann der Restaurationszeit.* Veröffentlichungen aus den Archiven preussischer Kulturbesitz, vol. 17. Cologne and Vienna, 1981.

Bury, J.P.T. "The End of the Napoleonic Senate." *Cambridge Historical Journal*, IX no. 2 (1948), 165–189.

Colenbrander, Herman Theodor. *Vestiging van het Koninkrijk 1813–1815.* Amsterdam, 1927.

Corti, Egon Cäsar Conte. *Metternich und die Frauen.* 2 vols. Zurich and Vienna, 1948–1949.

Craig, Gordon A. "Wilhelm von Humboldt as Diplomat." In *Studies in International History*, edited by K. Bourne and D. C. Watt. London, 1967.

Dard, Emile. *Napoleon und Talleyrand*. Translated by Willy Grabert. Giessen and Berlin, 1938.

Delbrück, Hans. "Friedrich Wilhelm III. und Hardenberg auf dem Wiener Kongress." *Historische Zeitschrift*, LXIII (1889), 242–265.

Diefendorf, Jeffry M. *Businessmen and Politics in the Rhineland, 1789–1834*. Princeton, N.J., 1980.

Dietrich, Julius Reinhart. "Hessen-Darmstadt auf dem Wiener Kongress und die Erwerbung Rheinhessens." *Quellen und Forschungen zur hessischen Geschichte*, IV (1917), 147–294.

Doeberl, Michael. *Entwicklungsgeschichte Bayerns*. 3 vols. Munich, 1908–1931.

Dökert, Walter. *Die englische Politik auf dem Wiener Kongress*. Ph.D. dissertation, University of Leipzig, 1911.

Dommermuth, Nikolaus. *Das angebliche europäische Garantierecht über den deutschen Bund von 1815 bis 1866*. Ph.D. dissertation, University of Frankfurt, 1928.

Dorpalen, Andreas. "The German Struggle against Napoleon: The East German View." *Journal of Modern History*, XLI (1969), 485–516.

Dunk, Hermann von der. *Der deutsche Vormärz und Belgien 1830–1848*. Veröffentlichungen des Instituts für europäische Geschichte, Mainz. Abteilung Universalgeschicte, vol. 41. Wiesbaden, 1966.

Dupuis, Charles. *Le ministère de Talleyrand en 1814*. 2 vols. Paris, 1919–1920.

Dyroff, Hans-Dieter, ed. *Der Wiener Kongress 1814/15. Die Neuordnung Europas*. Nördlingen, 1966.

Egloffstein, Hermann von. *Carl August auf dem Wiener Kongress*. Beiträge zur neueren Geschichte Thüringens, vol. 3. Jena, 1915.

Emerson, Donald. *Metternich and the Political Police: Security and Subversion in the Habsburg Monarchy*. The Hague, 1968.

Epstein, Klaus. "Stein in German Historiography." *History and Theory*, V (1966), 241–274.

Fehrenbach, Elisabeth. *Vom Ancien Régime zum Wiener Kongress*. Munich and Vienna, 1981.

Feine, Hans Erich. *Das Werden des deutschen Staates seit dem Ausgang des heiligen römischen Reiches 1800 bis 1933. Eine verfassungsgeschichtliche Darstellung*. Stuttgart, 1936.

Feldmann, Roland. *Jacob Grimm und die Politik*. Kassel, 1970.

Ferrero, Guglielmo. *The Reconstruction of Europe: Talleyrand and the Con-*

gress of Vienna 1814–1815. Translated by Theodore R. Jaickel. New York, 1941.

Fournier, August. *Napoleon I. A Biography*. Translated by Annie Elizabeth Adams. New York, 1915.

Gagern, Hans Christoph von. *Mein Antheil an der Politik*. 4 vols. Stuttgart, 1823–1833.

Gebhardt, Bruno. *Wilhelm von Humboldt als Staatsmann*. 2 vols. 1899. Reprint. Aalen, 1965.

Gembruch, Werner. *Freiherr vom Stein im Zeitalter der Restauration*. Wiesbaden, 1960.

Gerhard, Dietrich. *England und der Aufstieg Russlands*. Munich, 1933.

Gerschler, Walter. *Das preussische Oberpräsidium der Provinz Jülich-Kleve-Berg in Köln*. Edited by Walther Hubatsch. Studien zur Geschichte Preussens, vol. 12. Cologne and Berlin, 1967.

Gerstner, Hermann. *Die Brüder Grimm*. Gerabronn and Crailsheim, 1970.

Glaser, Marie. "Die badische Politik und die deutsche Frage zur Zeit der Befreiungskriege und des Wiener Kongresses." *Zeitschrift für die Geschichte des Oberrheins*, n. s. XLI (1928), 268–317.

Goerdeler, Marianne. *Die Reichsidee in den Bundesplänen und ihr geistiger Hintergrund*. Ph.D. dissertation, University of Leipzig, 1943.

Goldmann, Karl. *Die preussisch-britischen Beziehungen in den Jahren 1812–1815*. Würzburg, 1934.

Gollwitzer, Heinz. *Europabild und Europagedanke. Beiträge zur deutschen Geistesgeschichte des 18. und 19. Jahrhundert*. Munich, 1951.

———. *Die Standesherren. Die politische und gesellschaftliche Stellung der Mediatisierten, 1815–1918. Ein Beitrag zur deutschen Socialgeschichte*. Göttingen, 1964.

Gooch, George Peabody. *Studies in German History*. London and New York, 1948.

Griewank, Karl. "Preussen und die Neuordnung Deutschlands." *Forschungen zur brandenburgischen und preussischen Geschichte*, LII (1940), 234–279.

———. "Preussische Neuordnungspläne für Mitteleuropa aus dem Jahre 1814." *Deutsches Archiv für Landes- und Volksforschung*, VI (1942), 342–360.

———. *Der Wiener Kongress und die Neuordnung Europas 1814–1815*. Leipzig, 1942.

Grimsted, Patricia Kennedy. *The Foreign Ministers of Alexander I. Political Attitudes and the Conduct of Russian Diplomacy, 1801–25*. Berkeley, 1969.

Grosjean, George. *La politique extérieure de la restauration et l'Allemagne*. Paris, 1930.

Grube, Walter. *Der Stuttgarter Landtag 1457–1957. Von den Landständen zum demokratischen Parlament.* Stuttgart, 1957.

Gruner, Justus von. "Justus Gruner und der Hoffmannsche Bund." *Forschungen zur brandenburgischen und preussischen Geschichte,* XIX (1906), 485–507.

Gruner, Wolf D. "Der deutsche Bund—Modell für eine Zwischenlösung?" *Politik und Kultur,* IX, no. 5 (1982), 22–42.

———. "Europäischer Friede als nationales Interesse. Die Rolle des deutschen Bundes in der britischen Politik 1814–1832." *Bohemia, Jahrbuch des Collegium Carolinum,* XVIII (1977), 96–128.

———. "Die Interaktion von britischer Deutschland- und Europapolitik zur Zeit des Wiener Kongresses und in der Anfangsphase des deutschen Bundes." In *Grossbritannien und Deutschland. Europäische Aspekte der politisch-kulturellen Beziehungen beider Länder in Geschichte und Gegenwart,* edited by O. Kuhn. Munich, 1974.

Gulick, Edward Vose. *Europe's Classical Balance of Power: A Case History of the Theory and Practice of One of the Great Concepts of European Statecraft.* Ithaca, N.Y., 1955.

Haas, Arthur G. *Metternich, Reorganization and Nationality 1813–1818. A Story of Foresight and Frustration in the Rebuilding of the Austrian Empire.* Veröffentlichungen des Instituts für europäische Geschichte, Mainz. Abteilung Universalgeschichte, vol. 28. Wiesbaden, 1963.

Hammer, Karl. *Die französische Diplomatie der Restautation und Deutschland 1814–1830.* Pariser Historische Studien, vol. 2. Stuttgart, 1963.

Hantsch, Hugo. *Die Geschichte Österreichs.* 2 vols. Graz and Vienna, 1937–1950.

Hartmann, Hans-Joachim. *Das Schicksal der preussisch-österreichischen Verfassungsvorschläge insbesondere des Entwurfs vom 14. Oktober 1814 auf dem Wiener Kongress.* Ph.D. dissertation, University of Göttingen, 1964.

Hartung, Fritz. *Das Grossherzogtum Sachsen unter der Regierung Carl Augusts 1775–1828.* Weimar, 1923.

Hausherr, Hans. *Hardenberg. Eine politische Biographie.* Edited by Karl Erich Born. Kölner historische Abhandlungen, vol. 8. Cologne, 1963.

———. "Stein und Hardenberg." *Historische Zeitschrift,* CXC (1960), 267–289.

———. *Die Stunde Hardenbergs.* Hamburg, 1943.

Headlam-Morley, James. *Studies in Diplomatic History.* London, 1930.

Heffter, Heinrich. *Die deutsche Selbstverwaltung im 19. Jahrhundert. Geschichte der Ideen und Institutionen.* Stuttgart, 1950.

Heilmann, Johann. *Feldmarschall Fürst Wrede.* Leipzig, 1881.

Helleiner, Karl F. *The Imperial Loans: A Study in Financial and Diplomatic History.* Oxford, 1965.

Himly, August. *Histoire de la formation territoriale des états de l'Europe centrale.* 2 vols. 2nd ed. Paris, 1894.

Hölzle, Erwin. *Württemberg im Zeitalter Napoleons und der deutschen Erhebung.* Stuttgart and Berlin, 1937.

Hoff, Johann Friedrich. *Die Mediatisiertenfrage in den Jahren 1813–1815.* Abhandlungen zur mittleren und neueren Geschichte, no. 46. Berlin and Leipzig, 1913.

Huber, Ernst Rudolf. *Deutsche Verfassungsgeschichte seit 1789.* 5 vols. Stuttgart, Berlin, Cologne, and Mainz, 1957–1978.

Ilse, Leopold Friedrich. *Geschichte der deutschen Bundesversammlung insbesondere ihres Verhaltens zu den deutschen Nationalinteressen.* 3 vols. 1861–1862. Reprint. Hildesheim, 1971–1972.

Kaehler, S. A. *Wilhelm von Humboldt und der Staat. Ein Beitrag zur Geschichte deutscher Lebensgestaltung um 1800.* 2nd ed. Göttingen, 1963.

Kaltenborn, Karl von. *Geschichte der Deutschen Bundesverhältnisse und Einheitsbestrebungen von 1806 bis 1856.* 2 vols. Berlin, 1857.

Kann, Robert A. "Metternich: A Reappraisal of his Impact on International Relations." *Journal of Modern History,* XXXII (1960), 333–339.

Keerl, Erich. *Herzog Ernst I von Sachsen-Coburg zwischen Napoleon und Metternich. Ein deutscher Kleinstaat im politischen Kräftespiel der Grossmächte 1800–1830.* Erlangen, 1973.

Keil, Walter. "Die Beeinflussung des Wiener Kongresses durch Bayern unter dem Ministerium Montgelas." Ph.D. dissertation, University of Erlangen, 1950.

Kielmansegg, Peter von. *Stein und die Zentralverwaltung 1813/14.* Stuttgart, 1964.

Kircheisen, Friedrich M. *Napoleon.* Translated by H. St. Lawrence. New York, 1932.

Kissinger, Henry A. *A World Restored. Metternich, Castlereagh, and the Problems of Peace 1812–1822.* London, 1957.

Klein, August. *Friedrich Graf zu Solms-Laubach, preussischer Oberpräsident in Köln, 1815–1822.* Veröffentlichungen des Kölnischen Geschichtsvereins, vol. 13. Cologne, 1936.

Klein, Ernst. *Von der Reform zur Restauration. Finanzpolitik und Reformgesetzgebung des preussischen Staatkanzlers Karl August von Hardenberg.* Veröffentlichungen der Historischen Kommission zu Berlin beim Friedrich-Meinecke-Institut der Freien Universität Berlin, vol. 16. Berlin, 1965.

Klemmer, Lieselotte. *Aloys von Rechberg als Bayerischer Politiker (1766–1849).* Miscellanea Bavarica Monacensia, vol. 60. Munich, 1975.

Klingenburg, E. M. *Die Entstehung der deutsch-niederländischen Grenze.* Leipzig, 1940.

Koch, Rainer, "Ständische Repräsentation oder liberale Repräsentativverfassung? Die Constitutions-Ergänzungs-Acte der freien Stadt Frankfurt als historischer Kompromiss." *Zeitschrift für historische Forschung,* v (1978) 187–214.

Kohlschmidt, Walter. *Die sächsische Frage auf dem Wiener Kongress und die sächsische Diplomatie dieser Zeit.* Aus Sachens Vergangenheit, no. 6. Dresden, 1930.

Kraehe, Enno E. "Austria and the Problem of Reform in the German Confederation, 1851–1863." *American Historical Review,* LVI (1950–1951), 276–294.

———. "Foreign Policy and the Nationality Problem in the Habsburg Monarchy, 1800–1867." *Austrian History Yearbook,* III, pt. 3 (1967), 3–36.

———. "From Rheinbund to Deutscher Bund: The Road to European Equilibrium." *Proceedings of the Fourth Annual Consortium for Revolutionary Europe,* 163–175. Tallahassee: Florida State University Press, 1977.

———. "Idéologie et raison d'état dans la politique allemande de Metternich, 1809–1820." *Revue d'histoire moderne et contemporaine,* XIII (1966), 181–195.

———. "The Origins of the Carlsbad Decrees: Some Perspectives." Paper read before the American Historical Association, New York, 28 December 1971.

———. "The United Nations in the Light of the Experiences of the German Confederation." *South Atlantic Quarterly,* XLIX (1950), 138–149.

Krausnick, Kurt. *Ernst Graf von Münster in der europäischen Politik 1806–1815.* Ph.D. dissertation, University of Berlin, 1936.

Krones, Franz. *Geschichte der Neuzeit Oesterreichs vom achtzehnten Jahrhundert bis auf die Gegenwart.* Berlin, 1879.

Kuchnawe, Hugo and Veltze, Alois. *Feldmarschall Karl Fürst zu Schwarzenberg, der Führer der Verbündeten in den Befreiungskriegen.* Vienna and Leipzig, 1913.

Kukiel, Marian. *Czartoryski and European Unity 1770–1861.* Princeton, N.J., 1955.

Landauer, Robert. "Die Einverleibung Salzburgs durch Österreich 1816. Ein Kapitel aus Metternichs deutsche Politik." *Mitteilungen der Gesellschaft für Salzburger Landeskunde,* LXXIII (1933), 1–38.

Lange, Günther. "Die Rolle Englands bei der Wiederherstellung und Vergrösserung Hannovers 1813–1815." *Niedersächsisches Jahrbuch für Landesgeschichte,* XXVIII (1956), 73–175.

Lauber, Emil. *Metternichs Kampf um die europäische Mitte. Struktur seiner Politik von 1809 bis 1815.* Vienna and Leipzig, 1939.

Lautzas, Peter. *Die Festung Mainz im Zeitalter des Ancien Regime, der Französischen Revolution, und der Empire (1763–1814). Ein Beitrag zur Militärstruktur des Mittelrheim-Gebietes.* Geschichtliche Landeskunde, vol. 8. Wiesbaden, 1973.

Ley, Francis. *Alexander Ier et sa Sainte-Alliance (1811–1825).* Paris, 1975.

Liebeschütz, Hans, and Paucker, Arnold, eds. *Das Judentum in der deutschen Umwelt 1800–1850.* Schriftenreihe wissenschaftlicher Abhandlungen des Leo Baeck Instituts, no. 35. Tübingen, 1977.

Lipgens, Walter. *Ferdinand August Graf Spiegel und das Verhältnis von Kirche und Staat 1789–1835. Die Wende vom Staatskirchentum zur Kirchenfreiheit.* 2 vols. Veröffentlichungen der Historischen Kommission Westphalens, vol. 18. Münster in Westphalia, 1965.

Losch, Philipp. *Geschichte des Kurfürstentums Hessen 1803 bis 1866.* 1922. Reprint. Cassel, 1972.

Macartney, C. A. *The Habsburg Empire 1790–1918.* London, 1968.

McGuigan, Dorothy Gies. *Metternich and the Duchess.* New York, 1975.

Madelin, Louis. *Le consulat et l'empire.* 2 vols. Paris, 1932–1933.

Mager, Wolfgang. "Das Problem der landständischen Verfassungen auf dem Wiener Kongress 1814/15." *Historische Zeitschrift,* CCXVII (1973), 296–346.

Markert, Werner. *Osteuropa und die abendländische Welt. Aufsätze und Vorträge.* Göttingen, 1966.

Mauersberg, Hans. "Rekonstruktionsprojekte deutscher Staaten auf dem Wiener Kongress und die ihr dienlichen bevölkerungsstatistischen und sonstigen Unterlagen nach den Gesandtschaftsberichten des kgl. britischen und hannöverschen Bevollmächtigten, des Grafen Münster." In *Wirtschaft, Geschichte und Wirtschaftsgeschichte. Festschrift zum 65. Geburtstag von Friedrich Lütge,* edited by Wilhelm Abel et al. Stuttgart, 1966.

Maurois, André. "Metternich." *La revue de Paris,* LXIII (July 1956), 5–17.

Mayr. Josef K. "Aufbau und Arbeitweise des Wiener Kongresses." *Archivalische Zeitschrift,* XLV, 64–127.

———. *Geschichte der österreichischen Staatkanzlei im Zeitalter des Fürsten Metternichs.* Inventare des Wiener Haus-, Hof- und Staatsarchiv, vol. 2. Vienna, 1935.

———. *Metternichs geheimer Briefdienst, Postlagen und Postkurse.* Inventare des Wiener Haus-, Hof- und Staatsarchivs, vol. 3. Vienna, 1935.

Meinecke, Friedrich. *Das Leben des Generalfeldmarschalls Hermann von Boyen.* 2 vols. Stuttgart, 1899.

————. *Weltbürgertum und Nationalstaat.* 5th ed. Munich and Berlin, 1919.

Meister, Robert, *Nassau und die Reichsritterschaft vom Reichsdeputationshauptschluss bis zum Wiener Kongress (1803–1815).* Historische Studien, no. 153. Berlin, 1923.

Merkle, J. *Katherina Paulowna, Königin von Württemberg.* Stuttgart, 1889.

Meyer, A. O. "Der Streit um Metternich." *Historische Zeitschrift,* CLVII (1937), 75–84.

Molden, Ernst. *Zur Geschichte des österreichisch-russischen Gegensatzes.* Vienna, 1916.

Mommsen, Wilhelm. *Stein, Ranke, Bismarck. Ein Beitrag zur politischen und sozialen Bewegung des 19. Jahrhunderts.* Munich, 1954.

————. "Zur Bedeutung des Reichsgedankens." *Historische Zeitschrift,* CLXXIV (1952), 385–415.

Mueller, Adolf. *Bayerische Politik und bayerische Diplomaten zur Zeit Carl Theodors und Max Josephs. Aus dem Leben des Gesandten und General-Majors Joseph F. von Sulzer.* Schriftenreihe zur bayerischen Landesgeschichte, vol. 49. Munich, 1954.

Mueller, Christine L. "The Estates of Styria, 1740–1848: A Century of Transition." Ph.D. dissertation, University of Virginia, 1980.

Müller, Heinrich. *Der letzte Kampf der Reichritterschaft um ihre Selbständigkeit (1790–1815).* Historische Studien, no. 77. Berlin, 1910.

Näf, Werner. *Zur Geschichte der heiligen Allianz.* Berner Untersuchungen zur allgemeinen Geschichte, vol. 1. Bern, 1928.

Nicolas, Mikhailovich, Grand Duke of Russia. *Le Tsar Alexander Ier.* Translated by Baroness N. Wrangel. Paris, 1931.

Nicolson, Harold. *The Congress of Vienna. A Study in Allied Unity 1815–1822.* New York, 1946.

Nørregaard, Georg. *Danmark og Wienerkongressen.* Copenhagen, 1948.

Obenaus, H. "Verwaltung und ständische Repräsentation in den Reformen des Freiherrn vom Stein." *Jahrbuch für die Geschichte Mittel- und Ostdeutschlands,* XVIII (1969), 130–179.

————. "Finanzkrise und Verfassungsgebung. Zu den sozialen Bedingungen des frühen deutschen Konstitutionalismus." In *Gesellschaft, Parlament, und Regierung,* edited by G. A. Ritter. Düsseldorf, 1974.

Obermann, Karl. "Der Wiener Kongress 1814/1815." *Zeitschrift für Geschichtswissenschaft,* XIII (1965), 474–492.

Olshausen, Klothilde von. *Die Stellung der Grossmächte zur sächsischen Frage auf dem Wiener Kongress und deren Rückwirkung auf die Gestaltung der preussischen Ostgrenze.* Munich, 1933.

Oman, Carola. *Napoleon's Viceroy Eugène de Beauharnais.* New York, 1966.

Oncken, Wilhelm. *Das Zeitalter der Revolution, des Kaiserreichs, und der Befreiungskriege.* 2 vols. Berlin, 1886.

Palmer, Alan. *Metternich.* London, 1972.

Pertz, Georg Heinrich. *Das Leben des Ministers Freiherrn vom Stein.* 6 vols. 2nd ed. Berlin, 1850–1854.

———, and Delbrück, H. *Das Leben des Feldmarschalls Grafen Neithardt von Gneisenau.* 5 vols. Berlin, 1864–1880.

Pfister, Albert. *Aus dem Lager der Verbündeten 1814 und 1815.* Stuttgart, 1897.

Pflugk-Harttung, Julius von. "Die Gegensätze zwischen England und Preussen wegen der Bundestruppen 1815." *Forschungen zur brandenburgischen und preussischen Geschichte,* XXIV, no. 2 (1911), 125–180.

Phillips, Walter Alison. *The Confederation of Europe: A Study of the European Alliance, 1813–1823, as an Experiment in the International Organization of Peace.* London and New York, 1914.

Pirenne, Jacques-Henri. *La Sainte-Alliance: Organisation européenne de la paix mondiale.* 2 vols. Neuchâtel, 1946–1949.

Posch, Andreas. "Die kirchenpolitische Einstellung Metternichs." *Religion, Wissenschaft, Kultur,* XIII (1962), 119–127.

Price, Arnold H. *The Evolution of the Zollverein: A Study of the Ideas and Institutions Leading to German Economic Unification between 1815 and 1833.* University of Michigan Publications in History and Political Science, vol. 17. Ann Arbor, 1949.

Prössler, Helmut. "Die politische Freundschaft zwischen Freiherr vom Stein und Friedrich zu Solms-Laubach von 1813–1812." *Archiv für hessische Geschichte,* n.s. XXVI (1958), 103–138.

Prokesch-Osten, Anton von. *Denkwürdigkeiten aus dem Leben des Feldmarschalls Fürsten Carl zu Schwarzenberg.* Vienna, 1861.

Quint, Wolfgang. *Souveränitätsbegriff und Souveränitätspolitik in Bayern. Von der Mitte des 17. bis zur ersten Hälfte des 19. Jahrhunderts.* Schriften zur Verfassungsgeschichte, vol. 15. Berlin, 1971.

Radvany, Egon. *Metternich's Projects for Reform in Austria.* The Hague, 1971.

Raumer, Kurt von. *Deutschland um 1800. Krise und Neugestaltung 1789–1815.* Handbuch der deutschen Geschichte, vol. 3, pt. 1. New edition edited by Leo Just. Constance, n.d.

Real, Willy. *Die deutsche Verfassungsfrage am Ausgang der napoleonischen Herrschaft bis zum Beginn des Wiener Kongresses.* Leipzig, 1935.

———. "Von Bemühungen um die Errichtung eines Bundesgerichts zur Zeit des Wiener Kongresses." *Zeitschrift für die Geschichte des Oberrheins,* n. s. XLIX (1935), 214–228.

Reinerman, Alan J. *Austria and the Papacy in the Age of Metternich*. Washington, D.C., 1979.

Renier, Gustaaf Johannes. *Great Britain and the Establishment of the Kingdom of the Netherlands, 1813–1815: A Study in British Foreign Policy*. London, 1930.

Rheindorf, Kurt. "Englische Rheinpolitik 1813–1815." *Elsass-Lothringen Jahrbuch*, VII (1928), 158–193.

Rie, Robert. *Der Wiener Kongress und das Völkerrecht*. Bonn, 1957.

Rieben, Hans. *Prinzipiengrundlage und Diplomatie in Metternichs Europapolitik 1815–1848*. Berner Untersuchungen zur allgemeinen Geschichte, vol. 12. Aaron, 1942.

Ritter, Gerhard. *Stein. Eine politische Biographie*. 2 vols. 1931. Rev. ed. in 1 vol. Stuttgart, 1958.

Rössler, Hellmuth. *Graf Johann Philipp Stadion, Napoleons deutscher Gegenspieler*. 2 vols. Vienna and Munich, 1966.

———. *Österreichs Kampf um Deutschlands Befreiung. Die deutsche Politik der nationalen Führer Österreichs 1805–1815*. 2 vols. Hamburg. 1940.

———. *Zwischen Revolution und Reaktion. Ein Lebensbild des Reichsfreiherrn Hans Christoph von Gagern, 1766–1852*. Veröffentlichungen der historischen Kommission für Nassau, vol. 14. Göttingen, Berlin, and Frankfurt, 1958.

Rohden, Peter Richard. *Die klassische Diplomatie von Kaunitz bis Metternich*. Leipzig, 1939.

Ruck, Erwin. *Die römische Kurie und die deutsche Kirchenfrage auf dem Wiener Kongress*. Basel, 1917.

Sahrmann, Adam. *Pfalz oder Salzburg? Geschichte des territorialen Ausgleichs zwischen Bayern und Österreich, 1813–1819*. Munich and Berlin, 1921.

Sarholz, Hans. "Das Herzogtum Nassau 1813–1815. Ein Beitrag zur Geschichte des Rheinbundes und der Befreiungskriege." *Nassauische Annalen*, LVII (1937), 55–119.

Schaffstein, Friedrich. *Wilhelm von Humboldt. Ein Lebensbild*. Frankfurt am Main, 1952.

Schaumann, A. H. "Geschichte der Bildung des deutschen Bundes auf dem Wiener Kongress." *Historisches Taschenbuch*, 3rd ser., vol. 1 (1850), 151–280.

Schiemann, Theodor. *Geschichte Russlands unter Kaiser Nikolaus I*. Vol. I: *Kaiser Alexander I und die Ergebnisse seiner Lebensarbeit*. Berlin, 1904.

Schilder, Nikolai Karlovich. *Imperator Aleksandr Pervyi ego zhizn'i tsarstvovanie*. 4 vols. 2nd ed. St. Petersburg, 1904–1905.

Schlegel, Friedrich. *Kritische Friedrich-Schlegel-Ausgabe*. Edited by Ernst

Behler. Vol. VII: *Studien zur Geschichte und Politik*. Munich, Paderborn, and Vienna, 1966.

Schmidt, W. A. *Geschichte der deutschen Verfassungsfrage während der Befreiungskrieg und des Wiener Kongresses*. Edited by Alfred Stern. Stuttgart, 1890.

Schnabel, Franz. *Deutsche Geschichte im neunzehnten Jahrhundert*. 4 vols. Freiburg, 1929–1937.

Schneider, Franz. *Pressefreiheit und politische Öffentlichkeit; Studien zur politischen Geschichte Deutschlands bis 1848*. Neuwied and Berlin, 1966.

Schröder, Richard. *Lehrbuch der deutschen Rechtsgeschichte*. Leipzig, 1902.

Schulte, Aloys. *Der deutsche Staat. Verfassung, Macht und Grenzen, 919–1914*. 1933. Reprint. Aalen, 1968.

Schwarz, Wilhelm. *Die Heilige Allianz. Tragik eines europäischen Friedensbundes*. Stuttgart, 1935.

Schwarzenberg, Karl Fürst. *Feldmarschall Fürst Schwarzenberg. Der Sieger von Leipzig*. Vienna and Munich, 1964.

Schwemer, Richard. *Geschichte der freien Stadt Frankfurt am Main (1814–1866)*. 3 vols. Frankfurt am Main, 1910–1915.

Sherwig, John M. *Guineas and Gunpowder: British Foreign Aid in the Wars with France 1793–1815*. Cambridge, Mass., 1969.

Simon, Walter. *The Failure of the Prussian Reform Movement 1807–1819*. Ithaca, N.Y., 1955.

———. "Prince Hardenberg." *Review of Politics*, XVIII (1956), 88–99.

Sorel, Albert. *L'Europe et la révolution française*. 8 vols. Paris, 1885–1904.

Srbik, Heinrich von. *Deutsche Einheit. Idee und Wirklichkeit vom Heiligen Reich bis Königgrätz*. 4 vols. Munich, 1935–1942.

———. "Der Ideengehalt des 'Metternichsystems.'" *Historische Zeitschrift*, CXXXI (1925), 240–262.

———. *Metternich der staatsmann und der Mensch*. 3 vols. Munich, 1925–1954.

———. "Metternichs Plan der Neuordnung Europas 1814/15." *Mitteilungen des Instituts für österreichische Geschichtsforschung*, XL (1925), 109–126.

Stählin, Karl. *Geschichte Russlands von den Anfängen bis zur Gegenwart*. 4 vols. in 5. Königsberg and Berlin, 1923–1939.

Stern, Alfred. *Geschichte Euorpas seit den Verträgen von 1815 bis zum Frankfurter Frieden von 1871*. 10 vols. Berlin, 1894–1924.

Strathmann, Friedrich. *Altständischer Einfluss auf die deutschen Territorial-Verfassungen der Jahre 1814 bis 1819; ein Beitrag zum Problem der Kontinuität der deutschen Verfassungsgeschichte*. Mainz, 1955.

Straus, Hannah Alice. *The Attitude of the Congress of Vienna toward Na-*

tionalism in Germany, Italy, and Poland. Studies in History, Economics, and Public Law, no. 558. New York, 1949.

Sweet, Paul R. *Friedrich von Gentz, Defender of the Old Order.* 1941. Reprint. Westport, Conn., 1970.

———. *Wilhelm von Humboldt: A Biography.* 2 vols. Columbus, Ohio, 1978–1980.

Temperley, Harold William, and Penson, Lillian M. *Foundations of British Foreign Policy from Pitt (1792) to Salisbury (1902).* Cambridge, 1938.

Thackeray, Frank W. *Antecedents of Revolution: Alexander I and the Polish Kingdom, 1815–1825.* East European Monographs, no. 47. Boulder and New York, 1980.

Thielen, Peter Gerrit. *Karl August von Hardenberg 1750–1822: Eine Biographie.* Cologne and Berlin, 1967.

Thiry, Jean. *Le sénat de Napoléon (1800–1814).* Paris, 1932.

Tiedemann, Helmut. *Der deutsche Kaisergedanke vor und nach dem Wiener Kongress.* Breslau, 1932.

Treitschke, Heinrich von. *Treitschke's History of Germany in the Nineteenth Century.* Translated by Eden and Cedar Paul. 7 vols. New York, 1915–1919.

Tritsch, Walther. *Metternich und sein Monarch. Biographie eines seltsamen Doppelgestirns.* Darmstadt, 1952.

Ulmann, Heinrich. "Der Beitritt Hessen-Darmstadts zu dem Wiener Geheimvertrag vom 3. 1815." *Archiv für hessische Geschichte und Altertumskunde,* n. s. XI (1915), 309–320.

———. *Denkwürdigkeiten aus dem Dienstleben des Freiherrn der Thil 1803–1848.* Leipzig and Stuttgart, 1921.

———. "Zur Entstehung der Kaisernote der 29 Kleinstaaten vom 16. November 1814." *Historische Zeitschrift,* CXVI (1916), 459–483.

Valjavec, Fritz. *Die Entstehung der politischen Strömungen in Deutschland 1770–1815.* Munich, 1951.

Vierhaus, Rudolf. "Eigentumsrecht und Mediatisierung. Der Kampf um die Rechte der Reichsritterschaft 1803–1815." In *Eigentum und Verfassung. Zur Eigentumsdiskussion im ausgehenden 18. Jahrhundert,* edited by Rudolf Vierhaus. Veröffentlichungen des Max-Planck-Instituts für Geschichte, vol. 37. Göttingen, 1972.

Völker, Karl. "Metternichs Kirchenpolitik." *Zeitschrift für Kirchengeschichte,* XLIX (1930), 222–246.

Waliszewski, K. *La Russie il y a cent ans. La règne d'Alexandre Ier,* 3 vols. Paris, 1924.

Walter, Gero. *Der Zusammenbruch des Heiligen Römischen Reiches deutscher Nation und die Problematik seiner Restauration in den Jahren 1814/15.*

Studien und Quellen zur Geschichte des deutschen Verfassungs-rechts, series A, vol. 12. Heidelberg and Karlsruhe, 1980.

Ward, A. W., and Gooch, G. P. *The Cambridge History of British Foreign Policy.* 3 vols. New York, 1923.

Webster, Charles K. *The Congress of Vienna 1814–1815.* 1919. Reprint. New York, 1963.

———. "England and the Polish-Saxon Problem at the Congress of Vienna." *Transactions of the Royal Historical Society,* 3rd ser. VII (1913), 49-102.

———. *The Foreign Policy of Castlereagh.* Vol. I: *1812–1815. Britain and the reconstruction of Europe.* London, 1931.

Weil, M. H. "Le revirement de la politique autrichienne à l'égard de Joachim Murat et les négotiations secrètes entre Paris et Vienne (12 Novembre 1814–4 Mars 1815)." *Biblioteca di Storia Italiana Recente (1800–1850),* II (1909), 391–438.

Weis, Eberhard. "Die Begründung des modernen bayerischen Staates unter König Max I. 1799–1825." In *Handbuch der bayerischen Geschichte,* edited by Max Spindler. Munich, 1974.

———. "Zur Entstehungsgeschichte der bayerischen Verfassung von 1818." *Zeitschrift für bayerische Landesgeschichte,* XXXIX (1976), 412–444.

Weiss, Eva. "The Vienna Conference of 1819–1820: Metternich and Article 19 of the Federal Act." Ph.D. dissertation, McGill University, 1979.

Wertheimer, Eduard. "Fürst Metternich und die Staatskonferenz." *Oesterreichische Rundschau,* X (1907), 41–54 and 111–128.

Wettig, Gerhard. *Zur russischen Aussenpolitik gegenüber Deutschland vom Wiener Kongress bis zur Gegenwart.* Cologne and Ehrenfeld, 1969.

Windelband, Wolfgang. *Die auswärtige Politik der Grossmächte in der Neuzeit von 1494 bis zur Gegenwart.* 5th ed. Essen, 1942.

Winkler-Seraphim, Brigitte. "Das Verhältnis der preussischen Ost-provinzen, insbesondere Ostpreussens, zum Deutschen Bund im 19. Jahrhundert." *Zeitschrift für Ostforschung,* IV (1955), 321–350.

Winter, Alexander. *Karl Philipp Fürst von Wrede als Berater des Königs Max Joseph und des Kronprinzen Ludwig von Bayern (1813–1825).* Miscellanea Bavarica Monacensia, no. 7. Munich, 1968.

Wintterlin, Friedrich. "Die württembergische Verfassung 1815–1819." *Württembergische Jahrbücher für Statistik und Landeskunde* (1912), 47–83.

Wolff, Karl. *Die deutsche Publizistik in der Zeit der Freiheitkämpfe und des Wiener Kongresses.* Plauen, 1934.

Woynar, Karl. "Österreichs Beziehungen zu Schweden und Dänemark

1813 und 1814." *Archiv für österreichischen Geschichte*, LXXVII (1891), 377–542.

Wunder, Bernd. "Landstände und Rechtsstaat. Zur Entstehung und Verwirklichung des Art. 13 DBA." *Zeitschrift für historische Forschung*, V (1978), 139–185.

Zak, L. A. "Die Grossmächte und die deutschen Staaten am Ende der napoleonischen Kriege." *Zeitschrift für Geschichtswissenschaft*, XIX (1971), 1536–1547.

———. "Iz istorii diplomaticheskoi bor'bi na Venskom Kongresse." *Voprosy istorii*, III (1966), 70–82.

———. *Monarkhi Protiv Narodov*. Moscow, 1966.

NOTE: The following valuable studies came to my attention too late for inclusion above:

Derndarsky, Michael. "Österreich und der deutsche Bund 1815–1866." In *Österreich und die deutsche Frage im 19. und 20. Jahrhunderts*, edited by Heinrich Lutz and Helmut Rumpler. Vienna, 1982.

Duchhardt, Heinz. *Gleichgewicht der Kräfte, Convenance, Europäisches Konzert, Friedenskongresse, und Friedensschlüsse vom Zeitalter Ludwig XIV bis zum Wiener Kongress*. Darmstadt, 1976.

Gruner, Wolf D. "Der Deutsche Bund als 'Centralstaat von Europa' und die Sicherung des Friedens. Aspekte Britisch-deutscher Beziehungen in der internationalen Krise von 1819/20." In *Studien zur Geschichte Englands und der deutsch-britischen Beziehungen. Festschrift für Paul Kluke*, edited by Lothar Kettenacker, Manfred Schlenke, and Hellmut Seier. Munich, 1981.

———. "Grossbritannien, der deutsche Bund, und die Struktur des europäiscjen Friedens im frühen 19. Jahrhundert. Studien zu den britisch-deutschen Beziehungen in einer Periode des Umbruchs 1812–1820." Unpublished *Habilitationsschrift*, University of Munich, 1979.

INDEX

431

Library of Congress Cataloging in Publication Data

(Revised for vol. 2)

Kraehe, Enno E.
Metternich's German policy.

Includes bibliographies and indexes.
CONTENTS—v. 1. The contest with Napoleon, 1799–1814.
—v. 2. The Congress of Vienna, 1814–1815.
1. Metternich, Clemens Wenzel Lothar, Fürst von,
1773–1859. 2. Austria—Foreign relations—1789–1900.
DB80.8.M57K7   943.6'03'0924   63-9994
ISBN 0-691-05186-0 (v. 2)
ISBN 0-691-10133-7 (v. 2, lim. pbk. ed.)

Enno E. Kraehe is William W. Corcoran Professor of History at the University of Virginia. Besides writing Volume I of this study, Professor Kraehe is the editor of *The Mettternich Controversy* (1971) and author of many articles on German, Austrian, and European diplomatic history.